D1252330

Humans at the End of the Ice Age

The Archaeology of the Pleistocene–Holocene Transition

INTERDISCIPLINARY CONTRIBUTIONS TO ARCHAEOLOGY

Series Editor: Michael Jochim, *University of California, Santa Barbara*
Founding Editor: Roy S. Dickens, Jr., *Late of University of North Carolina, Chapel Hill*

A *Chronological Listing of Volumes in this series appears at the back of this volume.*

A Continuation Order Plan is available for this series. A continuation order will bring delivery of each new volume immediately upon publication. Volumes are billed only upon actual shipment. For further information please contact the publisher.

Humans at the End of the Ice Age

The Archaeology of the Pleistocene–Holocene Transition

Edited by

LAWRENCE GUY STRAUS
University of New Mexico
Albuquerque, New Mexico

BERIT VALENTIN ERIKSEN
University of Åarhus
Højbjerg, Denmark

JON M. ERLANDSON
University of Oregon
Eugene, Oregon

and

DAVID R. YESNER
University of Alaska
Anchorage, Alaska

PLENUM PRESS • NEW YORK AND LONDON

Library of Congress Cataloging-in-Publication Data

Humans at the end of the Ice Age : the archaeology of the Pleistocene
  -Holocene transition / edited by Lawrence Guy Straus ... [et al.].
      p.   cm. -- (Interdisciplinary contributions to archaeology)
  Includes bibliographical references and index.
  ISBN 0-306-45177-8
  1. Man, Prehistoric. 2. Man--Influence of climate.
3. Agriculture--Origin. 4. Paleoecology--Holocene.
5. Paleoecology--Pleistocene. 6. Glacial epoch.   I. Straus,
Lawrence Guy. II. Series.
GN741.H85 1996
930.1--dc20   96-8914
                                                            CIP

ISBN 0-306-45177-8

© 1996 Plenum Press, New York
A Division of Plenum Publishing Corporation
233 Spring Street, New York, N. Y. 10013

10 9 8 7 6 5 4 3 2 1

Printed in the United States of America

Contributors

C. Melvin Aikens • Department of Anthropology, University of Oregon, Eugene, Oregon 97403-1218

Takeru Akazawa • University Museum, University of Tokyo, Tokyo 113, Japan

Jim Allen • Department of Archaeology, La Trobe University, Bundoora, Victoria 3083, Australia

David G. Anderson • National Park Service, Atlanta, Georgia 30303

Ofer Bar-Yosef • Department of Anthropology, Peabody Museum, Harvard University, Cambridge, Massachusetts 02138

Robson Bonnichsen • Department of Anthropology, Oregon State University, Corvallis, Oregon 97331

Luis Alberto Borrero • Prehistoric Studies Program, University of Buenos Aires, 1039 Buenos Aires, Argentina

Angela E. Close • Department of Anthropology, University of Washington, Seattle, Washington 98195

Pavel M. Dolukhanov • Department of Archaeology, University of Newcastle, Newcastle-upon-Tyne NE1 7RU, United Kingdom

Berit Valentin Eriksen • Department of Prehistoric Archaeology, University of Åarhus, Moesgaard, 8270 Højbjerg, Denmark

Jon M. Erlandson • Department of Anthropology, University of Oregon, Eugene, Oregon 97403-1218

George C. Frison • Department of Anthropology, University of Wyoming, Laramie, Wyoming 82071

Albert C. Goodyear • Institute of Archaeology and Anthropology, University of South Carolina, Columbia, South Carolina 29208

Michael A. Jochim • Department of Anthropology, University of California, Santa Barbara, California 93106

Peter Kershaw • Department of Geography and Environmental Science, Monash University, Melbourne 3168, Australia

Peter J. Mitchell • Pitt Rivers Museum Research Centre, University of Oxford, Oxford OX2 6PN, United Kingdom

Dan F. Morse • Arkansas Archeological Survey, State University, Arkansas 72467

Madonna L. Moss • Department of Anthropology, University of Oregon, Eugene, Oregon 97403-1218

John E. Parkington • Department of Archaeology, University of Cape Town, Rondebosch 7700, Cape Town, South Africa

Surin Pookajorn • Faculty of Archaeology, Silpakorn University, Bangkok 10200, Thailand

William R. Powers • Department of Anthropology, University of Alaska, Fairbanks, Alaska 97707

Romuald Schild • Institute of Archaeology and Ethnology, Polish Academy of Sciences, 00-140 Warsaw, Poland

Lawrence Guy Straus • Department of Anthropology, University of New Mexico, Albuquerque, New Mexico 87131

Royden Yates • Department of Archaeology, University of Cape Town, Rondebosch 7700, Cape Town, South Africa

David R. Yesner • Department of Anthropology, University of Alaska, Anchorage, Alaska 99508

Preface

This book is about the diverse responses of human societies worldwide to the environmental changes of the Pleistocene–Holocene transition between 13,000 and 8,000 years ago. Those changes were extreme in many regions, especially at the middle and high latitudes, and attenuated in equatorial regions. But in all inhabited continents, there were shifts in climate, seasonality, sea levels, ice cover, vegetation, fauna, and soils across the Last Glacial–Interglacial boundary. Just as some aspects of environmental change were abrupt and others more gradual, so too were the adaptive reactions of human forager groups around the world. This book chronicles and explores the significance of the variety of cultural responses.

The transition from the Last Glacial to the Present Interglacial, centered on 10,000 BP and now known in great detail, was just one of a couple of dozen such transitions that have occurred since the Cenozoic Ice Ages began some 2.5 million years ago. Yet only at this last glacial–interglacial boundary were there *anatomically modern humans living on all the continents and major islands* (except Antarctica and Greenland), at relatively high densities in some regions, and in some cases at fairly high latitudes. And only shortly after *this* glacial–interglacial transition did many human groups find it necessary or at least very useful to adopt food production, shifting from a 5-million-year-old universal subsistence strategy of pure exploitation of wild food resources that had involved gathering, scavenging, hunting, and eventually fishing. What was it about the last glacial–interglacial transition that was different? What was this transition so significant in the history of our hominid family? A subtext of this book is this question: Why was agriculture adopted quickly thereafter in some regions but not in others? Why did hunter–gatherers successfully adapt as such in many regions and in some cases survive into the twentieth century?

This volume includes chapters by specialists in the Late Last Glacial prehistory of many of the most-studied regions of the world. Each addresses in his or her own way the specific nature and consequences of the environmental changes of the end of the Pleistocene, detailing the nature, speed, and magnitude of the cultural changes that occurred in the chosen regions. Continental overviews and comparisons are provided throughout by the volume's editors and in a general concluding chapter by series editor Michael Jochim, himself a specialist in hunter–gatherer ecology and in the prehistory of the transition in Germany.

The volume had its origin in and is the first publication of a Working Group on Archeology of the Pleistocene–Holocene Transition, established by Hans-Jurgen Müller-

Beck, President of the International Union for Quaternary Research (INQUA) Commission for the Paleoecology of Early Man. Preliminary versions of the chapters were presented at the 1994 meeting of the Society for American Archaeology in Anaheim, California, with financial support from Müller-Beck and the International Research and Exchanges Board.

LAWRENCE GUY STRAUS
Chair of the INQUA Working Group

Contents

Chapter 8. The Pleistocene–Holocene Transition on the East European Plain 159

Pavel M. Dolukhanov

PART IV. ASIA AND AUSTRALIA DURING THE PLEISTOCENE–HOLOCENE TRANSITION 171

Jon M. Erlandson

Chapter 9. The Pleistocene–Holocene Transition in Greater Australia 175

Jim Allen and Peter Kershaw

Chapter 10. Human Activities and Environmental Changes during the Late Pleistocene to Middle Holocene in Southern Thailand and Southeast Asia 201

Surin Pookajorn

Humans at the End of the Ice Age

The Archaeology of the Pleistocene–Holocene Transition

PART I

INTRODUCTION

Chapter **1**

The World at the End of the Last Ice Age

LAWRENCE GUY STRAUS

Since hominids began producing archeologically recognizable stone tools about 2.5 million years ago in tropical Africa, the world has undergone some two dozen transitions between glacial and interglacial conditions. (Shackleton and Opdyke 1973). Each time, there were major increases in global temperature, whole-scale shrinkage of continental and montane glaciers, rises in sea level of more than 100 m, significant changes in weather patterns and precipitation, and massive shifts in vegetation types and faunas. With each glacial–interglacial transition, the world was in effect remodeled, with the most striking changes occurring in the middle latitudes.

For about the first 1.5 million years of the Paleolithic, stone-tool-making hominids apparently dealt with these fluctuations only within the latitudinal confines of Africa (36°N–35°S). After about 1 million years ago, *Homo erectus* expanded its range to first include southwestern, southern, and eastern Asia, then some time (100–500,000 years) thereafter, southern, western, and central Europe. There have been a dozen glacial/interglacial cycles over the past million years and a half-dozen over the past half-million years (Martinson et al. 1987). At present, there is no credible evidence that humans inhabited the continental core of Eurasia (i.e., Siberia), Greater Australia, or the Americas during the penultimate glacial–interglacial transition around 129–125 thousand years ago. It is even questionable that humans were living in northerly regions of oceanic western Europe or eastern Asia during any but the last few glacial-interglacial cycles of the late Middle Pleistocene (Roebroeks et al. 1992). In short, *only during the last transition* from full glacial to full interglacial conditions, 13,000–8,000 years ago, were there humans living on all the world's continents and major islands (except Antarctica and Greenland). And for the first time ever, the hominids coping with the massive changes in their world were anatomically modern *Homo sapiens sapiens* and

LAWRENCE GUY STRAUS • Department of Anthropology, University of New Mexico, Albuquerque, New Mexico 87131.

Humans at the End of the Ice Age: The Archaeology of the Pleistocene–Holocene Transition, edited by Lawrence Guy Straus, Berit Valentin Eriksen, Jon M. Erlandson, and David R. Yesner. Plenum Press, New York, 1996.

culturally highly complex hunter–fisher–gatherers. Finally, only immediately or quite soon after the transition between Oxygen Isotope Stages 2 and 1 did humans in many regions of the world, often distantly separate regions, invent or adopt food-production strategies, that is, agriculture or animal husbandry or both.

What happened around the globe between 13,000 and 8,000 years ago that led to the creation of the world of humankind as we know it in the present interglacial? What were the variations of environmental and resource changes in, and human responses to, the last glacial–interglacial transition around the globe? Which changes in human culture would seem to be directly or indirectly correlated with (and possibly caused by) the environmental changes and which other factors (e.g., demography, historical trajectories) may have been involved in the sometimes sweeping adaptive changes that occurred about 10 millennia ago? And what of regions where change was neither abrupt nor major at the Pleistocene–Holocene transition? Why did the environmental transition cause such major changes in some regions and only more subtle change in others? There are some of the questions addressed by the various contributions to this volume.

Two (relatively recent) periods in the Earth's Quaternary climatic history have been especially intensively studied and are thus well documented: the Last Glacial Maximum centered on 18,000 radiocarbon years ago and the Pleistocene–Holocene transition (i.e., the Last Glacial [also known as Oxygen Isotope Stage 2]–Postglacial [also known as Oxygen Isotope Stage 1] boundary or "termination") centered on 10,000 radiocarbon years ago (= 11,500 calibrated calendar years ago). This documentation is the result of the work of the CLIMAP (e.g., CLIMAP 1976) and COHMAP (e.g., COHMAP 1988) teams in synthesizing the abundant, relatively detailed oceanic and terrestrial proxy indicators, respectively, for large-scale environmental conditions at these two periods. Deep-sea oxygen isotope evidence—coupled with geomorphological, palynological, and paleontological data—provides us with pictures of continental and regional *variations* in conditions at the height of the Upper Pleniglacial and during the course of the Tardiglacial–early Postglacial climatic amelioration.

Because of generally good chronological control (especially through radiocarbon dating) and because of a relative wealth of archeological sites, these "time slices" lend themselves to broad comparative study. Such was the aim of two recent volumes of *The World at 18,000 BP* (Gamble and Soffer 1990; Soffer and Gamble 1990). A first, limited attempt to survey part of the world at the end of the Last Glacial began the task of documenting and contrasting the variety of human reactions—some marked and others subtle—to the environmental perturbations in different regions of Africa, Southwest Asia, and Europe (Straus 1986). In the past decade, the pace of research—chronometric, paleoenvironmental, and archeological—has accelerated, not only in the Old World, but also in the New Worlds. This fact amply justified the creation of a working group on the archeology of the Pleistocene–Holocene transition within the International Union for Quaternary Research (INQUA) Commission for the Paleoecology of Early Man, of which H. J. Müller-Beck is President. The first collective activity of this group was a double symposium at the 1994 meeting of the Society for American Archaeology in Anaheim, California. Foreign (i.e., non–United States) participation was partially funded by grants from INQUA and from the International Research and Exchanges Board (IREX).

The Pleistocene–Holocene transition was a play in several acts. Like a play by Shakespeare, it is seemingly familiar and well known. Overconfidence stemming from its relative recency, however, may lead to "translation" errors, and significant gaps in the record do exist. Many alternative interpretations are possible. Just as Shakespeare's identity and authorship remain somewhat unclear, debates rage over the cause(s) of the climatic fluctuations that eventually resulted in the Holocene interglacial. And this play, like *King Lear* or *Taming of the Shrew*, has universal validity, despite the existence of translated versions or variant adaptations.

The prologue to this play consists of the full and near-full glacial conditions of the period between about 25,000 and 13,0000 years ago, generally manifested by lowered temperatures and precipitation, albeit with significant fluctuations and regional variations. This period is known as the Upper Pleniglacial plus Early Tardiglacial (a.k.a. Dryas I in Europe).

Act I plays out in scenes of a sharp rise in temperatures, migration of ocean currents, inception of full-scale deglaciation, and, in many regions that had earlier had open herbaceous vegetation, the spread of woodlands. Sometimes and in some proxy records, this climatic amelioration is interrupted by a brief retreat to more glacial conditions. In the "classic" region of northwestern Europe, this act is known as Bölling–Dryas II–Alleröd; a term such as "Tardiglacial Interstadial" would seem appropriate, especially when the interruption is subtle or patently absent.

Act II is a return—brief, yet marked, abrupt, and seemingly widespread—to near glacial conditions, with significant changes in ocean currents, lowered temperatures, glacier readvance, woodland retreat, and other vegetational (and faunal) perturbations. Known in the classic region (and, by extension, elsewhere especially at the middle and higher latitudes) as Dryas III (= Younger Dryas), this event is traditionally dated between about 11,000 and 10,000 radiocarbon years ago.

Act III is the irrevocable arrival of near-full interglacial conditions. Admittedly, even the period between 10,000 and 8,000 BP witnessed limited fluctuations in temperature and precipitation, as well as significant successional changes in vegetation and continued rise in sea level.

The Epilogue is the Postglacial Optimum (= Atlantic period), from about 8,000 to 5,000 radiocarbon years ago. There is still a denouement to come, as sea levels rose above modern limits, some regions became hyperarid while others experienced increased precipitation, and temperatures were generally higher than today, with consequent shifts in biotopes.

There can be little doubt that the basic phenomenon—the waning of Ice Age conditions—was the result of Milankovich phenomena: the orbital and tilt relationships between the Earth and the Sun (A. Berger 1986; Imbrie and Imbrie 1979). However, increasing evidence for a generalized (universal?) manifestation of the brief return to near full-glacial conditions in Dryas III has stimulated a major debate over the possible causes and speed (of onset and end) of this remarkable phenomenon (e.g., Alley et al. 1993; W. Berger 1990; W. Berger and Labeyrie 1987; Dansgaard et al. 1989; Johnsen et al. 1992; Lehman and Keigwin 1992; Taylor et al 1993; Veum et al 1992). The likelihood that the climates of especially the middle and higher latitudes could have suffered sharp reverses within the span of a few decades raises the obvious questions as to how humans (as individuals and as groups) perceived and dealt with environments (and hence resource bases) that were visibly changing within the time frame of a few generations or maybe even a single generation. There is growing evidence that dramatic events in North Atlantic ocean temperatures and currents at the end of the Pleistocene had worldwide climatic effects.

Accustomed to the slow pace and vast scale of even Quaternary geological time, prehistorians are faced with chronometric problems more familiar to archeologists working in recent periods. What do we mean in practice by diachronism vs. synchronism in the archeological record of a period in which change is so rapid and marked? How can be compare archeological phenomena that were contemporaneous (and hence pertained to the same basic set of environmental conditions) to those that may have been only slightly separated in time and yet pertained to significantly different worlds of climate, vegetation, and fauna even within the same region? Startling new developments in the ability to dendrochronologically calibrate radiocarbon dates (with oaks and pines entombed in the muds of the Rhine and Danube—and with Swiss lake varves) call into question our ability to confidently use radiocarbon to accurately measure time precisely during the millennia of the Pleistocene–Holocene transition, centered on the Dryas III event (e.g., Becker and Kromer 1986, 1991; Kromer and Becker 1993; Lotter 1991). The upshot of this research is that there were four radiocarbon plateaus between 10,000 and 8,200 BP, making precise archeological correlation and comparison dicey, despite the apparent advantage of being well within the feasible range of ^{14}C dating and in the first period of prehistory that is replete with determinations from most regions of the world. This fact must be kept in mind when drawing the interim conclusion that two assemblages or sites appear either contemporaneous or separated in time according to their radiocarbon dates. Nevertheless, it is comforting to see good agreement between radiocarbon calibrations based on dendrochronology and those based on uranium series dating of marine corals. Both show that at circa 10,000 radiocarbon years ago, real ages are about 1,500 years older (Bard et al. 1990).

Finally, it may be timely to inquire whether archeology should continue to invest in the study of human–land relations in this age of renewed emphasis on social and ideological issues in prehistory. While this volume does not advocate unreconstructed environmental determinism and while many of its chapters suggest the importance of cultural–historical trajectories (i.e., archeological "traditions") in determining certain (stylistic) aspects of the artifactual record, it does overtly focus on exploring the role (or, in some cases, the lack of a role) of specific aspects of environmental change, occurring within specific regions, in culture change. There can be no doubt that local shifts in such phenomena as temperature, precipitation (rain and snow), seasonality, coastline, glaciers, vegetation, and fauna can and do directly and immediately affect the ability or success of hunter–fisher–gatherers in procuring food (and shelter) and hence in reproducing themselves and in surviving. Directly or indirectly, the local/regional physical environment impacts all aspects of human adaptations, including the forms of social organization, artistic expression, and ideology that were previously practiced. Without a realistic, detailed understanding of the interfaces between humans and their environments (including the structure of their resource bases), little progress can be made in terms of reconstructing the variety of social and ideological aspects of past human culture and their roles. None of the authors in this volume would deny the importance of stylistic trajectories in the prehistoric record of the terminal Pleistocene and initial Holocene that, under the relevant conditions, may have been more or less reinforced by continental or regional environmental factors leading to diverse phenomena, some of which are migration into heretofore unoccupied habitats, population packing, changes in subsistence strategies and tactics, mobility patterns, and territory size.

This volume seeks to be global in its scope and scale, yet the record of human responses to the manifestations of the last glacial–interglacial transition are regional and highly diverse. It is not the case that this global environmental "event" was universally catastrophic or cataclysmic, or even that it was necessarily transcendental in terms of all human adaptive patterns. In some regions, despite noticeable (albeit relatively subtle) environmental changes centered on 10,000 BP, there is strong evidence for considerable cultural *continuity* across the transition. Yet in many other regions, but for often vastly divergent reasons (e.g., melting of glaciers, reforestation of steppe-tundras, inundation of continental shelves, greening of deserts), the adaptive changes were very abrupt and sweeping—even "brutal" in some specific cases, such as when a key food resource was suddenly extirpated. It is this *diversity* of regional environmental manifestations of the Pleistocene–Holocene boundary and of human reactions that is the central theme of this volume. After all, each region's cultural–ecological trajectory across the period from about 13,000 to 8,000 BP engendered the subsequent history of methods of food production (if any) adopted. The nature of the Pleistocene–Holocene transition in each region was the essential background for any Neolithic cultural developments. Environmental *and* cultural history mattered very much.

This volume is organized along continental lines, beginning in the continent longest inhabited by humans (Africa), proceeding via the Near East to Europe, Asia, and Australia, and ending in the most recently occupied continents (the Americas). Hence Part II consists of chapters on two of the best-studied subcontinental regions of Africa: southern (Chapter 2 [Mitchell, Yates, and Parkington]) and northern (Chapter 3 [Close]). There are also the parts of Africa in which the environmental changes at the end of the Pleistocene were most marked. We have also opted to place the Levant (Southwest Asia) (Chapter 4 [Bar-Yosef]) in this Part, since this region is the biogeographic bridge between Africa, Europe, and Asia.

Europe is of course the continent in which the paleoenvironmental and archeological records have been longest and most intensively studied. In Part III, Chapters 5 (Straus), 6 (Eriksen), 7 (Schild), and 8 (Dolukhanov) reflect this history and the diversity of national research traditions in Europe and provide the most detailed interregional comparisons and contrasts.

Asia is still relatively poorly known in this Quaternary period (and in others). Part IV includes Chapter 10 (Pookajorn) on Southeast Asia (with examples from Thailand), Chapter 12 (Powers) on Siberia—clearly to be read in conjunction with Chapter 13 (Yesner) on Alaska and the Yukon in Part V—and Chapter 11 (Aikens and Akazawa) on Japan (where there is an extraordinarily rich record pertaining to the unusual Jomon culture, analogous in several respects to the Natufian of the Levant). Part IV also includes Chapter 9 (Allen and Kershaw) on greater Australia (Sahul), which draws sweeping comparisons among the highly varied environments spanning the range between present-day New Guinea and Tasmania.

The Americas, like Sahul, constitute a somewhat different case from Africa, Europe, and Asia per se, in that they were occupied late in the Upper Pleistocene. Indeed, the traditional view (and still the majority view) is that the Americas were significantly settled by humans only within a very few thousand years of the end of the Pleistocene. Because of the relatively short history of New World human occupation, population densities were generally low, and many of the adaptive changes that occurred after circa 10,000 BP can be attributed to environmental causes—including particularly severe faunal extinctions as well as other changes in biomes that, while perhaps less well known than those that happened in Europe, were of great significance to forager lifeways. This diversity is reflected in Part V by Chapters 13 (Yesner), 14 (Erlandson and Moss), 15 (Frison and Bonnichsen), 16 (Morse, Anderson, and Goodyear), and 17 (Borrero).

Obviously many important regions of the world could not be represented, either for lack of space or because invited authors were not able to provide manuscripts within the deadlines we imposed. Nonetheless, we hope we have provided a fairly representative sample of the range of environmental changes and human responses across the Pleistocene–Holocene boundary—not focusing simply on the few "classic" regions such as western Europe or the Levant (though some of the latest work in these regions is also represented herein).

The authors were urged to present broadly synthetic, comparative chapters and to eschew unnecessary detail and specifics, except for particularly illustrative case studies. In those regions in which the record is perhaps less well known to a general North American and European readership, however, more emphasis is given to documenting the empirical record. In all cases, the reader is urged to consult the references for more detailed publications of sites. Each editor has taken the responsibility of introducing a continental section, and Michael Jochim has graciously provided the concluding overview Chapter 18.

REFERENCES

Alley R., Meese, D., Shuman, C., Gow, A., Taylor, K., Grootes, P., White, J., Ram, M., Waddington, E., Mayewski, P., and Zielinski, G., 1993, Abrupt Increase in Greenland Snow Accumulation at the End of the Younger Dryas Event, *Nature* 362:527–529.

Bard, E., Hamelin, B., Fairbanks, R., and Zindler, A., 1990, Calibration of the ^{14}C Timescale over the Past 30,000 Years Using Mass Spectrometric U-Th Ages from Barbados Corals, *Nature* 345:405–410.

Becker, B., and Kromer, B., 1986, Extension of the Holocene Dendrochronology by the Preboreal Pine Series, 8800 to 10,100 BP, *Radiocarbon* 28:961–967.

Becker, B., and Kromer, B., 1991, Dendrochronology and Radiocarbon Calibration of the Early Holocene, In N. Barton, A. Roberts, and D. Roe, eds., *The Late Glacial in North-West Europe*, Council for British Archaeology, London, pp. 22–24.

Berger, A., ed., 1986, *Milankovitch and Climate*. Reidel, Dordrecht, The Netherlands.

Berger, W., 1990, The Younger Dryas Cold Spell—A Quest for Causes. *Palaeogeography, Palaeoclimatology, Palaeoecology* 89:219–237.

Berger, W., and Labeyrie, L. eds., 1987, *Abrupt Climatic Change*. Reidel, Dordrecht, The Netherlands.

CLIMAP, 1976, The Surface of the Ice-Age Earth, *Science* 191:1131–1137.

COHMAP, 1988, Climatic Changes of the Last 18,000 years, *Science* 241:1043–1052.

Dansgaard, W., White, J., and Johnsen, S., 1989, The Abrupt Termination of the Younger Dryas Climate Event, *Nature* 339:532–534.

Gamble, C., and Soffer, O., eds., 1990, *The World at 18,000 BP*, Volume 2. Unwin Hyman, London.

Imbrie, J., and Imbrie, K., 1979, *Ice Ages: Solving the Mystery*. Enslow, Short Hills, NJ.

Johnsen, S., Clausen, H., Dansgaard, W., Fuhrer, K., Gundestrup, N., Hammer, C., Iversen, P., Jouzel, J., Stauffer, B., and Steffensen, J., 1992, Irregular Glacial Interstadials Recorded in a New Greenland Ice Core, *Nature* 359:311–313.

Kromer, B., and Becker, B., 1993, German Oak and Pine ^{14}C Calibration, 7200–9439 BC, *Radiocarbon* 35:125–135.

Lehman, S., and Keigwin, L., 1992, Sudden Changes in North Atlantic Circulation during the Last Deglaciation, *Nature* 356:757–762.

Lotter, A., 1991, Absolute Dating of the Late-Glacial Period in Switzerland using Annually Laminated Sediments, *Quaternary Research* 35:321–330.

Martinson, D., Pisias, N., Hays, J., Imbrie, J., Moore, T., and Shackleton, N., 1987, Age Dating and the Orbital Theory of the Ice Ages, *Quaternary Research* 27:1–29.

Roebroeks, W., Conard, N., and van Kolfschoten, T., 1992, Dense Forests, Cold Steppes, and the Paleolithic Settlement of Northern Europe, *Current Anthropology* 33:551–586.

Shackleton, N. J., and Opdyke, N. D., 1973, Oxygen Isotope and Paleomagnetic Stratigraphy of Equatorial Pacific Core V28-238, *Quaternary Research* 3:39–55.

Soffer, O., and Gamble, C., 1990, *The World at 18,000 BP*, Volume 1. Unwin Hyman, London.

Straus, L. G., ed., 1986, *The End of the Paleolithic in the Old World*. British Archaeological Reports, Oxford.

Taylor, K., Lamorey, G., Doyle, G., Alley, R., Grootes, P., Mayewski, P., White, J., and Barlow, L., 1993, The "Flickering Switch" of Late Pleistocene Climate Change, *Nature* 361:432–436.

Veum, T., Jansen, E., Arnold, M., Beyer, I., and Duplessy, J.-C., 1992, Water Mass Exchange between the North Atlantic and the Norwegian Sea during the Past 28,000 Years, *Nature* 356:783–785.

PART II

THE PLEISTOCENE–HOLOCENE TRANSITION IN AFRICA AND THE NEAR EAST

Alone among the continents, Africa is centered symmetrically on the Equator and extends no more than about 10 degrees to the north or south of the Tropics. Logically, it should have undergone the least severe environmental changes across the Pleistocene–Holocene transition. This is true, however, only if one concentrates solely on temperature, for Africa underwent enormous changes in precipitation between 13,000 and 8,000 years ago, and these changes were not synchronous throughout the continent. Throughout Africa, however, human groups responded by means of demographic adjustment (i.e., population growth or reduction by various means), migration (i.e., range expansion or contraction), and changes in subsistence strategies and technologies. Some of these changes in precipitation and consequent adjustments were among the most dramatic to have occurred anywhere in the world circa 10,000 BP—despite Africa's equable geographic position.

Ironically, the regions that are paleoenvironmentally and archeologically best known for the Pleistocene–Holocene transition are the southern and northern ends of Africa, those regions where the environmental changes were the most marked. Although the tropical rain forests of central Africa are known to have significantly expanded after the Upper Pleniglacial, the archeological records are simply still very sparse for this period outside the Republic of South Africa and its immediate neighbors and outside the Maghreb, Sahara, and lower Nile regions of northern Africa. Thus, the chapters in this part concentrate on the rich records from southern and northern Africa.

In Chapter 2, the sweeping *tour d'horizon* of Mitchell, Yates, and Parkington highlights the degree of variability in environmental and archeological changes across the southern African subcontinent, from north to south, east to west, coast to interior, lowland to upland. A complex series of climatic and hence floral and faunal changes is beginning to be revealed for this region through the course of the transition, with evidence of significant fluctuations in precipitation that markedly affected human distributions in the Terminal Pleistocene and early Holocene. Nonetheless, the authors acknowledge and explore a variety of other possible explanations for observed changes in the dense technological and subsistence record of the recent Later Stone Age that are encapsulated in such normative concepts as "Robberg," "Albany/Oakhurst," and "Wilton." These explanations include Parkington's well-known sampling bias, lithic raw material, and "change of place" models, as well as L. Wadley's social exchange model. This chapter constitutes a sophisticated, multicausal approach to a complex problem of well-documented, apparently vectored culture change.

The Sahara—our modern image of a prototypical desert—is the subject of Chapter 3, by Angela Close, which shows us graphically how much this vast region changed between circa 13,000 and 8,000 BP. Based on extensive palynological, geological, paleontological and archeological research by scientists principally from France, United States, Belgium and Poland, we know of the astounding greening of especially the western Sahara caused by relaxation of the trade winds and northward migration of the summer monsoons beginning ca. 10,000 BP and ending ca. 7000 BP. Where before (and after) the Sahara (especially its lowlying basins) had been essentially abiotic, ponds, marshes and streams, savanna and woodlands appeared due to dramatic increases in rainfall. This led to impressive migrations (mainly from the Maghreb—as documented by physical anthropology). These populations at first sustained themselves by hunting, gathering and fishing, but when aridification began they took up cattle pastoralism and home-grown agriculture, which they eventually took with them into the Sahel and beyond when the desert finally reclaimed the region in the mid-Holocene.

Less marked than the rainfall changes in the western Sahara were those in the eastern Sahara, but equally significant (and truly dramatic) were the perturbations of the Nile, the lifeblood of Egypt and Sudan, during the transition. As this chapter carefully documents, our period began around 12,500 BP with the so-called "Wild Niles" (with high rainfall in the Nile's highland source areas of east Africa and continued hyperaridity in the eastern Sahara) and a time of crisis for Nilotic human populations with nowhere to go, leading, no doubt, to the massacres at Jebel Sahaba. At times circa 10,500 BP, the Nile almost ceased to flow and human occupation of at least sectors of its valley became scarce or absent, while the desert became relatively attractive. Out of this complex, stressful situation arose early experiments in cattle domestication and at least intensive wild harvesting of native cereals. Chapter 3 shows how adjacent habitats—the Nile Valley and the flanking deserts—could have environmental histories, and consequently cultural trajectories, that were out of synchrony, causing striking contradictions in the archeological record.

The Near East (a.k.a. southwest Asia) is a crossroads between the great continental landmasses of Africa and Eurasia. The Levant specifically is one of the great biogeographic corridors of the world, and, being located in the lower middle latitudes at the eastern end of the Mediterranean, it underwent significant but controversial fluctuations in precipitation and seasonality at the end of the Last Glacial. Ofer Bar-Yosef, in his masterful synthesis in Chapter 4, summarizes the main features of the paleoclimatic and vegetational records. He then brings in the complex, now-classic cultural sequence and makes a clear case for much of the temporally vectored archeological variation being the direct result of changes in subsistence, settlement, and mobility strategies, in turn governed by changing distributions and compositions of vegetation zones tied closely to the vicissitudes of precipitation in this fragile, topographically tightly compartmentalized region. Here, the effects of migrating biotopes were critical in the early coevolutionary development of human groups and native cereal grains, a process brought to fruition in the crisis of Dryas III. The exact nature of the quick-time responses within a few generations of late Natufian survivors during the Dryas III drought remains one of the most fascinating test cases for the detailed study of why and how people actually go about the adoption of agriculture.

These three case studies set the stage for worldwide complexity across the transition.

LAWRENCE GUY STRAUS

Chapter **2**

At the Transition

The Archaeology of the Pleistocene–Holocene Boundary in Southern Africa

PETER J. MITCHELL, ROYDEN YATES,
AND JOHN E. PARKINGTON

INTRODUCTION

Southern Africa is a subcontinent of contrasts, not only in climate and ecology, which encompass summer, year-round, and winter rainfall regimes and a variety of distinct biotic communities, but also in extent of archaeological coverage. While some areas (the Western and Eastern Cape Provinces of South Africa) have been quite intensively investigated, others (e.g., Botswana, Mozambique, and northern Namibia) remain largely unexplored. Our chapter reflects this difference. In general terms, the northern half of the subcontinent is a savanna region populated by browsing and mixed feeding ungulates. The east is mostly covered by grasslands suitable for large, gregarious grazers, while the west trends into sparsely vegetated scrub or desert with a reduced diversity of large game; browsers are found in large numbers in a heathland (*fynbos*) along the southwestern margins of the subcontinent. We use these broad ecozonal distinctions (De Vos 1975) as a framework for our discussion.

PALAEOENVIRONMENTAL BACKGROUND

Knowledge of southern Africa's palaeoenvironmental history is vital to understanding human adaptations across the Pleistocene–Holocene boundary, but is unfortunately still

PETER J. MITCHELL • Pitt Rivers Museum Research Centre, University of Oxford, Oxford OX2 6PN, United Kingdom.   **ROYDEN YATES and JOHN E. PARKINGTON** • Department of Archaeology, University of Cape Town, Rondebosch 7700, Cape Town, South Africa.

Humans at the End of the Ice Age: The Archaeology of the Pleistocene–Transition, edited by Lawrence Guy Straus, Berit Valentin Eriksen, Jon M. Erlandson, and David R. Yesner. Plenum Press, New York, 1996.

marked by extremely patchy spatiotemporal coverage. While post–Last Glacial Maximum (LGM) warming began earlier in the southern than in the northern hemisphere (J. Deacon and Lancaster 1988:157), frost-shattered debris at Wonderwerk, Northern Cape Province (Figure 1) (Beaumont et al., 1984), suggests that it remained considerably colder than today until 11,500 BP. Observations from several areas further indicate that cool conditions persisted to circa 10,000 BP (Scholtz 1986; Scott 1982; Tusenius 1989), but quantifying these observations has been only rarely attempted. The factor analysis by J. F. Thackeray (1987) of micromammalian frequencies at several sites suggests that at some (e.g., Byneskranskop, Cape ecozone), maximum Holocene temperatures were reached only after 8,000 BP.

Since precipitation, not temperature, is the major limiting factor for vegetation in most of the subcontinent today, gauging relative aridity plays an important part in palaeoclimatic studies. Within the winter rainfall area of the Western Cape Province, for example, the mean size of dune molerats (*Bathyergus suillus*) at Elands Bay Cave suggests that conditions remained relatively dry until 12,000 BP, but were then moister until 8,000 BP (Klein 1991). Eastward expansion of the winter rainfall regime is indicated, however, by micromammal, pollen, and charcoal studies at Boomplaas, southern Cape, between 14,000 and 12,000 BP (Avery 1982; H. J. Deacon et al. 1984; Scholtz 1986), when this region experienced its wettest conditions of the last 70,000 years; from 10,000 BP, a shift to a drier climate is indicated, with rainfall increasingly concentrated in summer.

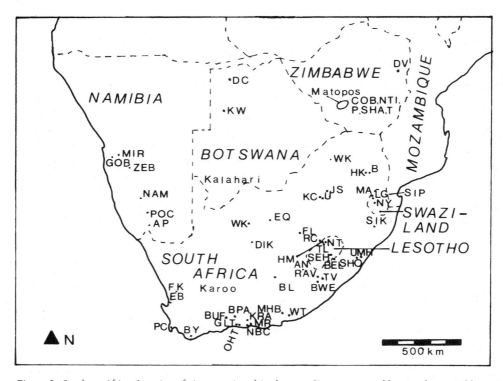

Figure 1. Southern Africa: Location of sites mentioned in the text. Site names are abbreviated as in Table 1.

Within the modern summer rainfall area, a coherent pattern is more difficult to discern. The Wonderkrater pollen sequence (Scott 1982, 1989) suggests that drier, warmer conditions prevailed in central and northern South Africa after 9,500 BP, as indicated by the replacement of open grassland by Kalahari-type bushveld savanna, and Dowson's (1988) analysis of charcoal at Jubilee Shelter also shows bushveld present in this region by 8,500 BP. Charcoals at Siphiso, Swaziland, indicate, however, that wetter conditions persisted through the early Holocene (Prior and Price-Williams 1985), a pattern largely confirmed by work in the Caledon Valley. Here, though, a trend toward less, possibly more solely summer precipitation is evident by 11,000 BP at its northern end (Scott 1986), or from circa 10,000 BP in the northern Eastern Cape Province (Tusenius 1989). More severely arid conditions set in only toward the very end of our period (Esterhuysen and Mitchell in press). Over the northern half of the subcontinent, high lake and pan levels in the Kalahari indicate increased moisture availability until 11,000 BP (J. Deacon and Lancaster 1988:78–79), as do diatoms in the Nswatugi cave deposits at 10,265 BP (Walker 1980). Drier conditions prevailed in both the Kalahari and the Namib by 10,000 BP (J. Deacon and Lancaster 1988:53), but various indicators suggest to Beaumont et al. (1984) that conditions in the Northern Cape Province became progressively warmer and wetter after 10,500 BP.

Few studies have detected more closely dated environmental fluctuations. The analysis by Coetzee (1967) of pollen from Aliwal North (Basutolian ecozone) documents several short-lived oscillations between grassland (implying cooler, moister conditions) and more xeric karroid plant communities (implying drier, warmer communities) between 12,600 or earlier and 9,600 BP; she equates the second of these karroid events (11,650–11,250 BP) with the Allerød interstadial of northern Europe. More recently, evidence has emerged from oxygen isotope analysis of seashells for the identification of the Younger Dryas (Cohen et al. 1992), now also detected in the terrestrial record (J. Lee Thorp personal communication). Given the complexity of the better-known northern hemisphere record, however, we are reticent about too readily equating short-lived climatic oscillations in southern Africa with those marking the Pleistocene–Holocene boundary in Europe.

The Cape ecozone shows the greatest differences between LGM and Holocene conditions and allows environmental change across the Pleistocene–Holocene transition to be tracked most closely. Pre-12,000 BP archaeozoological assemblages dominated by large, gregarious grazers (Klein 1972, 1978; Klein and Cruz-Uribe 1987) imply the existence of substantially more open grassland in the late Pleistocene. In contrast, the region's historic ungulate faunas were dominated by smaller, browsing species characteristic of the modern closed *fynbos* shrub. As the relationship between change in large mammal faunas and other aspects of the archaeological record is central to some models (Ambrose and Lorenz 1990; H. J. Deacon 1976; J. Deacon 1984b) that seek to explain changes in lithic technology, settlement pattern, and social organization across the Pleistocene–Holocene boundary, we return to this issue later on, but make the preliminary observation that faunal analyses elsewhere (e.g., Heuningneskrans Shelter, Mpumalanga [Klein 1984a]) show much less pronounced change at this time.

An additional aspect of these faunal changes is the extinction of a number of large ungulate species. Some, such as the giant buffalo (*Pelorovis antiquus*), giant hartebeest (*Megalotragus priscus*), southern springbok (*Antidorcas australis*), and Cape horse (*Equus capensis*), disappear from Cape faunas by 9,500 BP at the latest, as part of the general faunal replacement already noted. However, extinction was not restricted to the Cape ecozone: The most recent record for both *E. capensis* and *M. priscus* is in early Holocene contexts at Wonderwerk (Beaumont and Morris 1990), and Bond's springbok (*Antidorcas bondi*) is known as late as 7,600 BP at Kruger Cave, Gauteng (Brown and Verhagen 1985). Such data suggest that extinction was a regionally variable phenomenon and that there is no close connection with changes in stone tool assemblages such as might imply the adoption of an improved projectile technology (the bow and arrow). Although Klein (1984b) argues that increased hunting pressure *was* a factor in driving these species below reproductive thresholds and thus facilitating their extinction, we lack firm evidence for suggesting that the terminal Pleistocene–Holocene transition was ecologically identical to previous glacial–interglacial transitions, and the role of environmental change may thus have been greater than generally estimated. In this regard, we note that those species that became extinct are the most specialized grazing forms present (J. S. Brink personal communication) and that some (e.g., Cape horse, giant hartebeest, and Bond's springbok) may have been interlinked in grazing successions (Klein 1980). Furthermore, Churcher and Richardson (1978) suggest for at least one (the Cape horse) that it evolved into a still extant species (Grevy's zebra, *Equus grevyi*), and Peters et al. (1994) have recently made the same case for *Pelorovis antiquus*, reducing it to the status of a chronosubspecies of the modern Cape buffalo (*Syncerus caffer*). We propose that the jury should stay out on the extent to which humans contributed to these late Quaternary extinctions, more particularly as there is little evidence for their selective hunting and a complete absence of major kill sites on the North American or European model.

The Cape is also that part of southern Africa most affected by sea-level changes, since the continental shelf is shallowest between the Cape of Good Hope and Cape St. Francis. This question relates to that of faunal change, as reconstructions of the shelf's lithology and vegetation suggest that it was largely covered by open grassland (Van Andel 1989). The progressive flooding of the shelf after 13,000 BP (J. Deacon and Lancaster 1988) can be monitored at present-day coastal sites, particularly Elands Bay Cave (EB). Here, successive changes in site catchment are documented by shifts in the balance and composition of the terrestrial, estuarine, and littoral resources exploited by people (Parkington 1987, 1990; Poggenpoel 1987). For example, the first shellfish appear in the EB sequence around 11,000 BP and are dominated by limpets (*Patella* spp.). A subsequent shift in emphasis to black mussels (*Choromytilus meridionalis*), a cold-water species, suggests that upwelling of cold water in the Benguela Current was reinitiated by 10,000 BP (Parkington 1986), while a near-modern coastal configuration had been achieved by 9,000 BP (Dingle and Rogers 1972). Archaeologically, the significance of these changes lies not only in the "changes of place" (*sensu* Parkington 1980) that sites at or near the modern coast underwent, but also in the loss of potentially important aspects of Terminal Pleistocene settlement systems and of evidence for earlier coastal resource exploitation.

THE CULTURAL–STRATIGRAPHIC FRAMEWORK

Radiocarbon dating forms the basis for our chronology (Table 1), but no southern African dates from the period reviewed have yet been calibrated; as in Europe (Mellars 1990), it seems likely that this calibration will affect our understanding of rates of cultural and environmental change and that, even if relative chronologies are largely preserved intact, some patterning may become less distinct.

Three technological traditions are generally recognized within the 13,000–8,000 BP period. In reviewing the southern African Later Stone Age (LSA), Janette Deacon (1984a,b) distinguished early microlithic, terminal Pleistocene–early Holocene nonmicrolithic and Holocene microlithic assemblages; Wadley (1993) also employs the first two of these terms. Other writers (e.g., H. J. Deacon 1976; Inskeep 1978; Sampson 1974) prefer the terms Robberg, Oakhurst, and Wilton after localities in which the type assemblages were first recovered. Cultural systematics is an issue examined later in greater depth; here, we briefly describe these three complexes.

Early microlithic assemblages have few retouched pieces (<1% of all flaked stone), although naturally backed knives (NBKs), scrapers, and rare adzes and backed microliths do occur (J. Deacon 1984a: Figure 2). Their most "formal" component is the production of unretouched bladelets, often from distinctive forms of bladelet core, presumed to have been used in composite artifacts such as knives and projectile weapons (Mitchell 1988). Particularly where quartz was a favored raw material, cores are often bipolar (J. Deacon 1984a; Parkington 1984). Artifacts of bone as well as ostrich eggshell (OES) and bone ornaments are found, but generally not in frequencies as high as in succeeding Holocene occurrences; data from Boomplaas (J. Deacon 1984b: Figure 103) and EB suggest that this difference may partly be due to differential preservation.

Early microlithic assemblages occur in a broad swath in and coastward of the Great Escarpment of southern Africa, extending inland to include the Caledon Valley (Wadley 1993; Mitchell 1994) and, apparently, the Northern Cape Province (Beaumont and Morris 1990); with one possible exception (Walker and Wadley 1984), however, they do not occur in Zimbabwe. Associated radiocarbon dates show that the same tradition was present at some of these sites at the LGM, but it is represented at more, and more widespread, sites between 13,000 and 12,000 BP (Figure 2). In an earlier review, J. Deacon (1984b) argued that it disappeared quite abruptly around 12,000 BP, but more recent observations suggest that bladelet technology may have persisted rather longer in southeastern southern Africa (Barham 1989a; Kaplan 1990; Mitchell and Vogel 1994; Opperman 1987); regional variability within these assemblages has otherwise been little addressed.

Sampson (1974) grouped nonmicrolithic assemblages of the terminal Pleistocene–early Holocene into the Oakhurst Industrial Complex, within which several regional industries are recognized: the Albany in the Western and Eastern Cape Provinces (H. J. Deacon 1976; J. Deacon 1984a,b), the Kuruman in the Northern Cape Province (Humphreys and Thackeray 1983), and the Pomongwan in southwestern Zimbabwe (Walker 1980); "Oakhurst-like" assemblages have been noted elsewhere (e.g., Wadley 1987, 1993). Associated dates range from just before 12,000 to about 8,000 BP, although the many open sites are dated only typologically and some Oakhurst assemblages fall within the 8th millennium BP (e.g., Cable et al. 1980). In the north of the subcontinent, informal macrolithic assemblages have been excavated by Yellen et al. (1987) at Kwihabe (Botswana) and by Wendt (1972) in southern Namibia. The wider affiliations of these occurrences are unknown, but they, at least the latter, are similar to those known there at the LGM, suggesting that Namibia remained outside the interaction network represented by Early Microlithic assemblages south of the Orange River. Because of a lack of relevant observations, it is almost impossible to state the extent to which the northern third of our region is part of developments further south, but we note that the Oakhurst Complex is unknown north of the Matopos (J. Deacon 1984a); ongoing research should pay dividends here (Robbins 1990).

Table 1.   Radiocarbon Dates from Southern African Sites Occupied between 13,000 and 8,000 BP[a]

Site abbreviation (ecozone[b])	Name and uncalibrated dates BP	References[c]
AP (Karoo-Namaqualian)	Apollo 11 9,430 ± 90 (KN-I-610) 10,420 ± 80 (KN-I-611) 12,500 ± 120 (Pta-1021) 13,000 ± 120 (Pta-1010)	Wendt (1972, 1976), Freundlich et al. (1980), Vogel and Visser (1981)
B (Transvaalian)	Bushman Rock Shelter 9,570 ± 55 (GrN-5874) 9,510 ± 55 (GrN-4854) 9,940 ± 80 (GrN-4813) 12,090 ± 95 (GrN-4814) 12,310 ± 120 (Pta-1175) 12,160 ± 95 (GrN-4815) 12,470 ± 120 (Pta-1176) 12,510 ± 105 (GrN-4816) 12,800 ± 75 (Pta-1177) 12,950 ± 40 (Pta-1178)	Plug (1981)
BEL (Basutolian)	Belleview 8,650 ± 80 (Pta-359)	Carter and Vogel (1974)
BPA (Cape)	Boomplaas 9,100 ± 135 (UW-306) 10,425 ± 125 (UW-411) 12,060 ± 105 (Pta-1828) 12,480 ± 130 (UW-412)	Fairhall et al. (1976), J. Deacon (1984b)
BUF (Cape)	Buffelskloof 8,960 ± 80 (Pta-1484) 11,875 ± 115 (Pta-1805)	Opperman (1978)
BWE (Basutolian)	Bonawe 8,040 ± 100 (Pta-1709)	Opperman (1987)
BY (Cape)	Byneskranskop 9,760 ± 85 (Pta-1857) 12,730 ± 185 (I-7948)	Schweitzer and Wilson (1982)
COB (Zambezian)	Cave of Bees 9,130 ± 90 (Pta-3459) 10,500 ± 100 (Pta-2578) 11,000 ± 100 (Pta-2586) 12,800 ± 120 (Pta-2585)	Vogel et al. (1986), Walker (1987)
DC (Kalaharian)	Depression Cave 10,900 ± 420 (Beta-2281)	Robbins (1990)
DIK (Karoo-Namaqualian)	Dikbosch 8,010 ± 60 (Pta-3411) 12,450 ± 100 (Pta-1067)	Humphreys (1974), Vogel et al. (1986)
DV (Zambezian)	Diana's Vow 10,650 ± 80 (Pta-1857)	Cook (1979), Vogel et al. (1986)

(continued)

Table 1. *(Continued)*

Site abbreviation (ecozone[b])	Name and uncalibrated dates BP	References[c]
EB (Karoo-Namaqualian)	Elands Bay Cave	Fairhall et al. (1976), Parkington (1977, 1980, 1986, 1992)
	8,000 ± 95 (Pta-1829)	
	8,110 ± 90 (AA-5832)	
	8,340 ± 80 (Pta-1871)	
	8,860 ± 90 (Pta-5305)	
	9,600 ± 90 (Pta-0686)	
	9,640 ± 90 (Pta-5306)	
	9,800 ± 160 (OxA-456)	
	9,750 ± 100 (Pta-3086)	
	9,950 ± 270 (Pta-2592)	
	10,000 ± 90 (Pta-2481)	
	10,460 ± 80 (Pta-5336)	
	10,660 ± 100 (Pta-5369)	
	10,840 ± 70 (AA-5833)	
	10,640 ± 110 (Pta-732)	
	10,700 ± 100 (Pta-737)	
	10,600 ± 100 (Pta-5361)	
	10,090 ± 165 (UW-193)	
	11,070 ± 140 (UW-192)	
	10,860 ± 180 (OxA-478)	
	11,415 ± 80 (AA-5834)	
	12,450 ± 280 (GaK-4335)	
EQ (Karoo-Namaqualian)	Equus Cave	Vogel et al. (1986)
	10,800 ± 270 (Pta-4052/57)	
FK (Karoo-Namaqualian)	Faraoskop	Manhire (1993)
	10,810 ± 100 (Pta-4816)	
	11,550 ± 120 (Pta-4817)	
FL (Basutolian)	Florisbad	Kuman and Clarke (1986)
	11,700 ± 110 (Pta-3643)	
GOB (Karoo-Namaqualian)	Gobabeb	Vogel and Visser (1981)
	12,800 ± 140 (Pta-2596)	
HK (Transvaalian)	Heuningneskrans	Beaumont (1981)
	9,110 ± 110 (LJ-3199)	There is also a date of 7,200 ± 70
	9,480 ± 120 (LJ-3198)	BP (Pta-112) from the same layer.
	9,780 ± 85 (Pta-099)	
	10,430 ± 150 (Pta-114)	
	12,590 ± 130 (LJ-3150)	
HM (Basutolian)	Ha Makotoko	Mitchell (1993a)
	8,370 ± 80 (Pta-5191)	
	8,950 ± 80 (Pta-5192)	
	9,290 ± 90 (Pta-5204)	
	9,970 ± 90 (Pta-5205)	
JS (Basutolian)	Jubilee Shelter	Wadley (1987)
	8,500 ± 240 (Wits-1436)	

(continued)

Table 1. *(Continued)*

Site abbreviation (ecozone[b])	Name and uncalibrated dates BP	References[c]
KC (Basutolian)	Kruger Cave 9,100 ± 90 (Pta-1273) 10,150 ± 90 (Pta-1272) 10,310 ± 150 (Wits—not published) 10,430 ± 150 (Wits—not published)	Mason (1988), Vogel et al. (1986)
KRA (Cape)	Kangkara 9,260 ± 90 (Pta-2307) 12,250 ± 110 (Pta-782) 12,330 ± 130 (Pta-782)	J. Deacon (1984b) Two different chemical fractions of the same sample.
KW (Kalaharian)	Kwihabe 12,200 ± 150 (SI—no lab. no. given)	Yellen et al. (1987)
LC (Transvaalian)	Lion Cavern 9,640 ± 80 (Y-1713)	Dart and Beaumont (1968)
MA (Transvaalian)	Mlaula 9,370 ± 160 (Y-1996) 9,570 ± 450 (Pta-004)	Beaumont and Vogel (1972)
MHB (Cape)	Melkhoutboom 10,500 ± 150 (GaK-1538)	H. J. Deacon (1976)
MIR (Karoo-Namaqualian)	Mirabib 8,200 ± 80 (Pta-1013) 8,410 ± 80 (Pta-1368)	Sandelowsky (1977), Vogel and Visser (1981)
MR (Cape)	Matjes River 9,450 ± 55 (GrN-5886) 9,580 ± 85 (GrN-5872) 10,500 ± 400 (L-336G) 11,250 ± 400 (L-336H) 9,780 ± 60 (GrN-5061) 10,030 ± 55 (GrN-5871)	Louw (1960), Vogel (1970)
NAM (Karoo-Namaqualian)	Namtib 8,230 ± 70 (KN-2143)	Freundlich et al. (1980)
NBC (Cape)	Nelson Bay Cave 9,080 ± 185 (UW-179) 8,070 ± 240 (UW-181) 8,570 ± 170 (UW-184) 8,990 ± 80 (Pta-391) 10,256 ± 210 (Q-1085) 10,540 ± 110 (UW-178) 10,150 ± 90 (Pta-392) 10,180 ± 85 (UW-164) 11,505 ± 110 (UW-162) 11,950 ± 150 (UW-177) 11,080 ± 260 (I-6515) 10,600 ± 150 (UW-218)	J. Deacon 1984b There is also a date of 6,070 ± 125 BP (UW-222) for the same layer.

(continued)

Table 1. *(Continued)*

Site abbreviation (ecozone[b])	Name and uncalibrated dates BP	References[c]
NT (Basutolian)	Ntloana Tsoana 8,780 ± 30 (Pta-5238) 9,690 ± 120 (Pta-5207) 9,420 ± 110 (Pta-5237) 10,200 ± 100 (Pta-5208) 12,110 ± 120 (Pta-5236)	Mitchell (1993a)
NTI (Transvaalian)	Nswatugi 9,220 ± 90 (Pta-3116) 9,790 ± 90 (Pta-1771) 10,270 ± 90 (Pta-2218)	Walker (1980)
NY (Transvaalian)	Nyonyane 8,080 ± 160 (Tx-5633) 8,880 ± 140 (TX-5634) 9,310 ± 90 (TX-5635) 10,080 ± 430 (TX-5636) 10,970 ± 480 (TX-5367)	Barham (1989a)
OHT (Cape)	Oakhurst 8,950 ± 90 (Pta-410) 8,270 ± 55 (Pta-375) 9,100 ± 90 (Pta-3724)	Schrire (1962), Patrick (1989)
P (Transvaalian)	Pomongwe 8,420 ± 80 (Pta-3470) 8,540 ± 90 (Pta-2306) 9,500 ± 120 (Pta-3117) 11,020 ± 60 (Pta-2300) 12,300 ± 100 (Pta-3118) 13,000 ± 120 (Pta-3119)	Vogel et al. (1986), Walker (1980, 1987)
RAV (Basutolian)	Ravenscraig 10,000 ± 80 (Pta-3194) 10,200 ± 100 (Pta-3451)	Opperman (1987)
RC (Basutolian)	Rose Cottage Cave 8,380 ± 70 (Pta-5600) 8,600 ± 100 (Pta-2067) 8,614 ± 40 (Pta-5560) 8,600 ± 100 (Pta-2067) 9,250 ± 70 (Pta-5599) 12,690 ± 120 (Pta-5593)	Vogel et al. (1986), Wadley (1991), Wadley and Vogel (1991)
SEH (Basutolian)	Sehonghong 9,280 ± 45 (Pta-6368) 9,740 ± 140 (Pta-6057) 11,090 ± 230 (Pta-6065) 12,180 ± 110 (Pta-6282)	Carter and Vogel (1974), Carter et al. (1988), Mitchell and Vogel (1994), Vogel (pers. comm.) A date of 6,960 ± 40 BP (Pta-6354) comes from immediately below this. This unit also produced a date of 6,270 ± 50 BP (Pta-6076).

(continued)

Table 1.   (*Continued*)

Site abbreviation (ecozone[b])	Name and uncalibrated dates BP	References[c]
SEH (Basutolian) (*cont.*)	12,250 ± 300 (Q-3175)	
	12,200 ± 250 (Q-3176)	
	12,410 ± 45 (Pta-6062)	
	12,470 ± 100 (Pta-6058)	
	12,800 ± 250 (Q-3173)	
	13,000 ± 140 (Pta-884)	
SHA (Transvaalian)	Shashabugwa	Vogel et al. (1986), Walker (1987)
	8,920 ± 80 (Pta-2569)	
SHO (Transvaalian)	Shongweni	Davies (1975), Vogel et al. (1986)
	11,870 ± 130 (Pta-682)	
SIK (Transvaalian)	Sikhanyisweni	Mazel (1988)
	9,700 ± 100 (Pta-3782)	
	10,000 ± 100 (Pta-3780)	
SIP (Transvaalian)	Siphiso Shelter	Barham (1989b)
	9,380 ± 90 (TX-5628)	
	8,700 ± 120 (Pta-3540)	
	8,860 ± 180 (TX-5630)	
	9,360 ± 190 (TX-5629)	
	9,370 ± 160 (Y-1996)	
	9,570 ± 450 (Pta-004)	
	10,050 ± 160 (TX-5782)	
	11,820 ± 300 (TX-5631)	
	11,990 ± 270 (TX-5783)	
T (Transvaalian)	Tshangula	Cooke (1979), Vogel et al. (1986)
	8,560 ± 80 (Pta-2472)	
	9,760 ± 90 (Pta-2473)	
TL (Basutolian)	Tloutle	Mitchell (1993b)
	8,680 ± 70 (Pta-5172)	
TV (Basutolian)	Te Vrede	Opperman (1987)
	8,100 ± 80 (Pta-3204)	
	10,000 ± 120 (Pta-3203)	
U (Basutolian)	Uitkomst	Mason (1962)
	11,250 ± 200 (Y-1324)	
	9,844 ± 200 (Lab no. not given)	
	9,000 ± 200 (Lab no. not given)	
UMH (Transvaalian)	Umhlatuzana	Kaplan (1990)
	9,180 ± 90 (Pta-4307)	
	9,870 ± 90 (Pta-4631)	Note that this date is below one of >13,000 BP and therefore seems unlikely to be correct.
WK (Karoo-Namaqualian)	Wonderwerk	Humphreys and Thackeray (1983),
	8,000 ± 80 (Pta-3366)	Beaumont and Morris (1990),
	9,130 ± 90 (Pta-2546)	Wadley (1993)

(*continued*)

Table 1. (*Continued*)

Site abbreviation (ecozone[b])	Name and uncalibrated dates BP	References[c]
WK (Karoo-Namaqualian)	10,200 ± 90 (Pta-2786)	
(*Cont.*)	10,000 ± 70 (Pta-2790)	
	9,030 ± 90 (Pta-3439)	
	9,760 ± 120 (Pta-2852)	
	10,130 ± 110 (SI-2032B)	
	12,160 ± 115 (SI-3561)	
	12,370 ± 180 (Pta-3441)	
	12,380 ± 95 (Pta-2141)	
WT (Cape)	Wilton	J. Deacon (1972)
	8,260 ± 720 (GaK-1541)	
ZEB (Kalaharian)	Zebrarivier	Vogel and VIsser (1991)
	11,900 ± 90 (Pta-1996)	

The following sites are also mentioned in the text and located in Figure 1:

AN	Aliwal North	Coetzee (1967)
BL	Blydefontein	Bousman (1989)
GLT	Glentyre	Fagan (1960)
PC	Peers Cave	Rightmire (1984)
POC	Pockenbank	Freundlich et al. (1980), Vogel and Visser (1981), Wendt (1972)
WK	Wonderkrater	Scott (1982)

[a]Dates are listed in stratigraphic sequence within individual sites.
[b]Ecozone names are after De Vos (1975).
[c]Only the most essential references are given.

On the South Africa interior plateau, hundreds of open sites are included within the Lockshoek Industry as a further aspect of this nonmicrolithic tradition (Sampson 1974). Parkington (1984) argued against this interpretation, citing the presence of NBKs both in the Lockshoek and in some Robberg assemblages as a link between them and suggesting that the former is an interior contemporary of the latter, differing because of situational variability in raw material availability (hornfels in the interior and principally quartz toward the coast). The absence of distinctively Lockshoek assemblages in Lesotho, where hornfels is abundant, militates against this argument (Mitchell 1988), as do the few radiocarbon dates now available for the Lockshoek (Bousman 1989; Kuman and Clarke 1986).

Characteristic of terminal Pleistocene–early Holocene nonmicrolithic assemblages (J. Deacon 1984a: Figure 4) are the absence or extreme rarity of bladelet production and a shift toward using materials, often coarser-grained, that occur naturally in larger preforms (such as hornfels, quartzite, and sandstone); flakes are often sidestruck. Formal tools, especially backed microliths, remain rare, and scrapers, varied in form, are generally larger than before or later; a wider, more sophisticated range of bone tools is found at some sites (J. Deacon 1984b; Parkington 1986; Plug 1982). J. Deacon (1984a) notes that elongated end-scrapers with steep adze-like retouch down one or both lateral sides are prevalent in southern Cape assemblages after 9,000 BP; the same phenomenon is apparent in the northern Eastern Cape Province and Lesotho (Mitchell 1994; Opperman 1987), but is less common in the Western Cape Province at Byneskranskop (Schweitzer and Wilson 1982) and Elands Bay Cave. In all

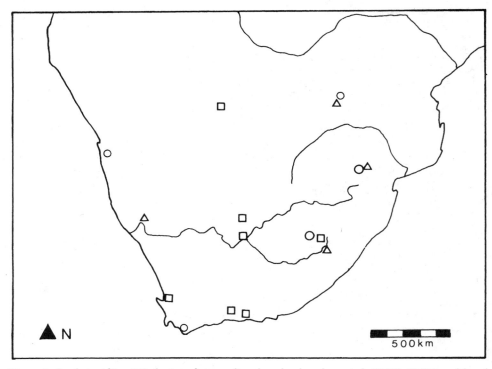

Figure 2. Southern Africa: Distribution of sites radiocarbon-dated to the periods 13,000–12,500 BP (O) and 12,500–12,000 BP (□). (△) Sites with dates for both periods.

these areas, however, the phenomenon signals a marked increase in the frequency and formality of retouched artifacts.

Across southern Africa, microlithic assemblages are found in the middle Holocene, but they appear before 8,000 BP at some sites. Overall patterning in associated dates is consistent with a north-to-south diffusion of a technology (J. Deacon 1984a: Figure 5) featuring increased use of finer-grained rocks, a marked increase in formal tool frequencies, and systematic production of backed microliths, especially segments, and smaller, often thumbnail-shaped scrapers. During the period under review, such assemblages, grouped within the Wilton Complex, are found in Zimbabwe (Cooke 1979; Walker 1980) and southern Namibia (Freundlich et al. 1980; Wendt 1972, 1976); only after 8,000 BP do they occur south of the Limpopo and Orange Rivers (J. Deacon 1984a: Table 2a).

SUBSISTENCE

Plant food availability in southern Africa varies between major biomes. In the Basutolian, Karoo-Namaqualian, and Cape ecozones, most are geophytes and have carbohydrate-rich underground storage organs. To the north, in the Transvaalian and Zambezian ecozones, fruiting trees provide the bulk of the plant foods within savanna vegetations. Geophyte exploitation is now documented in southern Africa before the LGM (Opperman 1992; Opperman and Heydenrych 1990), but after 13,000 BP, we begin to obtain increasing evidence for the human use of plant foods. Some of the best data come from the Transvaalian ecozone, where seeds of several later staples are preserved at Bushman Rock Shelter (Plug 1981; Wadley 1987), Heuningneskrans (Beaumont 1981), Kruger Cave (Mason 1988), and Umhlatuzana (Kaplan 1990); at Bushman Rock, the stratigraphic distributions of marula (*Sclerocarya birrea*) seeds and *Hypoxis* corms are mutually exclusive, suggesting a shift in diet as climate alternated between warmer and colder conditions (Wadley 1987). Other plant foods for which we have evidence are !nara melon seeds (*Acanthosicyos horrida*) at Zebrarivier and Mirabib, Namibia (Sandelowsky 1977; Wendt 1976), of which modern foragers eat both the flesh and the seeds, and several fruiting species at Byneskranskop in the Cape (Schweitzer and Wilson 1982). There is no direct evidence, however, for geophyte use in the Cape ecozone before 8,000 BP, despite their later importance. Increasingly refined recovery techniques (e.g., Hather 1991) may help assess whether this absence of evidence is genuine, though H. J. Deacon (1993) argues from the occurrence of sites in the Cape Fold Mountains and the stratigraphic makeup of individual excavated layers that people have exploited geophytes in this region from at least the Last Interglacial.

Faunal remains are generally much better preserved, and we have already commented on the trend from grazers to browsers in the Cape ecozone across the Pleistocene–Holocene boundary. While this trend seems relatively rapid at some sites (e.g., Boomplaas [Klein 1978]), at others browsers dominate only from 6,000 BP (e.g., Byneskranskop [Schweitzer and Wilson 1982] and possibly Melkhoutboom [H. J. Deacon 1976]). The shift to a diet in which meat was largely derived from hunting and trapping small bovids may thus have been a regionally variable phenomenon within the Cape, although a comparable change is evident in the Caledon Valley around 9,000 BP (Plug and Engela 1992; Mitchell 1993a). It can be discerned to a lesser degree in areas of greater environmental stability (Mpumalanga [Klein 1984a; Plug 1981]), but in the northern Eastern Cape Province, the shift in emphasis to small ungulates is a late Holocene phenomenon (Opperman 1987).

Much increased exploitation of r-selected animal resources (Jochim 1976) is visible at some sites during the period reviewed, particularly those on the modern coast. At EB, for example, the period 11,000–9,000 BP witnessed massively increased consumption of tortoises and ostrich eggs, the former so common that "pavements" of tortoise carapaces were noted in excavation (Parkington 1990). It is unclear whether the resumption of evidence in the archaeological record for the eating of shellfish and other marine foods (fish, rock lobsters, marine birds) is part of this same process or only a reflection of the regression of the shoreline so that some of our surviving samples of sites now occur at economically viable exploitation distances from the coast. Changes in sea levels, marine temperatures, salinity, and current strengths, however, will all have affected resource densities (Van Andel 1989), and it cannot be assumed that shellfish availability, for example, was as high during the Last Glacial as in the Holocene.

ART, PERSONAL ORNAMENT, AND BURIAL

While southern Africa's parietal art remains largely undated, painted spalls at sites in the Matopo Hills indicate that the tradition may extend back into the terminal Pleistocene, at least in this part of Zimbabwe (Walker 1987). Bearing in mind the possibility that spalls may migrate through deposits (cf. Richardson 1992), arguably more convincing evidence of the presence of art in our period comes from Wonderwerk, Northern Cape Province, where an engraved dolomite slab dating to 10,200 ± 90 BP (Pta-2786) depicts an unfinished mammal (A. I. Thackeray et al. 1981). More widely distributed are the fragments of ostrich eggshell incised with simple geometric patterns found at a number of sites, including Boomplaas (J. Deacon 1984b), Byneskranskop (Schweitzer and Wilson 1982), and Wonderwerk (Beaumont and Morris 1990).

Jewelry in various forms, but most typically as OES beads, is found increasingly in southern African sites from 13,000 BP onward, but occurs regularly only after 11,000–10,000 BP. Beads were also made from bone, and occasional bone pendants are known, as at Matjes River (Louw 1960). Increasing use of marine molluscs as ornaments is documented by, among other findings, a cowrie shell bead at Matjes River (Wadley 1993) and by the regular presence of *Nassarius kraussianus* beads and fragments of *Donax serra* shell at Boomplaas, 80 km inland, after 12,000 BP (J. Deacon 1984b). The most impressive evidence for long-distance movement of items during this period, however, is the presence of *Nassarius kraussianus* and *Nerita* sp. shell ornaments at sites in Lesotho that are 180–300 km from the Indian Ocean (Mitchell 1993a, 1996) and of marine shell fragments, including at least one pendant, at Apollo 11 in southern Namibia, 130 km or more inland of the Atlantic coast (Wendt 1972).

Human burials are unknown in southern Africa during the late Pleistocene, with the possible exception of one skeleton from Peers Cave near Cape Town (Rightmire 1978). Although most LSA burials are of middle or recent Holocene age, some older examples are known. Almost all are from rock shelters in the southern Cape coastal forelands, a spatial concentration remarked on by Inskeep (1986), which perhaps indicates that the processes responsible for it were already operating in the early Holocene (Hall and Binneman 1987). Relevant sites include Matjes River (Louw 1960), Oakhurst (Goodwin 1937; Inskeep 1986), Glentyre (J. Deacon 1979; Fagan 1960) and Wilton (J. Deacon 1972). Outside this area, the only known burials come from EB, Western Cape Province (Parkington 1992), and Nswatugi, Zimbabwe (Walker 1980); interestingly, the latter was covered with one or more stones or slabs, like that from Wilton and the majority of those at Oakhurst and Matjes River (Inskeep 1986:230). Grave goods are extremely rare in these early burials, but red ocher is associated with some of those from Oakhurst (Goodwin 1937) and Matjes River (Louw 1960).

CHANGES IN HUMAN SETTLEMENT PATTERNS, DEMOGRAPHY, AND INTERACTION

Using the available radiocarbon determinations, we have analyzed site distributions within each 500-year segment of the period reviewed (Figures 3–6). Even though deposits have not always been dated systematically through individual sequences, some sites (notably the many open sites of the Lockshoek Industry) are undated, and southern African radiocarbon determinations have not yet been calibrated, we believe this exercise is a useful first approximation to changes in regional demography across the Pleistocene–Holocene boundary. H. J. Deacon and Thackeray (1984), J. Deacon (1984a), and Wadley (1993) have all commented on the increase in dated sites that marks the period 13,000–12,000 BP relative

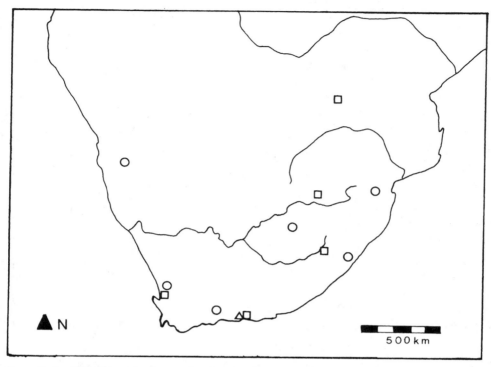

Figure 3. Southern Africa: Distribution of sites radiocarbon-dated to the periods 12,000–11,500 BP (○) and 11,500–11,000 BP (□). (△) Sites with dates for both periods.

to the several millennia between it and the LGM. Our closer analysis, however, suggests another "leap" in site numbers after 10,500 BP (Figure 7), perhaps coinciding with the end of the Younger Dryas; some areas, however (such as the Richtersveld in the northwestern Western Cape Province [Webley 1992]), remained unoccupied until the recent Holocene. Arguably, the total number of observations is too small to discuss the comparative advantages and disadvantages of particular regions, except to note that Mazel (1989) has proposed that only in the Holocene did hunter–gatherers, possibly moving inland from the more coastal parts of KwaZulu/Natal, colonize the Thukela Basin, and that the period after 10,500 BP is marked by a much more sustained occupation of the eastern half of the Basutolian eco-zone. H. J. Deacon (1993) has isolated plant staple distributions—correctly, we believe—as a key factor in understanding regional population histories, but we are still woefully ignorant of the climatic constraints operating on these species and have only an impressionistic understanding of precipitation levels. What we are seeing, however, is in general terms probably a combination of population increase and the infilling of a wider range of environments as biotic diversity increased and climate ameliorated from the Late Glacial on. Brooks and Robertshaw (1990) remind us that an additional factor may be changes in settlement strategy that resulted in increased archaeological visibility in some localities without concomitant changes in population numbers.

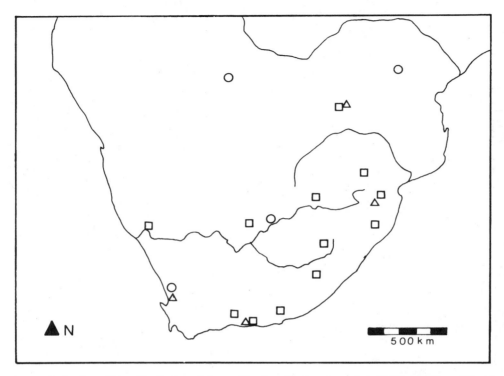

Figure 4. Southern Africa: Distribution of sites radiocarbon-dated to the periods 11,000–10,500 BP. (O) and 10,500–10,000 BP (□). (△) Sites with dates for both periods.

Within individual regions, settlement patterns appear to have been structured differently in the terminal Pleistocene–early Holocene than in the more recent Holocene. Thus, in the Phuthiatsana-ea-Thaba Bosiu Basin of western Lesotho, occupation between 12,000 and 5,000 BP focused on large rock shelters (Mitchell 1994). In the recent Holocene, a very different settlement signature is indicated by more ephemeral occupation of large shelters, coupled with widespread use of small overhangs and boulders that form rocky backdrops to surface artifact scatters. Larger group sizes and fewer residential shifts may perhaps be inferred for the pre–5,000 BP period. Results from the exhaustive survey by Sampson (1985a) of the Seacow Valley in South Africa's Karoo region also indicate differences between early (Lockshoek) and later Holocene settlement systems. The latter, attributed to the Interior Wilton Industry, is less closely tied to spring eyes, perhaps indicating greater use of OES water containers, and favors hillsides and ridge crests with commanding views; however, it still "best fits a model of circulating mobility from one waterpoint to the next" (Sampson 1985a:69). We return later to differences between late Pleistocene and Holocene patterns.

Down to circa 12,000 BP, similarities in artifact assemblages define three broad divisions across southern Africa: (1) In South Africa, Lesotho, and Swaziland, early microlithic

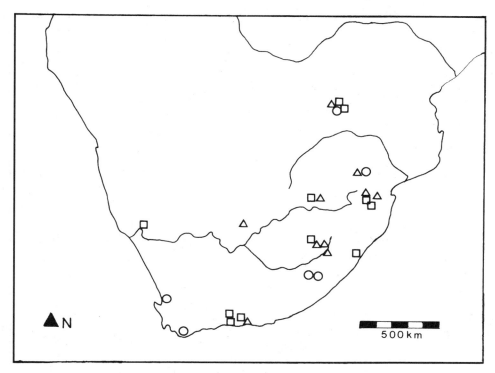

Figure 5. Southern Africa: Distribution of sites radiocarbon-dated to the periods 10,000–9,500 BP (○) and 9,500–9,000 BP (□). (△) Sites with dates for both periods.

assemblages share an emphasis on systematic bladelet production and a tendency to use quartz or other fine-grained rocks; (2) in southern Namibia, the Pockenbank and Apollo 11 assemblages are more macrolithic and lack any bladelet emphasis (Wendt 1972); (3) in Zimbabwe, the Maleme Industry, which has relict Middle Stone Age (MSA) features (Walker 1990), forms a third province. These three groupings define regions of interaction sharing common features of lithic technology and, by implication, methods and strategies of artifact production and use. They are, in the terms of Clarke (1968), "technocomplexes," but our limited number of observations makes it impossible as yet to detect lower-level groupings within them, other than those relating to a contrast between quartz-dominated and opaline-dominated bladelet-rich assemblages (Mitchell 1988). The deeply incised spirals common to bone ornaments from Bushman Rock Shelter (Plug 1982), Nelson Bay Cave, and Boomplaas (J. Deacon 1984b), but absent from Elands Bay Cave, at the end of the Pleistocene may be a further indicator of open, extended interaction networks (Wadley 1993) that facilitated coping with the constraints of reduced population densities and greater resource scarcity and unpredictability imposed by Last Glacial conditions.

We detect through the period reviewed a progressive trend toward greater regionalization of material culture. We have already noted that scrapers with adze-like lateral retouch

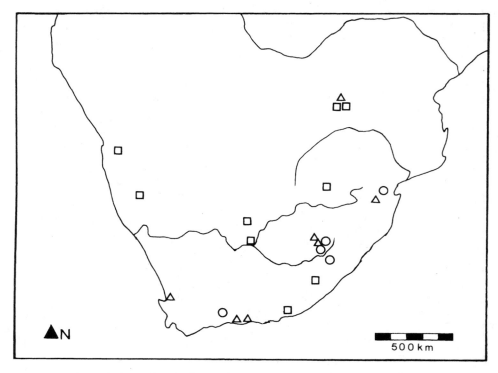

Figure 6. Southern Africa: Distribution of sites radiocarbon-dated to the periods 9,000–8,500 BP (○) and 8,500–8,000 BP (□). (△) Sites with dates for both periods.

are found in high numbers in Lesotho, the northern Eastern Cape Province, and the southern Cape after 9,000 BP and consider the distribution of this formally designed artifact type to be a potential indicator of one such social network. At a smaller scale, analysis of the movements of OES beads and seashells in southeastern southern Africa distinguishes the Thukela Basin, the Pietermaritzburg/Durban area, the Lesotho highlands, the northern Eastern Cape Province, and the eastern Free State (Mitchell 1996). Within some of these areas, the use of particular lithic materials was also emphasized, even though the various alternatives are all commonly available. For example, assemblages from both western and southeastern Lesotho between 9,500 BP and 8,000 BP are dominated by opalines, even though hornfels and dolerite are also widely available there. It is the latter or other coarse-grained rocks, however, that were preferred choices in the eastern Free State (Wadley and Vogel 1991) and the northern Eastern Cape Province (Opperman 1987); Mitchell and Vogel (1992), as well as Mazel (1989) in the Thukela Basin and Hall (1990) in the Eastern Cape Province, suggest that such choices were deliberate and used to signal social differences. Other trends, such as identical trajectories in mean OES bead size across the Pleistocene–Holocene boundary in sites as far apart as Elands Bay Cave (Western Cape Province) and Sehonghong (Lesotho), suggest continued far-reaching interactions, which we are only beginning to explore.

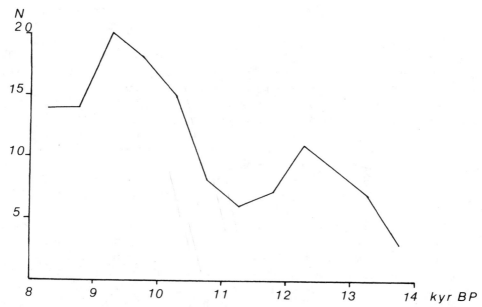

Figure 7. Southern Africa: Frequency distribution of sites dating to the period 13,000–8,000 BP. Only one radiocarbon determination per 500 years is used for each site.

DISCUSSION

The study by H. J. Deacon (1972) of post-Pleistocene adaptations initiated the modern examination of changes in southern Africa's archaeological record across the Pleistocene–Holocene boundary. In that study and elsewhere (e.g., H. J. Deacon 1976), he drew a distinction between late Pleistocene and Holocene adaptations: The former, with a subsistence economy based on hunting large, migratory game, was correlated with low population densities, large group sizes, long-distance residential shifts, and an absence of territoriality; the latter, linked to a subsistence base stressing plant foods and small game, was correlated with the reverse of this pattern. Cultural change was conceptualized cybernetically, with each of the three successive industries recognized in the Eastern Cape Province (the Robberg, Albany, and Wilton) described as a homeostatic plateau, within which changes were minor and self-regulating; briefer episodes of more rapid positive feedback and structural change separated the plateaus (H. J. Deacon 1976). While the position of the Albany, a third industry within an essentially dichotomous subsistence–settlement model, was anomalous (Parkington 1980:81), the emphasis placed upon links between technology, subsistence, social organization, and environmental change significantly affected subsequent research.

Addressing the relationship between cultural change and environmental shifts, the analysis by Janette Deacon (1984b) of the artifact sequences from three southern Cape sites demonstrated that the replacement of a Robberg technology by the Albany Industry occurred some 2000 years *after* the onset of post-LGM climatic amelioration. Positing a connection with the shift from an economy based on hunting large game to one in which smaller bovids, and other resources, became increasingly important, she essentially pushed backward the contrast between Pleistocene and Holocene adaptations previously mentioned. Her argument was more subtle, however, in that, borrowing from the ideas of Deetz (1977) about the "deep structure" of a culture, she argued against any directly functional explanation and in favor of shifts in lithic assemblages (e.g., scraper and flake size) being indicators of the "social stress" produced by adaptations to changing environmental circumstances (J. Deacon 1984b). More recently, Ambrose and Lorenz (1990:24) have placed the Robberg–Albany transition in a broader theoretical and comparative framework, arguing that the shifts in raw material usage between the two indicate a breakdown of a nonlocal lithic resource procurement system "as mobility and exchange decreased, and possibly as territoriality increased in response to resource-base enrichment at the Pleistocene/Holocene boundary"; they propose that a wide range of locally available rocks were increasingly used instead.

Not fully taken on board by these models are the discontinuous nature of our stratigraphic sequences (Parkington 1980; Sampson 1985b), which automatically enhances the contrasts between compared assemblages, and the scale, both spatial and temporal, at which observations are made and explanations formulated. Thus, in critiquing the J. Deacon (1984b) model of the Robberg–Albany transition, Mitchell (1988) argued that a model linking faunal and technological change in the southern Cape, even if valid there, could not account for the *subcontinent-wide* disappearance of a bladelet-rich microlithic technology circa 12,000 BP, given that data from other regions (Klein 1984a; Opperman 1987) did not support the case for major faunal change, but yet showed a similar pattern of technological reorganization. Instead, he suggested that the introduction of the bow and arrow as a replacement for multibarbed spears might account for the widespread, rapid disappearance of bladelet technology and proliferation of bone points at this time, while recognizing that this disappearance left other changes in lithic technology unexplained (Mitchell 1988). The much fuller model of Ambrose and Lorenz (1990) attempts to combat this problem, but we lack detailed evidence as to which raw materials are truly "exotic" and over what distances they were obtained (compare J. Deacon [1984b] with Inskeep [1987]). More far-reachingly, the call by H. J. Deacon (1993) for reassessment of the previously underemphasized role of plant foods in late Pleistocene diets suggests that differences from Holocene foragers in group size and territorial behavior may have been overdramatized. Contrary to the implications of some syntheses (e.g., Wadley 1993), we even lack hard evidence (e.g., from taphonomic studies) that pre-9,000 BP faunas dominated by large game *do* derive from hunting. Nor do we know how, if at all, Robberg–Oakhurst and MSA hunters differed in hunting strategies or technologies; the date at which the bow and arrow came into use also continues to elude us.

The Elands Bay Cave sequence has been the subject of a markedly different kind of explanation. Eschewing cultural labels, Parkington (1986, 1987, 1990, 1992) emphasizes how interlocking shifts in lithic assemblages, the frequency and variety of OES and bone artifacts, the introduction of marine foods, and other variables document the rescheduling of the role of this site within a broader settlement system as it moved from expedient short-term use (perhaps as a largely male-occupied hunting station) to home-base status. Viewing these changes within a model of "place" (Parkington 1980) lays greater stress on underlying continuities in cultural systems, especially stone tool assemblages; we think here particularly of the more informal nature of Robberg *and* Oakhurst technologies compared to that of the Wilton. If we seek the emergence of a new cultural system within the southern African LSA, then arguably it is to the adoption of a microlithic technology that regularly produces formal tools *and* is associated with a much greater variety of material culture, possibly signifying the adoption of a recognizably modern pattern of seasonal aggregation and dispersal (Wadley 1987), that we should look (cf. Humphreys and Thackeray 1983); perhaps the appearance of formally designed scrapers circa 9,000 BP (J. Deacon 1984a; Mitchell 1994) marks the beginning of this trend before the latter adoption of segments as arrow or knife armatures.

A "change of place" model for the EB sequence, while potentially generalizable to other present-day coastal sites, still makes it difficult to account for similar social and technological changes at the broader southern African scale. This is the first point we wish to stress: We need to begin distinguishing those changes and variables that are of local or regional significance from those that are subcontinental in scale and seek explanations that take these differences into account. In so doing, we shall doubtless find, as the Annalistes and others have argued (Bailey 1983; Braudel 1972), that different processes are most in evidence at different spatiotemporal scales (cf. H. J. Deacon 1980; Parkington 1980). The possibility that bladelet technology persisted well after 12,000 BP in the southeast of the subcontinent provides one important example of spatial variation in cultural process that would require explanation; equally, this possibility may be a product of "sample error" in research coverage and dating programs or of differences in the resolution with which cultural–stratigraphic units are defined elsewhere. It thus also emphasizes the need for much more basic fieldwork.

Largely because of advances in rock art research pioneered by David Lewis-Williams (1981), Stone Age archaeology in southern Africa has shifted increasingly over the past decade toward a concern with social processes and a historical–materialist explanatory framework. Both Wadley (1987, 1993) and J. Deacon (1990) take up these points in commenting on the Pleistocene–Holocene transition. Seasonal aggregation and dispersal and the different sociostructural poses characterizing these phases, as well as the practice of reciprocal gift exchange (*hxaro*), are seen as central to San gatherer–hunter social relations. Wadley (1987) has identified them in mid-Holocene Wilton contexts, but they become increasingly difficult to trace further backward in time. The comparatively small number of bone points and beads (popular contemporary *hxaro* gifts) in Robberg assemblages may indicate that gift exchange was only weakly developed, or absent, in the late Pleistocene, becoming more common, possibly as an information-sharing aid and economic insurance policy for territorial expansion and recolonization, after 12,000 BP (cf. Gamble 1982). Similarly, aggregation/dispersal is difficult to establish in Robberg sites, which show no sign of such differentiation (but how many have been excavated on a sufficiently large scale?) and are restricted to widely dispersed rock shelters. The site of Faraoskop, Western Cape Province (Manhire 1993), does show, however, that not only large shelters were used in the late Pleistocene. The appearance of a much wider variety of sites, including open-air locations, by 12,000 BP may thus help document social relations more similar to those of modern San (J. Deacon 1990; Wadley 1993), though Lewis-Williams (1984), discussing the much older Apollo 11 art (Wendt 1976), argues for ideological continuity among southern African hunters–gatherers over at least the last 26,000 years; we agree with Mazel (1989) that this latter claim requires much fuller substantiation than is at present available. Furthermore, while accepting that the *surviving* Robberg settlement pattern is quite different from that of the Holocene, we must also be aware that all pre–10,000 BP settlement patterns close to the modern coast are probably partial remnants of systems that once included now-drowned locations (Parkington 1990). As such, they cannot represent the full range of activities or sites, and if we wish to contrast late Pleistocene and Holocene settlement more effectively, we should focus on areas such as the eastern Transvaal or the southern Drakensberg, where sea-level changes had little or no impact.

Linking back to our earlier comments on explaining change without resorting to the use of cultural labels (cf. Inskeep 1967), the adoption of this "historical narrative" alternative requires a shift in archaeological methodology toward the recovery of more finely resolved spatiotemporal patterning and the handling of small samples. The extent of our success in attempting this for the Pleistocene–Holocene boundary remains to be seen, but it seems a precondition for successfully tackling those models that "situate the motivation for change in the social rather than the ecological realm" (Parkington 1993:96). It should be factored into future research strategies that seek to fill many of the blanks (geographic and chronological) still present on the archaeological map of southern Africa between 13,000 BP and 8,000 BP as well as into those that aim to assess the validity of the explanations already advanced. In both respects, as well as in refining our still broad-brush palaeoenvironmental knowledge, hunter–gatherer archaeology in our region stands at its own transition.

ACKNOWLEDGMENTS

We would like to thank R. Inskeep, N. Barton, and L. Straus for their reading of a first draft of this paper and C. Mitchell for help with references. Grants from the British Academy, the Prehistoric Society, and the University of Wales made possible participation in the Symposium on the Archaeology of the Pleistocene–Holocene Transition at the 1994 meeting of the Society for American Archaeology, at which this chapter was first presented.

REFERENCES

Ambrose, S. H., and Lorenz, K., 1990, Social and Ecological Models for the Middle Stone Age in Southern Africa, in: *The Emergence of Modern Humans* (P. Mellars, ed.), Edinburgh University Press, Edinburgh, pp. 3–33.

Avery, D. M., 1982, Micromammals as Palaeoenvironmental Indicators and an Interpretation of the Late Quaternary in the Southern Cape Province, *Annals of the South African Museum* 85:185–374.

Bailey, G. N., 1983, Concepts of Time in Quaternary Prehistory, *Annual Review of Anthropology* 12:165–192.

Barham, L. S., 1989a, A Preliminary Report on the Later Stone Age Artifacts from Siphiso Shelter in Swaziland, *South African Archaeological Bulletin* 44:33–43.

Barham, L. S., 1989b, Radiocarbon Dates from Nyonyane Shelter, Swaziland, *South African Archaeological Bulletin* 44:117–118.

Beaumont, P. B., 1981, The Heuningneskrans Shelter, in: *Guide to Archaeological Sites in the Northern and Eastern Transvaal* (E. A. Voight, ed.), Southern African Association of Archaeologists, Pretoria, pp. 133–145.

Beaumont, P. B., and Morris, D., 1990, *Guide to Archaeological Sites in the Northern Cape*, McGregor Museum, Kimberly, South Africa.

Beaumont, P. B., and Vogel, J. C., 1972, On a New Radiocarbon Chronology for Africa South of the Equator, Parts 1 and 2, *African Studies* 31:66–89, 155–181.

Beaumont, P. B., Van Zinderen Bakker, E. M., and Vogel, J. C., 1984, Environmental Changes since 32,000 BP at Kathu Pan, Northern Cape, in: *Late Cainozoic Palaeoclimates of the Southern Hemisphere* (J. C. Vogel, ed.), A. A. Balkema, Rotterdam, pp. 329–338.

Bousman, B., 1989, Implications of Dating the Lockshoek Industry from the Interior Plateau of Southern Africa, *Nyame Akuma* 32:30–33.

Braudel, F., 1972, *The Mediterranean World in the Age of Philip II*, Collins, London.

Brooks, A. S., and Robertshaw, P., 1990, The Glacial Maximum in Tropical Africa: 22,000 to 14,000 BP, in: *The World at 18,000 BP*, Volume 2, Low Latitudes (C. Gamble and O. Soffer, eds.), Unwin Hyman, London, pp. 121–169.

Brown, A. J. V., and Verhagen, B. T., 1985, Two *Antidorcas bondi* Individuals from the Late Stone Age Site of Kruger Cave 35/83, Olifantsnek, Rustenburg District, South Africa, *South African Journal of Science* 81:102.

Cable, J. H. C., Scott, K., and Cater, P. L., 1980, Excavations at Good Hope Shelter, Underberg District, Natal, *Annals of the Natal Museum* 24:1–34.

Carter, P. L., and Vogel, J. C., 1974, The Dating of Industrial Assemblages from Stratified Sites in Eastern Lesotho, *Man* 9:557–570.

Carter, P. L., Mitchell, P. J., and Vinnicombe, P., 1988, *Sehonghong: The Middle and Later Stone Age Industrial Sequence from a Lesotho Rock-Shelter*, British Archaeological Reports, Oxford.

Churcher, C. S., and Richardson, M. L., 1978, Equidae, in: *Evolution of African Mammals* (V. J. Maglio and H. B. S. Cooke, eds.). Harvard University Press, Cambridge, pp. 379–422.

Clarke, D. L., 1968, *Analytical Archaeology*, Methuen, London.

Coetzee, J. A., 1967, Pollen Analytical Studies in East and Southern Africa, *Palaeoecology of Africa* 3:1–146.

Cohen, A. L., Parkington, J. E., Brundrit, G. B., and Van der Merwe, N. J., 1992, A Holocene Marine Climatic Record in Mollusc Shells for the Southwestern African Coast, *Quaternary Research* 38:379–385.

Cooke, C. K., 1979, Excavations at Diana's Vow Rock Shelter, Makoni District, Zimbabwe, Rhodesia, *Occasional Papers of the National Museum of Rhodesia A* 4:115–148.

Dart, R., and Beaumont, P. B., 1968, Ratification and Retrocession of Earlier Swaziland Iron Ore Mining Radiocarbon Dates, *South African Journal of Science* 63:264–267.

Davies, O., 1975, Excavations at Shongweni South Cave, *Annals of the Natal Museum* 22:627–662.

Deacon, H. J., 1972. A Review of the Post-Pleistocene in South Africa, *South African Archaeological Society Goodwin Series* 1:26–45.

Deacon, H. J., 1976, Where Hunters Gathered: A Study of Holocene Stone Age People in the Eastern Cape, *South African Archaeological Society Monograph Series* 1:1–231.

Deacon, H. J., 1980, Comment on Time and Place: Some Observations on Spatial and Temporal Patterning in the Later Stone Age Sequence in Southern Africa, *South African Archaeological Bulletin* 35:86–88.

Deacon, H. J., 1993, Planting an Idea: An Archaeology of Stone Age Gatherers in South Africa, *South African Archaeological Bulletin* 48:86–93.

Deacon, H. J., and Thackeray, J. F., 1984, Late Quaternary Environmental Changes and Implications for the Archaeological Record in Southern Africa, in: *Late Cainozoic Palaeoclimates of the Southern Hemisphere* (J. C. Vogel, ed.), A. A. Balkema, Rotterdam, pp. 375–390.

Deacon, H. J., Deacon, J., Scholtz, A., Thackeray, J. F., Brink, J. S., and Vogel, J. C., 1984, Correlation of Palaeoenvironmental Data from the Late Pleistocene and Holocene Deposits at Boomplaas Cave, Southern Cape, in: *Late Cainozoic Palaeoclimates of the Southern Hemisphere* (J. C. Vogel, ed.), A. A. Balkema, Rotterdam, pp. 339–352.

Deacon, J., 1972, Wilton: An Assessment after 50 years, *South African Archaeological Bulletin* 27:10–45.

Deacon, J., 1979, *A Guide to Archaeological Sites in the Southern Cape*, University of Stellenbosch, Stellenbosch, South Africa.

Deacon, J., 1984a, Later Stone Age People and Their Descendants in Southern Africa, in: *Southern African Palaeoenvironments and Prehistory* (R. G. Klein, ed.), A. A. Balkema, Rotterdam, pp. 221–328.

Deacon, J., 1984b, The Later Stone Age of Southernmost Africa, British Archaeological Report, Oxford.

Deacon, J., 1990, Changes in the Archaeological Record in South Africa at 18,000 BP, in: *The World at 18,000 BP*, Volume 2, *Low Latitudes* (C. Gamble and O. Soffer, eds.), Unwin Hyman, London, pp. 171–188.

Deacon, J., and Lancaster, N., 1988, *Late Quaternary Palaeoenvironments of Southern Africa*, Clarendon Press, Oxford.

Deetz, J., 1977, *In Small Things Forgotten: The Archaeology of Early American Life*, Doubleday, New York.

De Vos, A., 1975, *Africa, The Devastated Continent?* W. Junk, The Hague.

Dingle, R. V., and Rogers, J., 1972, Effects of Sea-Level Changes on the Pleistocene Palaeoecology of the Agulhas Bank, *Palaeoecology of Africa* 6:55–58.

Dowson, T. A., 1988, Shifting Vegetation Zones in the Holocene and Later Pleistocene: Preliminary Charcoal Evidence from Jubilee Shelter, Magaliesberg, Southern Transvaal, *Palaeoecology of Africa* 19:233–239.

Esterhuysen, A. B., and Mitchell, P. J., in press, Palaeoenvironmental and Archaeological Implications of Charcoal Assemblages from Holocene Sites in Western Lesotho, Southern Africa, *Palaeoecology of Africa* (submitted).

Fagan, B. M., 1960, The Glentyre Shelter and Oakhurst Re-examined, *South African Archaeological Bulletin* 15:80–94.

Fairhall, A. W., Young, A. W., and Erickson, J. L., 1976, University of Washington Dates IV, *Radiocarbon* 18:221–239.

Freundlich, J. C., Schwabedissen, H., and Wendt, W. E., 1980, Köln Radiocarbon Measurements II, *Radiocarbon* 22:68–81.

Gamble, C., 1982, Interaction and Alliance in Palaeolithic Society, *Man (NS)* 17:92–107.

Goodwin, A. J. H., 1937, Archaeology of the Oakhurst Shelter, George. Parts 1 and 2, *Transactions of the Royal Society of South Africa* 25:229–257.

Goodwin, A. J. H., and Van Riet Lowe, C., 1929, The Stone Age Cultures of South Africa, *Annals of the South African Museum* 27:1–289.

Hall, S. L., 1990, *Hunter–Gatherer–Fishers of the Fish River Basin: A Contribution to the Holocene Prehistory of Eastern Cape.* Unpublished Ph.D. thesis, University of Stellenbosch, Stellenbosch, South Africa.

Hall, S. L., and Binneman, J. N. F., 1987, Later Stone Age Burial Variability in the Cape: A Social Interpretation, *South African Archaeological Bulletin* 42:140–152.

Hather, J., 1991, The Identification of Charred Archaeological Remains of Vegetative Parenchymatous Tissues, *Journal of Archaeological Science* 18:661–675.

Humphreys, A. J. B., 1974, A Preliminary Report on Test Excavations at Dikbosch Shelter I, Herbert District, Northern Cape, *South African Archaeological Bulletin* 29:115–119.

Humphreys, A. J. B., and Thackeray, A. I., 1983, Ghaap and Gariep: Later Stone Age Studies in the Northern Cape, *South Africa Archaeological Society Monograph Series* 2:1–328.

Inskeep, R. R., 1967, The Late Stone Age, in: *Background to Evolution in Africa* (W. W. Bishop and J. D. Clark, eds.), Chicago University Press, Chicago, pp. 557–582.

Inskeep, R. R., 1978, *The Peopling of Southern Africa*, David Philip, Cape Town.

Inskeep, R. R., 1986, A Preliminary Survey of Burial Practices in the Later Stone Age, from the Orange River to the Cape Coast, in: *Variation, Culture and Evolution in African Populations* (R. Singer and J. K. Lundy, eds.), University of the Witwatersrand Press, Johannesburg, pp. 221–240.

Inskeep, R. R., 1987, *Nelson Bay Cave, Cape Province, South Africa*, British Archaeological Reports, Oxford.

Jochim, M. A., 1976, *Hunter–gatherer Settlement and Subsistence*, Academic Press, London.

Kaplan, J., 1990, The Umhlatuzana Rock Shelter Sequence: 100,000 Years of Stone Age History, *Natal Museum Journal of Humanities* 2:1–94.

Klein, R. G., 1972, The Late Quaternary Mammalian Fauna of Nelson Bay Cave (Cape Province, South Africa): Its Implications for Megafaunal Extinctions and Environmental and Cultural Change, *Quaternary Research* 2:135–142.

Klein, R. G., 1978, A Preliminary Report on the Larger Mammals from the Boomplaas Stone Age Cave Site, Cango Valley, Oudtshoorn District, South Africa, *South African Archaeological Bulletin* 33:66–75.

Klein, R. G., 1980, Environmental and Ecological Implications of Large Mammals from Upper Pleistocene and Holocene Sites in Southern Africa, *Annals of the South African Museum* 81:223–283.

Klein, R. G., 1984a, Later Stone Age Faunal Samples from Heuningneskrans Shelter, Transvaal, and Leopard's Hill Cave, Zambia, *South African Archaeological Bulletin* 39:109–116.

Klein, R. G., 1984b, Mammalian Extinctions and Stone Age People in Africa, in: *Quaternary Extinctions: A Prehistoric Revolution* (P. S. Martin and R. G. Klein, eds.), Arizona University Press, Tucson, pp. 553–573.

Klein, R. G., 1991, Size Variation in the Cape Dune Molerat (*Bathyergus suillus*) and Late Quaternary Climatic Change in the Southwestern Cape Province, South Africa, *Quaternary Research* 36:243–256.

Klein, R. G., and Cruz-Uribe, K., 1987, Large Mammal and Tortoise Bones from Eland's Bay Cave and Nearby Sites, Western Cape Province, South Africa, in: *Papers in the Prehistory of the Western Cape* (J. E. Parkington and M. Hall, eds.), British Archaeological Reports, Oxford, pp. 132–163.

Kuman, K., and Clarke, R., 1986, Florisbad—New Investigations at a Middle Stone Age Hominid Site in South Africa, *Geoarchaeology* 1:103–125.

Lewis-Williams, J. D., 1981, *Believing and Seeing: Symbolic Meanings in Southern San Rock Paintings.* Academic Press, London.

Lewis-Williams, J. D., 1984, Ideological Continuities in Prehistoric Southern Africa: The Evidence of Rock Art, in: *Past and Present in Hunter-Gatherer Studies* (C. Shrire, ed.), Academic Press, Orlando, FL, pp. 225–251.

Louw, J. T., 1960, The Prehistory of the Matjes River Shelter, *Memoirs of the National Museum, Bloemfontein* 1:1–143.

Manhire, A., 1993, A Report on the Excavations of Faraoskop Rock-Shelter in the Graafwater District of the South-Western Cape, *Southern African Field Archaeology* 2:2–23.

Mason, R. J., 1962, *Prehistory of the Transvaal*, University of the Witwatersrand Press, Johannesburg.

Mason, R. J., 1988, *Kruger Cave*, Archaeological Research Unit Occasional Paper 17, University of the Witwatersrand, Johannesburg.

Mazel, A. D., 1988, Sikhanyisweni Shelter: Report on Excavations in the Thukela Basin, Natal, South Africa, *Annals of the Natal Museum* 29:379–406.

Mazel, A. D., 1989, People Making History: The last 10,000 Years of Hunter–Gatherer Communities in the Thukela Basin, *Natal Museum Journal of Humanities* 1:1–168.

Mellars, P. A., 1990, A Major "Plateau" in the Radiocarbon Time-Scale at *c.* 9650 BP: The Evidence from Star Carr (North Yorkshire), *Antiquity* 64:836–841.

Mitchell, P. J., 1988, *The Early Microlithic Assemblages of Southern Africa*, British Archaeological Reports, Oxford.

Mitchell, P. J., 1992, Last Glacial Maximum Hunter–Gatherers in Southern Africa as an Example of a High-Technology Foraging System, unpublished paper presented to the Conference of the Society of Africanist Archaeologists, Los Angeles.

Mitchell, P. J., 1993a, Archaeological Investigations at Two Lesotho Rock-Shelters: The Terminal Pleistocene/Early Holocene Assemblages from Ha Makotoko and Ntloana Tsoana, *Proceedings of the Prehistoric Society* 59:39–60.

Mitchell, P. J., 1993b, The Archaeology of Tloutle Rock-Shelter, Maseru District, Lesotho, *Navorsinge van die Nasionale Museum, Bloemfontein* 9:77–132.

Mitchell, P. J., 1994, The Archaeology of the Phuthiatsana-ea-Thaba Bosiu Basin, Western Lesotho, Southern Africa: Changes in Later Stone Age Regional Demography, *Antiquity* 68:83–96.

Mitchell, P. J., 1996, Marine Shells and Ostrich Eggshell as Indicators of Prehistoric Exchange and Interaction in South-Eastern Southern Africa, *African Archaeological Review* 13:35–76.

Mitchell, P. J., and Vogel, J. C., 1992, Implications of Recent Radiocarbon Dates from Western Lesotho, *South African Journal of Science* 88:175–176.

Mitchell, P. J., and Vogel, J. C., 1994, New Radiocarbon Dates from Sehonghong Rock Shelter, Lesotho, *South African Journal of Science* 90:284–288.

Mitchell, P. J., Parkington, J. E., and Yates, R., 1994, The Recent Holocene Archaeology of Southern and Western Lesotho, *South African Archaeological Bulletin* 49:33–52.

Opperman, H., 1978, Excavations in the Buffelskloof Rock Shelter near Calitzdorp, Southern Cape, *South African Archaeological Bulletin* 33:18–28.

Opperman, H., 1987, *The Later Stone Age of the Drakensberg Range and Its Foothills*, British Archaeological Reports, Oxford.

Opperman, H., 1992, A Report on the Results of a Test Pit in Strathalan Cave B, Maclear District, North-Eastern Cape, *Southern African Field Archaeology* 1:98–102.

Opperman, H., and Heydenrych, B., 1990, A 22,000 year-old Middle Stone Age Camp Site with Plant Food Remains from the North-Eastern Capes, *South African Archaeological Bulletin* 45:93–99.

Parkington, J. E., 1977, *Follow the San*, unpublished Ph.D. thesis. University of Cambridge.

Parkington, J. E., 1980, Time and Place: Some Observations on Spatial and Temporal Patterning in the Later Stone Age Sequence in Southern Africa, *South African Archaeological Bulletin* 35:73–83.

Parkington, J. E., 1984, Changing Views of the Later Stone Age of South Africa, *Advances in World Archaeology* 3:89–142.

Parkington, J. E., 1986, Landscape and Subsistence Changes since the Last Glacial Maximum along the Western Cape Coast, in: *The End of the Palaeolithic in the Old World* (L. G. Straus, ed.), British Archaeological Reports, Oxford, pp. 201–227.

Parkington, J. E., 1987, Prehistory and Palaeoenvironments at the Pleistocene–Holocene Boundary in the Western Cape, in: *The Pleistocene Old World—Regional Perspectives* (O. Soffer, ed.), Academic Press, New York, pp. 343–363.

Parkington, J. E., 1990, A View from the South: Southern Africa before, during and after the Last Glacial Maximum, in: *The World at 18,000 BP, Volume 2, Low Latitudes* (C. Gamble and O. Soffer, eds.), Unwin Hyman, London, pp. 214–228.

Parkington, J. E., 1992, Making Sense of Sequence at the Elands Bay Cave, Western Cape, South Africa, in: *Guide to Archaeological Sites in the South-western Cape* (A. B. Smith and B. Mütti, eds.), Southern African Association of Archaeologists, Cape Town, pp. 6–12.

Parkington, J. E., 1993, The Neglected Alternative: Historical Narrative Rather than Cultural Labelling, *South African Archaeological Bulletin* 48:94–97.

Patrick, M. K., 1989, An Archaeological and Anthropological Study of the Human Skeletal Remains from the Oakhurst Rockshelter, George, Cape Province, Southern Africa, unpublished M.A. thesis, University of Cape Town.

Peters, J., Gautier, A., Brink, J. S., and Haenen, W., 1994, Late Quaternary Extinction of Ungulates in Sub-Saharan Africa: A Reductionist's Approach, *Journal of Archaeological Science* 21:17–28.

Plug, I., 1981, Some Research Results on the Late Pleistocene and Early Holocene Deposits of Bushman Rock Shelter, Eastern Transvaal, *South African Archaeological Bulletin* 36:14–21.

Plug, I., 1982, Bone Tools and Shell, Bone and Ostrich Egg Shell Beads from Bushman Rock Shelter (BRS), Eastern Transvaal, *South African Archaeological Bulletin* 37:57–62.

Plug, I., and Engela, R., 1992, The Macrofaunal Remains from Recent Excavations at Rose Cottage Cave, Orange Free State, *South African Archaeological Bulletin* 47:16–25.

Poggenpoel, C., 1987, The Implications of Fish Bone Assemblages from Eland's Bay Cave, Tortoise Cave and Diepkloof for Changes in the Holocene History of the Verlorenvlei, in: *Papers in the Prehistory of the Western Cape* (J. E. Parkington and M. Hall, eds.), British Archaeological Reports, Oxford, pp. 212–236.

Prior, J., and Price-Williams, D., 1985, An Investigation of Climatic Change in the Holocene Epoch using Archaeological Charcoal from Swaziland, Southern Africa, *Journal of Archaeological Science* 12:457–475.

Richardson, N., 1992, Conjoin Sets and Stratigraphic Integrity in a Sandstone Shelter: Kenniff Cave (Queensland, Australia), *Antiquity* 66:408–419.

Rightmire, G. P., 1978, Human Skeletal Remains from the Southern Cape Province and Their Bearing on the Stone Age Prehistory of South Africa, *Quaternary Research* 9:219–230.

Robbins, L. H., 1990, The Depression Site: A Stone Age Sequence in the Northwest Kalahari Desert, Botswana, *National Geographic Research* 6:329–338.

Sampson, C. G., 1974, *The Stone Age Archaeology of Southern Africa*, Academic Press, New York.

Sampson, C. G., 1985a, Atlas of Stone Age Settlement in the Central and Upper Seacow Valley, *Memoirs of the National Museum, Bloemfontein* 18:1–110.

Sampson, C. G., 1985b, Review Article of Janette Deacon's 1984 The Later Stone Age in Southernmost Africa, *South African Archaeological Bulletin* 40:56–68.

Sandelowsky, B. N., 1977, Mirabib: An Archaeological Study in the Namib, *Madoqua* 10:221–283.

Scholtz, A., 1986, Palynological and Palaeobotanical Studies in the Southern Cape, unpublished MA thesis, University of Stellenbosch.

Schrire, C., 1962, Oakhurst: A Re-examination and Vindication, *South African Archaeological Bulletin* 17:181–195.

Schweitzer, F. R., and Wilson, M. L., 1982, Byneskranskop 1: A Late Quaternary Living site in the Southern Cape Province, South Africa, *Annals of the South African Museum* 88:1–203.

Scott, L., 1982, A Late Quaternary Pollen Record from the Transvaal Bushveld, South Africa, *Quaternary Research* 17:339–370.

Scott, L., 1984, Palynological Evidence for Quaternary Palaeoclimates in Southern Africa, in: *Southern African Palaeoenvironments and Prehistory* (R. G. Klein, ed.), A. A. Balkema, Rotterdam, pp. 65–80.

Scott, L., 1986, Pollen Analysis and Palaeoenvironmental Interpretation of Late Quaternary Sediment Exposures in the Eastern Orange Free State, South Africa, *Palaeoecology of Africa* 17:113–170.

Scott, L., 1989, Climatic Conditions in Southern Africa since the Last Glacial Maximum, Inferred from Pollen Analysis, *Palaeoclimatology, Palaeogeography, Palaeoecology* 70:375–383.

Sealy, J., and Yates, R., 1994, The Chronology of the Introduction of Pastoralism to the Cape, South Africa, *Antiquity* 68:58–67.

Singer, R., and Inskeep, R. R., 1961, Review: Prehistory of the Matjes River Rock Shelter by J. T. Louw (1960), *South African Archaeological Bulletin* 16:29–31.

Thackeray, A. I., Thackeray, J. F., Beaumont, P. B., and Vogel, J. C., 1981, Dated Rock Engravings from Wonderwerk Cave, South Africa, *Science* 214:64–67.

Thackeray, J. F., 1979, An Analysis of Faunal Remains from Archaeological Sites in Southern South West Africa (Namibia), *South African Archaeological Bulletin* 34:18–33.

Thackeray, J. F., 1987, Late Quaternary Environmental Changes Inferred from Small Mammalian Fauna, Southern Africa, *Climatic Change* 10:285–305.

Tusenius, M. L., 1989, Charcoal Analytical Studies in the North-Eastern Cape, South Africa, *South African Archaeological Society Goodwin Series* 6:77–83.

Van Andel, T. H., 1989, Late Pleistocene Sea Levels and the Human Exploitation of the Shore and Shelf of Southern South Africa, *Journal of Field Archaeology* 16:133–155.

Vogel, J. C., 1970, Groningen Radiocarbon Dates IX, *Radiocarbon* 12:444–471.

Vogel, J. C., and Visser, E., 1981, Pretoria Radiocarbon Dates II, *Radiocarbon* 23:43–80.

Vogel, J. C., Fuls, A., and Visser, E., 1986, Pretoria Radiocarbon Dates III, *Radiocarbon* 28:1133–1172.

Wadley, L., 1987, *Later Stone Age Hunters and Gatherers of the Southern Transvaal: Social and Ecological Interpretations*, British Archaeological Reports, Oxford.

Wadley, L., 1991, Rose Cottage Cave: Background and a Preliminary Report on the Recent Excavations, *South African Archaeological Bulletin* 46:125–130.

Wadley, L., 1993, The Pleistocene Later Stone Age South of the Limpopo River, *Journal of World Prehistory* 7: 243–296.

Wadley, L., and Vogel, J. C., 1991, New Dates from Rose Cottage Cave, Ladybrand, Eastern Orange Free State, *South African Journal of Science* 87:605–608.

Wadley, L., Esterhuysen, A., and Jeannerat, C., 1992, Vegetation Changes in the Eastern Orange Free State: The Holocene and Late Pleistocene Evidence from Charcoal Studies at Rose Cottage Cave, *South African Journal of Science* 88:558–563.

Walker, N. J., 1980, Later Stone Age Research in the Matopos, *South African Archaeological Bulletin* 35:19–24.

Walker, N. J., 1987, The Dating of Zimbabwean Rock Art, *Rock Art Research* 4:137–149.

Walker, N. J., 1990, Zimbabwe at 18,000 BP, in: *The World at 18,000 BP*, Volume 2, *Low Latitudes* (C. Gamble and O. Soffer, eds.), Unwin Hyman, London, pp. 206–213.

Walker, N. J., and Wadley, L., 1984, Evidence for an Early Microlithic LSA Industry at Duncombe Farm, Zimbabwe, *Cookeia* 1:4–13.

Webley, L., 1992, The History and Archaeology of Pastoralist and Hunter–Gatherer Settlement in the Northwestern Cape, South Africa, unpublished Ph.D. thesis, University of Cape Town.

Wendt, W. E., 1972, Preliminary Report on an Archaeological Research Programme in South West Africa, *Cimbebasia B* 2:1–61.

Wendt, W. E., 1976, "Art Mobilier" from Apollo 11 Cave, South West Africa: Africa's Oldest Dated Works of Art, *South African Archaeological Bulletin* 31:5–11.

Yellen, J., Brooks, A. S., Stuckenrath, R., and Welbourne, R., 1987, A Terminal Pleistocene Assemblage from Drotsky's Cave, Western Ngamiland, Botswana, *Botswana Notes and Records* 19:1–6.

Chapter **3**

Plus Ça Change

The Pleistocene–Holocene
Transition in Northeast Africa

ANGELA E. CLOSE

INTRODUCTION

Northeast Africa is here taken to include Egypt and northern Sudan. It contains the arid heart of the Eastern Sahara, the driest region of the great desert, large parts of which now lie within the 0-mm isohyet. Across this desert, however, there flows the River Nile, one of the world's major rivers. The Nile is tightly confined within its steep-sided and cliff-lined valley, flowing through a land in which rainfall is a newsworthy event, so that the transition between the riverine valley and the desert proper is abrupt and measurable in meters. The modern environments of the valley and the desert could not be more different; similarly, the effects of the Pleistocene–Holocene transition upon these two zones could not have been more different.

At the end of the Pleistocene, the arrival of the rains meant that desert opened up, and vast areas that had been completely uninhabitable for tens of millennia became available for colonization by plants, followed by human and other animals. In the Nile Valley, on the other hand, the changes at the end of the Pleistocene led to the essential destruction of a long-established and stable environment, which had seen the development of an equally long-established, and rather complex, system of human adaptation. This destruction occurred under conditions that also left the inhabitants of this new and changed Nile Valley with nowhere else to go.

ENVIRONMENTS OF THE PLEISTOCENE–HOLOCENE TRANSITION

At lower latitudes, water tends to be a more critical factor in the transition from the Pleistocene to the Holocene than does temperature, and this is particularly true of northeast

ANGELA E. CLOSE • Department of Anthropology, University of Washington, Seattle, Washington 98195.

Humans at the End of the Ice Age: The Archaeology of the Pleistocene–Holocene Transition, edited by Lawrence Guy Straus, Berit Valentin Eriksen, Jon M. Erlandson, and David R. Yesner. Plenum Press, New York, 1996.

Africa, where water still remains a matter of great concern. The end of the Pleistocene saw temperatures rise a few degrees, but the cold had not been extreme even at the glacial maximum. It was changes in the regimen of the Nile and in local rainfall patterns—indeed, for much of this region, it was the actual advent of local rainfall—that led to such profound disturbance of regional and local environments.

The Nile Valley

The headwaters of the Nile lie in the highlands of East Africa. Late in the Pleistocene, there was considerably less rainfall than there is today, lake levels were lower, and, for at least part of this period, the course of the White Nile appears to have been blocked by dunes in southern Sudan (Williams and Adamson 1980), so that it did not reach the main Nile at all. Today, in the Blue Nile, there is much more difference between the high and low stages of the river in the volume of water flowing than there is in the White Nile (Wendorf and Schild 1989b: 769–771). (This is also true of the Atbara, but the Atbara is a relatively minor contributor to the main Nile as a whole.) The Blue Nile also carries much more sediment downstream than does the White Nile, from which most of the sediment load is lost as it wanders through the swamps of the Sudd. Thus, if the White Nile made no contribution to the main Nile near the end of the Pleistocene, then the main Nile, compared with its modern equivalent, would have been a river in which there flowed an absolutely lower amount of water (a difference that would have been aggravated by the lower rainfall in the headwaters as a whole), but in which there was a greater relative difference between the flood and low stages of the river, and in which there was a relatively greater amount of sediment. The amount of sediment carried downriver would have been further increased by the effects of temperature changes in the Nile headwaters. The East African highlands were 4°–8°C colder than today (Williams and Adamson 1980: 287), so that the tree line was probably some 1000 m lower (Livingstone 1980), vegetation cover was sparser, and there was a greater freeze–thaw effect at higher altitudes. There would thus have been more erosion than today, providing more sediment to be carried by the waters of the Blue Nile.

All these factors operating in the headwaters meant that downstream, in northeast Africa proper, the Late Pleistocene witnessed a very significant period of Nilotic aggradation. This aggradation, which has been called the Late Paleolithic Alluviation, began before 20,000 years ago and lasted until about 12,500 BP (Schild and Wendorf 1989:51–95). Throughout this period, the Nile brought considerably less water than today, but more sediment, which choked the valley and built up the floodplain until it was 25–30 m higher than the modern floodplain. Because of the nature of the Blue Nile (and the Atbara), the main Nile still bore a significant annual flood after the summer rains in the headwaters. For the rest of the year, however, the main Nile was probably not the single large channel that we see today, but rather a series of small, braided channels, wandering across a very wide and high floodplain. It is also very possible that in some seasons of some years, the Nile was not a flowing river at all. Since the fish fauna of the river survived, we may assume that even in the driest years, there were significant residual pools of water in the lowest parts of the river's channels, but the actual flow of river may at times have been interrupted (Wendorf and Schild 1989b:770–771).

This Nilotic regimen persisted for 8,000 years or more, with little variation and none of great significance. Change occurred only as we begin to approach the end of the Pleistocene.

Near, but not yet at, the end of the Pleistocene, the most significant change in the East African headwaters was an increase in the amount of rain falling over them. The dating of this increase is not very precise (most of the dates referred to here are not noticeably precise), but in East Africa, it probably occurred at about 12,500 BP (Gasse et al. 1980). The increase in rainfall in the headwaters meant that the Blue Nile and the Atbara contributed more water to the flow of the main Nile. It also gave the White Nile sufficient force to break through the dune barrier, which had blocked its course for several millennia (Williams and Adamson 1980:297–298), and join the main Nile, thus increasing the flow of the latter even more.

Downstream, where the valley was choked with the sediments of the Late Paleolithic Alluviation, there was, at about 12,500 BP, a brief period of extraordinarily high floods, which have been called, evocatively, the "Wild Nile" (Butzer 1980:272). The inhabitants of the valley, after 8 millennia or more, had doubtless become accustomed to sharing the valley with a rather sluggish river that flowed most of the time. The period of the Wild Nile, however, saw much greater quantities of water coming down in the annual flood, which deposited silts at higher elevations all along the valley than had ever been reached before (Butzer 1980; Paulissen 1986; Paulissen and Vermeersch 1987; Wendorf and Schild 1976). Unfortunately, at this time, the increased rainfall of the Final Pleistocene was still confined to East Africa. Along the course of the main Nile, there was still no local precipitation, and the desert remained completely arid and inhospitable. If the Wild Nile made conditions in the valley unfavorable or even impossible for its inhabitants, this catastrophe was doubly unfortunate in that they were also unable to move out of the valley into surrounding areas.

At this time in the headwaters of the river, temperatures were also rising slightly, leading to a denser vegetation cover, a higher tree line, and less effective frost action (Livingstone 1980). These factors lowered the amount of erosion in the highlands, in turn decreasing the amount of sediment being carried by the river. The main Nile downstream thus now had less sediment and considerably more water, so that it very soon began to downcut. The episode of downcutting had probably begun before 12,000 BP, and within a very few centuries, the main Nile had become a rather powerful stream, flowing in a single channel that was incised very deeply into its former floodplain. The effective floodplain was therefore very much narrower, and more prone to violent flooding, than it had been during the Late Paleolithic Alluviation.

Throughout this period of catastrophe in the Nile Valley, there was still no local rainfall. Only after the floods of the Wild Nile and after the recession was already well advanced do we find wadi silts interfingering with those of the river (Paulissen and Vermeersch 1987:47), showing that the local wadis had begun to flow again and that the rains had finally reached northeast Africa.

The Eastern Sahara

Within the desert of the Eastern Sahara, the environmental sequence of the Pleistocene–Holocene transition echoes that of the Nile Valley, except that there is no river. The Eastern Sahara saw several periods of noteworthy rainfall (probably in the region of 500 mm a year) in the earlier parts of the Last Interglacial (Wendorf et al 1993). The last of these periods ended before the end of the Middle Paleolithic, however, perhaps as early as 90,000 years ago and certainly by 50,000 years ago. The Eastern Sahara seems to have remained devoid of rainfall and of all life almost throughout the Last Glaciation and almost to the end of the Pleistocene. At the Last Glacial Maximum and for several millennia thereafter (Rognon 1976), the southern boundary of the desert was probably some 400–500 km south of where it now lies. Thus, whatever environmental change might occur in the desert at the Pleistocene–Holocene transition, it could not make worse a region that was already incapable of supporting life.

The increase in rainfall in East Africa, which occurred at about 12,500 years ago, was manifested in two different ways: Not only was there an absolute increase in the amount of rain, but also the monosoonal belt, within which the rain fell, itself expanded northward. The rate at which this northward expansion took place is not completely clear, but it seems likely that rainfall had reached northern Sudan and southern Egypt by about 11,000 BP (summarized in Close 1992). This timing also matches the approximate date at which the wadis started flowing into the Nile Valley.

At perhaps a comparable time, or more likely a little later, there was also a southward expansion across the desert of the winter rainfall belt from the Mediterranean (Petit-Maire et al. 1991). These two rainfall belts probably overlapped, although it is not known where the zone of overlap lay. Siwa (Hassan and Gross 1987) and the Fayum were within the winter-rainfall belt, and the occurrence of southern forms of plants as far north as Abu Ballas (Neumann, 1989:Tables 1 and 2a) suggests that that area lay within the monosoonal summer-rainfall belt. It is not clear what happened between these two latitudes.

Although rain had returned to the Eastern Sahara by about 11,000 years ago, there was not a great deal of it. Estimates of how much was falling have varied from less than 50 mm a year to as much as 200 mm a year. In light of the formation of playa lakes across much of southern Egypt, the latter figure seems more likely, but even 200 mm is not a very high annual precipitation rate. This paucity is reflected in the composition of the wild fauna found in the desert at this time, which consisted primarily of hare and small gazelle, with occasional oryx (Gautier 1984; Van Neer and Uerpmann 1989). All these are desert-adapted creatures, which can survive for long periods of time without actually drinking: Hare can obtain sufficient moisture from the dew that forms even in the desert, while gazelle and oryx obtain water from the vegetation they eat.

As well as being sparse, the rainfall was also highly seasonal. Over most of the area in question, the rain was strictly monoonal, falling during only a brief period each summer; in the north, it fell in winter, following the Mediterranean pattern. For the rest of the year and for most of the year, the desert would be, as before, without rain. Nonetheless, harsh though conditions remained in the Eastern Sahara, even after the advent of such rains as came with the Pleistocene–Holocene transition, the region had previously been utterly uninhabitable. Even a mere 200 mm of rain per annum represented a great improvement over earlier conditions and opened the area to colonization by plants and by human and other animals.

ARCHAEOLOGY OF THE PLEISTOCENE–HOLOCENE TRANSITION

The Nile Valley

In the Nile Valley, the period immediately before the environmental changes that marked the Pleistocene–Holocene transition was the final part of the Late Paleolithic.

Between about 13,000 BP and 11,500 BP, three, or perhaps four, industries, or variants of the Late Paleolithic, existed in the Nile Valley, for all of which the dating is somewhat problematical (Figure 1).

The known distribution of the *Afian* extends from the First Cataract (Wadi Kubbaniya) to just north of the Qena bend (Makhadma) (Close 1989; Close et al. 1979; Vermeersch et al. 1989; J. L. Phillips personal communication). Almost all the direct, or closely related, radiocarbon dates indicate that it spans most of the thirteenth millennium; there are two slightly older dates on shell from Kom Ombo.

The *Isnan* has a very similar distribution, extending from Wadi Kubbaniya to Dishna (Hassan 1974; Vermeersch et al 1989; Wendorf and Schild 1976, 1989a). It seems to be slightly younger than the Afian: The generally accepted dates are not earlier than 12,500 BP, and a site at El Kilh dates to about 11,600 BP, which is within the period of the Nile downcutting.

The *Qadan* has a more southerly orientation; most sites lie between the Second Cataract and Tushka, in southern Egypt (Irwin et al. 1968; Shiner 1968; Wendorf 1968a,b), with an outlier near the First Cataract, at Wadi Kubbaniya (Banks 1980). Most of the Qadan sites are undated, and a high proportion of the available dates seem less than reliable because of stratigraphic inconsistencies or the materials dated. The Qadan probably did not survive after 12,000 BP and probably did not begin much earlier than 13,000 BP; it is therefore similar in age to the Afian.

The *Sebilian* is known all the way from the Second Cataract to north of the Qena bend (Hassan 1972, 1974; Hassan and Wendorf 1974; Hill et al. 1989; Marks 1968; Wendorf 1968a; Wendorf and Schild 1976). It is thus the most widespread of the industries probably belonging to this period, but is also the least understood. The two radiocarbon dates of about 11,000 BP may well be too young because of inadequate pretreatment, and the little stratigraphic evidence at Ballana (Wendorf 1968a:807–831) suggests that the Sebilian is late in the Late Paleolithic Alluviation but earlier than the Qadan. The real problem with the Sebilian, however, is that its makers deliberately sought out blocks of quartzitic sandstones or volcanic rocks for the manufacture of large flakes, frequently using discoidal or Levallois techniques, and then often used the flakes as blanks for single or multiple truncations. This tradition is utterly alien to the Nilotic Late Paleolithic, which for millennia had used homogeneous, fine-grained raw materials to produce microlithic flakes and bladelets, some of which were used as blanks for backed pieces or geometrics. The scattering of small Sebilian sites over much of the lower Nile Valley, the complete incompatibility of the Sebilian with the established Late Paleolithic artifactual tradition, and the apparent difference in economy (there are no grinding stones or fish in Sebilian sites) have led to the suggestions that the Sebilian either might represent intrusive groups from farther south in Africa, moving down the rejuvenated river (Wendorf 1968c:1048; Wendorf and Schild 1989b:814), or might be a part of the Middle Paleolithic (Paulissen and Vermeersch 1987:52).

No sites of this period (or, indeed, from this period until well into the Holocene) are known from the Nile Valley north of the area of the Qena bend (Figure 1). That they are not is usually attributed to the burial of the deposits of this age deep beneath the modern floodplain. What is much more surprising is that there are also no sites known from the area of the Second Cataract southward. In fact, the complete lack of archaeological remains would suggest that that part of the central Nile Valley was unoccupied for tens of millennia

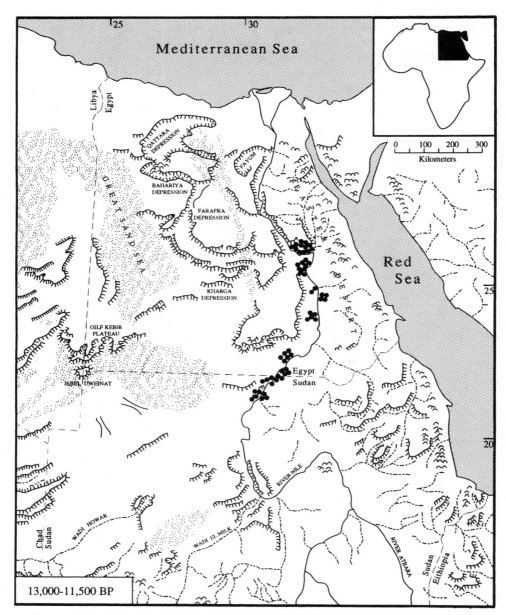

Figure 1. Distribution of archaeological sites in northeast Africa most probably dating between circa 13,000 BP and 11,500 BP. All are confined to the Nile Valley between the area of the Second Cataract and Asyut.

during the Late Pleistocene (Marks et al. 1987:137–138). Plausible explanations for this hiatus have not been forthcoming.

The three mainstream Late Paleolithic variants seem all to have practiced the same kind of subsistence economy as had existed in the lower Nile Valley from the beginning of the Late Paleolithic Alluviation (Wendorf et al. 1989a,b). A major source of animal protein was fish, which were seasonally harvested in huge quantities when they followed the flood to the edge of the floodplain in order to spawn. Catfish are very common in some of the Isnan sites (Vermeersch et al 1989) and in some of the Qadan sites that are set back in wide embayments of the floodplain (Greenwood 1968), while tilapia predominate in at least one Afian site, Makhadma-4 (Vermeersch et al 1989). Although claims that fish were routinely decapitated may have been exaggerated because of the differentially good preservation and identification of the head bones of catfish (Gautier and Van Neer 1989:148–151), fish were nevertheless taken in such large quantities in the short period during and after the flood that some kind of preservation and storage for future use seems very likely. This is also indicated by what may be drying or smoking pits in sites at Makhadma (Vermeersch et al 1989).

Some Isnan (Gautier 1976a:362) and Afian sites (Butzer and Hansen 1968:172) also yielded large quantities of shells of the Nile oyster (*Unio* sp.), which would have been collected in spring, during the lowest stage of the river. Other sites of the Qadan and Afian variants (Ballmann 1980) also contained the bones of waterfowl that today are winter visitors to the Nile Valley.

All the Late Paleolithic variants (including the Sebilian, which seems to have done little else) hunted the standard trio of herbivores in the lower Nile Valley: wild cattle, hartebeest, and gazelle (Gautier 1968, 1976a,b; Gautier and Van Neer 1989). Hippopotamus remains occur in some sites, but are never common, and quite understandably, the creature seems not to have been hunted regularly.

The other major component of diet was undoubtedly plant foods, although direct evidence is frustratingly lacking for this phase of the Late Paleolithic. Many of the sites (but no Sebilian sites), however, contain large numbers of grinding stones, from which we may infer that plants played a significant role in the economy. Plant remains from earlier Late Paleolithic sites in Wadi Kubbaniya (Hillman et al. 1989) show that people were making extensive use of wetland plants, particulary—but not only—the tubers of purple nut-grass (*Cyperus rotundus*) and club-rush seeds (*Scirpus* sp.). Chemical analysis of grinding stones from the same sites suggests their use in processing the tubers (Jones 1989), which would otherwise have been too toxic to consume in quantity. Such practices cannot be documented for the final Late Paleolithic, but the overall distribution of the grinding stones themselves does suggest that they were still being used for wetland plants: Grinding stones are common only in sites in wide floodplain embayments, where wetland plants would have grown best; such artifacts are otherwise rare or absent. Nut-grass tubers would have been a seasonally abundant and easily stored food.

While grass seeds might have been collected in the Late Paleolithic, there is no evidence that they were. Investigations of the "sickle gloss" claimed for some Isnan and Qadan artifacts have shown that it is actually a polish that results from sawing an (unidentified) hard and gritty material (Becker and Wendorf 1993; Juel Jensen et al. 1991), while the finds of a "cereal-type" pollen reported in preliminary form from Isna (Wendorf and Schild 1976:73–74) could not be duplicated and the pollen grains were most probably those of ordinary grasses only (Wendorf and Schild 1989b:817).

The abundance and accessibility of most of these resources—the wetland plants, the spawning fish, and the waterbirds—are closely dependent upon the existence of a very wide and flat floodplain, with a river that was generally sluggish but nonetheless provided significant floods every year, thus creating and maintaining large areas of wetland and marshes. The economic system, and the environmental system that sustained it, were established and essentially unvarying for thousands of years.

Shortly before the end of the Pleistocene, however, all this was effectively ended when there was a period of very high and very violent floods, the Wild Nile, immediately after which the river began to incise its channel deeply into its former floodplain. This downcutting greatly reduced the extent of the wetlands and the availability of their resources, on which people had long depended for much of their immediate, and perhaps storable, food. Since the Nile still flowed through a rainless desert, there was no other place to which people could escape and they were thus compelled to remain in the valley and deal with the catastrophe that had overtaken them.

One course of action pursued by at least some groups was to obey the apparently ancient economic truism that the most efficient way of acquiring goods is to take them from someone else. Although it is not precisely dated, the graveyard of Jebel Sahaba falls within the general period of the end of the Late Paleolithic. This is the burial site of 59 people, of whom 24 showed definite evidence of violent death, in the form of artifacts embedded in the bones, or inside the skull, or bones with severe cut marks (Wendorf 1968b). Such deaths were inflicted regardless of age or sex, and given the variety of violent deaths that can leave no trace on the bones, this proportion of some 40% must be regarded as minimal; it is likely that the actual proportion who died violently was much higher. The stone artifacts used as armatures for the weapons would be assigned to the Qadan industry; we do not know what kind of artifacts were made by those who died.

In light of the environmental crisis at this time, it is not surprising to find evidence of such extreme intergroup conflict. Life in the Nile Valley had become very difficult—so difficult, in fact, that between 11,500 BP and 10,000 BP, the only sites known are a small cluster of scatters of stone artifacts near the Second Cataract (the Arkinian) (Schild et al 1968) and an even smaller cluster on the Atbara (Marks et al. 1987) (Figure 2). In both cases, the faunas are dominated by large bovids, primarily aurochs and hartebeest; fish are very rare, winter birds are absent, and there are no (the Atbara) or almost no (the Second Cataract) grinding stones. The Nilotic adaptations of the Late Paleolithic were evidently no longer practiced.

After 10,000 years ago, no more sites are known from the lower Nile Valley until almost 8,000 BP (Connor and Marks 1986:172–178); even then, the archaeological record is little richer than it had been for the 11th millennium (Figures 3 and 4). Clusters of small sites are known from the Fayum (the Qarunian) (Wendorf and Schild 1976; Wenke et al. 1988), from Upper Egypt (the Elkabien) (Vermeersch 1978), and from around the Second Cataract (the Shamarkian) (Schild et al. 1968). Elkabian and Shamarkian subsistence practices seem to have been essentially like those of the Arkinian, with a primary dependence upon large herbivores and little evidence for wetland or specifically riverine exploitation. Fishing, probably seasonal, was much more important to the Qarunian peoples living around the shores of the Fayum lake, but their economy was otherwise little different from that of their few contemporaries in the lower Nile Valley proper.

Thus, in the lower Nile Valley, the Pleistocene–Holocene transition is recorded,

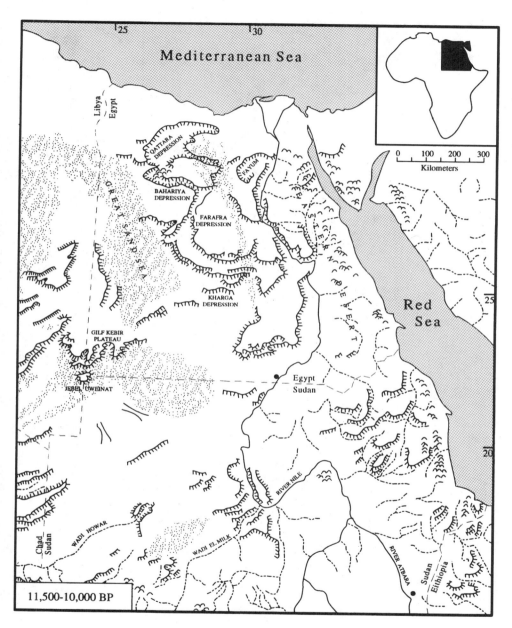

Figure 2. Distribution of archaeological sites in northeast Africa most probably dating between circa 11,500 BP and 10,000 BP. Only two small clusters are known: near the Second Cataract and on the Atbara.

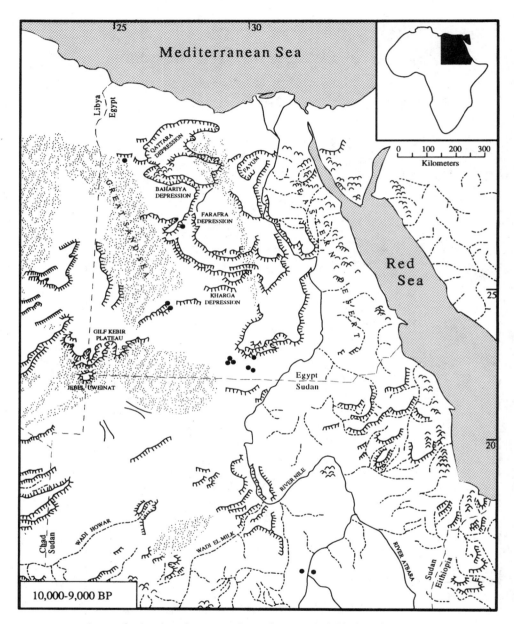

Figure 3. Distribution of archaeological sites in northeast Africa most probably dating between circa 10,000 BP and 9,000 BP. The only Nilotic sites are near Khartoum, but occupation of the Eastern Sahara was beginning.

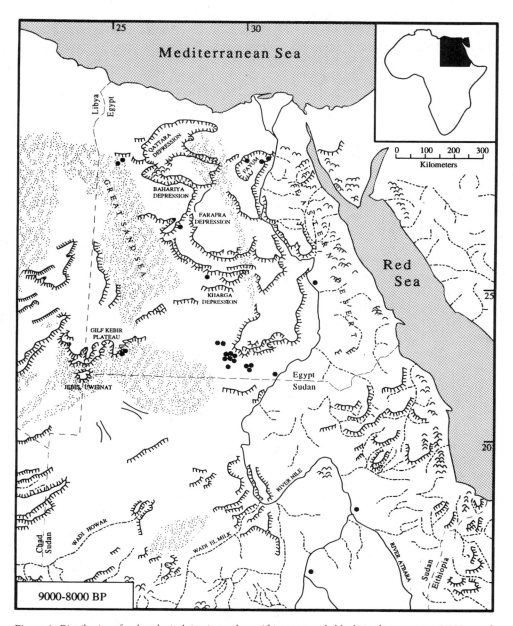

Figure 4. Distribution of archaeological sites in northeast Africa most probably dating between circa 9,000 BP and 8,000 BP. Sites were still very rare in the Nile valley, but denser in the desert.

archaeologically, by a sequence beginning with numerous large sites that were part of a sophisticated Nilotic adaptation that had endured for millennia. After 11,500 BP, this record contracts to a few very small sites of rather generic hunter–gatherers, while after 10,000 BP, the record becomes so thin as to be invisible until almost 8,000 BP. For the inhabitants of the lower Nile Valley, the Pleistocene–Holocene transition would seem to have been an unmitigated diaster.

In the central Nile Valley, the sequence is very different. The archaeological record is nonexistent almost down to the very end of the Pleistocene (there are only the few sites on the Atbara, noted above), but somewhat before 9,000 BP, the Khartoum Mesolithic suddenly appeared in the area around Khartoum (Figure 3), full-blown and without local antecedents, but with a highly developed and economically important ceramic technology. Although much has been made of the supposed sedentism of Khartoum Mesolithic groups (Caneva 1988; Haaland 1992), a pattern of seasonal movement and reoccupation of the same sites seems more probable.

Unlike the Arkinian and later groups in the lower Nile Valley, and also unlike their immediate predecessors on the Atbara, Khartoum Mesolithic groups along the Nile made significant use of the resources of the river—fish, molluscs, and reptiles (Peters 1991)—and much of the fishing involved the same techniques of floodplain fish harvesting as occurred in the Late Paleolithic of the lower Nile Valley (Peters 1991:38–39). Their riverine adaptation differs, however, from that of the Late Paleolithic in the use of the technology to take deepwater fish, including ceramic and stone net-sinkers and barbed bone points (fish gorges were known in the Late Paleolithic) and, by implication, boats or rafts. Khartoum Mesolithic sites also include a very wide array of land mammals, principally of medium and large antelopes and other large bovids, but extending all the way up to elephants (Gautier 1989: Table 1). This wider range of prey is primarily due to the occurrence of significant local rainfall, which, in the early Holocene, is estimated to have been about 500 mm per annum, which would maintain a wooded savannah even away from Nile Valley (Wickens 1975).

An a priori assumption that plants were important in the diet seems to be supported by the numerous grinding stones. Direct evidence is remarkably rare, however, only Haaland reporting *Setaria*, *Celtis*, and *Zizyphus* from sites on the Atbara (Haaland 1987:49, 1992: 48). These are savannah and Sahelian plants, two of them (*Setaria* and *Zizyphus*) also being important in the Eastern Sahara at this time, rather than the wetland plants used by the more northerly inhabitants of the Pleistocene Nile Valley.

The Eastern Sahara

Rainfall had returned to the Eastern Sahara probably by about 11,000 BP. Despite one or two outlying radiocarbon dates (Gabriel 1986:11; C. V. Haynes, personal commnication), however, people seem not to have reoccupied the desert in detectable numbers before about 9,500 BP. In the southern part of the desert, they seem to have come from the east, from the Nile Valley (there are some similarities in artifacts between the very earliest sites and the Arkinian of the Second Cataract), since there is no evidence for earlier occupation in the desert or along the coast to the north, or in the desert to the west, or, surprisingly, in the desert or Sahel to the south. In northwestern Sudan, there are almost no sites older than 9,000 years, and very few older than 8,000 years (Kuper 1988; Richter 1989). One unpublished site west of Merga is typologically similar to the Atbara sites dating to before

10,000 BP (Close 1992: Fig. 2; Marks et al. 1987), but comparable artifacts have not been found in more northerly sites. It would seem, then, that people were not migrating northward and following the expansion of the rainfall belt.

All the Saharan sites earlier than 9,000 BP and most of those earlier than 8,000 BP (Figures 3 and 4) seem to be typical, short-term camps of small groups of hunters–gatherers characterized by flaked stone, some ground stone, mammal bones, ostrich eggshell, occasional potsherds, and charcoal (Barich and Hassan 1990; Hassan and Gross 1987; Kuper 1988; McDonald 1990; Wendorf and Schild 1980:103–128; Wendorf et al. 1984). Except in the great oases, where there was permanent water, dwelling structures were quite insubstantial and all the evidence suggests a strictly nomadic way of life. The largest sites (and those richest in artifacts), which are presumably those used for the longest periods, are in the lower parts of playa basins. Since these sites were seasonally flooded, they were also seasonally abandoned; other sites were even more ephemeral. If the Masara stone circles on the edge of Dakhla oasis are indeed older than 8,000 BP (they are not directly dated) (McDonald 1990), then they might suggest less extreme mobility than was practiced in the high desert; even here, however, full sedentism seems improbable.

In the southern part of the Eastern Sahara, almost all the faunal collections of any size (>40 identifiable specimens) include a few bones of cattle, which have been presumed to be domestic (Close and Wendorf 1992) (but for arguments to the contrary, see, for example, Clutton-Brock 1989; A. B. Smith 1984). The argument for their status as domesticates is an ecological one, in that cattle, which must drink every other day if they are to survive and every day if they are to thrive, would not be found naturally in an environment that otherwise supported only such desert-adapted forms as hare, gazelle, and oryx—nondrinkers all. The absence of intermediate-size antelopes, especially hartebeest, an animal that always occurs with gazelle and wild cattle in the valley, emphasizes how anomalous would be the presence of wild cattle in this setting. Pastoralists, however, could force their stock to move into an unlivable environment and, once they were there, could help ensure their survival. After 8,500 BP, there is considerable evidence for the digging of wells in the desert, some of them with a shallow side basin (Close 1984: Figure 12.6), such as today are used to water camels along the caravan routes. Before 8,500 BP, it is possible that people spent the driest seasons of the year in the valley, coming into the desert only during and immediately after the summer rains.

The rarity of cattle bones in all Saharan sites until the mid-Holocene would suggest that almost all meat was obtained by hunting hare and gazelle, while the cattle were kept as living producers of protein in the forms of milk and blood. Some modern Sahelian pastoralists live for several months of each year on little except milk and milk products (S. E. Smith 1980). The Eastern Sahara immediately after the Pleistocene–Holocene transition was as unforgiving as the present-day Sahel, and the domestication of cattle may have provided the insurance that permitted people to colonize, and to survive in, this very precarious environment. This comparison with modern African pastoralists also raises the possibility that the socially ascribed importance of cattle may have seemed as great to their herders as their economic role. This possibility becomes more apparent later in the Holocene, when we find individual animals buried intact under stone-covered mounds (A. Applegate personal communication).

Grinding stones are present in even the earliest, and some of the most ephemeral, Holocene sites in the Sahara, indicating a not unexpected reliance on plant foods. Remains of such foods have been recovered in quantity only from one site, at Nabta, where they are securely dated to about 8,000 BP (Wendorf et al. 1992). The most common varieties were *Zizyphus* fruits and grains of sorghum, which was morphologically wild although its lipid chemistry suggests the possibility of cultivation. Although domesticated sorghum, which must have come from Africa, was present in eastern Arabia by 5,000 BP and possibly earlier (Potts 1993:180, 182), there is no early evidence for it in Africa itself. Even in the Nile Valley, there is nothing more than a few impressions of (wild) grains in potsherds from 6th- and 5th-millennium sites near Khartoum (Stemler 1990). This is not conclusively negative evidence, however, since sorghum could have been long cultivated and yet remained morphologically wild, depending on the techniques of harvesting and sowing (Stemler 1984). The Nabta site provides by far the earliest evidence for intensive collecting of sorghum.

At Nabta, there was also a range of other wild, Sahelian grasses (mostly *Panicum, Setaria,* and *Echinochloa*), seeds of legumes, seeds probably of the mustard and caper families, unidentified tubers, and other, less frequent types (Wasylikowa 1992). Harlan (1989), summarizing the ethnographic evidence for the use of wild grasses by Saharan and sub-Saharan groups in the 19th and 20th centuries, has observed that in marginal areas—a category that would certainly include the Early Holocene Eastern Sahara—wild plants were more important and more reliable sources of food than were domesticated forms and that wild-grass seeds are more nutritious than domesticated cereals. In fact, there is no evidence for the Southwest Asian cereals in northeastern Africa until about 6,000 BP at Merimde and in the Fayum (Hassan 1988), and they would not, in any case, have grown well under the regimen of strictly summer rainfall that obtained farther south. It is thus likely that the tens of thousands of grinding stones occurring in Holocene sites in the Sahara were used with local, and probably wild, plant foods, and bear no relation to the later farming of the introduced crops upon which Pharaonic civilization was based.

CONCLUSION AND AFTERMATH

The major environmental changes in northeast Africa, occurring somewhat before the actual transition to the Holocene proper, were an increase in the competence of the Nile, resulting from an increase in rainfall in the river's headwaters in East Africa, and the expansion of this higher ranfall belt northward into what had been high desert. These two changes were not synchronous, the former occurring perhaps 1,500 years before the latter. The effects of these changes on the human inhabitants of northeast Africa could not have been more profound, or more different.

In the lower Nile Valley, a pattern of wetland exploitation, which had been established for some 8,000 years, rapidly became untenable as the Nile destroyed the wetlands of its own floodplain. There is evidence for violent conflict between groups as their customary subsistence base disappeared, and populations then became so sparse as to be archaeologically invisible for more than 2 millennia. In the central Nile Valley, where there is no evidence for anyone before the Pleistocene–Holocene changes, semi-sedentary groups of fisher–gatherer–hunters suddenly appeared, as if from nowhere, to occupy the valley and its rich Sahelian hinterland. In the Eastern Sahara, the complete absence of human occupation late in the Pleistocene was probably as real as it is apparent. However, the encroachment of the northern edge of the monsoon rainfall belt permitted new immigrants to colonize this vast area, where they thrived by a combination of intensive collecting of plant foods, including some later domesticated in Africa, hunting of the restricted desert fauna, and the keeping of domestic cattle. The Eastern Sahara was never lush, and making a living may at times have been precarious, but this strategy enabled people to survive there through the early millennia of the Holocene.

In northeast Africa, unlike most regions of the world, the drastic environmental changes of the Pleistocene–Holocene transition had been effectively reversed by the mid-Holocene. After the virtual depopulation of the valley in the millennia before 8,000 BP, the Nile began once more to aggrade. In the north, by 6,000 BP, local groups had begun to practice food production, using the southwest Asian suite of domestic species. These species, combined with the incredible fertility of the Nile Valley as agricultural land, permitted the dense populations upon which Pharaonic and all later Egyptian societies have been based. To the west, in the Sahara, Nature was less kind. The rainfall decreased and the monosoonal belt began to retreat toward the south. By about 5,500 BP, rain had ceased to fall over southern Egypt and northern Sudan, and the desert was once more empty.

As northeast Africa was through most of the Late Pleistocene, so again it is now: a densely populated Nile Valley dependent upon the resources of the river and the adjacent Sahara, uninhabitable and uninhabited. The changes associated with the end of the Last Glaciation were indeed profound—but they did not last.

REFERENCES

Ballmann, P., 1980, Report on the Avian Remains from Sites in Egyptian Nubia, Upper Egypt, and the Fayum, in: *Loaves and Fishes: The Prehistory of Wadi Kubbaniya* (F. Wendorf and R. Schild, assemblers, and A. E. Close, ed.), Department of Anthropology, Institute for the Study of Earth and Man, Southern Methodist University, Dallas, pp. 307–310.

Banks, K. M., 1980, Report on Site E-78-10, in: *Loaves and Fishes: The Prehistory of Wadi Kubbaniya* (F. Wendorf and R. Schild, assemblers, and A. E. Close, ed.), Department of Anthropology, Institute for the Study of Earth and Man, Southern Methodist University, Dallas, pp. 217–228.

Barich, B. E., and Hassan, F. A., 1990, Il Sahara e le oasi: Farafra nel Deserto Occidentale Egiziano, *Sahara* 3:53–62.

Becker, M., and Wendorf, F., 1993, A Microwear Study of a Late Pleistocene Qadan Assemblage from Southern Egypt, *Journal of Field Archaeology* 20:389–398.

Butzer, K. W., 1980, Pleistocene History of the Nile Valley in Egypt and Lower Nubia, in: *The Sahara and the Nile* (M. A. J. Williams and H. Faure, eds.), Balkema, Rotterdam, pp. 253–280.

Butzer, K. W., and Hansen, C. L., 1968, *Desert and River in Nubia: Geomorphology and Prehistoric Environments at the Aswan Reservoir*, University of Wisconsin Press, Madison.

Caneva, I., 1988, The History of a Middle Nile Environment: A suggested cultural model, in: *El Geili: The History of a Middle Nile Environment 700 B.C.–A.D. 1500* (I. Caneva, ed.), British Archaeological Reports International Series 424, Oxford, pp. 359–377.

Close, A. E., 1984, Report on Site E-80-1, in: *Cattle-Keepers of the Eastern Sahara: The Neolithic of Bir Kiseiba* (F. Wendorf and R. Schild, assemblers, and A. E. Close, ed.), Department of Anthropology, Southern Methodist University, Dallas, pp. 251–297.

Close, A. E., 1989, Report on Site E-83-4: A Small Afian Surface Concentration in the Kubbaniya Dune Field, in: *The Prehistory of Wadi Kubbaniya Volume 3: Late Paleolithic Archaeology* (F. Wendorf and R. Schild, assemblers, and A. E. Close, ed.), Southern Methodist University Press, Dallas, pp. 697–703.

Close, A. E., 1992, Holocene Occupation of the Eastern Sahara, in: *New Light on the Northeast African Past: Current Prehistoric Research* (F. Klees and R. Kuper, eds.), Africa Praehistorica 5, Heinrich-Barth-Institut, Cologne, pp. 155–183.

Close, A. E., and Wendorf, F., 1992, The Beginnings of Food-Production in the Eastern Sahara, in: *Transitions to Agriculture in Prehistory* (A. B. Gebauer and T. D. Price, eds.), Prehistory Press, Madison, WI, pp. 63–72.

Close, A. E., Wendorf, F., and Schild, R., 1979, *The Afian: A Study of Stylistic Variability in a Nilotic Industry*, Department of Anthropology, Institute for the Study of Earth and Man, Southern Methodist University, Dallas.

Clutton-Brock, J., 1989, Cattle in Ancient North Africa, in: *The Walking Larder: Patterns of Domestication, Pastoralism and Predation* (J. Clutton-Brock, ed.), Unwin Hyman, London, pp. 200–206.

Connor, D. R., and Marks, A. E., 1986, The Terminal Pleistocene on the Nile: The Final Nilotic Adjustment, in: *The End of the Paleolithic in the Old World* (L. G. Straus, ed.), British Archaeological Reports International Series 284, Oxford, pp. 171–199.

Gabriel, B., 1986, Die östliche Libysche Wüste im Jungquartär. *Berliner Geographische Studien* 19, Institut für Physische Geographie der Technischen Universität Berlin, Berlin.

Gasse, F., Rognon, P., and Street, F. A., 1980, Quaternary History of the Afar and Ethiopian Rift Lakes, in: *The Sahara and the Nile* (M. A. J. Williams and H. Faure, eds.), Balkema, Rotterdam, pp. 361–400.

Gautier, A., 1968, Mammalian Remains of the Northern Sudan and Southern Egypt, in: *The Prehistory of Nubia* (F. Wendorf, ed.), Fort Burgwin Research Center and Southern Methodist University Press, Dallas, pp. 80–99.

Gautier, A., 1976a, Freshwater Mollusks and Mammals from Upper Palaeolithic sites Near Idfu and Isna, in *Prehistory of the Nile Valley* (by F. Wendorf and R. Schild), Academic Press, New York, pp. 349–364.

Gautier, A., 1976b, Animal Remains from Localities near Dishna, in: *Prehistory of the Nile Valley* (by F. Wendorf and R. Schild), Academic Press, New York, pp. 365–367.

Gautier, A., 1984, Archaeozoology of the Bir Kiseiba region, Eastern Sahara, in: *Cattle-Keepers of the Eastern Sahara: The Neolithic of Bir Kiseiba* (F. Wendorf and R. Schild, assemblers, and A. E. Close, ed.), Department of Anthropology, Southern Methodist University, Dallas, pp. 49–72.

Gautier, A., 1989, A General Review of the Known Prehistoric Faunas of the Central Sudanese Nile Valley. In: *Later Prehistory of the Nile Basin and the Sahara* (L. Krzyzaniak and M. Kobusiewicz, eds.), Polish Academy of Sciences, Poznan Branch, and Poznan Archaeological Museum, Poznan, pp. 353–357.

Gautier, A., and Van Neer, W., 1989, Animal Remains from the Late Paleolithic Sequence at Wadi Kubbaniya, in: *The Prehistory of Wadi Kubbaniya*, Volume 2, *Stratigraphy, Paleoeconomy, and Environment* (F. Wendorf and R. Schild, assemblers, and A. E. Close, ed.), Southern Methodist University Press, Dallas, pp. 119–161.

Greenwood, P. H., 1968, Fish Remains, in: *The Prehistory of Nubia* (F. Wendorf, ed.), Fort Burgwin Research Center and Southern Methodist University Press, Dallas, pp. 100–109.

Haaland, R., 1987, Problems in the Mesolithic and Neolithic Culture-History in the Central Nile Valley, Sudan. In: *Nubian Culture: Past and Present* (T. Hägg, ed.), Kungl. Vitterhets Historie och Antikvitets Akademien, Konferenser 17, Almqvist and Wiksell, Stockholm, pp. 47–74.

Haaland, R., 1992, Fish, Pots and Grain: Early and Mid-Holocene Adaptations in the Central Sudan, *African Archaeological Review* 10:43–64.

Harlan, J. R., 1989, Wild-Grass Seed Harvesting in the Sahara and Sub-Sahara of Africa, in: *Foraging and Farming: The Evolution of Plant Exploitation* (D. R. Harris and G. C. Hillman, eds.), Unwin Hyman, London, pp. 79–98.

Hassan, F. A., 1972, Note on Sebilian Sites from Dishna Plain, *Chronique d'Egypte* 47:11–16.

Hassan, F. A., 1974, The Archaeology of the Dishna Plain, Egypt: A Study of a Late Paleolithic Settlement, *Papers of the Geological Survey of Egypt 59*, Geological Survey of Egypt, Cairo.

Hassan, F. A., 1988, The Predynastic of Egypt, *Journal of World Prehistory* 2:135–185.

Hassan, F. A., and Gross, G. T., 1987, Resources and Subsistence during the Early Holocene at Siwa Oasis, Northern Egypt, in: *Prehistory of Arid North Africa: Essays in Honor of Fred Wendorf* (A. E. Close, ed.), Southern Methodist University Press, Dallas, pp. 85–103.

Hassan, F. A., and Wendorf, F., 1974, A Sebilian Assemblage from El Kilh, Upper Egypt, *Chronique d'Egypte* 49:211–221.

Hill, C. L., Wendorf, F., and Schild, R., 1989, Report on Site E-84-1: A multicomponent Paleolithic Site at Wadi Kubbaniya, in: *The Prehistory of Wadi Kubbaniya*, Volume 3, *Late Paleolithic Archaeology* (F Wendorf and R. Schild, assemblers, and A. E. Close, ed.), Southern Methodist University Press, Dallas, pp. 365–374.

Hillman, G., Madeyska, E., and Hather, J., 1989, Wild Plant Foods and Diet at Late Paleolithic Wadi Kubbaniya: The Evidence from Charred Remains, in: *The Prehistory of Wadi Kubbaniya*, Volume 2, *Stratigraphy, Paleoeconomy, and Environment* (F. Wendorf and R. Schild, assemblers, and A. E. Close, ed.), Southern Methodist University Press, Dallas, pp. 162–242.

Irwin, H. T., Wheat, J. B., and Irwin, L. F., 1968, University of Colorado Investigations of Paleolithic and Epipaleolithic Sites in the Sudan, Africa, *University of Utah Papers in Anthropology 90*, University of Utah Press, Salt Lake City.

Jones, C. E. R., 1989, Archaeochemistry: Fact or Fancy, in: *The Prehistory of Wadi Kubbaniya*, Volume 2, *Stratigraphy, Paleoeconomy, and Environment* (F. Wendorf and R. Schild, assemblers, and A. E. Close, ed.), Southern Methodist University Press, Dallas, pp. 260–266.

Juel Jensen, H., Schild, R., Wendorf, F., and Close, A. E., 1991, Understanding the Late Palaeolithic Tools with Lustrous Edges from the Lower Nile Valley, *Antiquity* 65:122–128.

Kuper, R., 1988, Neuere Forschungen zur Besiedlungsgeschichte der Ost-Sahara, *Archäologisches Korrespondenzblatt* 18:127–142.

Livingstone, D. A., 1980, Environmental Changes in the Nile Headwaters, in: *The Sahara and the Nile* (M. A. J. Williams and H. Faure, eds.), Balkema, Rotterdam, pp. 339–359.

Marks, A. E., 1968, The Sebilian Industry of the Second Cataract, in: *The Prehistory of Nubia* (F. Wendorf, ed.), Fort Burgwin Research Center and Southern Methodist University Press, Dallas, pp. 461–531.

Marks, A. E., Peters, J., and Van Neer, W., 1987, Late Pleistocene and Early Holocene Occupations in the Upper Atbara River Valley, Sudan, in: *Prehistory of Arid North Africa: Essays in Honor of Fred Wendorf* (A. E. Close, ed.), Southern Methodist University Press, Dallas, pp. 137–161.

McDonald, M. M. A., 1990. New Evidence from the Early to Mid-Holocene in Dakleh Oasis, South-Central Egypt, Bearing on the Evolution of Cattle Pastoralism, *Nyame Akuma* 33:3–9.

Neumann, K., 1989, Zur Vegetationsgeschichte der Ostsahara in Holozän. Holzkohlen aus Prähistorischen Fundstellen, in: *Forschungen zur Umweltgeschichte der Ostsahara* (R. Kuper, ed.), Africa Praehistorica 2, Heinrich-Barth-Institut, Cologne, pp. 13–181.

Paulissen, E., 1986, Characteristics of the "Wild Nile" stage in Upper Egypt, *Travaux et Documents de l'ORSTOM* 197:367–369.

Paulissen, E., and Vermeersch, P. M., 1987, Earth, man and climate in the Egyptian Nile Valley during the Pleistocene, in: *Prehistory of Arid North Africa: Essays in Honor of Fred Wendorf* (A. E. Close, ed.), Southern Methodist University Press, Dallas, pp. 29–67.

Peters, J., 1991, Mesolithic Fishing along the Central Sudanese Nile and the Lower Atbara, *Sahara* 4:33–40.

Petit-Maire, N., Burollet, H. P., Ballais, J.-L., Fontugne, M., Rosso, J. C., and Lazaar, A., 1991, Paléoclimats Holocènes du Sahara Septentrional, *C. R. Acad. Sciences Paris*, Série II, 312:1661–1666.

Potts, D. T., 1993, The Late Prehistoric, Protohistoric, and Early Historic Periods in Eastern Arabia (ca. 5000–1200 B.C.), *Journal of World Prehistory* 7:163–212.

Richter, J., 1989, Neolithic Sites in the Wadi Howar (Western Sudan), in: *Later Prehistory of the Nile Basin and the Sahara* (L. Krzyzaniak and M. Kobusiewicz, eds.), Polish Academy of Sciences, Poznan Branch, and Poznan Archaeological Museum, Poznan, pp. 431–442.

Rognon, P., 1976, Essai d'Interprétation des Variations Climatiques au Sahara Depuis 40000 ans, *Revue de Géographie Physique et de Géologie Dynamique* 18:251–282.

Schild, R., and Wendorf, F., 1989, The Late Pleistocene Nile in Wadi Kubbaniya, in: *The Prehistory of Wadi Kubbaniya*, Volume 2, *Stratigraphy, Paleoeconomy, and Environment* (F. Wendorf and R. Schild, assemblers, and A. E. Close, ed.), Southern Methodist University Press, Dallas, pp. 15–100.

Schild, R., Chmielewska, M., and Wieckowska, H., 1968, The Arkinian and Shamarkian Industries, in: *The Prehistory of Nubia* (F. Wendorf, ed.), Fort Burgwin Research Center and Southern Methodist University Press, Dallas, pp. 651–767.

Shiner, J. L., 1968, The Cataract tradition, in: *The Prehistory of Nubia* (F. Wendorf, ed.), Fort Burgwin Research Center and Southern Methodist University Press, Dallas, pp. 535–629.

Smith, A. B., 1984, The origins of food-production in northeast Africa, in: *Palaeoecology of Africa*, Volume 16 (J. A. Coetzee and E. M. van Zinderen Bakker, eds.), Balkema, Rotterdam, pp. 317–324.

Smith, S. E., 1980, The Environmental Adaptation of Nomads in the West African Sahel: A Key to Understanding Prehistoric Pastoralists, in: *The Sahara and the Nile* (M. A. J. Williams and H. Faure, eds.), Balkema, Rotterdam, pp. 467–487.

Stemler, A., 1984, The Transition from Food Collecting to Food Production in Northern Africa, in: *From Hunters to Farmers: The Causes and Consequences of Food Production in Africa* (J. D. Clark and S. A. Brandt, eds.), University of California Press, Berkeley, pp. 127–131.

Stemler, A., 1990, A Scanning Electron Microscopic Analysis of Plant Impressions in Pottery from the Sites of Kadero, El Zakiab, Um Direiwa and El Kadada, *Archéologie du Nil Moyen* 4:87–105.

Van Neer, W., and Uerpmann, H.-P., 1989, Palaeoecological Significance of the Holocene Faunal Remains of the B.O.S.-Missions, in: *New Light on the Northeast African Past: Current Prehistoric Research* (F. Klees and R. Kuper, eds.), Africa Praehistorica 5, Heinrich-Barth-Institut, Cologne, pp. 307–341.

Vermeersch, P. M., 1978, *Elkab II: Epipaléolithique de la Vallée du Nil Égyptien*, Universitaire Pers Leuven and Fondation Egyptologique Reine Elisabeth, Leuven and Brussels.

Vermeersch, P. M., Paulissen, E., and Van Neer, W., 1989, The Late Palaeolithic Makhadma Sites (Egypt), Their Environment and Subsistence, in: *Later Prehistory of the Nile Basin and the Sahara* (L. Krzyzaniak and M. Kobusiewicz, eds.), Polish Academy of Sciences, Poznan Branch, and Poznan Archaeologial Museum, Poznan, pp. 87–114.

Wasylikowa, K., 1992, Exploitation of Wild plants by Prehistoric Peoples in the Sahara, *Würzburger Geographische Arbeiten* 84:247–262.

Wendorf, F., 1968a, Late Paleolithic sites in Egyptian Nubia, in: *The Prehistory of Nubia* (F. Wendorf, ed.), Fort Burgwin Research Center and Southern Methodist University Press, Dallas, pp. 791–953.

Wendorf, F., 1968b, Site 117: A Nubian Final Paleolithic Graveyard near Jebel Sahaba, Sudan, in: *The Prehistory of Nubia* (F. Wendorf, ed.), Fort Burgwin Research Center and Southern Methodist University Press, Dallas, pp. 954–995.

Wendorf, F., 1968c, Summary of Nubian Prehistory, in: *The Prehistory of Nubia* (F. Wendorf, ed.), Fort Burgwin Research Center and Southern Methodist University Press, Dallas, pp. 1041–1060.

Wendorf, F., and Schild, R., 1976, *Prehistory of the Nile Valley*, Academic Press, New York.

Wendorf, F., and Schild, R., 1980, *Prehistory of the Eastern Sahara*, Academic Press, New York.

Wendorf, F., and Schild, R., 1989a, Report on Site E-81-5: A small Isnan assemblage, in: *The Prehistory of Wadi Kubbaniya*, Volume 3, *Late Paleolithic Archaeology* (F. Wendorf and R. Schild, assemblers, and A. E. Close, ed.), Southern Methodist University Press, Dallas, pp. 704–711.

Wendorf, F., and Schild, R., 1989b, Summary and Synthesis, in: *The Prehistory of Wadi Kubbaniya*, Volume 3, *Late Paleolithic Archaeology* (F. Wendorf and R. Schild, assemblers, and A. E. Close, ed.), Southern Methodist University Press, Dallas, pp. 768–824.

Wendorf, F., Schild, R. (assemblers), and Close, A. E. (ed.), 1984, *Cattle-Keepers of the Eastern Sahara: The Neolithic of Bir Kiseiba*, Department of Anthropology, Southern Methodist University, Dallas.

Wendorf, F., Schild, R., (assemblers), and Close, A. E. (ed.), 1989a, *The Prehistory of Wadi Kubbaniya*, Volume 2, *Stratigraphy, Paleoeconomy, and Environment*, Southern Methodist University Press, Dallas.

Wendorf, F., Schild, R. (assemblers), and Close, A. E. (ed.), 1989b, *The Prehistory of Wadi Kubbaniya*, Volume 3, *Late Paleolithic Archaeology*, Southern Methodist University Press, Dallas.

Wendorf, F., Close, A. E., Schild, R., Wasylikowa, K., Housley, R. A., Harlan, J. R., and Królik, H., 1992, Saharan Exploitation of Plants 8,000 Years BP, *Nature* 359:721–724.

Wendorf, F., Schild, R., Close, A. E., and associates, 1993, *Egypt during the Late Interglacial: The Middle Paleolithic of Bir Tarfawi and Bir Sahara East*, Plenum Press, New York.

Wenke, R. J., Long, J. E., and Buck, P. E., 1988, Epipaleolithic and Neolithic Subsistence and Settlement in the Fayyum Oasis of Egypt, *J. Field Archaeology* 15:29–51.

Wickens, G. E., 1975, Changes in the climate and vegetation of the Sudan since 20,000 B.P., *Boissiera* 24:43–65.

Williams, M. A. J., and Adamson, D. A., 1980, Late Quaternary Depositional History of the Blue and White Nile Rivers in Central Sudan, in: *The Sahara and the Nile* (M. A. J. Williams and H. Faure, eds.), Balkema, Rotterdam, pp. 281–304.

Chapter 4

The Impact of Late Pleistocene–Early Holocene Climatic Changes on Humans in Southwest Asia

OFER BAR-YOSEF

INTRODUCTION

The aim of this chapter is to provide basic evidence for the impact of climatic fluctuations on human cultures in southwest Asia during the terminal Pleistocene and early Holocene. Climatic evidence is drawn from deep sea cores in the eastern Mediterranean and terrestrial pollen records mainly from Turkey and northwest Iran, with fewer from Syria and Israel (Fontugne et al. 1994; van Zeist and Bottema 1991). Geomorphological and chemical information concerning paleolakes and river terraces is available from the Levant. Archaeological information comes from the most intensive archaeological investigations of this period conducted in the southern Levant (Israel and Jordan), with fewer data from the northern Levant (Lebanon and Syria) and fragmentary information from neighboring countries. It should therefore be noted that this geographic bias may impair the validity of the more general conclusions.

The archaeological attributes taken into account include the distribution of the Epi-Paleolithic and early Neolithic sites, their size, and the contents and volumes of sites in terms of architectural remains, mobile material culture, and ecofacts. Interpretation of archaeological records is based on what is generally known from studies of hunter–gatherers, farmers, and herders. Special attention is given to the geographic distribution of resources in the region as well as to the ways in which exploitation strategies could have been optimized.

Studies of responses to stress, either seasonal, annual, or decadal, on the part of hunter–gatherers, farmers, and herders form the bases for hypotheses concerning past

OFER BAR-YOSEF • Department of Anthropology, Peabody Museum, Harvard University, Cambridge, Massachusetts 02138.

Humans at the End of the Ice Age: The Archaeology of the Pleistocene–Holocene Transition, edited by Lawrence Guy Straus, Berit Valentin Eriksen, Jon M. Erlandson, and David R. Yesner. Plenum Press, New York, 1996.

responses and enable us to interpret archaeological remains. Stress could have been expressed as food shortages sometimes resulting in famine, failing health, or social conflicts, all of which could have led to major changes in social structure of individual groups or entire populations (Cohen 1989). Scholars often disagree about the causes of the archaeological or historically known changes. Abundant literature on diet, reproductive ecology, and disaster relief, however, may provide a basis for understanding the combined biological, social, and economic processes that result in cultural changes. Systematically gathered information following major disasters such as droughts surpasses that which is traditionally available from ethnohistorical sources alone (e.g., Glantz 1987, 1994).

The archaeological sequence of the Levant during the terminal Pleistocene–early Holocene is relatively well known, while information from the Zagros and the Taurus ranges remains scare. In contrast, the Neolithic period from the latter region and the Anatolian plateau is being better documented with major archaeological and chronological summaries (e.g., Bar-Yosef 1990, 1991; Bar-Yosef and Belfer-Cohen 1989b; Bar-Yosef and Meadow 1995; Byrd 1994; Cauvin 1994; Goring-Morris 1987; Henry 1989; Hole 1987; Mellaart 1975; Moore 1985) readily available and cited in the following discussion.

The archaeological attributes of both Epi-Paleolithic and Neolithic contexts, such as site size, thickness of deposits, building materials, architectural forms, and lithic and bone industries, are rarely a subject for major disagreements among scholars working in the region. Therefore, changes in settlement pattern such as the depopulation of large late Pre-Pottery Neolithic B (PPNB) settlements across the Levant (see below) and the reestablishment of small villages, hamlets, and farmsteads can be discussed in terms of social reaction to environmental calamities. While the basic subsistence strategies employed by late hunter–gatherers are generally understood, it is the reconstruction of the economy of the early Neolithic settlements that is still debated (for detailed accounts, see Bar-Yosef 1991; Bar-Yosef and Meadow 1995; Bar-Yosef et al. 1991; Cauvin 1994; Hillman and Davies 1990; Kislev 1989, 1992; van Zeist and Bakker-Heeres 1982/1985, 1984/1986; van Zeist and de Roller 1991/1992; D. Zohary 1992). Even if current interpretations diverge, one may find in the literature a growing awareness of the impact of climatic changes, especially on later civilizations with more complex social structure (e.g., Weiss et al. 1993). Rapid accumulation of solid data on climatic changes will enable us to rule out certain hypotheses and, more important, to attempt to understand the social processes at work.

THE REGION

The definition of the geographic region reviewed here needs clarification, since the term "southwest Asia" is ill-defined. While southwest Asia encompasses the area south of the Caucasus and the Caspian Sea to the Red Sea and the Arabian peninsula, scholars often refer to it as the "Near East" or "Middle East." In order to move away from the geopolitical connotations of these terms, I will adhere in this chapter to the geographic term.

The region of southwest Asia is characterized by a great variation in land forms and climate. The dominant topographic features are mountains (mostly of the Alpine Orogenesis), plateaus, and alluvial plains, with coastal plains often very narrow in comparison to those of other continents. The Anatolian plateau is bounded by the Pontain Mountains on the north and the Taurus Mountains on the south, each range extending about 1500 km, which join the northwestern end of the 1800-km-long Zagros Mountains. The Iranian plateau is bounded on the west and south by the Zagros Mountains, on the north by the Elburz and Kopet Dagh Mountains, and on the east by the Khurasan and Baluchistan Mountains, which separate this basin from the Nimruz basin in Afghanistan. The Mesopotamian plain stretches from the foothills of the Zagros and Taurus to the Persian Gulf and is bounded on the west by the Syro-Arabian Desert, which slopes into the Arabian peninsula (Figure 1). A special zone within the region is the Mediterranean Levant, which covers an area about 1100 km long and 250–350 km wide. Topographically, it includes the coastal mountain range (lower overall than the Taurus), the Orontes-Jordan Rift Valley, the inland mountain ranges, and the eastward-sloping desertic plateau, which is dissected by numerous wadis flowing eastward into the Syro-Arabian Desert.

The position of the region surrounded by the three landmasses of Europe, most of Asia, and Africa determines the prevailing atmospheric systems. The junction between the westerlies and the monsoonal regimes dictates the seasonal patterns of storm tracks. Although each of these atmospheric systems operates during successive seasons, winter and summer, they affect neighboring portions of the region, and their environmental impact depends on their strength. Thus, the confluence of the systems may shift position and cause climatic instability on both decadal and centennial scales.

The climate of present-day southwest Asia is dominated by two seasons: cool, rainy winters and hot, dry summers. Winter temperatures are higher in the coastal ranges and lower inland or at higher elevations. Precipitation is affected by distance from the sea and by altitude. The central Anatolian and Iranian plateaus, the Syro-Arabian Desert, and Mesopotamia are the driest zones. In the Mediterranean Levant, rainfall decreases in a north–south direction from the Taurus Mountains to the Sinai peninsula. This zone is characterized by Eu-Mediterranean vegetation comprised of woodlands or open parklands on and along the coastal ranges (M. Zohary 1973). In contrast, western Anatolia is covered by broadleaf and needleleaf trees and shrubs resistant to cold, and a cold-adapted deciduous broadleaf woodland characterizes the eastern mountains and large areas of the Zagros. Dwarf shrubland and steppic vegetation (Irano-Turanian) dominate the eastern Anatolian plateau and form a wide, arching belt south of the northern Levantine, Taurus, and northern Zagros hilly ranges. Farther south, open xeromorphic dwarf shrubland and desert plant associations (Saharo-Arabian) cover areas with an annual precipitation of less than 300–400 mm.

The current complex climatic system of southwest Asia makes it difficult to reconstruct the patterns of the past (Roberts and Wright 1993; Rognon and Wright 1982; Wigley and Farmer 1982; Wright 1993). At present, large annual rainfall fluctuations characterize the region, with storm tracks following various paths. Those that carry humidity along the Mediterranean Sea move in a more arid, southerly direction. Other storms descend from northern Europe and, while turning east over the Mediterranean Sea, leave most of the southern region dry.

These topographic contrasts between high and low altitudes, together with the effects of variable temperatures and rainfall, result in a rather varied, mixed pattern of vegetation belts and patchy environments, including oases in the Syro-Arabian desert, with a great variety of plant and animal resources exploitable by humans (M. Zohary 1973). The Terminal Pleistocene climatic changes that resulted in latitudinal, longitudinal, and altitudinal shifts of vegetation belts had direct effects on the distribution of resources and thus on relative densities of human population. In the current interpretation, the reconstructed

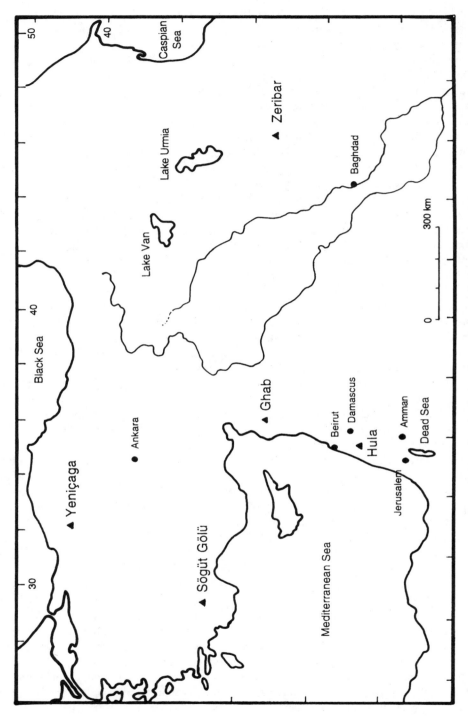

Figure 1. Map of southwest Asia showing locations of major pollen cores.

vegetation belts indicate the optimal location of the core area for the emergence of agriculture.

GENERAL CONSIDERATIONS IN RECONSTRUCTING THE PALEOCLIMATIC SEQUENCE OF SOUTHWEST ASIA

Reconstructions of past climates have traditionally been accomplished by correlating the oxygen isotope stages and the various terminations recognized in deep sea cores during the closing millennia of the Pleistocene with the terrestrial pollen record. A certain time lag between the oxygen isotope changes and vegetation shifts is to be expected. This lag becomes obvious when wetter periods are correlated with the expansion of forests. Reconstruction of the paleoclimates of southwest Asia was attempted by members of CLIMAP (1976) and COHMAP (1988), as well as by other scholars (e.g., Bar-Yosef and Belfer-Cohen 1992; Bintliff 1982; Butzer 1978; Goldberg and Bar-Yosef 1982; Henry 1986; Magaritz and Goodfriend 1987; Roberts and Wright 1993; Rognon 1982; van Zeist and Bottema 1991).

The present annual rainfall fluctuations in the Levant are considered to characterize the Holocene climate. The seasonal differences that mark the current climate originated in the Pleistocene, however, even if their strength and duration may have been different. Warm or hot summers with some rain and cold and mostly wet winters have persisted since the Lower Pleistocene, enabling the emergence of what is known as the Mediterranean vegetation belt (Suc 1984).

Today, two winter patterns of atmospheric systems prevail. The first is controlled by the storm tracks that carry humidity across the southern edge of the Mediterranean Sea, causing rain over the Negev and the Arabian Desert. The second storm track descends through Europe, leaving most of the southern Levant drier but bringing rain to the northern Levant and to the Taurus and Zagros Mountains. It is interesting to note that chemical studies of the Upper Pleistocene Lisan lake beds, which covered an area of about 2800 km^2 in the Jordan Valley, demonstrate that the geographic distribution of late Pleistocene rainfall was similar to that of today (Begin et al. 1980; Goodfriend 1990). Rather than temperature changes, trends of increasing or decreasing precipitation on decadal and centennial scales were responsible for the expansion and contraction of vegetation belts reflected in the palynological sequences and lake levels across southwest Asia (for details, see Roberts and Wright 1993; van Zeist and Bottema 1991; Yechieli et al. 1993). Despite controversy concerning the chronological interpretation of the pollen sequences (Baruch 1994; Baruch and Bottema 1991; Bottema 1987; Bottema and van Zeist 1981; van Zeist and Bottema 1982), most scholars agree that the dominant precipitation in the region was the winter rains. This view was supported by the tracing of rainstorm patterns in the study of Holocene land snails in the Negev (Goodfriend 1990). However, El-Moslimany (1982, 1994) has suggested on the basis of the relative frequencies of Poaceae pollen and its ratio to Chenopodiaceae and Artemisia (calculated from published information) that the early Holocene enjoyed summer rains. Although summer rains were probably less important than winter precipitation, their existence would have enhanced the presence of certain species of wild cereals such as diploid einkorn (Triticum boeticum) and would also explain the origin of the hexaploid wheats, considered hybrids of Aegilops squrrosa (found south of the Caspian) and Triticum diccocoides (which occurs in the Levant), which, due to summer rains, would have overlapped in their geographic distribution. The presence of the early Holocene sapropel indicates increased freshwater flooding in the Mediterranean from 9,000 to 6,000 BP (Fontugne et al. 1994) and also supports the latter scenario.

A climatic fluctuation that is currently receiving increased attention is the short, cold period of the Younger Dryas (11,000/10,800–10,300/10,000 BP) (Figure 2). The Younger Dryas was first identified as a global phenomenon on the basis of isotope values in deep sea cores in the Atlantic Ocean (Lehman and Keigwin 1992), in the Sulu Sea in the western tropical Pacific Ocean (Kudrass et al. 1991), off the coast of Japan (Kallel et al. 1988), in the northern Pacific Ocean, and in the Gulf of Mexico. Additional evidence has been retrieved from ice cores (Dansgaard et al. 1989) and recently from the advance of a glacier in New Zealand (Denton and Hendy 1994). These observations, which were gathered in distant regions, indicate that the Younger Dryas cooling was caused by changes in atmospheric circulation. Therefore, claims (e.g., van Zeist and Bottema 1991) for a lack of direct timing correlations of cold or humid spells between Europe and southwest Asia during the late Pleistocene and early Holocene cannot be substantiated.

When applied to southwestern Asia, the paleoclimatic data predict that due to topographic features, there was a time lag of up to several hundred years in the expansion of woodland and parkland belts between the coast and the inland mountain chains. In addition, the shifts in the boundary belt between the monsoonal summer rain system and the winter westerlies system meant that the southern reaches of the region could have been either arid or alternatively steppic similarly to the eastern Sahara (Neumann 1989).

Despite some apparent contradictions in the available literature, it is the author's opinion that the following summary represents a plausible reconstruction of the terminal Pleistocene–early Holocene paleoclimatic history of this region.

THE RECONSTRUCTED PALEOCLIMATIC SEQUENCE

During the Last Glacial Maximum (LGM) (24,000–16,000/14,000 BP), the climate of the entire region was cold and dry, although the coastal hilly areas enjoyed winter precipitation and were covered by forests. Precipitation across the region slowly increased from 14,000 BP onward, more rapidly from 13,500/13,000 BP to a peak around 11,500 BP. The decrease in rainfall from about 11,000 BP to 10,000 BP is correlated with the Younger Dryas.

Although there was a return to pluvial conditions around 10,000 BP, rainfall never again reached the levels of the previous peak in the southern Levant (Baruch and Bottema 1991), even though levels were higher in Anatolia and the Zagros Mountains (van Zeist and Bottema 1991). An early Holocene climate (10,000–8,000 BP) more moist than today's is recorded in pollen cores of the Levant and supported by global climatic models (COHMAP 1988).

The effects of these climatic fluctuations caused both large and small lakes in closed basins, such as Lake Lisan, to recede or dry up during the LGM. This retraction was followed by an expansion of water bodies from about 14,000 to 13,000 BP, with some fluctuations until 11,000 BP (e.g., Goldberg 1986), although the drier conditions of the Younger Dryas made certain parts of southwest Asia inhospitable. With the onset of the Holocene, certain lake levels were restored even if they did not reach previous altitudes. According to the model formulated by the COHMAP (1988) group, the Indian Ocean monsoonal system penetrated into the southern and eastern portions of southwest Asia during the period of

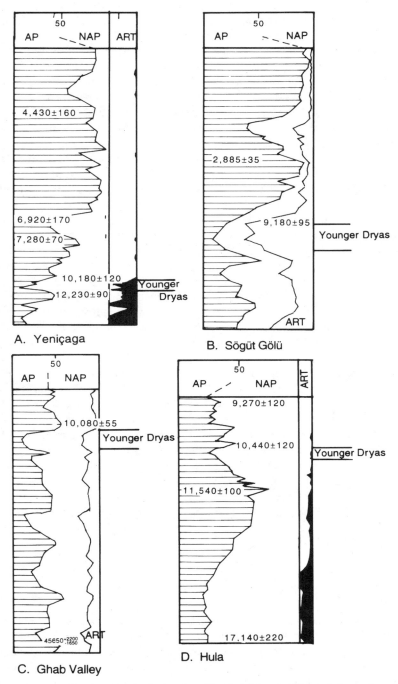

Figure 2. Major pollen diagrams for the late Last Glacial and Postglacial periods in southwest Asia.

12,000–9,000 BP (calendar years) and then retreated. The effects of such changes, mentioned above, would have meant that during several millennia the region enjoyed both winter rains and in some areas also summer rains or ephemeral summer storms. This rainfall would have increased grazing opportunities particularly in semiarid areas, but would have had little effect on the growth of the winter cereals that formed a principal base of early agriculture. The geomorphological expression for the northwest shift of the monsoonal system is recorded in the numerous paleolake deposits in Arabia with late PPNB sites and Pottery Neolithic age occurrences, which testify to wetter conditions in this arid zone.

The rise in seal level after the LGM was gradual and continued until the mid-Holocene. During the Holocene, the Levantine coastal plain from southeast Turkey to the Nile delta lost to the sea a stretch of land varying in width from 2 to 4 km along 600 km of coastline. Some of the best-documented cases for the sea rise are the PPNB site of Atlit-Yam (Galili et al. 1993) and the later Pottery Neolithic and Chalcolithic sites along the coast of Mount Carmel. Although such an inundation would have affected the territory size for both hunter–gatherers and early farmers, as this part of the Mediterranean Sea was particularly saline and therefore aquatic food resources were minimal, the main cultural impact would have been on the collection of marine shells used for decoration.

Early Holocene pluvial conditions may have fluctuated, but appear to have lasted through the Pre-Pottery Neolithic A (PPNA) and PPNB periods (10,300/10,000–9,500/300 and to 8,000 BP). The retreat of the monsoonal system around 9,000 BP is correlated with the uncalibrated date of 8,000/7,800 BP (Stuiver and Braziunas 1993) that marks the final phase of the Levantine PPNB. It is therefore not surprising that the "collapse" of the PPNB and the phase known as PPNC that designate a cultural change are correlated with a major climatic shift.

The entire terminal Pleistocene–early Holocene paleoclimatic sequence is supported by dated geomorphic events and paleosols (Goldberg 1986, 1994; Goodfriend and Magaritz 1988). Among the important changes was the main shrinkage of Lake Lisan from its maximum expansion at 180 m below sea level that occurred during the Kebaran (18,000/19,000–13,000 BP, uncalibrated) and before the early Natufian (13,000/12,800–11,000 BP, uncalibrated) (Bar-Yosef 1987). The entire valley floor was exposed, and the Jordan River, from its outlet in Lake Kineret, started incising its channel in the soft Lisan marls. The wetter and warmer period of the early Natufian, however, did not restore the full surface of the lake, and the Younger Dryas, correlated with the late Natufian, caused a major shrinkage. Thus, the PPNA site of Gesher, located in the Beith Shean (Beisan) basin, is situated at 245 m below sea level. This evidence makes untenable the reconstruction of Lake Beisan suggested by Koucky and Smith (1986).

THE IMPACT OF CLIMATIC CHANGES ON HUMANS

In studying human responses to natural disasters such as droughts and famines, researchers who work in relief programs have identified several aspects of interaction between societies and their environments. In analyzing the effects of stress or disaster, the following aspects are taken into account in an ascending order from a group level (band, macroband, tribe) through the regional scale that accommodates several populations (e.g., Copans 1983; Glantz 1987; Hewitt 1983):

1. Human ability to control such natural factors of production as, for example, the size of wild animal populations, the growth of certain wild stands of edible seeds or fruit trees, availability of water within the vicinity of the settlement, and the quality of cultivable land and pastures.
2. Social organization of foragers, farmers, and herders and the articulation between the social unit and the mode and structure of exploitation, including such factors as, for example, the social perception of the settlement, the home ranges, and the presence of sacred localities.
3. Knowledge on the part of local inhabitants that most natural disasters, such as droughts and their effects, are characteristic phenomena of marginal areas, with the level of preparedness for natural disasters depending on the degree of their relative rarity in the living memory of the social unit (e.g., Minc 1986).
4. The scale of an entire region, such as southwest Asia, and the existing variability of social organizations, alliances, and history of conflicts, as well as the different modes of food acquisition or production.

The reconstruction of the basic settlement patterns is taken to reflect the summary of lifeways of various populations of hunter–gatherers, farmers, and herders in southwest Asia. By recognizing the various modes of socioeconomic structure, we may identify the cultural filter used by each group to respond to a natural disaster. In evaluating the impact of sudden calamities or prolonged periods of food stress, we need to consider what is generally known about subsistence practices and social organization (including aspects of territorial perception, ritual, cosmology, and religion) of hunter–gatherers, farmers, and herders (e.g., Barnard 1992; Binford 1978; Glantz 1987; Hawkes and O'Connell 1992; Jochim 1981; Kent 1992). The application of this cummulative knowledge to the particular conditions of southwest Asia as summarized in the literature (e.g., Bar-Yosef and Belfer-Cohen 1989b, 1991, 1992; Bar-Yosef and Khazanov 1992; Bar-Yosef and Meadow 1995; Henry 1989) is the basis for the following interpretation of the archaeological record.

THE IMPACT OF CLIMATIC CHANGES ON CULTURAL ENTITIES

In the following pages, the impact of the climatic fluctuations on each of the known cultural entities is discussed. It is assumed that the reader is familiar with the archaeological definition of each entity. Archaeological summarizes, mostly mentioned above, take into account an entire set of archaeological aspects, including lithic industries, their manufacturing methods, tool hafting and retooling, function of artifacts as recorded by microwear and edge damage, different types of pounding and grinding stone tools, bone objects, their manufacturing process and use, the contents of sites (e.g., structures, silos, caches, special-purpose buildings, garbage areas), mortuary practices, and "art objects." The overall settlement pattern classified within a scale from high mobility to sedentary communities is defined essentially on the basis of biological remains. The combined features of well-defined archaeological entities indicate, similarly to genetic and linguistic studies (Sokal et al. 1991), that in future research we should expect to be able to identify boundaries between prehistoric populations.

The baseline for the current reconstruction is the time of the LGM. The evidence at hand indicates that the distribution of Kebaran sites and similar entities was limited to the coastal mountains in the Levant and a few oases (e.g., Bar-Yosef 1991; Byrd and Garrard 1990). Recent work in southwest Turkey (Yalçinkaya et al. 1995) hints of a similar situation there, while little is known about other areas such as the Zagros foothills (e.g., Smith 1986). One may expect that population densities dwindled toward the more arid high plateaus and the desert belt, and the evidence from the Sinai peninsula and the eastern Sahara supports this conclusion. Winter rains enabled the occupation of wadis flowing into oases such as the Azraq basin (Garrard et al. 1994).

Within the coastal zone, the settlement pattern seems to have been one of relatively low residential mobility. Estimates of carrying capacity within the Mediterranean vegetation belt and the margins of the Irano-Turanian vegetation belt indicate that 500–1000 km² would have been the area required to feed a band of hunter–gatherers, and thus marriage networks would have encompassed large territories. Poor chronological control of the period from 18,000 BP to 14,000 BP, however, prevents us from testing hypotheses correlating lithic variability, group size, settlement pattern, territorial perception, presence of sacred locals, and exogamous marriage ties.

The period beginning by 14,000 BP marks a period of population expansion that was facilitated, on the basis of pollen data, the $^{16/18}$O curves, and geomorphological evidence, by the expansion of the Mediterranean and Irano-Turanian vegetation belts. Increased precipitation rapidly enlarged potential hunting and gathering territories, thus allowing for the relaxation of reproductive restraints and resulting in a population increase. The presence of the Geometric Kebaran and Mushabian entities in Sinai and southern Jordan (Bar-Yosef and Belfer-Cohen 1989b, 1992; Henry 1989; Phillips and Mintz 1977) can be interpreted only as the opening of semiarid territories to exploitation. The sites in central Jordan (Wadi Jilat and the Azraq basin) not only are larger in surface area but also have thicker deposits (Byrd and Garrard 1990; Garrard et al. 1994).

The archaeological material culture, which in many sites is limited to lithic assemblages, does not permit us to answer the question of whether this expansion was also accompanied by technological innovations. Rather, it seems that systematically high frequencies of microliths in most assemblages and the appearance of similar types of microliths in diverse environments, although based on only a few microwear analyses, indicate that these retouched pieces served as parts of projectiles. The presence of the same types over time and space reflects continued technological traditions. We may imagine, however, that the population expansion into a rich steppic region during at least a thousand radiocarbon years allowed the splitting of groups and the movement of other groups from poorer areas into this zone. Thus, it is not surprising that although most groups exploited the same resources, some chose to use different types of composite projectiles or knives or both made of hafted microliths. The greatest technotypological variability is recorded in Jordan (Byrd and Garrard 1990; Garrard et al. 1988, 1994; Henry 1989).

A major change is expressed with the establishment of the early Natufian culture. The explanation preferred by the author is that this archaeological entity emerged as a socioeconomic response to stress on the part of hunter–gatherers who were already practicing anticipated mobility (for detailed explanations, see Bar-Yosef and Belfer-Cohen 1989b, 1991, 1992; Belfer-Cohen 1991; Belfer-Cohen and Bar-Yosef in press). Needless to say, other explanations are possible. For example, the Hula pollen core (Baruch and Bottema 1991; Weinstein-Evron 1990) suggests a rapid increase in precipitation around 13,000 BP. This change would have led to increase in carrying capacity of smaller territories, thus enabling a much shorter search for both animal and vegetable food. Therefore, a "pull" model might also explain the emergence of the early Natufian.

Although Natufian sedentism remains a subject for argument, it seems that the overwhelming biological evidence from various sites indicates that esoteric ethnographic comparisons are of limited value (e.g., Tchernov 1984, 1991, 1993; Lieberman 1993 contra Wyncoll and Tangri 1991). Although sedentism can be defined in various ways, in the context of the Levantine research it is understood as the presence of a base camp, or a hamlet, that is inhabited for at least 9 months during the year (Bar-Yosef and Belfer-Cohen 1992; Bar-Yosef and Meadow 1995). In the territory held by a certain group, not far from the base camp, one can find ephemeral camps or small temporary individual stations. An example is the Natufian occupation in Sefunim cave in the Mount Carmel area (Ronen 1984). Other examples are sites at which annual exploitation of cereals and other food sources, including hunting and trapping, took place. For the Natufian base camps on the western flanks of the Galilee–Judea hills, facing the coastal plain, such seasonal sites were in the Jordan Valley (Bar-Yosef 1975). The predicted time of their occupation, spring–summer, is supported by the analysis of cementum increments of gazelle teeth (Lieberman 1993). Somewhat similar distribution is predicted for the Jordanian plateau, from the Gebel Druze area (in southern Syria) to the Edom mountains. Sites such as Wadi Hammeh 27 could have been small base camps situated on the western slopes of the plateau and receiving the same amount of rain as Mount Carmel, while sites such as Azraq 18 (Garrard et al. 1994) could have been ephemeral sites occupied during one season. No doubt the diversity of Natufian sites (in terms of function, duration of occupation, subsistence, and cultural activities) is larger than this over simplified dichotomy (e.g., Byrd 1989).

It is well established that early Natufian sites and their contents differ in many aspects from the late Natufian, dated to 11,000–10,300 BP (Bar-Yosef and Belfer-Cohen 1989b; Belfer-Cohen 1991; Garrod 1957; Valla 1975, 1981). Although additional early Natufian sites are expected to be found in southern Syria, perhaps in the Damascus basin, the ephemeral occupation of Yabrud III (Rust 1950) indicates the exploitation of the more arid, higher areas.

The late Natufian is marked by wider geographic distribution of occupations. During this time, new sites were established in the Negev highlands, the Jordanian plateau, and as far as the valley of the middle Euphrates (Byrd 1989; Cauvin 1994; Henry 1989). The most interesting phenomenon is that farther north, at the flanks of the Taurus, similar villages were established by a population that carried the Zagros tradition of making microlithic stone tools dominated by triangles. The first site to be excavated there was Hallan Çemi, where rounded houses and a "plaza" were uncovered (Rosenberg 1994). The establishment of such village sites during the Younger Dryas means that more lush areas remained unaffected.

The increase in population during the early Natufian forced the social groups, whether large or small, to search for various options of local adaptations. Certain groups became mobile and thus returned to the old lifeways (for additional details, see Belfer-Cohen and Bar-Yosef in press). Others moved and established new, perhaps even smaller hamlets. Additional filed work in southeast Turkey should be expected to reveal new villages dated to this period (11,000–10,000 BP, uncalibrated) that would indicate that the role of the dry and cold climate of the Younger Dryas was ameliorated in the coastal northern hilly ranges.

The important role of the Younger Dryas in the Levant, and perhaps more particularly in the southern Levant that borders arid belts on two or three sides, can be traced in the archaeological record. As mentioned above, the harsher conditions forced late Natufians to change their lifeways. The Harifian culture in the Negev and northern Sinai (an area of about 30,000 km^2) is the archaeological expression of what economic stress can do (Bar-Yosef 1987; Goring-Morris 1987, 1991). The Harifian settlement pattern consists of small base camps, occupied during spring–summer and perhaps the fall, in the Negev highlands, and small ephemeral winter sites in the western lowlands. Such a settlement pattern provided sufficient amounts of plant food and game during the warmer part of the year when social agglomeration could have taken place, with social fissioning during the lean season, which in this region lasted from November through February. Obviously, biodata are needed in order to support this archaeological interpretation.

Other late Natufian groups opted for a different solution. The decreasing yields of collected cereals and other C$_3$ plant food resulting from the effects of the dry and cold years prompted them to compensate by enlarging their territories, moving the more permanent camps closer to the wild stands of cereals, and eventually to begin cultivating the cereals. The end result in terms of settlement pattern is that the larger PPNA sites are located in the Jordan Valley, where previously only rather small seasonal Natufian camps were found. In addition, referring to the argument concerning the morphological attributes of domestication of cereals (e.g., Kislev 1989, 1992 contra D. Zohary 1992), it is not impossible that the earliest PPNA villages and hamlets survived by hunting, trapping, and gathering wild fruits and vegetables, as well as by intensive harvesting of wild stands and not by cultivation, as is often claimed. This scenario is amenable to scientific testing, as the effects on the Younger Dryas have been documented through paleobotanical remains and especially by analyzing $^{16/18}$O ratios of noncarbonized seeds. Thus, chain decisions concerning site location and shifts in procurement strategies could have led to changes in the social realm and resulted in the emergence of farming or cultivating communities during this cold and dry period.

The PPNA economy spread rapidly through the "Levantine corridor" (Bar-Yosef and Belfer-Cohen 1989b, 1992) into southeast Turkey and resulted in the establishment of a specific pattern of site distribution also reflected in site size. Along the cultivated land, large communities were founded, while within both marginal areas, hunter–gatherers continued to practice the old subsistence strategies. Most early villages did not last more than several hundred radiocarbon years in one locale. Salinization and overexploitation of wild resources (both plant and animal), coupled with increasing population, forced them to shift site location and let nature restore the exhausted environments. Alluviation, and in some place also colluviation, caused the renewal of lowlands and alluvial fans, as well as the burial of sites or their lower levels as evidenced in Jericho, Netiv Hagdud, and Hatoula (Bar-Yosef 1986). It is not known whether small climatic fluctuations during this time span (10,300–9,500/9,300 BP) had any effect on settlement movements. In addition, a stable economy led to an increase in population size, and, as explained elsewhere (Bar-Yosef and Belfer-Cohen 1989a), this increase resulted in an entirely viable social group at one site that reduced the geographic spread of the mating system, thus leading to the emergence of local cultures, specific social structures, and particular rituals.

The PPNB, archaeologically and radiometrically defined as a longer period than the previous one (9,500/300–7,800/500 BP), is marked by the rapid distribution of farming communities into Anatolia. There, in the inland plateau and flat highland, the cereals that lacked natural rivals among the wild weeds enjoyed an overwhelming success. Communities became larger, and social structure developed to be more complex both within and among sites (Cauvin 1994) (compare, for example, Çayönü [Özdögan and Özdögan 1989], Çatal Hüyük [Mellaart 1967], and Asikli Hüyük [Esin et al. 1991]). The climatic crisis that came around 8,000 BP involved warming, seal-level rise, decreased winter rains, and the final retreat of the monsoonal system from the semiarid vast areas of the Arabian peninsula, and made it more difficult for the Levantine Neolithic people in the villages to subsist. The complex social structure that had developed during a millennium or more collapsed.

It has been suggested that the environmental degradation was caused by grazing animals and extensive wood-cutting (Rollefson and Köhler-Rollefson 1989; Simmons et al. 1988). Modern research on the role of goats and sheep in overgrazing does support the notion that PPNB herds caused the damage. The impact of cutting trees for firewood and for making lime has also been shown to be exaggerated, as recent research (Goren and Goldberg 1991) has demonstrated that only small quantities of lime are incorporated in the plaster floors. It therefore seems that a more regional cause led to the abandonment of many PPNB sites across the Levant. A climate change would have affected even the more mesic belt of the Mediterranean woodland zone. This change is reflected in a major shift in settlement pattern. The size hierarchy of PPNB villages, where the largest attained 12 hectares, was replaced by distribution of mostly hamlets and farmsteads over the entire region, occupying the same ecological niches (e.g., Banning et al. 1994; Bar-Yosef and Belfer-Cohen 1989a; Gopher and Gofna 1993).

The economic basis during the ensuing millennium (8,000–7,000 BP) remained the same as in the previous millennium: Cultivation of cereals, legumes, and flax and the herding of goats and sheep continued to be essential activities. Furthermore, cattle and pigs were introduced into the Levant from Anatolia, and the purposive tending of fruit trees became a systematic agricultural activity, as is apparent from the archaeobotanical remains. Olives, figs, and, later, dates and vines were grown. In sum, it seems that the climatic change did not drive the people out of the region. Rather, it may have enhanced earlier trends when regions such as Anatolia, certain areas in northern Mesopotamia, and the intermontane valleys of the Zagros became the center of agricultural and social development. One may even suggest that the PPNB collapse in the Levant marked the rapidly decreasing importance, on a regional scale, of this area in southwest Asia.

What followed was a warm period (the Atlantic) called the "altithermal" (or "Climatic Optimum") around 4,500 BP. The dominant source of precipitation was still the winter rains, and the contribution of the monsoonal system of summer rains finally ceased. Culturally, this was the time when the Mesopotamian civilizations flourished, when urban organization emerged, and pastoralism as a mode of life rapidly expanded. The climatic conditions enabled the establishment of mixed farming–herding economies on what today are the margins of the desert. One such well-studied cultural phenomenon is the Ghassulian in the Negev (Levy 1994).

CONCLUSION

This chapter argues that the climatic changes through the terminal Pleistocene and early Holocene were experienced through various cultural filters responsible for the emergence of agriculture and for the rise of pastoralism in the Syro-Arabian desert. We may view the social realignments and reorganizations in light of fluctuating environmental changes that several times broadened or constricted the size of areas suitable for productive hunting and gathering and later for cultivation and pastoralism. Nevertheless, one should not belittle the role that social decisions played in determining the economic outcome. Even a cursory survey of the literature concerning relief efforts may indicate the important role played by individuals, local chiefs, and governments. Many decisions are made, however, within the constraints of the social structure of the affected population as well as its religion and cosmological views. While several of these aspects are not easily reconstructed from the prehistoric records, Neolithic contexts in southwest Asia provide a wealth of information (e.g., Bar-Yosef and Alon 1988; Garfinkel 1994; Hole 1983; Rollefson 1983, 1986; Voigt 1983, 1991). Concerning these issues, we can also assume that decisions undertaken as a response to an abrupt climatic change or ecological disaster led to unintentional and unpredicted results. Thus, the decision to relocate a site during the Younger Dryas, or to cultivate, resulted in the domestication of cereals, legumes, and other plant foods. Similarly, penning herd animals such as goats and sheep resulted in their domestication. Recognizing the role of social forces and social decision, however, does not exclude the possibility that some of the more important cultural changes were triggered by an abrupt climatic change.

REFERENCES

Banning, R. B., Rahimi, D., and Siggers, J., 1994, The Late Neolithic of the Southern Levant: Hiatus, Settlement Shift or Observer Bias? *Paléorient* 20(2):151–164.

Barnard, A., 1992, *Hunters and Herders of Southern Africa: A Comparative Ethnography of the Khoisan Peoples*, Cambridge University Press, Cambridge.

Baruch, U., 1994, The Late Quaternary Pollen Record of the Near East, in: *Late Quaternary Chronology and Paleoclimates of the Eastern Mediterranean* (O. Bar-Yosef and R. Kra, eds.), Radiocarbon and the ASPR, Tucson, AZ, and Cambridge, MA, pp. 103–120.

Baruch, U., and Bottema, S., 1991, Palynological Evidence for Climatic Changes in the Levant ca. 17,000–9,000 B.P., in: *The Natufian Culture in the Levant*, International Monographs in Prehistory, Ann Arbor, pp. 11–20.

Bar-Yosef, O., 1975, The Epi-Palaeolithic in Palestine and Sinai, in: *Problems in Prehistory* (F. Wondorf and A. E. Marks, eds.), Southern Methodist University Press, Dallas, pp. 363–378.

Bar-Yosef, O., 1986, The Walls of Jericho: An Alternative Explanation, *Current Anthropology* 27:157–162.

Bar-Yosef, O., 1987, The Origins and Early Stages of Pastoral Societies in the Levant, *Israel-Am VeAretz (Annual of the Museum of Eretz Israel Tel Aviv)* 4:85–100 (in Hebrew).

Bar-Yosef, O., 1990, The Last Glacial Maximum in the Mediterranean Levant, in: *The World at 18,000 BP*, Volume 2, *Low Latitudes* (C. Gamble and O. Saffer, eds.), Unwin Hyman, London: pp. 58–72.

Bar-Yosef, O., 1991, The Early Neolithic of the Levant: Recent Advances, *Review of Archaeology* 12(2):1–18.

Bar-Yosef, O., and Alon, D., 1988, Excavations in the Nahal Hemar Cave, *Atiqot* 18:1–30.

Bar-Yosef, O., and Belfer-Cohen, A., 1989a, The Levantine "PPNB" Interaction Sphere, in: *People and Culture in Change*, British Archaeological Reports, International Series 508i, Oxford, pp. 59–72.

Bar-Yosef, O., and Belfer-Cohen, A., 1989b, The Origins of Sedentism and Farming Communities in the Levant, *Journal of World Prehistory* 3(4):447–498.

Bar-Yosef, O., and Belfer-Cohen, A., 1991, From Sedentary Hunter–Gatherers to Territorial Farmers in the Levant, in: *Between Bands and States* (S. A. Gregg, ed.), Center for Archaeological Investigations, Carbondale, pp. 181–202.

Bar-Yosef, O., and Belfer-Cohen, A., 1992, From Foraging to Farming in the Mediterranean Levant, in: *Transitions to Agriculture in Prehistory* (A. B. Gebauer and T. D. Price, eds.), Prehistory Press, Madison, Wisconsin, pp. 21–48.

Bar-Yosef, O., and Khazanov, A., ed., 1992, *Pastoralism in the Levant: Archaeological Materials in Anthropological Perspectives*, Prehistory Press, Madison.

Bar-Yosef, O., and Meadow, R. H., 1995, The Origins of agriculture in the Near East, in: *Last Hunters, First Farmers: New Perspectives on the Prehistoric Transition for Agriculture* (T. D. Price and G. Gebauer, eds.), School of American Research, Santa Fe.

Bar-Yosef, O., Gopher, A., Tchernov, E., and Kislev, M. E., 1991, Netiv Hagdud—An Early Neolithic Village Site in the Jordan Valley, *Journal of Field Archaeology* 18(4):405–424.

Begin, Z. B., Nathan, Y., and Erlich, A., 1980, Stratigraphy and Facies Distribution in the Lisan Formation: New Evidence from the South of the Dead Sea, *Israel Journal of Earth Sciences* 29:182–189.

Belfer-Cohen, A., 1991, The Natufian in the Levant, *Annual Review of Anthropology* 20:167–186.

Belfer-Cohen, A., and Bar-Yosef, O., in press, Early Sedentism in the Near East: A Bumpy Road to Village Life (13,000–8,000 B.P.). Paper presented at the 1993 Meeting of the Society for American Archaeology, Anaheim.

Binford, L. R., 1978, *Nunamiut Ethnoarchaeology*, Academic Press, New York.

Bintliff, J. L., 1982, *Palaeoclimatic Modelling of Environmental Changes in the East Mediterranean Region since the Last Glaciation*, British Archaeological Reports International Series 133, Oxford.

Bottema, S., 1987, Chronology and Climatic Phases in the Near East from 16,000 to 10,000 BP, in: *Chronologies in the Near East* (O. Aurenche, J. Evin, and F. Hours, eds.), British Archaeological Reports, International Series 379(i), Oxford, pp. 295–310.

Bottema, S., and Van Zeist, W., 1981, Palynological Evidence for the Climatic History of the Near East 50,000–6000 BP, in: *Prehistoire du Levant* (J. Cauvin and P. Sanlaville, eds.), Editions CNRS, Paris, pp. 111–132.

Butzer, K. W., 1978, The Late Prehistoric Environmental History of the Near East, in: *The Environmental History of the Near and Middle East since the Last Ice Age* (W. C. Brice, ed.), Academic Press, London, pp. 5–12.

Byrd, B. F., 1989, The Natufian: Settlement Variability and Economic Adaptations in the Levant at the End of the Pleistocene, *Journal of World Prehistory* 3(2):159–198.

Byrd, B. F., 1994, Late Quaternary Hunter–Gatherer Complexes in the Levant between 20,000 and 10,000 BP, in: *Late Quaternary Chronology and Paleoclimates of the Eastern Mediterranean* (O. Bar-Yosef and R. Kra, ed.), Radiocarbon and the ASPR, Tucson, AZ, and Cambridge, MA, pp. 205–226.

Byrd, B. F., and Garrard, A. N., 1990, The Last Glacial Maximum in the Jordanian Desert, in: *The World at 18,000 BP*, Volume 2, *Low Latitudes* (C. Gamble and O. Soffer, eds.), Unwin Hyman, London, pp. 78–92.

Cauvin, J., 1994, *Naissance des Divinités, Naissance de l'Agriculture*, CNRS, Paris.

CLIMAP, 1976, The Surface of the Ice-Age Earth, *Science* 191:1131–1137.

Cohen, M. N., 1989, *Health and the Rise of Civilization*, Yale University Press, New Haven.

COHMAP, 1988, Climatic Changes of the Last 18,000 Years: Observations and Model Simulations, *Science* 241:1043–1052.

Copans, J., 1983, The Sahelian Drought: Social Sciences and the Political Economy of Underdevelopment, in: *Interpretations of Calamity from the Viewpoint of Human Ecology* (K. Hewitt, ed.), Allen and Unwin Inc., Boston, pp. 83–97.

Dansgaard, W., White, J. W. C., and Johnsen, S. J., 1989, The Abrupt Termination of the Younger Dryas Climate Event, *Nature* 339:532–534.

Denton, G. H., and Hendy, C. H., 1994, Younger Dryas Age Advance for Franz Josef Glacier in the Southern Alps of New Zealand, *Science* 264:1434–1437.

El-Moslimany, A. P., 1982, The Late Quaternary Vegetational History of the Zagros and Taurus Mountains in the Regions of Lake Mirabad, Lake Zeribar, and Lake Van: A Reappraisal, in: *Plaeoclimates, Palaeoenvironments and Human Communities in the Eastern Mediterranean Region in Later Prehistory* (J. L. Bintliff and W. van Zeist, eds.), British Archaeological Reports International Series 133(ii), Oxford, pp. 343–351.

El-Moslimany, A. P., 1994, Evidence of Early Holocene Summer Precipitation in the Continental Middle East, in: *Late Quaternary Chronology and Paleoclimates of the Eastern Mediterranean* (O. Bar-Yosef and R. Kra, eds.), Radiocarbon and the ASPR, Tucson and Cambridge, pp. 121–130.

Esin, U., Biçakçu, E., Ösbasaran, M., Balkan Atli, N., Berker, D., Uagmur, I., and Korkurt Atli, A., 1991, Salvage Excavations at the Pre-Pottery Site of Asikli Hoyuk in Central Anatolia, *Anatolica* 27:124–174.

Fontugne, M., Arnold, M., Labeyre, L., Paterne, M., Calvert, S. E., and Duplessy, J.-C., 1994, Paleoenvironment, Sapropel Chronology and Nile River Discharge during the Last 20,000 Years as Indicated by Deep-Sea Sediment Records, in: *Late Quaternary Chronology and Paleoclimates of the Eastern Mediterranean* (O. Bar-Yosef and R. Kra, eds.), Radiocarbon and the ASPR, Tucson, AZ, and Cambridge, MA, pp. 75–88.

Galili, E., Weinstein-Evron, M., Hershkovitz, I., Gopher, A., Lernau, O., Kolski-Horwitz, L., and Lernau, H.,

1993, Atlit-Yam: A Prehistoric Site on the Sea Floor off the Israeli Coast, *Journal of Field Archaeology* 20(2): 133–157.

Garfinkel, Y., 1994, Ritual Burial of Cultic Objects: The Earliest Evidence, *Cambridge Archaeological Journal* 4(2):159–188.

Garrard, A. N., Betts, A., Byrd, B., and Hunt, C., 1988, Summary of Palaeoenvironmental and Prehistoric Investigations in the Azraq Basin, in: *The Prehistory of Jordan* (A. N. Garrard and H. G. Gebel, eds.), British Archaeological Reports, Oxford, pp. 311–337.

Garrard, A., Baird, D., and Byrd, B. F., 1994, The chronological basis and significance of the Late Paleolithic and Neolithic sequence in the Azraq Basin, Jordan, in: *Late Quaternary Chronology and Paleoclimates of the Eastern Mediterranean* (O. Bar-Yosef and R. Kra, eds.), Radiocarbon and the ASPR, Tucson, AZ, and Cambridge, MA, pp. 177–200.

Garrod, D. A. E., 1957, The Natufian Culture: The Life and Economy of a Mesolithic People in the Near East, *Proceedings of the British Academy* 43:211–227.

Glantz, M. H. (ed.), 1987, *Drought and Hunger in Africa*, Cambridge University Press, Cambridge.

Glantz, M. H. (ed.), 1994, *Drought Follows the Plow*, Cambridge University Press, Cambridge, UK.

Goldberg, P., 1986, Late Quarternary Environmental History of the Southern Levant, *Geoarchaeology* 1:225–244.

Goldberg, P., 1994, Interpreting Late Quarternary Continental Sequences in Israel, in: *Late Quarternary Chronology and Paleoclimates of the Eastern Mediterranean* (O. Bar-Yosef and R. Kra, eds.), Radiocarbon and the ASPR, Tucson, AZ, and Cambridge, MA, pp. 89–102.

Goldberg, P., and Bar-Yosef, O., 1982, Environmental and Archaeological Evidence for Climatic Change in the Southern Levant, in: *Paleoclimates, Palaeoenvironments and Human Communities in the Eastern Mediterranean Region in Later Prehistory* (J. L. Bintliff and W. van Zeist, eds.), British Archaeological Reports International Series 133(ii), Oxford, pp. 399–414.

Goodfriend, G. A., 1990, Rainfall in the Negev Desert during the Middle Holocene, Based on [13]C Organic Matter in Land Snail Shells, *Quaternary Research* 34:186–197.

Goodfriend, G. A., and Magaritz, M., 1988, Palaeosols and Late Pleistocene Rainfall Fluctuations in the Negev Desert, *Nature* 332:144–146.

Gopher, A., and Gophna, R., 1993, Cultures of the Eighth and Seventh Millennium BP in Southern Levant: A Review for the 1990's, *Journal of World Prehistory* 7(3):297–351.

Goren, Y., and Goldberg, P., 1991, Petrographic Thin Sections and the Development of Neolithic Plaster Production in Northern Israel, *Journal of Field Archaeology* 18:131–138.

Goring-Morris, A. N., 1987, *At the Edge: Terminal Pleistocene Hunter-Gatherers in the Negev and Sinai*, British Archaeological Reports, Oxford.

Goring-Morris, A. N., 1991, The Harifian of the Southern Levant, in: *The Natufian Culture in the Levant* (O. Bar-Yosef and F. R. Valla, eds.), International Monographs in Prehistory, Madison, pp. 173–216.

Hawkes, K., and O'Connell, J., 1992, On Optimal Foraging Models and Subsistence Transitions, *Current Anthropology* 23(1):63–66.

Henry, D. O., 1986, The Prehistory and Palaeoenvironments of Jordan: An Overview, *Paléorient* 12(2):5–26.

Henry, D. O., 1989, *From Foraging to Agriculture: The Levant at the End of the Ice Age*, University of Pennsylvania Press, Philadelphia.

Hewitt, K. (ed.), 1983, *Interpretations of Calamity from the Viewpoint of Human Ecology*, Allen and Unwin, Inc., Boston.

Hillman, G. C., and Davies, M. S., 1990, Measured Domestication Rates in Wild Wheats and Barley under Primitive Implications, *Journal of World Prehistory* 4(2):157–222.

Hole, F., 1983, Symbols of Religion and Social Organization at Susa, in: *Prehistoric Archaeology Along the Zagros Flanks* (L. Braidwood, J. R. Braidwood, B. Howe, C. A. Reed, and P. J. Watson, eds.), Oriental Institute, Chicago, pp. 315–331.

Hole, F., 1987, Archaeology of the Village Period, in: *The Archaeology of Western Iran* (F. Hole, ed.), Smithsonian Institution Press, Washington, DC, pp. 29–78.

Jochim, M. A., 1981, *Strategies for Survival: Cultural Behavior in an Ecological Context*, Academic Press, New York.

Kallel, N., Labeyrie, L. D., Juillet-Leclere, A., and Duplessy, J.-C., 1988, A Deep Hydrological Front between Intermediate and Deeper-Water-Masses in the Glacial Indian Ocean, *Nature* 333:651–655.

Kent, S., 1992, The current forager controversy: Real versus ideal views of hunter–gatherers, *Man* 27(1):45–70.

Kislev, M. E., 1989, Pre-Domesticated Cereals in the Pre-Pottery Neolithic A Period, in: *People and Culture in Change* (I. Hershkovitz, ed.), British Archaeological Reports, International Series 508i, Oxford, pp. 147–152.

Kislev, M. E., 1992, Agriculture in the Near East in the VIIth Millennium B.C., in: *Préhistoire de l'Agriculture: Nouvelles Approches Experimentales et Ethnographiques* (P. C. Anderson, ed.), Editions du CNRS, Paris, pp. 87–93.

Koucky, F. L., and Smith, R. H., 1986, Lake Beisan and Prehistoric Settlement of the Northern Jordan Valley, *Paléorient* 12(2):27–36.

Kudrass, H. R., Erlenkeuser, H., Vollbrecht, R., and Weiss, W., 1991, Global Nature of the Younger Dryas Cooling Event Inferred from Oxygen Isotope Data from Sulu Sea Cores, *Nature* 349:406–409.

Lehman, S. J., and Keigwin, L. D., 1992, Sudden Changes in North Atlantic Circulation during the Last Deglaciation, *Nature* 356:757–762.

Levy, T., ed., 1994, *The Archaeology of Society in the Holy Land*, Pinter Publishers, London.

Lieberman, D. E., 1993, The Rise and Fall of Seasonal Mobility among Hunter–Gatherers, *Current Anthropology* 34(5):599–631.

Margaritz, M., and Goodfriend, G. A., 1987, Movement of the Desert Boundary in the Levant from the Latest Pleistocene to the Early Holocene, in: *Abrupt Climatic Changes* (W. H. Berter and L. D. Labeyrie, eds.), D. Reidel Publishing, Dordrecht, pp. 173–183.

Mellaart, J., 1967, *Catal Hüyük, A Neolithic Town in Anatolia*, Thames and Hudson, London.

Mellaart, J., 1975, *The Neolithic of the Near East*, Thames and Hudson, London.

Minc, L. D., 1986, Scarcity and Survival: The Role of Oral Tradition in Mediating Subsistence Crisis, *Journal of Anthropological Archaeology* 5(1):39–113.

Moore, A., 1985, The development of Neolithic Societies in the Near East, in: *Advances in World Archaeology* (F. Wendorf and A. E. Close, eds.), Academic Press, New York, pp. 1–69.

Neumann, K., 1989, Holocene Vegetation of the Eastern Sahara: Charcoal from Prehistoric Sites, *The African Archaeological Review* 7:97–116.

Özdögan, M., and Özdögan, A., 1989, Çayönü, a Conspectus of Recent Work, *Paléorient* 15(1):65–74.

Phillips, J. L., and Minz, E., 1977, The Mushabian, in: *Prehistoric Investigations in Gebel Meghara, Northern Sinai* (O. Bar-Yosef and J. L. Phillips, eds.), Hebrew University, Jerusalem, pp. 149–183.

Roberts, N., and Wright, Jr., H. E., 1993, Vegetational, Lake Level, and Climatic History of the Near East and Southwest Asia, in: *Global Changes Since the Last Glacial Maximum* (H. E. Wright, Jr., J. E. Kutzbach, T. Web III, F. Ruddiman, F. A. Street-Perrott, and P. J. Bartlein, eds.), University of Minnesota Press, Minneapolis, pp. 194–220.

Rognon, P., 1982, Modifications des Climats et des Environments en Afrique du Nord et au Moyen Orient depuis 20,000 BP, in: *Palaeoclimates, Palaeoenvironments and Human Communities in the Eastern Mediterranean Region in Later Prehistory* (J. L. Bintliff and W. van Zeist, eds.), British Archaeological Reports International Series 133(i), Oxford, pp. 67–97.

Rollefson, G. O., 1983, Ritual and Ceremony at Neolithic 'Ain Chazal (Jordan), *Paleorient* 9(2):29–38.

Rollefson, G. O., 1986, Neolithic 'Ain Ghazal (Jordan): Ritual and Ceremony II, *Paléorient* 12:45–52.

Rollefson, G. O., and Köhler-Rollefson, I., 1989, The Collapse of Early Neolithic Settlements in the Southern Levant, in: *People and Culture in Change* (I. Hershkovitz, ed.), British Archaeological Reports International Series 508i, Oxford, pp. 73–89.

Ronen, A., 1984, *Sefunim Prehistoric Sites, Mount Carmel, Israel*, British Archaeological Reports International Series 230, Oxford.

Rosenberg, M., 1994, Hallan Çemi Tepesi: Some Further Observations Concerning Stratigraphy and Material Culture, *Anatolica* 20:121–140.

Rust, A., 1950, *Die Höhlenfunde von Jabrud (Syrien)*, Karl Wacholtz Verlag, Neumünster.

Simmons, A. H., Köhler-Rollefson, I., Rollefson, G. O., Mandel, R., and Kafafi, Z., 1988, 'Ain Ghazal: A Major Neolithic Settlement in Central Jordan, *Science* 240:35–39.

Smith, P. E. L., 1986, *Palaeolithic Archaeology in Iran*, The American Institute of Iranian Studies, University of Pennsylvania, Philadelphia.

Sokal, R. R., Oden, N. L., and Wilson, C., 1991, Genetic Evidence for the Spread of Agriculture in Europe by Demic Diffusion, *Nature* 351:143–145.

Stuiver, M., and Braziunas, T. F., 1993, Modeling Atmospheric ^{14}C Influences and ^{14}C Ages of Marine Samples to 10,000 BC, *Radiocarbon* 35(1):137–189.

Suc, J.-P., 1984, Origin and Evolution of the Mediterranean Vegetation and Climate in Europe, *Nature* 307(2): 429–432.

Tchernov, E., 1984, Commensal Animals and Human Sedentism in the Middle East, in: *Animals and Archaeology* (J. Clutton-Brock and C. Grigson, eds.), British Archaeological Reports International Series 202, Oxford, pp. 91–115.

Tchernov, E., 1991, Biological Evidence for Human Sedentism in Southwest Asia during the Natufian, in: *The Natufian Culture in the Levant* (O. Bar-Yosef and F. R. Valla, eds.), International Monographs in Prehistory, Ann Arbor, pp. 315–340.

Tchernov, E., 1993, The effects of Sedentism on the Exploitation of the Environment in the Southern Levant, in: *Exploitation des animaux Sauvages a Travers le Temps* (J. Desse and F. Audoin-Rouzeaur, eds.), APDCA, Juan-les-Pins, pp. 137–159.

Valla, F. R., 1975, *Le Natoufien: Une Culture Préhistorique en Palestine*, Gabalda, Paris.

Valla, F. R., 1981, Les Establissements Natoufiens dans le Nord d'Israel, in: Préhistoire du Levant (J. Cauvin and P. Sanlaville, eds.), CNRS, Paris, pp. 409–420.

van Zeist, W., and Bakker-Heeres, J. A. H., 1982/1985, Archaeobotanical Studies in the Levant 1. Neolithic Sites in the Damascus Basin: Aswad, Ghoraifé, Ramad, *Palaeohistoria* 24:165–256.

van Zeist, W., and Bakker-Heeres, J. A. H., 1984/1986, Archaeobotanical Studies in the Levant, 3. Late Palaeolithic Mureybit, *Palaeohistoria* 26:171–189.

van Zeist, W., and Bottema, S., 1982, Vegetational History of the Eastern Mediterranean and the Near East during the Last 20,000 Years, in: *Palaeoclimates, Palaeoenvironments and Human Communities in the Eastern Mediterranean Region in Later Prehistory* (J. L. Bintliff and W. van Zeist, eds.), British Archaeological Reports, Oxford, pp. 231–277.

van Zeist, W., and Bottema, S., 1991, *Late Quaternary Vegetation of the Near East*, Dr. Ludwig Reichert Verlag, Weisbaden.

van Zeist, W., and de Roller, G. J., 1991/1992, The Plant Husbandry of Aceramic Çayönü, Southeast Turkey, *Palaeohistoria* 33/35:65–96.

van Zeist, W., and de Roller, G. J., 1993, Plant remains from Maadi, a Predynastic site in Lower Egypt, *Vegetation History and Archaeobotany* 2:1–14.

Voigt, M. M., 1983, *Hajji Firuz Tepe, Iran: The Neolithic Settlement*, The University Museum, Philadelphia.

Voigt, M. M., 1991, The Goddess from Anatolia: An Archaeological Perspective, *Oriental Rug Review* 11(2):32–39.

Weinstein-Evron, M., 1990, Palynological History of the Last Pleniglacial in the Levant, *Etudes et Recherches Archaeologiques de l'Université de Liège* 42:9–25.

Weiss, H., Courty, M.-A., Wetterstrom, W., Guichard, F., Senior, L., Meadow, R., and Curnow, A., 1993, The genesis and collapse of third millennium north Mesopotamian civilization, *Science* 261:995–1004.

Wigley, T. M. L., and Farmer, G., 1982, Climate of the Eastern Mediterranean and Near East, in: *Palaeoclimates, Palaeoenvironments and Human Communities in the Eastern Mediterranean Region in Later Prehistory* (J. L. Bintliff and W. van Zeist, eds.), British Archaeological Reports International Series 133, Oxford, pp. 3–37.

Wright, K., 1993, Early Holocene Ground Stone Assemblages in the Levant, *Levant* 25:93–111.

Wyncoll, G., and Tangri, D., 1991, Origins of Commensalism and Human Sedentism, *Paléorient* 17(2):157–159.

Yalçinkaya, I., Léotard, J.-M., Kartal, M., Otte, M., Bar-Yosef, O., Carmi, I., Gautier, A., Gilot, E., Goldberg, P., Kozlowski, J., Liberman, D., Lopez-Bayon, I., Pawlikowski, M., Thiebault, S., Ancion, V., Paton, M., Barbier, A., and Bonjean, D., in press, Les Occupations Tardiglaciaires du Site d'Ökuzini (Sud-Ouest de la Turquie): Résultats Preliminaires des Derniers Récherches, *L'Anthropologie* 100 (4):562–585.

Yechieli, Y., Magaritz, M., Levy, Y., Weber, U., Kafri, U., Woelfi, W., and Bonani, G., 1993, Late Quaternary Geological History of the Dead Sea Area, Israel, *Quaternary Research* 39:59–67.

Zohary, D., 1992, Domestication of the Neolithic Near East Crop Assemblage, in: *Préhistoire de l'Agriculture* (P. C. Anderson, ed.), Éditions du CNRS, Paris, pp. 81–86.

Zohary, M., 1973, *Geobotanical Foundations of the Middle East*, Springer Verlag, Stuttgart.

PART III

THE PLEISTOCENE–HOLOCENE TRANSITION IN EUROPE

Though a small continent, Europe is complex in its relief, coastlines, climates, and biota. Ranging between the middle and upper latitudes, dissected by major mountain ranges and rivers, bounded by seas to the south and north, by the Atlantic with its interglacial Gulf Stream to the west, and by the vast continental plains of Asia to the east, Europe was a diverse arena for human adaptations across the Pleistocene–Holocene transition. Some regions witnessed abrupt, marked changes in environments and cultural responses, while others saw only gradual, subtle shifts. In general, the severity of changes increased along a south-to-north cline.

Large parts of northern Europe were devoid of human settlement during the last Pleniglacial. More than half the area was covered by extensive inland glaciers, and the remaining part was severely affected by accompanying periglacial phenomena, such as permafrost, high winds, loess blowout and deposition, cryoclastic erosion, and solifluction. In contrast, though colder than at present, the mountainous southern peninsular regions of Europe continued to harbor diverse plant and animal resources, including a wealth of coastal and marine species. The rich resources of southern France and Iberia, together with their abundant caves and rock shelters, made these favored zones of habitation by late Upper Paleolithic hunter–gatherer societies.

At 18,000 BP the ice-free corridor in central Europe was a truly inhospitable region, characterized by a markedly arctic–continental climate and covered with treeless tundra and loess-steppe. It was very sparsely populated the predominant life forms being roaming herds of mammoth and perhaps woolly rhinoceros. The absence of archaeological finds may to some extent be due to inadequate conditions for preservation caused by various peri-glacial phenomena and extremely sparse vegetation. In any case, though, population density was close to an absolute minimum.

By 13,000 BP, the picture had changed dramatically. The northwest European lowland, from the British Isles in the west to the Russian plain in the east, had by then become the destination of many hunter–gatherer groups—immigrating from their probable late Pleistocene *refugia* in the southwest (Jochim 1987; Straus 1991) or the southeast (Soffer 1987). The immigrations, or reimmigrations, increased markedly around 12,000 BP when the climatic amelioration had finally established itself, being manifested, for example, in the incipient regeneration of the Central European forest.

By the onset of the Holocene at approximately 10,000 BP, hunter–gatherer groups had expanded throughout all of Europe, including probably even northernmost Norway. Subsistence-economic activities were still exclusively based on hunting and gathering, but within the next few millennia, groups in the southeast would already be engaged in incipient food-production activities, namely, stock raising and crop cultivation.

In northern Europe, cultural changes in the period 13,000–8,000 BP are very distinct. In his *Mesolithic Prelude*, Grahame Clark (1980:38) explains that this distinctness came about because the transition from Pleistocene to Holocene conditions was most sharply defined here. Inhabitants of this region thus had to make the most radical adjustments to adapt to the new conditions. Consequently, the Pleistocene–Holocene transition in northern Europe is also generally considered to mark the borderline between Paleolithic and Mesolithic hunter–gatherer societies. Nevertheless, the Mesolithic is perceived of as the economic, technological, and social continuation into the Holocene of the "Paleolithic way of Living."

In southern Europe, cultural changes in the late Pleistocene–early Holocene appear to be rather more complex. Unfortunately, this complexity is also reflected in archaeological terminology. Confusion is introduced by inconsistent use of the terms Mesolithic and Epipaleolithic in much of the literature. The use and significance of these terms depend on each individual author and his or her idea of the sociocultural or chronological significance of individual phases (Bietti 1981; Thévenin 1982:14f). Here too, however, the socioeconomic continuity across the Pleistocene–Holocene boundary remains generally unquestioned.

The four chapters in this section represent a fine selection of recent research efforts considering the Pleistocene–Holocene transition in Europe. Geographically, they are slightly biased toward northern and central Europe. In their generally multidisciplinary approach, however, they are highly representative of the state and level of current research directions.

At a descriptive level, they offer first-hand regional summaries of the most recent research with respect to the Iberian peninsula and Aquitaine, Germany and Denmark, the Northwest European plain, and the Russian plain. These chapters all aim at a synthesis of paleoenvironmental and archaeological data. Discussions consider geochronological issues and long-term effects of paleoclimatic change while focusing on adaptive changes with respect to subsistence behavior and settlement patterns.

Southwestern Europe obviously saw great interregional variability in human responses to environmental changes during the period 13,000–8,000 BP. In Chapter 5, Straus carefully illustrates how in some regions major climatic, vegetative, and faunal disruptions led to abrupt, significant changes in settlement–subsistence systems, while the opposite was true in other regions. In Iberia (Vasco-Cantabria, Levante, and Portugal), subsistence intensification (including *both* overall diversification and situational specialization) began early, and climatic fluctuations after 16,000 BP were relatively attenuated. Adaptive changes were accordingly gradual. In southern France, however, general specialization in herd ungulate hunting (e.g., reindeer) and open vegetation conditions ended abruptly, with marked consequences for humans.

In Chapter 6, dedicated to resource exploitation and subsistence strategies, Eriksen examines the gradual northward migration of flora, fauna, and people into the virgin areas of northwest Europe. In the ice-free corridor of central Europe, fauna development during the period in question is characterized by a general decrease in species diversity. In southern Scandinavia, however, a considerable increase in overall biological productivity, including the amount and diversity of available game resources, is observed. The chapter illustrates how late Paleolithic–early Mesolithic hunters in northwest and central Europe adapted to the changing environment by incorporating new technology such as domesticated wolves and the bow and arrow.

In Chapter 7, Schild convincingly demonstrates how in the late Pleistocene and early Holocene, the North European plain underwent several profound environmental changes that deeply affected cultural and demographic systems of the time. Evidently, the most dramatic shift in the cultural system took place in the early Holocene, around 9,600–9,500 BP. It was expressed by demographic movements, basic changes in technologies, and raw material economies, as well as by a reduction in information networks. A relative stabilization of the system took place circa 9,300 BP.

Moving further eastward, Dolukhanov explicates in Chapter 8 that three consecutive waves may be distinguished in the initial late Pleistocene settlement of the Russian plain. The first two occurred during Bølling-Allerød, the last one during the Younger Dryas. All three waves resulted from the overflow of surplus population in the late Pleistocene refuge areas in Atlantic (western) Europe and in the periglacial zone of eastern and central Europe. The subsequent socioeconomic development in northeast Europe proceeded as a gradual adaptation to the increasingly forested environment of the early Holocene.

Late Pleistocene and early Holocene hunter–gatherers were very mobile, and intergroup contact networks seem to have covered distances of 800–1000 km. For a general study of cultural change, detailed regional analyses are thus imperative for a proper distinction between local causal relationships and regional relationships, the latter being significant only with respect to a larger geographic region (Jochim 1987). The chapters in this section illustrate the marked spatial and temporal diversity in the archaeological record, and they enable us to examine valid interpretations in a wider geographic context. They allow for an overall comparison, while recognizing a full range of past ethnogeographic variability that must be considered, understood, and incorporated in our reconstruction of past human adaptations.

BERIT VALENTIN ERIKSEN

REFERENCES

Bietti, A., 1981, The Mesolithic Cultures in Italy: New Activities in Connection with Upper Paleolithic Cultural Traditions, in: *Mesolithikum in Europa* (B. Gramsch, ed.), Veröffentlichungen des Museums für Ur- und Frühgeschichte Potsdam, Band 14/15, VEB Deutscher Verlag der Wissenschaften, Berlin.

Clark, G., 1980, *Mesolithic Prelude: The Palaeolithic–Neolithic Transition in Old World Prehistory*, Edinburgh University Press, Edinburgh.

Jochim, M., 1987, Late Pleistocene Refugia in Europe, in: *The Pleistocene Old World: Regional Perspectives* (O. Soffer, ed.), Plenum Press, New York, pp. 317–331.

Soffer, O., 1987, Upper Paleolithic Connubia, Refugia, and the Archaeological Record from Eastern Europe, in: *The Pleistocene Old World: Regional Perspectives* (O. Soffer, ed.), Plenum Press, New York, pp. 333–348.

Straus, L. G., 1991, Human Geography of the Late Upper Paleolithic in Western Europe: Present State of the Question, *Journal of Anthropological Research* 47/2:259–278.

Thévenin, A., 1982, *Rochedane: L'Azilien, l'Epipaléolithique de l'Est de la France et les Civilisations Épipaléolithiques de l'Europe Occidentale*, Mémoires de la Faculté des Sciences Sociales Ethnologie 1. Tome I-II. Université des Sciences Humaines de Strasbourg, Strasbourg.

Chapter 5

The Archaeology
of the Pleistocene–Holocene
Transition in Southwest Europe

LAWRENCE GUY STRAUS

INTRODUCTION

The general image of the end of the Pleistocene (i.e., end of the Last Glacial) in Europe is one of brutal changes in climate, landscape, vegetation, fauna, and, consequently, in human strategies for survival in a new world that came into being around 10,000 years ago. The break between Magdalenian horse, reindeer, and bison hunters on the periglacial steppe-tundra and Mesolithic forest foragers and fishers is often generalized as being sharp and abrupt, and sometimes characterized as "degenerative," especially in the realm of artistic production.

The point of this chapter is to show that whatever validity this stereotype might have, it is decreasingly accurate the farther one moves toward the south in western Europe. In the Iberian peninsula (36–43°N latitude) (Figure 1), the record of the Pleistocene–Holocene transition is one more of *continuity* than of rupture in resources and adaptations, despite changes in temperature, precipitation, extent of arboreal vegetation, coastlines, and ice cover across the period of the late Tardiglacial and early Postglacial, 13,000–8,000 BP.

In contrast, north of the Pyrenees in southern France (43–46°N latitude), the nature of the transition was already considerably different, with growing evidence of sometimes earlier, more mosaic, sharper change at the close of the Würm Glacial. I argue that the contrast between Iberia and Aquitaine can be largely explained by differences in topography and in the principal Ice Age game species exploited by humans in each region (see Straus 1983, 1986, 1992a,b, 1995a,b).

LAWRENCE GUY STRAUS • Department of Anthropology, University of New Mexico, Albuquerque, New Mexico 87131.

Humans at the End of the Ice Age: The Archaeology of the Pleistocene–Holocene Transition, edited by Lawrence Guy Straus, Berit Valentin Eriksen, Jon M. Erlandson, and David R. Yesner. Plenum Press, New York, 1996.

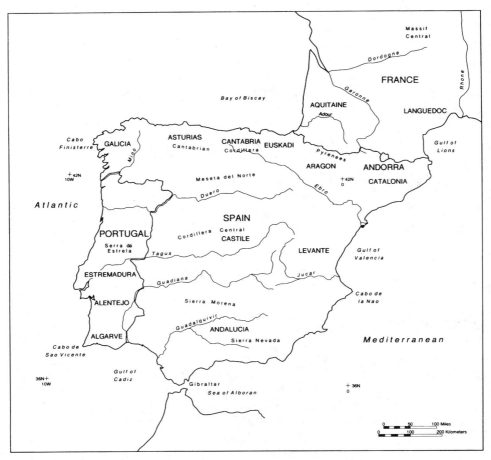

Figure 1. Southwest Europe: Portugal, Spain, Andorra, and southern France, showing major regions mentioned in the text.

CHRONOSTRATIGRAPHIC AND PALEOCLIMATIC BACKGROUND

The principal climatic phase designations shown in Table 1 are generally accepted for southwest Europe, even though they were originally developed through pollen analyses in northwest Europe (Barton et al. 1991; Dupré 1988; Evin 1979; Leroi-Gourhan and Renault-Miskovsy 1977; Renault-Miskovsky and Leroi-Gourhan 1981; Watts 1986). The temporal boundaries of these phases are defined by large numbers of radiocarbon dates from both pollen cores and archaeological sites, although recent calibration studies using German pines and oaks indicate the existence of radiocarbon plateaus around 10,000 BP (Becker and Kromer 1991) that should make us view the *absolute* accuracy of the dates for this period with some skepticism. Dates given here are uncalibrated.

Table 1. Late Glacial and Early Postglacial Chronoclimatic Phases for Southwest Europe

Pollen zone	Radiocarbon age[a]	Major stage
Atlantic	8,000–5,000 BP	Postglacial
Boreal	9,000–8,000 BP	
Preboreal	10,200–8,700 BP	Oxygen Isotope Stage 1
Dryas III	10,800–10,200 BP	
Alleröd	11,800–10,800 BP	Tardiglacial
Dryas II	12,400–11,800 BP	
Bölling	13,000–12,400 BP	
Dryas I	17,000–13,000 BP	Oxygen Isotope Stage 2
Lascaux	18,000–17,000 BP	
Last Glacial Maximum	22,000–18,000 BP	Upper Pleniglacial
Tursac	24,000–22,000 BP	
Maisières/Kesselt	30,000–27,000 BP	
		Interpleniglacial Oxygen Isotope Stage 3

[a]Approximate uncalibrated dates.

Following the cold, dry maximum (20,000–16,000 BP) of the Upper Pleniglacial, conditions remained very rigorous, with generally open herbaceous environments during the three millennia of Dryas I, there being only subtle change in environments, particularly centered on the Lascaux, Angles, and Prebölling oscillations. At around 13,000 BP, however, temperatures and humidity increased markedly, with significant increases in arboreal pollen throughout Spain and southern France. There is microfaunal and macrobotanical evidence of significant reforestation in south central Portugal replacing more steppic biotopes as early as 14,000 BP and becoming dominant by 11,500 BP (Bicho 1993; Povoas et al. 1992).

The Bölling phase, with parklands that included significant stands of pine, hazel, juniper, and even, in some regions, oak, lasted until around 12,000 BP and represented the noticeable beginning of the end of the Glacial. The mountainous terrain of southwest Europe (Massif Central, Corbières, Pyrenees and Cantabrian, Central/Estrela, Iberic, Morena, and Penibetic/Nevada Sierras) served as *refugia* for trees (including thermophile taxa) during the Pleniglacial, so their rapid spread during the Bölling amelioration is not surprising. This period corresponds to reestablishment of the northeastward flow of the Gulf Stream toward northwest Europe, dramatic decrease in North Atlantic sea ice, great increase in ocean water temperature in the Bay of Biscay, and major retreat of mountain and continental glaciers (see Duplessy et al. 1981; Ruddiman and McIntyre 1981).

There is disagreement among types of proxy evidence (e.g., pollen vs. geology vs. deep sea cores), among regions, and among specialists concerning the existence or severity of the

Dryas II climatic downturn. In general, in southwest Europe, there seems to have been a mild cooling trend with a decrease in arboreal vegetation, but without noticeable decrease in ocean water temperature, between about 12,200 BP and about 11,900 BP. The climatic amelioration continued in Alleröd until about 11,000 BP. In some regions, arboreal pollen percentages reached 30–50%, with numerous thermophile taxa, although pine still generally dominates the spectra. More or less open parklands with significant areas of wood characterized many of the landscapes of southwest Europe during Alleröd.

As elsewhere around the middle and upper latitudes of the northern hemisphere, the marked trend toward interglacial conditions was brusquely interrupted in southwest Europe by the Dryas III cold event, the cause or causes of which, possibly at least in part related to changes in North Atlantic currents provoked by glacial meltwater, are at present under debate (e.g., papers in Berger 1990; Berger and Labeyrie 1987). Temperatures, having nearly reached Holocene levels in Alleröd, fell back on the order of 8–15°C (less in the Mediterranean basin), with half this brutal decline possibly occurring within decades (Berger 1990). The Polar Front in the North Atlantic redescended to the level of Cabo Finisterre in northwest Spain, and glaciers readvanced in the high mountain chains. With respect to temperature, the setback to full glacial conditions was nearly complete. By 10,200 BP, Dryas III was over, but during its few centuries (possibly 40–45 human generations), woodlands were drastically reduced and the distribution of thermophile taxa retreated southward or into favored microhabitats. Humidity generally remained relatively high in the Atlantic regions, while it seems to have been somewhat lower in the western Mediterranean (Dupré 1988; Pons et al. 1987; cf. Watts 1986).

As fast as it began, Dryas III ended, and temperatures rose dramatically in the Preboreal, usually considered to be the first climatic phase of the Holocene, from 10,200 BP to 8,700 BP. Rich, dense Mediterranean woodlands with pines and numerous thermophile taxa (e.g., oaks, ash, olive, pistachio) spread across eastern and southern Spain and southern and central Portugal, with some indications of relatively dry conditions. Varying quantities of hazel, birch, oak, and elm, accompanying pine, made up the forests of northern Spain, the Pyrenees, and southwest France. Abundant ferns testify to often high humidity in these Atlantic regions (Bicho 1993 with references; Duprè 1988). Pine and hazel, together with oaks, dominated the spreading Mediterranean woodlands, as shown by both pollen and charcoal studies of the Preboreal–Boreal transition layer at Sota Palau in Catalunya (Carbonell et al. 1985). Sea level, which had been rising fast since Bölling times, reached essentially its present height by the end of this period (Ters 1973), cumulatively resulting in a loss of present-day flooded inner continental shelfland that may have been inhabited by Tardiglacial humans.

Mixed deciduous forests continued their growth under warmer and often relatively dry conditions of the Boreal until about 8,000 BP, which was the beginning of the Postglacial Optimum or Atlantic phase, with a general increase in humidity. The extension of these forests was checked throughout southwest Europe only by Neolithic (i.e., anthropic) deforestation, followed by slightly declining temperatures and humidity in the Subboreal.

In sum, the transition from a very cold, relatively dry southwest Europe with generally open, herbaceous vegetation to a relatively warm, forested southwest Europe, humid along the Atlantic facade and drier along the Mediterranean, was accomplished over the course of some 5,000 years and was characterized by numerous fluctuations, the sharpest of which occurred at the beginning and end of the Dryas III "catastrophe."

TRADITIONAL CULTURAL–HISTORICAL FRAMEWORKS

Aquitaine and Vasco-Cantabria

Table 2 presents the generally accepted cultural–historical frameworks for southwest France, Cantabrian and Levantine Spain, and Portugal, with approximate radiocarbon ages. The Upper Magdalenian of southwest France and Cantabrian Spain is in part defined by the frequent presence of antler harpoons that seem to have been invented circa 13,000 BP. It is further characterized (especially in Aquitaine) by generally rich, diverse assemblages of lithic tools, including a variety of types of burins, end-scrapers, perforators, backed blades and bladelets, and points. In some sites, microlithic backed bladelets make up around half (or more) of the retouched lithic assemblage, indicative of the existence of composite projectiles formed of multiple lithic elements hafted as tips, cutting edges, or barbs to antler or wood points. Antler points (*sagaies*)—some grooved for bladelet insertion—perforated antlers (*bâtons de commandement*), spear-throwers, spatulas, wands, bone needles, awls, and works of mobile art are widely distributed and in certain sites very abundant. In certain cases (Niaux, El Castillo [Valladas et al. 1992]), Pyrenean and Cantabrian cave art has been radiometrically proven to date to the Upper Magdalenian, although much of the art pertains to the earlier Magdalenian.

Classic Magdalenian industries developed into Azilian industries during the period between Alleröd and Preboreal (roughly between 12,000–9,000 BP). The Azilian is technologically and typologically clearly derived from the late Magdalenian. The transition was not simultaneous between regions (i.e., southwest France and Cantabrian Spain) or even within regions. There is some evidence that the trend toward simplification and microlithization took place earlier in some parts of Aquitaine than in most of Vasco-Cantabria, while other zones of southwest France (i.e., along the Pyrenees) witnessed relatively late "survival" of

Table 2. Late Paleolithic and Mesolithic Cultural–Stratigraphic Subdivisions[a]

Aquitaine	Vasco-Cantabria	Levante	Portugal
Sauveterrian 9,000–6,500 BP	Asturian/Geometric Epi-Paleolithic 9,000–6,500 BP	Geometric Epi-Paleolithic 8,000–7,000 BP	Mesolithic 8,500–6,000 BP
Azilian 11,000–9,000 BP	Azilian 10,500–9,000 BP	Microlaminar Epi-Paleolithic 10,500–8,000 BP	Final Magdalenian/ Epi-Paleolithic 10,500–8,500 BP
Upper Magdalenian 13,000–11,000 BP	Upper Magdalenian 13,000–10,500 BP	Upper Magdalenian 13,000–10,500 BP	Late Magdalenian 12,500–10,500 BP
Lower + Middle Magdalenian 18,000–13,000 BP	Lower Cantabrian Magdalenian 17,000–13,000 BP	Solutreo-Gravettian + Early Magdalenian 17,500–13,000 BP	"Magdalenian" 18,000–12,500 BP
Solutrean 21,000–18,000 BP	Solutrean 21,000–17,000 BP	Solutrean 21,000–17,500 BP	Solutrean 21,000–18,000 BP

[a]Radiocarbon ages are uncalibrated and approximate; there is considerable temporal overlap between most adjacent pairs of cultural–stratigraphic units.

Magdalenian-style technology (Straus 1985). The Azilian is generally characterized by a (perhaps functionally related) decrease in burins (now rarely outnumbering end-scrapers) and bone artifacts (e.g., Fernández 1980). As categorized by the standard de Sonneville-Bordes/Perrot typology, the numbers of lithic tool types are often reduced vis-à-vis those of Magdalenian assemblages. This decrease is also true of bone/antler artifacts; *sagaies* and decorated objects are rare and harpoons generally less elaborately worked and very rarely decorated. Numerically abundant artifact assemblages are rarer than in the Upper Magdalenian of southwest France and Cantabrian Spain; occupied site areas sometimes seem to be smaller (though size is hard to judge accurately, since almost all known sites are in caves). "Artistic" representations expressed on durable media seem to become far less frequent, naturalistic images virtually disappear in favor of geometric designs, and cave art seems to come to an end in the Azilian.

During the course of the Preboreal and Boreal, industries characterized by high relative frequencies of microlithic artifacts (*armatures*) develop in southwest France and the Basque country. In France, these artifacts can include increasing representations of obliquely truncated points, Sauveterre points, and triangles, with evidence of use of the microburin technique on bladelet blanks (Rozoy 1978). Geometric microliths (notably triangles of both "French" and "Mediterranean" La Cocina types) were also added onto an Azilian (Epi-Paleolithic) artifact substrate in the Basque region of France and Spain, with similar further decreases in burins and osseous artifacts (Arias 1991; Berganza 1990). Further to the west, in Santander and Asturias Provinces, most Boreal-age assemblages lie within the Asturian technocomplex, characterized by heavy-duty cobble picks, choppers, minimally or unretouched flakes, and a bone industry limited to a few awls and simply modified antlers. In apparent parallel with the Asturian, which is a "Mesolithic" coastal shell-midden phenomenon, are a few sites in the Cantabrian interior with microliths (including geometrics such as triangles) that may be indicative of predominant hunting activities (as opposed to gathering of shellfish and vegetal foods) (Arias 1991; Clark 1983; González Morales 1982). It is into the Mesolithic and geometric Epi-Paleolithic milieux that ceramics and domesticated animals were introduced in the middle Atlantic period.

Levante

The Tardiglacial and early Postglacial cultural sequence for eastern Spain has recently been synthesized by Aura and Pérez (1992, 1995), based on recent excavations and (re)analyses of several key sites distributed among Catalunya in the north, Pais Valenciano in the center, and Andalusia in the south. Following Fortea (1973), Aura and Pérez Ripoll divide the cultural manifestations corresponding to the transition into Mediterranean Upper Magdalenian, Microlaminar, and Geometric complexes. The second gradually and irregularly replaced the first throughout the Levantine region between circa 12,000 and 10,000 BP, and the third replaced the second between circa 10,000 and 8,000 BP, with a sharper break seeming to occur in the radiocarbon record between the Upper Magdalenian and the Microlaminar (at circa 11,000 BP) than between the Microlaminar and Geometric complexes.

The Mediterranean Upper Magdalenian already includes a significant bladelet component, including pointed bladelet armatures and backed bladelets. Burins are abundant, either surpassing or equaling end-scrapers, but there are few perforators and variable percentages of truncated, denticulated, and notched pieces. The osseous component is relatively rich and includes points, a few harpoons, decorated wands, and bipointed "fish gorges." Mobile art objects (especially engraved stone plaquettes) are abundant (notably at Parpalló in Valencia) and widespread. Assemblages clearly derived from the Magdalenian technological tradition include microlamina-rich assemblages (mostly backed bladelets with rare geometric microliths) that have few or very few burins and many or very many end-scrapers—a nature and range of compositional variability similar to that of the Azilian. Osseous artifacts (except bipointed fish gorges and awls) all but disappear. As in the Azilian of the Atlantic world, there are some painted cobbles, but few other mobile art manifestations. A certain amount of the interassemblage variability within the Mediterranean Upper Magdalenian and Microlaminar complexes is attributed to functional causes, while the rest might be reflections of different regional "traditions," as well as the results of technological evolution, according to Aura and Pérez Ripoll (1992). There are clear parallels with the transition from the classic Magdalenian to the Azilian of southwest France and Vasco-Cantabria: decrease in burins, osseous artifacts, art, and artifact size; relative increase in backed bladelets and end-scrapers; apparent reduction in numbers of specialized tools in favor of potentially multifunctional, hafted, replaceable microlithic elements; and continued absence or rarity of geometrics.

The Mediterranean Geometric Epi-Paleolithic consists of a pair of facies typified by assemblages from the sites of Filador (Barcelona) and La Cocina (Valencia). The former has about equal amounts of end-scrapers, denticulates/notches, and geometrics (especially triangles and segments) made on backed bladelets. There is also a trend toward an increasing representation of macrolithic tools (as at Sota Palou [Girona], where at circa 8,800 BP there are backed bladelets, burins, end-scrapers, denticulates, splintered pieces/bipolar cores, large worked cobbles, several harmmerstones, anvils, and abundant debitage [Carbonell et al. 1985]). The Cocina facies has many microlithic trapezes, with varying percentages of end-scrapers and notches/denticulates. The strong emphasis on projectile tips/barbs is clear. There is definite intergradation in Levantine Spain between the lithic armatures of the last Epi-Paleolithic hunter–gatherers and those of the first Neolithic pastoralist–farmers, despite the appearance of sickle blades and ceramics in the latter around 7,000 BP (Aura and Pérez 1995).

Portugal

Not until recently has Portugal (notably the south central Portuguese province of Estremadura)—by far the least-known region of southwest Europe in terms of the adaptive transformations of the Pleistocene–Holocene transition—seen such a renaissance of archaeological research and the creation of an independent cultural sequence and chronostratigraphy. This renaissance has largely been the work of Zilhão (e.g., Zilhão 1992), Marks (Marks et al. 1994), and Marks's student, Bicho (1992, 1993).

The so-called "Magdalenian" of Portugal developed in the millennium between 17,000 and 16,000 BP, as in Vasco-Cantabria, with the replacement of Solutrean foliate and tanged lithic points by backed bladelets as weapon tips. Osseous artifacts are rare, however, and harpoons are totally absent. (With more trees in the Tardiglacial environment of south central Portugal, wood may have been used more than bone or antler for point shafts and other artifacts.) Double-backed bladelet points are frequent in one facies, while lightly, inversely retouched (Dufour) bladelets are abundant in another. The facies rich in backed bladelets (with little use of the microburin technique and few geometrics) seems to have lasted from circa 16,000 to 9,000 BP, while the Dufour bladelet–rich facies (with many carinate core/scrapers resultant from the production of the bladelet blanks) seems to have lasted from circa 12,000 to 8,400 BP. Burins are rare, as are other specialized lithic tools. There is a distinct trend toward microlithization and simplification among assemblages dated between circa 9,000 and 8,000 BP, such as Ponta da Vigia and Escravelheira, with small end-scrapers and perforators, truncated and backed bladelets, notched, denticulated, and retouched flakes/blades, and occasional geometrics. Cobble tools also occur (Carvalho et al. 1989; Zilhão et al. 1987). Works of mobile art are absent so far in the Magdalenian/Epi-Paleolithic, and Portugal's only cave art site, Escoural, may have been decorated during Solutrean times (since it contains Solutrean artifacts, but no Magdalenian ones [Otte et al. no date]).

It was between circa 8,000 and 7,000 BP that the microburin technique and (consequently) geometric microliths (notably triangles) became common (Araújo 1993; Vierra 1992). Heavy-duty picks and "hoes" made on large cobbles are found associated sometimes with limited numbers of backed bladelets, notably in coastal contexts such as the Mirian site of Palheirões do Alegre in Alentejo (but also inland) (Raposo et al. 1989). The famous Atlantic period shell middens of the Tagus, Sado, and Mira estuaries are characterized by rich geometric microlith assemblages accompanied by expedient, often large-size flake and cobble tools (Roche 1972a). It is into this milieu that Neolithic ceramic technology and food production were introduced in south central Portugal circa 6,500 BP (Zilhão 1993a).

RESOURCES AND SUBSISTENCE STRATEGIES

Southwest France

Magdalenian Aquitaine was a land of reindeer and reindeer hunters, with ancillary subsistence mainstays being horse, bison, ibex, and salmon. Early in the Tardiglacial, saiga antelope was a significant game species on the steppe-vegetated plains of this region, and late in the period, red deer began to displace reindeer (Bahn 1984; Delpech 1983). Except for specialized ibex-hunting sites in the Pyrenees (e.g., La Vache-Monique, Les Eglises), most pre-Alleröd Magdalenian sites are highly dominated by reindeer, suggesting the continuation of a very specialized subsistence system (begun at least during the Last Glacial Maximum) that included the interception and massive slaughter of migrating *Rangifer* herds, as well as more individualized killing on summer and winter pastures. It is during Alleröd that the rich, diverse, gregarious Last Glacial fauna (notably reindeer) begins to disappear, to be displaced or replaced by ungulates that prefer somewhat or much more temperate and often wooded habitats (red deer, roe deer, boar). In some habitats, such as the valley of the Dronne at the site of Pont d'Ambon, this change seems to have occurred relatively early; at others (e.g., La Madeleine, La Gare de Couze), reindeer continued to be overwhelmingly the dominant game species apparently through Alleröd; at still others (Le Morin, La Faurélie, Duruthy, Dufaure), reindeer continued to be dominant, but red deer (plus some boar and red deer) were beginning to make significant inroads during Alleröd times.

Typologically, the artifact assemblages from La Madeleine, La Gare de Couze, Le Morin, Duruthy, and Dufaure are classified as Upper/Final Magdalenian (but often with some "Azilian" characteristics, notably Azilian points). The Pont d'Ambon assemblages, however, are attributed to the Azilian (Laville et al. 1980). The "Magdalenian" artifact assemblages are associated with reindeer-dominated faunas (and frequently with relatively abundant salmon remains as well) and are often found in much larger sites or occupation horizons than Azilian ones. Whether "Azilian" artifact assemblages appear early (Alleröd) or late (Dryas II or Preboreal), they seem to be associated with faunal assemblages dominated by red deer together with roe deer and boar—less gregarious species than reindeer that may have been more usually hunted singly or in small numbers by stalking, beating, or surrounding. A functional relationship is suggested.

The case of the rock-shelter sites lining the south-southwest-facing Pastou Cliff on the boundary of Les Landes and French Basque country is significant in documenting the regional variability in the timing and nature of subsistence change near the end of the Last Glacial. Duruthy, Dufaure, and le Grand Pastou all indicate a substantial degree of specialization in the hunting of reindeer during repeated cold-season occupations throughout the Final Magdalenian (Altuna et al. 1991; Delpech 1978; Lalande 1988). At the first two sites, the most massive evidence of reindeer hunting comes from deposits attributed clearly to Alleröd by radiocarbon dates and by palynology (Arambourou 1978; Straus 1995b). The wealth of *Rangifer* remains occurs in a context of parkland indicated by high arboreal pollen percentages. It has been hypothesized by Delpech (1983) and supported subsequently by Altuna and Mariezkurrena (1995) that a separate Pyrenean population (herd) of reindeer managed to survive the warmer conditions of Alleröd through its ability to migrate altitudinally between low winter and high summer pastures. Migrating bands seem to have been intercepted along traditional routes, such as the Gave d'Oloron, at strategic chokepoints, such as the base of the Pastou Cliff. Having mastered the strategy, tactics, organizational and planning aspects, and weaponry required for the large-scale slaughter and processing of reindeer, the "Magdalenians" of the western Pyrenean region seem to have continued this practice even though the *Rangifer* population may have already been under considerable environmental or subsistence stress or both. It is even conceivable that the humans contributed to the eventual extermination of a viable reindeer population in the Pyrenees. At Dufaure, we have been able to document that red deer were making steady inroads in reindeer territory throughout the course of Alleröd (Altuna et al. 1991).

The high degree of dependence on and specialized hunting of reindeer at the Pastou sites crashed, ironically, in Dryas III, under colder (albeit humid) conditions. And the replacement of reindeer by red deer (plus small quantities of roe deer and boar) occurred simultaneously with the change from Magdalenian to Azilian technology (the latter clearly derived from the former, but with simplification of assemblage composition, microlithization, virtual disappearance of osseous artifacts and burins, a notable shift in lithic raw material procurement patterns, and drastic reduction of the inhabited area at the Pastou sites). A few reindeer survived (and were probably hunted singly or in very small groups like other woodland deer) through Dryas III and into Preboreal at both Duruthy and Dufaure (Altuna and Mariezkurrena 1995; Delpech 1978). There are no more of the large overwintering residential aggregations along the base of the cliff with their extensive cobblestone pavements and other features. One can hypothesize that Azilian bands were smaller and possibly covered far less extensive annual territories than the Magdalenian bands (their "ancestors"), which probably had moved up into the Pyrenees from the Aquitaine lowlands in summer.

One constant of the Pyrenean (and Cantabrian) regions was the presence of specialized ibex- (and sometimes chamois-) hunting sites (e.g., Les Eglises, La Vache, La Balma Margineda, Bolinkoba, Ekain, Ermittia, Abauntz, El Rascaño, Collubil) in *both* Magdalenian and Azilian times. Some of these upland or cliffside sites were utilized at various seasons (including fall–winter, when they may have been logistical localities *sensu* Binford [1983]), while others seem to have been used more strictly residentially in the warm season (Straus 1987).

Cantabrian Spain

Magdalenian subsistence in Cantabrian Spain was characterized by both circumstantial specialization in the hunting of red deer or ibex *and* overall diversification, with the significant exploitation of aquatic resources (estuarine and littoral molluscs and marine, estuarine, and riverine fish) and some birds (Altuna 1972, 1986, 1990, 1992; Freeman 1973, 1981; Straus 1977, 1983, 1992a,b; Straus and Clark 1986). There seem never to have been such large-scale slaughters of red deer in this region as there seem to have been of reindeer in Aquitaine, probably due to the much smaller herd sizes of the former cervid at any given season. There is an apparent trend toward the increased killing of young red deer and ibex (along with their mothers) throughout the late Magdalenian and Azilian (Altuna 1981, 1986; González Sainz 1989a,b; Straus and Clark 1986) that is a probable indicator of subsistence stress and intensification.

Indeed, at La Riera Cave and several other sites throughout the region, there is considerable evidence of *subsistence continuity* across the environmental fluctuations of the Tardiglacial and early Postglacial. Reindeer had never been a significant game species in Cantabrian Spain and disappeared after Dryas II. Bison was extirpated at about the same time, although horse continued to exist and was hunted well into Postglacial times (Altuna 1992). The hunting of roe deer and boar naturally increased because of both the extension of woodlands and the increased human need to diversify (coupled, at least in the case of boar, with an increased ability to hunt at safer distances with the invention of the bow and arrow). Intensification in the exploitation of aquatic resources is evidenced by the increasing amounts and variety of molluscs and in the decreasing size of the main species of limpets that had already been exploited systematically since Solutrean and early Magdalenian times. The numbers and variety of birds increased in final Magdalenian and Azilian times (Dryas III/Preboreal). Marine fish and seals were occasionally added to the catch that already included salmon and trout, probably from estuaries and rivers. New species and new habitats were being exploited, and pressure was being brought to bear on old food sources.

These trends culminated in the late Preboreal and Boreal with the formation in cave mouths of large shell middens, especially in western Santander and eastern Asturias provinces—the Asturian "culture"—but also in eastern Santander (e.g., El Perro) and in Vizcaya (e.g., Santimamiñe) (Clark 1976, 1983; González Morales 1982, 1990; Ortea 1986; Straus and Clark 1986). The middens are composed of a broad diversity of molluscan species, but with usually one or two (limpet, topshell, or oyster) highly dominant. Remains of deer and boar are also present in generally small quantities. Oxygen isotope analyses point to cold-season collection of limpets at several Asturian sites (Deith 1983;

Deith and Shackleton 1986; González Morales personal communication). Less is known about the subsistence activities of penecontemporaneous sites in the interior, although a series of Epi-Paleolithic sites in the Basque region are highly dominated by red deer, followed by roe deer and boar, with small numbers of caprids and only traces of bovines (probably aurochs) (Altuna 1990). Domesticated animals (sheep/goat, cattle, pig) begin to appear in Vasco-Cantabria (first and most convincingly in the eastern/Basque sector) only by 5,500–6,000 BP, but the construction of megalithis throughout the region suggests major socioeconomic change sometime thereafter (Arias 1991; Straus 1992a).

Levantine Spain

The faunal spectra of the Mediterranean zone of Spain are generally similar to those of Vasco-Cantabria: Red deer and ibex alternate as the dominant large game species, depending on the local orography surrounding each site. Rabbit remains, however, are often extremely abundant (and associated with small numbers of hare bones) (Aura and Pérez Ripoll 1992; Davison 1989; Estévez 1979, 1987; Freeman 1981). Although horse is still relatively abundant in Magdalenian contexts in Catalonia (northeast Spain), there are no Nordic or now-extinct species in the archeofaunas of the Mediterranean zone, though they are present in some much older deposits in the region. (The few reindeer antlers from the final Magdalenian of Bora Gran at Serinya near the French border in Gerona [Catalonia] are shed and may have been brought from the north for artifactual purposes [Canal and Carbonell 1989:346].)

Bird and fish bones and molluscs are present at numerous sites from Catalonia to Andalusia in Solutrean, Magdalenian, and Epi-Paleolithic times. Both riverine and marine fish are found. Unfortunately, the shallow continental shelf along the Levantine coast is generally quite broad (in contrast to that of the Cantabrian Sea), so many sites (notably those at which the most substantial amount of Last Glacial marine subsistence information would have been found) have been lost. The shelf off Andalusia is narrow, however, so that even during the late Tardiglacial, the site of Nerja (Málaga) was no more than 4 km from the shore (Aura et al. 1989). Already by Upper Magdalenian times, shellfishing was a major subsistence activity, leading to the formation of a shell midden, with dominant clams plus a wide variety of other molluscs. Mussels then replace clams at the end of the Last Glacial and in the Holocene, due to changes in the shoreline and its habitats. Echinoderms and crustaceans, as well as a variety of marine fish, are also found in the Epi-Paleolithic midden, along with rare seal remains (Alcalá et al. 1987; Aura and Pérez Ripoll 1992; Aura et al. 1989). There is also evidence for use of vegetal foods throughout the Nerja sequence (Aura and Pérez 1992:37). The overall picture of subsistence across the Pleistocene–Holocene transition in Levante is one of continued intensification of a broad spectrum of hunted, fished, and collected wild foodstuffs.

South Central Portugal

Very little is known about subsistence in the period 13,000–8,000 BP in Portugal. The Solutrean faunal record is dominated by red deer and ibex, including many young animals in Caldeirão Cave (Estremadura). Rabbit remains are also very abundant at this site and others (Zilhão 1987, 1991). Ibex and chamois drop out (presumably because they moved into the mountains of northern Portugal) in the Tardiglacial, but boar and roe deer are added to the

Caldeirão fauna in the "Magdalenian," and rabbit becomes even more common (Zilhão 1993b). The Magdalenian of Suão Cave (closer to the shore: 15 km at present) actually yielded marine and estuarine molluscs and fish remains, as well as red deer, ibex, horse, and boar (Roche 1982). Horse and aurochs are present along with deer and boar in the initial Holocene Epi-Paleolithic site of Bocas (Rio Maior, Estremadura) (Bicho 1993). In this same time period (≈9,800–8,800 BP), sites that are on the present coast of Estremadura (Vale da Mata, Magoito, Sao Julião) and even one over 40 km from it (Papagaio) have major shell midden deposits. There are several nongeometric Epi-Magdalenian sites on the Estremadura coast (e.g., Ponta da Vigia—8,700 BP [Zilhão et al. 1987], Escravelheira [Carvalho et al. 1989]). A millennium later, in the early Atlantic (7,300 BP), there is a *concheiro* now associated with a geometric microlithic industry at Forno da Telha (Rio Maior), 25 km from the Obidos Lagoon shore (Araújo 1993).

The phenomenon of coastal/estuarine shell middens continued and grew more common throughout the Preboreal and Boreal and into the Atlantic period. The huge, well-known *concheiros* of the Muge and the less spectacular ones of the Sado and Mira valleys and of the northern Alentejo coast consist of vast quantities of limpets, cockles, clams, scallops, oysters, topshells, mussels, crabs, and others. Fish remains are also abundant (including both shallow ocean and estuarine species), as are marine and land birds. Mammalian fauna include red and roe deer, aurochs, horse, boar, hedgehog, rabbit, hare, rodents, and small carnivores (Arnaud, 1986, 1987, 1989; Lentacker 1986, 1991; Roche 1972a,b; Straus et al. 1990). The Muge sites may have had (semi)sedentary human settlements, while those of the Sado (also with large cemeteries, but so far without dug-out structures like those of the Moita do Sebastião on the Muge), Mira, and Alentejo coast may have been seasonal residential sites (possibly involving short moves between the coast in summer and the near interior in winter). The broad-spectrum subsistence base of the Portuguese Mesolithic was clearly a continuation of the trend toward intensified diversification begun as early as the Magdalenian, with many of the same major mammalian species being hunted. Use of marine resources was clearly already well established in Tardiglacial times, as in Cantabria and Levante. The spread of wooded parklands with oaks, olives, strawberry bushes, and other arbored species as early as the Alleröd and then the flourishing of oak woodlands in the initial Holocene must have meant the existence of abundant nuts, berries, tubers, and other plant foodstuffs in Portugal (Bicho 1993). Again, continuity was the order of the day, with no clear break at circa 10,000 BP.

CONCLUSIONS

Southern Fance and the coastal peripheries of the Iberian peninsula had been rather densely populated refuge areas for humans during the Last Glacial Maximum, characterized by Solutrean technology, notably foliate, shouldered, or tanged lithic points at least sometimes delivered by another Solutrean invention, the atlatl. Toward the end of this period, technologies based on backed bladelets and antler points and other artifacts developed (Lower/Middle Magdalenian). Antler harpoons were invented at the close of Dryas I, and proliferated in the regions of Aquitaine and Vasco-Cantabria with salmon rivers. Limited numbers of harpoons have also been found in Mediterranean Spain, but not in Portugal. The lithic tools of southwest France are noted for a high degree of specialization in this period.

Otherwise, there are broad similarities among the industries of all these regions in the Upper/Final Magdalenian.

At many sites along the rivers of the plateaus and Pyrenees of southwest France, subsistence strategies became highly specialized in the hunting of reindeer or ibex, supplemented with salmon fishing and other means. Consequently, very structured patterns of mobility and site function seem to have developed. The reindeer-dependent adaptations of Gironde, Lot, and Périgord seem to have crashed in Alleröd times with the extirpation of *Rangifer*. The highly mobile, territorially extensive "Magdalenian" system, with its diverse, specialized tools and weapons, evolved into the Azilian, with more restricted mobility and territories, simpler, more generalized tool kits, and possibly smaller co-resident groups at least most of the year. The adaptive changes related to the exploitation of less gregarious, less mobile, and often smaller-body-size game in the new woodlands also seem to have led to profound changes in ideologies, as reflected by the abrupt disappearance of Magdalenian mobile and cave art.

In the region along the northern flank of the Pyrenees, however, an isolated reindeer population survived through the whole of Alleröd and seems to have been *increasingly* hunted by humans (even though the species may have been under considerable stress, including competition from the invading red deer). At the Pastou sites, the classic Magdalenian technologies and intensive reindeer hunting during large-scale cold-season occupations all crashed at the *end* of Alleröd, although small numbers of surviving reindeer continued to be killed along with red and roe deer and boar by small bands of humans with "Azilian" technology in Dryas III and Preboreal. The dense Boreal woodlands of southwest France seem to have been lightly populated by small bands of hunters with "Sauveterrian" microlithic technology and most probably the bow and arrow. The abrupt cultural break had come, however, at different times between 12,000 and 10,500 BP and in different places (plateaus vs. mountains/piedmont) in Aquitaine with the reindeer crash that caused complete readjustment of subsistence strategies, technologies, mobility and territory patterns, social arrangements, and ideologies.

The picture is quite different around the Iberian peninsula. Instead of following the strategy of specializing mainly in the hunting of one mammalian game species, subsistence intensification in Vasco-Cantabria, Levante, and Portugal involved broad-spectrum diversification in some cases as early as the Solutrean (despite technological similarities with southern France—no doubt in part reflections of indirect or direct inter-regional social contacts). Although red deer and ibex were obviously key species during the Magdalenian of Iberia, several other ungulates were also hunted (including true woodland species such as roe deer, board, and chamois). But more significantly, riverine, estuarine, and marine resources, as well as birds, were exploited, sometimes in substantial quantities. "Mesolithic"-type broad-spectrum subsistence was being practiced during the Tardiglacial (and even Pleniglacial). No major food sources became extinct in Iberia (and even the coldwater periwinkles were immediately replaced by topshells). Subsistence intensification through diversification simply continued across the Pleistocene–Holocene boundary in Iberia with no abrupt break in resources or strategies, despite expansion of woodlands and sea-level rise.

The Azilian of Cantabria developed almost imperceptibly and rather late out of the relatively nonspecialized Magdalenian of that region (with only the notable change from circular- to flat-section harpoons), and there are even continuities in the geometric motifs on some mobile art objects, although the cave art disappeared. Coastal midden sites continue to grow, but are only part of a system that contined to emphasize hunting and presumably plant food collection. Geometric microliths make only late and spotty appearances in this region, and even the late introduction of ceramics and domesticated animals may not have fundamentally changed the economics of the mixed subsistence base for many centuries.

Levantine Spain also saw considerable technological overlap and continuity across the Pleistocene–Holocene transition. In fact, with a lesser emphasis on osseous artifacts than along the Bay of Biscay facade and with very few antler harpoons, the continuity between the so-called Mediterranean Magdalenian and Microlaminar Epi-Paleolithic seems even greater. The environmental shifts (particularly south of Catalonia) were subtle, and subsistence practices emphasizing diversification that included red deer and ibex hunting, lagomorph snaring (?), fishing, and mollusc collection simply continued and expanded. The Geometric Epi-Paleolithic may signify the introduction of the bow and arrow, although there may have been an earlier invention thereof during the Solutrean, suggested by the tanged points of Parpalló. The significant break here (although even it involved a major degree of population and lithic technological continuity) was the relatively early introduction of ceramics and of Near Eastern cultigens and domesticated animals via the sea and shore.

The Portuguese records of technology and subsistence are also ones of continuity, again emphasizing, respectively, backed bladelets and diversified terrestrial and aquatic foods. These trends culminated in the formation of the vast (semi)sedentary *concheiros* of Ribatejo and Alentejo based on the extremely rich resources of the Atlantic period (high-sea-level) estuaries. So successful were these diversified strategies that they continued for several centuries even after the introduction of Neolithic lifeways in Estremadura circa 6,500 BP.

Although the end of the Last Glacial of the Pleistocene saw significant changes in the extent of woodlands and in the location of coastlines around the Iberian Peninsula, it was not an abrupt or even major development for Iberian hunter–gatherer–fishers, since their resource bases remained essentially intact and their long-term strategy of diversification continued to be successful. Thus, despite sharing technological and artistic traditions, despite geographical proximity, and despite undoubted social links, the trajectories of southern France and Iberia diverged when the more Ice Age–like world of the former, with its large reindeer herds, abruptly disappeared, while the latter underwent more subtle, gradual changes in environments and resources, allowing the inhabitants of Iberia to readjust by following the same basic strategies they had long pursued. The determination of this divergence is a classic example of the value of controlled comparison in anthropology.

REFERENCES

Alcalá, L., Aura, J., Jordá, J., and Morales, J., 1987, Ejemplares de Foca en los niveles Epipaleolíticos y Neolíticos de Nerja, *Cuaternario y Geomorfología* 1:15–26.

Altuna, J., 1972, Fauna de Mamíferos de los Yacimientos Prehistóricos de Guipúzcoa, *Munibe* 24:1–464.

Altuna, J., 1981, Restos Óseos del Yacimiento Prehistórico del Rascaño, in: *El Paleólitico Superior de la Cueva del Rascaño* (J. González Echegaray and I. Barandiarán, eds.), Centro de Investigación y Museo de Altamira, Santander, pp. 223–269.

Altuna, J., 1986, The Mammalian Faunas From the Prehistoric Site of La Riera, in: *La Riera Cave* (L. Straus and G. Clark, eds.), Anthropological Research Papers 36, Tempe, pp. 237–274, 421–480.

Altuna, J., 1990, La Caza de Herbívoros durante el Paleolítico y Mesolítico del País Vasco, *Munibe* 42:226–240.

Altuna, J., 1992, El medio ambiente durante el Pleistoceno superior en la región Cantábrica con referencia especial a sus faunas de mamíferos, *Munibe* 44:13–29.

Altuna, J., and Mariezkurrena, 1995, Les Restes Osseux de Macromammifères, in: *Les Derniers Chasseurs de Rennes du Monde Pyrénéen: L'Abri Dufaure, Un Gisement Tardiglaciaire en Gascogne* (L. Straus, ed.), Mémoire de la Société Préhistorique Française, 22, Paris, pp. 181–211.

Altuna, J., Eastham, A., Mariezkurrena, K., Spiess, A., and Straus, L., 1991, Magdalenian and Azilian Hunting at the Abri Dufaure, SW France, *Archaeozoologia* 4(2):87–108.

Arambourou, R., 1978, *Le Gisement Préhistorique de Duruthy*, Mémoires de la Société Préhistorique Française, 13, Paris.

Araújo, A., 1993, A Estaçao Mesolítica do Forno da Telha, *Trabalhos de Antropologia e Etnologia* 33:15–44.

Arias, P., 1991, *De Cazadores a Campesinos*, Universidad de Cantabria, Santander.

Arnaud, J., 1986, Post-Glacial Adaptations in Southern Portugal. Paper presented at the First World Archaeological Congress, Southampton (Preprint).

Arnaud, J., 1987, Os concheiros Mesolíticos dos Vales do Tajo e Sado: Semelanças e Diferenças, *Arqueologia* 15: 53–64.

Arnaud, J., 1989, The Mesolithic Communities of the Sado Valley, Portugal, in Their Ecological Setting, in: *The Mesolithic in Europe* (C. Bonsall, ed.), John Donald, Edinburgh, pp. 614–631.

Aura, J., and Pérez Ripoll, M., 1992, Tardiglaciar y Postglaciar en la Región Mediterránea de la Península Ibérica, *Saguntum* 25:25–47.

Aura, J., and Pérez Ripoll, M., 1995, Características Culturales y Económicas del Holoceno Inicial en el Mediterráneo Español, in; *Los Ultimos Cazadores* (V. Villaverde, ed.), Instituto Gil Albert, Alicante, pp. 119–146.

Aura, J., Jordá, J., and Rodrigo, M., 1989, Variaciones en la Linea de Costa y su Impacto en la Explotación de los Recursos Marinos en el Limite Pleistoceno–Holoceno, in: *Actas de la Segunda Reunión del Cuaternario Ibérico*, Instituto Geológico y Minero de España, Madrid, pp. 1–13.

Bahn, P., 1984, *Pyrenean Prehistory*, Aris & Philips, Warminster,

Barton, N., Roberts, A., and Roe, D., 1991, *The Late Glacial in North-west Europe*, Council for British Archaeology Report 77, London.

Becker, B., and Kromer, B., 1991, Dendrochronology and Radiocarbon Calibration of the Early Holocene, in: *The Late Glacial in North-west Europe* (N. Barton et al., eds.), CBA Report No. 77, London, pp. 22–24.

Berganza, E., 1990, El Epipaleolítico en el País Vasco, *Munibe* 42:81–89.

Berger, W., 1990, The Younger Dryas Cold Spell—A Quest for Causes, *Palaeogeography, Palaeoclimatology, Palaeoecology* 89:219–237.

Berger, W., and Labeyrie, L., 1987, *Abrupt Climatic Change*, D. Reidel, Dordrecht.

Bicho, N., 1992, Technological Change in the Final Upper Paleolithic of Rio Maior, Portuguese Estremadura. Unpublished Ph.D. dissertation, Southern Methodist University Department of Anthropology.

Bicho, N., 1993, Late Glacial Prehistory of Central and Southern Portugal, *Antiquity* 67:761–775.

Binford, L., 1983, *Working at Archaeology*, Academic Press, New York.

Canal, J., and Carbonell, E., 1989, *Catalunya Paleolítica*, Patronat Francesc Eiximenis, Girona, Spain.

Carbonell, E., et al., 1985, *Sota Palou*, Diputació de Girona, Girona, Spain.

Carvalho, E., Straus, L., Vierra, B., Zilhão, J., and Araújo, A., 1989, More Data for an Archaeological Map of the County of Torres Vedras, *Arqueologia* 19:16–33.

Clark, G., 1976, *El Asturiense Cantábrico*, Bibliotheca Praehistórica Hispana, Madrid.

Clark, G., 1983, *The Asturian of Cantabria*, Anthropological Papers of the University of Arizona, Tucson.

Davidson, I., 1989, *La Economía del Final del Paleolítico en la España Oriental*, Servicio de Investigación Prehistórica, Valencia.

Deith, M., 1983, Seasonality of Shell Collecting, Determined by Oxygen Isotope Analysis of Marine Shells from Asturian Sites, in: *Animals and Archaeology*, Volume 2 (C. Grigson and J. Clutton-Brock, eds.), British Archaeological Reports S-183, Oxford, pp. 67–76.

Deith, M., and Shackleton, N., 1986, Seasonal Exploitation of Marine Molluscs, in: *La Riera Cave* (L. Straus and G. Clark, eds.), Anthropological Research Papers, Tempe, pp. 299–314.

Delpech, F., 1978, Les Faunes Magdaléniennes et Azilienne du Gisement de Duruthy, in: *Le Gisement Préhistorique de Duruthy* (R. Arambourou, ed.), Mémoire de la Société Préhistorique Française 13, Paris, pp. 110–116.

Delpech, F., 1983, *Les Faunes du Paléolithique Supérieur dans le Sud-Ouest de la France*, CNRS, Paris.

Duplessy, J., Delibrias, G., Turon, J., Pujol, C., and Duprat, J., 1981, Deglacial Warming of the Northeastern Atlantic Ocean, *Palaeogeography, Palaeoclimatology, Palaeoecology* 35:121–144.

Dupré, M., 1988, *Palinología y Paleoambiente: Nuevos Datos Españoles*, Servicio de Investigación Prehistórica, Valencia.

Estévez, J., 1979, La Fauna del Pleistoceno Catalán. Unpublished doctoral dissertation, Universitat de Barcelona.

Estévez, J., 1987, La fauna de l'Arbreda, *Cypsela* 6:73–88.

Evin, J., 1979, Réflexions Générales et Données Nouvelles sur la Chronologie Absolue ^{14}C des Industries de la Fin du Paléolithique et du Début du Mésolithique, in: *La Fin des Temps Glaciaires en Europe* (D. de Sonneville-Bordes, ed.), CNRS, Paris, pp. 5–13.

Fernández Tresguerres, J., 1980, *El Aziliense en las Provincias de Asturias y Santander*, Centro de Investigación y Museo de Altamira, Santander.

Fortea, J., 1973, *Los Complejos Microlaminares y Geométricos del Epipaleolítico Mediterráneo Español*, Universidad de Salamanca, Salamanca.

Freeman, L., 1973, The Significance of Mammalian Faunas from Paleolithic Occupations in Cantabrian Spain, *American Antiquity* 38:3–44.

Freeman, L., 1981, The fat of the land: notes on Paleolithic diet in Iberia, in: *Omnivorous Primates* (R. Harding and G. Teleki, eds.), Columbia University Press, New York, pp. 104–165.

González Morales, M., 1982, *El Asturiense y Otras Culturas Locales*, Centro de Investigación y Museo de Altamira, Santander.

González Morales, M., 1990, La Prehistorica de las Marismas: Excavaciones en el Abrigo de la Peña del Perro, *Cuadernos de Trasmiera* 2:13–28.

González Sainz, C., 1989a, *El Magdaleniense Superior-Final de la Región Cantábrica*, Tantin, Santander.

González Sainz, C., 1989b, Notas sobre el Magdaleniense Superior–Final de la Región Cantábrica, in: *Le Magdalénien en Europe* (J. Rigaud, ed.), ERAUL 38, Liège, pp. 441–455.

Lalande, B., 1988, Les grands mammifères de l'abri du Grand Pastou, *Bulletin de la Sociètè de Borda* 113:3–12.

Laville, H., Rigaud, J.-Ph., and Sackett, J., 1980, *Rockshelters of the Périgord*, Academic Press, New York.

Lentacker, A., 1986, Preliminary Results of the Fauna of Cabeço de Amoreira and Cabeço de Arruda, *Trabalhos de Antropologia e Etnologia* 26:9–26.

Lentacker, A., 1991, Archeolzoölogisch Onderzoek van Laat-Prehistorische Vindplaatsen uit Portugal. Unpublished doctoral dissertation, Universiteit Gent.

Leroi-Gourhan, A., and Renault-Miskovsky, J., 1977, La Palynologie Appliquée à l'Archéologie, in: *Approche Ecologique de l'Homme Fossil* (H. Laville and J. Renault-Miskovsky, eds.), Supplément au Bulletin de l'Association Française pour l'Etude du Quaternaire 47:35–49.

Marks, A., Zilhão, J., Bicho, N., and Ferring, R., 1994, Upper Paleolithic prehistory in Portuguese Estremadura: Preliminary Results, *Journal of Field Archaeology* 21:53–68.

Ortea, J., 1986, The malacology of La Riera Cave, in: *La Riera Cave* (L. Straus and G. Clark, eds.), Anthropological Research Papers, Tempe, pp. 289–298.

Otte, M., Silva, A. C. da, and Lejeune, M., no date, Portuguese Palaeolithic Art: New Research. Manuscript in possession of the author.

Pons, J., Beaulieu, J. de, Guiot, J., and Reille, M., 1987, The Younger Dryas in Southwestern Europe: An Abrupt Climate Change as Evidenced from Pollen Records, in: *Abrupt Climate Change* (W. Berger and L. Labeyrie, eds.), Reidel, Dordrecht, pp. 195–208.

Puvoas, L., Zilhão, J., Chaline, J., and Brunet-Leconte, P., 1992, La faune de Rongeurs du Pleistocéne Supérieur de la Grotte de Caldeirão, *Quaternaire* 3:40–47.

Raposo, L., Penalva, C., and Pereira, J., 1989, Notícia da Desoberta da Estaçao Mirense de Palheirões do Alegra, Cabo Sardão, in: *Actas de la Segunda Reunión del Cuaternario Ibérico*, Instituto Geológico y Minero de España, Madrid, pp. 25–29.

Renault-Miskovsky, J., and Leroi-Gourhan, A., 1981, Palynologie et archéologie: Nouveaux Résultats du Paléolithique Supérieur au Mésolithique, *Bulletin de l'Association Française pour l'Etude du Quaternaire* 1981:121–128.

Roche, J., 1972a, Les amas coquilliers (concheiros) mésolithiques de Muge, *Fundamenta* B3(VII):72–107.

Roche, J., 1972b, *Le Gisement Mésolithique de Moita do Sebastião*, Instituto de Alta Cultura, Lisbon.

Roche, J., 1982, A Gruta Chamada Lapa do Suão, *Arqueologia* 5:5–18.

Rozoy, J., 1978, *Les Derniers Chasseurs*, Société Archéologique Champenoise, Charleville.

Ruddiman, W., and McIntyre, A., 1981, The North Atlantic Ocean during the Last Deglaciation, *Palaeogeography, Palaeoclimatology, Palaeoecology* 35:145–214.

Straus, L., 1977, Of Deerslayers and Mountain Men: Paleolithic Faunal Exploitation in Cantabrian Spain, in: *For Theory Building in Archaeology* (L. Binford, ed.), Academic Press, New York, pp. 41–76.

Straus, L., 1983, Terminal Pleistocene Faunal Exploitation in Cantabrian Spain and Gascony, in: *Animals and Archaeology*, Volume 1 (J. Clutton-Brock and C. Grigson, eds.), British Archaeological Reports S-163, Oxford, pp. 209–225.

Straus, L., 1985, Chronostratigraphy of the Pleistocene-Holocene Transition: The Azilian Problem in the Franco-Cantabrian region, *Palaeohistoria* 27:89–122.

Straus, L., 1986, The End of the Paleolithic in Cantabrian Spain and Gascony, in: *The End of the Paleolithic in the Old World*, L. Straus, ed., British Archaeological Reports S-284, Oxford, pp. 81–116.

Straus, L., 1987, Upper Paleolithic Ibex Hunting in SW Europe, *Journal of Archaeological Science* 14:163–178.

Straus, L., 1992a, *Iberia before the Iberians*, University of New Mexico Press, Albuquerque.

Straus, L., 1992b, To Change or Not to Change: The Late and Post-Glacial in SW Europe, *Quaternaria Nova* 2: 161–185.

Straus, L., 1995a, Diversity in the face of adversity, in: *Los Ultimos Cazadores* (V. Villaverde, ed.), Fundación Gil Albert, Alicante, pp. 9–22.

Straus, L., 1995b, *Les Derniers Chasseurs de Rennes du Monde Pyrénéen: L'Abri Dufaure, un Gisement Tardiglaciaire en Gascogne*, Mémoires de la Société Préhistorique Française, 22, Paris.

Straus, L., and Clark, G., 1986, *La Riera Cave*, Anthropological Research Papers 36, Tempe.

Straus, L., Altuna, J., and Vierra, B., 1990, The concheiro at Vidigal: A contribution to the late Mesolithic of southern Portugal, in: *Contributions to the Mesolithic in Europe* (P. Vermeersch and P. Van Peer, eds.), Katholieke Universiteit, Leuven, pp. 463–474.

Ters, M., 1973, Les Variations du Niveau Marin Depuis 10,000 ANS, le Long du Littoral Atlantique Français, in: *Actes du 9ième Congrès International de l'INQUA*, CNRS, Paris, pp. 114–135.

Valladas, H., Cachier, H., Maurice, P., Bernaldo de Quirós, F., Clottes, J., Cabrera, V., Uzquiano, P., and Arnold, M., 1992, Direct Radiocarbon Dates for Prehistoric Paintings at the Altamira, El Castillo and Niaux Caves, *Nature* 357:68–70.

Vierra, B., 1992, Subsistence Diversification and the Evolution of Microlithic Technologies: A Study of the Portuguese Mesolithic. Unpublished Ph.D. dissertation, University of New Mexico Department of Anthropology.

Watts, W., 1986, Stages of Climatic Change from Full Glacial to Holocene in Northwest Spain, Southern France and Italy, in; *Current Issues in Climate Research* (A. Ghazi and R. Fantechi, eds.), Reidel, Dordrecht, pp. 101–112.

Zilhão, J., 1987, *O Solutrense da Estremadura Portuguesa*, Trabalhos de Arqueologia 4, Lisbon.

Zilhão, J., 1991, Le Solutréen du Portugal, in: *Feuilles de Pierre* (J. Kozłowski, ed.), ERAUL 42, Liège, pp. 485–501.

Zilhão, J., 1992, *Gruta do Caldeirão, O Neolítico Antigo*, Trabalhos de Arqueologia 6, Lisbon.

Zilhão, J., 1993a, The Spread of Agro-Pastoral Economies across Mediterranean Europe: A View from the Far West, *Journal of Mediterranean Archaeology* 6:5–63.

Zilhão, J., 1993b, O Paleolítico Superior em Portugal, in *O Quaternario em Portugal, Balanço e Perspectiva*, Colibri, Lisbon, pp. 163–172.

Zilhão, J., Carvalho, E., and Araújo, A., 1987, A Estaçao Epipaleolítica da Ponta da Vigia, *Arqueologia* 16:8–18.

Chapter 6

Resource Exploitation, Subsistence Strategies, and Adaptiveness in Late Pleistocene–Early Holocene Northwest Europe

Berit Valentin Eriksen

INTRODUCTION

Throughout western Europe, the Pleistocene–Holocene transition is characterized by marked environmental and cultural changes. Following the gradual retreat of the Weichselian glacier, large areas in the north and northeast were again—or at last—made available to human settlement. Obviously, then, this period is one of great archaeological significance. The settling of the north following the retreat of the ice must have been a major challenge, demanding a high degree of past human adaptivity. An examination of the gradual northward migration of flora, fauna, and people into the virgin areas of southern Scandinavia is thus of general methodological interest. Most important, it enables us to examine the nature and timing of possible relationships between long-term environmental and cultural change throughout a geographically extensive region.

Much archaeological research on the Pleistocene–Holocene transition has focused on geographically rather limited areas. However, given the environmental conditions and the marked seasonal variation in climate, flora, and fauna, it is obvious that mobility must have been high and that mobility and settlement patterns must have been accordingly complex at the time. Moreover, mobility and settlement patterns are likely to have changed a lot in the course of this 5000- to 7000-year-long period. If the geographic area of investigation is too

BERIT VALENTIN ERIKSEN • Department of Prehistoric Archaeology, Univeristy of Åarhus, Moesgaard, 8270 Højbjerg, Denmark.

Humans at the End of the Ice Age: The Archaeology of the Pleistocene–Holocene Transition, edited by Lawrence Guy Straus, Berit Valentin Eriksen, Jon M. Erlandson, and David R. Yesner. Plenum Press, New York, 1996.

limited, we will miss the overall context within which to interpret these patterns, and we may even miss vital aspects of the patterns themselves—such as, for instance, the cultural, socioeconomic, and perhaps even ethnic relationships that may have existed between hunter–gatherer groups of the northwestern lowland and the mountainous areas in the south. Over the years, many prominent researchers have argued in favor of such direct relationships (Rust 1937; Schwabedissen 1954; Sturdy 1975; Taute 1969), and this study presents a welcome opportunity to reexamine the substance of these asserted connections.

The general climatic amelioration during the late Pleistocene and early Holocene led to considerable changes in biological productivity, including the amount and general diversity of available food resources (as will be illustrated by Tables 1–3 and Figures 5 and 6). Obviously, these changes were of essential importance to contemporary hunters and gatherers, and this chapter therefore focuses on subsistence strategies and the exploitation of the various—and varying—faunal resources in the period in question.

GEOGRAPHIC STUDY AREAS

Unfortunately, a large-scale, interregional study is severely hampered by the geographically and chronologically very uneven distribution of well-documented sites and especially of sites with organic remains. For methodological and source-critical reasons, this chapter will therefore focus on sites associated with the following three main regions in central and northwest Europe (Figure 1):

1. The Jurassic limestone formation (Alb highland) and its immediate surroundings in northwest Switzerland and southwest Germany.
2. The Thuringian Basin in Central Germany.
3. The lowland area of Denmark and northwest Germany.

The main geomorphological differences between these regions relate to topography and geology. The two southernmost areas are both situated in (or on the edge of) the so-called "ice-free corridor" in continental Europe. The northernmost area, however, was for the main part covered by ice during the last pleniglacial. Moreover, this area was characterized by a very turbulent coastline history during the period in question. Thus, from an ecological perspective, these three regions appear highly different. Obviously, this difference would also have applied to paleoenvironmental and paleoclimatic conditions.

GEOCHRONOLOGICAL FRAMEWORK—CLIMATE AND VEGETATION

To facilitate comparison between the regions, it is necessary to operate in a very generalized chronological framework. Names and datings of chronozones are thus kept identical even if the descriptive characteristics may vary substantially (Tables 1–3). Most of the climatic events occurring in the late Pleistocene–early Holocene are not synchronous throughout northwest Europe. The differences observed, however, are of minor importance with respect to the general comparative approach adopted here.

Geochronologically, we are dealing with the late Pleistocene chronozones of Bølling, Allerød, and Younger Dryas and the early Holocene chronozones of the Preboreal and Boreal. The existence of an Older Dryas climatic retreat is highly disputed and rather

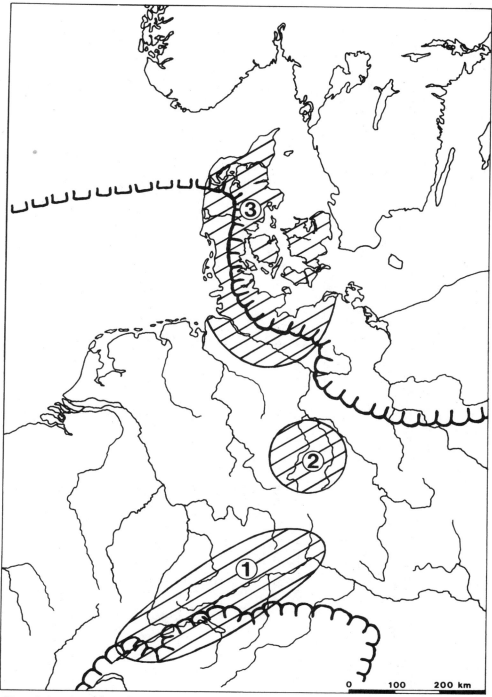

Figure 1. Location of the study areas in central and northwest Europe. Maximal extent of the Weichselian glacier at 20,000 BP.

Table 1. Schematic Outline of Geochronology, Climate, and Vegetation in Southwest Germany and Northwest Switzerland

Years BP	Chronozones	Climate	Vegetation	Archaeological cultures
8,000				
	Boreal	Warm temperate Increasing oceanic	Boreal forest (oak, elm, alder, lime, ash)	
9,000				Beuronian
	Preboreal	Temperate	Light, open forest (pine, birch, hazel)	
10,000				
	Dryas III	Cool temperate continental	Sparse forest and park-tundra (pine–birch, willow, herbs)	
11,000				Late Paleolithic and Fürsteiner
	Allerød	Temperate	Sparse forest (pine–birch, sea buckthorn, grasses, herbs)	
12,000	–(Dryas II)–	Increasing oceanic		
	Bølling (sensu lato)	Cool temperate	Park-tundra and sparse forest (birch, juniper, willow, [pine], grasses, herbs)	
13,000				Magdalenian (sensu lato)
	Dryas I	Subarctic Marked continental	Tundra and park-tundra (dwarf birch, willow, juniper, rock rose, sea-grape)	
14,000				

Table 2. Schematic Outline of Geochronology, Climate, and Vegetation in the Thuringian Basin (Central Germany)

Years BP	Chronozones	Climate	Vegetation	Archaeological cultures
8,000				
	Boreal	Temperate	Open, boreal forest (hazel, elm, oak, alder, aspen, ash)	Early Mesolithic
9,000				
	Preboreal	Temperate	Light, open forest (pine, birch, hazel)	
10,000				
	Dryas III	Cool temperate continental	Sparse forest and park-tundra (birch–pine, willow)	
11,000				Late Paleolithic
	Allerod	Temperate	Sparse forest and scrub steppe (pine–birch, wormwood, grasses, herbs)	
12,000	–(Dryas II)–	Increasing oceanic		
	Bölling (sensu lato)	Cool temperate	Park-tundra, sparse forest and steppe (birch, juniper, [pine], grasses, herbs)	
13,000				Magdalenian (sensu lato)
	Dryas I	Cold subarctic	Tundra (dwarf birch, sea buckthorn, herbs)	
14,000				

Table 3. Schematic Outline of Geochronology, Climate, and Vegetation in Denmark and Northwest Germany

Years BP	Chronozones	Climate	Vegetation	Archaeological cultures
8,000				
	Boreal	Warm temperate	Boreal forest (hazel, elm, oak, alder, aspen, ash)	Maglemose
9,000				
	Preboreal	Cool temperate Continental	Light, open forest (birch, pine, aspen, juniper, crowberry)	Barmose-group
10,000				
	Dryas III	Subarctic Oceanic	Park-tundra (willow, dwarf birch, juniper, wormwood, crowberry, grasses, sedges)	Ahrensburgian
11,000				
	Allerød	Cool temperate	Park-tundra and sparse forest (birch, rowan, juniper, aspen, willow, [pine], grasses, herbs)	Bromme and Federmesser
12,000	–(Dryas II)–	Increasing oceanic		
	Bølling (sensu lato)	Cool temperate	Park-tundra (birch, rowan, willow, wormwood, grasses, herbs)	Hamburgian
13,000				
	Dryas I	Subarctic Continental	Tundra and park-tundra (dwarf birch, willow, wormwood, rock rose, sea buckthorn, grasses, herbs)	
14,000				

uncertain in central Europe (Ammann et al. 1984:70; Beaulieu et al. 1984; Watts 1980:20; Welten 1982) and frequently questioned even in northwest Europe (Kolstrup 1991 with further references). As a consequence, the "Older Dryas" is here included in the Bølling *sensu lato*.

Apart from the northern area (3 in Figure 1), only the southernmost part of area (1) was covered by ice during the last glaciation. The Scandinavian as well as the alpine glacier retreated rapidly during early Oldest Dryas, and thus both areas were ice-free before Bølling (Berglund 1979; Frenzel 1983). Throughout most of the late Pleistocene, these virgin young morainic areas were characterized by a typical arctic–subarctic tundra vegetation with dwarf birch, arctic and herbaceous willow, and a multitude of sedges, grasses, and herbs. The landscape of the ice-free corridor would have presented a more varied picture. The mountainous highland surrounding the Thuringian basin as well as the Jura Alb was generally covered by tundra, park-tundra, or grass steppe. The river valleys would have been covered with willow scrub and juniper and during the warmer periods of Bølling and Allerød even with light open birch and pine forests (especially those made up of *Betula pubescens* and *Pinus silvestris*) (Frenzel 1983; Mania 1973). The climate was continental, though in Bølling and Allerød increasingly oceanic and cool temperate.

The climatic deterioration of the Younger Dryas was distinct and well-documented in central Europe (Watts 1980), although it was far from as marked as in the north. The worsening of the climate set in about 10,800 BP and was most significant in the high-lying western and southwestern part of the area (notably the Swiss Jura, the Black Forest, and the Vosges) (Frenzel 1983). Summers were now probably colder and wetter than during Bølling–Allerød (Ammann et al. 1984; Frenzel 1983), but as a whole climatic change was gradual. Even the beginning of the Preboreal had the character of a smooth transition from Younger Dryas. The southernmost area was now covered by an open pine–birch or birch–pine forest. There was also a marked rise in the pollen curve for hazel and a corresponding fall in the curve for willow. Toward the end of the Preboreal, hazel became more and more dominant. Birch and pine receded, and there was an increase in oak and elm (Firbas 1949; Rösch 1985).

The regeneration of the forest that began during Bølling was now at an end. In the Boreal, there was dense, impenetrable deciduous forest everywhere—on the Alb highland as well. During this period, even the Swabian Alb was dominated by hazel scrub. In addition, a mixed oak forest with elm, alder, lime, and ash began to spread (Firbas 1949; Rösch 1985).

Throughout the period in question, the northern study area was characterized by a turbulent coastline history that had a marked effect on climate and vegetation (Petersen 1984, 1985). Following the retreat of the glaciers, the sea level rose, but at the same time land that had been weighed down by the ice slowly began to rise. During the Oldest Dryas and Bølling, the ice melted away rapidly, and there was a corresponding rapid rise in sea level (Figure 2). From this period, there are many marine deposits on present-day dry land. Large parts of northern Jutland appear to have been flooded first by the arctic Yoldia Sea of the Oldest Dryas and later by the slightly more temperate Zirphaea Sea of the Bølling. In the Allerød and Younger Dryas, however, the upheaval of land took the lead (Figure 3). As a consequence, the North Sea and most of the Baltic coastline of that time are today submerged.

The enormous amount of meltwater from the retreating glacier led to the formation of the great Baltic Ice Lake. This lake was blocked by surrounding land and ice and had only

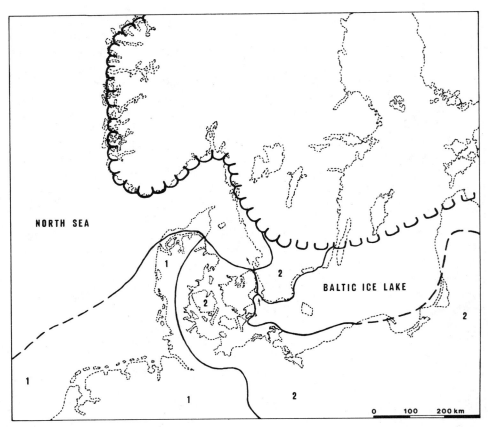

Figure 2. South Scandinavian land and sea configuration in Bølling (ice margin at 12,500 BP): (1) tundra; (2) park-tundra with birch groves (vegetational zones cf. Huntley and Birks 1983).

few and insufficient outlets. Toward the end of the Younger Dryas, the glacier had come to a stop in Central Sweden, and only the mountain of Billingen then separated the ice lake from the North Sea. The surface of the lake was by then some 26 m above sea level (Björck and Digerfeldt 1984:46). When the temperature again rose markedly at the onset of the Preboreal, it caused a dramatic draining of the lake. The "deluge" appears to have taken place in several stages (Björck and Digerfeldt 1984), but even so it must have been a major ecological disaster, destroying and disrupting plantlife and wildlife over a large area.

This event marks the beginning of the Preboreal in northern Europe. In a short time, the open park-tundra was transformed into a light open birch forest with pine, aspen, juniper, and crowberry.

Obviously, the vegetational history of the north is significantly delayed compared to that of the southern areas. Hazel, for instance, does not immigrate until early Boreal, and even then we find it only in the southeastern part of the area. It takes another 700 years to spread to the northwest. This difference not only illustrates the climatic variation through-

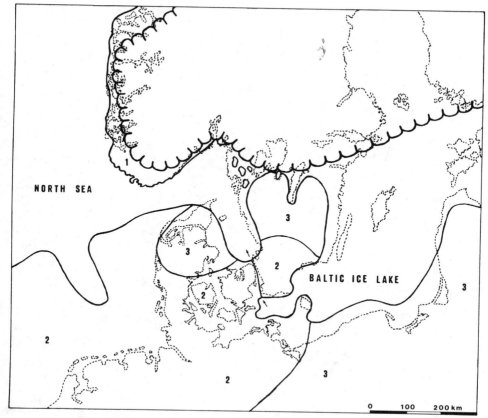

Figure 3. South Scandinavian land and sea configuration in Dryas III (ice margin at 10,000 BP): (1) tundra; (2) park-tundra with birch groves; (3) sparse birch and pine forest (vegetational zones cf. Huntley and Birks 1983).

out the region, but also indicates that there probably were different mechanisms operating with respect to the migration of hazel. Due to the weight of the fruits, hazel does not by itself spread as quickly as, for example, pine and birch, the lightweight fruits of which are spread by the wind. A likely explanation (first expressed by Firbas 1949) thus is that the collecting, storing, and transporting of hazelnuts by prehistoric man was an important factor in the early Boreal spread of hazel in the southeastern part of the region. The following spread to the northwest, on the other hand, might reflect natural, that is, more slowly operating, migration mechanisms.

By late Boreal, the forest was dominated by hazel and pine, but soon elm, oak, alder, aspen, and ash would immigrate and cover the landscape with a stable primeval forest. Meanwhile, in southern and central Sweden, the isostatic upheaval of land continued, and once again the Baltic was cut off from the North Sea (Figure 4). The Boreal is the time of the Ancylus lake. The climate was warm, temperate, and—because of the North Sea land bridge between Denmark and Great Britain—mostly continental.

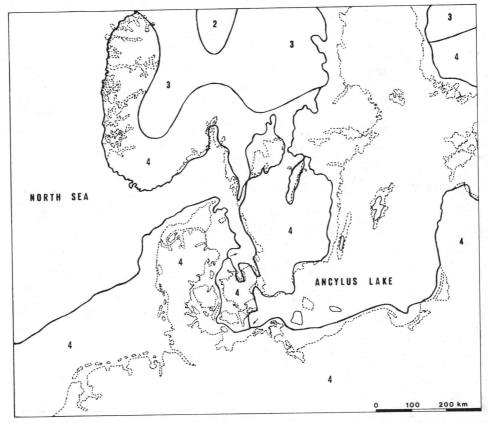

Figure 4. South Scandinavian land and sea configuration in early Boreal (8,000 BP): (2) park-tundra with birch groves; (3) sparse birch and pine forest; (4) mixed deciduous forest (vegetational zones cf. Huntley and Birks 1983).

THE FAUNAL REMAINS—SOURCE EVALUATION AND FAUNA HISTORY

Changes in fauna are closely related to changes in climate and vegetation. Unfortunately, though, the fauna of the two southernmost study areas is known almost exclusively from archaeological sites and thus presents many interpretational problems (Eriksen 1991a; Koenigswald 1976). Moreover, the distribution of late Pleistocene sites with faunal remains in northwest Switzerland and southwest Germany displays a severe bias with respect to general find context. In this area, the vast majority of sites are caves and rock shelters. Open-air sites constitute fewer than 10%, but this scarcity is most likely due to a number of secondary factors influencing their preservation and discovery (Eriksen 1991a, in press). It does not reflect any prehistoric reality, but it does result in a major interpretational problem. In short, a cave site usually represents the actual occupation area containing a selection of organic remains, whereas an open-air site with preserved organic remains generally (i.e., with rather few exceptions) can be taken as a refuse area.

Other problems pertain to the interpretation of occasional finds of single bones from otherwise rare species. Such a find is especially problematic as regards the so-called "old fauna elements" (Table 4). The possible value of these elements with respect to the dating of inventories has in some cases been extremely overestimated (Weniger 1982:21f). It is obvious (cf. Table 4) that many of the central European Magdalenian inventories with old fauna elements are very likely mixed. Moreover, mammoth is often present only in the form of ivory fragments. Woolly rhinoceros, giant deer, cave lion, cave hyena, and other species are also often present only in the form of occasional bones or teeth. Obviously, such isolated specimens have very limited source value.

. The asserted coexistence of boreal forest and high-arctic species such as roe deer and wild boar with mammoth and woolly rhinoceros (Musil 1992) is thus considered highly improbable. Nevertheless, it is true that environmental conditions at the time were very different from present-day subarctic or arctic conditions. The late Pleistocene of central Europe displayed a variety in habitat that is absolutely unparalleled in any present-day environment, and many allopatric species apparently coexisted here.

In Figure 5 (which summarizes the faunal evidence from the southernmost study area), we notice the probable extinction of the typical Ice Age fauna (e.g., woolly rhinoceros, mammoth, reindeer, cave bear, cave lion) in late Bølling. However, a recent find of a reindeer metatarsus in an early Mesolithic settlement horizon from Rottenburg-Siebenlinden I (Hahn et al. 1993) indicates that this species might have survived quite a while as a relict population in mountainous areas like the Black Forest or the Swiss Jura. The find circumstances of the reindeer metatarsus are meticulously documented and raise no doubt with respect to the early Holocene age of the piece. The archaeological dating has also been confirmed by a radiocarbon analysis indicating an absolute age of 9,110 ± 80 BP (ETH 8265) (Hahn et al. 1993). The origin of the animal presents more of a question. The nearest contemporary, that is, early Boreal, reindeer population is probably located in central Scandinavia. A Scandinavian origin, however, appears rather unlikely—partly because of the distance and partly because of the lack of other evidence of mutual early Holocene connections between these two regions. The proposed existence of a relict population, on the other hand, corresponds well with the assumption that late Pleistocene reindeer in southwest Germany made short seasonal migrations within a fairly limited area (Eriksen 1991a; Hahn 1979; Weniger 1982).

Other arctic species, including, for instance, musk ox, arctic fox, and wolverine, might also have survived awhile as relict populations in mountainous areas. In the sense of important game fauna, however, these species were not present after Bølling.

In early Bølling, the first cold-tolerating forest species such as elk (*Alces alces*), red fox, lynx, polecat, and badger began to immigrate, and the more ubiquitous species (i.e., red deer, wolf, brown bear) increased in numbers and frequency. In Allerød, then, a truly warmth-loving species, the roe deer, made its first appearance.

Obviously, late Pleistocene–early Holocene fauna development in central Europe was very gradual. The most important changes occurred during Bølling and Allerød (Koenigswald 1976, 1983). Throughout most of the late Pleistocene, the fauna were characterized by species displaying a varied spectrum of biotope preferences. Arctic-mountainous, steppe, and temperate-forest species seem to have co-existed in an environment characterized by a patchwork of different ecological niches.

In the Thuringian basin, the typical Ice Age fauna seem to have persisted much longer than in the south. This persistence is due to the influence of an extensive subarctic loess-

Table 4. Central European Magdalenian Inventories Containing 'Old Fauna Elements'[a]

Sites	Old fauna elements						Recent fauna elements								
	Mammoth	Woolly rhinoceros	Giant deer	Cave lion	Cave hyena	Cave bear	Roe deer	Wild boar	Pine marten	Wild cat	Beaver	Caper-caillie	Elk	Aurochs	Badger
Thierstein (1890–1906)						+		(7/3)	1/1	1/1					2/1
Kohlerhöhle (1934–1938)	+					+									
Kesslerloch, Yellow layer (1873–1903)		–/1					–/1				–/1			+	
Freudenthal (1874)	+					+	+	+		+			+		+
Teufelsküche, B.C. (1925–1926)	i	–/4								–/1					–/4
Munzingen (1914–1915)	i														
Petersfels, cave (1927–1928)	i	.													
Petersfels, P3, AH4-5 (1974–1976)	i			–/1			–/6	+		+	–/1	+			+
Zigeunerfels, F-G-H (1971–1972)	++			+							+		?		
Napoleonskopf (1906)	+	+	–/1												
Sirgenstein, Iα (1906)	1/1					++						1/1			
Brillenhöhle, IV (1955–1963)		+				15/4				+					
Haldensteinhöhle, IV (1936)					+	+									
Hohlenstein Stadel, III (1908–1961)	i			14/–	3/–	936/–			1/–	2/–			3/–		
Hohlenstein Kl. Scheuer (1908–1974)				+						+					
Vogelherd, II-III (1931)	–/1	–/3		2/–		–/2			1/–						
Spitzbubenhöhle, AH2 (1970–1971)		1/1										–/1			
Kl. Scheuer Rosenstein, I-II (1916–1919)						+			+						
Kleine Ofnet, 1 (1934–1936)	+/i	1/1	1/1		–/2	–/2									
Kaufertsberg, 1 (1913)	+					+									
Kastlhänghöhle, V (1888–1900)						+									+
Oelknitz (1957–1967)	1/–	1/–						1/–		1/–					
Lausnitz (1928, 1960)	1/1	(1/1)					2/1								
Teufelsbrücke, 3 (1970–1972)	7/1						1/1								

[a]Numbers are NISP/MNI. Data from Andree (1939), Bandi (1947), Eriksen (1991a), Feustel et al. (1963), Koken (1912), Musil (1980, 1985), Pasda (1992), and Sarasin (1918). (i) Ivory only.

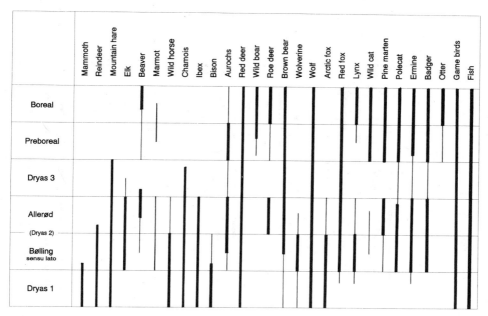

Figure 5. Schematic outline of probable or definite presence of various game animals in southwest Germany and northwest Switzerland.

steppe immediately east of this area. Clear steppe elements include the presence of saiga antelope and the considerable amount of wild-horse hunting being done here (cf. below).

Considering the faunal development in northwest Europe (Figure 6), we observe a clear delay in the disappearance of arctic fauna elements (especially reindeer), together with a marked delay in the immigration of warmer species. On the whole, we find in this area a much more explicit distinction between cold late Pleistocene and warm early Holocene game fauna.

Fortunately, the picture here is complemented by a number of bog finds and other naturally deposited faunal remains. We thus know from marine deposits in northern Jutland that the ice sea sustained a rich marine fauna with seals, whales, fish, and even polar bear (Aaris-Sørensen 1989; Aaris-Sørensen and Petersen 1984; Møhl 1971). Hunter–gatherer groups of southern Scandinavia may be expected to have visited the coasts—perhaps even on a regular basis—but as the coastline is now mostly submerged, there is only scant evidence of probable coastal exploitation (Nilsson 1989).

As regards the possible fauna of the Baltic Ice Lake, we have no reliable evidence. It has been argued that the lake was almost dead due to a thick surface layer of meltwater, but it has also been argued that during Allerød the lake was in fact a salt sea with direct access to the White Sea in the northeast as well as Skagerak in the west (the discussion is quoted in Møhl 1971:328). If this is true, then Allerød man would have had rich opportunity to hunt and fish from the coasts. For the time being, though, we have neither direct nor indirect evidence of coastal hunting in the Baltic region.

In conclusion, it is widely accepted to conceive of fauna development during the late Pleistocene and early Holocene in terms of a general decrease in species diversity (Koenigs-

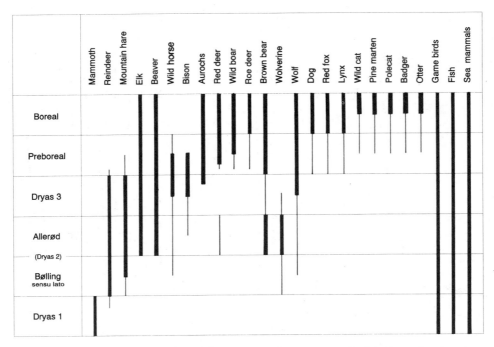

Figure 6. Schematic outline of probable or definite presence of various game animals in Denmark and northwest Germany.

wald 1976; Musil 1992; Stewart and Jochim 1986). Obviously, this applies primarily to the southernmost study area (see Figure 5). On the other hand, changes here seem to have taken place rather gradually, both climatically and with regard to vegetation and fauna. Considering all available food resources (plant and animal), the general impression thus is that the early Holocene environment would have been different from, but no less varied than, the late Pleistocene environment.

In the north, in the young morainic areas, species diversity increased markedly in the early Holocene (see Figure 6). Here, then, the general climatic amelioration led to a considerable increase in biological productivity, including the amount and overall diversity of available food resources.

EXPLOITING THE FAUNAL RESOURCES—SUBSISTENCE ANALYSES

Due to the chronological and spatial extent of this study, the archaeological sites examined belong to a number of different technocomplexes, cultures, and culture phases. Absolute chronologies are summarized in Tables 1–3. For a thorough presentation of relative chronologies (including the lithic and organic inventories), the reader may refer to the extensive literature on this topic. Examples of general overviews are Burdukiewicz (1986), Clark (1975), Eriksen (1991a), Jensen (1982), Schild (1984), Weniger (1989), and Wyss (1973).

It is very unfortunate that data from the Thuringian basin are available only with respect to late Pleistocene subsistence strategies, data from early Holocene sites with organic remains having yet to be reported from this area. Furthermore, we find in all study areas a general lack of sites belonging to the period from late Allerød throughout Younger Dryas and early Preboreal. The question is whether this lack reflects prehistoric reality, that is, an actual decrease in settlement, or whether it is rather a reflection of inadequate embedding and preservation of archaeological horizons from the period in question (Eriksen 1991a). Methodological problems pertaining to radiocarbon dating may also be in part responsible for the pattern observed.

Since the primary issue is subsistence strategies, all sites examined have organic (mostly faunal) remains. It follows that a fair number of samples have been radiocarbon dated in the past. Still, precise dating is a rather relativistic concept, and it is in general highly problematic to discuss the absolute as well as the relative contemporaneity of sites. However, if we assume that the sites in individual chronozones are archaeologically contemporary, and that their patterning is persistent within a broad chronological framework, we find it quite promising, after all, to make a comparative analysis of the three study areas.

Late Pleistocene Subsistence Strategies

Twenty years ago, it was still widely accepted to conceive of late Pleistocene subsistence economy more or less exclusively in terms of reindeer hunting. More than a decade of intensive research, however, has contributed to a new understanding of especially the Magdalenians and Hamburgians as being highly adaptive and generally opportunistic hunters who had the choice of a variety of game animals. This variety is very clearly illustrated by analyses of faunal inventories from the southernmost study area (Eriksen 1991a).

It is true that the reindeer was the dominant game animal in many Swabian and Swiss fauna inventories, but both the minimum number of individuals and the number of fragments are generally low, and a balance, or even dominance, of wild horse or other species (e.g., mountain hare, ibex, and grouse) is frequent (Eriksen 1991a). The few sites in which vast amounts of reindeer bones have been found are all situated in the vicinity of the extensive young morainic areas in Oberschwaben, that is, areas that would have favored a sustained tundra vegetation throughout the late Pleistocene. Topographically, these finds (Petersfels, Kesslerloch, Schweizersbild, and Schussenquelle) represent a rather special situation compared to the other sites of the region; their uniqueness is therefore not due solely to some extremely suitable conditions for preservation. It should be noted, however, that these inventories (except for Schussenquelle) also contain a number of other species and that wild horse, mountain hare, and grouse in particular are very well represented.

The size of these large inventories may be interpreted as a result of many repeated occupations. Petersfels in particular may be interpreted as a repeatedly visited kill site (Albrecht 1984; Albrecht and Berke 1987), and it is reasonable, at least to a certain degree, to extend this interpretation to include the other sites as well. On the other hand, complementary analyses of settlement dynamics and mobility patterns also indicate the probable existence of a flexible settlement structure with periodic aggregation camps in this specific area (Eriksen 1990, 1991a; Weniger 1982).

Moreover, it is likely that late Pleistocene reindeer made seasonal migrations within a fairly limited area and thus, for example, spent the summer in small dispersed groups in the

Alb highlands, while during winter they may have congregated in larger herds in the young moraine areas (Eriksen 1991a). Accordingly, this region might at times (i.e., during Bølling) have allowed more extensive habitations with respect to length of stay or number of inhabitants or both—for example, by permitting storage of meat from mass killings of reindeer.

Fortunately, we have a reasonable number of seasonal determinations to complement the evidence on subsistence economy. The map in Figure 7 synthesizes the location and presumed seasonal determination of 20 Magdalenian sites in southwest Germany and northwest Switzerland. In the Swabian Alb proper, we observe a distinct polarization between the northeast and the southwest. In the Ostalb and Mittlere Alb, spring and summer habitations predominate, whereas autumn and winter indications are rare. In the southwest (Hegaualb and Randen), autumn and winter habitations are most prominent, while spring and summer indications are rather infrequent. The Federsee area (i.e., Schussenquelle) occupies a geographically and seasonally intermediate position. The Swiss finds, too, display a clear polarization with respect to Hegau. In the Swiss Jura, summer and autumn habitations predominate, whereas spring and especially winter habitations are rare.

In trying to interpret this pattern, we face a number of methodological problems— partly because of the reliability of the seasonal determinations and partly because the map represents a compressed view of a long time span. If we assume, however, that the determinations are reliable, that the sites are archaeologically contemporary, and that their patterning is persistent within a broad chronological framework, we find clear agreement with a model of interpretation initially proposed by Hahn (1979) and further elaborated by Weniger (1982). The elaborate model assumes short seasonal movements between spring and summer residential camps in the Alb valleys and autumn and winter aggregation camps in the surrounding lowlands. Considering the map, though, we should add to this model the possibility that certain groups might have been able to remain within fairly limited parts of the area, in the northeast or in the southwest, throughout the year (Eriksen 1991a). In any case, the evidence suggests that the Magdalenian hunters stayed within the region throughout the year. There is nothing to support the model proposed by Sturdy (1975), according to which the Magdalenians undertook comprehensive transregional migrations between summer occupations in the Swabian Alb and winter occupations in the northwest European lowland.

Marked seasonal differences in the environment generally area of great importance to hunter–gatherer groups. There are examples from ethnography of people who show such extreme seasonal variation in their behavior that one single group will act as several completely different groups at different times of the year. This is not the case, however, in late Pleistocene northwest and central Europe. This study deals with discrete, regionally delimited, social and cultural groups of which only the groups from the two southernmost areas appear to have had some kind of direct connections with one another (Eriksen in press).

What, then, is the situation in the other study areas?

In the Thuringian Basin, evidence on subsistence economy comes from eight Magdalenian sites of a reasonable, though varied, quality (Table 5). As mentioned, these finds are characterized by a prevalence of steppe elements with wild horse as the preferred game. Other species have been hunted or trapped as well, including, for example, reindeer, hare, arctic fox, and grouse. The number of different species, however, is extremely low. In two

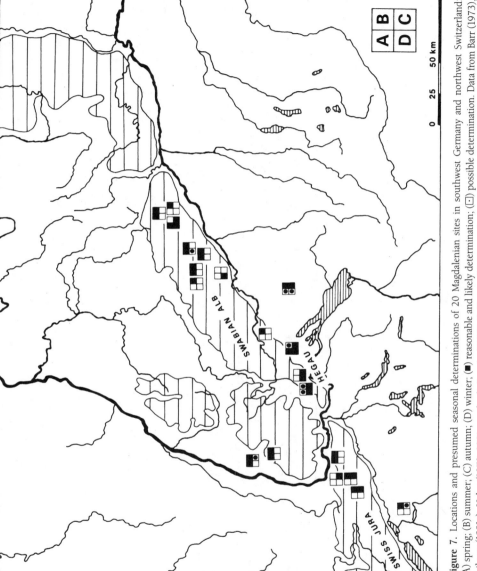

Figure 7. Locations and presumed seasonal determinations of 20 Magdalenian sites in southwest Germany and northwest Switzerland: (A) spring; (B) summer; (C) autumn; (D) winter; (■) reasonable and likely determination; (⊡) possible determination. Data from Barr (1973), Eriksen (1991a), Hahn (1979, 1981, no date), Sarasin (1918), Sedlmeier (1982, 1989), Weniger (1982).

Table 5. Late Pleistocene Fauna Inventories from the Thuringian Basin[a]

Site	Mammoth	Reindeer	Bovids	Wild horse	Hare	Saiga	Brown bear	Dog (?)	Wolf	Fox	Grouse
Bad Frankenhausen				886/12							
Saaleck				–/20							1/–
Oelknitz		118/27	10/2	3866/127	201/29		4/2	2/1		35/12	
Lausnitz		11/3		476/15	12/2					25/4	
Kniegrotte VIII	1/1	–/9		–/42	–/18	–/5	–/2	–/4		–/25	–/6
Bärenkeller		3/1		200/5			+				
Teufelsbrücke 3	7/1	86/5		242/17	214/23	5/1	7/1	9/1		49/8	10/2
Teufelsbrücke 4		70/3	1/1	546/30	57/6		4/1	4/2	9/1	13/2	1/1

[a]Numbers are NISP/MNI. Data from Andree (1939), Feustel and Musil (1977), Feustel et al. (1963, 1971), Musil (1974, 1980, 1985), and Teichert (1971).

inventories, horse is the only species present; in all other inventories, horse is one way or another the dominant prey. At Kniegrotte VIII, the MNI of reindeer is based on bone counts. In antler is included, the MNI of this species would be 92. For methodological reasons, however, the bone counts are considered more reliable.

In four inventories, we also note the presence of probably domesticated wolves. The difficulties of distinguishing early domestic dogs and wolves in late Pleistocene and early Holocene find contexts have been dealt with in numerous papers. For summaries of the discussion relating to the European find material, the reader may refer to such publications as Benecke (1987), Clutton-Brock (1969), Degerbøl (1961), Nobis (1986), and Zeuner (1963).

Reliable paleozoological evidence of late Pleistocene domesticated wolves or dogs from central Europe is rare. The Thuringian finds are supplemented merely by a probable, though not quite unambiguous, Magdalenian dog of early Bølling age from Bonn-Oberkassel (Nobis 1986) and a pre-Allerød (Dryas II) dog from Bettenroder-Berg I (Staesche 1993). The latter was found in a Federmesser horizon immediately below and thus sealed by the Laacher tephra and appears very convincing.

Thus, by reference to the dog from Bettenroder-Berg I, it appears safe to credit the domestication of wolves in the Thuringian Magdalenian. In this discussion, however, the term *domesticated or humanly controlled wolf* will be preferred. The dog, as we know it in the sense of "man's best friend," is a very late phenomenon. In the late Mesolithic, the dog had reached a high status as a domestic animal, as clearly demonstrated by the number of dog burials in the late Mesolithic cemetery at Skateholm in southern Sweden (Larsson 1990). At that time, the dog must have been an almost invaluable hunting companion, but as regards the previous early Mesolithic and late Paleolithic periods, the dog or the domesticated wolf should rather be regarded as a weapon, and the act of domestication may be likened to the introduction of a new technology.

In southern Scandinavia, there are plenty of dog remains from the earliest Mesolithic and onward (Benecke 1987). In southwest Germany and Switzerland, however, dogs are not reported until much later (the find from Gnirshöhle being omitted here due to problematic find circumstances [cf. Albrecht et al. 1977:175]). Apparently not everybody was in need of this new development—and why not? Rather, why would they need it in the Thuringian Magdalenian?

Inspired by the "dog" remains from Kniegrotte, Musil (1974:52) suggested a very interesting explanation—namely, that these tame wolves were used to hunt horses. Hunting horses is very difficult. The animals are wary and will flee long before the hunter is close enough to harm them. Unless the hunter himself is mounted or equipped with firearms, the best way of hunting horses is to wait for them at a waterhole or to drive them into an ambush or a trap. Horses, however, are not easy to drive: Not only are they wary, but also they move fast, and the stallion, when threatened, may even stand and fight off the aggressor rather than run away. Still, given a suitable topographical situation, a viable group of hunters might successfully drive a group of horses over shorter distances (Olsen 1989). A few domesticated wolves would be of good use in such a situation—for example, by keeping the stallion occupied. Thus, the obvious success of horse hunting in the Thuringian Magdalenian may be directly linked with the presence of domesticated wolves. In a number of finds, the faunal remains are also supplemented by engravings of horses (Feustel 1980:78f). Some of these engravings even seem to portray horses with arrows protruding from their necks (Hanitzsch

1972). These sites may indeed represent the remains of relatively specialized horse hunters. Unfortunately, though, we have only scant evidence on the seasonality of the sites, and it is impossible to say whether we are dealing with a seasonal (which is most likely) or a year-round type of specialization.

Incidentally, it may be only a question of time before remains of late Pleistocene "dogs" or domesticated wolves are found in southwest German or Swiss find contexts (cf. Gnirshöhle). It will be interesting to see whether they too will appear in close association with horse remains.

Turning to northwest Europe, we find that our knowledge of late Pleistocene subsistence strategies in this area is based on the organic remains from a very few, and in part unique, sites. By a reasonable estimate, there are some 100 late Pleistocene settlement sites in the area, of which just 12 have yielded faunal remains. Half of these inventories are very small and very problematic, and for methodological reasons they are excluded from further analyses. The characteristics of the remaining six substantially and chronologically disparate inventories are presented in Table 6. These six comprise three Bølling inventories belonging to the Hamburgian culture: two Allerød inventories, one each belonging to the Federmesser and the Bromme culture; and one Younger Dryas inventory of the Ahrensburgian culture.

The Bølling and Younger Dryas inventories are all very large and have a very pronounced (almost 100%) dominance of reindeer. The Allerød inventories, on the other hand, are small and have an asserted, though very problematic, dominance of elk. The rich faunal remains from Meiendorf, Poggenwisch, and Stellmoor led to an initial interpretation of the Hamburgian and Ahrensburgian groups as being highly specialized reindeer hunters, whereas the Federmesser and Bromme people were believed to be specialized elk hunters. Today, however, there is a general consensus that the limited species composition at these few sites presents a picture of late Pleistocene subsistence strategies that is interesting but not very representative and not very reliable (Aaris-Sørensen 1989; Bratlund 1993; Eriksen 1991b; Grønnow 1987; Larsson 1991). Obviously, the hunters of Bølling and Younger Dryas had an opportunity to practice periodic mass killings of reindeer—an opportunity the Allerød hunters do not seem to have had—but it is very unlikely that they subsisted exclusively (year-round) on reindeer.

Evidence of hunting strategies is, of course, incomplete, but nevertheless displays demonstrable differences between Bølling and Younger Dryas. Recent analyses of faunal remains from the Hamburgian levels of Meiendorf and Stellmoor (Bratlund 1990, 1993; Grønnow 1987) indicate that these sites were repeatedly visited, residential camps occupied in late autumn–early winter. Hamburgian hunters here apparently stalked reindeer and used every bit of the killed animals. There is no evidence of communal drive hunts from Bølling (Bratlund 1990). The Ahrensburgian finds from Stellmoor, on the other hand, may be interpreted as the probable remains of an aggregation camp at which communal drive hunts of reindeer took place (Bokelmann 1991; Bratlund 1991). Meat supplies were correspondingly abundant, and only the best parts of the animals were used.

The differences in hunting strategies are accompanied by possible differences in hunting gear (Bokelmann 1991). Excavators found 105 wooden arrows or arrow fragments in the Ahrensburgian levels at Stellmoor and probably missed many more (Bokelmann 1991; Rust 1943). Thus, we know that the Ahrensburgians had the bow and arrow at their disposal, whereas the Hamburgians may have been equipped with spears and spear throwers only. The question remains, however, whether this is merely a reflection of inadequate find

Table 6. Late Pleistocene Fauna Inventories from Denmark and Northwest Germany[a]

Era	Site	Reindeer	Elk	Wild horse	Hare	Beaver	Wolf	Red fox	Wolverine	Grouse	Aquatic birds
Dryas III / Allerod	Stellmoor, upper	17,083/300	9/2	4/1	4/1		3/1			26/3	15/5
	Klein-Nordende		59/2								
	Bromme	2/–	37/–			2/–			3/–		2/–
Bolling	Meiendorf	1,931/69		7/1	23/2			2/1	1/–	33/5	45/12
	Stellmoor, lower	1,904/41			3/1					3/1	10/6
	Poggenwisch	250/15								+	+

[a]Numbers are NISP/MNI. Data from Bokelmann et al. (1983), Bratlund (1993), Herre and Requate (1958), Krause (1937), Krause and Kollau (1943), and Mathiassen (1946).

circumstances and conditions for preservation. The composite arrows found in the Ahrensburgian levels at Stellmoor surely are the refined products of a long history of development. Moreover, recent experiments have shown that even the rather heavy Bromme points may have been used as arrowheads (Fischer et al. 1984).

It is tempting to compare evidence on Hamburgian subsistence strategies in northern Germany with contemporary Magdalenian subsistence strategies in southwest Germany and northwest Switzerland. For methodological and source-critical reasons, however, such a comparison must be confined to a very general level, such as, for instance, the question of specialization vs. opportunism. The settling of the north following the retreat of the ice must have been a major challenge, demanding a very high degree of adaptivity. Specializing in one single game species would have been a most dangerous strategy under the prevailing circumstances. Given the marked seasonal differences in the surrounding environment, it is evident (not least by analogy with the more exhaustive evidence from the southernmost study area) that Hamburgian subsistence economy must have been much more varied and much more opportunistic than indicated by the few available finds.

Magdalenian hunters were able to practice periodic mass killings of reindeer to an extent that was not quite paralleled by the Hamburgians in the north. Approximately a thousand years later, however, the Ahrensburgian hunters seem to have enjoyed corresponding possibilities for supporting periodic aggregation camps. Despite the spatial and temporal variations, though, we observe that finds containing large amounts of reindeer bones as a rule are situated very close to or in the virgin lands of the Weichselian moraine. The interjacent ice-free corridor seems to have been "horse country" in Bølling (cf. also the evidence from the Rhine valley).

Early Holocene Subsistence Strategies

From early Holocene northwest Europe, evidence for subsistence strategies is plenty and reliable. In the Thuringian Basin, there are no well-documented early Mesolithic sites with organic remains, but evidence from southwest Germany is again plentiful and in complete agreement with the data from northwest Europe (Eriksen 1991a).

Fishing, fowling, and gathering are now much in evidence. Due to generally unsatisfactory conditions for preservation, however, food gathering especially is very much underrepresented in the settlement remains. Animal and plant foods that have been collected include birds' eggs, river mussels, hazelnuts, blackberries, round-leaved sorrel, and seeds of yellow water lily. Obviously, though, in comparing these items with pollen-analytical evidence, we find that they very likely represent a minute array of what was originally collected.

The gathering of hazelnuts is especially important, and as mentioned, it is probable that the collecting, storing, and transporting of these fruits by early Holocene man was partly responsible for the early Boreal spread of hazel to the north. The Duvensee sites in northern Germany thus document an intensive autumn exploitation of hazelnuts, even as early as the late Preboreal, that is, approximately 500 years before the pollen-analytical hazel maximum (Bokelmann 1980; Bokelmann et al. 1981). The nutshells are often charred and in some cases even appear to have been roasted in special fireplaces (Bokelmann 1980; Bokelmann et al. 1981). If hazelnuts are stored dry, further preservation is generally unnecessary. The roasting thus most likely would have been to improve the taste. At any rate, though, hazelnuts probably made up an important part of winter supplies. For this reason, they are considered fairly problematic as seasonal indicators.

The hunting of big game (aurochs, elk, red deer, wild boar) and trapping of fur-bearing carnivores (e.g., red fox, badger, pine marten) was also important. Some outstanding bog finds of complete skeletons of aurochs suggest how this big game was hunted (Aaris-Sørensen and Petersen 1986; Aaris-Sørensen 1989; Hartz and Winge 1906; Ströbel 1959). It seems to have been a kind of "tour de force" hunt, an endurance test of hunter and prey, in which hunting dogs probably played an important part in chasing and tracking down the game. Elk was presumably hunted in a similar way. This game animal, too, is known from some outstanding bog finds in the northern study area. Two finds (Skottemarke and Faurbo) may be interpreted as winter kill sites (Møhl 1980; Sørensen 1980). Here, too, the hunting dog very likely played an important part in the chase and perhaps even helped carry the meat back to the base camp.

In the early Holocene, seasonal fluctuations in climate, flora, and fauna are likely to have been fairly marked, albeit less so than in the late Pleistocene. The increased density of boreal vegetation probably led to an increased residential mobility throughout time (Eriksen 1991a; Kelly 1983). By comparison to those in the late Pleistocene, the seasonal mobility patterns thus now presumably would have been less pronounced. Unfortunately, though, evidence concerning seasonality is inconclusive in both study areas. Spring and summer datings are most in evidence, whereas especially winter datings are exceedingly rare. In the northern study area, specific seasonal findings may be lacking because that part of the year was spent at the coasts, which are now submerged. As the same seasons are missing in the south and the north, however, it might also be a simple question of which kind of evidence is more likely to be preserved. Moreover, if people lived on stored food during winter, these settlements would show up as autumn sites in the record.

As a consequence, we should refrain from proposing any particular model of interpretation with respect to early Holocene seasonal settlement and mobility patterns. On the other hand, it is important that the seasonal evidence is in no way inconsistent with an assumption of increased residential mobility in the period in question.

CONCLUSION

Environmental change is neither synchronous nor identical in the three study areas. In the south, we observe a very gradual development of climate, flora, and fauna. In the north, environmental changes appear to have been more abrupt, and we find a clear distinction between cold late Pleistocene and warm early Holocene fauna.

In the study areas, the cultural developments in the period in question are conceived of as continuous and highly endogenous. They were all settled in the late Pleistocene (the north obviously some thousand years later than the south) and developed culturally from that point. Of course, there would have been significant influence from and contact with neighboring regions. Neither in the south nor in the north, however, is there any evidence of renewed waves of immigration at the onset of the Holocene.

Due to environmental and probably also cultural differences, socioeconomic develop-

Table 7. Schematic Outline of 'Subsistence Economic Trajectories' in Central and Northwest Europe

Era	Southwest Germany	Thuringian Basin	South Scandinavia
Boreal	*Early Mesolithic:* Stalking and trapping of various game animals. Gathering very important. Increased residential mobility.	No evidence	*Early Mesolithic:* Opportunistic stalking, trapping, gathering, etc. Boats (dugouts) probably available. Increased residential mobility.
Preboreal	*Early Mesolithic:* Stalking and trapping of various game animals. Increased importance of gathering.	No evidence	*Early Mesolithic:* Opportunistic stalking of elk, aurochs, etc., probably with hunting dogs. At the end of this period, increased importance of gathering.
Dryas III	*Late Paleolithic:* Probably very opportunistic hunting, possibly with bow and arrow. Rather insufficient evidence.	No evidence	*Ahrensburgian:* Possibility for periodic mass killing of reindeer. Bow and arrow hunting. At least one possible aggregation camp.
Allerød	*Late Paleolithic:* Possibly increased importance of fishing (and fowling). Opportunistic stalking and trapping of various game animals.	*Late Magdalenian:* Probably seasonal specialization in horses, possibly with domesticated wolves in a combination of stalking, driving, and ambushing.	*Bromme* and *Federmesser:* Opportunistic stalking of, e.g., elk. Rather insufficient evidence.
Bølling	*Magdalenian:* In young moraine areas, possibility for periodic mass killings of reindeer and aggregation camps. Opportunistic hunting of various game animals.	*Magdalenian:* Probably seasonal specialization in horses, possibly with domesticated wolves in a combination of stalking, driving, and ambushing.	*Hamburgian:* Probably seasonal specialization in reindeer. Probable stalking with spears and spear-throwers?! Bow and arrow questionable.

ment followed different trajectories. We do find some marked similarities along these trajectories (summarized in Table 7), however, especially at the beginning (Bølling) and at the end (Boreal).

In a preliminary analysis dealing with the late Pleistocene and early Holocene of the Swabian Alb, the difference in subsistence economy throughout time was reduced to a mere difference of degree (Eriksen 1991a). Contrary to prevailing assumptions, there was found to be no demonstrable increase in importance of small game in the early Mesolithic, nor was there any increased importance of fishing. On the other hand, there are possible indications of an increased importance of fishing (and perhaps also fowling) as early as Allerød, as people *seem to* have moved out from the Alb area into the open morainic lowland and settled around the lakes there (Eriksen in press).

Evidence from all three study areas clearly suggests that people of late Pleistocene western Europe were flexible, mobile, and generally opportunistic hunters who knew how to successfully exploit the rich and varied resources of their environment. Given the proper circumstances, they would specialize—sometimes in reindeer, sometimes in horse—incorporating new technology (such as the domesticated wolf or the bow and arrow) when necessary. The succeeding early Holocene hunter–gatherer groups lived in perfect agreement with these traditions. Obvious changes in their subsistence economies relate partly to a changing environment and partly to internal dynamic processes. Future studies should especially address the influence of the latter.

ACKNOWLEDGMENTS

I wish to thank Lawrence G. Straus for his energetic efforts in organizing the symposia meetings in Anaheim. Critical comments by Michael Jochim and Lawrence G. Straus on earlier drafts of this chapter were of great help. However, nobody is to blame for the flaws of the text but myself. The financial support of the Danish Research Council for the Humanities is gratefully acknowledged. The chapter is dedicated to Normann for his enthusiastic confidence in and support of my work.

REFERENCES

Aaris-Sørensen, K., 1989, *Danmarks Forhistoriske Dyreverden*, Gyldendal, Copenhagen.

Aaris-Sørensen, K., and Petersen, K. S., 1984, A Late Weichselian Find of Polar Bear (*Ursus Maritimus* Phipps) from Denmark and Reflections on the Paleoenvironment, *Boreas* 13:29–33.

Aaris-Sørensen, K., and Petersen, E. B., 1986, The Prejlerup Aurochs—an Archaeozoological Discovery from Boreal Denmark, *STRIAE* 24:111–117.

Albrecht, G., 1984, Intensive Fall Hunting at Petersfels during the Magdalénien: Questions Concerning the Motives, in: *Jungpaläolithische Siedlungsstrukturen in Europa* (H. Berke, J. Hahn, and C.-J. Kind, eds.), Urgeschichtliche Materialhefte 6, Archaeologica Venatoria, Tübingen, pp. 99–102.

Albrecht, G., and Berke, H., 1987, Das Brudertal bei Engen/Hegau—Beispiel für eine Arealnutzung im Magdalénien, *Mitteilungsblatt der Archaeologica Venatoria* 12:1–11.

Albrecht, G., Drautz, D., and Kind, J., 1977, Eine Station des Magdalénien in der Gnirshöhle bei Engen-Bittelbrunn im Hegau, *Archäologisches Korrespondenzblatt* 7:161–179.

Ammann, B., Chaix, L., Eicher, U., Elias, S. A., Gaillard, M.-J., Hofmann, W., Siegenthaler, U., Tobolski, K., and Wilkinson, B., 1984, Flora, Fauna and Stable Isotopes in Late-Würm Deposits at Lobsigensee (Swiss Plateau), in: *Climatic Changes on a Yearly to Millennial Basis* (N.-A. Mörner and W. Karlén, eds.), D. Reidel Publishing Company, Dordrecht, pp. 69–73.

Andree, J., 1939, *Der eiszeitliche Mensch in Deutschland und seine Kulturen*, Stuttgart: Ferdinand Enke Verlag.

Bandi, H.-G., 1947, *Die Schweiz zur Rentierzeit*, Huber, Frauenfeld.

Barr, J. H., 1973, *The Late Upper Paleolithic Site of Moosbühl: An Attempt to Analyze Some of Its Problems*, University of Bern, Ph.D. Thesis.

Beaulieu, J.-L. de, Clerc, J., and Reille, M., 1984, Late Weichselian fluctuations in the French Alps and Massif Central from Pollen Analysis, in: *Climatic Changes on a Yearly to Millennial Basis* (N.-A. Mörner and W. Karlén, eds.), D. Reidel Publishing Company, Dordrecht, pp. 75–90.

Benecke, N., 1987, Studies on Early Dog Remains from Northern Europe, *Journal of Archaeological Science* 14:31–49.

Berglund, B. E., 1979, The Deglaciation of Southern Sweden 13,500–10,000 B.P., *Boreas* 8:89–117.

Björck, S., and Digerfeldt, G., 1984, Climatic Changes at Pleistocene/Holocene Boundary in the Middle Swedish Endmoraine Zone, Mainly Inferred from Stratigraphic Indications, in: *Climatic Changes on a Yearly to Millennial Basis* (N.-A. Mörner and W. Karlén, eds.), D. Reidel Publishing Company, Dordrecht, pp. 37–56.

Bokelmann, K., 1980, Duvensee, Wohnplatz 6: Neue Befunde zur Mesolithischen Sammelwirtschaft im 7. Vorchristlichen Jahrtausend, *Die Heimat* 87(10):320–330.

Bokelmann, K., 1991, Some New Thoughts on Old Data on Humans and Reindeer in the Ahrensburgian Tunnel Valley in Schleswig-Holstein, Germany, in: *The Late Glacial in North-West Europe: Human Adaptation at the End of the Pleistocene* (N. Barton, A. J. Roberts and D. A. Roe, eds.), CBA Research Report No. 77, Alden Press, Oxford, pp. 72–81.

Bokelmann, K., Averdieck, F.-R., and Willkomm, H., 1981, Duvensee, Wohnplatz 8, Neue Aspekte zur Sammelwirtschaft im Frühen Mesolithikum, *Offa* 38:21–40.

Bokelmann, K., Heinrich, D., and Menke, B., 1983, Fundplätze des Spätglazials am Hainholz-Esinger Moor, Kreis Pinneberg, *Offa* 40:199–239.

Bratlund, B., 1990, Rentierjagd im Spätglazial: Eine Untersuchung der Jagdfrakturen an Rentierknochen von Meiendorf und Stellmoor, Kreis Stormarn, *Offa* 47:7–34.

Bratlund, B., 1991, A Study of Hunting Lesions Containing Flint Fragments on Reindeer Bones at Stellmoor, Schleswig-Holstein, Germany, in: *The Late Glacial in North-West Europe: Human Adaptation at the End of the Pleistocene* (N. Barton, A. J. Roberts and D. A. Roe, eds.), CBA Research Report No. 77, Alden Press, Oxford, pp. 193–207.

Bratlund, B., 1993, *Senglacialtidens Jagtøkonomi—En Zooarkæologisk Undersøgelse af Faunamaterialet fra Renjæger-stationerne Meiendorf og Stellmoor*, University of Aarhus, Ph.D. Thesis.

Burdukiewicz, J. M., 1986, *The Late Pleistocene Shouldered Point Assemblages in Western Europe*, E. J. Brill, Leiden.

Clark, G., 1975, *The Earlier Stone Age Settlement of Scandinavia*, Cambridge University Press, London.

Clutton-Brock, J., 1969, The Origins of the Dog, in: *Science in Archaeology* (D. Brothwell and E. Higgs, eds.), Thames and Hudson, London, pp. 303–309.

Degerbøl, M., 1961, On a Find of a Preboreal Domestic Dog (*Canis familiaris L.*) from Star Carr, Yorkshire, with Remarks on Other Mesolithic Dogs, *Proceedings of the Prehistoric Society* 27:35–55.

Eriksen, B. V., 1990, Cultural Change or Stability in Prehistoric Hunter–Gatherer Societies. A Case Study from the Late Paleolithic–Early Mesolithic in Southwestern Germany, in: *Contributions to the Mesolithic in Europe* (P. M. Vermeersch and P. Van Peer, eds.), Leuven University Press, Leuven, pp. 193–202.

Eriksen, B. V., 1991a, *Change and Continuity in a Prehistoric Hunter–Gatherer Society: A Study of Cultural Adaptation in Late Glacial–Early Postglacial Southwestern Germany*, Archaeologica Venatoria 12, Archaeologica Venatoria, Tübingen.

Eriksen, B. V., 1991b, Den Naturmæssige Baggrund for den Senglaciale Bromme Bosættelse i Sydskandinavien, *LAG* 2:5–29.

Eriksen, B. V., n.d., Settlement Patterns, Cave Sites and Locational Decisions in Late Pleistocene Central Europe, in: *The Human Use of Caves* (C. Bonsall and C. Smith, eds.), in press.

Eriksen, B. V., in press, Fossil Mollusks and Exotic Raw Materials in Late Glacial and Early Postglacial Find Contexts—a Complement to Lithic Studies, to be published in: *Lithic Raw Material Economy in Late Glacial and Early Postglacial Western Europe* (B. V. Eriksen and L. E. Fisher, eds.).

Feustel, R., 1980, *Magdalenienstation Teufelsbrücke* (I-II). Weimarer Monographien zur Ur- und Frühgeschichte 3, Museum für Ur- und Frühgeschichte, Weimar.

Feustel, R., and Musil, R., 1977, Der Bärenkeller bei Königsee-Garsitz, eine jungpaläolithische Kulthöhle (II), *Alt-Thüringen* 14:60–81.

Feustel, R., Teichert, M., and Unger, K. P., 1963, Die Magdalénienstation Lausnitz in der Orlasenke, *Alt-Thüringen* 6:57–103.

Feustel, R., Kerkmann, K., Schmid, E., Musil, R., and Jacob, H., 1971, Der Bärenkeller bei Königsee-Garsitz, eine jungpaläolithische Kulthöhle (I), *Alt-Thüringen* 11:81–130.

Firbas, F., 1949, *Spät- und nacheiszeitliche Waldgeschichte Mitteleuropas nördlich der Alpen*, Gustav Fisher, Jena.

Fischer, A., Hansen, P. V., and Rasmussen, P., 1984, Macro and Micro Wear Traces on Lithic Projectile Points: Experimental Results and Prehistoric Examples, *Journal of Danish Archaeology* 3:19–46.

Frenzel, B., 1983, Die Vegetationsgeschichte Süddeutschlands im Eiszeitalter, in: *Urgeschichte in Baden-Württemberg* (H. Müller-Beck, ed.), Konrad Theiss Verlag, Stuttgart, pp. 91–166.

Grønnow, B., 1987, Meiendorf and Stellmoor Revisited: An Analysis of Late Palaeolithic Reindeer Exploitation, *Acta Archaeologica* 56(1985):131–166.

Hahn, J., 1979, Essai sur l'écologie du Magdalénien dans le Jura souabe, in: *La Fin des Temps Glaciaires en Europe* (D. de Sonneville-Bordes, ed.), Colloques Internationaux CNRS No. 271, Centre National de la Recherche Scientifique, Paris, pp. 203–211.

Hahn, J., 1981, Zur Abfolge des Jungpaläolithikums in Südwest-Deutschland, *Kölner Jahrbuch für Vor- und Frühgeschichte* 15(1975–1977):52–67.

Hahn, J., n.d., *Die Buttentalhöhle-eine spät-jungpaläolithische Abristation im Oberen Donautal*, Unpublished manuscript, Tübingen.

Hahn, J., Kind, C.-J., and Steppan, K., 1993, Mesolithische Rentierjäger in Südwestdeutschland? Der Mittelsteinzeitliche Freilandfundplatz Rottenburg "Siebenlinden I" (Vorbericht), *Fundberichte aus Baden-Württemberg* 18:29–52.

Hanitzsch, H., 1972, *Groitzsch bei Eilenburg: Schlag- und Siedlungsplätze der späten Altsteinzeit*, VEB Deutscher Verlag der Wissenschaften, Berlin.

Hartz, N., and Winge, H., 1906, Om Uroxen fra Vig, Saaret og Dræbt med Flintvaaben, *Aarbøger for Nordisk Oldkyndighed og Historie* 1906:225–236.

Herre, W., and Requate, H., 1958, Die Tierreste der Paläolithischen Siedlungen Poggenwisch, Hasewisch, Borneck und Hopfenbach bei Ahrensburg, in: *Die jungpaläolithischen Zeltanlagen von Ahrensburg* (A. Rust), Offa-Bücher 15, Karl Wachholtz Verlag, Neumünster, pp. 23–27.

Huntley, B., and Birks, H. J. B., 1983, *An Atlas of Past and Present Pollen Maps for Europe: 0–13000 Years Ago*, Cambridge University Press, Cambridge.

Jensen, J., 1982, *The Prehistory of Denmark*, Methuen, London.

Kelly, R. L., 1983, Hunter–Gatherer Mobility Strategies, *Journal of Anthropological Research* 39:277–306.

Koenigswald, W. von, 1976, Der Austausch der Säugetierfauna an der Pleistozän-Holozän-Grenze, *Zentralblatt für Geologie und Paläontologie* II, 5/6:452–456.

Koenigswald, W. von, 1983, Die Säugetierfauna des Süddeutschen Pleistozäns, in: *Urgeschichte in Baden-Württemberg* (H. Müller-Beck, ed.), Konrad Theiss Verlag, Stuttgart, pp. 167–216.

Koken, E., 1912, Die Geologie und Tierwelt der paläolithischen Kulturstätten Deutschlands, in: *Die diluviale Vorzeit Deutschlands* (R. R. Schmidt), Schweizerbartsche Verlagsbuchhandlung, Nägele und Dr. Sproesser, Stuttgart, pp. 159–228.

Kolstrup, E., 1991, Palaeoenvironmental developments during the Late Glacial of the Weichselian, in: *The Late Glacial in North-West Europe: Human Adaptation at the End of the Pleistocene* (N. Barton, A. J. Roberts and D. A. Roe, eds.), CBA Research Report No. 77, Alden Press, Oxford, pp. 1–6.

Krause, W., 1937, Die Eiszeitlichen Knochenfunden von Meiendorf, in: *Das altsteinzeitliche Rentierjägerlager Meiendorf* (Rust A.), Karl Wachholtz Verlag, Neumünster, pp. 48–61.

Krause, W., and Kollau, W., 1943, Die Steinzeitlichen Wirbeltierfaunen von Stellmoor, in: *Die alt- und Mittelsteinzeitlichen Funde von Stellmoor* (Karl Wachholtz Verlag, Neumünster, pp. 49–59.

Larsson, L., 1990, Dogs in Fraction—Symbols in Action: in: *Contributions to the Mesolithic in Europe* (P. M. Vermeersch and P. Van Peer, eds.), Leuven University Press, Leuven, pp. 153–160.

Larsson, L., 1991, The Late Palaeolithic in Southern Sweden: Investigations in a Marginal Region, in: *The Late Glacial in North-West Europe: Human Adaptation at the End of the Pleistocene* (N. Barton, A. J. Roberts, and D. A. Roe, eds.), CBA Research Report No. 77, Alden Press, Oxford, pp. 122–127.

Mania, D., 1973, Eiszeitliche Landschaftsentwicklung im Kartenbild, Dargestellt am Beispiel des Mittleren Elbe-Saale-Gebietes, *Jahresschrift für Mitteldeutsche Vorgeschichte* 57:17–47.

Mathiassen, T., 1946, En Senglacial Boplads ved Bromme, *Aarbøger for Nordisk Oldkyndighed og Historie* 1946:121–197.

Møhl, U., 1971, Fangstdyrene ved de Danske Strande, *Kuml* 1970:297–329.

Møhl, U., 1980, Elsdyrskeletterne fra Skottemarke og Favrbo: Skik og Brug ved Borealtidens Jagter, *Aarbøger for Nordisk, Oldkyndighed og Historie* 1978:5–29.

Musil, R., 1974, Tiergesellschaft der Kniegrotte, in: *Die Kniegrotte: Eine Magdalénien-Station in Thüringen* (R. Feustel, ed.), Hermann Böhlaus Nachfolger, Weimar, pp. 30–95.

Musil, R., 1980, Die Großsäuger und Vögel der Teufelsbrücke, in: *Magdalenienstation Teufelsbrücke II* (R. Feustel, ed.), Weimarer Monographien zur Ur- und Frühgeschichte 3, Museum für Ur- und Frühgeschichte, Weimar, pp. 5–59.

Musil, R., 1985, *Die Fauna der Magdalénien-Siedlung Oelknitz*, Weimarer Monographien zur Ur- und Frühgeschichte 17, Museum für Ur- und Frühgeschichte, Weimar.

Musil, R., 1992, Changes in Mammalian Communities at the Pleistocene–Holocene Boundary, *Annales Zoologic Fennici* 28:241–244.

Nilsson, T., 1989, Senglacial Bosættelse i Vendsyssel, *Kuml* 1987:47–75.

Nobis, G., 1986, Die Wildsäugetiere in der Umwelt der Menschen von Oberkassel bei Bonn und das Domestikationsproblem von Wölfen im Jungpaläolithikum, *Bonner Jahrbücher* 186:367–376.

Olsen, S. L., 1989, Solutré: A Theoretical Approach to the Reconstruction of Upper Palaeolithic Hunting Strategies, *Journal of Human Evolution* 18:295–327.

Pasda, C., 1992, *Das Magdalénien in der Freiburger Bucht*, University of Tübingen, Ph.D. Thesis.

Petersen, K. S., 1984, Late Weichselian Sea-Levels and Fauna Communities in Northern Vendsyssel, Jutland, Denmark, in: *Climatic Changes on a Yearly to Millennial Basis* (N.-A. Mörner and W. Karlén, eds.), D. Reidel Publishing Company, Dordrecht, pp. 63–68.

Petersen, K. S., 1985, The Late Quaternary History of Denmark: The Weichselian Icesheets and Land/Sea Configuration in the Late Pleistocene and Holocene, *Journal of Danish Archaeology* 4:7–22.

Rösch, M., 1985, Ein Pollenprofil aus dem Feuenried bei Überlingen am Ried, in: *Berichte zu Ufer- und Moor-siedlungen Südwestdeutschlands 2* (B. Becker et al.), Materialhefte zur Vor- Und Frühgeschichte in Baden-Württemberg Hefte 7, Konrad Theiss Verlag, Stuttgart, pp. 43–79.

Rust, A., ed., 1937, *Das altsteinzeitliche Rentierjägerlager Meiendorf*, Karl Wachholtz Verlag, Neumünster.

Rust, A., 1943, *Die alt- und mittelsteinzeitlichen Funde von Stellmoor*, Karl Wachholtz Verlag, Neumünster.

Sarasin, F., 1918, *Die steinzeitlichen Stationen im Birstal zwischen Basel und Delsberg*, Neue Denkschriften des Schweizerischen Naturforschungs Gesellschaft 54/2, Zürich.

Schild, R., 1984, Terminal Paleolithic of the North European Plain: A Review of Lost Changes, Potentials, and Hopes, *Advances in World Archaeology* 3:193–274.

Schwabedissen, H., 1954, *Die Federmessergruppen des nordwesteuropäischen Flachlandes*, Karl Wachholtz Verlag, Neumünster.

Sedlmeier, J., 1982, *Die Hollenberghöhle 3: Eine Magdalénien-Fundstelle bei Arlesheim, Kanton Basel-Landschaft*, Basler Beiträge zur Ur- und Frühgeschichte 8, Habegger Verlag, Derendingen-Solothurn.

Sedlmeier, J., 1989, *Jungpalaeolithikum und Spaetpalaeolithikum in der Nordwestschweiz*, University of Bern, Ph.D. Thesis.

Sørensen, I., 1980, Datering af elsdyrknoglerne fra Skottemarke og Favrbo, *Aarbøger for nordisk Oldkyndighed og Historie* 1978:33–43.

Staesche, U., 1993, Ein Spätpaläolithischer Hund aus dem Abri Bettenroder Berg I im Leinebergland Südlich von Göttingen, Niedersachsen, *Zeitschrift für Archäologie* 27(1):1–7.

Stewart, A., and Jochim, M., 1986, Changing Economic Organization in Late Glacial Southwest Germany, in: *The End of the Palaeolithic in the Old World* (L. G. Straus, ed.), British Archaeological Reports, International Series 248, Oxford, pp. 47–62.

Ströbel, R., 1959, Tardenoisspitze in einem Bovidenknochen von Schwenningen am Neckar (Kr. Rottweil), *Fundberichte aus Schwaben*, Neue Folge 15:103–106.

Sturdy, D. A., 1975, Some reindeer economies in prehistoric Europe, in: *Palaeoeconomy* (E. S. Higgs, ed.), Cambridge University Press, Cambridge, pp. 55–95.

Taute, W., 1969, Großwildjäger der späten Eiszeit, *Bild der Wissenschaft* 1969:1203–1211.

Teichert, M., 1971, Die Knochenreste aus der Wildpferdjägerstation Bad Frankenhausen, *Alt-Thüringen 11*: 227–234.

Watts, W. A., 1980, Regional Variation in the Response of Vegetation to Lateglacial Climatic Events, in: *Studies in the Lateglacial of North-West Europe* (J. J. Lowe, J. M. Gray, and J. E. Robinson, eds.), Pergamon Press, Oxford, pp. 1–21.

Welten, M., 1982, *Vegetationsgeschichtliche Untersuchungen in den westlichen Schweizer Alpen: Bern-Wallis*, Denk-schriften des Schweizerischen Naturforschungs Gesellschaft 95, Basel.

Weniger, G.-C., 1982, *Wildbeuter und ihre Umwelt*, Archaeologica Venatoria 5, Archaeologica Venatoria, Tübingen.

Weniger, G.-C., 1989, The Magdalenian in Western Central Europe: Settlement Pattern and Regionality, *Journal of World Prehistory* 3:323–372.

Wyss, R., 1973, Zum Problemkreis des Schweizerischen Mesolithikums, in: *The Mesolithic in Europe* (S. K. Kozlowski, ed.), Warsaw University Press, Warszawa, pp. 613–649.

Zeuner, F., 1963, *A History of Domesticated Animals*, Hutchinson & Co., London.

Chapter *7*

The North European Plain and Eastern Sub-Balticum between 12,700 and 8,000 BP

ROMUALD SCHILD

INTRODUCTION

More than a decade has passed since I published an overview of the Terminal Paleolithic of the North European Plain (Schild 1984). During this time, several new prehistoric sites appeared, but my early statement that the North European Plain was not the promised land for archaeologists, particularly those interested in the Terminal Paleolithic, seems to be still valid. Stratified sites with good organic preservation remain rare commodities. Only the pace of destruction of sites increased exponentially. Indeed, during this period, there was no major breakthrough in prehistoric research in the North European Plain that would dramatically alter our ideas about the past. On the other hand, it would not be right to say that nothing has happened. The necessary rethinking of old ideas, however, has come from paleoclimatology, dendrochronology, isotope dating, and paleobiology, rather than from archaeology.

PALEOECOLOGY

Combined evidence based on northern Atlantic foraminifera (Bard et al. 1987), Greenland oxygen isotope and dust records (Dansgaard and Oeschger 1989), and European pollen, oxygen isotope, and beetle studies (Amman and Lotter 1989; Atkinson et al. 1987; Siegenhalter et al. 1984), strongly suggests a considerable revision of late Glacial–early

ROMUALD SCHILD • Institute of Archaeology and Ethnology, Polish Academy of Sciences, 00-140 Warsaw, Poland.

Humans at the End of the Ice Age: The Archaeology of the Pleistocene–Holocene Transition, edited by Lawrence Guy Straus, Berit Valentin Eriksen, Jon M. Erlandson, and David R. Yesner. Plenum Press, New York, 1996.

Holocene paleoclimatology. An abrupt warming in the northern Atlantic at around 12,700 BP[1] was terminated at 10,800 BP by a sudden cooling that preceded an abrupt warming at about 10,000 BP. The latter marks the beginning of the Holocene.

The first warming, from 12,700 to 10,800 BP, combines the two mild intervals of yesteryear, the Bölling and the Alleröd. The cooling is that of the Younger Dryas, and it is now clear that its significance is global (Kudras et al. 1991). The position and importance of the Older Dryas are still debated. The oscillation seems to be well recorded in continental sedimentological signals, particularly in dune deposition (Nowaczyk 1986). Mörner (1993) sees it as a setback in a warming trend that is also accompanied by a minor glacial readvance (Berger 1990).

A short, rapid climatic amelioration of the Younger Dryas–Preboreal boundary at the beginning of the Holocene, at 10,000 BP, is then followed by a cooling event of the Piottino Oscillation placed between circa 9,900 and 9,700 BP (Mörner 1993:249). A rapid warm event occurs between 9,700 and 9,500 BP, after which the climate stabilizes, showing, however, small-amplitude oscillations. A third major warming step is seen at circa 8,000 BP, at the Boreal–Atlantic boundary (Berger 1990).

Accelerator and conventional radiocarbon dating of macrofloral remains from varved lake deposits (Broecker 1992; Goslar et al. 1992; Lotter 1991) and tree-ring records (Becker 1992; Becker and Kromer 1993; Becker et al. 1991; Goslar 1990; Stuiver et al. 1991) permit a very attractive calibration of ^{14}C measurements as well as estimation of the duration of climatic episodes.

In the varves of Rotsee in Switzerland, the length of the traditional chronozone of Bölling is estimated at circa 800 calendar years vs. 1,000 ^{14}C years; the Alleröd chronozone is of only 400 calendar years duration vs. 1,000 ^{14}C years; and the Younger Dryas extends for 900 calendar years vs. 1000 ^{14}C years (Lotter 1991). The duration of the Younger Dryas in the varve count of Lake Gościąż in Poland, on the other hand, is estimated at circa 1250 calendar years (Goslar et al. 1992:828).

Two pronounced radiocarbon age plateaus occur at circa 10,000 BP and 12,800 BP. Tree-ring calibration for continental Europe, almost continuous after 10,000 BP, places the end of the 10,000 BP plateau at circa 11,000 calendar years BP (Becker 1992).

The early part of the late Glacial warming (Bölling *sensu lato*) in the North European Plain is characterized by open landscapes. Shrub and park-tundra dominate. The regional response to local conditions is of considerable magnitude (e.g., Berglund 1971; Lowe et al. 1994; Pennington 1977). The Alleröd portion of the warming shows dominance of birch forest in the early part, followed by pine. Clear woodland and gallery woods in the valleys are dominant in the north. In the Younger Dryas, the return of the scrub and park-tundras in the plain and the park forests in the piedmont is witness to the abrupt cooling (Walker et al. 1994).

The Holocene warming of the Preboreal sees a succession of mixed pine–birch forest with *Ulmus* and later with hazel, *Ulmus*, and *Alnus*. In the Boreal, assemblages composed of pine, birch, hazel, and *Alnus* dominate.

The fauna spectra from Bölling reflect a landscape with reindeer, horse, and steppe bison as major megafauna components. Rare Alleröd fauna remains include red deer, elk, *Megaloceros giganteus* (Bratlund 1994). beaver, and other typical forest elements. The return of wooded tundra on the plain during the Younger Dryas cooling brings back open

---

[1]Unless stipulated to the contrary, dates in this chapter are expressed in conventional ^{14}C radiocarbon years before present (BP).

landscape assemblages with reindeer and aurochs in the woods along the river valleys. Again, the Holocene warming sees the restitution of forest megafauna.

LATE GLACIAL CULTURAL TAXONOMY

After many years of often heated technical discussion on typology and stylistics of the lithic assemblages of the late Glacial and Holocene, a consensus view has slowly emerged.

Hamburgian–Creswellian Technocomplex

The oldest late Glacial Technocomplex of the plain extends from southwest England to western Poland (Burdukiewicz 1987), southern Denmark (Fischer 1993; Holm and Rieck 1992), and Sweden (Larsson 1993) in the north (Figure 1). No sites of any kind dating to Bölling are known from the areas to the east of western Poland. The lithic manufacturing is based on blade technology with pre-prepared opposed- and single-platform cores. The toolkit includes shouldered points, backed and truncated blades, tanged Havelte points, and Zinken groovers, as well as the usual burins and end-scrapers.

The most reliable ^{14}C age estimates place this technocomplex between circa 12,800 BP and circa 12,000 BP (Gough's Cave, England) for the Creswellian (Jacobi 1986, 1988), as well as between circa 12,700 BP at Olbrachcice, Poland (Burdukiewicz 1987:98), and circa 12,200 BP at Stellmoor, Schleswig Holstein, for the Hamburgian (Fischer and Tauber 1986). The surprisingly late radiocarbon measurements from Oldeholtwolde, Holland, of circa 11,650 BP (Stapert 1992; Stapert and Krist 1987), need additional confirmation, particularly in the light of the geological situation of the site (Figure 2).

Arch Backed Piece Technocomplex

In the Alleröd and early Younger Dryas, the Arch Backed Piece (ABP) Technocomplex occupies almost the entire western end central part of the North European Plain. It spreads from probably as far west as England (Jacobi 1988:438), across the Low Countries, lower Germany, and southern Denmark (Fischer 1993), to the Vistula Valley in the east. There are a few isolated sites on the eastern bank of the Vistula, as at Cekanowo, near Płock (Sulgo-stowska 1989:63). To the south, the ABP stretches out beyond the geographic limits of the North European Plain. It extends along the footslopes of the Tatra (Valde-Nowak 1991) and the Alps (Brunnacker et al. 1988; Taute 1975; Eriksen 1991) as well as the hills of southeast France (Thévenin 1982, 1988), where it merges into the final Magdalenian, *Aziloid* units (Figure 3). Several local names for the ABP Technocomplex entities (e.g., Tjongerian, Federmesser, Witowian) reflect national preferences.

Technologically, the ABP lithics are characterized by single- and opposed-platform cores for heavy blades and flakes often exploited with hard hammer. Pointed, arch-backed pieces are a quite characteristic component, as are numerous short end-scrapers and heavy, blunt burins.

Radiochronology of the ABP in the west (Figure 3) is quite complicated by the dispersal of estimates stretching over 4,000 years (Schild 1989). Stratigraphic placement of the cultural beds just underneath, in, and slightly above the Usselo paleosoils (Arts 1988) indicates Alleröd and early Younger Dryas (?) age of this taxonomic unit.

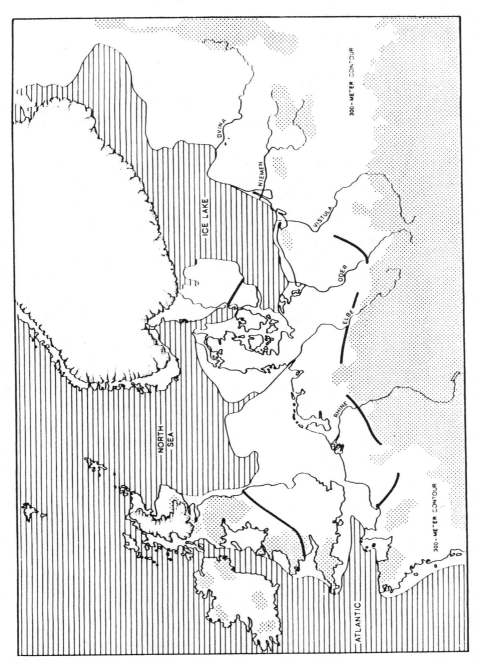

Figure 1. Areal extension of Hamburgian and Creswellian sites (demarcated by the discontinuous line). Shorelines and ice sheets of Europe are as in the Younger Dryas.

In the central section of the plain, in Poland, chronological assignment of the complex is very firm (Figure 4). The ^{14}C estimates range from circa 11,700 BP (Całowanie Level III) to circa 10,800 BP (Witów) and 10,750 BP (Rydno-Mine). The biostratigraphic emplacements of ABP assemblages at the stratified sites indicate almost the entire Alleröd and the very beginning of the Younger Dryas chronozones.

TECHNOCOMPLEX WITH PEDUNCULATED POINTS

Early Units

In Denmark (Andersen 1988; Fischer and Sonne Nielsen 1987; Mathiassen 1948), southern Sweden (Salomonsson 1964; Larsson 1993), and perhaps as far south as Schleswig Holstein, where it overlaps with the ABP units, a technocomplex characterized by the presence of tanged projectile points (Fischer 1989) appears in the Alleröd (see Figure 3). The technology of these early sites is based on single-platform cores, rarely opposed-platform ones, exploited with heavy hammer. Resulting thick blanks give a heavy appearance to the end-scrapers, burins, and tanged points. These assemblages are known under the name of Brommian. Both the palynology at Bromme (Iversen 1946) and the radiochronology at Trollesgave (Fischer 1978) indicate the Alleröd age for the Brommian (see Figure 2).

Largely similar assemblages with heavy tanged points and hard hammer technique of flint knapping are known from central Poland (Schild 1975), northern Byelorussia (Kudriashov and Lipnitskaya 1994), and Lithuania (Rimantiene 1971). In Poland, at Cało-wanie (Schild 1975), an assemblage clearly within the Bromme style is bio- and radiocarbon-dated to Alleröd (Figure 4).

Late Units

In the Low Countries and the German Plain (Figure 5), a late tanged point complex, known under the general name of Ahrensburgian, is characterized by single- and opposed-blade core technology, often with extensive pre–core preparation. Tanged points, micro-truncations, subtriangles, and backed pieces, primarily in the western portion of the Ahrensburgian territory, form the most characteristic group, which is accompanied by end-scrapers and burins (Taute 1968).

Although largely confined to the areas below the 300-m contour line (Taute 1968), the Ahrensburgian in the south seems to occasionally penetrate valleys of the upper Rhine area (Cziesla 1992). To the east, Ahrensburgian elements cross the Oder Valley and form an overlap zone with the Masovian on both sides of the valley and well beyond it (Kobusiewicz and Kabaciński 1992; Kobusiewicz et al. 1987). In the north, Ahrensburgian-like finds reach southern Jutland (Andersen 1988:535) and eastern Denmark (Vang Petersen and Johansen 1993).

Biostratigraphy places the Ahrensburgian in the Younger Dryas. The ^{14}C estimates for the unit are rare (see Figure 2) and confined to a few sites (compare Fischer and Tauber 1986). The most reliable results bracket the Ahrensburgian between circa 10,550 BP at Schlaatz, near Potsdam, in Germany (Gramsch 1987a) and 9800 BP at Gramsbergen, Holland (Lanting and Mook 1977). The measurement of almost 11,000 BP at Geldrop 1 (Lanting and Mook 1977) is certainly too old.

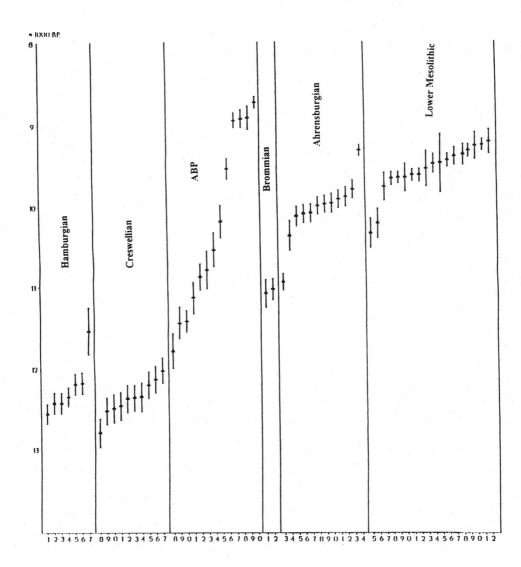

Another large taxonomic unit with tanged projectile points is known under the name of Masovian or Swiderian. The assemblages classified within this entity occur in the central part of the North European Plain, in Poland (Schild 1984); Byelorussia and Ukraine (Zalizniak 189); southeast Sub-Balticum, in Lithuania (Rimantiene 1971) and Latvia (Zagorska 1994); as far south as the Polish Carpathians (Valde-Nowak 1991); the Tatra Mountains (Barta 1980); the upper Dniester, in Ukraine (Zalizniak 1989); and as far southeast as the Crimea (Janevich 1993; Schild 1965).

Willow leaf and tanged projectile points with inverse, invasive retouch of the stem are the most characteristic element for the unit. Elaborate, preshaped opposed-platform cores for blades, exploited with light hammer and punch techniques, are the trademark of the unit. Microtruncations are occasional. The end-scrapers and usually elongated burins form the backbone of the toolkit. The biostratigraphy of the Masovian (Schild 1979), as well as the radiochronology, place it in the entire Younger Dryas and the beginning of Preboreal, in the Piottino Oscillation, from circa 10,800 to 9,700 BP (see Figure 4).

EARLY HOLOCENE CULTURAL TAXONOMY

Early Maglemose Technocomplex

The western and central sections of the North European Plain (Figure 6) see in the early part of the lower Holocene a seemingly abrupt change of lithic technocomplex. The blanks

←_____

Figure 2. Selected radiochronology of the terminal Paleolithic and early Mesolithic of the western section of the North European Plain. Hamburgian: (1) Poggenwisch (K-4332); (2) Poggenwisch (K-4331), (3) Poggenwisch (K-4577), (4) Meiendorf (K-4329), (5) Stellmoor (K-4261), and (6) Stellmoor (K-4328) according to Fischer and Tauber (1986), (7) Oldeholtwolde (GrN-19274) according to Stapert and Kirst (1987). Creswellian: (8) Gough's Cave (OxA-592), (9) Sun Hole (OxA-587), (10) Gough's Cave (OxA-592), (11). Gough's Cave (OxA-464), (12) Gough's Cave (OxA-463), (13) Gough's Cave (OxA-590), (14) Gough's Cave (OxA-465), and (15) Sun Hole (OxA-535) according to Jacobi (1986); (16) Presle II, Bed II, according to Leotard and Otte (1988); (17) Gough's Cave (OxA-588) according to Jacobi (1986). Arch Backed Pieces (ABP) Technocomplex: (18) Westerkappeln C (Kl-271), (19) Rissen 14-14A (M-75-68), (20) Budel 11 (GrN-1675), (21) Duurswoude I (GrN-4871), (22) Usselo (Y-139-2), (23) Duurswoude I (GrN-607), (24) Rissen 14-14A (Y-157-A), (25) Westerkappeln A (Kl-270), (26) Nedeerwert (GrN-908), (27) Meer I (GrN-4961), (28) Meer I (GrN-4960), (20) Meer I (GrN-7939), and (30) Meer II (GrN-5706) according to Lanting and Mook (1977). Brommean: (31) Trollesgave and (32) Trollesgave according to Fischer (1978). Ahrensburgian: (33) Geldrop 1 (GrN-1059) according to Lanting and Mook (1977); (34) Remouchamps (Lv 535) according to Dewez (1988); (35) Stellmoor (K-4326), (36) Stellmoor (K-4262), (37) Stellmoor (K-4581), (38) Stellmoor (K-4325), (39) Stellmoor (K-4581), (40) Stellmoor (K-4579), (41) Stellmoor (K-4323), (42) Stellmoor (K-4324), and (43) Stellmoor (K-4580) according to Fischer and Tauber (1986)]; (44) Gramsbergen (GrN-7793) according to Lanting and Mook (1977). Early Mesolithic: (45) Thatcham 3 (Q-659), (46) Thatcham 3 (Q-658) and (47) Thatcham 5 (Q-677) according to Gob (1988); (48) Friesack, Bed 10a-Xe (Bln-3036), and (49) Friesack, Bed 10a-Xe, according to Gramsch (1987b); (50) Thatcham 5 (Q-650) according to Gob (1988); (51) Friesack, Bed 9b (Bln-3020), and (52) Friesack, Bed 9a (Bln-3019), according to Gramsch (1987b); (53) Star Carr (Q-14) according to Gob (1988); (54) Friesack, Bed 9a (Bln-2753), according to Gramsch (1987b); (55) Star Carr (C-353) according to Gob (1988); (56) Friesack, Bed 9a (Bln-1914), (57) Friesack, Bed 8b-Xc (Bln-2760) according to Gramsch (1987b) and (58) Draved Mose 604 (K-1466) according to Gob (1988); (59) Friesack, Bed 8b-Xc (Bln-3025) according to Gramsch (1987b); (60) Draved Mose 604 (K-1605) according to Gob (1988); (61) Friesack, Bed 8b-Xc (Bln-3000) according to Gramsch (1978b), (62) Klosterlund (K-1317) according to Gob (1988).

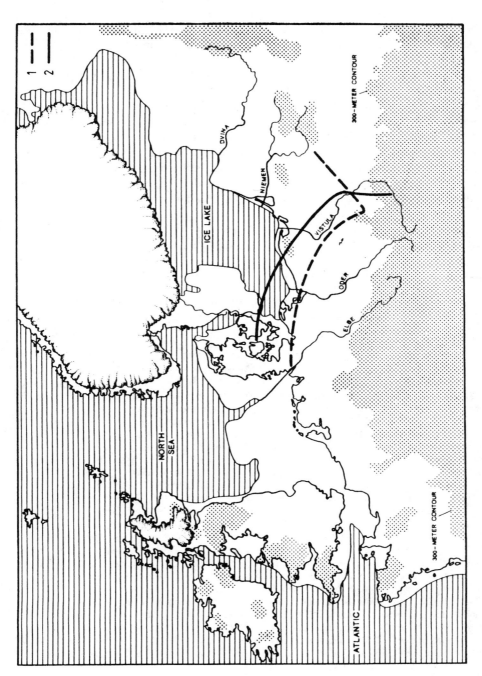

Figure 3. Areal extension of ABP and Older Tanged Point sites. Shorelines and ice sheets are as in the Younger Dryas. (1) Approximate southern limit of the Older Tanged Point sites; (2) approximate northern and eastern limits of the ABP sites and the zone of overlap with Older Tanged Point occurrences.

and tools are often slightly reduced in size and contain numerous geometrics such as isosceles and scalene triangles, straight and arched, pointed backed pieces, usually proximal microtruncations, double-backed pieces, and others. Short end-scrapers and burins on flakes form the usual background. Flake adzes and bifacial axes are common. The technology is based on single- and opposed-platform blade and flake cores, as well as on flake cores with changed orientation.

Several sites with good preservation of the organics, particularly in Denmark and Germany, yielded a quite impressive bone and antler toolkit associated with this new technocomplex. It includes various simple and barbed bone points, chisels, awls, and other tools, as well as perforated antler "adzes" and hafting equipment. Rare wood artifacts include arrowheads, fragments of spears, bows, and other items.

It seems that within the early Maglemose technocomplex, there are several local stylistic units, the boundaries of which are never sharp. Local terminology (e.g., Maglemose, Duvensee, Boberg, Komornica, Narvian) may easily overlap with stylistic boundaries (for examples of terminology, see Kozłowski and Kozłowski 1979).

Biochronology and, particularly, radiochronology (see Figures 2 and 4) of the earliest sites of this technocomplex were not entirely clear until very recent years. Biostratigraphically, the earliest sites are obviously Preboreal in age, but most probably later than the cool Piottino Oscillation. Radiocarbon estimates, after rejuvenation of the unusually old dates at Thatcham, England (Figure 2, Nos. 45 and 46) (Healy et al. 1992), place the earliest sites between just after 9,700 and 9,400 BP (Bokelmann 1992; Gramsch 1987b; Kobusiewicz and Kabaciński 1993; Schild 1990). The closing age estimates for the technocomplex are debatable, but should be placed near 8,000 BP.

Kunda Technocomplex

The southeastern shores of the Baltic reveal in the early Holocene quite distinctive lithic assemblages, together with rich and variable bone and antler inventory preserved in biogenic sediments. The most characteristic technological trait of this unit is the presence of the pressure flaking technique, used both in obtaining blades from single-platform cores and in (often diagonally) retouching elaborate tools, among them tanged projectile points. The tool kit includes svelte tanged points with very small stems, rare geometrics (Sulgostowska personal communication), and delicately backed bladelets among other, background tools.

The earliest site, at Pulli, Estonia, is in an organic-rich bed of Preboreal age. Two radiocarbon measurements, on biogenic materials, are between 9,700 and 9,600 BP (Jaanits 1981; Jaanits and Jaanits 1975, 1978). The samples seems to come from the top of the lower section of artifact-bearing, biogenic bed (Gurina 1989:49), thus suggesting yet an earlier than 9,700 ^{14}C age for the beginning of the Kunda occupation at Pulli.

THE EARLY HOLOCENE CHANGE

The very first glimpse at the early Holocene flint and bone and antler products seemingly shows dramatic differences from those of the late Glacial and Younger Dryas–Preboreal boundary. These perceptible differences were at the very root of the concept of

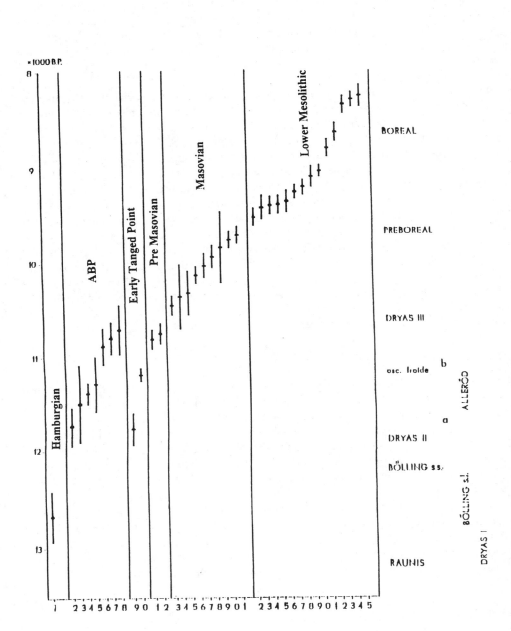

Mesolithic as a technological stage in the history of humankind (see Price 1987; Westropp 1866).

Technological changes, however, need to be explained in terms of socioeconomic, biological, and environmental transformations, far beyond the simplistic proposition of the new environmental adaptation, for every human culture is adapted to its environment. Perhaps a closer examination of the changes in human behavior in the North European Plain in the late Glacial and the Holocene will help to understand these changes.

The operation must begin with establishment of a fine-resolution chronological boundary between the terminal Paleolithic and Mesolithic assemblages of the plain. Only in this context can we understand the changes and look for continuity or discontinuity among the cultural phenomena (see also Newell and Constandse-Westermann 1985).

Fine-Resolution Chronology of the Terminal Paleolithic–Mesolithic Transition

Until recently, it seemed obvious that even on the macroscale of the entire North European Plain, a clear-cut hiatus occurred between the late Ahrensburgian and Masovian vs. early Maglemose-like units (Price 1987). Recent ^{14}C measurements permit clarification of this assumption.

The plots of ^{14}C measurements from the entire western and central portion of the North European Plain show a macroscale continuity between the terminal Paleolithic and early Mesolithic within one standard deviation (see Figures 2 and 4). On the medium scale of the Polish part of the plain, the results seem to be similar, a continuity of dates within one sigma (Figure 7). The clustering of the same dates, however, indicates four distinctive groups: the early and late Tanged Point Technocomplex and the early and late Narvian (Figure 8).

A plot of the same dates on the calibration curve based on dendrochronology (Becker et al. 1991) reveals a few interesting points (Figure 9). First of all, the latest Tanged Point age estimates pass the 10,000 BP plateau and are in a rapidly descending section, where the ^{14}C years are longer than the dendroyears. The earliest Mesolithic date of circa 9,550 BP from

---

Figure 4. Selected radiochronology of the terminal Paleolithic and early Mesolithic of Poland. Hamburgian: (1) Olbrachcice 8 (Lod-11) according to Burdukiewicz (1987). ABP Technocomplex: (2) Całowanie, Cut X, Bed III (Gd-4165), and (3) Zalasie (GrN-8519) according to Bocheński et al. (1985); (4) Całowanie, Cut X, Bed III (GrN-5967), and (5) Mosty B (Lod-107) according to Cyrek (1986); (6) Rydno-Mine, Vut III/79 (Gd-713), and (7) Witów, Houses (Gro-828) according to Chmielewska (1978); (8) Rydno-Mine, Cut III/79 (Gd-714), Older (Early) Tanged Point assemblages: (9) Całowanie, Peat Cut IX, Bed IV (Gd-2882), (10) Całowanie, Peat Cut IX, Bed IV (GrN-5410), Pre-Masovian (early Masovian): (11) Całowanie, Bed V (GrN-5253), and (12) Całowanie, Bed V (GrN-4966), Masovian: (13) Całowanie, Peat Cut IX, Bed VI (GrN-5409), (14) Rydno-Mine, Cut I/77, Pit 1 (Gd-710), (15) Kochlewo (Lod-142) according to Cyrek (1983); (16) Całowanie, Bed VI (Gd-1648), (17) Całowanie, Bed VI (Gd-2174), (18) Całowanie, Bed VI (GrN-5254), (19) Rydno-Mine, Cut III/79 (Gd-719), (20) Całowanie, Bed VI (Gd-1662), and (21) Całowanie, Bed VI (Gd-1717), Early Narvian: (22) Chwalim (Bln-1766) according to Kobusiewicz and Kabacinski (1993); (23) Całowanie, Beds VII and VIII (Gd-2734), (24) Całowanie, Beds VII and VIII (Gd-1721), (25) Całowanie, Beds VII and VIII (Gd-1719), (26) Całowanie, Beds VII and VIII (Gd-2198), (27) Całowanie, Bed VII (GrN-5251), (28) Całowanie, Bed VII (GrN-5442), (29) Całowanie, Beds VII and VIII (Gd-2149), (30) Całowanie, Beds VII and VIII (Gd-3041), (31) Całowanie, Beds VII and VII (Gd-1667), (32) Całowanie, Beds VII and VIII (Gd-1668), (33) Całowanie, Bed VIII (GrN-5960), (34) Całowanie, Beds VII and VIII (Gd-1670), and (35) Całowanie, Beds VII and VIII (Gd-2146).

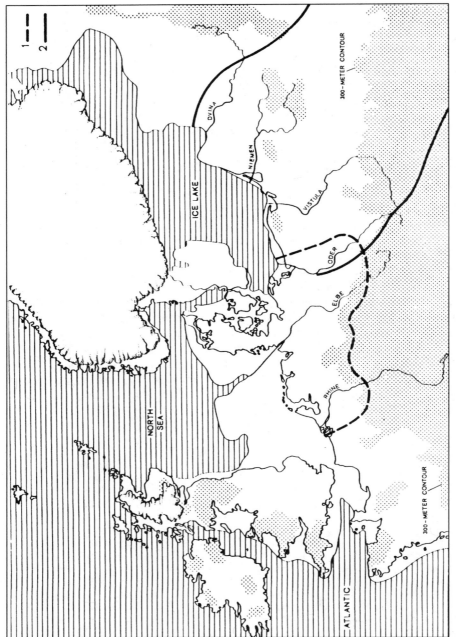

Figure 5. Areal extension of Ahrensburgian and Masovian sites. Shorelines and ice sheets are as in the Younger Dryas. (1) Approximate western, southern, and eastern limits of Ahrensburgian sites; (2) approximate eastern and western limits of Masovian sites.

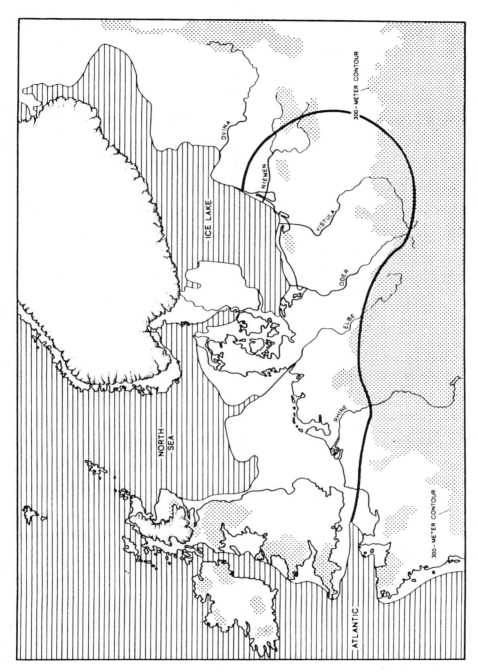

Figure 6. Approximate southern and eastern limits of the early Maglemose-like Mesolithic. Shorelines and icesheets are as in the Younger Dryas.

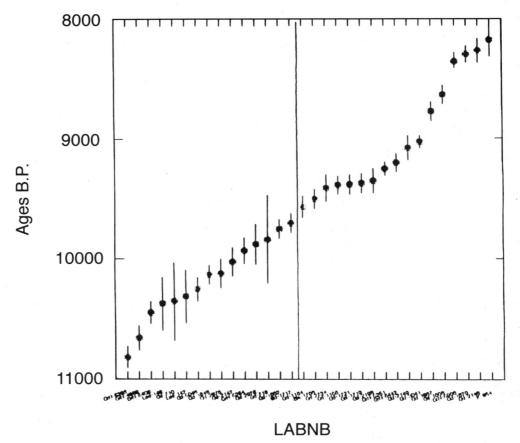

Figure 7. Late Terminal Paleolithic (left panel) and Narvian (early mesolithic) (right panel) radiocarbon age estimates from Poland.

Chwalim, in western Poland, is again at a small plateau and may be freely moved between slightly before circa 11,150 BP and 10,500 dendroyears BP, not counting the standard deviation. Depending on the placement of the ^{14}C measurements within the circa 9,600- to 9,500-year plateau on the calibration curve, one may suggest either lack or presence of a hiatus between the latest terminal Paleolithic and the earliest Mesolithic occupants in western Poland. A number of other early Mesolithic sites (e.g., Duvensee 9, in Schleswig Holstein) show ^{14}C age estimates clearly within the 9,600- to 9,500-year plateau (Bokelmann 1992:86).

Placement on the same calibration curve of the earliest ^{14}C measurements from the lower Mesolithic site of Friesack, in Brandenburg, eastern Germany, indicates a very different picture, even though Friesack is located just a few hundred kilometers west of Chwalim.

At Friesack, the lowermost series of four dates from Bed 10a/Xe place the earliest

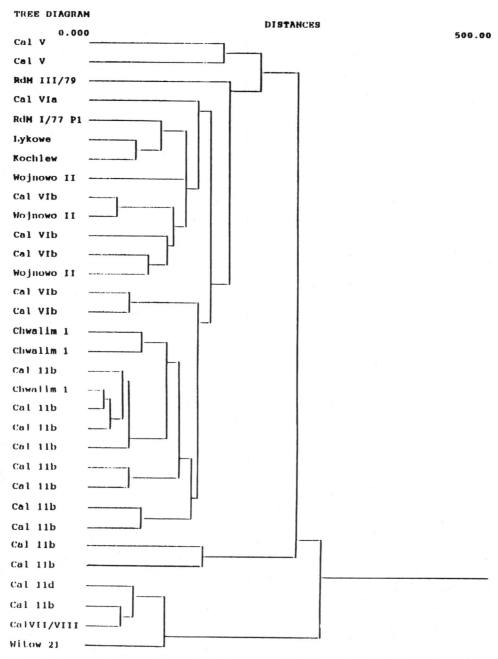

Figure 8. Clustering (nearest-neighbor method) of late terminal Paleolithic and early Mesolithic radiocarbon age estimates from Poland. All Mesolithic dates cluster below Cal VIb (Całowanie, Bed VI), the latest terminal Paleolithic measurement from Poland.

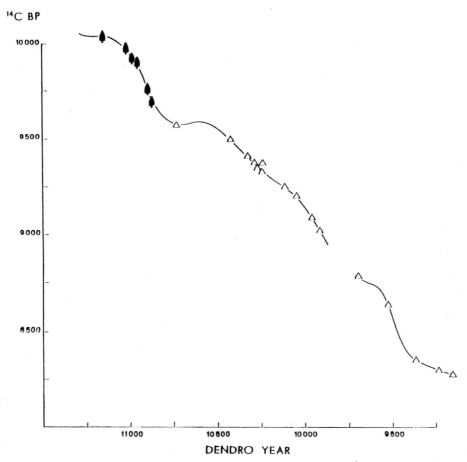

Figure 9. Simplified calibration curve (after Becker et al. 1991) and latest Masovian (◆) and early Mesolithic (△) radiocarbon age estimates.

occupation at circa 9,600–9,700 BP (Gramsch 1987b); that is within the rapidly descending section of the calibration curve, clearly before the 9,600–9,500 plateau. When calibrated, these earliest dates are right at the very end of the latest Ahrensburgian and Masovian age estimates, circa 11,150 dendroyears BP (compare with the curve in Figure 9). In the macroscale of the central North European Plain, the calibration of the dates does not show a hiatus between the terminal Paleolithic and early Mesolithic.

The problem looks different at the microscale, that is, in the regions of Wojnowo, in western Poland, and at Całowanie, near Warsaw, the two best-dated terminal Paleolithic–early Mesolithic complexes of settlements on the plain. In the Wojnowo area, the latest Mazovian radiocarbon age estimate is at 9,880±170 BP (Gd-5045) (Kobusiewicz 1993) and near the beginning of the sharply descending dendroyear curve (Figure 9). The earliest Mesolithic age estimate is at 9565±90 BP (Gd-1164) (Kobusiewicz and Kabaciński 1993:77) and beyond one sigma of the Gd-5045 measurement.

On the calibrated curve, the size of the hiatus depends on the placement of the Gd-1164 measurement within the 9,600 to 9,500-year plateau. If located in the earliest section of the plateau, as suggested by the estimate, the hiatus is on the order of circa 150 dendroyears and within one standard deviation of both estimates. If, on the other hand, the early Mesolithic sample has been moved to the later section of the plateau, the gap will increase to slightly over 300 dendroyears, and well beyond one sigma (compare Figure 9).

At Całowanie, the gap is evident. The latest of the several terminal Paleolithic radio-carbon measurements is at circa 9,700, while the earliest Mesolithic one is at circa 9,400 and also beyond one sigma. On the calibrated curve, the gap is over 500 dendroyears (Figure 9) and already well beyond one sigma.

In summary, there is a chronological continuum between Terminal Paleolithic and the early Maglemose technocomplex on the macroscale of the western and central portion of the North European Plain. In the eastern peripheries of the technocomplex, however, where the dating is continuous, the hiatus is significant. There, the calibration curve suggests considerable increase in the gap toward the east.

Comparing Late Glacial and Early Holocene Adaptations

Subsistence

It is now clear that most of the late Glacial technocomplexes are basically zone-transgressive. They certainly occupy various landscapes, however, showing certain similarities on the macroscale. The best-known, late Tanged Point Technocomplex, particularly the Mazovian, occupies in the late Younger Dryas the tundra and park-tundra in the central and northern zone, the coniferous forest (?) in the east, a clear birch–pine forest along the north Carpathian piedmont in the south, and the cold steppe in the Dnester basin and the Crimea (compare also Sulgostowska 1989). Perhaps the only technocomplex that seems to be associated with a largely uniform landscape is the one represented by the early tanged point assemblages that are found in the northern birch forests and park forests of the Alleröd.

The extreme scarcity of Terminal Paleolithic sites with good organic preservation in the plain prevents meaningful examination of hunting and foraging strategies. We know, however, that, for example, the faunas from the Ahrensburgian site at Stellmoor in the north (Rust 1943) and from Remouchamps (Dewez et al. 1974) and Hohlen Stein (Andree 1931, 1935) in the hills of the southern fringe of the plain are different. This difference is not only a product of contrast in the local environment (tundra in the north and forest in the southern fringes of the plain), but also a result of discrete functional and sedimentological character of the sites.

Because of the geographic differences, the southern Ahrensburgian faunal assemblages are much more temperate in character. On the other hand, we know today that the Hamburgian and Ahrensburgian occurrences of the Stellmoor Valley, so spectacularly dominated by the reindeer, represent repetitive specialized, seasonal hunting episodes (Bratlund 1990, 1991, 1993; Grønnow 1987).

Recent, very detailed studies of the famous Meiendorf and Stellmoor Hamburgian and Ahrensburgian kill and butchery sites by Grønnow (1987) and Bratlund (1990, 1991, 1993) have radically changed earlier interpretation of the finds (Schild 1984; Sturdy 1975). The analysis of hunting lesions and butchering marks led Bodil Bratlund (1990, 1991, 1993) to a number of very important conclusions.

At the Hamburgian Meiendorf site, the hunt took place in September–October. The reindeer were killed during drives of small herds and stalking. The treatment of the killed animals was extremely economical. Almost all the available meat was consumed.

At the Ahrensburgian Stellmoor site, the reindeer (650 MNI) were killed during communal drive-hunts. In contrast to Meiendorf, butchering was very selective, and the low-quality body parts were abandoned (Bratlund 1991; Grønnow 1987). Clearly, both sites represent a palimpsest of similar-function hunting episodes.

The butchery and kill sites of the Hamburgian and Ahrensburgian in the Stellmoor Valley represent only a fraction of the seasonal strategies of hunting and other resource exploitation that were employed. At Potsdam-Schlaatz (Gramsch 1987a,c; Gustavs 1987), in eastern Germany, a single aurochs was probably stalked, killed, and butchered at a meander of the small River Nuthe during a mid-Younger Dryas summer (Weisse 1987).

In the late Younger Dryas–early Preboreal waterlogged Masovian bed (9b, Cultural Layer VIb) of Całowanie, near Warsaw, flotation revealed fragments of charred tubers of as yet unspecified water plants (Kubiak-Martens personal communication).

Almost nothing is known of the subsistence strategies of the ABP Technocomplex in the plain. The site of Bromme, in Denmark, on the other hand, yielded a significant spectrum of exploited fauna by Early Tanged Point people.

Despite the meagerness of data concerning exploitation of food resources on the plain, a new picture slowly emerges. It appears that instead of being highly specialized hunters, the inhabitants of the latest Ice Age communities were broad-spectrum, very opportunistic users of the environment.

Studies on the settlement pattern and intrasite spatial variability are at an initial stage and cannot yet be considered as relevant. A few anecdotal facts, however, have been known for some time. The presence of large houses at certain sites (Rydno), sometimes accompanied by distinct patterning of tools (Całowanie Level IV), indicates base camps that were used semipermanently or repeatedly or both. Others are clearly temporary camps (Schild 1980; Schild and Królik 1981).

At a few occurrences, very careful refitting of lithics permits estimation of the number of knappers and circulation of the artifacts in and out of the camp. The pattern suggests repetitive settling of sites by the same group (Fiedorczuk 1992). Evidently, the intraunit spatial analyses of sites without organic preservation, although very instructive, will never provide deep insight into the economic system of past societies.

A slightly larger number of the early Maglemose-like sites with good preservation of organics give better insight into the adaptation to the pine and birch–pine forest of the Preboreal. It is again a broad-spectrum, opportunistic seasonal exploitation of forest resources, with concentration on megafauna, as shown at the earliest sites: Star Carr (Legge and Rowley-Convy 1988, 1989), Friesack (Gramsch 1987b; Gramsch and Kloss 1989), and Chwalim (Gautier 1993).

More intensive fishing is a later phenomenon as demonstrated at Friesack (Gramsch and Kloss 1989; Kernchen and Gramsch 1989). Seasonality of occupations is evident, that is, spring at Friesack (Gramsch 1987b; Gramsch and Kloss 1989) and Całowanie (Kubiak-Martens personal communication) and late spring and summer at Starr Carr (Legge and Rowley-Convy 1988, 1989). Some of the preferred seasonal spots span probably repetitive occupations for more than 1,000 years (Schild 1989), as at Całowanie (1,100 ^{14}C years or circa 950 dendroyears).

Edible floral macroremains have seldom been reported from early Mesolithic sites, partially an instrument of sampling procedures. At Całowanie, however, the late Preboreal–early Boreal Mesolithic beds yielded strawberry seeds, most probably concentrated in the bio-anthropogenic deposits via digestive tracks (Kubiak-Martens personal communication).

Social Structure

It is believed that people of the early Maglemose Technocomplex were organized into typical band societies. This proposition is based on the grouping of certain decorative elements judged to be sensitive evidence for an exogamic network of marriages and information, both of ethnic importance (Constandse-Westermann and Newell 1988, 1989; Newell et al. 1990). The rather imprecise clustering of a number of stylistic and technological attributes of early Mesolithic lithic industries into smaller taxonomic entities may also, in some instances, suggest closed mating networks (Price 1981:228) or a population in a biological sense. The problem, however, appears to be much more complicated (Schild 1984:261). Similar social structuring is postulated for late Glacial sociotechnocomplexes (Schild 1984:259).

Continuity

The recent archaeological data at hand suggest cultural and demographic continuity between the terminal Paleolithic and early Mesolithic in the Northwest European Plain. Among these data, three areas of evidence seem to be the most important: continuity of ^{14}C ages for the period of transition, an impressive number of typological and technological similarities between the two entities, and an obvious compatibility of the forest adaptation in the southern fringe of the terminal Paleolithic world of the plain with that of the early Preboreal.

The hypothesis of continuity between the terminal Paleolithic and early Mesolithic in the western part of the North European Plain has been postulated already for some time, for example, by Fischer (1978), Gob (1988), Newell and Constandse-Westermann (1991), and Rozoy (1978). On the other hand, the situation in the eastern area of the early Maglemose Technocomplex, that is, in the central part of the North European Plain, in Poland, is not so straightforward.

Signals of Early Holocene Stress

Several behavioral signals during the early Mesolithic in the Polish section of the plain indicate serious stress and discontinuity immediately after the Piottino Oscillation, an idea already suggested by fine-resolution chronology. The discontinuity of cultural tradition is best seen in two areas: the raw material economy of the early Mesolithic and the use of the ochre mine and aggregation complex of Rydno, in central Poland.

Raw Material Economy

Raw material economy in the Alleröd and Younger Dryas shows a high degree of complexity, reflecting large dense information networks that indicate not only movements of bands, but also their intensive interaction. The best test case is the use of the chocolate flint in the late Glacial of central Poland, in the Vistula Basin.

The chocolate flint of the northeastern footslopes of the Holy Cross Mountains in central Poland, was mined at least from middle Paleolithic times (Schild and Sulgostowska 1988) onward (Schild 1976). This flint was also collected on the surface in the same area and to the south of its outcrops, where it had been redeposited by the glaciations preceding Saale. The flint is of excellent quality.

During Alleröd, the population of the ABP Technocomplex used the chocolate flint heavily. Some of the sites in the Vistula Valley located as far as circa 100 km from the source area contain over 90% of this flint, despite the availability of the local erratic, Cretaceous flint that occurs in the river gravels and nearby tills (compare Schild 1976, 1987).

In the Younger Dryas, the exploitation and distribution of the chocolate flint is at its peak. Several changes in the technological indices of lithic assemblages relate strictly to the distance from the source area, reflecting complex reduction and curation processes of the elaborate raw material economic system (Figure 10).

The falloff effect in the chocolate-flint-dominated assemblages in the northern Vistula Valley occurs at about 200 km from the source area. Isolated imports, on the other hand, are

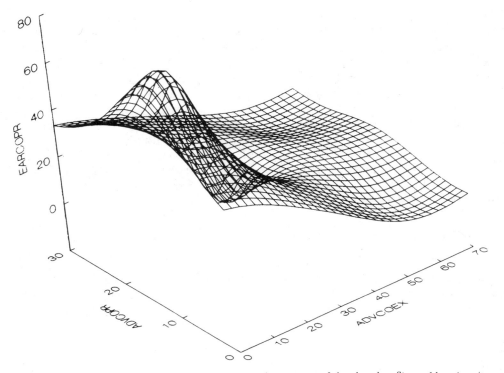

Figure 10. Three-dimensional model of conservation and processing of the chocolate flint at Masovian sites showing high incidence of early (EARCOPR) and advance core preparation (ADVCOPR) at sites located at mines and their vicinity vs. advance core exploitation (ADVCOEX) at occurrences up to 200 km from the source area.

found as far as 500 km from source (Schild 1976). Recently, several tools and blades of chocolate flint have been reported from the Site of Lauskola on the Daugava, some 750 km to the northeast of the outcrops (Sulgostowska 1990:320; Zagorska 1994 personal communication). It has been suggested that the distance of the falloff effect reflects amplitudes of band seasonal movement (Schild 1976) or range of the intermarriage networks, for example, close information networks as defined by the intensity of groups' interaction.

Raw material distribution and curation changed abruptly in the early Mesolithic, even though the technological requirements for good-quality flint were still quite high. Yet the use of chocolate flint almost entirely ended. In the early Mesolithic of Całowanie (≈100 km from the source), where the preceding Masovian assemblages had been made almost entirely of this flint, it now accounts for only a fraction of the percentage.

A similar situation is seen in early Mesolithic inventories some 20 km farther to the north, but still in the Warsaw basin (Więckowska 1985). Even at the chocolate flint mine of Tomaszów, a small early Mesolithic assemblage is made on surface-collected, erratic Cretaceous and chocolate flints (Schild et al. 1985).

The raw material economy of early Mesolithic Poland suggests that the tradition of chocolate flint use and exploitation was completely forgotten. It appears that the early Holocene population had no knowledge of the places where it occurred and could have been mined. Yet the early Mesolithic technology required a good-quality stone that was still sought out, as shown by the erratic flint exploitation areas in western Poland (Kobusiewicz 1989). Only as late as in the late Mesolithic did the distribution and mining of chocolate flint see a revival.

The Ochre Mine at Rydno and Surrounding Aggregation Grounds

In generally the same region as the chocolate flint outcrops is a unique Paleolithic red ochre mine surrounded by hundreds of Stone Age sites. The complex was functioning from circa 20,000 BP until the Neolithic. Its blossoming falls between 12,000 and 9,700 BP (compare Schild and Królik 1981).

In the vicinity of the mine are 34 recorded ABP assemblages. Many occurrences are very rich and contain remains of basin huts (Figure 11), sometimes arranged (Figure 12) in a planned, village-like pattern (Schild and Królik 1981). The rich sites always contain exotic raw materials from the south, coming from as far as Hungary, as well as those from northern areas of the plain.

The Masovian camps are best represented at Rydno. In total, there are 66 Masovian assemblages. Several yield man-made features such as pits, tent basins, and a pit house with tunnel entrance. A number of Masovian occupations are large workshops that base their production on the chocolate flint that outcrops slightly over 10 km to the north. Also, the Masovian sites are characterized by the common presence of exotic raw materials.

The Narvian (early Maglemose Technocomplex) is extremely rare at Rydno. There are no more than 14 assemblages exclusively represented by poor, small concentrations (the richest of which contains 39 tools), as well as isolated finds. None of the excavated mining pits has been dated to this period. On the other hand, the late Mesolithic is much more numerous (33 assemblages), and the sites are richer. They often contain traces of dwellings and exotic imports.

The density and variability of Terminal Paleolithic occurrences are the rest of very

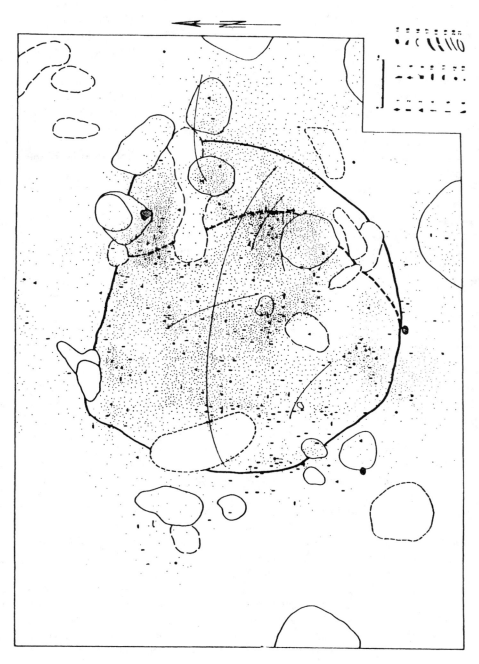

Figure 11. ABP basin house from Rydno III/77. After Schild and Krolik (1981). (1) Cores; (2) end-scrapers; (3) burins; (4) burin spalls; (5) perforators and groovers; (6) backed pieces; (7) truncations; (8) pedunculated points; (9) *raclettes*; (10) denticulates; (11) retouched pieces; (12) *varia*; (13) débitage; (14) stones; (15) ground blades and flakes; (16) articulations (some); (17) area of heavy ochre admixture and limits of the basin; (18) light ochre admixture within basin; (19) tree-fall pits; (20) recent pits; (21) gravel heaves.

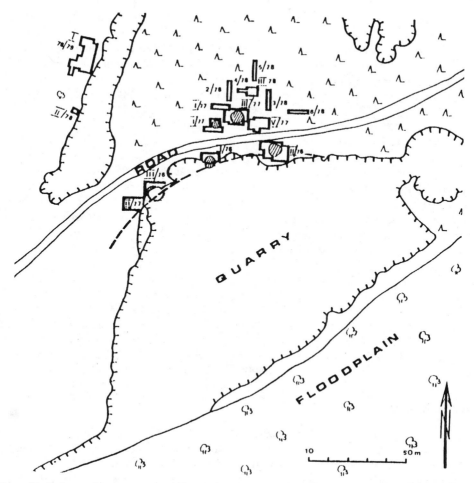

Figure 12. Rydno sand quarry area. Distribution of cuts and basin houses (hachured) after the 1979 field season according to Schild and Królik (1981).

frequent encampment in the area. The sites were used for longer times and frequently reused (Fiedorczuk 1992). The very high variability in the quantitative and qualitative content of assemblages and imported materials probably indicates different ownership status of the dwellers.

All the evidence at Rydno points to the special character of this complex in the late Glacial. Rydno was not simply a locality at which red ochre could be easily mined; it was also a place for the exchange of goods and for aggregation of social groups and bands.

It is estimated that the late Glacial assemblages of Rydno, totaling over a hundred, accumulated over a span of 1,500 years (calibrated), while the few early Mesolithic assemblages came into existence over almost 1,700 dendroyears. Obviously, the importance of the

Rydno mine, and particularly its socioeconomic character, was lost between the terminal Paleolithic and the Mesolithic.

Yet red ochre was still intensively used in the early Mesolithic (Marciniak 1993; Sulgo-stowska 1990). Then, however, it was most probably obtained from glacial deposits. With the changes in raw material economy and use of aggregation complexes like Rydno, a cultural tradition as long as the entire late Glacial was dramatically broken.

THE NEW ARRIVALS

The chronological and cultural data from the central part of the North European Plain, particularly from Poland, suggest that the early Mesolithic was a cultural entity that had no ties with the late Glacial societies of this territory. The Masovian had not contributed to the early Narvian. This proposition is also corroborated by the fact that the area of Narvian occurrence overlaps only partially with that of the Masovian (see Figures 5 and 6). The question of what happened to the Masovian population, however, is an entirely different one.

The southeastern shores of the Baltic, which were occupied by the Kunda assemblages in the early Holocene, show almost no traces of earlier occupations except for a few northernmost Masovian finds on the Daugava River, in Latvia (Zagorska 1994). The Kunda stone technology represents a totally different approach to blank manufacturing, largely based on the pressure technique. The pressure treatment of cores is not known in the late Glacial North European Plain. It is common, however, in late Glacial Siberia, where it reaches at least as far back as circa 16,000 BP (Larichev et al. 1992; Vasil'ev 1992).

ACKNOWLEDGMENTS

Participation of the author in the Symposium SAA/INQUA at Anaheim, California, was sponsored by a grant from the State Committee for Scientific Research, Poland, awarded to Romuald Schild and by another grant awarded to Lawrence Straus by IREX, USA. The research was supported by another grant (1163 91 02) from SCSR awarded to Romuald Schild and Kazimierz Tobolski.

REFERENCES

Ammann, B., and Lotter, A. F., 1989, Late-Glacial Radiocarbon and Palynostratigraphy on the Swiss Plateau, *Boreas* 18:109–126.

Andersen, S. H., 1988, A Survey of the Late Palaeolithic of Denmark and Southern Sweden, in: *De la Loire à l'Oder: Les Civilisations du Paléolithique Final dans le Nord-Ouest Européen*, Volume 2 (M. Otte, ed.), British Archaeological Reports International Series, Oxford, 444(II), pp. 523–566.

Andree, J., 1931, Die frühmesolitische Fauna aus dem Hohlen Stein bei Callenhardt (Kreis Lippstadt), *Abhandlungen aus dem westfälischen Provinzialmuseum für Naturkunde* 2:5–15.

Andree, J., 1935, Mittelsteinzeitliche Funde aus dem Hohlen Stein bei Callenhardt in Westfalen, *Aus der Vorzeit in Rheinland und Westfalen* 2:129–136.

Arts, N., 1988, A Survey of Final Palaeolithic Archaeology in the Southern Netherlands, in: *De la Loire à l'Order: Les Civilisations du Paléolithique Final dans le Nord-Ouest Européen*, Volume 1 (M. Otte, ed.), British Archaeological Reports International Series 444(I), Oxford, pp. 287–356.

Atkinson, B., Briffa, K. R., and Coope, G. R., 1987, Seasonal Temperatures in Britain during the Past 22,000 Years, Reconstructed Using Beetle Remains, *Nature* 325:587–591.

Bard, E., Arnold, M., Maurice, P., Duprat, J., Moyes, J., and Duplessy, J. C., 1987, Retreat Velocity of the North Atlantic Polar Front during the last Deglaciation Determined by [14]C Accelerator Mass Spectrometry, *Nature* 328:791–794.

Barta, J., 1981, Wielki Sławków—Pierwsza Osada Kultury Świderskiej na Słowacji, *Acta Archaeologica Carpathica* 20:5–17.

Becker, B., 1992, The History of Dendrochronology and Radiocarbon Calibration, in: *Radiocarbon after Four Decades: An Interdisciplinary Perspective* (R. E. Taylor, A. Long, and R. S. Kra, eds.), Springer-Verlag, New York, pp. 34–47.

Becker, B., and Kromer, B., 1993, The Continental Tree-Ring Record—Absolute Chronology, [14]C Calibration and Climatic Change at 11 ka, *Palaeogeography, Palaeoclimatology, Palaeoecology* 103:67–71.

Becker, B., Kromer, B., and Trimborn, P., 1991, A Stable-Isotope Tree-Ring Timescale of the Late Glacial/Holocene Boundary, *Nature* 353:647–649.

Berger, W. H., 1990, The Younger Dryas Cold Spell—A Quest for Causes, *Palaeogeography, Palaeoclimatology, Palaeoecology* 89:219–237.

Berglund, B., 1971, Late Glacial Stratigraphy and Chronology in South Sweden in the Light of Biostratigraphic Studies at Kullen, Scania, *Geologiska Föreningens I Stockholm Förhandlingar* 93:11–45.

Bocheński, Z., Ginter, B., Kozłowski, J. K., Mook, W. G., Muszyński, M., Nadachowski, A., Stworzewicz, E., and Szyndlar, Z., 1985, Badanie Osadów Schronisk Podskalnych w Zalasie, k. Krakowa, *Folia Quaternaria* 56: 3–56.

Bokelmann, K., 1992, Duvensee, Wohnplatz 9: Ein präborealzeitlicher Lagerplatz in Schleswig-Holstein, *Offa* 48:75–114.

Bratlund, B., 1990, Rentierjagd im Spätglazial: Eine Untersuchung der Jagdfrakturen an Rentierknochen von Meiendorf und Stellmoor, *Offa* 47:7–34.

Bratlund, B., 1991, Die Spätglaziale "Opfertiere" von Meiendorf und Stellmoor, Kreis Stormarn: Neue Ansätze zur Interpretation alter Funde, *Offa* 48:41–73.

Bratlund, B., 1993, Tanged Point Cultures in Central and Eastern Europe: A Survey of the Ahrensburgian Hunting Economy at Stellmoor, *Symposium, Tanged Point Cultures, Lublin 1993, Abstracts*, pp. 4–5.

Bratlund, B., 1994, Ein Riesenhirschschädel mit Bearbeitungsspuren aus Lüdersdorf, Kreis Grevesmühlen, *Offa* 49/50:7–14.

Broecker, W. S., 1992, Defining the Boundaries of the Late-Glacial Isotope Episodes, *Quaternary Research 38*: 135–139.

Brunnacker, K., von Koenigswald, W., Rähle, W., Schweingruber, F. H., Taute, W., and Wille, W., 1982, Die Sedimente der Burghöhle Dietfurt, *Kölner Jahrbuch für Vor-und Frühgeschichte* 15:86–160.

Burdukiewicz, J. M., 1987, Późnoplejstoceńskie Zespoly z Jednozadziorcami w Europie Zachodniej, *Studia Archeologiczne 14.*

Chmielewska, M., 1978, *Późny Paleolit Pradoliny Warszawsko-Berlińskiej*, Ossolineum, Wrocław.

Constandse-Westermann, T. S., and Newell, R. R., 1988, Patterns of Extraterritorial Ornaments Dispersion: An Approach to the Measurement of Mesolithic Exogamy, *Supplemento della Rivista di Antropologia* 66:75–126.

Constandse-Westermann, T. S., and Newell, R. R., 1989, Social and Biological Aspect of the Western European Mesolithic Population Structure: A Comparison with the Demography of North American Indians, in: *The Mesolithic in Europe* (C. Bonsall, ed.), John Donald Publishers, Edinburgh, pp. 106–115.

Cyrek, K., 1983, Późnopaleolityczne Obozowisko I Pracownia Krzemieniarska w Kochlewie, woj Sieradzkie, *Prace i Materiały Muzeum Archeologicznego i Etnograficznego w Łodzi, Seria Archeologiczna* 30:5–81.

Cyrek, K., 1986, Magdaleńskie obozowisko w Górach Świętokrzyskich (Mosty, Stanowisko B), *Acta Archaeologica Carpathica* 25:11–55.

Cziesla, E., 1992, Ahrensburger Jäger in Südwestdeutschland, *Archäologisches Korrespondenzblatt* 22:13–26.

Dansgaard, W., and Oeschger, H., 1989, Past Environmental Long-Term Records from the Arctic, in: *The Environmental Record in Glaciers and Ice Sheets* (H. Oeschger and C. C. Langway, Jr., eds.), Wiley, New York, pp. 287–318.

Dewez, M., 1988, Ahrensbourgien, Creswellien et Magdalénien an Belgique, in: *De la Loire à l'Oder: Les Civilisations du Paléolithique Final dans le Nord-Ouest Européen*, Volume 1 (M. Otte, ed.), British Archaeological Reports International Series 444(I), Oxford, pp. 179–187.

Dewez, M., Alexandre-Pyre, S., Brabant, H., Bouchud, J., Callut, M., Damblon, F., Degerbøl, M., Ek, C., Frére, H.,

Gilot, E., Glbert, M., and Juvigné, E., 1974, Nouvelles Recherches a la Grotte de Remouchamps, *Bulletin de la Société Royale Belge d' Anthropologie et de Préhistoire* 85:1–160.

Eriksen, B. V., 1991, *Change and Continuity in a Prehistoric Hunter–Gatherer Society: A Study of Cultural Adaptation in Late Glacial–Early Postglacial Southwestern Germany*, Verlag Archaeologica Venatoria, Tübingen.

Fiedorczuk, J., 1992, Późnopaleolityczne Zespoly Krzemienne ze Stanowiska Rydno IV 57 w Świetle Metody Składanek, 1992, *Przeglad Archaeologiczny* 39:13–65.

Fischer, A., 1978, På Sporet af Overgangen Mellem Palaeoliticum og Mesoliticum i Sydskandinavien, *Hikuin* 4: 27–50.

Fischer, A., 1989, Hunting with Flint-Tipped Arrows: Results and Experiences from Practical Experiments, in: *The Mesolithic in Europe* (C. Bonsall, ed.), John Donald Publishers, Edinburgh, pp. 29–39.

Fischer, A., 1993, The Late Palaeolithic, in: *Digging into the Past: 25 Years of Archaeology in Denmark* (S. Hvass and B. Storgaard, eds.), The Royal Society of Northern Antiquaries and Jutland Archaeological Society, Aarhus, pp. 51–56.

Fischer, A., and Sonne Nielsen, F. O., 1987, Senistidens Bopladser ved Bromme. En Genbearbejdning af Westerby's og Mathiassen's Fund, *Aarbøger* 1986:5–42.

Fischer, A., and Tauber, H., 1986, New C-14 Datings of Late Palaeolithic Cultures from Northwestern Europe, *Journal of Danish Archaeology* 5:7–13.

Gautier, A., 1993, The Faunal Remains, in: *Chwalim, Subboreal Hunter–Gatherers of the Polish Plain* (M. Kobusiewicz and J. Kabacinski, eds.), Institute of Archaeology and Ethnology, Polish Academy of Sciences, Poznań, pp. 79–89.

Gob, A., 1988, L'Ahrensbourgien de Fonds-de-Forêt et sa place dans le processus de mésolithisation dans le nord-ouest de l'Europe, in: *De la Loire à l'Oder: Les Civilisations du Paléolithique Final dans le Nord-Ouest Européen*, Volume 1 (M. Otte, ed.), British Archaeological Reports International Series 444(I), Oxford, pp. 259–285.

Goslar, T., 1990, Pomiary Naturalnych Aktywności ^{14}C o Podwyższonej Dokładności I Zmiany Koncentracji ^{14}C w Atmosferycznym CO_2 na Przełomie X I XI Tysiąclecia BP, *Geochronometria* 7.

Goslar, T., Kuc, T., Pazdur, M. F., Ralska-Jasiewiczowa, M., Różański, K., Szeroczyńska, K., Walanus, A., Wicik, B., Więckowski, K., Arnold, M., and Bard, E., 1992, Possibilities for Reconstructing Radiocarbon Level Changes during the Late Glacial by Using a Laminated Sequence of Gościąż Lake, *Radiocarbon* 34:826–832.

Gramsch, B., 1987a, Zeugnisse menschlicher Aktivitäten in Verbindung mit dem Spätglazialzeitlichen Ur-Fund am Schlaatz bei Potsdam, *Veröffentlichungen des Museums für Ur- und Frühgeschichte Potsdam* 21:47–51.

Gramsch, B., 1987b, Ausgrabungen auf dem mesolithischen Moorfundplatz bei Friesack, Bezirk Potsdam, *Veröffentlichungen des Museums für Ur- und Frühgeschichte Potsdam* 21:75–100.

Gramsch, B., 1987c, Betrachtungen zum Ur-Fund am Schlaatz bei Potsdam, *Veröffentlichungen des Museums für Ur- und Frühgeschichte Potsdam* 21:69–74.

Gramsch, B., and Kloss, K., 1989, Excavations near Friesack: An Early Mesolithic Marshland Site in the Northern Plain of Central Europe, in: *The Mesolithic in Europe* (C. Bonsall, ed.), John Donald Publishers, Edinburgh, pp. 313–324.

Grønnow, B., 1987, Meiendorf and Stellmoor Revisited: An Analysis of Late Paleolithic Reindeer Exploitation, *Acta Archaeologica* 56:131–166.

Gurina, N. N., 1989, Mezolit Latvii i Estonii, in: *Mezolit SSSR* (L. V. Koltsov, ed.), Nauka, Moscow, pp. 46–54.

Gustavs, S., 1987, Das Ur-Skelett von Potsdam-Schlaatz: Der Archäologische Befund, *Veröffentlichugen des Museums für Ur- und Frühgeschichte Potsdam* 21.

Healy, F., Heaton, M., and Lobb, S. J., 1992, Excavations of a Mesolithic Site of Thatcham, Berkshire, *Proceedings of the Prehistoric Society* 58:41–76.

Holm, J., and Rieck, F., 1992, Istidsjægere ved Jelssøerne, *Skrifter fra Museumsrådet for Sønderjyllands Amt* 5.

Iversen, J., 1946, Geologisk Datering af en Senglacial Boplads ved Bromme, *Aarbøger* 1946:198–231.

Jaanits, K., 1981, Die Mesolithischen Siedlungsplätze mit Feuersteininventar in Estland, *Veröffentlichungen des Museums für Ur- unf Frühgeschichte Potsdam* 14/15:389–400.

Jaanits, L., and Jaanits, K., 1975, Frühmesolithische Siedlung in Pulli, *Eesti NSV Teaduste Akadeemia Toimetised* 24(1):64–70.

Jaanits, L., and Jaanits K., 1978, Ausgrabungen der Frühmesolithischen Siedlung von Pulli, *Eesti NSV Teaduste Akadeemia Toimetised* 27(1):56–63.

Jacobi, R. M., 1986, A. M. S. Results from Cheddar Gorge—Trodden and Untrodden, in: *Archaeological Results from Accelerator Dating*, Oxford University Committee for Archaeology, Oxford, pp. 81–86.

Jacobi, R. M., 1988, Towards a British Lateglacial Archaeology, in: *De la Loire à l'Oder: Les Civilisations du Paléolithique Final dans le Nord-Ouest Européen*, Volume II (M. Otte, ed.), British Archaeological Reports International Series 444(II), Oxford, pp. 427–446.

Janevich, A., 1993, The Swiderian Sites of the Crimea, *Symposium, Tanged Point Cultures, Lublin 1993, Abstracts*, p. 16.

Kernchen, I., and Gramsch, B., 1989, Mesolithische Netz- und Seilreste von Friesack, Bezirk Potsdamn und ihre Konservierung, *Veröffentlichungen des Museums für Ur- und Frühgeschichte Potsdam* 23:23–27.

Kobusiewicz, M., 1989, Procurement of Flint in the Mesolithic of the Polish Plain, in: *The Mesolithic in Europe* (C. Bonsall, ed.), John Donald Publishers, Edinburgh, pp. 442–446.

Kobusiewicz, M., 1993, Tanged Point Cultures of Great Poland: 25 Years from the First Approach, *Symposium, Tanged Point Cultures, Lublin 1993, Abstracts*, p. 17.

Kobusiewicz, M., and Kabaciński, J., 1992, Late Paleolithic Site at Wojnowo, Zielona Góra Voivodeship, *Fontes Archaeologici Posnanienses* 37:23–39.

Kobusiewicz, M., and Kabaciński, J., 1993, *Chwalim: Subboreal Hunter-Gatherers of the Polish Plain*, Institute of Archaeology and Ethnology, Polish Academy of Sciences, Poznań.

Kobusiewicz, M., Nowaczyk, B., and Okuniewska-Nowaczyk, I., 1987, Late Vistulian Settlement in the Middle Odra Basin, in: *Late Glacial in Central Europe: Culture and Environment* (J. M. Burdukiewicz and M. Kobusiewicz, eds.), Polska Akademia Nauk, Oddział we Wrocławiu, Prace Komisji Archaeologicznej 5, Ossolineum, Wrocław, pp. 165–182.

Kozlowski, J. K., and Kozlowski, S. K., 1979, Upper Palaeolithic and Mesolithic in Europe, *Taxonomy and Palaeohistory*, Prace Komisji Archaeologicnej 18, Ossolineum, Wrocław.

Kudras, H. R., Erlenkeuser, H., Vollbrecht, R., and Weiss, W., 1991, Global Nature of the Younger Dryas Cooling Event Inferred from Oxygen Isotope Data from Sulu Sea Cores, *Nature* 349:406–409.

Kudriashov, V., and Lipnitskaya, O., 1994, Kamiennaia Industria v Raionie Krasnoselskikh Kremmieobrabotyvaiushtshikh Shakht, *Symposium, Recent Research on the Stone and Early Bronze Ages in the South-Eastern Subbalticum, Supraśl, Poland 1994*.

Lanting, J. N., and Mook, W. G., 1977, *The Pre- and Protohistory of the Netherlands in Terms of Radiocarbon Dates*, Rijksuniversiteit Groningen, Groningen.

Larichev, V., Khol'ushkin, U., and Laricheva, I., 1992, The Upper Paleolithic of Northern Asia: Achievements, Problems and Perspectives. III. Northeastern Siberia and the Russia Far East, *Journal of World Prehistory* 6: 441–476.

Larsson, L., 1993, Neue Siedlungsfunde der Späteiszeit im südlichen Schweden, *Archäologisches Korrespondenzblatt* 23(3):275–283.

Legge, A. J., and Rowley-Convy, P. A., 1988, *Star Carr Revisited: A Re-Analysis of the Large Mammals*, Centre for Extra-Mural Studies, University of London, London.

Legge, A. J., and Rowley-Convy, P. A., 1989, Some Preliminary Results of a Re-Examination of the Star Carr Fauna, in: *The Mesolithic in Europe* (C. Bonsall, ed.), John Donald Publishers, Edinburgh, pp. 225–230.

Leotard, J.-M., and Otte, M., 1988, Occupation Paléolithique Final aux Grottes de Presle; Fouilles de 1983–1984 (Aiseau-Belgique, Pl. 1), in: *De la Loire à l'Oder: Les Civilisations du Paléolithique Final dans le Nord-Ouest Européen*, Volume 1 (M. Otte, ed.), British Archaeological Reports International Series 444(I), Oxford, pp. 189–215.

Lotter, A. F., 1991, Absolute Dating of the Late-Glacial Period in Switzerland Using Annually Laminated Sediments, *Quaternary Research* 35:321–330.

Lowe, J. J., Amman, B., Birks, H. H., Björck, S., Coope, G. R., Cwynar, L., de Beaulieu, J. L., Mott, R. J., Peteet, D. M., and Walker, M. J. C., 1994, Climatic Changes in the Areas Adjacent to the North Atlantic during the Last Glacial–Interglacial Transition (14–9 ka BP): A Contribution to IGCP 253, *Journal of Quaternary Science* 9: 185–198.

Marciniak, M., 1993, Mesolithic Burial and Dwelling Structure from the Boreal Period Excavated at Mszano Site 14, Torun District, Poland: Preliminary Report, *Mesolithic Miscellany* 14(1/2):7–11.

Mathiassen, T., 1948, En Senglacial Boplads ved Bromme, *Aarbøger* 1946:121–196.

Mörner, N. A., 1993, Global Change: The High-Amplitude Changes 13–10 ka Ago—Novel Aspect, *Global and Planetary Change* 7(1/2):243–250.

Newell, R. R., and Constandse-Westermann, T. S., 1985, Reflection on the Transition from the Late Palaeolithic to the Mesolithic in Western Europe, *Palaeohistoria* 27:123–127.

Newell, R. R., and Constandse-Westermann, T. S., 1991, "The Mesolithic of Western Europe" reviewed: An Appraisal of Bouquet, Clarity, Body and Price, *Helinium* 31(1):138–151.

Newell, R. R., Kielman, D., Constandse-Westermann, T. S., van Gijn, A., and van der Sanden, W. A. B., 1990, *An Inquiry into the Ethnic Resolution of Mesolithic Regional Groups: A Study of their Decorative Ornaments in Time and Space*, E. J. Brill, Leiden.

Nowaczyk, B., 1986, *Wiek Wydm w Polsce*, Wydawnictwo Naukowe UAM, Poznan.

Pennington, W., 1977, The Late Devensian Floras and Vegetation of Britain, *Philosophical Transactions of the Royal Society of London, Series B* 280:247–271.

Price, T. D., 1981, Regional Approaches to Human Adaptation in the Mesolithic of the North European Plain, *Veröffentlichunden des Museums für Ur- und Frühgeschichte Potsdam* 14/15:217–234.

Price, T. D., 1987, The Mesolithic of Western Europe, *Journal of World Prehistory* 1:225–305.

Rimantiene, R. K., 1971, *Paleolit i Mezolit Litvy*, Mintis, Vilnius.

Rozoy, J. G., 1978, *Les Dernier Chasseurs*, Société Archéologique Champenoise, Reims.

Rust, A., 1943, *Die Alt- und Mittelsteinzeitlichen Funde von Stellmoor*, Karl Vachholtz Verlag, Neumünster.

Salomonsson, B., 1964, Découverte d'une Habitation du Tardiglaciaire a Segebro, Scanie, Suède, *Acta Archaeologica* 38(1):11–21.

Schild, R., 1965, Późny paleolit Krymu a cykl mazowszański, *Archeologia Polski* 10(2):31–73.

Schild, R., 1975, Późny Paleolit, in: *Prahistoria Ziem Polskich*, Volume I (W. Chmielewski and W. Hensel, eds.), Ossolineum, Warszawa–Wrocław, pp. 159–338.

Schild, R., 1976, Flint Mining and Trade in Polish Prehistory as Seen from the Perspective of the Chocolate Flint of Central Poland. A Second Approach, *Acta Archaeologica Carpathica* 16:147–177.

Schild, R., 1979, Chronostratigraphie et Environnement du Paléolithique Final en Pologne, in: *Colloques Internationaux C.N.R.S. No. 271, La Fin des Temps Glaciaires en Europe* (D. de Sonneville-Bordes, ed.), CNRS, Paris, pp. 799–819.

Schild, R., 1980, Introduction to Dynamic Technological Analysis of Chipped Stone Assemblages, in: *Unconventional Archaeology: New Approaches and Goals in Polish Archaeology* (R. Schild, ed.), Ossolineum, Wrocław, pp. 57–85.

Schild, R., 1984, Terminal Paleolithic of the North European Plain: A Review of Lost Chances, Potential and Hopes, in: *Advances in World Archaeology*, Volume III (F. Wendorf and E. Close, eds.), Academic Press, New York, pp. 193–275.

Schild, R., 1987, The Exploitation of Chocolate Flint in Central Poland, in: *The Human Uses of Flint and Chert* (G. de G. Sieveking and M. H. Newcomer, eds.), Cambridge University Press, Cambridge, pp. 137–149.

Schild, R., 1989, The Formation of Homogeneous Occupation Units ('Kshemenitsas') in Open Air Sandy Sites and its Significance for the Interpretation of Mesolithic Flint Assemblages, in: *The Mesolithic in Europe* (C. Bonsall, ed.), John Donald Publishers Edinburgh, pp. 89–98.

Schild, R., 1990, Datowanie Radioweglowe otwartych Stanowisk Piaskowych Późnego Paleolitu i Mezolitu, *Geochronometria* 6:153–163.

Schild, R., and Królik, H., 1981, Rydno: A Final Paleolithic Ochre Mining Complex, *Przegląd Archeologiczny* 29: 53–100.

Schild, R., and Sulgostowska, Z., 1988, The Middle Paleolithic of the North European Plain at Zwoleń, in: *L'Homme de Néandertal* (M. Otte, ed.), Volume 8, University of Liege, Liege, pp. 149–167.

Schild, R., Królik, H., and Marczak, M., 1985, *Kopalnia Krzemienia Czekoladowego w Tomaszowie*, Ossolineum, Wrocław.

Siegenhalter, U., Eicher, U., and Oeschger, H., 1984, Lake Sediments as Continental $\delta^{18}O$ Records from the Glacial/Post-Glacial Transition, *Annals of Glaciology* 5:149–152.

Stapert, D., 1992, *Rings and Sectors: Intrasite Spatial Analysis of Stone Age Sites*, Riksuniversiteit Groningen, Groningen.

Stapert, D., and Krist, J. S., 1987, Oldeholtwolde, a Hamburgian Site in the Tjonger Valley (Prov. Friesland, the Netherlands), in: *Late Glacial in Central Europe: Culture and Environment* (J. M. Burdukiewicz and M. Kobusiewicz, eds.), Polska Akademia Nauk, Oddział we Wrocławiu, Prace Komisji Archaeologicznej 5, Ossolineum, Wrocław, pp. 67–94.

Stuiver, M., Braziunas, T. F., Becker, B., and Kromer, B., 1991, Climatic, Solar, Oceanic, and Geomagnetic Influences on Late-Glacial and Holocene Atmospheric $^{14}C/^{12}C$ Change, *Quaternary Research* 35(1):1–24.

Sturdy, D. A., 1975, Some Reindeer Economies in Prehistoric Europe, in: *Palaeoeconomy* (E. S. Higgs, ed.), Cambridge University Press, Cambridge, pp. 55–95.

Sulgostowska, Z., 1989, *Prahistoria międzyrzecza Wisły, Niemna i Dniestru u schylku plejstocenu*, Pństwowe Muzeum Archeologiczne, Warszawa.

Sulgostowska, Z., 1990, Occurrence and Utilization of Local Ochre Resources During the Early Holocene in the Oder and Vistula River Basins, in: *Contributions to the Mesolithic in Europe* (P. M. Vermeersch and P. Van Peer, eds.), Leuven University Press, Leuven, pp. 317–321.

Taute, W., 1968, *Die Stielspitzen-Gruppen in nördlichen Mitteleuropa*, Böhlau Verlag, Cologne.

Taute, W., 1975, Ausgrabungen zum Spätpaläolithikum und Mesolithikum in Süddeutschland, in: *Ausgrabungen in Deutschland*, Volume 1 (K. Böhner, ed.), Deutsche Forschungsgemeinschaft, Mainz, pp. 64–73.

Thévenin, A., 1982, Rochedane: L'Azilien, l'Epipaléolithique de l'Est de la France et les Civilisations Épipaléolithiques de l'Europe Occidentale, *Mémoire n. 1 de la Faculté des Sciences Sociales, Ethnologie*, Faculté des Sciences humaines de Strasbourg, Strasbourg.

Thévenin, A., 1988, Le Paléolithique superieur final du nord-est de la France, in: *De la Loire à l'Oder. Les Civilisations du Paléolithique Final dans le Nord-Ouest Européen*, Volume 1 (M. Otte, ed.), British Archaeological Reports International Series 444(I), Oxford, pp. 125–135.

Valde-Nowak, P., 1991, Studies in Pleistocene Settlement in the Polish Carpathians, *Antiquity* 65:593–606.

Vang Petersen, P., and Johansen, L., 1993, Sølbjerg I—An Ahrensburgian Site on a Reindeer Migration Route through Eastern Denmark, *Journal of Danish Archaeology* 10:20–37.

Vasil'ev, S. A., 1992, The Late Paleolithic of the Yenisei: A New Outline, *Journal of World Prehistory* 6:337–383.

Walker, M. J. C., Bohncke, S. J. P., Coope, G. R., O'Connel, M., Usinger, H., and Verbguggen, C., 1994, The Devensian (Weichselian) Late Glacial in Northwest Europe (Ireland, Britain, North Belgium, The Netherlands, Northwest Germany), *Journal of Quaternary Science* 9:109–118.

Weisse, R., 1987, Zur Entstehung von Oberflächenformen und Sedimenten an der Fundstelle des Ur-Skeletts am Schlaatz bei Potsdam, *Veröffentlichungen des Museums für Ur- und Führgeschichte Potsdam* 21:53–64.

Westropp, H., 1866, Analogous Forms of Implements Among Early and Primitive Races, *Memoirs of the Anthropological Society* 2:288–293.

Więckowska, H., 1985, *Osadnictwo póznopaleolityczne i mezolityczne nad dolna, Narwią*, Ossolineum, Wrocław.

Zagorska, I., 1994, Salaspils Laukskolas Akmens Laikmeta Apmetne, *Archeologija un Etnografija* 16:14–28.

Zalizniak, L. L., 1989, *Okhotniki na Svernego Oleniia Ukrainskogo Pol'esia Epokhi Finalnogo Paleolita*, Naukova Dumka, Kiev.

Chapter **8**

The Pleistocene–
Holocene Transition
on the East European Plain

PAVEL M. DOLUKHANOV

INTRODUCTION

The territory of the East European (Russian) Plain is a terrain highly suitable for the study of the Pleistocene–Holocene transition and its effects on social and environmental processes. Consideration of the Russian Plain in terms of the area directly affected by the Last (Valdai) glaciation and the extraglacial part is of key importance in this respect; this chapter is mainly restricted to the analysis of the former area.

The time span under discussion is chronologically subdivided into two units: (1) late Glacial (15,000–10,000 BP) and (2) early Holocene, which includes the Preboreal and Boreal periods (10,000–8,000 BP). All radiocarbon dates given in the text are in uncalibrated years BP.

For each of these two chronological periods, the following topics are discussed: (1) paleoenvironment (most based on pollen and paleohydrological data), (2) settlement (archaeological data), and (3) interpretation (the assessment of the socioeconomic development of local communities based on the interaction of environmental and archaeological data).

PAVEL M. DOLUKHANOV • Department of Archaeology, University of Newcastle, Newcastle-upon-Tyne NE1 7RU, United Kingdom.

Humans at the End of the Ice Age: The Archaeology of the Pleistocene–Holocene Transition, edited by Lawrence Guy Straus, Berit Valentin Eriksen, Jon M. Erlandson, and David R. Yesner. Plenum Press, New York, 1996.

LATE GLACIAL (15,000–10,000 BP)

Paleoenvironment

According to present-day estimates based on numerous radiocarbon measurements of pollen profiles in the Russian Plain, the following chronological divisions are distinguishable in the late Glacial:

Older Dryas (Dr-1):	15,000–12,800 BP
Bølling (BØ):	12,800–12,000 BP
Middle Dryas (Dr-2):	12,000–11,800 BP
Allerød (AL):	11,800–11,000 BP
Younger Dryas (Dr-3):	11,000–10,800 BP

The main features of paleoenvironmental development of the Russian Plain during the course of the late Glacial included: rapid recession and oscillations of the ice sheet; formation of a new hydrological network, which included ice-dammed lakes and interconnecting channels; fluctuations of climate and changes in the vegetation, the aeolian activity. The recession of ice was particularly rapid during the warmer stages, the Bølling and Allerød, and led to the greater part of Russian being virtually freed of ice during the greater part of this period.

New data suggest the complex character of late Glacial climatic phases. The pollen data for Latvia (Stelle et al. 1987) indicate two warm substages in the Allerød separated by a cooler episode at 11,300–11,000 BP. July temperature during the Alleroød optimal episodes, according to the estimates of Klimanov (1985), were 2–3°C below present values, the precipitation equal to or slightly above present values. During the warm stages of the Allerød, the greater part of the East European Plain was woodland. According to reliable reconstructions in Central Russia (Zelikson, in press), these woodlands were dominated by spruce, with larch becoming more common farther east. Pine forests were omnipresent on sandy soils, becoming more numerous in the western areas. The presence of warm-loving, broadleaf trees is attested in the Western Dvina catchment. Dwarf shrub heath and open grassland prevailed in low-lying waterlogged areas. Khotinsky et al. (1991) view the occurrence of this vegetation, as well as the wide proliferation of spruce forests, as resulting from the thawing of the upper levels of permafrost inherited from the pleniglacial. Steppe vegetation covered the hilltops.

The Younger Dryas (11,000–10,800 BP) marked the reestablishment in Europe of an extremely cold "pleniglacial" climate, basically similar to that of the Glacial Maximum. According to the estimates of Klimanov (1985), the July temperature at that time was 6–8°C below present values, with precipitation about 250 mm less than now. In the East European Plain, this interval featured the decrease of spruce woodlands restricted to permafrost-affected areas and the pronounced increase of grassland with *Artemisia* and Chenopodiaceae. The occurrence of ruderal herbs, which included *Artemisia*, Chenopodiaceae, *Urtica*, and other species, was a typical feature of the late Glacial vegetation (Dilukhanov in press).

The greater part of Allerød and Younger Dryas periods corresponded to the existence of the Baltic Ice Age connected to numerous local ice-dammed lakes. The level of the latter was subject to fluctuations related to the altitude of the drainage thresholds (Kvasov 1975).

Hence, the existence of a complex network of waterways was the most typical feature of late Glacial landscapes.

The formation of huge parabolic dunes was yet another feature of the late Glacial environment. The development of these huge landforms was particularly active during the colder (Dryas) stages. According to available estimates (Drenova et al in press), the velocity of dune-forming winds of predominantly westerly direction could reach 6–7 m/sec.

Settlement

According to reliable evidence, the greater part of the ice-freed East European Plain was uninterruptedly occupied by dynamic human groups in the course of the Late Glacial. This occupation is attested to by regular occurrences of artifacts idenfiable with the Hamburgian-, Ahrensburgian-, and Lyngby-related cultural units, covering the time span from the Older Dryas to the final Younger Dryas (Figure 1). Triangular points typical of the Hamburgian have been identified at the sites in the Neman catchment (Rimantiene 1971), in the Upper Pripet (Isaenko 1977), and in the Lower Pripet (Zaliznjak 1989).

Rimantiene (1971) identified the Lyngbian tradition in a group of sites near Vilnius, Lithuania. Lyngby points have been reported from several sites in the catchment of the Upper Dnieper and Sozh in northern Ukraine and Blelarus (Kopytin 1979; Isaenko 1977). The site of Anosovo in the Upper Dnieper valley (Gurina 1965) is of particular significance

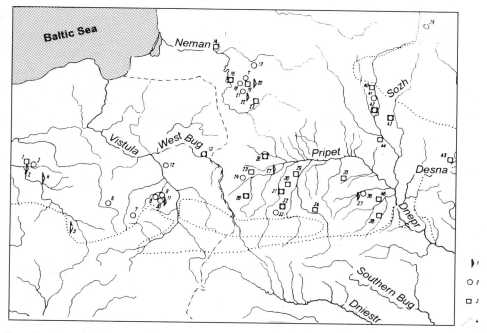

Figure 1. Sites with the points of Hamburg, Ahrensburg, and Lyngby types. After Zaliznjak (1989). (1) Hamburgian points; (2) Lyngby points; (3) Ahrensburg points; (4) limits of the loess.

in this respect. Lyngby points were found there in the context of an archaic Paleolithic assemblage that included single- and double-platform cores, endscrapers, and burins.

Rimantiene (1971) distinguished several Ahrensburgian sites in the area of Vilnius (Vilnius, Ilgis, Mitriskes 6A, and others). Kopytin (1979) and Zaliznjak (1989) reported the Ahrensburg-type points at several sites in the catchment of the Upper Dnieper, Pripet, and Desna. In some cases, Ahrensburg and Lyngby points were found together within the same assemblages, as in the archaic assemblage of Anosovka in the Upper Dnieper valley (Gurina 1965).

Yet the most intensive settlement of the Northeastern European Plain corresponded to the spread of Swiderian assemblages during the course of the Younger Dryas. Sites of this type were originally identified in southern Poland. In light of recent research, the Polish sites located in the catchment of the Vistula and Odra (Schild 1975) comprise only the western sector of the total Swiderian distribution area. A large cluster of Swiderian sites has been found in the catchment of the Neman, in Lithuania and north-west Belarus (Charnyavski 1979; Rimantiene 1971). Another large concentration of Swiderian sites lies in the valley of Pripet (Zaliznjak 1989). Yet another cluster of Swiderian sites is situated in the catchment of the Upper Dnieper, including the valleys of the Desna and Sozh (Bud'ko 1970). The northwestern limits of the penetration of the Swiderian groups correspond to the catchment of the Western Dvina. The assemblages containing Swidry points were found within the depression of Usvyaty Lake in the southern part of the Pskov district (Dolukhanov 1978; Dolukhanov and Miklyayev 1986). In that area, the clusters of stone and bone artifacts have been found on the dunes, which had developed on the shores of an ice-dammed lake allegedly of Allerød–Younger Dryas age. These materials included both Swidry points and two-sided harpoons. Assemblages with Swidry points in similar geomorphic conditions were found in the Upper Volga catchment (Kol'tsov 1989).

A large concentration of late Paleolithic sites is located in the area of Polesye, the terraced accumulative valley of the Pripet, in the border area between Ukraine and Belarus. During late Glacial times, it was one of the main channels of drainage for the Upper Neman ice-dammed lake into the Dnieper catchment (Kvasov 1975). Several sites of late Glacial age in the Pripet catchment feature the presence of Lyngby points: Opol 2, Veliky Midsk, Tur, Pribor. Ahrensburg points have been identified at several sites in the same area (Zaliznjak 1989). Yet the greater number of late Glacial sites in Polesye are clearly attributable to the Swiderian tradition. Sites of this type have been found on the dunes developed on the sandy terraces of the Pripet and its tributaries. The northeasternmost point in the distribution of Swiderian-like assemblages is located at the mouth of the Western Dvina, at the site of Salaspils in Latvia (Zagorska 1994).

In practically all cases, the cultural deposits of late Glacial sites are associated with sand dunes developed on the terraces of rivers and residual ice-dammed lakes. Recent studies have confirmed that the massive formatoin of aeolian sand sheets and dunes was actively under way during the course of the colder late Glacial stages, mostly in the Older and the Middle Dryas (Drenova et al. in press). Yet considerable differences are observable in the geomorphic position of Swiderian sites. Most known sites are found in or above the dunes developed on the surface of the second and the third river terraces, or on the terraces of ice-dammed lakes, in both cases at a considerable altitude above the water. There are reasons to suggest that these sites at the time of their existence were at a considerable distance from the channels. Few sites, usually of smaller size, are found on the lower levels, less than 3 m above the present water level. Larger sites often include several clusters of archaeological materials; five such clusters, each 10 m in diameter, have been found at the site of Pribor 13, in the Pripet catchment (Zaliznjak 1989), where lenses of charcoal-rich sand could be identified.

Interpretation

There exist several hypotheses concerning the origins of the Swiderian tradition. Basing his view on the typological similarity of Swidry points with leaf-shaped Upper Paleolithic implements, Schild saw the roots of the Swiderian in the Central European Upper Paleolithic (Schild 1975, 1984). Using the same criteria, Gurina (1965) has identified the origins of the Swiderian in the assemblage of Borshevo II on the River Don. The stratified site of Grensk on the river Sozh (Bud'ko 1980) seems to support the case for the local development of the Swiderian. The lower level of the site contains implements similar to those of the Upper Paleolithic sites situated in the same basin (e.g., Yudinovo, Gontsy). Hence, one may conclude that the Swiderian assemblages in the Northern and Northeast European Plain resulted mostly from gradual movements of social groups from the main areas of Upper Paleolithic settlement in the periglacial zone of Central and Eastern Europe, and particularly from the catchments of the Dnieper and the Don.

Recent studies of the Hamburgian and Ahrensburgian sites at Meiendorf and Stellmoor (Bratlund 1990, 1992; Grønnow 1987) suggest a broad-spectrum economy, the hunting of reindeer being but a seasonal strategy. Yet seasonal movements of groups of various composition are hardly questionable.

In discussing interpretive scenarios, one should especially bear in mind the vulnerability of late Glacial landscapes containing large areas of barren ground and permafrost at a low depth. The regular occurrence of pollen indicative of disturbed ground (e.g., *Artemisia*, *Rumex acetosa*) may have resulted from both human and animal interference and may have led to a rapid depletion of natural resources within the catchment area of a social group.

Following Zaliznjak (1989:127), one may suggest the occurrence of two types of dwelling sites: spring–summer and autumn–winter ones (Zaliznjak writes about a third type, the year-round settlement, which is questionable in my opinion). The smaller sites of the first type were located closer to the water and were mostly oriented toward the procurement of aquatic resources. Larger settlements of the second type were located further inland; subsistence in this case was based mostly on reindeer hunting. This pattern of two types of sites may be supported by analogies with ethnographic records for permafrost areas of the North American Plain indicative of the occurrence of light warm-weather houses of highly mobile groups, contrasted to more permanent winter houses with much higher artifact densities (Binford 1993). This pattern usually results in a circulating settlement system, with each group repeatedly visiting the same site following a regular seasonal round, yet the vulnerability of late Glacial landscapes makes return to the same site unlikely. General unidirectional migration along waterways following a repeating parabolic seasonal trajectory seems to be a more plausible scenario (Figure 2).

While retaining their cultural identity, the Swiderian groups were in constant contact with economically and socially similar groups of different origin within the greater area of the North European Plain. These contacts are documented by the occurrence of different

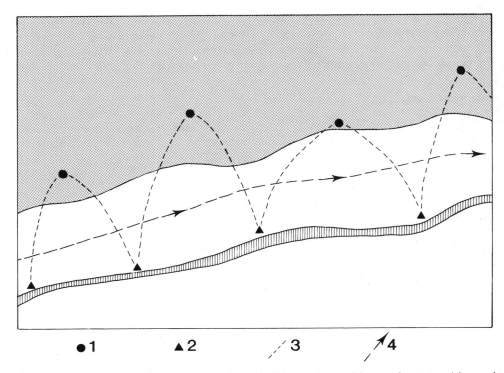

Figure 2. Late Glacial migrations. (1) Autumn–winter sites; (2) summer sites; (3) seasonal trajectory; (4) general trajectory.

types of tanged points (Lyngby, Ahrensburg) in the Swiderian-dominated area. Thus, the entire North European Plain in the late Glacial may be seen as a single economic zone within which several distinct cultural traditions were in constant interaction.

EARLY HOLOCENE (10,000–8,000 BP)

Paleoenvironment

The Younger Dryas–Preboreal transition at circa 10,000 BP marked an increase in temperature and rainfall, followed by the massive spread of forest vegetation. Birch–conifer tundra-type woodlands were dominant throughout the area, with elements of mixed broadleaf forests appearing in Belarus and Ukraine by the end of the stage. For the Preboreal, Khotinsky et al. (1991) have distinguished the Polovetsk warm stage (12,000–10,000 BP) followed by the Pereyaslavl' cool substage (10,000–9,300 BP). The latter took the form of a reduction of forests and a renewed expansion of the treeless pelniglacial-type tundra. The Boreal period corresponded to a further consolidation of forests, dominated by pine with an

increased participation of elements of mixed broadleaf woodland. The forest-steppe formations advanced to the north, reaching the southern confines of the Middle Russian Upland.
The latest evidence (Khotinsky et al. 1991) suggests the occurrence of two cooler substages,
Boreal-1 (9,300–8,900 BP) and Boreal-3 (8,300–8,000 BP), separated by a minor thermal
optimum, Boreal-2 (8,900–8,300 BP). According to computer simulation estimates, at that
time the mean annual temperature was about 1°C above the present value, while the rainfall
was less than now.

Changes no less important occurred in the Baltic littoral area. The combined effect of
the eustatic rise in sea level and the isostatic rebound of the earth's crust led to the
establishment of the Yoldia Sea in the Baltic basin. The continuous crustal uplift in central
Scandinavia eventually resulted in the isolation of the Baltic and the emergence of the
freshwater Yoldia Lake circa 9,300–9,200 BP. The rise in the eustatic sea level that started
worldwide at about 8,000 BP eventually led to the establishment of the Baltic connection
with the ocean via the Danish Straits and the emergence of the Litorina Sea. All these basins
included brackish and freshwater lagoons and estuaries in which specific biomass-rich
ecotones developed. With the transition to the Holocene, there occurred a massive reduction in the area taken up by late Glacial lakes, their levels falling and their margins turning
into mires and bogs. Together with the estuaries of the Yoldia Sea and Ancylus Lake, early
Holocene lakeshore ecotones were exceedingly rich in biomass.

Settlement

Throughout the Preboreal, Boreal, and early Atlantic (including the early Atlantic
climatic optimum), Mesolithic hunter–gatherer communities settled in various parts of the
temperate forest zone of Europe. The main feature of the postglacial Mesolithic settlement
in that part of Europe was a marked intensification and widening of the spectrum of foraging
strategies, based on the effective exploitation of ever more diverse wildlife resources.

Two principal types of Mesolithic settlements may be distinguished in the East European Plain: (1) riverine settlements and (2) estuarine-lacustrine settlements.

Riverine Settlements

The largest areas of concentration of riverine sites are known to exist in the catchment
of the Pripet, Neman, and Upper Volga. The locations of the sites are generally similar to
those of the late Glacial period; the sites are usually found on dunes developed along the
fringes of lower terraces. The larger sites often include remains of dwellings usually
rectangular in shape and about 4 m long. Numerous lenses of charcoal-rich sand up to 1.7 m
in diameter have been identified at the sites in the Pripet catchment (Zaliznjak 1991).
In cases of good preservation, the animal remains include moose, wild boar, roe deer, beaver,
and reindeer (the latter rarely and only in northern Russia).

The analysis of the lithic material by Zaliznjak (1991) suggests that the Mesolithic
groups identifiable in the Pripet, Neman, and Upper Volga catchment developed from the
local Swiderian units. At the same time, there occurred a constant influx from the west
identifiable in the lithic assemblages. Basing his analysis on the sites in the Pripet catchment,
Zaliznjak (1991) distinguished the following cultural groups:

1. Kudlavian—featuring the points of Kudlaevka-Stawinoga type and closely related to the Duvensee cultural area (Figure 3).
2. Janislawice Culture—an eastern extension of the cultural tradition from the core area in the Vistula network.
3. Pesochnorovian—viewed as a further development of Ahrensburgian and Lyngbian traditions.
4. Kukrekian—revealing typological similarities with the sites in the Lower Don and the Crimea.

Estuarine-Lacustrine Sites

The earliest indication of human presence in the coastal area of the northeastern Baltic comes from the Russian–Finnish border area. A bark float, part of the Mesolithic assemblage found in the lacustrine deposits near Antrea-Korpilahti, east of Viborg in Russian Karelia, was radiocarbon-dated to 9,230 ± 210 BP (Luho 1967). An early Mesolithic layer was found in the stratified deposits of a Yoldia Sea lagoon at Sindi near the town of Pärnu in Estonia (Jaanits and Jaanits 1975). Samples of wood from the peat deposits yielded dates of 9,600 ± 120 and 9,300 ± 75 BP. The largest Mesolithic site in Estonia—Kunda—was situated on Lammasmägi Island within an inshore lagoon that was in existence during the Yoldia Sea and succeeding Ancylus Lake. The Lower Mesolithic layer of the site was dated to 8340 ± 210 BP (Ilves et al. 1974). Another Mesolithic site in Estonia—Narva—was located on the southern shore of another lagoon. A series of radiocarbon dates obtained for various samples from that site range between 7,700 and 5,000 BP (Ilves et al. 1974).

Together with the coastal area, lake depressions remained the main arena of Mesolithic settlement. A number of Mesolithic sites are located in the depression of Lubana Lake in eastern Latvia. An earlier site—Sulgalis—which corresponded to a transgression of a local lake, was radiocarbon-dated to 9570 ± 80 BP (Loze 1988). A later Mesolithic site, which also corresponded to a new rise of the lake level, was dated by a series of radiocarbon measurements to 7,000–6,500 BP (Zagorskis 1967). As follows from the analysis of faunal remains (Paaver 1965), the bulk of the meat diet was procured by the hunting of moose, supplemented by red deer and boar. The percentage of the latter two species increased in later stages. Seal hunting was an important source of meat at the coastal sites.

A number of Mesolithic sites have been found in deposits of the residual ice-dammed lakes in the Upper Volga catchment: Ivanovskoye 3, Ivanovskoye 7, and Berendeyevo 3 (Krainov 1978; Khotinsky 1978). The faunal remains include the bones of moose, red deer, brown bear, beaver, and wolf, as well as numerous birds and fish. Several radiocarbon measurements, combined with the pollen data, clearly place the Upper Volga Mesolithic sites in the time span of 8,900–8,000 BP. The presence of the so-called "post-Swiderian points" in the lithic assemblages of all these sites clearly suggests their local origins, developed from local Swiderian variants.

Interpretation

Summing up the existing evidence, one may suggest the occurrence of two major zones in the early Holocene East European Plain featuring differences in the mode of life. The first zone includes riverine sites in the catchment of the Pripet, Neman, and Upper Volga, where

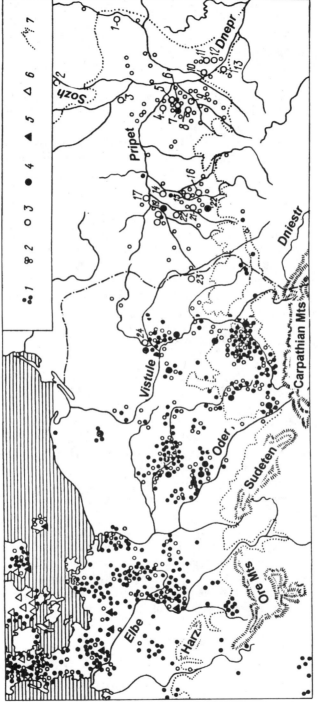

Figure 3. Sites with Komornica and Kudlaevka-Stawinoga points in central eastern Europe. After Zaliznjak (1991). (1) Komornica points; (2) Kudlaevka-Stawinoga; (3) Kudlaevian sites; (4) Komornica-related sites; (5) Duvensee sites; (6) Melsted sites; (7) 200-m contour.

the adaptation was a direct continuation of that of the late Glacial. A seasonally circulating settlement pattern included ephemeral summer sites close to waterways and more permanent winter dwellings farther inland. Taking into account the more stable character of Preboreal and Boreal landscapes, a more fixed seasonal cycle may be ascertained. The constant influx of population from the west and south is well attested by archaeological documents.

The second zone consists of estuarine and riverine settlements in the peri-Baltic area and Upper Volga basin. One may suggest that the rich diversity of wildlife resources available in these ecotones resulted in a more sedentary type of settlement. The peopling of this area mainly proceeded via a northward expansion of Post-Swiderian groups. Once established there, the groups of foragers modified their economic strategy by increasingly relying on the exploitation of marine and lacustrine resources. This broad-spectrum economy, based on the optimized exploitation of wild resources, resulted in the increasingly sedentary character of local groups and in the crystallization of comparatively large base camps with indices of prolonged (permanent or semipermanent) occupation (e.g., Kunda).

Basing their conclusions predominantly on typological grounds, researchers tend to distinguish several archaeological "cultures" with boundaries that are often ill-defined. The Mesolithic sites in Estonia, Latvia, and neighboring regions of the St. Petersburg and Pskov districts are regarded as belonging to the Kunda archaeological "culture." A different archaeological tradition—Nemanian—was identified in Lithuania and in the neighboring regions of northwest Belarus. In discussing the origins of both the Kunda and the Nemanian Mesolithic, scholars seem to be unanimous in identifying their source in local variants of the late Glacial Swiderian tradition (Kol'tsov 1989).

CONCLUSIONS

1. The initial penetration of human groups into ice-freed areas of eastern Europe occurred during the entire late Glacial period, becoming more intense in the Younger Dryas. Small social units were moving, following a seasonally oscillatory trajectory along the waterways. The presence of ruderal herbs identifiable in the pollen spectra suggests the disturbance of unstable landscapes in the vicinity of dwelling sites.

2. The early Holocene amelioration of climate and the massive spread of coniferous forests resulted in a crystallization of two major zones of settlement. The first, restricted to river floors, featured a seasonally radiating settlement system and remained the recipient of surplus population from the west and south. The second, more self-sustained zone included comparatively large settlements of permanent and semi-permanent character in Baltic lagoons and inland lacustrine depressions, with an economy based on the exploitation of a wide spectrum of wildlife resources. Both zones formed contact–exchange networks, resulting in the emergence of loose local cultural units.

REFERENCES

Binford, L. R., 1993, Bones for Stones: Considerations of Analogues for Features Found on the Central Russian Plain, in: *From Kostenki to Clovis: Upper Palaeolithic—Palaeo-Indian Adaptations* (O. Soffer and N. D. Praslov, eds.), New York & London: Plenum, p. 101–124.

Bratlund, B., 1990, Rentierjagd im Spätglazial, *Offa* 47:7–34.

Bud'ko, V. D., 1980, Paleolit, in: *Ocherki po Arkheologii Belorussii* (V. F. Isaenko, ed.), Nauka i Technika, Minsk, pp. 9–48.

Charnyavski, M. M., 1979, *Nealit Ponyamonn'a*, Nauka i Technika, Minsk.

Dolukhanov, P. M., 1978, *Ecology and Economy in the Neolithic Eastern Europe*, Duckworth, London.

Dolukhanov, P. M., in press, The Mesolithic–Neolithic Transition in the Boreal East European Plain, in: *Landscape in Flux* (J. Chapman and P. Dolukhanov, eds.), Oxbow, Oxford.

Dolukhanov, P. M., and Miklyayev, A. M., 1986, Prehistoric Lacustrine Pile Dwellings in the North-Western Part of the USSR, *Fennoscandia Archaeologica* 3:81–89.

Drenova, A. N., Timireva, S. N., and Chikolini, N. I., in press, Late Glacial Dune-building in the Russian Plain, in: *Late Quartenary Russian Plain* (A. A. Velichko, N. Rutter, and P. Dolukhanov, eds.),.

Grønnow, B., 1987, Meiendorf and Stellmoor Revisited: An Analaysis of Late Palaeolithic Reindeer Exploitation, *Acta Archaeologica* 56:131–166.

Gurina, N. N., 1965, Novye Dannye o Kamennon Veke Severo-Zapadnoi Belorussii, *Materialy i Issledovanija po Archeologii SSSR* 131:141–203.

Ilves, E., Liiva, A., and Punning, J.-M., 1974, *Radiouglerodnyi Metod i Ego Promenenie v Chetvertichnoi Geologii i Archeologii Estonii*, Akademija Nauk Estouskoi SSR, Tallinn.

Isaenko, V. F., 1977, Mezolit Pripjatskogo Poles'ja, *Kratkie Soobschenija Instituta Archaeologii AN SSSR* 149:53–59.

Jaanits, L., and Jaanits, K., 1975, Frühmesolithische Siedlung von Pulli, *Eesti NSV Teaduste Akadeemia Toimetised* 24(1):64–70.

Khotinsky, N. A., Aleshinskaja, Z. V., Guman, M. A., Klimanov, V. A., and Cherkinsky, A. E., 1991, Novaja Shema Periodizatsii Landshaftno-Klimaticheskih Izmenenij v Golocene, *Izvestija Akademii Nauk SSSR Serija Geograficheskaja*, No. 3, pp. 30–41.

Klimanov, V. A., 1985, Nekotorye Paleoklimatichekie Kharakteristiki Pozdnelednikov'ja na Russkoi Ravine, in: *Kraevye Obrazovanija Materikovyh Oledenenii*, Nauka, Moscow, pp. 214–216.

Kol'tsov, L. V., 1989, *Mezolit SSSR—Archeologija SSSR*, Nauka, Moscow.

Kopytin, V. F., 1979, Mezolit Poselenija Gorki v Posozh'e, *Kratkie Soobshchenija Institua Archeologii AN SSSR* 157: 27–32.

Krainov, D. A., 1978, Hronologicheskie Ramki Neolita Verhnego Povolzh'ja, *Kratkie Soobshchenija Instituta Archeologii AN SSSR* 153:57–62.

Krainov, D. A., and Khotinsky, N. A., 1977, Verhnevolzhskaja Archaeologicheskaja Kul'tura, *Sovetskaja Archeologija* 1977/3:42–68.

Kvasov, D. D., 1975, *Pozdnechetvertichnja Istorija Krupnyh Ozjor i Vnutrennih Morei Vostochnoi Noi Evropy*, Nauka, Leningrad.

Loze, I. A., 1988, *Poselenija Kamennogo veka Lubanskoi Niziny: Mezolit, Rannii i Srednii Neolit*, Zinatne, Riga.

Luho, V., 1967, Die Suomusjarvi-Kultur—Die Mittel- and Spatmesolithische Zeit in Finland, *Suomen Muinais nuistoyhdistyksen Aikakauskirja*, 66, Helsinki.

Paaver, K., 1965, *Formirovanie Terriofauny i Izmenchivost' Mlekopitajushchih Pribaltiki v Golocene*, Akademija Nauk Estonskoi SSR, Tallinn.

Rimantiene, R. K., 1971, *Paleolit i Mezolit Litvy*, Mintis, Vilnius.

Schild, R., 1975, Późny Paleolit, in: *Prahistoria Ziem Polskich*, 1, Ossolineum, Warsaw–Wroclaw, pp. 191–338.

Schild, R., 1984, Terminal Paleolithic of the North European Plain: A Review of Lost Chances, Potential and Hopes, in: *Advances in World Archaeology*, Volume 3 (F. Wendorf and E. Close, eds.), Academic Press, New York, pp. 193–274.

Stelle, V. J., V. Veksler, and Seglinš, 1987, Problemy Raschlenenija i Oatorovanija Otlozhenii Allerøda Na Territorii Latvii, in: *Metody izotopnoi geologii*, Volume 2, Nauka, Moscow, pp. 289–291.

Zagorska, I., 1994, Salaspils Lakslokas Akmens Laikmeta Apmente, *Archeologija un Etnografija*, 16:14–28.

Zagorskis, F., 1967, *Rannii i Razvitoi Neolit Vostochnoi Latvii*, Riga.

Zaliznjak, L. L., 1989, *Ohotniki na Severnogo Olenja Ukrainskogo Poles'ja Epohi Final'nogo Paleolita*, Naukova Dumka, Kiev.

Zaliznjak, L. L., 1991, *Naselenie Poless'ja v Mezolite*, Naukova Dumka, Kiev.

Zelikson, E. M., in press, Kharakteristike flory i rastitel'nosti Evropy v allerøde, in: *Late Quaternary Russian Plain* (A. A. Velichko, N. Rutter, and P. Dolukhanov, eds.).

PART IV

ASIA AND AUSTRALIA DURING THE PLEISTOCENE– HOLOCENE TRANSITION

The continents of Asia and Australia, along with their associated islands, encompass roughly 120 degrees of latitude (82°N to 43°S) and 165 degrees of longitude (170°W to 26°E), stretching nearly halfway around the world in both directions. This vast expanse of land and water—bounded by the Arctic Ocean on the north, the Pacific Ocean on the east, and the Indian Ocean on the south—contains a remarkable diversity of habitats, environments, and cultures. Even in East Asia and the greater Australia region (a.k.a. Sahul) alone, latitudinal variation and topographical relief ensure tremendous environmental differences: from the steaming jungles of Southeast Asia to the frozen steppes of northern Siberia, from the tropical coral-fringed islands of Sumatra and the Solomons to the cool oceanic archipelagoes of Japan and the Kurile Islands, and from the high alpine zones of the Himalayas to the scorched coastal deserts of western Australia. Average January temperatures in these diverse habitats vary from −48°C (−54°F) in northern Siberia to +31°C (+88°F) in northwest Australia. Precipitation patterns vary just as dramatically, averaging 5–10 cm per year in high- and low-latitude arid regions vs. 250 cm or more in some rain forest or montane settings.

For as long as people have occupied various parts of this immense landscape, human population densities and ecological adaptations have varied in response to such environmental variation. The adaptive diversity evident in the archaeological record of East Asia and Greater Australia is not simply the result of local or regional variation in the natural environment, however, for the nature and distribution of habitats have changed dramatically through time. Some of the most dramatic environmental changes took place across the Pleistocene–Holocene transition, between about 13,000 and 8,000 years ago. This was a time when postglacial climates were generally ameliorating, sea levels were rising rapidly, glaciated areas (small compared to European and North American examples) were contracting, and floral and faunal communities were adjusting to new climatic and geographic regimes. In some areas, significant mammalian extinctions accompanied these transitions, but in the more temperate or tropical parts of Southeast Asia and Sahul, such extinctions seem to have been less dramatic than those documented for many other parts of the world.

The people who occupied virtually the entire expanse of East Asia and Greater Australia (including most of the more substantial offshore islands) by the end of the Last Glacial entered the Pleistocene–Holocene transition with a diverse range of adaptations designed to cope with very different environmental circumstances. The diversity of these cultural adaptations reflects not only the immense variability in Asiatic and Sahulian environments, but also differences in the length of human occupation in various regions and the very different (and in some cases very long) cultural traditions they descended from. The sweeping geographic changes that took place between 13,000 and 8,000 years ago posed new challenges, however, for virtually all these diverse hunting and gathering peoples, challenges that provoked a variety of cultural responses.

As it is elsewhere in the world, the record of environmental and cultural changes associated with the Pleistocene–Holocene transition in East Asia and Greater Australia is somewhat spotty. The four chapters in this section, however, summarize the data available from several of the better-known regions: the Greater Australian area (Allen and Kershaw), Southeast Asia (Pookajorn), Japan (Aikens and Akazawa), and Siberia (Powers). Each of these chapters examines the relationships between environmental changes and human adaptations associated with the Pleistocene–Holocene transition. In an area as culturally and environmentally diverse as East Asia and Australian Sahul, of course, variation in both the magnitude of environmental change and the range of human responses is to be expected. In fact, while there are common threads in the interpretation of various regional patterns (the impact of sea-level change, for instance), each chapter also comes to somewhat different conclusions about the role that environmental changes played in the cultural developments of this vital period in human prehistory.

The discussion begins with Allen and Kershaw's summary in Chapter 9 of cultural and environmental changes of the Pleistocene–Holocene transition in New Guinea, New Britain and New Ireland, Australia, and Tasmania. The authors document the presence of a remarkable array of human adaptations in Greater Australia between about 15,000 and 7,000 years ago. Much of this adaptive diversity has deep roots and is related to local and regional environmental variability. It is now known that humans occupied this entire region (except for very arid desert areas) by at least 35,000 years ago, and the first settlement of Sahul is now thought by some to have occurred 50,000 or more years ago (Roberts et al. 1990). On a continental scale, environmental changes of the Pleistocene–Holocene transition are seen as intensifying an already established diversity of human adaptations to local differences in geography. Regional shifts in climate, sea level, and habitat stimulated a variety of cultural responses, however, varying from the early development of agriculture in New Guinea, to the intensification of maritime adaptations in some coastal areas, to the abandonment of southwest Tasmania as dense rain forests encroached. For Tasmania and New Guinea, rising sea levels flooded land connections with Australia, isolating the inhabitants of each area from Holocene cultural developments in adjacent areas.

In Chapter 10, Pookajorn focuses on recent research at two caves in southern Thailand to examine the transition from the late Paleolithic (Hoabinhian) to the Neolithic. Comparing technological and paleoenvironmental information from Moh Khiew Cave and Sakai Cave to data recovered in other Southeast Asian sites, Pookajorn documents the transition from broad-spectrum hunting and gathering during the late Pleistocene to the appearance of pottery, ground stone adzes, and rice grains in Neolithic levels dated between about 7,000 and 9,000 radiocarbon years ago. Pookajorn proposes that the appearance of agriculture in Thailand is not necessarily associated with significant climatic changes. Variations in the abundance and nature of marine faunal remains in various levels of the caves suggest, however, that fluctuating sea levels radically altered the distance of the caves from the coastline through time. Pookajorn believes these changes had the most dramatic impact on people occupying southern Thailand during the Pleistocene–Holocene transition. Similar patterns of environmental change and human adaptive response have been documented in a variety of coastal areas around the world (see Parkington 1981; Shackleton and van Andel 1980). Binford (1968), in fact, regarded postglacial sea-level rise as an important source of population pressure that may have contributed to the development of agriculture in certain key areas.

In Chapter 11, Aikens and Akazawa examine the environmental and cultural changes that took place in Japan during the Pleistocene–Holocene transition. These authors empha-size a number of environmental and archaeological similarities between Japan and Northeast Asia prior to about 13,000 years ago, particularly in the sequential appearance of Upper Paleolithic blade, bifacial, and microblade technologies (see also Aikens and Dumond, 1986; Aikens and Higuchi 1982). With the end of the Pleistocene, however, rising sea levels transformed Japan from a peninsular extension of Asia to a relatively isolated island chain with convoluted coastlines. These dramatic changes in geography were accompanied by the gradual northward expansion of temperate oak woodlands between 12,000 and 8,000 years ago. These environmental changes seem to have increased the diversity and productivity of both marine and terrestrial resources, leading to the development of broad-spectrum Jomon subsistence, increased residential sedentism, and early pottery and intensive plant use. In a case of closely related cultural and environmental changes, the northward spread of Jomon technologies and adaptations appears to be intimately linked to changes in Japanese coastlines and the northward shift of oak woodlands during the Pleistocene–Holocene transition.

In Chapter 12, Powers summarizes environmental and cultural changes occurring across the vast expanse of Siberia between about 13,000 and 8,000 years ago. His review is particularly welcome because so much recent Siberian research remains largely inaccessible to Western scholars. Due to their sensitivity to the climatic changes of the Pleistocene–Holocene transition, arctic and subarctic paleosol, pollen, and faunal records can provide relatively detailed environmental data. Combined with archaeological data on human settlement, subsistence, and technology, these records may yield detailed information on the relationships between environmental changes and human adaptations. As Powers notes, such a synthesis for Siberia is hindered by the dearth of stratified and well-dated sites and by the descriptive and cultural–historical focus of most archaeological reports. Nonetheless, Powers identifies some general patterns in Siberian settlement, technology, and subsistence that seem to be related to the environmental changes of the Pleistocene–Holocene transi-tion. These patterns include a general trend toward the diversification of subsistence through time, with evidence for intensive fishing appearing only after 10,000–12,000 years ago. Although Pitul'ko (1993) recently documented the occupation of high arctic (76°N) coasts almost 8,000 years ago, a major lacuna in Siberian research on the Pleistocene–Holocene transition is the dearth of early coastal sites comparable to several 9,000- to 10,000-year-old examples from the Pacific coast of North America (see Erlandson [1994] and Chapter 14). The flooding of Beringia clearly isolated late Glacial peoples of northeast Siberia from their North American counterparts, but the specific effects of postglacial sea-level rise on the archaeological record of Siberia remain largely unknown.

In sum, the authors of these chapters on East Asia and Australia–Sahul have written current and stimulating syntheses for four very different but equally interesting regions. Specific patterns of cultural and environmental changes associated with the Pleistocene–Holocene transition vary between regions and within each region. Clearly, however, the ecological changes that affected Asian and Australian landscapes during this dynamic period posed new and significant challenges to people living throughout this vast area. The four chapters that follow provide comparative models that may guide ongoing paleoecological and archaeological research in the regions they summarize, as well as surrounding regions.

Jon M. Erlandson

REFERENCES

Aikens, C. M., and Dumond, D. E., 1986, Convergence and common heritage: Some parallels in the archaeology of Japan and North America, in: *Windows on the Japanese Past: Studies in Archaeology and Prehistory* (R. J. Pearson, ed.), Center for Japanese Studies, University of Michigan, Ann Arbor, pp. 163–178.

Aikens, C. M., and Higuchi, T., 1982, *Prehistory of Japan*, Academic Press, New York.

Binford, L. R., 1968, Post-Pleistocene adaptations, in: *New Perspectives in Archaeology* (S. R. Binford and L. R. Binford, eds.), Aldine, Chicago, pp. 313–341.

Erlandson, J. M., 1994, *Early Hunter–Gatherers of the California Coast*, Plenum Press, New York.

Parkington, J., 1981, The Effects of Environmental Change on the Scheduling of Visits to the Elands Bay Cave, Cape Province, S.A., in: *Patterns of the Past* (I. Hodder, G. Isaac, and N. Hammond, eds.), Cambridge University Press, Cambridge, pp. 341–359.

Pitul'ko, V. V., 1993, An Early Holocene Site in the Siberian High Arctic, *Arctic Anthropology* 30(1):13–21.

Roberts, R. G., Jones, R., and Smith, M. A., 1990, Thermoluminescence Dating of a 50,000-year-old Human Occupation Site in Northern Australia, *Nature* 345:153–156.

Shackleton, J. C., and van Andel, T. H., 1980, Prehistoric Shell Assemblages from Franchthi Cave, *Nature* 288: 357–359.

Chapter **9**

The Pleistocene–Holocene Transition in Greater Australia

JIM ALLEN AND PETER KERSHAW

OVERVIEW

Greater Australia is the most popular of a range of names (Ballard 1993) given to the single Pleistocene landmass that connected New Guinea to the Australian mainland across Torres Strait and the Arafura Sea, and Tasmania to Australia across Bass Strait. Other smaller, now offshore, islands were also incorporated (Figure 1). This vast Pleistocene continent stretched from almost exactly the Equator to nearly 44°S and from ≈112°E to ≈154°E at its widest point, near the Tropic of Capricorn.

While Greater Australia was immense in size, it was (and is in its Holocene configuration) a land characterized by low physical relief. New Guinea has a mountainous spine running east–west that is in places over 4000 m.a.s.l., climbing at one point to more than 5000 m.a.s.l., but Australia is particularly flat, its highest mountain being only 2230 m.a.s.l. in the southeastern Australian Alps, with much more than half the remainder being less than 400 m.a.s.l. Thus, the Pleistocene in Greater Australia was not an epoch particularly distinguished by glaciations as it was in the northern hemisphere. Glacial activity was very geographically limited, and the Pleistocene continent was most affected by global climate and sea-level changes. During the Pleistocene–Holocene transition, the almost total disappearance of glaciers was a much less important event than the marine transgression that created the three major landmasses.

Humans arrived in Greater Australia only in the late Pleistocene and by 35,000 BP[1] had occupied every major environmental zone from north to south, with the possible exception of the arid center. Despite an assumed common Southeast Asian origin for the original

[1]All ^{14}C dates in this chapter are uncalibrated.

JIM ALLEN • Department of Archaeology, La Trobe University, Bundoora, Victoria 3083, Australia.   **PETER KERSHAW** • Department of Geography and Environmental Science, Monash University, Melbourne 3168, Australia.

Humans at the End of the Ice Age: The Archaeology of the Pleistocene–Holocene Transition, edited by Lawrence Guy Straus, Berit Valentin Eriksen, Jon M. Erlandson, and David R. Yesner. Plenum Press, New York, 1996.

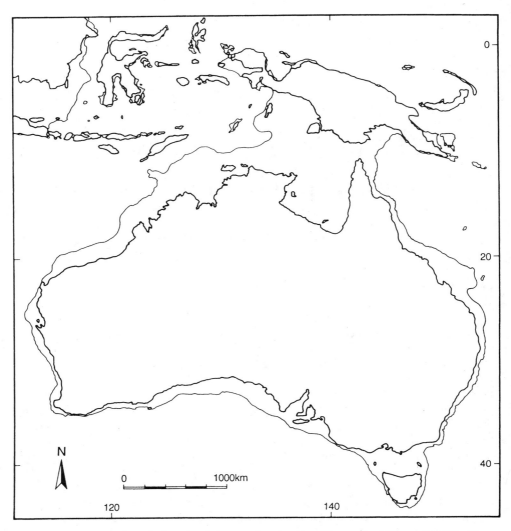

Figure 1. Greater Australia at the last Glacial Maximum based on the −30-m sea level (Chappell and Shackleton 1986).

colonists of each of the major regions of the single landmass, it is now being demonstrated in the archaeological record that different behavioral adaptations and probably distinct cultural patterns had developed by the terminal Pleistocene. That these developments facilitated different human behavioral trajectories after the separation of the three major Holocene landmasses seems probable, but may not entirely explain these separate Holocene histories; both diffusion and isolation may also be invoked, even if they are neither yet accurately quantified nor sufficiently explained.

Archaeologists continue to be wary of the utility of a traditional Pleistocene–Holocene divide at circa 10,000 BP as a useful way of structuring Australian archaeology. Pardoe (1993) has warned against creating an intellectual disjunction between the two, suggesting that the consequences include methodological and intellectual restrictions that inhibit reconstructions of past behaviors and biological histories. Frankel (1993:26–27), in particular, denies any utility in a division in local prehistory at 10,000 BP, suggesting that it is merely a methodological inheritance from Europe. Frankel argues that we cannot assume that either environments or human behaviors were distinctly different across this divide. The Australian terminal Pleistocene–early Holocene archaeological record remains a predominantly lithic record that, in general typological terms, continued unaltered across this boundary. Although many species of large marsupials apparently became extinct in the late Pleistocene, the archaeological association of humans and megafauna remains elusive, and explicit evidence implicating humans in these extinctions is nonexistent (although the implicit logic of the arguments for a human role remains persuasive). In the terminal Pleistocene–early Holocene, as Frankel points out, Australia witnessed neither any equivalent to the Mesolithic or Epi-Paleolithic nor the evolution of new sociocultural forms.

While change in Greater Australia cannot be sensibly pinned to a date of 10,000 BP and while it may not have followed northern hemisphere trajectories, fundamental change did occur. Between circa 16,000 BP and 7,000 BP, Greater Australia was reduced in area by more than 3,000,000 km^2 (an area much larger than Mexico). Three major landmasses existed where previously there had been one; thus, physical barriers or boundaries were created. Coastal sites were either submerged or preserved on islands, while sites of the former arid interior became coastal; coastlines were extended. In inland areas, concomitant environmental changes saw lakes become semiarid plains and glaciated mountains and valleys become new pastures for game. Changes so widespread and of such magnitude obviously caused behavioral realignments, some of which are reviewed here. The point is that evidence of these responses is often reflected only indirectly in the archaeological record and rarely in the technological or typological record of stone tools, possibly simply because many of the subsistence transformations in Greater Australia were not as pronounced as elsewhere.

Because the separation of Australia, Tasmania, and New Guinea led to quite separate behavioral trajectories in each place, we can legitimately ask whether differences had already developed in these regions prior to separation and whether the climatic shifts and rising seas exacerbated and hastened these differences or created new ones or had both effects. In this summary chapter, we contrast the changes in each of these regions by examining aspects of the Pleistocene–Holocene transition in each.

ENVIRONMENTAL CONDITIONS

The period 15,000–7,000 BP in the Australia–New Guinea region represents the transition from full glacial conditions to conditions broadly similar to those of today (Figure 2). There is general consensus that during the height of the last glacial, precipitation was substantially lower than today with estimates varying from 30% to 50% of present-day mean annual precipitation (Ross et al. 1992). This relative aridity resulted in the regional replacement of coastal and subcoastal sclerophyll forests and rainforests by more arid-adapted communities (Figure 2A). In the northern part of Australia, open woodlands were predomi-

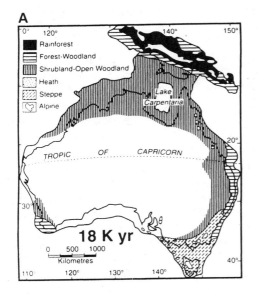

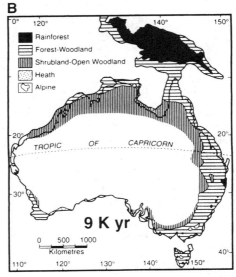

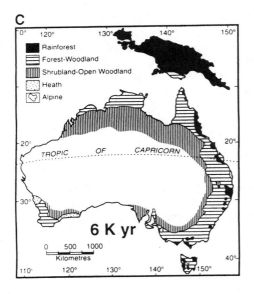

Figure 2. Reconstruction of vegetation changes for Greater Australia and Australia and New Guinea across the Pleistocene–Holocene transition. From Markgraf et al. (1992).

nant and, from pollen evidence preserved in Lake Carpentaria (Torgerson et al. 1988), covered the exposed continental shelf areas between northern Australia and New Guinea, as well as present terrestrial landscapes. In the southeast of the continent, steppe vegetation, with no modern analogue, was extensive and interspersed with shrublands. In the interior of the continent and extending in places to coastal locations, evidence for active desert dunes indicates a sparse vegetation cover and high wind speeds, probably 120% to 150% higher than today (Wasson 1989). In New Guinea and in southeastern Australia, snowlines were depressed by about 1000 m, suggesting a temperature depression in mountain areas at least of some 6°C (Colhoun et al. 1991; G. S. Hope and Peterson 1975). Lowland parts of southeast Australia experienced a similar degree of temperature lowering, but there is little temperature information from the northern lowlands.

The only reliably dated and continuous records of environmental change through much or all of the transition from the last Glacial to the mid-Holocene are derived from pollen and associated analyses of lake and swamp sites restricted to particular areas within the more humid margins of the continent (Figure 3). Regional climatic reconstructions for each of these areas are shown in Figure 4.

In all records providing some evidence for temperature changes, temperatures began to rise from between about 15,000 BP and 14,000 BP, reaching present-day levels by about 10,000 BP. At this time, ice had essentially disappeared from the mountains of the region except for the glaciers that still survive in the Carstanz area of West Irian (the western half of the island of New Guinea, now part of Indonesia), and alpine grasslands and herbfields had become much reduced in area. Patterns of vegetation change associated with the rise in tree lines could be interpreted as indicating a stepwise temperature increase.

Regional forest expansion in southeastern Australia occurred as early as 14,000 BP in wetter lowland areas, but later at higher altitudes. In drier areas, there is evidence for an increase in drier communities, including chenopodiaceous shrublands, between about 15,000 BP and 11000 BP before any forest expansion, suggesting a decrease in precipitation during this period. The most likely explanation for this decrease is that temperatures rose at a greater rate than precipitation, with the lag related to the slow rise in sea levels effectively reducing moisture levels. A similar explanation may account for reduced effective precipitation at a similar time in northeastern Australia and between about 13,000 BP and 11,500 BP in New Guinea.

Around 10,000 BP, all areas show further increases in temperature, precipitation, or both that resulted in expansion of forest vegetation. In southeast Australia, there is increasing evidence for the attainment of maximum Holocene temperature levels, possibly 1–2°C higher than those of today, between about 10,000 BP and 8,000 BP (Kershaw 1993). After this time, moisture levels peaked as a result of an absolute increase in precipitation, a decrease in temperature, or perhaps increased cloudiness that effectively reduced radiation and evaporation levels. The timing of this moisture peak appears regionally variable. In Tasmania, temperate rain forests achieved their maximum extent between 8,000 BP and 6,000 BP; in southeast mainland Australia, highest lake levels and maximum expansion of wet sclerophyll forest and rain forest occurred between about 7,000 BP and 5,000 BP. In New Guinea, the greatest development of forests occurred between 8,000 and 5,000 BP; in northeast Queensland, rain forest expansion is evident after 8,500 BP, reaching maximum extent between about 6,000 BP and 3,500 BP. Elsewhere in northern Australia, present-day conditions were established by about 7,000 BP.

REGIONAL TRANSITIONS: NEW GUINEA

We review two transitions in Papua New Guinea, the first in the highland valleys and the second in the large offshore islands to the east of New Guinea itself. In both cases, the separation of these areas from island Southeast Asia by a total absence of relevant data from

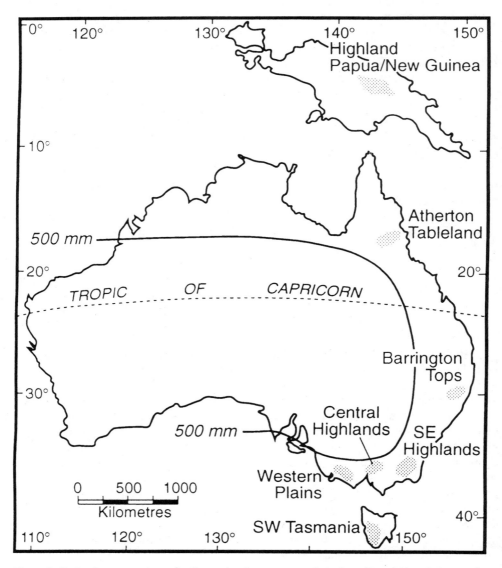

Figure 3. Regional concentrations of pollen and sedimentary records in Australia and New Guinea used to construct the climate curves in Figure 4.

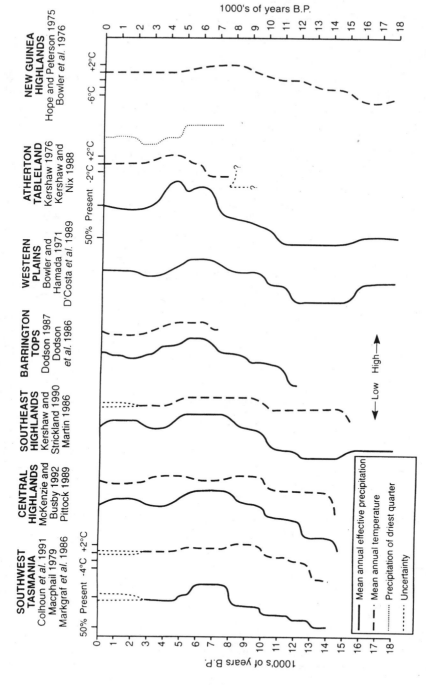

Figure 4. Best-estimate regional temperature and precipitation curves inferred from late Quaternary pollen and sedimentary records from Australia and New Guinea. Modified from McGlone et al. (1992).

West Irian hampers assessment of possible diffusions of ideas and technologies from the west. In both case study areas, however, researchers have steadily moved away from diffusionist explanations over recent decades.

Highlands (Figure 5)

Terminal Pleistocene assemblages show few major changes from the previous 10,000–20,000 years. Significant data points are often individual ones: claims for houses at Wañlek at 12,000–15,000 BP (Bulmer 1977:65) and at the Eastern Highlands site NFX at perhaps 18,000 BP (Watson and Cole 1978:35–40, 125, 132, 194–195); the claimed presence of pigs (certainly nonindigenous and probable reflectors of horticultural activities) at Kiowa and Yuku at 9,000–10,000 BP (Bulmer 1975:18–19; White and O'Connell 1982:187–189); marine shells transported inland more than 120 km to Kafiavana at 9,000 BP (White 1972:93). At the same time, from circa 14,000 BP onwards, new sites were occupied and previously occupied sites appear to have been more heavily used—or at least discard rates increased (Allen 1993:141). An older settlement pattern of occupying the midmontane

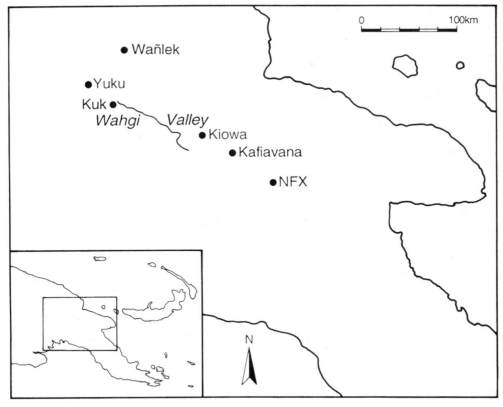

Figure 5. New Guinea Highlands sites mentioned in the text.

forests in order to access resources in higher- and lower-altitude areas may have been somewhat relaxed at this time, although the data are very unclear.

Despite sketchy data, some researchers now suggest that longer trajectories, still barely perceived in the archaeological record and as yet poorly understood, are more important than these terminal Pleistocene changes. New Guinean sites of this period away from the coast reflect the absence of large game animals and contain mainly rats, bats, reptiles, bandicoots, echidnas, and phalangers—none of which is much larger than a large domestic cat. It has long been recognized, however, that restricted availability of game is compensated by a large range of endemic edible plants. These plants include important plants of Gondwanaland origin and natural colonizations that occurred when the Australasian and Laurasian plates collided between 3 and 15 million years ago. Yen (1982, 1989, 1990, 1991), in particular, has elaborated the evidence that has altered the dominant view of a decade or so ago that the principal Melanesian food plants (pre– and post–established agriculture) had all been introduced by humans from Southeast Asia (see also Groube 1989:294). The food plants involved include a range of tubers, leaf vegetables, fruits, nuts, and the starchy pith of sago palms. Additionally, Golson (1989:678) has observed that since it was thought that Southeast Asia rice agriculture was preceded by the cultivation of such tubers and fruit and nut trees, the presence of these same species in Melanesia implied the diffusion of both the plants and associated horticultural practices. In short, however, both diffusionist aspects of the beginnings of New Guinean agriculture are now widely rejected in favor of the hypothesis of independent origins.

Botanical reconstructions thus now allow that incoming humans into the northern part of Greater Australia encountered familiar edible plant species, especially in coastal and lowland forests, and similar plants in the montane forests. Palynological evidence suggests human clearance of forest patches as early as 30,000 BP (G. S. Hope 1982), but it is uncertain whether this clearance reflects firing as a hunting technique or, alternatively, "wild plant-food production" as defined by Harris (1989). Large hafted stone tools found commonly in New Guinean sites from 40,000 BP onward have been interpreted by Groube (1989) as forest-clearance implements used to create open patches to facilitate and promote the useful food plants. In Kilu Cave in the northern Solomons Islands, to the east of New Guinea (see Figure 6), starch grains and crystalline raphides on stone tools indicate the processing of root vegetables and, in particular, the taro genus *Colocasia* at 29,000 BP (Wickler 1990:140). Arboriculture, often underrated in world views but still today a cornerstone of Melanesian agriculture, is reflected in the archaeological record by domesticated species of pandanus in the Highlands at 10,000 BP and domesticated species of the now-widespread food nut *Canarium* in the lowland Sepik-Ramu Basin by 14,000 BP (Yen 1990:262 and refs).

The agricultural transition in New Guinea, while coincident with the Pleistocene–Holocene transition, is thus seen as the intensification of long-term trajectories begun with initial colonization. At the same time, we are not looking at steady-state evolutionary growth in this period. By 9,000 BP, swamp agricultural systems involving both water retention and removal were in use in the Highlands Wahgi Valley at Kuk (Golson 1990) (see Figure 5). The structural features recorded there involve small basins interconnected with channels that are simpler than the uniform and linear features that overlie them. Golson suggests that these garden constructions allowed for varying soil and moisture requirements and thus the intercropping of various plant species.

Two important implications from the Kuk data are noted by Golson and others. First,

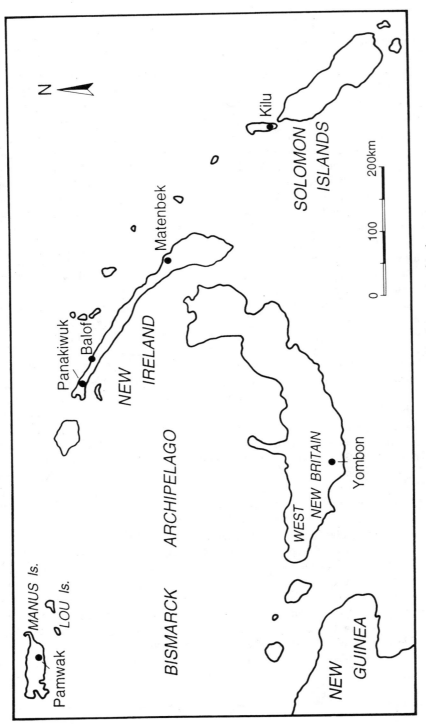

Figure 6. Melanesian islands sites and localities mentioned in the text.

swamp agriculture is often a part of a wider system that also involves extensive dry-land gardening on surrounding slopes, so that Kuk may be only the archaeologically visible tip of more widespread gardening in these Highlands valleys. Second, if Kuk at 9,000 BP is a product of intensifying the use of endemic New Guinean plant staples, then agriculture must have also been practiced at lower altitudes at this time, especially in the midaltitude regions, where, Yen (1982:292) suggests, many of the initial domestications occurred (although certainly not all [see Yen 1990:261]). That Kuk comes on line only at the time when the ameliorating climate first permits the cultivation of root crop staples such as taro at these higher altitudes is seen as no coincidence (Groube 1989:298).

To summarize: The case for independent origins of agriculture in New Guinea is strong. The endemic plant base was extensive geographically and varied in composition; meat protein away from the coast was likely to have been expensive in terms of caloric costs for hunters (for an ethnographic example that may have general comparability, see Dwyer 1974). Diffused agriculture from elsewhere, in terms of either the plant register or gardening technology (as far as the latter can be determined) was not necessary for agriculture to develop in New Guinea, nor is such diffusion reflected at the Pleistocene–Holocene transition (or earlier) in the archaeological record in any recognizable way. Later transfers (sometimes two-way) of plants and other things (genes, language, technology) between New Guinea and island Southeast Asia do not diminish the immediate argument. Climatic amelioration seems to be a primary basis for agricultural intensification in New Guinea at the Pleistocene–Holocene transition, but this brings us no closer to explaining why. Postulating demographic increase also begs the question. As in other parts of the world, we lack testable behavioral explanations to link climatic change as cause and agriculture as result.

We also need to note the important corollary: Although agriculture developed in fertile upland valleys of New Guinea as early as elsewhere in the world, the sometimes perceived inevitable consequences of agricultural development—cities, state formations, and central-ized authorities—did not. Explanations for this failure range from the inability to store, for any long time, an agricultural surplus of tubers or sago starch (except by maintaining large pig populations and converting this surplus to meat protein) to the significantly limiting controls on both demographic growth and local and long-distance population movement imposed by malaria, almost certainly from Pleistocene times onward (Groube 1993). Whether a lack of population pressure is a sufficient explanation for the subsequent inability of rice cereal agriculture (and the concomitant sociocultural forms it might have sustained) to spread into New Guinea from the adjacent islands of Southeast Asia is a question beyond our brief in this chapter.

Islands (Figure 6)

People crossed onto the large islands of New Britain and New Ireland immediately east of New Guinea some time before 36,000 BP and moved into zoologically more pauperate regions. Today, New Guinea is home to the following marsupial species: 2 anteaters, 4 tree kangaroos, 7 bandicoots, 9 wallabies, and 27 phalangers. These species diminish to 1 bandicoot, 1 wallaby, and 2 species of phalanger across this single water barrier (Brendan Marshall personal communication). Bird species across this gap reduce from 265 to 80 (Green 1991:494).

Compared with the trajectory toward more specialized and intensive subsistence activities in the Highlands, coastal groups may have been more mobile, geographically diffused, and broad-spectrum in their subsistence activities. Basic to this notion, late Pleistocene coastal and offshore canoe travel was likely neither infrequent nor haphazard. Manus Island is 200 km from its nearest neighbor island group, and its colonization necessitated the longest known sea voyage in Pleistocene history, where no land could be seen in any direction for 60–90 km. Irwin (1991, 1992) argues against the accidental colonization of Manus, but even allowing that initial settlement was accidental, from 12,000 BP onward, the archaeological record at Pamwak (Fredericksen et al. 1993) demonstrates both local and offshore sailing, the former to procure obsidian from Lou Island, 35 km to the south, and the latter to introduce a species of bandicoot and *Canarium* nuts from New Guinea. Similar sorts of evidence come from the cave site of Matenbek on southern New Ireland. There, at 20,000 BP, obsidian sourced to West New Britain was moved over a straight-line distance of 350 km. Since it probably traveled along coasts, across a 30-km water gap, and overland from source to site, the actual distance was likely significantly greater (Allen and Gosden in press; Summerhayes and Allen 1993). The same levels in Matenbek contain bones of another animal introduction to New Ireland, the phalanger.

Such data hint at an early development of low-level and generalized exchanges of food and raw materials to underwrite successful tropical foraging on islands with limited natural resources. In such a model, both a dependence on marine resources such as fish, shellfish, crustaceans, and turtle and access to coastal transport and communication may have kept people mainly coastal, with limited inland forays for hunting or to exploit stone sources.

The Pleistocene–Holocene transition is reflected here in a number of ways. The effects of changing resource location, accessibility, and centrality caused by sea-level rise are invoked as explanation for changes at Pamwak by Fredericksen et al. (1993:149–151), although they acknowledge that necessary complementary regional explanations of change are hampered by lack of data. On New Ireland, "inland" sites such as Panakiwuk and Balof (Marshall and Allen 1991; White et al. 1991) were initially but minimally used during the post glacial period from circa 14,000 BP onward, and another coastal site (Gosden and Robertson 1991) was reoccupied. The general implication is that there were more people in the Bismarcks at this time than earlier; at least, discard rates in the sites rose dramatically. Panakiwuk and Balof were most intensively occupied between circa 10,000 BP and circa 8,000 BP. In Panakiwuk, 70% of all artifacts were deposited in this period and marine shells occurred for the first time, indicating a significant change in site use that aligned it much more directly with coastal activities. In both sites, phalanger bones were discarded regularly for the first time, and further animal transpositions occurred, with the large rat, *Rattus praetor*, appearing at Panakiwuk and the thylogale, *Thylogale brunii*, appearing at Balof. In the midst of this activity, human occupation effectively ceased at Panakiwuk at 8,000 BP and diminished at Balof.

Between 9,000 BP and 6,000 BP, Matenbek deposits reflect much higher rates of deposition than in the underlying Pleistocene layers. Imported obsidian occurs in significantly greater amounts and supplants the use of local lithic materials in this site. Pig is present in the site shortly after 8,000 BP (Allen and Gosden in press). In the Solomons, the Kilu site was reoccupied circa 9,000 years ago, and domesticated species of *Canarium* occur from this time onward. A single phalanger bone from the site is the same age.

The transfer of nondomesticated animals into new habitats was relatively widespread in island Melanesia during the terminal Pleistocene–early Holocene (Allen 1993; Allen and Gosden in press; Flannery et al. 1988). The variation in both species and times of introduction argues that this was an accidental process rather than deliberate stocking of empty landscapes, with animals probably being moved as pets or to keep the meat fresh or for both reasons. The important point here is that the evidence of increasing transport of animals and obsidian and the spread of *Canarium* strongly implies that the early diffusion of lowlands agriculture into island Melanesia was both possible and probable. It provided the ability to maintain stable populations on islands with reduced natural resources, and it is no coincidence that smaller coral atolls in the region were occupied by the mid-Holocene. Unfortunately, prior to this period, our only archaeological windows are caves and rock shelters in which early indicators of agriculture exist only in the fauna, such as Matenbek pig, or in the stone and shell tools, such as the terminal Pleistocene edge-ground tools from Pamwak, seen as possible forest-clearance tools (Fredericksen et al 1993:150). On the larger islands during the Holocene, the use of these caves is much reduced and probably functionally different. While these changes suggest people moving to sedentary agricultural villages, so far we have only one open site in the islands older than the mid-Holocene, the quarry site of Yombon in west New Britain (Pavlides 1993; Pavlides and Gosden 1994).

REGIONAL TRANSITIONS: THE AUSTRALIAN MAINLAND

A Continent of Hunter–Gatherers

Before the arrival of European colonists 200 years ago, Australia remained the only continent without agriculturalists. Explanations for the failure of Aboriginal groups to invent or adopt agriculture—mostly untestable—have included a lack of suitable plant domesticates, poor soils and other environmental impediments, lack of contact with horticulturalists, deep cultural conservatism, no population pressure to induce subsistence intensification, a more plentiful supply of game, especially compared with New Guinea, general hunter–gatherer affluence, and cultural choice. Not all these explanations are mutually exclusive, and some subsume more particular explanations: The malaria thesis of Groube (1993), for example, argues that before the formation of the Arafura Sea–Torres Strait boundary, the plain linking New Guinea and north Australia may have formed a marked malaria gradient between the two, forming a zone that was largely depopulated. Thus, there existed between the two areas a parasitological boundary that was merely reinforced by the creation of the relatively trivial Holocene water barrier (Groube 1993:181–183). While this theory provides a reason for lack of contact rather than simply proposing it, none of these prime-mover explanations is without exceptions when viewed closely. Certain diffusions from Indonesia and across the Torres Strait did occur (Flood 1989:232–233). The provision of examples by Europeans for more than a century has also failed to persuade traditional Aboriginal groups of any virtues of agriculture (Chase 1989:51–53), even though many of the plants seen to be a sufficient basis for independent New Guinean horticulture are also endemic to north Australia (Golson 1971; Yen 1990). Jones and Meehan (1989) list in detail plants known to and used by the Gidjingali, an Arnhem Land coastal group, but note that some species that are agriculturally important in Southeast Asia and New Guinea are only marginally important to the Gidjingali. Plants available include yams, taro, wild rice, bush potato (*Ipomoea* spp.), Polynesian arrowroot, a wide variety of fruit and nut trees, and pith from palm trees. The Gidjingali detoxify some nuts such as cycads to remove neurotoxins and carcinogenic cycasin (Jones and Meehan 1989:123–124) and engage in other aspects of wild plant-food production, such as firing the landscape, replanting tubers, and loosening the soil. A second major set of potential domesticates, the grass seeds, will be looked at below.

The degree to which a lack of agricultural development and a lack of change in Australian lithic assemblages across the Pleistocene–Holocene boundary might be related has not been explored; no radical changes in stone tools take place in Australian mainland assemblages until widespread point and microlithic industries appear after 5,000 BP. Whether these industries developed independently or reflect diffusion from elsewhere is still uncertain. That diffusion contributed to change in the Holocene is best demonstrated by the introduction to Australia of the dingo, some time after 4,000 BP (Gollan 1982).

Coastal Responses (Figure 7)

In places around the Australian coast, the postglacial marine transgression reduced the width of the coastal plain by up to several hundred kilometers, thus presumably drowning

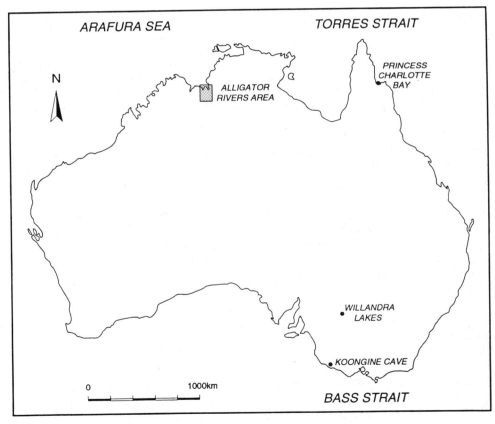

Figure 7. Australian sites and localities mentioned in the text.

many terminal Pleistocene sites in the process. This view has as its corollary a model of coastal dwellers retreating in the face of the inexorable rising seas. In a provocative counter-argument, Beaton (1985) suggested that continuously unstable sea levels prior to 6,000 BP may have resulted in a less productive coastal food base and many fewer coastal dwellers before stabilization. This model best fits coasts such as Beaton's research area at Princess Charlotte Bay, north Queensland, where the low gradient of the continental shelf resulted in extraordinary rates of shoreline displacement. Beaton (1985:12) cites geomorphologists suggesting extreme rates of 10–15 m per day in such locations in late Glacial times. Beaton argues that shell populations requiring calm and shallow waters above sandy or muddy floors could have developed only after sea-level stability was reached, and perhaps several millennia after, in the quantities required to provide a reliable food source. Beaton (1985:18) concedes that elsewhere where rocky platform gastropods predominate, such a lag may not have occurred. Those regions where the continental shelf was narrow must also have experienced different histories.

The main point, however, is that significant coastal realignments of human populations took place. Few reports of terminal Pleistocene–early Holocene sites near present coasts do not reflect or invoke as explanation the early Holocene marine transgression. Two examples must suffice. In the Alligator Rivers area on the western border of Arnhem Land, what had previously been inland river valleys were inundated between circa 8,000 BP, when seas were ≈12 m below their present height, and circa 6,800 BP. In the South Alligator, this new intertidal zone was rapidly colonized by a huge mangrove swamp, more than 80,000 hectares in area (Woodroffe et al. 1988:101), and similar transformations took place along the East Alligator River and the Magela Creek (Figure 8). Nearby rock shelters also containing Pleistocene deposits reflect these changes with upper intertidal species shell middens in their upper levels. The earliest dates for these middens match the chronology of environmental change well: 7,110 ± 130 BP at Nawamoyn, 5,980 ± 140 BP at Malangangerr, and 6,360 ± 100 BP at Malakunanja II (Gillespie and Temple 1977:34; Schrire 1983:85, 118). Woodroffe et al. (1988:98) report a buried midden scatter at Kapalka Landing, 62 km from the mouth of the South Alligator River, dated to 6,240 ± 100 BP. This site was within 300 m of the landward margin of mangrove forests circa 6,000 BP.

At the other end of the continent in South Australia, Frankel (1986:81–83) argues that Koongine Cave (see Figure 7), which had functioned in an inland economic system for 1,000–2,000 years, was abandoned circa 8,000 BP because a changing local environment associated with the approaching sea left the site between the focus of the inland economy, which had moved farther inland, and coastal camps, which would have been nearer the sea in coastal dunes.

Inland Responses

Inland, Pleistocene–Holocene transitions are also seen in terms of environmental change. Continent-wide models of arid-zone use by humans during the climatically fluctuating period from the last Glacial maximum until the late Holocene (O'Connor et al. 1993; Veth 1989) perhaps suffer from too little data, too few sites, and insufficient radiometric dating (Frankel 1993:27–29). In the absence of temporally limited lithic types and clear faunal changes, radiometric dating remains the primary organizing mechanism for Australian archaeology, but a survey of 149 Greater Australian Pleistocene sites by Smith and Sharp (1993:48) shows that fewer than 25% have more than 10 radiometric dates, while 40%

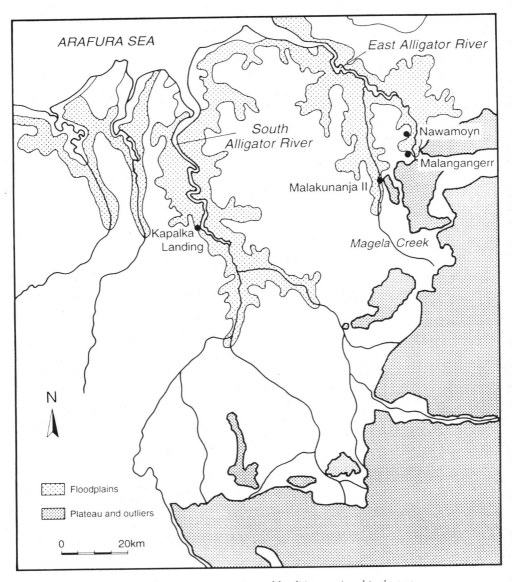

Figure 8. Alligator Rivers area sites and localities mentioned in the text.

have 3 or fewer dates. Despite the deficiencies of the data, O'Connor et al. (1993:102) find that after circa 15,000 BP, discard densities increase significantly in arid sites, and they suggest that populations increased and areas previously abandoned because of greater aridity at the glacial maximum were reoccupied.

The most concerted arid-area research has been carried out in western New South Wales, where various Pleistocene lake systems were fed by snow melt from the mountains to the east during the late Pleistocene. As Johnston (1993:197–198, 202) points out, the popular image of full lakes and abundant resources, both lacustrine (fish, shell fish, waterfowl) and terrestrial (kangaroos and other animals focused on the water source), may be distorted. However, freshwater mussel middens are common from 36,000 BP onward (J. Hope 1993). The Willandra Creek lake system (see Figures 7 and 9) is thought to have been completely dry at the height of the last Glacial and full between 16,000 BP and 15,000 BP before drying for the last time (Bowler 1980). In other "nearby" systems, 150–200 km away, lake-full conditions continued to 13,000 BP (J. Hope 1993:191). The unsurprising correlation between high lake levels and mussel midden accumulation episodes is quite clear, but, complementing this, when the lakes were dry, human use of the region appears to have been too infrequent to accumulate archaeological deposits. J. Hope (1993:194) argues on the basis of the radiocarbon dates that as the large lakes dried, people shifted their focus of activities to smaller lakes and the large rivers, where lowering discharge rates allowed easier access to riverine mussels and concomitant resources.

The division between large lake and riverine shell middens is emphasized by the distribution of grindstones in these sites. Balme (1991:6) recorded grindstones at only 1 of 14 lake sites, but at 27 of 33 riverine sites of terminal Pleistocene age. While Balme argues that these grindstones might be later Holocene artifacts, J. Hope (1993:194) proposes that their frequency at these sites equally suggests that they are Pleistocene in age. Grindstones dated between 15,000 BP and 12,000 BP were previously claimed for the Willandra by Allen (1972), who saw them as seed grinders that reflected the intensification of seed processing in the terminal Pleistocene. Allen (1990) is now more equivocal about the data and this interpretation. Elsewhere in Australia, expedient grindstones have been recorded in Pleistocene contexts (Smith 1986:37).

The intensive use of a wide range of tree and grass seeds in arid and semiarid Australia is widely recorded (for a summary see Smith 1986). Processes of intensification such as broadcasting seed, introducing seed to new areas, damming streams to flood wider areas, and storing seed against shortage indicate the importance of seed processing. Of 140 food plant species in central Australia, 50% are collected for their seeds (Latz 1982; Smith 1986:30). Smith (1986) argues, however, that the intensive patterns of seed use recorded ethnographically can be traced back only to 3,000–4,000 BP, before which grindstones lack the specialization of ethnographic seed grinders; he thus rejects a late Pleistocene development of "seed-gathering economies" as a response to increasing aridity circa 15,000 BP (Smith 1986:29), although he allows that seed processing may have been a component of terminal Pleistocene subsistence activities (Smith 1986:37). For the Willandra case, J. Hope (1993:195) points out that the grindstones were imported over distances of 50–300 km and concludes that uses apart from seed grinding that could account for the large numbers of these tools are not obvious. Overall, it seems likely that the intensive and elaborate seed-processing activities of the late Holocene have their antecedents in the simpler but no less important adjustments to changing resource availability that were made at the Pleistocene–Holocene transition.

REGIONAL TRANSITIONS: TASMANIA

Southern Tasmania divides into two distinct ecological zones: in the west, a fold-structured geology underlies temperate rain forest; in the east, dry sclerophyll vegetation grows on a fault-structured geology. During the terminal Pleistocene in the west, herbfields

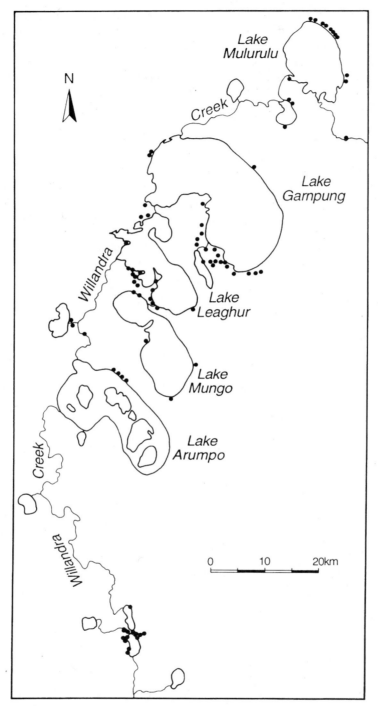

Figure 9. Pleistocene Willandra Lakes system, western New South Wales, showing shell midden locations recorded by Clark (1987).

and grasslands on limestone valley soils were increasingly invaded by tree and shrub species, while the climate was warmer and more moist than at the glacial maximum. In the east at this time, rainfall was lower and sand dune development took place (Cosgrove et al. 1990:60–62). There is a clear division between archaeological sites across southern Tasmania, with no Pleistocene sites yet found in the southeast and no early to mid-Holocene sites in the southwest.

At ≈43°S, Tasmania represents the southern edge of late Pleistocene human expansion, with occupation of the limestone valleys of southwest Tasmania by 35,000 BP. The presumed seasonal use of valley caves was maintained in this periglacial region throughout the glacial maximum. The climate was drier than today, but mean average annual temperature was likely only ≈0–4°C at this time. A number of caves, excavated in the last decade, are very rich in lithics and faunal remains (Figure 10). These sites have allowed initial regional paleoecological reconstructions of the prehistory of this period that are more detailed than those permitted by the Pleistocene data base elsewhere in Australia (Cosgrove et al. 1990; McNiven et al. 1993).

It is envisaged that the climatic amelioration that accompanied the Pleistocene–Holocene transition in Tasmania was more dramatic than in most other parts of Australia. Permanent ice on the highest mountains disappeared, as did glaciers in the higher valleys. In the southwest, temperate rain forest moved out of lower refuges into higher elevations. Almost all excavated sites in this region reflect increased deposition rates beginning circa 17,000–16,000 BP. The nature of deposition also seems to change. The more intact faunal remains at this time might merely be reflecting more rapid deposition. In the lithics, however, distinctive small circular tools labeled thumbnail scrapers, unlike anything in contemporary mainland assemblages, are ubiquitous in this period, and Darwin glass, an impactite with restricted distribution in the west, occurs in sites in straight-line distances of up to 100 km from source. The earlier view was that since these two elements appeared unexpectedly and simultaneously at 17,000 BP at Kutikina (Kiernan et al. 1983), they might reflect a general cultural replacement at this time (Jones 1990:281). The situation is now understood to be more complicated: While they occur infrequently and separately at various sites some millennia before the glacial maximum (Cosgrove et al. 1990:71), nonetheless there is no doubt that the peak frequency of these items is after 17,000 BP.

Paradoxically, in the midst of this heightened activity, occupation at all sites so far excavated ceased before circa 12,000 BP. Various explanations involving changed land-use patterns and a transfer from cave to open sites have been proposed (McNiven et al. 1993:218; Thomas 1993), but no open sites of the relevant age have yet been found, despite efforts to do so (Cosgrove et al. 1994). Most parsimoniously, it seems probable that as the encroaching rain forest drove out the game, so did humans abandon the region. The amelioration of glacial–arid conditions farther east may have meant that transferring activities out of the southwest was the most efficient response. Late Holocene and ethnographic incursions into the fringes of the southwest (Freslov 1993; Freslov personal communication on chronology) do not detract from the fact that southwest Tasmania is possibly the only region of its size (≈20,000 km^2) anywhere in the world to be occupied by humans throughout the terminal Pleistocene and abandoned during the Holocene.

In the central northern Forth River Valley, recent excavations of the Parmerprar Meethenar rock shelter by Cosgrove and Murray have produced the only Tasmanian sequence so far that spans the Pleistocene–Holocene transition. At this site, the terminal Pleistocene layers reflect the southwestern sequence just described, in terms of the presence

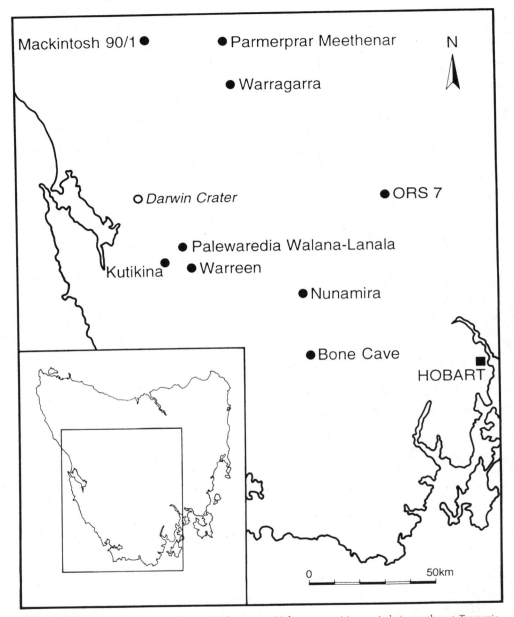

Figure 10. Cave sites of the Pleistocene and Pleistocene–Holocene transition periods in southwest Tasmania.

of many thumbnail scrapers, although the site lacks Darwin glass and the faunal suite may be different (Cosgrove and Murray personal communication). Deposition rates at the site fall dramatically after 12,000 BP, and the thumbnail scraper as a type disappears. Deposition rates do not increase until the late Holocene. In an adjacent valley, the site of Warragarra was under ice until circa 9,000 BP, after which its occupation profile mirrors that at Parmerprar Meethenar (Lourandos 1983).

Subsequent to being isolated from the Australian mainland by the marine transgression, Tasmanian prehistory took a necessarily different trajectory through the Holocene. Tasmanians were the only significant human group on earth who existed for 12,000 years without external contact. When reunited with the world by European colonial expansion at the end of the 18th century, they differed from mainland Aborigines in respect of language, diet, and material culture.

CONCLUSIONS

This review suggests the following conclusions:

1. While a precise boundary between the Pleistocene and Holocene at, say, 10,000 BP is unwarranted, significant geomorphological and climatic changes took place between 15,000 BP and 7,000 BP that altered human behavioral patterns in most locations in Greater Australia and caused significant disruptions of or changes in human lifeways in some places.

2. The physical changes in each of the three major landmasses may have intensified, rather than provoked, differences in human trajectories in the three areas. In other words, long-term patterns of behavior show adaptations that reflect ecosystemic differences among these three areas before the Pleistocene–Holocene transition, some of which were accentuated by the transition. This explanation seems clearest for the move to agriculture in New Guinea, less clear but apparent in some of the Australian examples, and least clear in Tasmania, where the extent of ecological change was perhaps greatest in local terms and where choices for human response were perhaps most restricted.

3. Change in socioeconomic systems in all areas was more gradual than revolutionary, although transformations occurred. Agricultural intensification at Kuk at 9,000 BP is one such transformation; the abandonment of southwest Tasmania over circa 2,000 years probably represents another, but currently we do not have sufficient information about the ways in which people there responded to the environmental shift to temperate rain forest.

4. The north–south gradient of degree of change might be viewed as a gradient of the possibilities of agricultural intensification, but this seems too gross a simplification. The Holocene histories of New Guinea, Australia, and Tasmania also present a gradient of increasing isolation from north to south that might imply a concomitant social conservatism, but the surviving material culture, including rock art, informs such matters little, if at all.

5. Hovering over all this are questions of demographic increase that have interested most Australian archaeologists over the last 20 years but are equally elusive in the archaeological record. If numbers of contemporaneous sites and rates of discard equal people, then increases in the numbers of people through the Pleistocene–Holocene transition (and into the late Holocene) take place in most regions for which data exist. Again, this growth seems gradual, and seems as much the effect of the changes we can recognize as the cause of them.

REFERENCES

Allen, H., 1972, *Where the Crow Flies Backwards: Man and Land in the Darling Basin*. Unpublished Ph.D. thesis. Canberra: Department of Prehistory, Research School of Pacific Studies, Australian National University.

Allen, H., 1990, Environmental history in southwestern New South Wales during the Pleistocene, in: *The World at 18,000 BP*, Volume 2, *Low Latitudes* (C. Gamble and O. Soffer, eds.), Unwin Hyman, London, pp. 296–321.

Allen, J., 1993, Notions of the Pleistocene in Greater Australia, in: *A Community of Culture: The People and Prehistory of the Pacific*, Occasional Papers in Prehistory, No. 21, (M. Spriggs, D. E. Yen, W. Ambrose, R. Jones, A. Thorne, and A. Andrews, eds.), Department of Prehistory, Research School of Pacific Studies, Australian National University, Canberra, pp. 139–151.

Allen, J., and Gosden, C., in press, Spheres of Interaction and Integration: Modeling the Culture History of the Bismarck Archipelago, in: *Pacific Culture History: Essays in Honour of Roger Green* (J. Davidson, G. Irwin, and A. Pawley, eds.).

Ballard, C., 1993, Stimulating Minds to Fantasy? A critical etymology for Sahul, in: *Sahul in Review*, Occasional Papers in Prehistory, No. 24 (M. A. Smith, M. Spriggs, and B. Fankhauser, eds.), Research School of Pacific Studies, Australian National University, Canberra, pp. 17–23.

Balme, J., 1991, The Antiquity of Grinding Stones in Semi-Arid Western New South Wales, *Australian Archaeology* 32:3–9.

Beaton, J. M., 1985, Evidence for a Coastal Occupation Time-Lag at Princess Charlotte Bay (North Queensland) and Implications for Coastal Colonization and Population Growth Theories for Aboriginal Australia, *Archaeology in Oceania* 20(1):1–20.

Bowler, J., 1980, Quaternary Chronology and Palaeohydrology in the Evaluation of Mallee Landscapes, in: *Aeolian Landscapes in the Semi-arid Zone of South Eastern Australia* (R. R. Storrier and M. E. Stannard, eds.), Australian Society of Soil Science, Wagga Wagga, pp. 17–36.

Bowler, J. M., and Hamada, T., 1971, Late Quaternary Stratigraphy and Radio Carbon Chronology of Water Level Fluctuations in Lake Keilambete, Victoria, *Nature* 232:330–332.

Bowler, J. M., Hope, G. S., Jennings, J. N., Singh, G., and Walker, D., 1976, Late Quaternary Climates of Australia and New Guinea, *Quaternary Research* 6:359–394.

Bulmer, S., 1975, Settlement and Economy in Prehistoric Papua New Guinea: A Review of the Archaeological Evidence, *Journal de la Société des Océanistes* 31:7–75.

Bulmer, S., 1977, Between the Mountain and the Plain: Prehistoric Settlement and Environment in the Kaironk Valley, in: *The Melanesian Environment* (J. H. Winslow, ed.), Australian National University Press, Canberra, pp. 61–73.

Chappell, J., and Shackleton, N. J., 1986, Oxygen Isotopes and Sea Level, *Nature* 324:137–140.

Chase, A. K., 1989, Domestication and Domiculture in Northern Australia: A Social Perspective, in: *Foraging and Farming: The Evolution of Plant Exploitation* (D. R. Harris and G. C. Hillman, eds.), Unwin Hyman, London, pp. 42–75.

Clark, P. M., 1987, Willandra Lakes World Heritage Area Archaeological Resource Study, unpublished report to the New South Wales Department of Planning and the Western Lands Commission.

Colhoun, E. A., van de Geer, G., and Fitzsimons, S. J., 1991, Late Glacial and Holocene Vegetation History at Governor Bog, King Valley, Western Tasmania, Australia, *Journal of Quaternary Science* 6:55–66.

Cosgrove, R., Allen, J., and Marshall, B., 1990, Palaeo-ecology and Pleistocene human occupation in south central Tasmania, *Antiquity* 64(242):59–78.

Cosgrove, R., Allen, J., and Marshall, B., 1994, Late Pleistocene Human Occupation in Tasmania: A Reply to Thomas, *Australian Archaeology* 38:28–35.

D'Costa, D. M., Edney, P., Kershaw, A. P., and DeDeckker, P., 1989, Late Quaternary Palaeoecology of Tower Hill, Victoria, Australia, *Journal of Biogeography* 16:461–482.

Dodson, J. R., 1987, Mire Development and Environmental Change, Barrington Tops, New South Wales, *Quaternary Research* 27:561–585.

Dodson, J. R., Greenwood, P. W., and Jones, R. L., 1986, Holocene Forest and Wetland Dynamics at Barrington Tops, New South Wales, *Journal of Biogeography* 15:589–602.

Dwyer, P. D., 1974, The price of protein: Five Hundred Hours of Hunting in the New Guinea Highlands, *Oceania* 44(4):278–293.

Flannery, T. F., Kirch, P. V., Specht, J., and Spriggs, M., 1988, Holocene Mammal Faunas from Archaeological Sites in Island Melanesia, *Archaeology in Oceania* 23(3):89–94.

Flood, J., 1989, *Archaeology of the Dreamtime* (Revised Edition 1989). Collins, Sydney.

Frankel, D., 1986, Excavations in the Lower Southeast of South Australia: November 1985, *Australian Archaeology* 22:75–87.

Frankel, D., 1993, Pleistocene chronological structures and explanations: A Challenge, in: *Sahul in Review* (M. A. Smith, M. Spriggs, and B. Fankhauser, eds.), Occasional Papers in Prehistory, No. 24, Department of Prehistory, Research School of Pacific Studies, Australian National University, Canberra, pp. 24–33.

Fredricksen, C., Spriggs, M., and Ambrose, W., 1993, Pamwak Rockshelter: A Pleistocene Site on Manus Island, Papua New Guinea, in: *Sahul in Review* (M. A. Smith, M. Spriggs, and B. Fankhauser, eds.), Occasional Papers in Prehistory, No. 24, Department of Prehistory, Research School of Pacific Studies, Australian National University, Canberra, pp. 144–152.

Freslov, J., 1993, The Role of Open Sites in the Investigation of Pleistocene Phenomena in the Inland Southwest of Tasmania, in: *Sahul in Review*, Occasional Papers in Prehistory, No. 24 (M. A. Smith, M. Spriggs, and B. Fankhauser, eds.), Department of Prehistory, Research School of Pacific Studies, Australian National University, Canberra, pp. 233–239.

Gillespie, R., and Temple, R. B., 1977, Radiocarbon Dating of Shell Middens, *Archaeology and Physical Anthropology in Oceania* 12(1):26–37.

Gollan, J. K., 1982, *Prehistoric Dingo*, unpublished Ph.D. thesis, Department of Prehistory, Research School of Pacific Studies, Australian National University, Canberra.

Golson, J., 1971, Australian Aboriginal Food Plants: Some Ecological and Culture–Historical Implications, in: *Aboriginal Man and Environment in Australia* (D. J. Mulvaney and J. Golson, eds.), Australian National University Press, Canberra, pp. 196–238.

Golson, J., 1989, The Origins and Development of New Guinea Agriculture, in: *Foraging and Farming: The Evolution of Plant Exploitation* (D. R. Harris and G. C. Hillman, eds.), London, Unwin Hyman, pp. 678–687.

Golson, J., 1990, Kuk and the Development of Agriculture in New Guinea: Retrospection and Introspection, in: *Pacific Production Systems: Approaches to Economic Prehistory—Papers from a Symposium at the XVth Pacific Science Congress, Dunedin, New Zealand, 1983*, Occasional Papers in Prehistory, No. 18 (D. E. Yen and J. M. J. Mummery, eds.), Department of Prehistory, Research School of Pacific Studies, Australian National University, Canberra, pp. 139–147.

Gosden, C., and Robertson, N., 1991, Models for Matenkupkum: Interpreting a late Pleistocene Site from Southern New Ireland, Papua New Guinea, in: *Report of the Lapita Homeland Project*, Occasional Papers in Prehistory, No. 20 (J. Allen and C. Gosden, eds.), Department of Prehistory, Research School of Pacific Studies, Australian National University, Canberra, pp. 20–45.

Green, R. C., 1991, Near and Remote Oceania—disestablishing "Melanesia" in culture history, in: *Man and A Half: Essays in Pacific Anthropology and Ethnobiology in Honour of Ralph Bulmer*, The Polynesian Society Memoirs, No. 48 (A. Pawley, ed.), The Polynesian Society, Auckland, pp. 491–502.

Groube, L., 1989, The taming of the rain forests: A model for late Pleistocene forest exploitation in New Guinea, in: *Foraging and Farming: The Evolution of Plant Exploitation* (D. R. Harris and G. C. Hillman, eds.), Unwin Hyman, pp. 292–317.

Groube, L., 1993, Contradictions and Malaria in Melanesian and Australian Prehistory, in: *A Community of Culture: The People and Prehistory of the Pacific* (M. Spriggs, D. E. Yen, W. Ambrose, R. Jones, A. Thorne, and A. Andrews, eds.), Occasional Papers in Prehistory, No. 21, Canberra: Department of Prehistory, Research School of Pacific Studies, Australian National University, Canberra, pp. 164–186.

Harris, D. R., 1989, An Evolutionary Continuum of People–Plant Interaction, in: *Foraging and Farming: The Evolution of Plant Exploitation* (D. R. Harris and G. C. Hillman, eds.), Unwin Hyman, London, pp. 11–26.

Hope, G. S., 1982, Pollen from Archaeological Sites: A Comparison of Swamp and Open Archaeological Site Pollen Spectra at Kosipe Mission, Papua New Guinea, in: *Archaeometry: An Australian Perspective* (W. Ambrose and P. Duerden, eds.), Department of Prehistory, Research School of Pacific Studies, Australian National University, Canberra, pp. 211–219.

Hope, G. S., and Peterson, J. A., 1975, Glaciation and Vegetation in the High New Guinea Mountains, *Bulletin of the Royal Society of New Zealand*, 13:155–162.

Hope, J., 1993, Pleistocene Archaeological Sites in the Central Murray–Darling Basin, in: *Sahul in Review* (M. A. Smith, M. Spriggs, and B. Fankhauser, eds.), Occasional Papers in Prehistory, No. 24, Department of Prehistory, Research School of Pacific Studies, Australian National University, Canberra, pp. 183–196.

Irwin, G., 1991, Pleistocene Voyaging and the Settlement of Greater Australia and its Near Oceanic Neighbours, in: *Report of the Lapita Homeland Project* (J. Allen and C. Gosden, eds.), Occasional Papers 20, Department of Prehistory, Research School of Pacific Studies, Australian National University, Canberra, pp. 9–19.

Irwin, G., 1992, *The Prehistoric Exploration and Colonisation of the Pacific*, Cambridge University Press, Cambridge.

Johnston, H., 1993, Pleistocene Shell Middens of the Willandra Lakes, in: *Sahul in Review*, Occasional Papers in Prehistory, No. 24 (M. A. Smith, M. Spriggs, and B. Fankhauser, eds.), Department of Prehistory, Research School of Pacific Studies, Australian National University, Canberra, pp. 197–203.

Jones, R., 1990, From Kakadu to Kutikina: the southern continent at 18,000 years ago, in: *The World at 18,000 BP: Volume 2, Low Latitudes*, Unwin Hyman, London, pp. 264–295.

Jones, R., and Meehan, B., 1989, Plant Foods of the Gidjingali: Ethnographic and Archaeological Perspectives from Northern Australia on Tuber and Seed Exploitation, in: *Foraging and Farming: The Evolution of Plant Exploitation* (D. R. Harris and G. C. Hillman, eds.), Unwin Hyman, London, pp. 120–135.

Kershaw, A. P., 1976, A Late Pleistocene and Holocene Pollen Diagram from Lynch's Carter, Northeast Queensland, Australia, *New Phytologist* 77:469–498.

Kershaw, A. P., 1993, Quantitative Palaeoclimatic Estimates from Bioclimatic Analyses of Taxa Recorded in Pollen Diagrams, *Quaternary Australasia* 11(1):61–64.

Kershaw, A. P., and Nix, H. A., 1988, Quantitative Paleoclimatic Estimates from Pollen Taxa Using Bioclimatic Profiles of Extent Taxa, *Journal of Biogeography* 15:589–602.

Kershaw, A. P., and Strickland, K. M. 1989, The Development of Alpine Vegetation on the Australian Mainland, *The Scientific Significance of the Australian Alps* (R. Good, ed.), Australian Academy of Science, Canberra, pp. 113–126.

Kiernan, K., Jones, R., and Ranson, D., 1983, New evidence from Fraser Cave for glacial age man in Southwest Tasmania, *Nature* 301:28–32.

Latz, P. K., 1982, Bushfires and Bushtucker: Aborigines and Plants in Central Australia, Unpublished M.A. thesis, University of New England, Armindall, New South Wales.

Lourandos, H., 1983, 10,000 Years in the Tasmanian Highlands, *Australian Archaeology* 16:39–47.

Macphail, M. K., 1979, Vegetation and Climates in Southern Tasmania since the Last Glaciation, *Quaternary Research* 11:306–341.

Markgraf, V., Bradbury, J. P., and Busby, J. R., 1986, Palaeoclimates in Southwestern Tasmania during the Last 13,000 Years, *Palaios* 1:368–380.

Markgraf, V., Dodson, J. R., Kershaw, A. P., McGlone, M. S., and Nicholls, N., 1992, Evolution of Late Pleistocene and Holocene Climates in the Circum-Pacific Land Areas, *Climate Dynamics* 6:193–211.

Marshall, B., and Allen, J., 1991, Excavations in Panakiwuk Cave, New Ireland, in: *Report of the Lapita Homeland Project*, Occasional Papers 20 (J. Allen and C. Gosden, eds.), Department of Prehistory, Research School of Pacific Studies, Australian National University, Canberra, pp. 59–91.

Martin, A. R. H., 1986, Late Glacial and Holocene Alpine Pollen Diagrams from the Kosciusco National Park, New South Wales, Australia. *Review of Palaeobotany and Palynology* 47:367–409.

McGlone, M. S., Kershaw, A. P., and Markgraf, V., 1992, El Niño/Southern Oscillation Climatic Variability in Australasian and South American Palaeoenvironmental Records, in: *El Niño: Historical and Palaeoclimatic Aspects of the Southern Oscillation* (H. F. Diaz and V. Markgraf, eds.), Cambridge University Press, Cambridge, pp. 435–462.

McKenzie, G. M., and Busby, J. R., 1992, A Quantitative Estimate of Holocene Climate Using a Bioclimatic Profile of *Nothofagus cunninghamii* (Hook) Oerst., *Journal of Biogeography* 19:531–540.

McNiven, I., Marshall, B., Allen, J., Stern, N., and Cosgrove, R., 1993, The Southern Forests Archaeological Project: An Overview, in: *Sahul in Review*, Occasional Papers in Prehistory, No. 24 (M. A. Smith, M. Spriggs, and B. Fankhauser, eds.), Department of Prehistory, Research School of Pacific Studies, Australian National University, Canberra, pp. 213–224.

O'Connor, S., Veth, S., and Hubbard, N., 1993, Changing Interpretations of Postglacial Human Subsistence and Demography in Sahul, in: *Sahul in Review*, Occasional Papers in Prehistory, No. 24 (M. A. Smith, M. Spriggs, and B. Fankhauser, eds.), Department of Prehistory, Research School of Pacific Studies, Australian National University, Canberra, pp. 95–105.

Pardoe, C., 1993, The Pleistocene Is Still with us: Analytical Constraints and Possibilities for the Study of Ancient Human Remains in Archaeology, in: *Sahul in Review*, Occasional Papers in Prehistory, No. 24 (M. A. Smith, M. Spriggs, and B. Fankhauser, eds.), Department of Prehistory, Research School of Pacific Studies, Australian National University, Canberra, pp. 81–94.

Pavlides, C., 1993, New Archaeological Research at Yombon, West New Britain, Papua New Guinea, *Archaeology in Oceania* 28:55–59.

Pavlides, C., and Gosden, C., 1994, 35,000-Year-Old Sites in the Rainforests of West New Britain, Papua New Guinea, *Antiquity* 68:604–610.

Pittock, J., 1989, *Palaeoenvironments of the Mt. Disappointment Plateau (Kinglake West, Victoria) from the Late Pleistocene.* Unpublished B.Sc. (Hons) Thesis, Department of Geography and Environmental Science, Monash University, Melbourne.

Ross, A., Donnelly, T., and Wasson, R., 1992, The Peopling of the Arid Zone: Human–Environment Interactions, *The Naive Lands* (J. Dodson, ed.), Longman Cheshire, Melbourne, pp. 76–114.

Schrire, C., 1983, *The Alligator Rivers: Prehistory and Ecology in Western Arnhem Land*, Terra Australis 7, Canberra: Department of Prehistory, Research School of Pacific Studies, Australian National University.

Smith, M. A., 1986, The Antiquity of Seedgrinding in Central Australia, *Archaeology in Oceania* 21(1):29–39.

Smith, M. A., and Sharp, N. D., 1993, Pleistocene Sites in Australia, New Guinea and Island Melanesia: Geographic and Temporal Structure of the Archaeological Record, in: *Sahul in Review*, Occasional Papers in Prehistory, No. 24, (M. A. Smith, M. Spriggs, and B. Fankhauser, eds.), Department of Prehistory, Research School of Pacific Studies, Australian National University, Canberra, pp. 37–59.

Summerhayes, G., and Allen, J., 1993, The Transport of Mopir Obsidian to Pleistocene New Ireland, *Archaeology in Oceania* 29(3):144–148.

Thomas, I., 1993, Late Pleistocene Environments and Aboriginal Settlement Patterns in Tasmania, *Australian Archaeology* 36:1–11.

Torgerson, T., Luly, J., De Decker, P., Jones, M. R., Searle, D. E., Chivas, A. R., and Ullman, W. J., 1988, Late Quaternary Environments of the Carpentaria Basin, Australia, *Palaeogeography, Palaeoclimatology, Palaeoecology* 67:245–261.

Veth, P., 1989, Islands in the Interior: A Model for the Colonization of Australia's Arid Zone, *Archaeology in Oceania* 24(3):81–92.

Wasson, R., 1989, Desert dune-building, dust raising and palaeoclimate in the Southern Hemisphere during the last 280,000 years, in: *CLIMANZ 3* (T. Donnelly and R. Wasson, eds.), Canberra, CSIRO, pp. 123–137.

Watson, V. D., and Cole, J. D., 1978, *Prehistory of the Eastern Highlands of New Guinea*, Australian National University Press, Canberra.

White, J. P., 1972, *Ol Tumbuna*, Terra Australis 2, Department of Prehistory, Research School of Pacific Studies, Australian National University, Canberra.

White, J. P., and O'Connell, J. F., 1982, *A Prehistory of Australia, New Guinea and Sahul*, Academic Press, Sydney.

White, J. P., Flannery, T. F., O'Brien, R., Hancock, R. V., and Pavlish, L., 1991, The Balof Shelters, New Ireland, in: *Reports of the Lapita Homeland Project*, Occasional Papers 20, (J. Allen and C. Gosden, eds.), Department of Prehistory, Research School of Pacific Studies, Australian National University, Canberra, pp. 46–58.

Wickler, S., 1990, Prehistoric Melanesian Exchange and Interaction: Recent Evidence from the Northern Solomon Islands, *Asian Perspectives* 29(2):135–154.

Woodroffe, C. D., Chappell, J., and Thom, B. G., 1988, Shell Middens in the Context of Estuarine Development, South Alligator River, Northern Territory, *Archaeology in Oceania* 23(3):95–103.

Yen, D. E., 1982, The History of Cultivated Plants, in: *Melanesia: Beyond Diversity*, Vol. 1 (R. J. May and H. Nelson, eds.), Department of Prehistory, Research School of Pacific Studies, Australian National University, Canberra, pp. 281–295.

Yen, D. E., 1989, The Domestication of Environment, in: *Foraging and Farming: The Evolution of Plant Exploitation* (D. R. Harris and G. C. Hillman, eds.), Unwin Hyman, London, pp. 55–75.

Yen, D. E., 1990, Environment, Agriculture and the Colonisation of the Pacific, in: *Pacific Production Systems: Approaches to Economic Prehistory. Papers from a Symposium at the XVth Pacific Science Congress, Dunedin, New Zealand, 1983*, Occasional Papers in Prehistory, No. 18 (D. E. Yen and J. M. J. Mummery, eds.), Department of Prehistory, Research School of Pacific Studies, Australian National University, Canberra, pp. 258–277.

Yen, D. E., 1991, Domestication: The lessons from New Guinea, in: *Man and a Half: Essays in Pacific Anthropology and Ethnobiology in Honour of Ralph Bulmer*, The Polynesian Society Memoir No. 48 (A. Pawley, ed.), The Polynesian Society, Auckland, pp. 558–569.

Chapter **10**

Human Activities and Environmental Changes during the Late Pleistocene to Middle Holocene in Southern Thailand and Southeast Asia

SURIN POOKAJORN

LOCATION AND GEOLOGICAL SETTING OF THE SITES

The Pleistocene–Holocene transition is best known in southern (peninsular) Thailand from two cave sites, one in the coastal lowlands and the other at a higher elevation in the interior. The first, Moh Khiew Cave, is situated in an isolated hill of Permian limestone in northern Krabi Province, southern Thailand (Figure 1). It is located about 10 m above mean sea level. In front of the cave, there is a small stream, Klong Krabi Noi, running north–south toward the sea, which is about 13 km from the site. The area surrounding the hill is covered with Quaternary sediments. The cave resembles a rock shelter, measuring 3 m wide by 30 m long, with its axis lying in an east–west direction. The cave entrance faces northward, and the entire area can be divided into three sections:

- The first section is the widest part of the rock shelter.
- The second section is a chamber, east of the first section, with an area of 9 m².
- The third section is a chamber, west of the first section, measuring about 12 m².

SURIN POOKAJORN • Faculty of Archaeology, Silpakorn University, Bangkok 10200, Thailand.

Humans at the End of the Ice Age: The Archaeology of the Pleistocene–Holocene Transition, edited by Lawrence Guy Straus, Berit Valentin Eriksen, Jon M. Erlandson, and David R. Yesner. Plenum Press, New York, 1996.

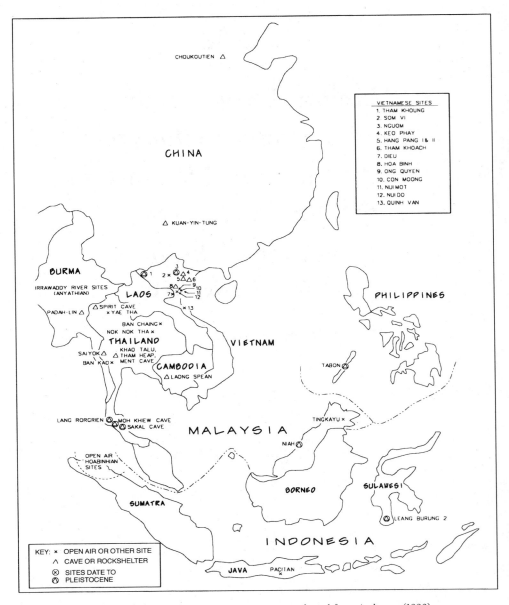

Figure 1. Archaeological sites of Southeast Asia. Adapted from Anderson (1990).

The area of Moh Khiew Cave has been severely disturbed by the villagers, who have collected the surface soil to be used as fertilizer. This cave was excavated to a depth of about 410 cm below the present surface.

Sakai Cave is situated in Palian district, Trang Province (Figure 1). It is in fact a rock shelter located in a limestone range, about 200 m above sea level. The depth of the cave is 5–9 m, and the ceiling height is about 8 m. The length from north to south is about 31 m. Near the entrance of the rock shelter, the ground surface slopes up at 35–40°. The nearest stream is about 200 m to the north of the rock shelter. Because the Sakai group uses this cave as a shelter, frequenting it only once a year during the rainy season, there are scattered fireplaces on the cave floor. Next to every hearth is a pallet about 10 cm high on which the inhabitants sit or lie. Given the size of the rock shelter, it is habitable by about 15–20 people. This cave was excavated to a depth of circa 175 cm below the present cave floor (Chaimanee 1994; Pookajorn 1991; Sinsakul 1994).

ARCHAEOLOGICAL CONTENT OF MOH KHIEW CAVE

The cultural deposit of Moh Khiew Cave can be divided into five levels. They are discussed in the following sections in order from bottom to top.

First Cultural Level

This level is predominantly characterized by the appearance of unifacial and bifacial core tools, made both by direct hard hammer percussion and by indirect percussion with bone punch. The number of stone tools of both techniques is 102, while 721 fragments of flake tools and 367 waste flakes were also found. The results of functional morphological analysis and microwear analysis show that most of the tools from Level 1 were used not only for direct hunting of large animals (Table 1) such as *Babalus bubalis* linneaus (Lekagul and McNeely 1989), *Sus* sp., and *Muntiacus muntjak*, but also for woodworking or making wooden traps for catching small animals such as *Presbytis* sp., *Macaca* sp., *Aonyx cinera*,

Table 1.   List of Faunal Remains from Moh Khiew Cave, 1991

1. *Babalus bubalis* kinnaeus	Wild water buffalo	14. *Arctogalidia trivirgata*	Civet
2. *Sus* sp.	Wild pig	15. *Callosciurus* sp.	Squirrel
3. *Muntiacus muntjak*	Barking deer	16. *Leopoldamys* sp.	Mouse and rat
4. *Presbytis* sp.	Langurs	17. *Hylobates* sp.	Gibbon
5. *Macaca* sp.	Monkey	18. *Martes flavigular*	Marten
6. *Aonyx cinera*	Otter	19. *Arctonyx collaris*	Badger
7. *Cynocephalus variegatus*	Flying lemur	20. *Paradoxurus hermaphroditus*	Civet
8. *Rhizomys* sp.	Bamboo rat	21. *Hylopetes phayrei*	Flying squirrel
9. *Hystrix* sp.	Porcupine	22. *Petaurista petaurista*	Flying squirrel
10. *Helarctos malayanus*	Bear	23. *Myotis* sp.	Bat
11. *Cervus* sp.	Deer	24. *Tapirus indicus*	Tapir
12. *Tragulus javanicus*	Mouse deer	25. *Hipposideros lylei*	Insectivore–bat
13. *Bos* sp.	Bovid		

Cynocephalus variegatus, *Callosciurus* sp., *Rhizomys* sp., and *Hystrix* sp., and fish (Chaimanee 1994). Some of the unifacial tools from this cultural level are similar in technique of manufacturing to those from Khao Talu, Ment, and Heap Caves and Ban Kao sites, Kanchanaburi Province (Pookajorn 1985, 1988), and Spirit and Banyan Valley Caves in Mae Hong Sorn Province, western and northwestern Thailand (Gorman 1969, 1971, 1972; Thosarat 1982). Compared to the unifacial tools recovered elsewhere in Thailand and at other sites in Southeast Asia, however, the unifacial tools from Moh Khiew Cave are smaller, but more multifunctional than those found in Kota Tampan (Malaysia) (Collings 1938; Majid and Tjia 1990; Sieveking 1958; Walker and Sieveking 1962) and the tools found at Spirit and Banyan Valley Caves (Gorman 1972) and at Sai Yok Cave (Heekeren 1969). The typology and raw material of bifacial tools from this cultural level are almost the same as those of tools found from nearby Lang Rongrien Rock Shelter, which is older than 37,000 BP (Anderson 1990).

Burial No. 1, found at the boundary of Cultural Levels 1 and 2, is a skeleton of an adult female, age about 35–40 years. The ^{14}C age at the boundary of Cultural Levels 1 and 2 of Moh Khiew Cave is only 25,800 ± 600 BP (TK-933 Pr). This date can be correlated with sites in Southeast Asia, such as Tabon Cave in Palawan, Philippines (Fox 1970); Niah Cave, Sarawak, Malaysia (Harrisson et al. 1961); and Nguom Rock Shelter (Ha Van Tan 1976, 1985). According to Ha Van Tan (1985:81–86), the climate in Vietnam and in Southeast Asia was very cold and arid during the period 30,000–23,000 BP, and after 23,000 years BP, there was a return to a humid and temperate climate. The existence of this cold and dry climate phase in the upper Pleistocene is not a phenomenon limited to Vietnam or to the Southeast Asian mainland, but can also be recognized on the islands of Southeast Asia.

On the basis of results of ^{14}C dating and stone tool typology, faunal remains, human skeleton analysis, and floral remains, all comparable to other sites in Southeast Asia, such as Lang Rongrien Rock Shelter (Anderson 1990), Tabon Cave (Fox 1970), Niah Cave [(Harrisson 1975; Harrisson et al. 1961), and Nguom Rock Shelter (Ha Van Tan 1976, 1985), this cultural level can be attributed to the late Paleolithic.

Second Cultural Level

In this level, core tools, flake tools, and waste flakes made of fine-grained stone such as chert, chalcedony, and geyserite are distinguished, while in the first cultural level there is more siliceous shale than other types of raw material. This evidence shows that prehistoric men of Moh Khiew Cave collected the raw materials from quarries located only 2 km to the southeast of the cave. There are 70 core tools, 3714 flake tools, and 1787 waste flake pieces. More than 60% of the flake tools were utilized. Most of the core tools are bifacial, mostly made by indirect percussion with bone punch, rather than by direct percussion with hard hammer. Functional, morphological, and high-power microwear analyses of the flake tools revealed that they were used for woodworking. This finding means that the prehistoric people of this level used stone tools not only for directly hunting large animals such as *Helarctos malayanus*, *Sus* sp., *Cervidae*, *Muntiacus muntjak*, *Tragulus javanicus*, and *Bos* sp., but also for making wooden tools or wooden traps for catching small animals such as *Presbytis* sp., *Macaca* sp., *Arctogalidia trivirgata*, *Callosciurus* sp., *Leopoldamys* sp., *Rhizomys* sp., and *Hystrix* sp., and fish (Chaimanee 1994). Some of the stone tools of this level are very similar to those of Lang Rongrien Rock Shelter (Anderson 1990), which is about 8 km from Moh Khiew Cave.

The results of palynological analysis show that *Brownlowia*, *Cardamine*(?), *Ammania*,

Quercus, Lagerstroemia, and Polypodiaceae (Wattanasak 1994) were deposited in Cultural Levels 2 and 3. Results of molluscan analysis of Level 2 indicate the presence of the following species: *Andanara granosa, Brotia* sp., *Nautilus* sp., *Brotia costura costura, Uniandra contradens rusticoides, Uniandra* sp., *Pseudodon vendembuchinus chaperi, Pila ampullacea, Polymesoda (gelonia) galathea, Spiphonocyclus tener, Trocholetopoma aspirans, Telescopum telescopium, Filopaludina (siamopaludina) martensi, Thais* sp., Pulmonata, *Perna viridis,* and *Crassostrea cucullata* (Vaisayadamrong 1993). These molluscs were not found in Level 1. More than 60% of the shells from Level 2 were cooked, either by boiling or roasting (40% of them were carbonized).

Third Cultural Level

The most important remains from this level are three human skeletons. One of them, Burial No. 2, was in a flexed position and associated with unifacial and bifacial cobble tools. The unifacial tools are similar to the ones found in Hoabinhian sites of Vietnam (Ha Van Tan 1976; Hoang Xuan Chinh 1989), especially at Con Moong Cave (Nguyen Lan Cuong 1986: 11–17; Pham Huy Thong et al. 1980); where a flexed burial was also recovered in association with unifacial tools.

The stone implements, core tools of both unifacial and bifacial type, are found in association with flake tools and waste flakes. The number of stone tools is 61, while there are 4760 flake tools and 2049 waste flake pieces. Most of the lithic artifacts from this level were made of chalcedony, chert, and geyserite. However, some very fine sandstone and siliceous shale were also used. Artifact-manufacturing techniques used in Level 3 are direct percussion with hard hammer and indirect percussion with bone punch. The results of functional and high-power microwear analyses, together with the results of lithic experiments, confirm that some tools were used for drilling and scraping wood. The results of faunal analysis showed that trapped species included *Hylobates* sp., *Presbytis* sp., *Macaca* sp., *Martes flavigular, Arctonyx collaris, Paradoxurus hermaphroditus, Arctogalidia trivirgata, Sus* sp., *Callosciurus* sp., *Hylopetes phayrei, Petaurista petaurista, Leopoldamys* sp., *Rhizomys* sp., *Hystrix* sp., and fish, while hunted animals were *Helarctos malayanus, Bos* sp., *Muntiacus muntjak,* and *Tragulus javanicus* (Chaimanee 1994).

In addition, the results of shell analysis showed the following molluscan species: *Andanara granosa, Nerita* sp., *Nerita planospira, Nautilus* sp., *Crassostrea* sp., *Brotia (brotia) costura costura, Brotia (brotia) costura peninsularis, Uniandra contradens rusticoides, Uniandra* sp., *Pseudodon vendembuchinus chaperi, Pila ampullacea, Polymesoda (geloina) galathea, Cyclophorus* sp., *Cyclophorus speciosus, Spiphonocyclus tener, Trocholeptopoma aspirans, Amphidromus* sp., *Cerithidea (cerithidae) weyersi, Telescopum telescopium, Filopaludina (siamopaludina) martensi, Thais* sp., *Perna viridis,* and *Crassostrea cucullata.* More than 50% were cooked by boiling or roasting. The prehistoric people of this level were procuring more marine food than in the previous Cultural Levels, because this level dates to the early Holocene, with a climate changing from that of the late Pleistocene. In general, climate in the late Pleistocene period was cooler and drier than in the Holocene period (Flenley 1979). Chaimanee et al. (1993) show that climatic changes in the Pleistocene especially affected small mammals (notably rodents), because small mammals are more sensitive than are large mammals (Chaimanee 1994).

The radiocarbon dates from this level are: 10,530 ± 100 BP (OAEP-1283), 11,020 ± 150 BP (OAEP-1284), 10,470 ± 80 BP (OAEP-1281), 9,670 ± 100 BP (OAEP-1280), 8,420 ± 90

BP (OAEP-1292), and 9,770 ± 100 BP (OAEP-1279). This range of dates can be compared to other sites in Southeast Asia with similar tool types and ^{14}C dates. The Lang Rongrien Rock Shelter is dated to about 9,655 ± 70 BP (Anderson 1990), Mai Da Nouc and Mai Da Sieu are dated to about 10,000 BP (Nguyen Lan Cuong 1986), and Con Moong Cave is dated to about 12,021 ± 70 BP (Pham Huy Thong et al. 1980). Therefore, Cultural Level 3 can be attributed to the early Holocene Pre-Neolithic period.

Fourth Cultural Level

This level contains, in relative quantity, unifacial and bifacial axes associated with unpolished axe blanks, as well as flake tools. There are 27 core tools, 2591 flake tools, and 2049 waste flakes. The major raw material for making lithic tools is siliceous shale. This kind of rock seems to have been preferred to other types of stone such as sandstone, geyserite, and chert. The technique for making tools in this level was direct percussion by hard hammer. Functional analysis showed that some of the tools were used to hunt large animals such as *Helarctos malayanus*, *Muntiacus muntjak*, *Bos* sp., and *Tragulus javanicus*, while most show evidence of use in making wooden tools, probably including traps. The bones of large animals decreased in number, while the animals hunted by trapping were *Hylobates* sp., *Presbytis* sp., *Macaca* sp., *Arctonyx collaris*, *Paradoxurus hermaphroditus*, *Sus* sp., *Rhizomys* sp., fish, and lizard. Remains of marine molluscs and mangrove shells increased vis-à-vis the lower levels. These shells include *Andanara granosa*, *Brotia* sp., *Nerita* sp., *Nerita planospira*, *Nautilus* sp., *Crassostrea* sp., *Brotia* (*brotia*) *costura costura*, *Brotia* (*brotia*) *costura peninsularis*, *Uniandra contradens rusticoides*, *Uniandra* sp., *Pila ampullacea*, *Polymesoda* (*geloina*) *galathea*, *Cyclophorus tener*, *Trocholeptopoma*, *Amphidromus* sp., *Cerithidea weyersi*, *Telescopum telescopium*, *Filopaludina* (*siamopaludina*) *martensi*, *Thais* sp., *Perna viridis*, and *Crassostrea cucullata*. Food processing practices of prehistoric humans, as interpreted from the evidence, included cooking the shellfish with fire before eating. Shell remains such as *Brotia* sp., show that they had been cut for convenience in eating.

The global sea-level change that occurred during the middle Holocene period influenced the sea level at Thailand as well. The sea level near Phang-Nga and Krabi Bay rose to 5 m above present sea level (Sinsakul 1990), corresponding to the sea level on the lower Khong River in Vietnam (Ky 1988) and along Malaysia's shoreline (Tjia 1987). During this marine transgression at 6,000–6,500 BP, Moh Khiew Cave was only 2 km from the coast (now it is more than 4 km). Doubtless, prehistoric people from this site hunted and gathered food in the coastal area.

The most important artifacts that distinguish this level are fragments of pottery and polished adzes. Carbon-14 dates for Cultural Level 4 are 6,090 ± 150 BP (OAEP-1278), 7,060 ± 100 BP (OAEP-1277), 5,590 ± 70 BP (OAEP-1291), and 5,940 ± 140 BP (OAEP-1289). These dates and the typology of stone tools and ceramics are very similar to those of Gua Cha Cave in Malaysia, which has been dated to 6,300 ± 170 BP. Therefore, this cultural level can be attributed to the middle Holocene–early Neolithic.

Fifth Cultural Level

This level is unfortunately only 20 cm thick, because at least 40 cm of topsoil had been removed by villagers for use as fertilizer. There are 20 core tools, 818 flake tools, and 438 waste flakes. These lithic artifacts are very similar in typology and technique to those found in Cultural Level 4. However, polished adzes and axes, as well as fragments of pottery, are found in greater numbers than in Cultural Level 4. Bone tools are also present. The fauna includes Myotis sp., Hylobates sp., Presbytis sp., Macaca sp., Arctonyx collaris, Cynocephalus variegatus, Sus sp., Rhizomys sp., Hystrix sp., fish, and lizard, all small animals that were probably trapped in wooden traps, while large animals such as Tapirus indicus and Bos sp. were perhaps hunted. The results of molluscan analysis show that in this level there are fewer species of shells than in Levels 3 and 4. In addition, in this level, the quantities of carbonized and boiled shells are less than in the underlying level.

This level has been radiocarbon-dated to 4,240 ± 150 BP (OAEP-1290). The polished adzes and axes can be compared to those found at other sites, such as Gua Cha Cave (Adi 1985:35), which was dated to 3,700 ± 250 BP, and the Lue and Bang Sites, Kanchanaburi Province (Sørensen 1967:110–111), dated to 3,720 ± 140 BP. Therefore, Cultural Level 5 can be attributed to the middle or late Neolithic in the mid-Holocene.

ARCHAEOLOGICAL AND ETHNOARCHAEOLOGICAL CONTENT OF SAKAI CAVE

The cultural deposit in Sakai Cave is divided into three levels. They are discussed in the following sections in order from oldest to youngest.

First Cultural Level

Unifacial tools made on river cobbles are found in this level. The technique of direct hard hammer percussion was employed. These artifacts are similar to those obtained from Khao Talu, Ment, and Heap Caves in Kanchanaburi Province (Pookajorn 1985, 1988). The results of functional analysis suggest that the tools found in this level were little utilized. Some of them appear to be similar to Hoabinhian tools discovered in various sites in Southeast Asia (Adi 1985; Gorman 1972; Ha Van Tan 1976; Heekeren 1969; Hoang Xuan Chinh 1989; Matthews 1961, 1964, 1969; Pham Huy Thong et al. 1980; Pookajorn 1984, 1985, 1988; Thosarat 1982). The mammalian fauna (Table 2), which are relatively scarce, include Presbytis sp., Macaca sp., and Hystrix sp., while the molluscs include Brotia (brotia) costura peninsularis, Pseudodon sp., Cyclophorus speciosus, Pulmonata, Rhinostoma housei, Cypraea sp., and Perna sp. Most of the animals hunted by the occupants of in this level were small and might have been taken with wooden traps. The molluscs, notably Cypraea sp. and Perna sp., are marine species, although Sakai Cave is very far from the sea. This means that these types of shells, obtained from the sea, probably had great value for the inhabitants. These rare types of shells are ornamental items at this site. Fire pits were found,

Table 2.   List of Faunal Remains from Sakai Cave, 1991

1. Presbytis sp.	Langur	5. Sus sp.	Wild pig
2. Maccaca sp.	Monkey	6. Ratufa bicolor	Squirrel
3. Hystrix sp.	Porcupine	7. Hylopetes phayrei	Flying squirrel
4. Arctonyx collaris	Badger		

making it possible to argue that the people occupying Cultural Level 1 might have used this cave as a temporary camp and workshop. This level is radiocarbon-dated from 9,280 ± 180 BP (OAEP-1371) to 9,020 ± 360 BP (OAEP-1371). Based on that fact and given the similarity of its tools to the Hoabinhian types at other sites in Southeast Asia, this level can be identified as Pre-Neolithic of early Holocene age.

Second Cultural Level

On the basis of the presence of two burials, polished adzes, pottery, and shell beads, it seems that this cultural level was a primary burial ground. Burial rituals that included putting tools and other possessions with the body were practiced.

The polished adzes found in this level showed evidence of being used, and many pieces had been resharpened. Pottery was associated with animal bones and rice grains. These offerings may have been given by prehistoric people to the dead as a part of ceremonial rites. Thin, polished shell beads are similar to those generally found in other Neolithic burial sites in Thailand and Southeast Asia.

Faunal remains include *Presbytis* sp., *Macaca* sp., *Arctonyx collaris*, *Sus* sp., *Ratufa bicolor*, *Hylopetes phayrei*, fish, and turtle. The results of shell sample analysis yielded *Brotia* spp., *Nerita planospira*, *Brotia* (*brotia*) *costura peninsularis*, *Pseudodon* sp., *Pila angelica*, *Polymesoda* sp., *Cyclophorus speciosus*, *Pulmonata*, *Rhinostoma housei*, *Cypraea* sp., and *Perna* sp. Since most of the animals were small, it can be argued that they were caught in wooden traps. As in Cultural Level 1, the seashells *Cypraea* sp. and *Perna* sp. are present and probably had high value as ornaments. This cultural level yielded more evidence of fire pits, each associated with three rocks for supporting a pottery vessel during cooking. This is a method of cooking similar to that used nowadays by the Sakai or Aranag Asli hunter–gatherer groups, who live near the cave. It can be assumed that this level was used not only for habitation, but also as a burial site. The habitation area, especially around the fire pits, produced a very thick deposit, which means that Neolithic people probably settled in this site for long periods until a group member died. Then they moved to another place, and other groups may have come to replace them. I deduce this because the habitation area is found in the inner part of the cave, while the burials are found at the mouth. This level is radiocarbon-dated to 8,700 ± 190 BP (OAEP-1370), 7,869 ± 280 BP (OAEP-1366), 7,620 ± 160 BP (OAEP-1364), and 9,260 ± 55 BP (HD-14890/14409). If these ^{14}C dates are correct, the Neolithic period in Southeast Asia must be reconsidered. It can be observed, however, that the dating of this level by the Heidelberg laboratory (HD 14890/14409) is very close to the dates for Cultural Level 1 (OAEP-1373), which means that when Neolithic people buried the human body, they probably dug out some charcoal from the lower level and mixed it with the burial fill. Radiocarbon dating of bone collagen could help confirm this interpretation. On the basis of chronological and typological data, this level can be compared to other sites in Thailand (Sørensen 1967) and at Gua Cha, Malaysia (Adi 1985), and attributed to a mid-Holocene Neolithic.

Third Cultural Level

Most finds in Cultural Level 3 are related to the material culture used by the Sakai or Orang Asli nowadays. The habitation deposits are not less than 30–50 cm thick. This thickness indicates that the Sakai have resided in this cave for quite a long time until the present. The habitation of the Sakai would have occurred annually in the rainy season. The fauna included the mammals *Presbytis* sp., *Macaca* sp., and *Ratufa bicolor*, fish, and turtle, while the results of shell analysis included *Nerita planospira*, *Brotia* (*brotia*) *costura penin-sularis*, *Brotia* spp., *Pseudodon* sp., *Pila angelica*, *Cyclophorus speciosus*, *Rhinostoma housei*, *Cypraea* sp., and *Perna* sp. These animals and molluscs were common foods that the Sakai hunted and gathered historically. The weapon that they used for hunting was the bamboo blowpipe, and they used wooden sticks or polished bones for digging wild yams. The ethnographic studies of the Sakai living in this area document the techniques of food gathering, hunting, and other daily activities, including rules and rites, that have been used to interpret the archaeological record from Moh Khiew and Sakai Caves.

In addition, the bone tools of this cave were found in parallel with core tools, flake tools, and probably wooden tools from Cultural Levels 1–3. The tool-using tradition continued from prehistoric times up to now, as shown by the Sakai, especially in regard to bone tools such as polished bone adzes, bamboo blowpipes, and other artifacts.

DISCUSSION AND CONCLUSION

Faunal remains provide clues to environments that existed in the past, by the unifor-mitarian assumption that present-day animal preferences for climate and diet are the same as in the past. The bases for reconstructing past environmental conditions from faunal remains are the presence and absence of animals, their abundance in assemblages, and their body size. The animals discovered in one place cannot be assumed to have been living only in this place at the time. The local environment may have been especially suitable for these animals, or humans may have preferentially selected these animals for food. The absence or scarcity of large-mammal remains in these two caves may reflect a selection against such animals for hunting or, probably, the capacity of the tools and techniques of hunting (Chaimanee 1994). The paleoenvironments of Moh Khiew and Sakai Caves can be interpreted as having included a climate in late Pleistocene times that was cooler and drier than that of the present (Chaimanee 1994; Flenley 1979). Recent discussions of the problem of climatic changes in the late Pleistocene in Southeast Asia conclude that late Würm temperatures were only 3–5°C below present levels and may have had only a limited direct effect in depressing altitudinal vegetation zones in upland areas (Glover 1977:160). This conclusion has been confirmed by V. M. Sinitsyn (Sinitsyn 1962; Ha Van Tan 1976:180), who analyzed the Pleistocene flora of Indochina and divided it into three groups:

1. Dipterocarp forest in the humid tropical region of the coast.
2. Savanna and deciduous forest in the interior.
3. Dipterocarp inland forest.

Ha Van Tan (1976:183) has also concluded that the climate of Southeast Asia during the Pleistocene was already affected by monsoons that caused this region to have a tropical climate, and it was suggested that no great change of climate between the late Pleistocene and the Holocene took place in the region. In some areas of Thailand, however, most of the forests have been destroyed by the shifting cultivation of hill-tribe groups, affecting archaeo-logical interpretation in the future (Pookajorn 1988:250).

In the mid-Holocene, the sea invaded far inland, particularly in the lowland areas (Figure 2) (Sinsakul 1990). Sea level reached its maximum height at around 6,000 BP, with an elevation about 5 m above the present mean. The sea level fell to 1.5 m at around 4,700 BP, and from then onward, fluctuations occurred until the present sea level was reached at 1,500 BP. In the Krabi region, the Holocene sea had invaded most of the lowland area and old stream channels, the shore reaching a position about 5–8 km inland of the present shoreline. Marine sediments were deposited all over the coastal area within an elevation 5 m above present mean sea level (Sinsakul 1994). At that time, the sea level near Phang Nga and Krabi Bay rose 5 m above the present sea level (Sinsakul 1990), corresponding to the sea level at the lower Khong River in Vietnam (Ky 1988) and along the Malaysian shoreline (Tjia 1987) (Figure 3). The change in Holocene sea level would have affected prehistoric human life, especially in Cultural Level 4 of Moh Khiew Cave. This cultural level yielded increased evidence of sea food exploitation relative to Cultural Levels 1–3. It was sea-level change, rather than climatic, vegetational, or faunal change, that had the greatest impact on humans in southern peninsular Thailand, and the sea-level fluctuations were not limited to the period centered on 10,000 BP.

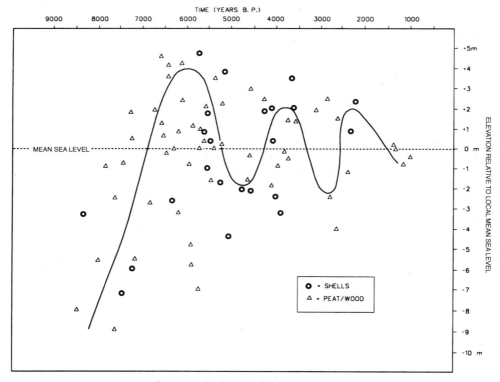

Figure 2. Holocene sea level curve of Thailand. After Sinsakul (1990).

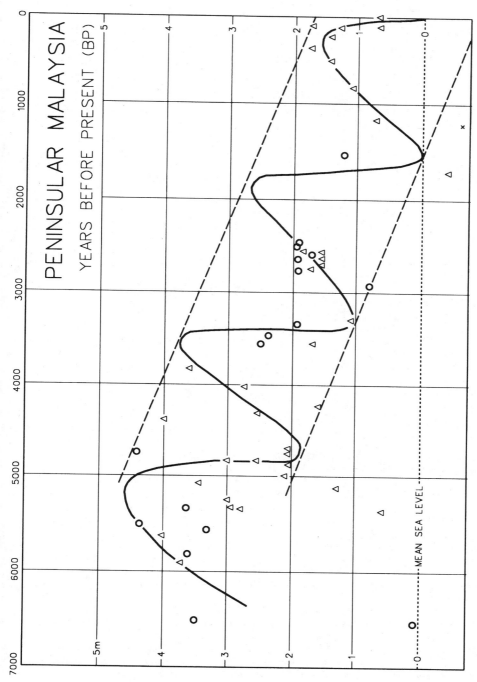

Figure 3. Radiocarbon ages of shoreline indicators from peninsular Malaysia. (△) Dates published earlier; (○) new dates; (×) shells from a depth of 2 m below sea level in the Beruas plain of Perak (Suntharalingam in press); (——) an interpretation of sea-level fluctuations. Note that the sea level rose gradually compared to sudden declines. After Tjia (1987).

ACKNOWLEDGMENTS

This study was made possible with the help of the Toyota Foundation, which supported a grant for my fieldwork in 1991. I owe thanks to many people, especially the scientists who helped me to analyze data from both archaeological and ethnographic projects. I wish to thank Prof. Dr. H.-J. Müller-Beck and Prof. Dr. Lawrence Guy Straus for providing me a grant to attend the S.A.A. Conference at Anaheim in 1994. Special thanks also go to Mr. Suraphol Nathapintu, Lawrence Guy Straus, and Jon M. Erlandson for improving my English grammar style.

REFERENCES

Adi, H. T., 1985, The Re-excavation of the Rockshelter of Gua Cha, Ulu Kelantan, West Malaysia, *Federal Museum Journal*, Volume 39, Muzim Negara, Kuala Lumpur, Malaysia.

Anderson, D., 1990, *Lang Rongrien Rockshelter: A Pleistocene–Early Holocene Archaeological Site from Krabi, Southwestern Thailand*, University of Pennsylvania Press, Philadelphia.

Chaimanee, Y., 1994, Mammalian Fauna from Archaeological Excavations at Moh Khiew Cave, Krabi Province and Sakai Cave, Trang Province, Southern Thailand, in: *Final Report: The Hoabinhian Research Project of Thailand (Phase 2)*, Silpakorn University Press, Bangkok.

Chaimanee, Y., Jaeger, J. J., and Suteethorn, S., 1993, Pleistocene Micro-Mammals of Thailand: Contribution to Palaeoenvironmental Changes, Biochronology and Biodiversity, in: *The International Symposium Biostratigraphy of Mainland Southeast Asia: Facies and Paleontology*, Chiang Mai University, Volume 1, pp. 125–136.

Collings, H. D., 1938, A Pleistocene Site in the Malay Peninsula, *Nature* 142:575.

Flenley, J. R., 1979, *The Equatorial Rain Forest: A Geological History*, University of Hull and Australian National University, Canberra.

Fox, R. B., 1970, *The Tabon Caves: Archaeological Explorations and Excavations in Palawan Island, Philippines*, National Museum, Manila.

Glover, I. C., 1977, The Hoabinhian: Hunter–Gatherers or Early Agriculturalists in Southeast Asia? in: *Hunter–Gatherers and First Farmers beyond Europe* (J. V. S. Megaw, ed.), Leicester University Press, Leicester, pp. 145–166.

Gorman, C. F., 1969, Hoabinhian: A Pebble Tool Complex with Early Plant Association in Southeast Asia, *Science* 163:671–673.

Gorman, C. F., 1971, The Hoabinhian and After: Subsistence Pattern in Southeast Asia during the Late Pleistocene and Early Recent Periods, *World Archaeology* 2(3):300–320.

Gorman, C. F., 1972, Excavation at Spirit Cave, North Thailand, *Asian Perspectives* 13:79–107.

Harrisson, T., 1975, Tampan: Malaysia's Palaeolithic Reconsidered, *Modern Quaternary Research in Southeast Asia*, 1: 53–71.

Harrisson, T. D., Hooijer, A., Lord Medway, 1961, An Extinct Giant Pangolin and Associated Mammals from Niah Cave, Sarawak, *Nature* 189:166.

Ha Van Tan, 1976, The Hoabinhian in the Context of Viet Nam, *Vietnamese Studies*, 46:127–197.

Ha Van Tan, 1985, The Late Pleistocene Climate in Southeast Asia: New Data from Vietnam, *Modern Quaternary Research in Southeast Asia*, 9:81–86.

Heekeren, H. R. V., 1969, The Thai Danish Prehistoric Expedition 1960–62, *Sai Yok*, Vol. 1, Munsgaard, Copenhagen.

Hoang Xuan Chinh, 1989, Van Hoa Hoa Binh O'Viet Nam, *Vien Khao CO Hoc*, Hanoi.

Ky, N. H., 1988, The Quaternary Geology of the Mekong Lower Plain and Islands in Southern Vietnam, *Proceedings of the Workshop on Correlation of Quaternary Succession in Southeast Asia*, pp. 215–241.

Lekagul, B., and McNeely, J. F., 1989, *Mammals of Thailand* (second edition), Bangkok: Darnsutha Press.

Majid, Z., and Tjia, H. D., 1990, The Tampanian Problem Resolved: Archaeological Evidence of a Late Pleistocene Lithic Workshop, *Modern Quaternary Research in Southeast Asia* 11:71–96.

Matthews, J., 1961, *A Checklist of Hoabinhian Sites Excavated in Malaysia 1860–1939*, Singapore: Eastern University Press.

Matthews, J., 1964, *The Hoabinhian in Southeast Asia and Elsewhere*, Ph.D. thesis, Australian National University, Canberra.

Matthews, J., 1969, A Review of the Hoabinhian in Indochina, in: *Asian Perspectives* 9:86–95.

Nguyen Lan Cuong, 1986, Two Early Hoabinhian Crania from Thanh Hoa Province, Vietnam, Stuttgart: Schweizerbartsche, Verlag Buchhandlung, pp. 11–17.

Pham Huy Thong et al., 1980, *Con Moong Cave*, Hanoi: Institute of Archaeology.

Pookajorn, S., 1984, *The Hoabinhian of Mainland Southeast Asia: New Data from the Recent Thai Excavation in the Ban Kao Area*, Bangkok: Thammasat University Press.

Pookajorn, S., 1985, *The Technological and Functional Morphology Analysis of the Lithic Tools from the Hoabinhian Excavation at Ban Kao Area*, Silpakorn University Press, Bangkok.

Pookajorn, S., 1988, *Archaeological Research of the Hoabinhian Culture or Technocomplex and Its Comparison with Ethnoarchaeology of the Phi Tong Luang, A Hunter–Gatherer Group of Thailand*, Institut für Urgeschichte, Universität Tübingen, Verlag Archaeologica Venatoria.

Pookajorn, S., 1991, *Preliminary Report of Excavation at Moh Khiew Cave, Krabi Province, Sakai Cave, Trang Province and Ethnoarchaeological Research of a Hunter–Gatherer Group, The So-Called "Sakai or Semang," at Trang Province*, Silpakorn University Press, Bangkok.

Sieveking, A. de G., 1958, The Palaeolithic Industry of Kota Tampan, Perak, Northwestern Malaysia, *Asian Perspectives* 2:91–102.

Sinitsyn, V. M., 1962, *Paleography of Asia*, Moscow-Leningrad.

Sinsakul, S., 1990, Evidence of Sea Level Changes in the Coastal Area of Thailand: A Review Workshop on Global Environmental Change, *The Role of the Geoscientist: Past, Present, and Future Sea Level Change*, Chiang Mai, Thailand.

Sinsakul, S., 1994, Environmental Geology of the Prehistoric Archaeological Site at Muang Krabi District, Krabi Province, in: *Final Report: The Hoabinhian Research Project of Thailand (Phase 2)*, Silpakorn University Press, Bangkok (in press).

Sørensen, P., 1967, *Archaeological Excavations in Thailand*, Volume 2, Ban Kao, Munksgaard, Copenhagen.

Thosarat, R., 1982, *Hoabinhian and Woodworking in Thailand*, M.Sc. research paper in anthropology, University of Pennsylvania, Philadelphia.

Tjia, H. D., 1987, Ancient Shoreline of Peninsular Malaysia, *Proceedings of SPAFA Seminar (T-W II) Thailand*, SPFA, Bangkok, pp. 239–257.

Vaisayadamrong, A., 1993, *The Result of Shell Samples Analysis from Moh Khiew and Sakai Caves*, B.A. thesis, Faculty of Archaeology, Silpakorn University, Bangkok.

Walker, D., and Sieveking, A. de G., 1962, The Paleolithic Industry of Kota Tampan, Perak, Malaysia, *Proceedings of the Prehistoric Society* 6:103–139.

Wattanasak, M., 1994, The Result of Archaeopalynological Analysis of Moh Khiew and Sakai Caves, in: *Final Report of the Hoabinhian Research Project of Thailand (Phase 2)*, Silpakorn University Press, Bangkok.

Chapter **11**

The Pleistocene–Holocene Transition in Japan and Adjacent Northeast Asia

Climate and Biotic Change, Broad-Spectrum Diet, Pottery, and Sedentism

C. Melvin Aikens and Takeru Akazawa

What we now call Japan was profoundly affected by the Pleistocene–Holocene transition, as rising sea levels transformed what had been a long appendage of the Asian continent into an archipelago, entirely separated from the mainland (Minato et al. 1965). The fossil record from Japan leaves no doubt that it was connected with the continent during much of the Pleistocene, though the active tectonism of the Pacific rim may have breached the connection at times. *Archidiskon, Stegodon, Parastegodon, Muntiacus,* and *Cervus,* elements of the Siva-Malayan and Sino-Malayan faunas, are all found in Early Pleistocene deposits of southern Japan. *Pinus koraiensis, Picea maximowiczii, Menyanthes trifoliata,* and *Phellodendron amurensis,* all endemic to Korea and northeast China, are known from Early Pleistocene fossil beds in central Japan. Continental connections during Middle Pleistocene time are indicated by widespread finds of *Paleoloxodon* in Japan, and Late Pleistocene connections are shown by *Megacervus* and *Mammuthus primigenius* finds in Hokkaido.

Pleistocene glaciation in Japan was apparently limited to the summit regions of the higher mountains in northern Honshu and Hokkaido, but there it is well attested by over 100 glacial cirques and a number of local moraine systems. Subarctic forest species, including *Picea, Larix,* and *Scabiosa,* are found in the *Egota* conifer bed near Tokyo, buried in the terminal Pleistocene Tachikawa Loam of about 33,000–10,000 BP.

C. Melvin Aikens • Department of Anthropology, University of Oregon, Eugene, Oregon 97403-1218.
Takeru Akazawa • University Museum, University of Tokyo, Tokyo 113, Japan.

Humans at the End of the Ice Age: The Archaeology of the Pleistocene–Holocene Transition, edited by Lawrence Guy Straus, Berit Valentin Eriksen, Jon M. Erlandson, and David R. Yesner. Plenum Press, New York, 1996.

Japan clearly participated in the worldwide transition from Pleistocene to Holocene climate (Figure 1). The nature of the Pleistocene–Holocene transition in Japan is most readily seen in pollen evidence synthesized by Tsukada (1986), which indicates a gradual northward expansion of temperate woodland in terminal Pleistocene–early Holocene times. He charts the first appearance of oak pollen in cores from numerous sites across Japan, from 31° to 44°N latitude. Starting from a *refugium* in southern Kyushu where they had existed before 20,000 BP, oaks spread from southern to central Honshu between about 14,500 and 11,000 years ago, thence northward into Hokkaido, which they reached about 8,500 BP. This evidence will be returned to below in a related discussion. On the adjacent continent, full-glacial vegetation was largely forest-steppe. But with Holocene warming, the forest-steppe retreated northward and the coastal zones were eventually covered by pines, firs, and birches, with deciduous oak, walnut, ash, and other species along the Amur River (Frenzel 1968).

With Holocene warming and rising sea levels, Japan became an island country. What the Pleistocene coasts may have looked like we do not know in any detail, but the new Holocene shores were deeply cut by innumerable small bays and inlets and fringed by broad tidal flats. These irregularities gave Holocene Japan a coastal zone of enormous length and biotic productivity. In the interior, a markedly rugged topography, with up to 3000 m of vertical relief between the seashore and the highest peaks along the mountainous spine of central Honshu, provided a physiographic context within which a comparably high degree of biotic diversity could develop under warmer Holocene conditions. While detailed comparisons of Pleistocene and Holocene biota in Japan remain to be developed, there is little doubt that the transition to warmer Holocene climatic conditions greatly enhanced overall biotic productivity.

TERMINAL PLEISTOCENE MACROBLADE AND MICROBLADE COMPLEXES

The lithic technologies of terminal Pleistocene Japan were distinctive (Akazawa et al. 1980), but ultimately related to the blade and microblade industries of the north Eurasian Upper Paleolithic (Table 1). The focus of this discussion is on Japan, but some reference is necessarily made to developments in Northeast Asia generally. This conjoint discussion helps to place the Japanese case in context and to offer a broader view of terminal Pleistocene and early Holocene lifeways than can be gained from Japanese data alone.

Large blades and microblades made from distinctive prepared cores have long been known from many Siberian sites. At Afontova Gora II, near Lake Baikal, large blades and cores were found in association with the bones of mammoth, reindeer, bison, horse, and saiga antelope. The famed nearby sites of Malta and Buryet yielded similar-blade-based tools and the bones of mammoth, rhino, and reindeer. These three sites are all ^{14}C-dated around 21,000 BP (Larichev et al. 1990:371–372). Verkholenskaia Gora, a site on the upper Angara River dated about 12,500 BP, contained large blades and prepared cores, but also micro-blades and wedge-shaped microcores (Chard 1974:28–33; Larichev et al. 1990:379). Barbed fish spears of bone and antler, and many salmon bones, show that fishing was well established there by at least 12,500 BP.

In Japan, large prepared-core flakes and blades, along with end-scrapers, burins, backed pieces, truncated pieces, points, and side-scrapers made on elongate flakes or

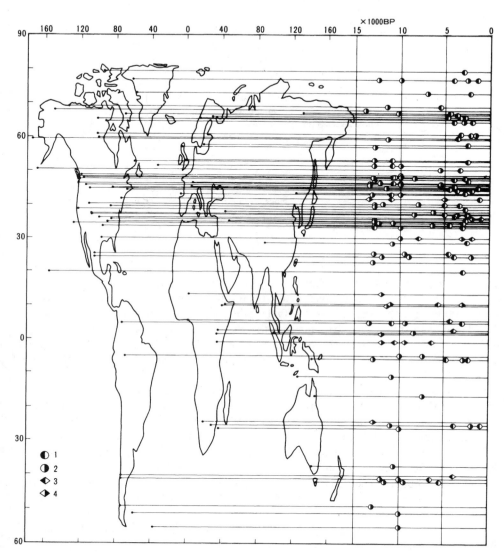

Figure 1. Turning points in global climate during final Pleistocene and Holocene times. The chart documents the onset of warming after 15,000 BP, a brief cool phase around 11,000 BP, continued warming during the interval 10,000–5,000 BP, and cooling after 5,000 BP. Symbols: (1) cooling; (2) warming; (3) drying; (4) becoming humid. Based on data from pollen studies, floral and faunal remains, sediments, sea level change, and oxygen isotope analysis. Modified from Sakaguchi (1984: Fig. 10-3).

Table 1.   Chronological Placement of Localities
Mentioned in the Text

Northeast Asia	Japan	^{14}C years BP
Kamchatka	—	4,500
Bel-Kachi	—	6,000
—	Yubetsu-Ichikawa	8,500–7,000
—	Aomori	8,600
—	Natsushima	9,500
Khabarovsk	—	12,000–10,500
—	Nishinodai	>12,000
—	Kamikuroiwa	12,200
Verkholenskaia Gora	—	12,500
—	Fukui Cave	12,700
Gasha	—	~12,960
Ushki Lake	—	13,000
Diuktai Cave	—	13,000
—	Araya	13,200
—	Nogawa, etc.	15,000–13,000
Malta/Buryet	—	21,000
Afontova II	—	21,000

blades, have been found at many sites. At Nogawa, on the campus of International Christian University in western Tokyo, a well-defined core-blade industry is dated between 18,000 and 15,000 BP. Heidaizaka, Tsukimino, Takaido-higashi, Suzuki, Nishinodai, Maehara, and ICU Locality 15 are other Tokyo-area sites that yield rich records of this same technology (Akazawa et al. 1980). Similar specimens are seen at many other Japanese sites as well, from Fukui Cave in southwestern Kyushu to the complex of sites at Shirataki in northeastern Hokkaido (Aikens and Higuchi 1982:25–94).

Microblades were subsequently added to an industry that included large blades and biface points, exemplified at Nishinodai, Shimbashi, and Suzuki in the Tokyo area; this complex is dated somewhat before 12,000 BP at Nishinodai (Akazawa et al. 1980:162–166, 188–191, 206–213). Microblades, microcores, and large blades have been found at many other sites, from Kyushu to Hokkaido (Hayashi 1968; Kamaki and Serizawa 1965; Oda and Keally 1975; Serizawa 1959; Sugihara and Ono 1965; Yoshizaki 1961). Araya, in north-western Honshu, documents the apparent integration of large blades and microblades within a single toolmaking activity. The distinctive Araya-type burins were made on large blades, and such burins were then evidently used to slot bone or antler hafts to receive microblade armatures. Microblades and wedge-shaped cores were abundant at the site, which is ^{14}C-dated to about 13,200 BP (Serizawa 1974).

MACROBLADES, MICROBLADES, AND POTTERY ACROSS THE PLEISTOCENE–HOLOCENE TRANSITION

Throughout Northeast Asia, a flaked-stone technology of large blades and microblades, and a bone and antler technology of harpoon points and fish hooks, persisted from the

Upper Paleolithic cultures of the terminal Pleistocene well into the Mesolithic or "Neolithic" cultures of early Holocene times. Despite major climatic and environmental change, in the farther north the earlier hunting–fishing practices and toolkit long remained appropriate and in use. At Ustinovka, on the Pacific coast, large blades and cores as well as microblades with wedge-shaped microcores were found in workshop assemblages apparently spanning the Pleistocene–Holocene transition. At Diuktai Cave were found large blades and disc cores, microblades and wedge-shaped cores, and leaf-shaped biface points, ^{14}C-dated about 13,000 BP. Ushki Lake has also yielded large blades, microblades, wedge-shaped microcores, and bifacially flaked stone points. These specimens are ^{14}C-dated between 14,000 and 10,000 BP. Associated with them were quantities of burned salmon bones, found in pithouse fireplaces dated to almost 11,000 BP (Dikov 1978; Powers 1973:78–93).

Inland and southward, the site of Bel-Kachi on the Aldan River shows that a blade and microblade complex lasted well into the middle Holocene. Large blades, blade-arrowheads, wedge-shaped microcores, and microblades found there were ^{14}C-dated to about 6000 BP. Novopetrovka, in the middle reaches of the Amur River, also produced large blade-arrowheads and wedge-shaped microcores (Derevianko 1969; Mochanov 1969). The same pattern is evident in northern Japan. On the island of Hokkaido, the contemporary blade technology was highly similar to that of Bel-Kachi on the mainland; at the site of Yubetsu-Ichikawa, the complex probably dates between 8,500 and 7,000 BP (Yubetsu-Ichikawa Survey Group 1973).

But in southern Japan, instead of such continuities across the Pleistocene–Holocene boundary, we see notable differences. In Kyushu, Shikoku, and southern Honshu, the blades and microblades that had also been widespread there during terminal Pleistocene times began to disappear with the onset of the Holocene. This disappearance was earliest in the south and later toward the north, and the blade technologies were progressively replaced in local assemblages by the new and different flake and ceramic technologies that would come to define the Jomon period. Put another way, we see in southern Japan the emergence of a new Holocene way of life that spread northward as the climate warmed, closely following a biota of southern character that was then expanding in the same direction.

These circumstances make it possible to link explicitly the conjoint appearance of a diversified Holocene biota, the Jomon broad-spectrum economy, a surprisingly early pottery industry, and the precocious residential sedentism that was so characteristic of the Jomon age. Restating the main theme of this volume, it is quite clear that there were, in Japan as elsewhere in Northeast Asia, strong connections between environmental and cultural change across the Pleistocene–Holocene boundary. It is further interesting that cultural changes were later and of lesser magnitude toward the north, probably related to the longer persistence in the higher latitudes of cooler climate and of biotic conditions less changed from those of the Pleistocene.

The earliest pottery so far known in Japan is ^{14}C-dated to about 12,700 BP at Fukui Cave, on the southern island of Kyushu (Figure 2). Microblades and wedge-shaped cores were found both in prepottery levels and in the strata that yielded the first potsherds, but blade technology soon dropped out of the sequence, to be replaced by a quite different lithic industry emphasizing broad, short flakes and ground stone tools (Serizawa 1974). At Kamikuroiwa, on the island of Shikoku, the earliest pottery found north of Fukui Cave was ^{14}C-dated to about 12,200 BP. In central Japan, the Natsushima site on Tokyo Bay gave a ^{14}C date of about 9,500 BP for a level slightly above that containing the earliest pottery.

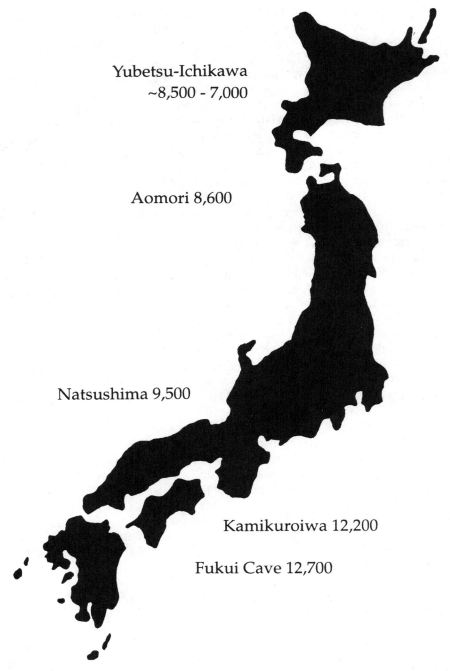

Figure 2. Dates for the first appearance of pottery at five sites in Japan. Chronology is based on radiocarbon years before present (BP). Data from Serizawa (1974) and Esaka (1986). Comparative stratigraphy and typology suggest a slightly earlier date than that of Fukui Cave for the nearby undated Sempukuji site and a date slightly earlier than Natsushima for the earliest pottery in the Tokyo region.

Pottery of the stratigraphically earlier Igusa type, its precedence established at undated sites elsewhere in the Tokyo area, predates the Natsushima finds by an unknown amount of time. Microblade technology was not found at either Kamikuroiwa or Natsushima, having already passed out of use by the time pottery appeared at those sites. In Aomori Prefecture, at the northern tip of Honshu, a ^{14}C date of 8,600 BP has been obtained for a soil layer that contained the earliest pottery found there. Finally, the earliest Jomon pottery in Hokkaido probably dates between 8,500 and 7,000 BP, as shown at the site of Yubetsu-Ichikawa, where pottery met and mingled with the previously mentioned long-persistent northern blade technology (Esaka 1986).

The same trend of decreasing age from south to north in the ^{14}C dates for earliest pottery is also indicated on the continent. A ^{14}C date of 12,960 BP at the Gasha or Sakachi Al'an site on the Middle Amur River is said to pertain to early pottery there, though contextual details remain unspecified (Derevianko 1989). Early pottery found near Khabarovsk occurs in a soil horizon thought to date between 10,500 and 12,000 BP. Farther west, excavations at the Ust'-Kyakhta site, south of Lake Baikal, produced pottery and a radiocarbon date of 11,500 BP. In all these cases, the first pottery is found with microblades, matching the case of Fukui cave in Japan. More to the north, the site of Bel-Kachi has given a ^{14}C date of about 6,000 BP for the earliest pottery known in Yakutia, where it was found along with a blade tool complex similar to that known from Yubetsu-Ichikawa in Hokkaido (Mochanov 1969). In Kamchatka, still farther north, pottery dates to about 4,500 BP (Ackerman 1989).

POTTERY, TEMPERATE WOODLAND, AQUATIC RESOURCES, AND SEDENTISM

What does the beginning of pottery use signify in terms of subsistence economics, and what are the environmental implications of the northward spread of pottery? Obviously, these questions are inseparable, as shown by the fact that pottery's northward movement followed closely the northward expansion of temperate forests (cf. Figures 2–4). Referring again to the work of Tsukada (1986), previously mentioned, a terminal Pleistocene–early Holocene expansion of temperate woodland is indicated by the progressively later appearance of oak and beech pollen in numerous localities distributed from 31° to 44°N latitude across the main islands of Japan. From a glacial *refugium* in southern Kyushu, where oak was present before 20,000 BP, it spread into southern Honshu by about 14,500 BP, then north and east along the archipelago to reach Hokkaido by about 8,500 BP (Figure 3). The spread of beech shows a similar pattern (Figure 4). The progressive south-to-north expansion of oak and beech parallels in a striking way the time-transgressive northward spread of pottery from Kyushu to Hokkaido, with pottery somewhat lagging the initial expansion of these mixed forest species. The earliest date for pottery in southern Kyushu is about 12,700 BP, while the earliest pottery in Hokkaido appears to date between 8,500 and 7,000 BP.

The critical connection between pottery and subsistence economies is illuminated by the dietary practices of the Ainu and other historic aborigines of Northeast Asia. The Ainu diet included such woodland game as deer, bear, boar, raccoon, otter, hare, wolf, and fox; fishes including river-run salmon and many littoral and marine species; birds of both shore and woodland; crabs, oysters, clams, mussels, scallops, and other species of the intertidal zone; and woodland fruits, berries, seeds, leaves, shoots, bulbs, roots, and fungi.

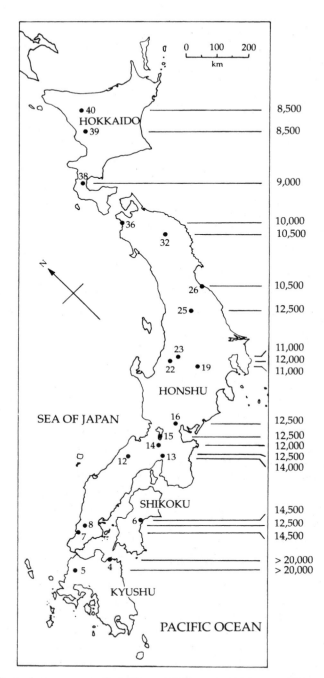

Figure 3. Dates for the first appearance of oak (*Quercus*) in 20 terminal Pleistocene–Holocene pollen sequences from Japan. Chronology is expressed in radiocarbon years before present (BP.); sites lacking ¹⁴C dates are placed by correlation, extrapolation, and interpolation. Ages are rounded to 500-year increments. Based on Tsukada (1986: Figures 1 and 8); site numbers in original.

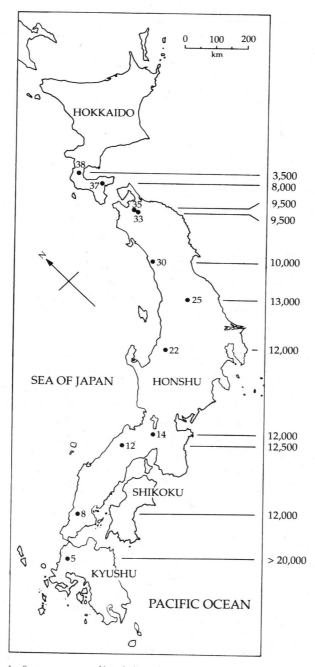

Figure 4. Dates for the first appearance of beech (*Fagus*) in 11 terminal Pleistocene–Holocene pollen sequences from Japan. Chronology is expressed in radiocarbon years before present (BP); sites lacking ^{14}C dates are placed by correlation, extrapolation, and interpolation. Ages are rounded to 500-year increments. Based on Tsukada (1986: Figures 1 and 9); site numbers in original.

As Batchelor (1927) reported, the prevalent method of cooking and eating these foods was by stewing them together in essentially any combination, according to their availability, in cooking pots that were kept going all the time. On the continental shore, the Goldi and Gilyak did much the same thing. Simply, but crucially, cooking vessels were fundamental to the preparation and eating of the highly varied diet of these broad-spectrum hunter–fisher–gathers.

Abundant archaeological evidence documents precisely this kind of diet as characteristic of Jomon culture from very early times. The shell mound of Natsushima, an Initial Jomon site previously mentioned, revealed a varied menu of food resources, which there included 34 shellfish species, 17 marine fish species, 11 species of mostly terrestrial mammals, and 7 avian species (Sugihara and Serizawa 1957). Such middens are a defining characteristic of Jomon culture and are known by the thousands all over the country. The importance of vegetal food resources to Jomon subsistence is also well documented. Stone grinding slabs, mortars, and pestles, as well as the shells of walnuts, acorns, chestnuts, and buckeyes, are commonplace in Jomon sites of almost any age, though the most dramatic examples currently known are from early and middle Jomon times. At Maeike in south central Honshu were found large, deep storage pits that had been filled with acorns and capped with clay. At Idojiri and other sites in highland central Honshu, many charred cakes of unidentified plant matter have been found. In all, at least 40 different species of edible plants have been recovered from Jomon sites, though hard-shelled nuts are most commonly preserved (Fujimori 1965; Watanabe 1975).

A distributional study of food-getting and processing technology by Akazawa (1986) and carbon-isotope studies on human bone by Minagawa and Akazawa (1992) and Chisholm et al. (1992) document the rich and regionally varied diets that Japanese societies began to develop from earliest Jomon times onward. As might be expected given the environmental variables, diets more heavily weighted toward aquatic resources are attested from sites in Hokkaido and northern Honshu, while plant foods are shown to have been more important farther to the south. Although the bulk of the available data do not come from the earliest phases of the Jomon tradition, these authors show that a significant degree of stability in regional diets extended over thousands of years, with some data (as well as environmental considerations) suggesting that the pattern goes back to earliest Jomon times. Obviously, further study of the critical Pleistocene–Holocene transitional period is needed, but currently available results are highly suggestive.

Finally, with the new broadly based, highly diversified Jomon economy came residential sedentism. Semisubterranean houses are known from Nishinojo, on Tokyo Bay, during the Igusa pottery phase of Initial Jomon. This timing would place them before (perhaps significantly before) 9,500 BP. Hanawadai and Hakeue, also in the Tokyo area, give further evidence for the building of quite substantial semisubterranean houses at this early period (Tsuboi 1971:114–115). By Early Jomon times, at least by 6,000 BP, this development had progressed so far that Jomon settlements of several different patterns and levels of complexity were established throughout the archipelago, and in northern Honshu were villages of many circular, single-family dwellings that clustered around one or a few very large communal longhouses (Kobayashi 1992).

The key to this flourishing Jomon sedentism is quite obviously the close juxtaposition in the Japanese landscape of wooded interior hills, stream and river valleys, bays, inlets, tidal flats, and open ocean, such that a great range of resources was to be had within relatively short distances of well-chosen central places. In such settings, human groups early developed logistical strategies for hunting, fishing, and harvest collecting that were centered on occupation sites from which forays could be mounted and in which diverse resources could be concentrated and stored (Aikens et al. 1986). A provocative "paleobiomass analysis" has been developed by Koike (1986, 1992), centered on just such a setting, using simulation modeling based on quantitative studies of contemporary populations of Jomon food species. This work, conducted in a locality off Tokyo Bay that has been continuously occupied since Early Jomon times, sheds light on the long-term dynamics of the Jomon subsistence pattern. The model successfully estimates the effects of sea-level change on deer and shellfish populations, as well as the effects of human hunting and collecting pressures on those populations. Koike's work sheds important light on the environmental basis of the Jomon subsistence pattern and on its essential long-term stability, though the critical earliest Jomon period remains to be studied in comparable terms. A bioarchaeological approach to analysis of similar cultural–environmental phenomena around Peter the Great Bay, near modern Vladivostok, points the way for future studies of the same kind in continental Northeast Asia—though again the currently available data are for periods significantly after the Pleistocene–Holocene transition (Brodianski and Rakov 1992).

CONCLUSIONS

The foregoing sketch links climatic change across the Pleistocene–Holocene transition with critical biotic changes that fostered the broad-spectrum economy of Holocene times, which was in turn helped to flourish by the advantages that pottery afforded in the cooking and storage of the newly diversified diet (see also Aikens 1995). Pollen evidence from Japan shows that the vegetable foods so important in the Jomon lifeway there would have been scarce in the preceding arctic and cold-temperate plant communities of the glacial age. Even considerably after the period of maximum cold, possibilities for gathering such plant foods as acorns, walnuts, and chestnuts—and the understory vegetation that these arboreal species imply—were limited to the Pacific coastal belt of southwestern Japan (Tsukada 1986:39). It was only with Holocene warming that temperate woodland became widespread in the Japanese archipelago, and as it did, the newly arrived biota increasingly fueled a new way of life based on a great diversity of subsistence resources. Equally, faunal evidence from shellmounds found everywhere on Japanese shores shows that exploitation of the highly productive coastline, newly established by rising sea levels, was also proceeding apace. Though evidence from the Northeast Asian mainland so far tells little of what was going on there during this crucial period, comparable developments seem indicated by the rich patterns that are documented for later times in the region (Brodianski and Rakov 1992; Chard 1974; Ye 1992).

Thus, we conclude that the crucial interval 13,000–8,000 BP saw established in Japan and adjacent Northeast Asia a new broad-spectrum hunting–fishing–gathering way of life, one that was to persist thereafter with great stability down to the time of agriculture, more than 5,000 years later. In the farthest north of Hokkaido, and beyond in continental Northeast Asia, comparable ways of life continued right down to modern times, protected from the destabilizing influence of agriculture by the rigorous climates of the north, last stronghold of the Ice Age.

REFERENCES

Ackerman, R. E., 1989, North Pacific Cultural Relationships: The Northern Northwest Coast of North America and Northeast Asia. Preprint proceedings of the Circum-Pacific Prehistory Conference, Seattle, Washington State University, Pullman.

Aikens, C. M., 1995, First in the World: The Jomon Pottery of Early Japan, in: *The Emergence of Pottery: Technology and Innovation in Ancient Societies* (W. K. Barnett and J. Hoopes, eds.), Smithsonian Institution Press, Washington, DC, pp. 11–21.

Aikens, C. M., Ames, K. M., and Sanger, D., 1986, Affluent Collectors at the Edges of Eurasia and North America: Some Comparisons and Observations on the Evolution of Society among North–Temperate Hunter–Gatherers, in: *Prehistoric Hunter–Gatherers in Japan: New Research Methods* (T. Akazawa and C. M. Aikens, eds.), University of Tokyo Press, Tokyo, pp. 3–26.

Aikens, C. M., and Higuchi, T., 1982, *Prehistory of Japan*, Academic Press, New York.

Akazawa, T., 1986, Regional Variation in Procurement Systems of Jomon Hunter–Gatherers, in: *Prehistoric Hunter–Gathers in Japan: New Research Methods* (T. Akazawa and C. M. Aikens, eds.), University of Tokyo Press, Tokyo, pp. 73–89.

Akazawa, T., Oda, S., and Yamanaka, I., 1980, *The Japanese Paleolithic*, Rippu Shobo, Tokyo.

Batchelor, J., 1927, *Ainu Life and Lore*, Japan Advertiser Press, Tokyo.

Brodianski, D. L., and Rakov, A. V., 1992, Prehistoric Aquaculture on the Western Coast of the Pacific, in: *Pacific Northeast Asia in Prehistory* (C. M. Aikens and S. N. Rhee, eds.), Washington State University Press, Pullman, pp. 27–31.

Chard, C. S., 1974, *Northeast Asia in Prehistory*, University of Wisconsin Press, Madison.

Chen, C., and Wang, X.-Q., 1989, Upper Paleolithic Microblade Industries in North China and Their Relationships with Northeast Asia and North America, *Arctic Anthropology* 26(2):127–156.

Chisholm, B., Koike, H., and Nakai, N., 1992, Carbon Isotopic Determination of Paleodiet in Japan: Marine Versus Terrestrial Sources, in: *Pacific Northeast Asia in Prehistory* (C. M. Aikens and S. N. Rhee, eds.), Washington State University Press, Pullman, pp. 69–73.

Crawford, G., and Hiroto, T., 1989, The Origins of Plant Husbandry in Northern Japan, Preprint Proceedings of the Circum-Pacific Prehistory Conference, Seattle, Washington State University, Pullman.

Derevianko, A. P., 1969, The Novopetrovka Blade Culture on the Middle Amur, *Arctic Anthropology* 6(1):119–127.

Derevianko, A. P., 1989, The Late Pleistocene Sites in the Selemdga River Basin and their Significance for Correlation of the Upper Paleolithic Complexes of the Pacific Ocean Basin. Preprint proceedings of the Circum-Pacific Prehistory Conference, Seattle, Washington State University, Pullman.

Dikov, N. N., 1978, Ancestors of Paleo-Indians and Proto-Eskimo-Aleuts in the Paleolithic of Kamchatka, in: *Early Man in America from a Circum-Pacific Perspective*, Occasional Papers 1 (A. L. Bryan, ed.), Department of Anthropology, University of Alberta, pp. 68–69.

Esaka, T., 1986, The Origins and Characteristics of Jomon Ceramic Culture: A Brief Introduction,, in: *Windows on the Japanese Past: Studies in Archaeology and Prehistory* (R. J. Pearson, G. L. Barnes and K. L. Hutterer, eds.), Center for Japanese Studies, The University of Michigan, Ann Arbor, pp. 223–228.

Frenzel, B., 1968, The Pleistocene Vegetation of Northern Eurasia, *Science* 161:637–649.

Fujimori, E. (ed.), 1965, *A Middle Jomon Culture from the Southern Foothills of Yatsugatake*, Chuo Koron Bijutsu Shuppan, Tokyo (in Japanese).

Hayashi, K., 1968, The Fukui Microblade Technology and Its Relationships in Northeast Asia and North America, *Arctic Anthropology* 5(1):128–190.

Kamaki, Y., and Serizawa, C., 1965, The Rockshelter of Fukui, Nagasaki Prefecture, *Kokogaku Syukan, Memoirs of the Tokyo Archaeological Society* 3(1):1–14 (in Japanese).

Kobayashi, T., 1992, Patterns and Levels of Social Complexity in Jomon Japan, in: *Pacific Northeast Asia in Prehistory* (C. M. Aikens and S. N. Rhee, eds.), Washington State University Press, Pullman, pp. 91–96.

Koike, H., 1986, Prehistoric Hunting Pressure and Paleobiomass: An Environmental Reconstruction and Archaeo-zoological Analysis of a Jomon Shellmound Area, in: *Prehistoric Hunter–Gatherers in Japan: New Research Methods* (T. Akazawa and C. M. Aikens, eds.), University of Tokyo Press, Tokyo, pp. 27–53.

Koike, H., 1992, Exploitation Dynamics During the Jomon Period, in: *Pacific Northeast Asia in Prehistory* (C. M. Aikens and S. N. Rhee, eds.), Washington State University Press, Pullman, pp. 53–57.

Larichev, V., Khol'ushkin, U., and Laricheva, I., 1990, The Upper Paleolithic of Northern Asia: Achievements, Problems, and Perspectives, II. Central and Eastern Siberia, *Journal of World Prehistory* 4(3):347–385.

Minagawa, M., and Akazawa, T., 1992, Dietary Patterns of Japanese Jomon Hunter-Gatherers: Stable Nitrogen and

Carbon Isotope Analyses of Human Bones, in: *Pacific Northeast Asia in Prehistory* (C. M. Aikens and S. N. Rhee, eds.), Washington State University Press, Pullman, pp. 59–67.

Minato, M., and Hunahashi, M. (eds.), 1965, *The Geological Development of the Japanese Islands*, Tokyo: Tsukiji Shokan.

Mochanov, I. A., 1969, The Bel'kachinsk Neolithic Culture on the Aldan, *Arctic Anthropology* 6(1):104–114.

Oda, S., and Keally, C. T., 1975, *Japanese Preceramic Cultural Chronology*, ICU Archaeology Research Center, International Christian University, Occasional Papers 2, Tokyo.

Powers, W. R., 1973, Paleolithic Man in Northeast Asia, *Arctic Anthropology* 10(2).

Sakaguchi, Y., 1984, Climatic Changes of Northern Area, in: *Natural Environments of Northern Area* (M. Fukuda, T. Koaze, and M. Nogami, eds.), Hokkaido University Press, Sapporo (in Japanese).

Serizawa, C., 1959, A New Microblade Industry Discovered at the Araya Site, and the Araya-type Graver, *Dai Yonki Kenkyu* 1(5):174–181 (in Japanese).

Serizawa, C., ed., 1974, *Ancient History Excavations I: The First Hunters*, Kodansha, Tokyo (in Japanese).

Sugihara, S., and Ono, S., 1965, Microlithic Culture of Yasumiba Sites, Shizuoka Prefecture, *Kokogaku Syukan, Memoirs of the Tokyo Archaeological Society* 3(2):1–33 (in Japanese).

Sugihara, S., and Serizana, C., 1957, *Shell Mounds of the Earliest Jomon Culture at Natsushima, Kanagawa Prefecture, Japan*, Meiji University, Tokyo (in Japanese).

Tsukada, M., 1986, Vegetation in Prehistoric Japan: The Last 20,000 Years, in: *Windows on the Japanese Past: Studies in Archaeology and Prehistory* (R. J. Pearson, G. L. Barnes, and K. L. Hutterer, eds.), Center for Japanese Studies, University of Michigan, pp. 11–56.

Tsuboi, K., 1971, A Discussion of Jomon Culture, in: *Nihon no Rekishi: Genshi Oyobi Kodai, I*, Iwanami Koza, Tokyo (in Japanese).

Watanabe, M., 1975, *Vegetable Foods of the Jomon Period*, Yuzankaku, Tokyo (in Japanese).

Ye, W., 1992, Neolithic Tradition in Northeast China, in: *Pacific Northeast Asia in Prehistory* (C. M. Aikens and S. N. Rhee, eds.), Washington State University Press, Pullman, pp. 139–156.

Yoshizaki, M., 1961, The Shirataki Site and Hokkaido's Aceramic Culture, *Minzokugaku Kenkyu* 26(1):13–23 (in Japanese).

Yubetsu-Ichikawa Survey Group 1973, *The Yubetsu-Ichikawa Site*. Yubetsu, Yubetsu-cho Kyoiku Iinkai (in Japanese).

Chapter **12**

Siberia in the Late Glacial and Early Postglacial

William R. Powers

INTRODUCTION

The problems of the peopling of Siberia and those of the peopling of the New World are one and the same. Regardless of when or how many times humans pressed north and east across this vast region, the successful solution to the adaptive problems they faced was an absolute precondition to their entry into the Western Hemisphere. During the last Glacial Maximum and spanning the late Glacial periods, lowered sea levels had united Asia and America at Beringia. Northern Asia experienced no continental glaciation, whereas northern North America was virtually locked in ice from the Pacific Ocean to the Atlantic Ocean. Large areas of eastern Beringia (Alaska and the northern part of the Yukon Territory) remained ice-free and may have been connected at times to interior North America through an ice-free corridor. But for all practical purposes, the unglaciated regions of northwest North America had become an extension of Asia and were virtually cut off from the rest of North America.

During the late Glacial period, biota profoundly different from that of today existed throughout north Eurasia, and the same floral and fauna associations existed in Beringia. The destruction of zonal biotic patterns during the onset of the last Glacial led to a merging of northern and southern elements, so that horse, bison, and steppe lemming could be found on the same periglacial landscapes as collared lemming, Arctic hare, and caribou. This merging was due in large part to the widespread replacement of the zonal taiga by combinations of tundra and steppe elements forming cold, dry northern steppes and tundras.

Such was the world in which humans existed during the last and late glacials, and their success in settling these landscapes determined their ability to occupy even higher latitudes and to pass into the New World.

WILLIAM R. POWERS • Department of Anthropology, University of Alaska, Fairbanks, Alaska 97707.

Humans at the End of the Ice Age: The Archaeology of the Pleistocene–Holocene Transition, edited by Lawrence Guy Straus, Berit Valentin Eriksen, Jon M. Erlandson, and David R. Yesner. Plenum Press, New York, 1996.

The reestablishment of zonal vegetation patterns and rising sea levels at the beginning of the postglacial led to the disintegration of the late glacial biotic patterns and intercontinental connections and introduced isolating mechanisms that affected human settlement and development.

The Siberian archaeological data dating to the late Glacial and early Postglacial have been organized within a regional climatostratigraphy that can be correlated with the Blytt–Sernander periods of climatic change (Bell and Walker 1992). Although this model has been simplified, or even abandoned (Price 1987; Roberts 1992), it is still in force for Russia. While regional terms are sometimes employed, the Blytt–Sernander model, through a prudent use of ^{14}C dating, has been extended across Siberia (Dolukhanov 1989; Khotinskii 1984; Medvedev et al. 1990; Tseitlin 1979).

In this chapter, I will attempt to determine possible changes in human adaptation in the face of changing environmental conditions during the late Glacial and early Postglacial periods. Radiocarbon-dated sites will be correlated to the climatostratigraphic framework just discussed. Where necessary, time slices of roughly a thousand years will be employed to help organize the information.

THE LATE GLACIAL

The time frame of interest to us began with the N'iapan Stade (15,000–13,000 BP = Oldest Dryas) of the Late Sartan Glaciation. This stage was followed by the Kokorevo warming (13,000–12,200 BP = Bölling). There followed a gap in the record of about 400 years in which there may have been a return to cooler conditions (Older Dryas) during which the Kokorevo soil was buried in loess. The Taimyr' warming (11,800–11,400 BP = Alleröd) followed this event and was terminated by a return to the colder conditions of the Nor'ilsk Stade (11,400–10,300 BP = Younger Dryas), the end of which brought the Pleistocene to a close (Tseitlin 1979).

Environments

In south Siberia, particularly on the Yenisei River, there is stratigraphic and geo-chronological evidence for the stade/interstade succession of the late Glacial; fortunately, this sequence has been found in archaeological sites. Here, two ^{14}C-dated buried soils exhibiting differing degrees of cryogenic disturbance form the stratigraphic basis for the Bölling and Alleröd warming periods. The Bölling soil is mildly disturbed and overlain by loess representing a cooler interval that is at present unnamed. During the Younger Dryas, the Alleröd soil was severely cryoturbated and fractured from ice-wedge formation deep enough to also penetrate the Bölling soil.

Even at the maximum spread of Sartan ice, the vast majority of Siberia was ice-free and available for habitation. Continental glaciation covered only the northern part of Western Siberia. Mountain glaciation was confined to the alpine regions of Eastern Siberia. Ice boundaries are generally mapped at minimum and maximum extents for continental glaciers, while mountain glaciers are simply indicated (Grichuk 1984). In a more extreme case, Laukhin (1990) maps a more extensive system of mountain glaciers for the northeast at the glacial maximum in which all the major highland regions are covered with ice. It is impossible, however, to establish the exact position of glacial margins for the late Glacial stades. We are probably safe in assuming that we are dealing with something near the minimum extent between 14,000 and 10,000 BP.

Due to lowered sea levels, Siberia was vastly enlarged in the northeast, and the exposed floors of the Chukchi and Bering Seas created Beringia, the bridge between the Old World and the New World that allowed the interchange of flora and fauna between the two continents. Beringia, likewise, was geographically critical for human migration during the late Glacial.

Late Glacial environments can be outlined following Khotinskii (1984). During the late Glacial, the climate was severe and continental. Hyperzonality, or zone mixing, resulted in mixtures of tundra, steppe, desert, and forest elements. Curious mixtures of *Artemisia*, Chenopodiaceae, *Betula nana*, and tundra species of *Lycopodium* and *Selaginella* became common as the zonal pattern of tundra, taiga, and steppe was rearranged; the steppe expanded northward and the tundra southward through a degraded forest zone. The result was a mosaic pattern with steppe on dry, well-drained south-facing slopes, divides, and terrace surfaces and tundra on cooler north-facing areas and poorly drained surfaces. Summers were short and hot, while winters were long and cold. There was considerable temperature variation and low precipitation. Although no modern analogue exists, there are still mixes of forest-tundra and steppe in central Yakutia and the continental Northeast (Yurtsev 1982).

The severe climatic conditions of the Sartan glaciation that maintained the cold steppes, tundras, and forest steppes were also responsible for the widespread occurrence of the Mammoth fauna, some of the main species of which were still common during the late Glacial. The reconstructed southern boundary of the colder adapted species (mammoth, woolly rhinoceros, musk ox) at 16,000 BP was still in southwestern Siberia, and these species were absent only in the uppermost reaches of the Yenisei and the Ob' and the upper portions of the Irtysh. By 13,000 BP, this boundary had shifted significantly to the northeast, forming a line running roughly diagonally across central Siberia from the mouth of the Ob' to the southern coast of the Sea of Okhotsk (Tseitlin 1979). Thus, a "warmer" fauna was distributed across south Siberia, and faunal remains in archaeological sites include horse, red deer, auroch or bison, reindeer, Asiatic wild ass, varying hare, argali sheep, Siberian goat, saiga antelope, fox, arctic fox, wolf, wolverine, various rodents, and some birds (Abramova 1979a,b; Larichev et al. 1988; Tseitlin 1979). Moose began to appear about 12,000 BP all across south Siberia (Abramova 1979a,b; Tseitlin 1979).

Between 12,000 BP and 10,000 BP, the south Siberian fauna was affected by climatic change and mixed forest and steppe faunal associations appeared: red deer, bison, roe deer, moose, goat, and bear. During the Younger Dryas, small, short-horned bison appeared in the south (Tseitlin 1979). The northern fauna was much the same as the southern fauna, with the possibility that mammoths were still on the landscape.

Archaeology

With few exceptions human—environmental interactions have not been central to Siberian Paleolithic research (for example, Dolukhanov and Khotinskii 1974, 1984). Though a great deal has been written about the Upper Paleolithic of Siberia, the main emphasis has always been on the stages preceding the late Glacial. Likewise, other than the attempt of Mockanov (1977) to delineate Western Afontova-Malta and Eastern Diuktai culture areas and the three-part English-language study of Larichev et al. (1988, 1990, 1992), there has been little true synthesis.

The late Glacial archaeological record is fairly impressive. For the Yenisei region alone, over 90% of the Paleolithic sites date to between 14,000 BP and 10,000 BP (Vasil'ev 1992). For the sake of greater precision, however, only those sites with ^{14}C dates and faunal remains will be included in this discussion.

Research to date has been intensively descriptive and focused on the identification of archaeological cultures distinguished by technology and diagnostic tool types or classes. Often, the defining characteristics of such cultures seem overly specific, especially when one considers the common technological and typological background of almost all the sites dating to this period of time. The study of the Siberian Upper Paleolithic has been affected by different emphases, and different criteria for defining units have been employed. We also must take note of whether a culture is being defined as a geographic or a stadial phenomenon.

Okladnikov (1968) once defined an Afontova-Oshurkovo culture for South Siberia that stretched from the Altai Mountains in Western Siberia to the Amur River. In the western sector of this zone, Abramova (1979a,b, 1984, 1989) isolated the Afontova and Kokorevo cultures. Later, Larichev et al. (1988) returned to Okladnikov's position in recognizing the cohesive unity of the Siberian late Upper Paleolithic. Vasil'ev (1992) recognized the tremendous complexity of the problem and retained the terms while stressing that they are variants of a single culture, with the Kokorevo culture compact on the Yenisei and the Afontova culture widespread across all of South Siberia.

Mochanov (1977) attempted to isolate a Diuktai culture area in Eastern Siberia and contrasted it to the Mal'ta-Afontova culture area that lay to the west and south. The concept of a Mal'ta-Afontova culture area basically reiterated Okladnikov's Afontova-Oshurkovo culture in both geography and time depth.

Most current researchers point out that regional differences, such as bifacial points in the Diuktai culture or large blade tools in the Kokorevo culture, are but local tendencies in an otherwise common technological and typological background that appears to have great time depth in northern Eurasia. Abramova (1989) retained the designators Kokorevo, Afontova, and Diuktai, but united them into her Stage III of the Siberian Upper Paleolithic. Stage III was preceded by the early Upper Paleolithic (macroblade technology), which in turn was preceded by the Mousterian. Stage III is characterized by the broad distribution of wedge-shaped microcores, microblades, and the composite inset technique. Alongside these miniature artifacts, we find large side-scrapers and choppers. Large blade tools in the Kokorevo culture, flake tools including microlithic in the Afontova culture, and bifacial knife blades in the Diuktai culture constitute cultural differences within this stage. The whole stage is also characterized by thin cultural layers, light surface dwellings, bone and antler implements, and decorative pieces. The one piece of representational art for this stage is an anthropomorphic statuette from the Maina site (Vasil'ev and Ermolova 1983). Overall, the record implies a high degree of mobility, and any tendency toward even seasonal sedentism remains undemonstrated.

Thus, it is the basic pattern of large chopping, cutting, and scraping tools side by side with a miniature toolkit including microblades that provides cohesion to the late Glacial

Siberian late Upper Paleolithic. Sites that do not conform to the basic pattern, Shikaevka in western Siberia and Layer VII at Ushki Lake in Kamchataka, lie, respectively, at the western and eastern extremities of Siberia.

14,000–13,000 BP

Sites dated, more or less, to this period are Shikaevka, Volch'ia Griva, Ust'-Kova, Kokorevo I, Maina, Golubaia I, Diuktai Cave, Berelekh, and Ushki 1, layer 7.

Shikaevka is one of two documented late Paleolithic sites truly in the heart of western Siberia. While there are no ^{14}C dates, the fauna and geological context indicate an age of about 13,000 BP. The tools do not fit the Siberian pattern. This is a blade industry with geometric microliths associated with mammoth, saiga, reindeer, hare, and mice. Pollen indicates a forest steppe (Larichev et al. 1988; Petrin 1986).

Volch'ia Griva (She-wolf Ridge) (14,200 ± 150) on the Baraba Steppe in western Siberia might have been a mammoth kill site or at least a mammoth butchering site, although natural catastrophe has been suggested as an explanation for this accumulation of mammoth bones. Only flakes were found, and there is abundant evidence that butchering did occur. The age conforms with existing information on the distribution of mammoth in south Siberia at this time (Larichev et al. 1988; Michael 1984).

Ust'-Kova (upper complex: 14,220 ± 100) on the middle Angara is the most northerly north site in the central Siberian region (59° north latitude). There are radial cores, parallel blade cores, blade tools, burins, and other tools, and bifacial points. This complex seems technologically intermediate between the Yenisei Paleolithic and the Diuktai culture. The fauna includes mammoth, reindeer, bison, moose, and horse. There is also a sculpted mammoth (Larichev et al. 1988; Vasil'evskii et al. 1988).

Kokorevo I ([Kokorevo culture] layer 2: 12,940 ± 270, 13,100 ± 500, 15,200 ± 200; layer 3: 13,500 ± 500, 13,330 ± 50, 14,450 ± 150, 15,900 ± 250), on the Yenisei, has a distinctive large-blade technology with burins and end-scrapers on blades. There are also wedges, side-scrapers, Mousterian-like points, antler points, dagger-like tools with unretouched microblade insets, and needle-like points. Well-constructed slab-lined hearths are also typical. Hunting concentrated overwhelmingly on reindeer and hare, but remains of horse, argali sheep, ass, Asiatic wild ass, roe deer, red deer, wolf, arctic fox, possibly dog, rodents, and birds were also found (Vasil'ev 1992).

Maina (layer 3: 12,120 ± 650, 13,900 ± 150; layer 4: 12,910 ± 100, 13,690 ± 390) is the main site for the Afontova culture in the upper Yenisei. Layers 2–4 contain a homogeneous assemblage. In this assemblage, 75–80% of the tools were made on flakes struck from large and mainly single-platform cores. Discoidal and Levallois cores are also present, as is a developed microblade technology based on wedge-shaped and end cores. Side- and end-scrapers are very common and represented by numerous types except end-scrapers on blades. Layers 2–4 also have broad bifacial tools. Burins are rare. There is also a well-developed bone and antler technology, with points, grooved points for insets, smoothers, fasteners, handles, needles, rods, and pendants. Red deer and Siberian wild goat are the dominant species. Other remains include auroch, argali sheep, moose, and hare. There are isolated finds of horse, fox, wolverine, and birds. This fauna reflects the more southerly position of the sites in mountainous topography (Vasil'ev 1992).

Golubaia I (layer 3: 12,900 ± 150, 13,050 ± 90, 12,980 ± 140, 13,650 ± 180) is an intrusive industry that disrupts the Afontova development in the upper Yenisei. Of the tools, 65% were made on blades and bladelets struck from end cores and flat cores. Some elements points to the Kokorevo culture; others harken back to earlier Upper Paleolithic techniques. The fauna includes red deer, auroch, Asiatic wild ass, hare, and birds (Vasil'ev 1992).

Diuktai Cave (layer 7b: 12,690 ± 120, 13,070 ± 90, 14,000 ± 100; layer 7c: 13,100 ± 90) is located in the Aldan Valley of eastern Siberia. The single ^{14}C date for Stratum 7c is probably too young, considering other lines of evidence and information from other sites (Michael 1984). Stratum 7b contains classic types for the Diuktai culture (see also Eliseev and Solov'ev 1992). Subdiscoidal, prismatic, and wedge-shaped core technologies are present, plus burins, insets, end-scrapers, and side-scrapers. Preforms for bifacial knives are present. The fauna includes mammoth (1 large fragment of scapula and 3 pieces of ivory), bison, horse, reindeer, moose, snow sheep (?), cave lion or tiger, fox, arctic fox, ground squirrel, marmot, beaver, hare, and various small rodents (Mochanov 1977).

Berelekh (12,930 ± 80, 13,220 ± 200) is the most northerly Paleolithic site in Siberia at 72° north latitude. It is probably a Diuktai culture site, as it contains both wedge-shaped core and bifacial point technology. Faunal remains from the cultural layer are dominated by varying hare, ptarmigan, and mammoth. Bison or horse, caribou, and fish are represented by a few bones each. Burned and broken mammoth bones were also found on the slope in front of the site (Mochanov 1977; Vereschagin and Mochanov 1972).

Ushki Lake 1 (layer 7: 13,600 ± 250, 14,300 ± 200) is located in central Kamchatka. This layer is an anomaly for the Siberian Upper Paleolithic, and relationships probably lie with Japan. A direct maritime connection through the Kuril Islands may have existed, although it is not necessarily implied. There are dwelling complexes, hearth stains, and a burial pit, although only red ocher, beads, and traces of bone have been preserved. The distinguishing characteristic is about 30 bifacial stemmed projectile points and fragments of other bifacial points. In addition, there are unifacial and bifacial knives, end-scrapers, side-scrapers, burins, burin-like points, and sandstone grinders. Microblades are present, but not wedge-shaped cores (Dikov 1979).

Bölling Warming: 13,000–12,000 BP

Sites dated to this period are Kokorevo III, Tashtyk I, Verkholenskaia Gora, Makarovo II, and Diuktai Cave, layer 7a.

Kokorevo III (12,690 ± 140), on the Yenisei, is a younger site of the Afontova culture. End-scrapers are the most common tool. There are also heavy bifacial side-scrapers, ungrooved antler points, bone needles, and a possible bâton de commandement. Reindeer, auroch, horse, argali sheep, and hare were found here (Abramova 1979b; Vasil'ev 1992).

Tashtyk I (upper layer: 12,180 ± 120), also on the Yenisei, is another site of the Afontova culture, although here several types of side-scrapers dominated the toolkit. End-scrapers are plentiful, and there are bifacial implements that appear to have been side-scrapers. There are also chipped adz and ax-like tools, antler points (ungrooved), awls, needles, rods, a large boar spear, and stone beads. Reindeer dominate the faunal remains, but horse, argali sheep, arctic fox, and willow ptarmigan also occur, as do rare finds of saiga, auroch, red deer, hare, marmot, cave lion, and wolf (Abramova 1979b; Vasil'ev 1992).

Verkholenskaia Gora I (layer III: 12,570 ± 180), on the Angara, is an important site that is usually classified as early Mesolithic, as it contains evidence of changes in the hunting economy (Aksenov 1980). While one might question the single date, geological studies at the site have confirmed the age (Tseitlin 1979). Layer III produced large knives with ovate edges, "ulu" knives, segment-like knives, large side-scrapers, wedge-shaped cores, micro-blades, Verkholenskaia burins (transverse), end-scrapers, micro-end-scrapers, choppers, and wedges. The small toolkit has several traits in common with that of the Diuktai culture, and the approximate parity of large and miniature tools remains typical for the Siberian late Upper Paleolithic. Antler and bone were used to make bilaterally barbed harpoons, which are extremely rare finds. There are also bilaterally slotted bone points for insets. A deer scapula was used as a digging tool. The fauna is comprised of red deer, horse, bison, roe deer, rodents, whitefish, sturgeon, pike, perch, and birds. Fish spearing together with the hunting of some forest species forms the basis for classifying this layer at the oldest phase of the Mesolithic period for the Angara region (Aksenov 1980).

Makarovo II (layer 4: 11,950 ± 50), on the upper Lena, contained wedge-shaped and prismatic cores, knives on blades, and a red deer antler point with bilateral alternating barbs. The fauna is comprised of horse and red deer (Aksenov 1974; Tseitlin 1979).

Diuktai Cave (layer 7a: 12,100 ± 120; 13,200 ± 250), on the Aldan, has the full range of characteristic technology and typology for the Diuktai culture. A good deal of the industry is typical for the late Siberian Upper Paleolithic. Distinctive features are the association of wedge-shaped cores (and debitage) and microblades with bifacial leaf-shaped points and transverse burins. There are also triangular and oval knives. Bone needles, rods, and a mallet comprise the bone industry. A rich faunal assemblage was recovered from the cave: mammoth ivory, bison, horse, reindeer, moose, snow sheep, wolf, fox, arctic fox, ground squirrel, pika, collared and Ob' lemming, gray vole, grouse, ducks, rock and willow ptarmigan, and several fish. Many of the broken long bones are probably mammoth. The most numerous remains, not counting mammoth, are of reindeer, moose, and hare (Mochanov 1977).

12,000–11,000 BP

This period encompasses a possible cooling between the Bölling and Alleröd warming trends, the Alleröd warming, and finally the onset of the Younger Dryas. Sites dated to this period are Novoselovo VI, Makarovo II, layer 3, and Studenoe I, layer 14.

Novoselovo VI (11,600 ± 500), on the Yenisei, is a Kokorevo industry with a typical hearth and the mandible of a woman. This was primarily a reindeer hunting site, but auroch, red deer, hare, wolf, arctic fox, and wolverine are also represented (Vasil'ev 1992).

Makarovo II, layer 3 (11,400 ± 500; 11,800 ± 200), on the upper Lena, contained mostly flakes and bone fragments, but prismatic cores, end-scrapers, and transverse burins are also present. There are also red deer antler points and fish spears, and a knife made from thin bone. The faunal remains include Asiatic wild ass, bison or auroch, horse, bison, wolf, deer, and arctic char (Tseitlin 1979).

The stratified Studenoe I site is remarkable for the stone dwelling foundations with central lined hearths in all levels. Layer 14 (10,975 ± 135; 11,395 ± 100) is typical late Siberian Upper Paleolithic without bifaces. The fauna is more exotic, with remains of Baikal yak, spiral-horned antelope, red deer, auroch or bison, and Siberian mountain goat (Abramova 1984; Larichev et al. 1990).

Younger Dryas: 11,000–10,000 BP

Only three radiocarbon-dated sites in Siberia appear to fall into this time period: Oshurkovo, Ushki Lake 1, layer 6, and Chernoozor'e II, although its date is too old.

Oshurkovo (10,900 ± 50), in the Trans-Baikal, is characterized by prismatic and wedge-shaped cores, pebble tools and choppers, large side-scrappers (sometimes bifacial), end-scrapers, and wedges. There are bone inset points, harpoons, and needles. Hearths contain an abundance of fish bones. The fauna here is comprised of small, short-horned bison, moose, red deer, reindeer, and hare (Okladnikov 1961).

Ushki Lake 1, layer 6 (10,360 ± 350; 10,760 ± 110) is an excellent example of a late Diuktai-like assemblage that forms an intermediary link between Siberia and the Denali Complex of Alaska. There are dwelling complexes and remains of reindeer, bison, horse, moose, and salmon. A dog burial is also reported. Pollens indicate a herbaceous tundra-steppe with stonepine (shrub), alder (shrub), and birch (most likely shrub or even dwarf forms) (Dikov 1979).

Chernoozer'e II (14,500 ± 500), near Omsk in western Siberia, produced a small assemblage containing cylindrical and conical prismatic cores for the removal of small blades. Wedge-shaped cores are absent. Artifacts are comprised of end-scrapers, wedges, perforators, and retouched blades. Of particular note is a large fragment of a bilaterally grooved "dagger" with quartzite insets. The faunal remains are moose, auroch, horse, fox, and varying hare (Petrin 1986). Geologic and faunal information indicates a Noril'sk Stade age for the site (Tseitlin 1979).

THE EARLY POSTGLACIAL

The early climatic episodes of the Holocene, again from the Blytt–Sernander model, are the Preboreal (10,300–9,700) and Boreal (9,700–8,200) periods (Dolukhanov 1984, 1989; Khotinskii 1984; Vorob'eva and Medvedev 1984a,b).

Environments

The transition to the Postglacial period was abrupt and lasted only a few centuries. The late Glacial hyperzonal pattern with meridional (north–south) circulation shifted to lati-tudinal vegetation zones (tundra, taiga, steppe) and zonal (west–east) circulation. Preboreal cooling is detectable in Siberia when late Glacial vegetation (grass and shrubs) appeared in the forests. Conditions were more severe to the east as *Artemisia* spread in the western Baikal region (Khotinskii 1984; Medvedev et al. 1990).

In the Boreal period, the general zonal pattern was similar to the present, although the taiga–tundra boundary was farther north and tundra expansion in the northeast was such that the southern boundary was 100–200 km farther north than at present.

Rising sea levels at the Pleistocene–Holocene transition began to breach the interconti-nental connection of Beringia and to enroach on the exposed continental shelf in northern Siberia, although the New Siberian Islands were still connected to the mainland. Both zonal vegetation patterns and rising sea levels must have been important isolating factors affecting human settlement, movement, and adaptation.

While vegetation zones were similar to the present, species composition was different. Spruce is absent or plays an insignificant role in the Siberian taiga today. During the Boreal period, a major zone of spruce (dark coniferous taiga) extended from the Urals to central Siberia, indicating a climate warmer and moister than present. In the Yenisei and Lena regions, spruce–larch forests were widespread. To the south, spruce–cedar (*Pinus sibirica*) and spruce–fir forests dominated. Significant stretches of steppe were present in the forests of central Yakutia. A cooling trend about 8,000 BP brought the Boreal Period to a close and began the reduction of the taiga to forest-tundra in the north. The dark coniferous taiga became degraded in the central zone (Khotinskii 1984).

The early Holocene fauna shows the effect of the drastic climatic reversal. Although some cold species continue, a mixture of taiga and steppe animals inhabit south Siberia and display regionalization. Horse, cattle, argali sheep, Siberian ibex, red deer, moose, reindeer, roe deer, wolf, and arctic hare are typical. In the Angara region, we find horse, steppe bison (*Bison priscus*), auroch, red deer, moose, reindeer, roe deer, red fox, brown bear, wolverine, and arctic hare. Horse, steppe bison, red deer, reindeer, and arctic fox constitute a cooler fauna. A reorganized early Holocene taiga fauna appears in the Lena basin: red deer, moose, reindeer, roe deer, brown bear, wolf, and hare (Klein 1971; Mochanov 1977). In the north, climatic changes at the end of the Pleistocene brought an end to mammoth, then bison, and finally horse as the dry tundra-steppe gave way to the wet, boggy tundra of the early Holocene. By the middle Holocene, only reindeer survived (Dikov 1979).

Archaeology

Of all the periods of Siberian prehistory, none is so poorly understood or studied as the Mesolithic (e.g., Epi-Paleolithic, Holocene Paleolithic, Pre-Ceramic period). In western Siberia, the complete absence of stratigraphic data and a meager level of geochronological information hinders synthesis. The situation in the Amur and Maritime Territory is little better. The stratigraphic data for south Siberia are significantly better, although the ^{14}C chronology could use improvement (Kol'tsov and Medvedev 1989).

In contrast, the stratigraphic and geochronological record improves in the north, and the single good sequence for the Postglacial period is located in the Lena basin (Mochanov 1973, 1977). In recent years, the Holocene complexes first defined in the Aldan basin have been found to occur over ever-expanding regions of eastern Siberia including the Arctic.

In the Baikal region, Late Paleolithic technology continues into the early Holocene as populations dealt with the environmental transition and reorganized forest-steppe landscapes. In the Lena basin, this period is marked by transition and technological change as populations adjusted to relictual steppe and expanding zonal taiga formations. In the northeast, there is direct continuity of the late Upper Paleolithic into the Holocene, at least in Kamchatka and the upper Kolyma (Aksenov 1980: Dikov 1979; Mochanov 1977).

The East Siberian North

The Sumnagin culture is known from over 30 sites in the Aldan Valley alone. This culture is well dated and is known from excellent stratigraphic contexts. While the main concentrations are on the Lena and Aldan, Sumnagin sites are known from the Olekma in the south, the Viliui to the west, the Okhotsk coast to the east, and in the north from the Taimyr' Peninsula, the Indigirka, and the Kolyma. The Sumnagin culture dates from about 10,500–6,000 BP and is internally consistent in time and space (Alekseev 1987; Argunov 1990; Kol'tsov 1989; Mochanov 1977).

The taiga hunting economy is exemplified by faunal remains of moose, red deer, roe deer, and brown bear. Moose account for two thirds of all remains. Reindeer were hunted in the mountain regions within the taiga and on the northern tundras and forest-tundras. Wolf or dog also occurs, as do forest and water fowl, voles, and a few fish remains.

Sites occur on terraces at headlands formed by the confluence of tributary streams and larger rivers. Finds are concentrated in oval patterns around hearths often lined with cobbles. There are remains of a dwelling in the oldest layer of the culture at Ust'-Timpton with a date of 10,650 ± 80.

Sumnagin is a blade culture. Blades removed from conical and cylindrical prismatic cores served as preforms for about 90% of the tools, and of these about half were made on microblades. These blade tools are insets that can account for 55–70% of all tools. There are also knives, end-scrapers, notched end-scrapers, notched blades, perforators, blades with beveled ends, lateral burins, and angle burins. Engravers (rezchiki) are characteristic. They have the same outline as angle burins except that the working edge is formed by retouch. Geometric microliths (parallelograms) were found at Bel'kachi and Ust'-Timpton and may indicate distant links with the west Eurasian Mesolithic. About 1.5–6.0% of tools were made on flakes and 0.5–3.5% from cobbles.

The bone tool inventory is composed of flat knifeblades with one slot for insets, unilaterally and bilaterally slotted points for insets, points with a split end for an inset, needles, and awls.

Bifacial working was utilized only for the manufacture of adzes, including eared forms, and axes. Notched stones possibly served as net sinkers.

In general, the Sumnagin culture appears to be intrusive from somewhere in the Yenisei region, although the immediate ancestor is unknown. There was some local continuity, since a few wedge-shaped cores were used in the early period of this culture (Mochanov 1973, 1977; Mochanov et al. 1983).

The late Ushki Upper Paleolithic (Kamchatka variant of Diuktai) continues into the Holocene. Finds from layer V at Ushki Lake, while few, are typical: leaf-shaped points and knives, wedge-shaped cores and microblades, burins, scrapers, and grooved abraders (Dikov 1979).

Dikov (1979) has proposed the Sibirdik culture on the basis of data from the Sibirdik and Kongo sites on the upper Kolyma. The early phase of this culture is known from the lower layer of the Kongo site (9,470 ± 130), where choppers, conical cores, burins, blades, and microblades were found. The late phase, based on material from the upper layer of Kongo (8,655 ± 220) and the third layer of Sibirdik (8,020 ± 80 and 8,480 ± 200), is Diuktai-like, with wedge-shaped cores, burins, scrapers, retouched blades, and choppers. Horse and reindeer remains are reported from Sibirdik. This culture appears to be an interface between Sumnagin and late Diuktai.

Finally, mention should be made of a site on Zhokov Island in the East Siberian Islands where a Mesolithic group hunted reindeer, polar bear, wolf, birds, walrus, and seal about 7,000–8,000 BP (Pitul'ko 1993; Pitul'ko and Makeyev 1991). While the New Siberian group was probably still connected to the mainland, Zhokov Island was not and lay about 150 km from the nearest land.

The East Siberian South

The Mesolithic period in the Baikal region is known from at least 52 sites, of which only a handful have good stratigraphic contexts. These sites occur in four geographic groups: the southern Angara (Ust'-Belaia, Sosnovyi Bor, Verkholenskaia Gora, Goreliy Les), the northwest coast of Lake Baikal (Lydar', Bazarnaia, Kurkut', Iterkhei, Ulan Khada, Kurla), Upper Lena (Makarovo I- and II, Kistenovo I–IV), and the northern Angara (Ust'-Kova, Chabodets).

The best-studied area is the Angara region, although there are now dated sequences for the western Cis-Baikal (Sagan-Nuge and Berloga) (Medvedev et al. 1990). The Angara Mesolithic is divided into three periods: Early (12,500–10,000 BP), Middle (10,000–8,000 BP), and Final (8,000–7,000 or 6,000 BP) (Kol'stov and Medvedev 1989; Medvedev et al. 1975).

Archaeological layers for the Early Mesolithic come from the previously discussed site of Verkholenskaia Gora (III: 12,570 ± 180) and Ust'Belaia (XIV–XVI); for the Middle Mesolithic from Verkholenskaia Gora (II), Sosnovyi Bor (IIIa-IIIg), and Ust'-Belaia (II–XIII; XIII: 9,800 ± 500, III–IV: 8,855 ± 300); and for the Final Mesolithic from Gorelyi Les (8,444 ± 300, 8,855 ± 300), Verkholenskaia Gora (I), Sosnovyi Bor (II), and Ust'-Belaia (I). The sites are on river terraces, with the majority on headlands at the mouths of tributary streams and, on Lake Baikal, in small bays.

General features of the Early Mesolithic are bifacial working, flat-faced cores, choppers, and side scrapers. Specific elements are wedge-shaped cores on bifaces and flakes, bifacial points, transverse burins on blades and flakes, bifacial knives and side-scrapers, unifacial and bifacial retouched blades and flakes, unifacial side-scrapers of quartzite and lidite, ordinary quartzite choppers with two or three edges, red deer antler harpoons, fishhooks, and bone and antler composite tools (knives and points). The ratio of blade to microblade is 4:1. Roe deer and fish predominate the fauna from Ust'-Belaia. The fauna for Verkholenskaia was listed above.

In the Middle Mesolithic, there was a standardization and refinement of core types. There are adzes and axes with polished bits, multifaceted burins, fishhooks, and a greater assortment of composite inset tools (knives, daggers, and points). The faunas from the different sites are moose, roe deer, goat, bear, auroch, fox, beaver, wolverine, birds, rodents, whitefish, sturgeon, and large arctic char. Dog burials are known. Fish and roe deer, however, predominate the faunal remains.

In the Final Mesolithic, there are practically no scrapers or choppers, transverse burins are sharply reduced in number, microblades and medium-size blades dominate, and microcores are of single- and double-platform varieties. Large blades are present, but the cores have not been found. Typical elements for this period are polyhedral burins and drills on specific preforms or cores, medial burins on blades, polished points, points on blades with edge retouch, adzes with notched edges, axes, polished slate fishhook shanks, bifacially retouched blade insets, and nonstandard bifacially retouched points. Bone and antler artifacts have not survived. If pottery were added to this complex, we would have an early

Neolithic assemblage. Faunal remains include moose, red deer, and fish, although roe deer predominate.

SUMMARY AND CONCLUSIONS

During the late Glacial period, hyperzonal biotic distributions affected human activity in the complex landscape of Siberia. The late Upper Paleolithic industries were geared to subsistence strategies designed to exploit the mosaic pattern of resources. Only specific trends stand out against this background of technological and typological diversity. In general, this diversity never exceeds the technological and typological standardization of the late Glacial industries; that is, there are few surprises.

Mesolithic stone and bone technologies are firmly rooted in the preceding late Upper Paleolithic. Microblades and the composite inset technique continued to be fundamental for projectile point and knife manufacture. Nonstandard bifacial projectile points, possibly arrow tips, make their appearance only during the Final Mesolithic period.

In general, settlement patterns were remarkably stable from the Late Upper Paleolithic through the northern Bronze Age. This stability is a specific adaptation to subarctic topography in which south-facing, well-drained locations near stream mouths were consistently sought for camping sites.

About 12,000 BP, however, climatic change and the biotic reorganization of the late Glacial landscapes forced an adaptive response that can be measured in the tool kits. Axes, adzes, and fishing gear become important for the first time. Both large herbivore numbers and species diversity were sharply reduced from late Pleistocene conditions, and hunting of large mammals was concentrated on mouse and caribou in the northern taiga and on moose, red deer, and roe deer in the southern taiga. This situation is most pronounced in the Baikal region and the Upper Lena. Caribou became the staple of life on the tundras. In the taiga–steppe borderlands, large-mammal populations were richer and more diversified.

During the early Holocene, large-scale patterns with low internal diversity emerge as an adaptation to the zonal requirements of taiga ecology. The Sumnagin culture is an excellent example of a pattern, with some 4,000 years of time depth adjusted to the warmer and moister taiga of the early Holocene.

Evidence for fishing is either absent, not preserved, or not recovered from the late Glacial sites and, in the north, early Holocene sites. We cannot assume a uniform hydrography or a large number of fish throughout the time period under consideration. Fishing becomes important only about 12,000 BP in the Baikal region and the Upper Lena. This may be the result of a subsistence shift or of fundamental changes in the hydrographic network with respect to water temperature and nutrient levels.

REFERENCES

Abramova, Z. A., 1979a, *Paleolit Yeniseia: Kokorevskaia Kul'tura* (*The Palaeolithic of the Yenisei: The Kokorevo Culture*), Nauka, Novosibirsk.

Abramova, Z. A., 1979b, *Paleolit Yeniseia: Afontovskaia Kul'tura* (*The Paleolithic of the Yenisei: The Afontova Culture*), Nauka, Novosibirsk.

Abramova, Z. A., 1984, Pozdnii Paleolit Aziatskoi Chasti SSSR (The Late Palaeolithic of the Asiatic Part of the USSR, in: *Paleolit SSSR: Arkheologiia SSSR (The Palaeolithic of the USSR: Archaeology of the USSR)* (P. I. Boriskovskii, ed.), Nauka, Moscow, pp. 302–346.

Abramova, Z. A., 1989, Pozdnii Paleolit Servernoi Azii (The Late Palaeolithic of Northern Asia), in: *Paleolit Kavkaza i severnoi Azii (The Palaeolithic of the Caucasus and Northern Asia)* (P. I. Boriskovskii, ed.), Nauka, Leningrad, pp. 168–240.

Aksenov, M. P., 1974, Mnogosloinyi Arkheologicheskii Pamiatnik Makarovo II (The Stratified Archaeological Site of Makarovo II), in: *Drevniaia Istoriia Narodov Iuga Vostochnoi Sibiri, I (The Ancient History of the Peoples of South Central Siberia I)* (M. P. Aksenov, V. V. Svinin, and I. L. Lezhenko, eds.), Irkutsk University, Irkutsk, pp. 91–126.

Aksenov, M. P., 1980, Arkheologicheskaia Stratigrafiia i Posloinoe Opisanie Inventaria Verkhlenskoi Gory I (The Archaeological Stratigraphy and Description of the Inventory by Layer of Verkholenskaia Gora I, in: *Mezolit Verkhnego Priangar'ia (The Mesolithic of the Upper Angara Region)* (M. P. Aksenov, ed.), Irkutsk University Press, Irkutsk, pp. 45–93.

Alekseev, A. N., 1987, *Kamennyi vek Olekma (The Stone Age of the Olekma)*, Irkutsk University, Irkutsk.

Argunov, V. G., 1990, *Kamennyi vek Severo-Zadapnoi Yakutii (The Stone Age of Northwest Yakutia)*, Nauka, Novosibirsk.

Bell, M., and Walker, M. J. C., 1992, *Late Quaternary Environmental Change: Physical and Human Perspectives*, Wiley, New York.

Dikov, N. N., 1979, *Drevnie Kul'tury Severo-Vostochnoi Azii (The Ancient Cultures of Northeast Asia)*, Nauka, Moscow.

Dolukhanov, P. M., and Khotinskii, N. A., 1974, Paleogeograficheskie Rubezhi Golotsena i Meso-Neoliticheskaia Istoriia Evropy (Paleogeographic Boundaries of the Holocene and the Meso-Neolithic History of Europe), in: *Pervobytnyi Chelovek, Ego Material'naia Kul'tura i Priorodnaia Sreda v Pleistotsene i Golotsene (Prehistoric Man, Material Culture and the Environment in the Pleistocene and the Holocene)* (I. P. Gerasimov, ed.), Institut Geografii, Akademiia Nauk SSSR, Moscow, pp. 211–216.

Dolukhanov, P. M., and Khotinskii, W. A., 1984, Human Cultures and the Natural Environment in the USSR during the Mesolithic and Neolithic, in: *Late Quaternary Environments of the Soviet Union* (A. A. Velichko, ed.), University of Minnesota Press, Minneapolis.

Dolukhanov, P. M., 1989, Priorodnye Usloviia Epokhi Mezolita na Territorii SSSR (The Environmental Conditions of the Mesolithic Epoch in the USSR) in: *Mezolit SSSR: Arkheologiia SSSR (The Mesolithic of the USSR. Archaeology of the USSR)* (L. V. Kol'tsov, ed.), Nauka, Moscow, pp. 11–17.

Eliseev, E. I., and Solov'ev, P. S., 1992, Novyi Pamiatnik Diuktaiskoi Kul'tury na Srednei Lene (A New Site of the Diuktai Culture on the Middle Lena), in: *Archaeologicheskie issledovaniia v Yakutii: Trudy Prilenskoi arkheologicheskoi ekspeditsii (Archaeological Research in Yakutiia: Transactions of the Lena Archaeological Expedition)* (A. Mochanov, ed.), Nauka, Novosibirsk.

Grichuk, V. P., 1984, Late Pleistocene Vegetation History, in: *Late Quaternary Environments of the Soviet Union* (A. A. Velichko, ed.), University of Minnesota Press, Minneapolis, pp. 155–178.

Khotinski, N. A., 1984, Holocene Vegetation History, in: *Late Quaternary Environments of the Soviet Union* (A. A. Velichko, ed.), University of Minnesota Press, Minneapolis, pp. 179–200.

Klein, R. G., 1971, The Pleistocene Prehistory of Siberia, *Quaternary Research* 1:133–161.

Kol'tsov, L. V., 1989, Mezolit Severa Sibiri i Dal'nego Vostoka (The Mesolithic of North Siberia and the Far East), in: *Mezolit SSSR: Arkheologiia SSSR (The Mesolithic of the USSR: Archaeology of the USSR)* (L. K. Kol'tsov, ed.), Nauka, Moscow, pp. 187–194.

Kol'tsov, L. V., and Medvedev, G. I., 1989, Mezolit Iuga Sibiri i Dal'nego Vostoka (The Mesolithic of South Siberia and the Far East), in: *Mezolit SSSR. Arkheologiia SSSR (The Mesolithic of the USSR: Archaeology of the USSR)* (L. K. Kol'tsov, ed.), Nauka, Moscow, pp. 174–186.

Larichev, V., Khol'ushkin, U., and Laricheva, I., 1988, The Upper Paleolithic of Northern Asia: Achievements, Problems, and Perspectives: I. Western Siberia, *Journal of World Prehistory* 2(4):359–396.

Larichev, V., Khol'ushkin, U., and Laricheva, I., 1990, The Upper Paleolithic of Northern Asia: Achievements, Problems, and Perspectives. II. Central and Eastern Siberia, *Journal of World Prehistory* 4(3):347–385.

Larichev, V., Khol'ushkin, U., and Laricheva, I., 1992, The Upper Paleolithic of Northern Asia: Achievements, Problems, and Perspectives. III. Northeastern Siberia and the Russian Far East, *Journal of World Prehistory* 6(4):441–476.

Laukhin, S. A., 1990, Paleogreorapicheskie Problemy Zaseleniia Severnoi Azii Paleolitcheskim Chelovekom i Migratsii Ego v Severnuiu Ameriku (Paleogeographical Problems in the Colonization of Northern Asia by Palaeolithic Man), in: *Khronostratigrafiia Paleolita Severnoi, Tsentral'noi i Vostochnoi Azii i Amerki (Doklady*

Mezhdunarodogo Simpoziuma). (*Chronostratigraphy of the Palaeolithic of North, Central and East Asia and America [Reports of an International Symposium]*), Novosibirsk: Institut Istorii i Institut Teplofiziki, Sibirskoe Otdeleniie, Akademiia Nauk SSSR, Novosibirsk, pp. 215–222.

Medvedev, G. I., Mikhniuk, G. N., and Shmygun, P. E., 1975, Mezolit Iuga Vostochnoi Sibiri (Mesolithic of the South of Eastern Siberia), in: *Drevniaia Istoriia Narodov Iuga Vostochnoi Sibiri 3* (*The Ancient History of the Peoples of the East Siberian South 3*) (I. L. Lezhenko, ed.), Irkutsk University Press, Irkutsk, pp. 74–80.

Medvedev, G. I., Savel'ev, N. A., and Svinin, V. V. (Eds.), 1990, *Stratigrafiia, Paleogeografiia and Arkheologiia Iuga Srednei Sibiri (K XIII Kongressu INKVA)* (*Stratigraphy, Paleogeograpy and Archaeology of South Central Siberia*), Irkutsk University Press, Irkutsk.

Michael, H. N., 1984, Absolute Chronologies of Late Pleistocene and Early Holocene Cultures of Northeastern Asia, *Arctic Anthropology* 21(2):1–68.

Mochanov, Iu. A., 1973, Severo-Vostochnaia Aziia v IX-V Tys. Do N.E. (Northeast Asia in the IXth to Vth Millennia B.C.), in: *Problemy Archaeologii Urala i Sibiri* (*Problems in the Archaeology of the Urals and Siberia*) (A. P. Smirnov, ed.), Nauka, Moscow, pp. 29–43.

Mochanov, Iu. A., 1977, *Drevneishie Etapy Zaseleniia Chelovekom Severo-Vostochnoi Azii* (*The Oldest Stages in the Human Colonization of Northeast Asia*), Nauka, Novosibirsk.

Mochanov, Iu. A., Fedoseeva, S. A., Alekseev, S. A., Kozlov, V. I., Kochmar, N. N., and Shcherbakova, N. M., 1983, *Arkheologichskie Pamiatkiki Yakutii (Basseiny Aldana i Olekmy)* (*Archaeological Sites of Yakutia [Aldan and Olekma bains]*), Nauka, Novosibirsk.

Okladnikov, A. P., 1961, The Paleolithic of Trans-Baikal, *American Antiquity* 26(4):486–497.

Okladnikov, A. P., 1968, Sibir' v Drevnekamennom Veke, Epokha Paleolita (Siberia in the Old Stone Age, The Paleolithic Epoch), *Istoriia Sibiri 1* (*The History of Siberia 1*), Nauka, Leningrad, pp. 37–72.

Petrin, V. T., 1986, *Paleoliticheskie Pamiatniki Zapadno-Sibirskoi Ravniny* (*Paleolithic Sites of the West Siberian Plain*), Nauka, Novosibirsk.

Pitul'ko, V. V., 1993, An Early Holocene Site in the Siberian High Arctic, *Arctic Anthropology* 30(1):13–21.

Pitul'ko, V., and Makeyev, V., 1991, Ancient Arctic Hunters, *Nature* 349:374.

Price, T. D., 1987, The Mesolithic of Western Europe, *Journal of World Prehistory* 1(3):225–305.

Roberts, N., 1992, *The Holocene: An Environmental History*, Blackwell, Oxford.

Tseitlin, S. M., 1979, *Geologiia Paleolita Severnoi Azii* (*Geology of the Palaeolithic of Northern Asia*), Nauka, Moscow.

Vasil'ev, S. A., 1992, The Late Palaeolithic of the Yenisei: A New Outline, *Journal of World Prehistory* 6(3):337–383.

Vasil'ev S. A., and Ermolova, N. M., 1983, Maininskaia stoianka—Novyi Pamiatnik Paleolita Sibiri (The Maina Site—a new Palaeolithic Site in Siberia), in: *Paleolit Sibiri* (*The Palaeolithic of Siberia*) (R. S. Vasil'evskii, ed.), Nauka, Novosibirsk, pp. 67–75.

Vasil'evskii, R. S., Burilov, V. V., and Drozdov, N. I., 1988, *Arkheologicheskie Pamiatniki Severnogo Priangar'ia* (*Archaeological Sites of the Northern Angara Region*), Nauka, Novosibirsk.

Vereshchagin, N. K., and Mochanov, Iu. A., 1972, Samie severnie v mire sledy verkhnego paleolita (Berelekhskoe mestonakhozhdenie v nizov'iakh r. Indigirki) (The Northernmost Traces of the Upper Palaeolithic in the World [The Berelekh Locality on the Lower Reaches of the Indigirka River]). *Sovetskaia arkheologiia* 1972(3):332–336.

Vorob'eva, G. A., and Medvedev, G. I., 1984a, *Pleistotsen–Golotsenovye Otlozheniia i Pochvy Arkheologicheskikh Pamiatnikov Iuga Srednei Sibiri* (*The Pleistocene–Holocene Deposits and Soils of the Archaeological Sites of South Central Siberia*), Irkutsk University Press, Irkutsk.

Vorob'eva, G. A., and Medvedev, G. I., 1984b, *Pleistotsen-Golotsenovye Otlozheniia Juga Srednei Sibiri i Arkheologicheskie Ostatki v Geologicheskikh Sloiakh* (*The Pleistocene–Holocene Deposits of South Central Siberia and the Archaeological Remains in the Geological Layers*), Irkutsk University Press, Irkutsk.

Yurtsev, B. A., 1982, Relicts of the Xerophyte Vegetation of Beringia in North-Eastern Asia, in: *Paleoecology of Beringia* (D. M. Hopkins, J. V. Mathews, Jr., C. E. Schweger, and S. B. Young, eds.), Academic Press, New York.

PART V

ENVIRONMENTS AND PEOPLES AT THE PLEISTOCENE–HOLOCENE BOUNDARY IN THE AMERICAS

The advent of warmer Holocene climatic conditions, with associated changes in flora and fauna, brought momentous change to the human populations that had only recently colonized the Americas. Throughout the Western Hemisphere, a series of demographic, technological, and economic changes began that ushered in the era that North American archaeologists label *Archaic* and South American archaeologists label *Preceramic*. In general, these periods are characterized by broad-spectrum or "diffuse" hunting and gathering economies, as well as by increased sedentism and population growth. What were the sources of these transformations? How pervasive were they, and how much variability attended this process throughout the Americas? The following comments, and the five chapters in this section, attempt to address some of these issues.

PALEOENVIRONMENTAL CHANGE AT THE PLEISTOCENE–HOLOCENE TRANSITION

Rising temperatures throughout the late Pleistocene finally ushered in an era that brought opportunities for colonization of new land areas (e.g., in the Arctic, Subarctic, and Subantarctic), but simultaneously offered severe economic challenges with the removal of the Pleistocene megafauna, the subsistence base of the original colonizers of the Americas. Among the more salient environmental changes associated with the Pleistocene–Holocene transition were the following: (1) recession of the Laurentide ice sheet in North America and of montane ice caps in the western coastal mountain ranges throughout the Americas; (2) inundation of the Bering Land Bridge due to glacial melt, severing a land connection with the Old World that had existed since at least 30,000 BP; (2) rising sea levels in areas south of the glacial margin, where isostatic rebound was minimal, resulting in inundation of formerly exposed coastal plains; (3) draining of late Pleistocene glacier-dammed lakes in high-latitude and montane environments; (4) shrinkage or disappearance of late Pleistocene pluvial lakes in western North America and the Andean region and simultaneous expansion of such lakes in northern South America (e.g., in the Venezuelan Ilanos); (5) revegetation of exposed glacial landscapes; (6) disappearance of the late Pleistocene "steppe-tundra" in Beringia and Tierra del Fuego and replacement by evergreen forest; (7) replacement of grasslands by piñon–juniper forest in the southern Great Plains and simultaneous replacement of spruce forest by grasslands in the northern Great Plains and Patagonia (Veblen and Markgraf 1988); (8) replacement of grassland and coniferous forest by deciduous forest in eastern North America; (9) shrinkage of savannas and replacement by subtropical forest in the highlands of Central America, northern South America (Venezuela, Surinam, and Guiana), and eastern Brazil; (10) replacement of savanna by tropical rain forest in Amazonia; (11) elevation of tree line throughout montane regions, resulting in expansion of montane forests and restriction of high-altitude grasslands; (12) extinction of many elements of the Pleistocene megafauna, including at least 30 genera of animals larger than 50 kg body weight (Martin 1967); (13) poleward and high-altitude contraction of tundra and boreal mammals (particularly small mammals) and simultaneous expansion of some deciduous forest genera (Graham et al. 1987); (14) shifts in the strength of nearshore upwelling systems and consequently changes in the productivity of coastlines resulting from changes in oceanic circulation patterns; (15) establishment of anadromous fish runs and shellfish beds following regional sea-level stabilization; (16) reconfiguration of sea mammal and seabird migration patterns following dissolution of land bridges and shifts in ocean circulation patterns; and (17) establishment of avian flyways following glacial recession.

Although it may be possible to list in this way some of the major environmental correlates of the Pleistocene–Holocene climatic shift in the Americas, it is also obvious that any such list is greatly affected by local variability in weather fronts and associated temperature and precipitation regimes. This pattern, which has been traced by Pielou (1991:270), resulted from an interaction between Milankovitch cycles and a host of processes including oceanic circulation patterns and geologic phenomena such as the disappearance of Beringia and establishment of the postglacial Great Lakes. For North America, this process resulted in a west-to-east pattern in the onset (or fullest development) of the postglacial thermal maximum (Figure 1). An early Holocene thermal maximum is evident in the pollen records from Alaska and British Columbia, with a slightly later maximum in much of the Great Basin, Pacific coast, and southwestern Untied States. In the plains–prairie regions, this phenomenon was retarded slightly—perhaps to 8,000 BP—whereas in eastern North America the maximum did not occur until some time between 4,000 and 7,000 BP. Local factors intervened as well in determining the nature of the Pleistocene–Holocene transition: photoperiodicity and seasonal variation in insolation, pedological factors, and the postglacial migration rates of key plant and animal species.

For South America, the picture appears even more complex (cf. Heusser 1987; Markgraf 1989; Markgraf and Bradbury 1983; Vuilleumier 1971). In the highlands of Venezuela and Guiana, as well as in the tropical lowlands to the south, cool, arid conditions of the late Pleistocene were replaced by moister, warmer conditions around 10,000 BP, conditions that lasted at least 2,000 years. In the northern and central Andes (extending from Colombia to northern Argentina), a southward movement of coastal mangrove forest occurred during the late Pleistocene, indicating either wetter conditions or increased runoff in coastal rivers due to accelerated glacial melt. In any case, these conditions were replaced by a dryer, warmer climate between 10,000 and 6,000 BP (with a possible intervening wet

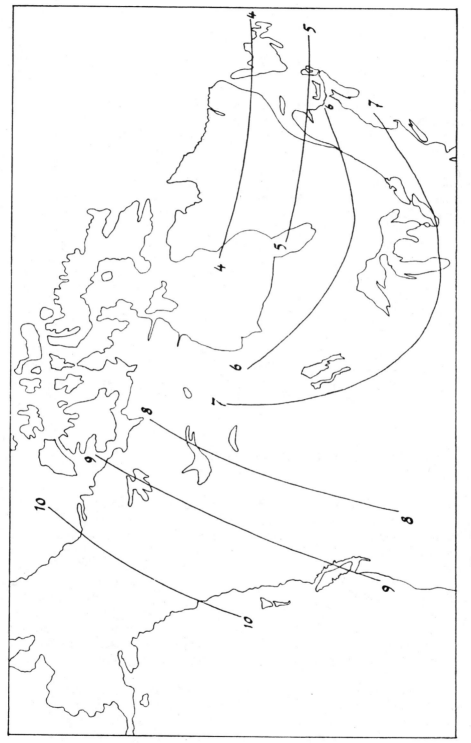

Figure 1. Progression of the climatic optimum in North America. From Pielou (1991:270).

period around 8,000 BP), with a postglacial thermal maximum between 7,500 and 6,500 BP (cf. Heusser 1987b). This increase in aridity may have been due to a shift in the position of the cold Humboldt Current, which had been well to the south along the west coast of South America during the late Pleistocene. As this current moved northward during the early Holocene, the North Pacific anticyclonic systems were displaced northward, creating rainfall reductions in the mountains and probably along the coast as well. In the southern Andes (Argentina and Chile), the situation was somewhat variable. In the northern portion of the area, warmer and relatively moist conditions prevailed, with a shift to more arid conditions between 8,500 and 6,500 BP. In the Patagonian desert, warmer and drier conditions occurred after 10,000 BP, culminating in a postglacial thermal maximum between 8,000 and 6,000 BP. In Tierra del Fuego and the Chilean archipelago, cooler and moister conditions occurred until 8,500 BP, with modern conditions established after 6,500 BP (Shackleton 1978).

In both North and South America, a strongly debated issue is the strength and importance of a brief (1,000-year?) episode of climatic deterioration during the terminal Pleistocene, possibly associated with the "Valders" glacial advance of the Laurentide ice in North America and the "El Abra" glacial advance in the Andes, and suggested to be linked to the "Younger Dryas" stage in the classic European climatic sequence. Pollen diagrams in a number of areas, ranging from Alaska to Tierra del Fuego, have been used to support this assertion (e.g., Markgraf 1991; Heusser and Robassa 1987) as has the record of loess deposition in interior Alaska (Bigelow et al. 1990). Haynes (1993) has suggested that a strongly arid climate prevailed in western North America during the Younger Dryas episode. Whether or not such interpretations are valid, and how much impact this brief climatic deterioration may have had on terminal Pleistocene human populations in the Americas, has yet to be determined.

IMPACT OF PALEOENVIRONMENTAL CHANGES ON HUMAN POPULATIONS

Nearly four decades ago, Joseph Caldwell (1958) suggested that the apparent paucity of early Holocene archaeological sites in eastern North America was due to the difficulties of adjustment to postglacial conditions, as the descendants of Paleoindians learned to adapt to newly forested environments. He referred to the process as one of developing "primary forest efficiency" and suggested that new technological developments were required to keep pace with postglacial environmental changes. Today, we recognize that part of the problem lies in the difficulty of discovering early Holocene sites. This difficulty is particularly true of sites in river valleys, buried by tons of alluvium deposited as river gradients lessened in response to eustatically rising sea levels of the early Holocene period. Part of the problem may also rest in the lower productivity of the early Holocene forests in places like eastern North America, in comparison with the high productivity "mast forests" of mid-Holocene times (Snow 1980).

At any rate, within ten years, the publication by Binford (1968) of a paper entitled "Post-Pleistocene Adaptations" initiated a paradigm shift that was more mechanistic and less teleological, in which postglacial environmental changes were viewed as neither permissive nor restrictive, but simply as requiring a set of technological changes (e.g., from "implements" to "facilities") and behavioral repertoires (e.g., smaller cooperative hunting groups) among those who survived the Pleistocene–Holocene transition. Binford (1983), Cohen (1975), Yesner (1980), and others emphasized the role of demographic factors in this process, and Hayden (1981) brought human decision making back into the process as well.

Current views of human response to the Pleistocene–Holocene transition in the Americas reflect some or all of these views, and it is certainly true that paleoenvironmental changes impacted human populations in diverse ways. One may isolate a number of key elements, however, that link the environmental changes to patterns of human subsistence and settlement. They may be expressed as a series of questions, as follows:

1. *The timing of human occupation of the Americas:* To what degree was the process of colonization of the Americas affected by the climatic changes occurring at the Pleistocene–Holocene transition? How did the disappearance of the Bering Land Bridge, the opening of the Western Canadian ("Ice-free") Corridor, dense forestation of the Panamanian isthmus, opening of the Magellan Straits, coastal changes related to isostatic rebound or sea-level rise, and patterns of glacial recession and vegetational change affect continued colonization of habitat in the Americas?

2. *Pleistocene megafaunal extinctions:* Was the process of terminal Pleistocene megafaunal extinction affected by climatic change at the Pleistocene–Holocene transition, or was it largely complete by this time? How much local variability occurred in this process? What role might humans be assigned in the process?

3. *Dietary diversity and technological change:* How diverse was the human diet at the Pleistocene–Holocene boundary in different parts of the Americas? To what degree did human populations attempt to continue to focus on large game animals by following them northward, by pursuing remnant populations in relict grassland areas, or by developing new technologies or hunting methods to intensify the exploitation of remnant populations? Alternatively, to what degree did populations shift to a broader spectrum of higher-cost, lower-return resources such as small game birds, fish, or shellfish?

4. *Use of coastal resources:* When did human use of marine resources begin? How are local variations in the timing of initiation of coastal exploitation to be explained? Can they be attributed primarily to changes in coastal geomorphology and marine productivity (the "pull" factor) or to population growth and impact on marine resources (the "push" factor)? Or are the observed patterns only an artifact of coastal site preservation?

5. *Environmental seasonality and "logistic" strategies:* In many areas, the substitution of forest for grassland resulted in the disappearance of large grazing animals. This process, however, also raised the diversity and biomass of edible plant resources, with the former emphasized in tropical areas and the latter in temperate ones. In tropical lowlands, although well-defined wet and dry seasons are present, there is relatively low seasonality in fruit and nut production, and there is a wider variety of resources available at all times of year. In temperate deciduous forests, however, there is a substantial seasonality in fruit and nut production, and in cooler areas some animals may hibernate, while others may be more difficult to obtain in winter. Storage practices and other "logistical" strategies concomitantly become more important. In open environments, an even greater use of "logistical" strategies

would have been necessitated by a shift from dependence on elephants and other species with short-term migrations (Churcher 1980) to caribou, bison, or camelids, which make migrations of greater distances. The impact of this shift toward exploiting migratory species would have been exacerbated by a simultaneous necessity to broaden the diet, requiring the use of intercept (as opposed to herd-pursuit) hunting methods. This process would have been most extreme in northern environments, where resource seasonality is greater, and most attenuated in the highlands of Central and South America. In the Andes, for example, because of the density of microenvironments within a restricted geographic region, changes in flora and fauna linked with changing tree lines could have been accommodated through short-distance "transhumance" and trade relations, hallmarks of the Andean Preceramic. This accommodation would have been particularly true along the central Andean coast, where highland, tropical lowland, coastal desert, and marine environments are juxtaposed within a relatively small area.

THE ARCHAEOLOGICAL RECORD AT THE PLEISTOCENE–HOLOCENE TRANSITION

The chapters in this section demonstrate some of the critical evidence that will allow us to address the questions raised above. My own Chapter 13 attempts to tackle several of the questions in examining the dynamics of the Pleistocene–Holocene boundary in the region of initial human occupation of the Americas: interior Alaska and the adjacent Yukon Territory. Current dating of sites in this region makes it apparent that there is no solid evidence for human occupation before circa 12,000 BP, and that conditions were probably inimical for human occupation before that time.

Two corollary points are readily apparent. First, the latest broadly accepted dates for mammoth and horse in interior Alaska either are coincident with or slightly precede the earliest dates for human occupation of the area (Dixon 1993). Thus, despite the popular model, there is no demonstrated evidence of humans killing mammoths in eastern Beringia; at the Broken Mammoth site, only mammoth tusk material was retrieved, apparently for tool manufacture. Here, the relationship of the early Holocene thermal maximum and the extinction of mammoth and horse is probably more than coincidental. That is to say, as obligate grazers of long, high-fiber grasses, such animals would have been much more subject to extinction as those grasses themselves began to disappear around 14,000 years ago and were replaced by an association of shorter grasses, sedges, and dwarf birch and willow, which supported the apparently surviving bison and elk populations. After 9,000 years ago, spruce forest (with cottonwood and alder) colonized the area, primarily as a result of tree migration rather than climatic warming. This forest would have had reduced carrying capacity for bison and elk, but would have created habitat for browsers and other boreal species, including moose and woodland caribou as well as small game. Continued exploitation of remnant bison populations in small *refugia* would have required more individualistic hunting strategies or the use of surround methods in valley bottoms. In interior Alaska, such methods would have necessitated some changes in settlement patterns, including abandoning overlook sites used for observation of large-game movement and initial processing of large-game kills, a process that seems to have taken place after 9,000 BP. In the process, the more fragmented, mobile microbands or household groups of the late Pleistocene would have been replaced by more sedentary riverine and lacustrine villages. Unfortunately, as indicated in Chapter 13, most such village sites are probably buried under tons of Holocene river valley alluvium.

Perhaps more important, the evidence from Broken Mammoth suggests that a wide diversity of small game, birds, and fish were exploited at the time of the Pleistocene–Holocene transition in addition to the bison, elk, caribou, moose, and possible camelid exploited at the site. In fact, the earliest occupation of the site (dating from circa 12,000 to 11,000 BP) is dominated by bird remains! This finding suggests that the North Pacific flyway had been reestablished and that a truly diverse subsistence base was exploited (fish were added to the repertory by 10,000 BP).

At the close of the Pleistocene, continual reductions in large-game populations may have forced the initial utilization of the coastline of northwestern North America. Although earlier authors (e.g., Aigner and Del Bene 1982; Laughlin et al. 1979) suggested that the southern coast of the Bering Land Bridge may have been occupied for 15,000 years, and although many still believe that the North Pacific coast could have served as a migration avenue for late glacial hunters, there is no evidence to suggest utilization of that coast before the earliest Holocene (≈9,000 BP). Before that time, ice tongues and icebergs in the Gulf of Alaska may have seriously impeded such a migration, and at best would have restricted the availability of food resources. A better avenue would have involved penetrating the coast in the region of the Alexander Archipelago in southeast Alaska. Here, too, however, the earliest dates are Holocene. The Hidden Falls site dates to circa 9,200 BP (Davis 1988), and Ackerman et al. (1979) estimate the Ground Hog Bay site to have a similar date. Earlier dates of circa 9,800 BP have been obtained from the Namu site on the British Columbia coast (Carlson 1991), and still older levels (as yet undated) were excavated during 1994. As Erlandson and Moss point out in Chapter 14, lack of intervening early archaeological assemblages in the Queen Charlotte Islands or northern British Columbia is likely a result of marine transgressions of terminal Pleistocene times, and undated intertidal assemblages may well date from this period. However, the appearance of microblade technology in the lowest levels of Ground Hog Bay, Hidden Falls, and now Namu (Carlson 1994 personal communication)—a technology that appears in the earliest sites in interior Alaska—suggests a pattern of southward coastal migration (of proto–Na Dene speakers?) during early Holocene times. If true, then these assemblages may predate the "Pebble Tool" or "Old Cordilleran" Tradition, even though the latter is represented in some of the intertidal assemblages. The "microblade people" appear to make their southernmost stand somewhere along the coast of British Columbia.

To date, no evidence has appeared to support the hypothesis of earlier coastal migrations put forth by Gruhn (1994). Farther south of British Columbia, the earliest coastal sites in California are found in the Channel Islands, including the Daisy Cave site reported by Erlandson and Moss, with dates of 10,200–10,400 BP, and the "Arlington Man" site, with dates of circa 10,000 BP. The tool assemblage described to date from Daisy Cave does not allow association with Clovis, "Old Cordilleran," or other early tool assemblages. By the time the evidence of coastal adaptation becomes more widespread—with the "Paleocoastal Tradition" postdating 10,000 BP (Moratto 1984)—bifacial industries linked to these traditions are well established.

Interestingly, the earliest coastal dates we have to the south of California—those along the coast of Peru and northern Chile—also date to earliest Holocene times (no older than 9,700 BP [cf. Richardson 1978]). As Erlandson and Borrero note, Pleistocene coastal productivities in both North and South America were probably lower than in the Holocene, which may help to account for this phenomenon. In this light, it is interesting that the places that have the record of some of the earliest Holocene coastal sites (the Aleutians, southern California, coastal Peru) are the places that today have the strongest upwelling systems and would therefore have had some of the few productive coastlines at the end of the Pleistocene—a point I made more than 15 years ago for other areas such as South Africa (Yesner 1980).

At any rate, the universality of early Holocene coastal dates—from the Aleutian Islands to the Chilean coast—suggests that this has more to do with the actual initiation of the use of coastal resources than simply with the preservation of coastal sites. If so, it may be viewed as an ultimate response to the extinction of large-game populations. Erlandson notes that late Paleoindians at Tule Lake in northern California were exploiting a diverse assemblage of resources, including aquatic resources. This diversity mirrors the diversity of terminal Pleistocene–earliest Holocene faunal assemblages at the Broken Mammoth site and at Charlie Lake cave in the interior of British Columbia. There are some suggestions as well (cf. Amick 1994) that faunal assemblages associated with the Folsom Paleoindians of the High Plains during the terminal Pleistocene–earliest Holocene period were more diverse than those associated with earlier Clovis Paleoindians.

How were the plains colonized? After decades of searching for early sites in the western corridor between the Laurentide and Cordilleran ice sheets in Alberta and British Columbia, little evidence of early usage of that area has been found. Charlie Lake Cave, at the southern end of the corridor, is terminal Pleistocene in date, and there is considerable evidence that the Peace River district to the north was as inimical to human occupation before that time as was interior Alaska. The excavators of the site (Fladmark et al. 1988) have suggested that it represents a northward movement of Paleoindians pursuing remnant bison herds at the close of the Pleistocene. Such a movement, if it occurred, might help to explain the existence of Paleoindian projectile points in both interior and northern Alaska—for example, at the Mesa site (Kunz and Reanier 1994)—in contexts best dated as early Holocene (around 10,000 BP).

In Chapter 15, Frison and Bonnichsen trace some additional effects of the Pleistocene–Holocene transition on the Plains and Rocky Mountains of North America. Although there were some minor shifts in vegetation zones and small-mammal populations before the end of the Pleistocene, these smaller-scale changes were replaced by strongly increasing temperature and aridity between 10,000 and 8,000 years ago, culminating in the conditions of the thermal maximum. As in interior Alaska, mammoth had become extinct and bison had become a less stable dependable resource, probably necessitating the use of different hunting techniques. More attention turned to small-game and plant resources (the latter being a solution not possible in Alaska). This change may have necessitated increased food storage, as well as increased transhumance to obtain mountain sheep and deer at higher altitudes. Again, as in Alaska, small *refugia* may have continued to exist where the old patterns of bison hunting remained possible.

Because of the acidic, podzolic soils associated with the forests of eastern North America, little bone preservation has occurred, except in unusual circumstances. As a result, most of the interpretations of shifting lifestyles at the Pleistocene–Holocene transition are focused on lithic assemblages and other archaeological features. In Chapter 16, Anderson, Morse, and Goodyear outline some of the changes that can be traced archaeologically. Except for the enigmatic earlier occupation of Meadowcroft Rock Shelter, early Paleoindian assemblages (11,900–10,750 BP), as in the Plains, were characterized by the fluted points of unknown ultimate origin. In late Paleoindian times of the terminal Pleistocene, these points were replaced by a more diverse lanceolate point assemblage, loosely grouped as the Dalton complex. By early Holocene times, these points were replaced by notched, bifurcate-based, and eventually stemmed points (after circa 8,000 BP). Regional localization of styles begins to take place, which (according to Morse and colleagues) may reflect reduction in territorial size. An alternative interpretation would be that this increased variability simply matches the increased diversity in the early Holocene environment itself.

The few faunal associations that are known suggest that caribou and possibly mammoth may have been a mainstay of earlier Paleoindians in northeastern North America, while mastodon, sloth, and peccary were favored in midlatitudes and mastodon, sloth, and camelids in the southeast United States region. With the climatic changes of the terminal Pleistocene, boreal forest withdrew into northeastern North America, supporting woodland caribou, moose, and probably elk, while white-tailed deer came to dominate farther south after the extinction of the Pleistocene megafauna. There may be some relationship between these faunal changes and the observed changes in projectile point styles, reflecting the necessities for different hafting regimes and possibly design changes in spear throwers. In addition, as in the Plains, plant resources would have formed a larger portion of the diet. As Flannery has argued for Mesoamerica, this switch would likely have resulted in more widely dispersed microbands, for whom resource "scheduling" would have been of greater concern. According to Morse and colleagues, this would have led to reduced archaeological visibility, which is the real reason for the apparent reduction in site numbers in the early Holocene period.

In South America, the level of human response to the Pleistocene–Holocene transition is still unclear, and was perhaps simply not as great as in North America. Thus, in Chapter 17, Borrero is able to conclude that "in most regions the transition produced no impact on human populations." There may be at least three major reasons that this is so. First, as Borrero notes, human populations in South America were still "beginning their process of adjustment to new environments," although colonization as far south as the Magellan Straits was certainly in place by 11,000 BP. Second, the transition appears less dramatic in South America because late Pleistocene populations there were already exploiting a more diverse food base than were similar peoples elsewhere in the Americas. This point is made separately by both Dillehay and Lynch, despite their differing views on the antiquity of colonization of South America. At the Monte Verde site in central Chile, local inhabitants—perhaps as early as 13,000 BP—were exploiting *both* mastodon and a diversity of other food resources, including a wide range of plant types (Dillehay 1989). The same could be said for the Guitarrero Cave site in the Peruvian highlands, dated some 3,000 years later (Lynch 1980). There, a wide variety of larger as well as smaller game and plants were utilized, and some of the first experiments with domestication were taking place as early as 9,000 BP among people with an otherwise Paleoindian-derivative technology and lifestyle. As Borrero notes, an increase in the "exploitation of a variety of food resources" did occur with the Pleistocene–Holocene transition in South America, particularly in response to the extinction of large game such as mastodon, sloth, and glyptodonts (the human role in this extinction being still unclear). The effect of this was apparently more marked in Patagonia (Miotti and Salemme 1995) than for South America as a whole; however, this process may have been less pronounced than in North America. On the basis of present data, it seems also to have been largely independent of the details of regional postglacial environmental changes outlined previously.

In addition, in the more open environments of Patagonia and the high Andes, wild camelids (guanaco and vicuna, respectively) continued to survive, serving as forerunners for domesticated camelids. Guanaco continued to be exploited by the Aonikenk (Tehuelche) and Selk'nam (Ona) people of southern Patagonia and northern Tierra del Fuego until historic times. Thus, there was a partial transfer of megafaunal hunting into postglacial times, analogous to the survival of bison on the Plains (and in interior Alaska?) or of various cervids in different parts of the Americas. Whether hunting techniques different from those used in Pleistocene times were applied to surviving camelid populations in South America is not yet clear.

Finally, as noted above, the initiation of the use of marine environments in South America, as in North America, began within 1,000 years of the Pleistocene–Holocene transition, particularly in the highly productive environment of the Peruvian coast, and was preceded by the still earlier coastal Paijan complex. By the time of the postglacial thermal maximum—ranging from 6,500 to 8,500 BP—coastal sites had become widespread, from the *sambaquis* of Brazil to the shores of the Beagle Channel in Tierra del Fuego. Much of the variability in this process had to do with sea level change (Isla 1989), as well as the dynamics of marine currents, local patterns of tectonic uplift, and even the frequency of tsunamis along tectonically active coasts.

In sum, the impact of the Pleistocene–Holocene transition on human populations in the Americas was highly variable and depended much on local patterns of climatic change, the diversity of available plant and animal species, and the responses of local flora and fauna to those climatic changes. As a whole, however, the patterns stand in contrast to those of the Old World and Australia, where human colonization had occurred much earlier and, one assumes, had developed a somewhat greater ability to adjust to the significant, if variable, impacts of these important climatic changes.

DAVID R. YESNER

REFERENCES

Ackerman, R. E., Hamilton, T. D., and Stuckenrath, R., 1978, Early Cultural Complexes on the Northern Northwest Coast, *Canadian Journal of Archaeology* 3:195–209.

Aigner, J. S., and Del Bene, T., 1982, Early Holocene Maritime Adaptation in the Aleutian Islands, in: *Peopling of the New World* (J. E. Ericson, R. E. Taylor, and R. Berger, eds.), Ballena Press, Los Altos, pp. 35–67.

Amick, D. F., 1994, Dietary Diversity among Folsom Paleoindian Populations. Paper Presented to the Annual Meeting of the Society for American Archaeology, Anaheim.

Bigelow, N. H., Beget, J. E., and Powers, W. R., 1990, Latest Pleistocene Increase in Wind Intensity Recorded in Aeolian Sediments from Central Alaska, *Quaternary Research* 34:160–168.

Binford, L. R., 1968, Post-Pleistocene Adaptations. in: *New Perspectives in Archaeology* (L. R. Binford and S. R. Binford, eds.), Seminar Press, New York, pp. 313–341.

Binford, L. R., 1983, *In Pursuit of the Past: Decoding the Archaeological Record*, Thames and Hudson, New York.

Caldwell, J. R., 1958, *Trend and Tradition in the Prehistory of the Eastern United States*, Society for American Archaeology, Menasha.

Carlson, R. L., 1991, The Northwest Coast before A.D. 1600, in: *The North Pacific to 1600* (A. E. Crounhart-Vaughan, eds.), Oregon Historical Society, Portland, pp. 109–136.

Churcher, C. S., 1980, Did the North American Mammoth Migrate? *Canadian Journal of Anthropology* 1:103–106.

Cohen, M. N., 1975, *The Food Crisis in Prehistory*, Yale University Press, New Haven.

Davis, S. D., 1988, *The Hidden Falls Site, Baranof Island, Alaska*, Alaska Anthropological Association, Anchorage.

Dillehay, T. D., 1989, *Monte Verde: A Late Pleistocene Settlement in Chile*, Smithsonian Institution Press, Washington, DC.

Dixon, E. J., 1993, *Quest for the Origins of the First Americans*, University of New Mexico Press, Albuquerque.

Fladmark, K. R., Driver, J. C., and Alexander, D., 1988, The Paleoindian Component at Charlie Lake Cave, British Columbia, *American Antiquity* 53:371–384.

Graham, R. D., Semken, H. A., and Graham, M. A., 1987, *Late Quaternary Mammalian Biogeography and Environments of the Great Plains and Prairies*, Illinois State Museum, Springfield.

Gruhn, R., 1994, The Pacific Coast Route of Initial Entry: An Overview, in: *Method and Theory for Investigating the Peopling of the Americas* (R. Bonnichsen and D. G. Steele, eds.), Center for the Study of the First Americans, Oregon State University, Corvallis, pp. 249–256.

Hayden, B. M., 1981, Research and Development in the Stone Age: Technological Transitions among Hunter–Gatherers, *Current Anthropology* 22:519–548.

Haynes, C. V., Jr., 1993, Clovis–Folsom Geochronology and Climatic Change, in: *From Kostenki to Clovis: Upper Paleolithic-Paleoindian Adaptations* (O. Soffer and N. D. Praslov, eds.), Plenum Press, New York, pp. 219–236.

Heusser, C. J., 1987a, Quaternary Vegetation of Southern South America, *Quaternary of South America and the Antarctic Peninsula* 5:197–222.

Heusser, C. J., 1987b, Fire History of Fuego-Patagonia, *Quaternary of South America and Antarctic Peninsula* 5: 93–109.

Heusser, C. J., and Rabassa, J., 1987, Cold Climatic Episode of Younger Dryas Age in Tierra del Fuego, *Nature* 328: 609–611.

Isla, F. I., 1989, Holocene Sea-Level Fluctuation in the Southern Hemisphere, *Quaternary Science Reviews* 8: 359–368.

Kunz, M. L., and Reanier, R. E., 1994, Paleoindians in Beringia: Evidence from Arctic Alaska, *Science* 263:660–662.

Laughlin, W. S., Jorgensen, J. B., and Frohlich, B., 1979, Aleuts and Eskimos: Survivors of the Bering Land Bridge Coast, in: *The First Americans: Origins, Affinities, and Adaptations* (W. S. Laughlin and A. B. Harper, eds.), Gustav Fisher, New York, pp. 91–104.

Lynch, T. F., 1980, *Guitarrero Cave*, Academic Press, New York.

Markgraf, V., 1989, Paleoclimates in Central and South America since 18,000 BP based on pollen and lake-level records, *Quaternary Science Reviews* 8:1–24.

Markgraf, V., 1991, Younger Dryas in Southern South America? *Boreas* 20:63–69.

Markgraf, V., and Bradbury, J. P., 1983, Holocene climatic history of North America, *Striae* 16:40–45.

Martin, P. S., 1967, Prehistoric Overkill, in: *Pleistocene Extinctions: The Search for a Cause* (P. S. Martin and H. E. Wrights, eds.), Yale University Press, New Haven, pp. 75–120.

Miotti, L., and Salemme, M., 1995, Biodiversity, Taxonomic Richness, and Generalists—Specialists during the Late Pleistocene/Early Holocene Times in the Pampas and Patagonia (Argentina, Southern South America). Paper presented at the International Quaternary Association, Berlin.

Moratto, M. J., 1984, *California Archaeology*, Academic Press, New York.

Pielou, E. C., 1991, *After the Ice Age: The Return of Life to Glaciated North America*, University of Chicago Press, Chicago.

Richardson, J. B., 1978, Early Man on the Peruvian North Coast, Early Maritime Exploitation, and the Pleistocene and Holocene Environment, in: *Early Man in America from a Circum-Pacific Perspective* (A. L. Bryan, ed.), Archaeological Researchers International, Edmonton, pp. 274–289.

Shackleton, N., 1978, Some Results of the CLIMAP Project, in: *Climatic Change and Variability: A Southern Perspective* (A. B. Pittock, L. A. Frakes, D. Jenssen, J. A. Peterson, and J. W. Ziliman, eds.), Cambridge University Press, Cambridge, pp. 69–76.

Snow, D. R., 1980, *The Archaeology of New England*, Academic Press, New York.

Veblen, T. T., and Markgraf, V., 1988, Steppe expansion in Patagonia? *Quaternary Research* 30:331–338.

Vuilleumier, B. S., 1971, Pleistocene Changes in the Fauna and Flora of South America, *Science* 173:771–780.

Yesner, D. R., 1980, Maritime Hunter–Gatherers: Ecology and Prehistory, *Current Anthropology* 21:727–750.

Chapter **13**

Human Adaptation at the Pleistocene–Holocene Boundary (circa 13,000 to 8,000 BP) in Eastern Beringia

DAVID R. YESNER

LATE PLEISTOCENE–EARLY HOLOCENE SITES IN ALASKA AND THE YUKON

During the past two decades, there has been a substantial evolution in thinking about the earliest human populations in Alaska. The advent of accelerator mass spectrometry (AMS) dating, enabling the dating of small amounts of remnant collagen in ancient bones, allowed the redating of the most diagnostic human implement from the Old Crow basin in the northern Yukon Territory—the famous caribou tibia flesher—from circa 28,000 BP to circa 1,800 BP. Coupled with demonstrations that other taphonomic agents—ranging from carnivores to ice push—could have been responsible for spiral fractures and polish found on the redeposited bones of the Old Crow River gravels, this redating took away the confidence of most Arctic archaeologists that such "preprojectile point" sites did in fact represent an earlier stage in the peopling of northern North America. Thus, Old Crow joined earlier constructions such as Sedna Creek, Engigstciak, and the British Mountain Complex of the North Slope of Alaska and the adjacent Mackenzie River drainage as representative elements of a hypothetical but unproven stage of occupation of northwest North America predating circa 13,000 BP.

Early cave sites in the north—ranging from the Trail Creek Caves on the Seward Peninsula of western Alaska to the Bluefish Caves of the Yukon Territory—have also provided

DAVID R. YESNER • Department of Anthropology, University of Alaska, Anchorage, Alaska 99508.

Humans at the End of the Ice Age: The Archaeology of the Pleistocene–Holocene Transition, edited by Lawrence Guy Straus, Berit Valentin Eriksen, Jon M. Erlandson, and David R. Yesner. Plenum Press, New York, 1996.

enigmatic data, since many of these early caves contain a record of animal bone deposits that can have resulted from multiple taphonomic agents. Many of these caves served as dens or lairs of Pleistocene carnivores including the cave lion and short-faced bear. Spiral fractures and impact points found on bones from such sites are no more clearly indicative of human workmanship than are the materials from the Old Crow basin. The Trail Creek caves, Upper Porcupine River caves, Lime Hills caves, and southeastern Alaskan caves may all fall into this category. Of all these sites, only the Bluefish Caves present a likely case for early human presence. There, a date on horse bone of circa 13,000 BP may provide the earliest unequivocal evidence for human evidence in the far north, assuming that the association of this material with the small artifactual assemblage, including a distal microblade segment, is valid (cf. Cinq-Mars 1979; Morlan and Cinq-Mars 1982).

After circa 12,000 BP, the record of human occupation of eastern Beringia becomes somewhat more abundant. For the period from circa 12,000 BP to 8,000 BP, it is possible to subdivide the archaeological record of eastern Beringia into four major segments: (1) northern Alaska, defined as the area north of the Yukon River drainage, including the region of continuous permafrost and tundra vegetation north of the Arctic Circle, as well as the Brooks Range; (2) interior Alaska, defined as the series of connected intermontane valleys ranging from the northern foothills of the Alaska Range north to the Yukon River; (3) southwest Alaska, including the Kuskokwim and other major river drainages lying in unglaciated territory; and (4) glaciated southern Alaska, a maritime region ranging from the Aleutian Islands in the west to the Alexander archipelago in the east. To some degree, different archaeological industries—and therefore possibly different ethnic traditions—characterized these regions.

In northern Alaska, a widespread fluted point industry is known from both surficial and buried contexts (Clark 1992) (cf. Figure 1). Fluted point assemblages are characterized by point typologies with linkages to the Agate basin and Goshen complexes of the northern Plains (Frison 1992, 1993). Although most dates associated with these industries are early Holocene rather than late Pleistocene, some earlier dates in the 11,000–12,000 BP region have been recorded from the Mesa site (Kunz and Reanier 1994; Reanier 1982) and the Putu site (Alexander 1987). Many of these sites are on bluffs, terraces, or mesas and represent probable "lookout" points for spotting and intercepting migratory herds of animals. Considering that boreal elements (i.e., spruce trees) came into this region late in the postglacial sequence (≈8,000 BP), reaching their maximum extension in the southern Brooks Range, it is likely that caribou and other species adapted to extreme cold, as well as to the utilization of lichens and other scanty vegetation, predominated throughout this period as they did in the later Holocene. In general, sites in this region are associated with relatively shallow soils, little paleosol formation, and relatively poor organic preservation (Hamilton 1994 personal communication), so that it is difficult to work out detailed artifact sequences or reconstruct prehistoric subsistence patterns.

In interior Alaska, the original archaeological constructs included a "Paleoarctic" tradition (Anderson 1970, 1984, 1988), initially based on materials from the Kobuk River in northwest Alaska; the "Denali Complex" (West 1967, 1974, 1975, 1980), based on sites in the northern foothills of the Alaska Range; and the "Chindadn Complex," best known from the Healy Lake village site in the southern Tanana Valley (Cook 1969, 1975). In all cases, these were assemblages that contained both biface production and microcore-and-blade technology; West (1981) has subsumed them under the "Beringian Tradition." Many of these

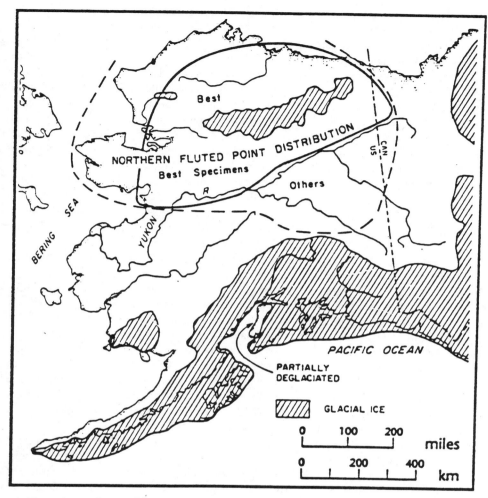

Figure 1. Distribution of fluted points in eastern Beringia. From Clark (1992). Used by permission.

sites suffered from interpretive problems due to geological contexts with thin soil formation and cryoturbation (Hamilton 1970; Schweger 1985; Thorson 1990).

The discovery of sites such as Dry Creek (Holmes 1974; Powers and Hamilton 1978; Powers et al. 1983), Walker Road (Powers et al. 1990), Panguingue Creek (Powers and Maxwell 1986), Moose Creek (Hoffecker 1985), and Owl Ridge (Phippen 1988) in the Nenana Valley south of Fairbanks, in contexts of thick loess deposits associated with glacial outwash streams (Thorson 1990; Thorson and Hamilton 1977), allowed finer separation of cultural components, often associated with paleosols representing stabilized land surfaces. Data from these sites have allowed the distinction of a late Pleistocene "Nenana Complex," based on a bifacial industry, and variously dated between 11,800 and 10,700 BP, from a terminal Pleistocene–early Holocene Denali Complex dominated by core and blade material (Powers and Hoffecker 1989; Powers et al. 1990; cf. Haynes 1990; Mobley 1991). Nenana Complex materials include teardrop-shaped "Chindadn" points, also known from Healy Lake (Cook 1969), and other projectile point types seen by the investigators as linked to Paleo-Indian industries south of the ice sheets (Goebel et al. 1991; Hoffecker et al. 1993). Preservation of intact paleosols within these loess deposits allows the reconstruction of discrete late Pleistocene activity areas, including simple dwellings, hearths, and discard areas. Unfortunately, however, the acidic nature of these soils, due to the podsolizaton associated with both tundra and coniferous forest, has generally limited organic preservation in these paleosols to carbonized wood and calcined bone fragments, except for very recent components (Yesner 1980, 1989). Like the north Alaskan sites, these sites appear universally to represent bluff-top encampments for spotting and intercepting animal migrations (Hamilton 1996; Hoffecker 1988). Only one archaeological site, however—the Dry Creek site, located in the Nenana Valley southwest of Fairbanks—has provided definitive evidence of fauna in a late Pleistocene–early Holocene context; this evidence is limited to tooth fragments of bison, wapiti, and mountain sheep (Guthrie 1983:211).

The discovery in 1989 of the "Broken Mammoth" site in the Shaw Creek Flats region of the central Tanana River valley of east central Alaska (Crossen et al. 1992; Holmes 1991; Holmes and Yesner 1992; Yesner 1994, 1996; Yesner and Crossen 1994; Yesner et al. 1993), and the subsequent discovery of the nearby Mead and Swan Point sites, have presented a new opportunity to evaluate the lifeways of early migrants into eastern Beringia. These sites, all found within an area known as "Shaw Creek Flats" (the catchment basin of the Shaw Creek drainage system), demonstrate unusually excellent preservation of organic materials within intact paleosols (former land surfaces) of late Pleistocene age. The source of this remarkable preservation is the matrix of highly calcareous loess sediments within which these paleosols are embedded. These sediments were derived in turn from glacial silts deposited in the floodplain of the nearby Tanana River, the ultimate source of these silts being limestone rocks eroded from the Alaska Range to the south.

Excavations at the Shaw Creek sites during the period from 1990 to 1993 have revealed the first well-preserved evidence of late Pleistocene human subsistence in eastern Beringia. Loess deposits at these sites contain a series of archaeological components, the earliest of which date to late Pleistocene and early Holocene times. These components are contained within paleosols that have preserved an excellent record of late Pleistocene–early Holocene human occupation. Included in these deposits are lithic artifacts and features referable to the Nenana Complex. Also included, however, are well-preserved organic materials, including bone artifacts and faunal remains (including mammal, bird, and fish bone; mammoth tusk fragments; mammal hair; avian feathers, gastroliths, and eggshell; terrestrial snail shell; and insect carapaces), as well as plant macrofossils.

The Broken Mammoth Site

The Shaw Creek sites, like those of the Nenana Valley, again represent "overlook" sites for spotting and intercepting animal migrations. The Broken Mammoth site, located on a 30-m bluff overlooking the confluence of Shaw Creek and the Tanana River (Figure 2), is typical of that pattern. The site was named for a number of mammoth tusk fragments found eroding from the bluff face during 1989, in association with other faunal remains, lithic

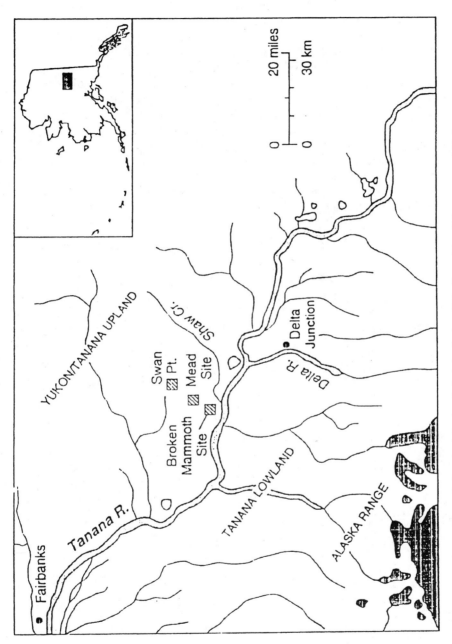

Figure 2. Location of archaeological sites in the middle Tanana River Valley, east central Alaska.

tools, and charcoal fragments. It has been preserved because of its proximity to the Tanana River, the major source of supply for aeolian sediments that entrain the occupations within paleosols (Thorson 1990:411). Also, because it is on a well-drained, south-facing slope that contains *Artemisia* (sage) and other elements of relict Beringian flora, it has apparently been little affected by cryoturbation. In fact, the late Pleistocene–early Holocene paleosols (and individual soil stringers within them) are extremely regular, flat-lying features that can be followed over tens of meters across the site surface. This lack of cryoturbation, coupled with the apparently rapid loess deposition sealing the late Pleistocene–early Holocene levels at the site has minimized taphonomic disturbance to these early occupations.

Basal paleosols at the Broken Mammoth site have preserved two archaeological components that have been labeled Cultural Zones 3 and 4 (Holmes and Yesner 1992; Yesner et al. 1993). *Cultural Zone 3* is separated from the upper cultural zones by 75–90 cm of culturally sterile loess and sands. It is associated with the "Middle Paleosol Complex" within the basal site stratigraphy and has provided radiocarbon dates ranging from 9,300 to 10,300 BP, including one hearth dated to 10,300 BP (Figure 3). Several large hearth smears with associated hearth stones, similar to Cultural Zone 2, were uncovered in Cultural Zone 3.

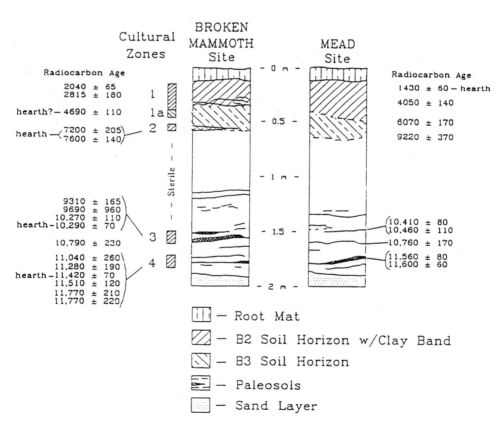

Figure 3. Generalized stratigraphy and radiocarbon dates from the Broken Mammoth and Mead sites.

Artifacts and butchered faunal material have been found scattered in and around the hearths. Several large workshop areas for artifact production, particularly utilizing Landmark Gap chert from the Tangle Lakes region, were exposed in this unit during the 1993 field season. Diagnostic artifacts include bifacial projectile points similar to Paleoindian forms, as well as bifacial knives, scrapers, and flake cores. Also found are choppers, hammerstones, and anvils. In addition, all the formal bone tools recovered from excavations at the Broken Mammoth site were found in this cultural zone. During the 1992 field season, clothing-related items were recovered from this unit, including an eyed bone needle and bone toggle or fastener. During the 1993 field season, a cache of mammoth ivory tools was recovered, including an ivory projectile point, curved shaft, and possible atlatl handle. The mammoth ivory point (Figure 4) appears to have been stained with red ocher, and is similar to others known from Paleoindian sites in the continental United States as well as from Siberian Upper Paleolithic sites.

Cultural Zone 4 at the Broken Mammoth site comprises the oldest cultural material found there. It is associated with the "Lower Paleosol Complex," located around 15–25 cm below Cultural Zone 3 and above a 50-cm-thick late Pleistocene sterile sand unit. Radiocarbon dates for Cultural Zone 4 range from 11,000 to 11,800 BP. Several large hearth smears were also excavated for Cultural Zone 4. Here, too, abundant butchered faunal remains, including a large number of avian remains, were found scattered in and around the hearths. Artifacts include various scrapers, flake cores, and other bifacial materials, as well as choppers, anvil, and hammerstones. Large workshop areas were also uncovered in this cultural zone, particularly for the reduction of local quartz ventifacts and river cobbles. No diagnostic bone tools have been recovered from this unit to date.

PALEOENVIRONMENTS AND ADAPTATIONS IN LATE PLEISTOCENE BERINGIA

Much debate has centered around the reconstruction of Beringian paleoenvironments, particularly concerning the biomass and diversity of flora and large-mammal fauna of the so-called "mammoth steppe" (Colinvaux and West 1984; Cwynar and Ritchie 1980; Guthrie 1968, 1982, 1985, 1990; Hopkins et al. 1982; Matthews 1982; Schweger 1982; Schweger and Habgood 1976; Wright 1991; Young 1976, 1982). Most of these models, however, have focused on paleoecological reconstructions of Beringia at the Last Glacial Maximum (LGM) (18,000–20,000 BP). In fact, the earliest archaeological sites in eastern Beringia were occupied during a period of climatic amelioration, particularly in interior Alaska. Indeed, the paleoenvironment of interior Alaska from circa 14,000 BP to 9,000 BP has been characterized as the "Birch Interval," during which scrub birch and willow colonized the xeric "tundra-steppe" of the LGM (Ager 1982, 1983; Ager and Brubaker 1985). This colonization probably resulted from a shift from more continental to maritime climate associated with inundation of the Bering Land Bridge (Young 1982), although recent data (Elias et al., 1992; Polyakova 1990) suggest that this process was not completed until after circa 12,500 BP. Young (1982:191) suggests that the birch–willow invasion "probably coincided with invasions of tussock tundra ... and sedge meadows [with] profound changes in soils and other features" of the landscape. Around 11,000 BP, these changes may have been followed by a temperature reversion of relatively short (500-year) duration, analogous to Younger Dryas

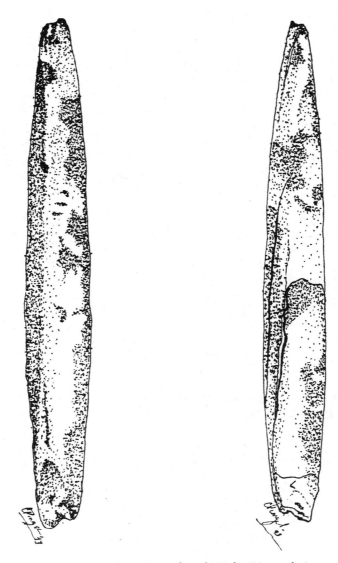

Figure 4. Mammoth Ivory point from the Broken Mammoth site.

events of the Old World (Bigelow et al. 1990a–c), but was followed by further climatic amelioration, leading to a xerothermic maximum circa 9,000 BP (Barnosky et al. 1987). At this time, the area was colonized first by poplar, then by spruce and alder (Ager 1983), after which modern boreal forest conditions developed.

The climatic and vegetational transformations of the Birch Interval, when humans apparently first colonized interior Alaska, resulted in "immediate and profound effects on the other elements of the ecosystem, including particularly the large mammals, and, presumably, the human cultures" (Young 1982:191). Unfortunately, the results of these events are somewhat difficult to judge, since most Pleistocene faunal assemblages in interior Alaska—including both coastal exposures (Guthrie 1968) and mining deposits (Porter 1979; Harington 1980)—tend to date to full-glacial times. Among the fossil remains known from late Pleistocene paleontological contexts, bison are the most abundant (Guthrie 1970, 1980; Matthews 1982:140). The late Pleistocene Trail Creek Cave deposits contain abundant evidence of bison, caribou, mammoth, bear, and mountain sheep (Vinson 1988). The deposits at Bluefish Cave also contain bison, caribou, mammoth, and sheep, as well as horse and wapiti (Cinq-Mars 1979); the latter is slightly larger than modern elk or wapiti (Guthrie 1966). Similar faunal assemblages are known from the Porcupine caves (Dixon 1993), dating to circa 9,000 BP. Both horse and mammoth seem to have survived into mid Birch Interval times at the time of the poplar invasion. The latest dates on mammoth are 10,050 BP at Lost Chicken Creek (Harington 1978) and 11,360 BP at Trail Creek caves (Vinson 1988). Nevertheless, mammoth extinction may have largely occurred shortly before human occupation of eastern Beringia: "Asian immigrants ... probably walked Alaskan mammoth trails that were still tracked and dusty" (Guthrie and Guthrie 1990:41). No postcranial mammoth remains have been recovered from late Pleistocene (or later) archaeological sites in Beringia.

In general, the scanty evidence currently available suggests that the landscape into which the earliest known hunters of interior Alaska moved was a mosaic of grassland and scrub birch, poplar, and willow, generally associated with more mesic precipitation and warmer temperatures than during the glacial maximum, and supporting a fauna of gregarious herd species such as bison and wapiti. These herd populations would have found *refugia* in areas such as the broad outwash floodplains of the Nenana and Tanana River valleys, where high-quality grazing forage would have been maintained and increasing snowfall would have been counteracted by high wind velocities. (These are the same areas in which bison have been successfully restocked today.) Nevertheless, the change from open savanna to scrub parkland in these areas may have been associated with changes in animal adaptations, including reductions in herd size and gregarious behavior, reductions in herd migration distances, and reductions in male aggressiveness and agonistic competition. All these changes can be expected to have had important impacts on human populations colonizing that landscape.

The Faunal Record from the Broken Mammoth Site

In addition to the artifactual remains, nearly 10,000 individual bone fragments have been recovered to date from excavations at the Broken Mammoth site, and an additional 1000 faunal elements from the Mead and Swan Point sites. Fully 70% of the entire faunal sample from these sites derives from the late Pleistocene–early Holocene strata, largely because of the better preservational conditions. The sample from the Broken Mammoth site, which has been best studied to date, includes a diverse spectrum of animal species, including large game, principally bison, wapiti, and caribou; small game, particularly hare, marmot, beaver, otter, ground squirrel, and Arctic fox; birds, principally waterfowl (swans, geese, and ducks), as well as ptarmigan; and fish, including a species of salmonid. Dall sheep and a large carnivore, possibly *Canis dirus*, are also represented by a few skeletal elements from the Pleistocene strata. Also present throughout the site are large numbers of rodent and insectivore bones, including three species of voles, as well as shrews, lemmings, and microtine rodents. Many of these remains are found articulated in krotavenas or in noncultural contexts, and none is burned, suggesting that these elements are intrusive. Ground squirrel bones occur in similar contexts, but are also found in association with occupation surfaces, and are sometimes burned, suggesting utilization.

Both mammal and bird remains from Cultural Zones 3 and 4 were characterized by a high degree of fragmentation, much of which appears to be intentional, since it is associated with impact marks on meat-bearing bones. Only about 15% of the faunal remains could be identified to taxon, primarily because of the high rate of fragmentation of both mammalian and avian remains. Approximately 80% of the mammal remains and 65% of the bird remains were long-bone diaphysis fragments or unidentifiable fragments of the pelvic and pectoral girdles. Despite this low rate of taxonomic identification, however, the species listed in Table 1 were attributable to Cultural Zones 3 and 4 at the Broken Mammoth site.

The faunal assemblage recovered to date from the Broken Mammoth site is nearly equally divided between Cultural Zones 3 and 4. The Cultural Zone 3 assemblage is dominated by large ungulates, as reflected by the dominance of large-mammal bone fragments from this unit (≈60% of both the identifiable and nonidentifiable specimens), followed by small-mammal and bird remains. Among the identifiable large-mammal remains, bison are numerically dominant (≈50%), followed by wapiti (35%) and caribou (15%). A single distal horn core attributable to bison was recovered from Component 3, measurements of which are compatible with *Bison priscus*. Somewhat less diagnostically, measurements of calcanei and astragali from this unit are also compatible with *Bison priscus*, and outside the modern range of *Bison bison*, including subspecies *athabascae*. Dall sheep (*ovis dalli*) and dire wolf (*Canis dirus*) were represented by single specimens (distal metacarpal and humerus, respectively). Small mammals contributed about 30% of the assemblage and were numerically dominated by Arctic ground squirrel (≈50% of the assemblage), followed by insectivores/rodents, hare, and hoary marmot. The lower assemblages, however, also contain the collared pika and Arctic fox, indicating that tundra elements were still extant in the local vegetation. At the same time, a few beaver and otter remains suggest the development of marshy habitat in the site vicinity (in Shaw Creek Flats?). Finally, birds contributed only about 10% of the assemblage and were attributable to three genera of waterfowl: dabbling ducks, geese, and brants.

Table 1. Species Attributable to Cultural Zones 3 and 4 at the Broken Mammoth Site

Latin name	Common name	Latin name	Common name
Sorex sp.	Shrews	*Bison* cf. *priscus*	Wisent (superbison)
Ochotona collaris	Collared pika	*Ovis* cf. *dalli*	Mountain sheep
Lepus arcticus	Arctic hare	*Mammothus pudnigenius*	Woolly mammoth
Marmota caligata	Hoary marmot	*Cygnus columbianus*	Tundra swan
Spermophilus parryi	Arctic ground squirrel	*Branta canadensis*	Canada goose
Microtus sp.	Voles	*Anser albifrons*	White-fronted goose
Alopex lagopus	Arctic fox	*Anser caerulescens*	Snow goose
Lutra canadensis	River otter	*Anas platyrhynchos*	Mallard
Canis cf. *dirus*	Dire wolf	*Anas acuta*	Pintail
Rangifer tarandus	Caribou	*Anas crecca*	Green-winged teal
Alces alces	Moose	*Lagopus lagopus*	Willow ptarmigan
Cervus cf. *elaphus*	Wapiti (elk)	Salmonidae	Unidentified salmonid fish

Salmonid fishes were also represented in Cultural Zone 3 by a dozen vertebral elements, as well as two fish scales. These may represent the Arctic grayling, a modern species in the area. If so, it may suggest that grayling populations had already become established in local streams, lakes, or backwater deposits by early Holocene times.

The character of the faunal assemblage from Cultural Zone 4 differs significantly from that of Cultural Zone 3. In particular, while only 20% of the taxonomically identifiable elements in Cultural Zone 3 were from birds, approximately 70% of the elements from Cultural Zone 4 were from birds. Thus, the Cultural Zone 4 assemblage was dominated by bird bones and bone fragments ($\approx$60% of both the identifiable and nonidentifiable specimens), followed by large-mammal remains ($\approx$25% of the assemblage) and small-mammal remains ($\approx$15% of the assemblage). Among the identifiable large-mammal remains, wapiti (elk) were numerically dominant ($\approx$65%), followed by bison (35%). No definitive elements of other large game species have been recovered, except for woolly mammoth, represented exclusively by ivory (tusk fragments). *Bison priscus* was represented by a complete innominate and nearly complete radioulna, as well as numerous fragmentary elements that were less diagnostic. The small-mammal assemblage was very similar to that of Cultural Zone 3, although some species such as the pika and otter were not represented (probably because of the somewhat smaller sample size). Small-mammal remains found in Cultural Zone 4 were numerically dominated by Arctic ground squirrel ($\approx$50% of the assemblage), followed by insectivores/rodents, hare, and hoary marmot. Carnivores include Arctic fox and a possible distal humerus of *Canis dirus*.

As noted above, birds contributed about 60% of the faunal assemblage in Cultural Zone 4 and represented a wider diversity of species than found in any of the other site components. The avian assemblage was dominated by the tundra (whistling) swan, *Cygnus columbianus*, which constituted 60% of identifiable bird remains. Since this was the only large bird represented in the assemblage (with the exception of a single distal mandible fragment that may be attributable to a large accipiter), it can be assumed that the large-bird long bone fragments that dominate the unidentifiable bird remains (also $\approx$60%) are similarly attributable to this species. Approximately 20% of the identifiable bird remains are attributable to three species of geese (*Branta canadensis*, *Anser albifrons*, and *Anser caerulescens*), 10% are attributable to three species of dabbling ducks (*Anas platyrhynchos*, *Anas acuta*, and *Anas crecca*). The willow ptarmigan (*Lagopus lagopus*). The abundant remains of waterfowl in Cultural Zone 4 at the Broken Mammoth site, including swans, geese, and ducks, as well as possibly related eggshells, testify to the fact that already by 12,000 BP, the North Pacific avian flyway had been reestablished, following the dissolution of the Bering Land Bridge (Hopkins 1992 personal communication) and perhaps that modern breeding areas had become established in backwater areas along the braided Tanana River floodplain. All the avian remains recovered in Cultural Zones 3 and 4 reflect extant species.

LATE PLEISTOCENE–EARLY HOLOCENE RESOURCE EXPLOITATION PATTERNS

Data from early sites spanning the Pleistocene–Holocene transition in the Tanana Valley of interior Alaska exhibit the following patterns of resource exploitation:

1. *Microenvironments utilized:* The taxa represented in the Broken Mammoth faunal assemblage indicate wide utilization of paleomicroenvironments adjacent to the Broken

Mammoth site: dry steppe-tundra (bison, elk, caribou), wetlands (fish, waterfowl, beaver, otter), and uplands (marmot, ground squirrel, Dall sheep, ptarmigan). As today, extensive wetlands were probably present in the Tanana Valley immediately below the site; their exact location and extent probably depended on the Postglacial dynamics of the Tanana River. Upland species would have been available to the north of the site, with more extensive areas to the south, in the foothills of the Alaska Range. Large grazing mammals were probably found both in the Tanana Valley floodplain and in adjacent Shaw Creek Flats, an important *refugium* for these taxa.

2. *Foraging strategies and dietary breadth:* Although analyses of faunal remains from the Broken Mammoth site remain incomplete, some general observations can be made about subsistence patterns and diet. The wide range of species represented at the Broken Mammoth site and other sites in the central Tanana Valley suggests a broad-spectrum diet that probably included most forms available to the human population. If the difference in the relative importance of large mammals and birds in Cultural Zones 3 and 4 is not attributable to shifts in avian flyways or changes in the location or flow patterns of the Tanana River or of the backwater lakes and tributaries within its floodplain, then it is most likely due to changes in foraging strategies, including seasonality of site occupation. In any case, the abundance of bird remains in Cultural Zone 4 suggests that this food resource may have been a key factor in attracting human populations to the site. In addition, the recovery of fish remains in Cultural Zone 3 suggests an even further broadening of the diet, a shift in seasonality of site occupation, the establishment of fish populations, or simply a sampling factor.

3. *Seasonality of site occupation:* The great abundance of mammalian teeth, particularly from the third component, allows establishment of seasonality of occupation of late Pleistocene populations at the Broken Mammoth site. Tooth eruption patterns from a juvenile bison mandible in that component are consistent with late fall–winter occupation, and this timing has been confirmed through sectioning of the large sample of mammalian teeth (including bison, wapiti, and caribou). Remains of migratory waterfowl from the fourth component, on the other hand, suggest either a spring or late summer–fall utilization of the site.

4. *Butchering patterns:* The abundant large-ungulate bones suggest that these species were of considerable importance as concentrated, storable, high-biomass resources. There is good evidence to suggest that some of the primary butchering of game, and much of the secondary butchering, took place on site. Although cranial fragments are not well represented, mandibles are well represented, along with axial skeletal elements (ribs and vertebrae), which are nearly as well represented as meat-bearing carcass segments. In addition, although hindlimbs are slightly better represented than forelimbs, the difference is not statistically significant. Elements frequently removed from kill sites (e.g., distal metapodials, carpals/tarsals, phalanges) are well represented. Cut marks are infrequent because of surface erosion of the bone, but spiral fractures and impact points are common. The high degree of comminution of large-mammal bones, particularly in the third component, suggests a major utilization of long bones, in particular, for tool production, marrow extraction, and bone grease/soup production. These activities may be correlated with the high number of large cobble tools known from the Broken Mammoth site (cf. Jody and Stanford, 1992). Eventually, refitting experiments will be necessary to reconstruct butchering and bone dispersal

patterns. The latter can be connected with feature patterns to discern whether bone dispersal reflects the characteristics of a "toss zone" (Binford 1978a,b), a household midden, or a palimpsest of bone accumulations in a deflated paleosol surface.

At present, the following tentative conclusions about the earliest archaeological record in interior Alaska may be offered:

1. Late Pleistocene–early Holocene occupations of blufftop sites such as the Broken Mammoth site represent segments of an annual round, during which activities relevant to intercepting large herbivore populations and exploiting local microenvironments—particularly wetlands—could be undertaken simultaneously.

2. Late Pleistocene–early Holocene occupations of these sites do not simply represent ephemeral encampments for scanning game for brief periods, nor are they long-term villages (base camps). Early site components should be expected to demonstrate distinct seasonality of occupation, but should also be expected to reflect a diversity of activities, including tool manufacture, mammal/bird butchery, food consumption, tool/food waste discard, hearth construction, tool maintenance (repair/replacement), small-scale caching of artifacts and food storage, hide preparation, skin sewing and clothing manufacture, and other "maintenance" activities. The range of activities undertaken is somewhat different in Cultural Zones 3 and 4, possibly related to differences in the seasonality of site occupation.

3. Late Pleistocene–early Holocene occupations of these sites contain large amounts of animal bone, but do not represent "kill" or "butchering" sites, even though numerous butchering activity areas are present. As noted above, elements frequently removed from kill sites are well represented at the Broken Mammoth site (cf. Todd 1987). Instead, it is now possible to verify the Guthrie (1983:212) hypothesis that sites such as Broken Mammoth are "spike camps" or processing stations to which "kills were brought to process the meat and hides for transport elsewhere." This function is indicated in part by the retrieval of both axial and meat-bearing segments of animal carcasses, indicating that some of the primary butchering and much of the secondary butchering took place on site.

4. Late Pleistocene–early Holocene site occupations of these bluff-top sites probably reflect the activities of supra–nuclear family groups (band segments or multiple household units). Because of the limited spatial scale of such units, periodic occupations do not cover the entire paleosol surface at any given time period (cf. Wilmsen 1974). In fact, paleosol surfaces containing occupational evidence represent a conflation of seasonal activities taking place over a period of decades to hundreds of years. This being the case, localized occupation of portions of the site will have occurred at discrete time intervals within the overall period of site occupation. These localized occupations appear to be characterized by discrete archaeological signatures, including formal artifact types, tool-manufacturing sequences, source materials for artifact production (local vs. long-distance), specific types of game exploited, patterns of tool/bone dispersal, and degree of permanence of occupation.

5. The technological inventories associated with these bluff-top site occupations reflect a combination of expedient and curated tool assemblages, but with a greater emphasis on the former. Indications of this emphasis include the use of a greater percentage of local stone sources for lithic tool manufacture, the use of heavy cobble industries for bone reduction for expedient tool manufacture (as well as for cooking, marrow extraction, and bone grease production), and the use of other readily available materials such as scavenged mammoth tusk for tool manufacture.

6. Foraging strategies of populations in the open parkland environments of the Birch Period probably continued to focus on large game whenever possible, following the tenets of foraging theory. By the time of occupation of the Broken Mammoth site, however, some obligate grazers such as the horse and mammoth may have been extinct. Other herd species such as bison and wapiti apparently survived in the *refugium* of the middle Tanana Valley, where wind-cleared grasslands would have been maintained on the floodplain outwash. Thus, some elements of the Pleistocene megafauna survived—at least until the early Holocene period—and had apparently not yet undergone substantial size diminution. Declining herd size and reduced herd gregariousness, however, would have increased search and pursuit times, and would therefore have decreased energetic return rates, of species such as bison and wapiti. The result of both of these phenomena would have been an increased relative advantage for use of smaller, higher-cost game and fish found in large seasonal aggregations. Increased exploitation of small game, birds, and fish would be expected (cf. Olsen 1990).

7. The major technique for obtaining herd species such as bison or wapiti would have involved the use of javelins or spears for taking individual animals, rather than the use of animal drives. No evidence is found at Broken Mammoth for large, catastrophic accumulations of animals, as reflected in numbers of bones, in unprocessed bone piles, or in animal age distributions (mortality profiles). "Opportunistic, heterogeneous hunting strategies" were probably used, rather than specialized techniques such as drives and impoundments (Guthrie 1983:265; cf. Frison 1991).

8. The season of the year most likely to have been favored for the exploitation of large game would have been autumn–winter, when migratory herds of species such as bison and wapiti could have been intercepted when they left their higher-altitude summer feeding grounds in the Alaska Range or Tanana Uplands to overwinter in the windy, relatively snow-free grasslands of the middle Tanana Valley. If the animals were taken with the use of coarse-grained "encounter" strategies (rather than drives), they would also have been easiest to hunt at this time of year (cf. Frison 1982, 1987; Todd 1991). In addition, they would have developed maximum concentrations of body fat, hides would have been in prime condition for winter clothing and skin tent manufacture, and limited frozen meat caches could have been developed. Fall–winter seasonality is tentatively indicated from the few bison teeth that have been examined to date. Other seasonally migratory species such as waterfowl could have been taken during the autumn as well, although spring may have been a more important season. Fish could have been taken in summer or autumn, while small game could have been taken year-round.

9. The overall settlement pattern in the middle Tanana Valley region during the late Pleistocene and early Holocene probably accords well with the Guthrie (1983:268) "orb model," which included "a moderately stable base camp and numerous outlier spike camps … in a radiating pattern away from the main hub" (Guthrie 1983:269; cf. also Binford 1978a,b; Kelly and Todd 1988; Wilmsen 1974). Such a base camp–"spike camp" model would have been appropriate for maximizing the use of large-game resources, which by the end of the Pleistocene were "thinly distributed [and] only moderately predictable" (Guthrie 1983:269), and at the same time a broader spectrum of lower-return but more predictable resources such as small game, birds, and fish. Unfortunately, the base camps in the Tanana Valley have probably been eroded or obscured by sediment deposition during the past 10,000 years, so that the only sites that remain visible are the "spike camps."

EFFECTS OF THE PLEISTOCENE–HOLOCENE TRANSITION

Faunal Extinction, Climatic Warming, and the Younger Dryas Question

The large size of both bison and wapiti remains from the Broken Mammoth site, including horn cores, metapodials, and tarsal bones (especially calcaneus and astragalus), suggests that these both represent larger Pleistocene forms (although the name *Cervus elaphus* is in use for both the slightly larger late Pleistocene and modern form of wapiti). The abundance of wapiti bones, particularly in Cultural Zone 3 at the Broken Mammoth site, suggests that even if major extinction events had been completed before 12,000 BP, large-scale shifts in species ranges were still in process, because the only living representatives of this species today occupy forest-edge settings several hundred miles to the south.

In addition, mammoth remains from the site clearly represent an extinct form. Whether these mammoth tusk fragments represent animals hunted by contemporaneous human populations remains an open question, however. Unless nontusk remains are eventually recovered, a competing argument may suggest scavenging of tusks from recently extinct animals. The recovery of the cache of mammoth ivory tools during 1993, as well as recovery in earlier seasons of mammoth ivory points, sections of split mammoth tusk, and a microchip embedded in a groove within one piece of mammoth ivory, suggests that mammoth tusks were being scavenged primarily for tool production. This is particularly suggested by the date of 15,800 BP obtained from AMS radiocarbon dating of the mammoth ivory tools recovered during 1993 and a date of 17,000 BP obtained from similar dating of mammoth ivory fragments recovered in 1990 from the Mead site. Alternatively, the hypothesis that mammoth postcranial material was not being retrieved from the kill site would fit recent ethnographic data from the Hadza of east Africa (O'Connell et al. 1988, 1990), who bone out large limb bones of elephants during the butchering process and leave the bones in the field. Although the overall pattern of late dates on mammoth and horse suggests earlier extinction (≈13,000–14,000 BP), probably related to climatic warming and replacement of the tundra-steppe of the glacial maximum with a scrub forest-steppe with fewer high-nutrient grazing opportunities, a later presence of mammoth cannot be ruled out. Dates as recent as 10,000–11,000 BP have been obtained on mammoth bone from the Trail Creek caves and the Lost Chicken Creek area of east central Alaska; both are exclusively paleontological sites. If not for these radiocarbon dates, the location of the mammoth ivory tools at the Broken Mammoth site at the top of Cultural Zone 4 and of some mammoth ivory fragments in Cultural Zone 3 at both the Broken Mammoth and Mead sites might be argued to represent extant animals. If humans played a role in woolly mammoth extinction, then the efficient three-part ivory atlatl uncovered in 1993 might be considered a reflection of that process.

The differences between the faunal assemblages in Cultural Zones 3 and 4 of the Broken Mammoth site include the following: (1) larger amounts of caribou and moose in Cultural Zone 3; (2) smaller amounts of wapiti in Cultural Zone 3; (3) greater representation of snowshoe hare, Arctic fox, marmot, and other small mammals in Cultural Zone 3; (4) presence of salmonid fish in Cultural Zone 3 but not in Cultural Zone 4; and (5) greatly reduced numbers of birds, particularly waterfowl, in Cultural Zone 3. Together, these data suggest a greater dietary diversity, perhaps following the extinction of key species such as mammoths and horses, in Cultural Zone 3. They also suggest (particularly the birds) some changes in seasonal utilization of the site. In addition, the larger amounts of caribou and moose and smaller amounts of wapiti in Cultural Zone 3 may also suggest some climatic cooling, but this hypothesis is very tentative and based on a very small sample. In fact, the overall exploitation pattern remains the same, and no major species appears to become extinct during Cultural Zone 3 times, attributed by some to a period of climatic deterioration equivalent to the "Younger Dryas" episode in Europe.

Artifact Assemblages and Human Migrations

Differences in artifactual assemblages between Cultural Zones 3 and 4 are somewhat difficult to judge, due to the small sample of formal artifacts; both assemblages are dominated by expedient tools with little retouch, and large amounts of debitage. Unifacial forms, however, including a large scraper-plane, are generally limited to Cultural Zone 4, which contains only a few examples of well-made bifaces. In contrast, the two basally thinned, edge-ground "Paleoindian" projectile points from the site (Figure 5) are both from Cultural Zone 3, along with a number of other examples of bifaces and bifacial thinning flakes. If the cultural units in the Tanana Valley are equivalent to those of the Nenana Valley, it would suggest a linkage between Cultural Zone 4 at Broken Mammoth and the Nenana Complex, which includes a unifacial industry, and between Cultural Zone 3 at Broken Mammoth and the Denali Complex, which includes a bifacial industry but is dominated by microblade technology.

In the central and lower Tanana Valley, two sites have produced evidence of early microblade technology: the Healy Lake site (Cook 1969) and the Swan Point site, both of which show associations with dates in excess of 11,000 BP. Either the criteria for the Nenana Complex must be rewritten to account for this fact or a new tack must be taken in utilizing microblade technology as an indicator of economic activities rather than ethnic identity. Such a position might suggest that inset microblades were used for specialized activities,

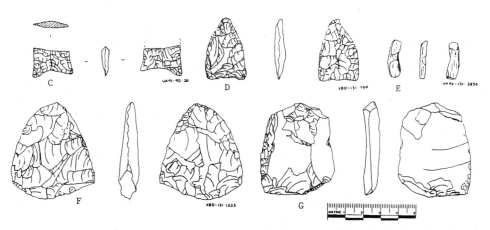

Figure 5. Lithic artifacts from Cultural Zones 3 and 4 at the Broken Mammoth Site (A–C) Bifaces from Cultural Zone 3; (D) bone fastener from Cultural Zone 3: (E) scraper from Cultural Zone 4.

such as hunting caribou (for which they may have been first developed in Europe), and that sites that contain them merely reflect that type of specialized activity.

If the differences between the oldest (late Pleistocene) and slightly younger (earliest Holocene) occupations of interior Alaska prove to be real, they may reflect something about the dynamics of early human population movement in (and through) Alaska. Early unifacial industries may well represent some of the earliest peoples to enter Alaska, exploiting remnant megafaunal populations during rapidly changing climatic conditions. If microblade industries do carry an ethnic signature, it is probably the ancestry of Na-Dene peoples who eventually became the modern Athapaskan, Tlingit, and Haida peoples of interior and southeast Alaska. The bifacial industries, including various versions of Paleoindian-style projectile points known from both northern and interior Alaska, may well represent a "backwash" of hunters retreating northward with remnant animal herds as the Laurentide ice melted and grass was replaced by forest in many parts of western North America.

THE END OF THE LATE PLEISTOCENE–EARLY HOLOCENE "TRANSITION"

After the earliest occupations ceased at the Broken Mammoth site at circa 9,000 BP, a high wind regime apparently developed, sealing the earlier layers and resulting in the deposition of 1 m of loess deposit at the Broken Mammoth site within a period of about 2,000 years. At the same time, the environment apparently became extremely arid, resulting in the precipitation of calcium carbonates that preserved the underlying organic remains at the site. These increasingly arid conditions, coupled with the increasingly forested environment following the end of the Birch Period, may have greatly affected local game populations and may be related to a decline in human populations in interior Alaska suggested by the relatively few sites that date from the early Holocene period. There is some evidence, however, that remnant bison and wapiti populations continued in the middle Tanana Valley *refugium* as late as 3,000 BP (Yesner et al. 1993).

UNRESOLVED ISSUES

Because of the loess record of interior Alaska, and on occasion the excellent organic preservation associated with it, we are well on our way to developing an understanding of the lifeways of the earliest people who utilized this environment in late Pleistocene–early Holocene times. It is clear that they were utilizing remnant populations of Pleistocene megafauna—particularly herd animals such as bison, wapiti, and caribou—in areas that formed *refugia* for these species in the rapidly changing environments of the "Birch Period," associated with climatic warming, perhaps increased precipitation, and significant vegetational changes. It is also clear that they utilized a diversity of available species, including small game, birds, and fish.

Less certain is the identity of these late Pleistocene–early Holocene occupants at various points in time. As noted above, the recent identification of an early (11,700 BP) microblade assemblage at the Swan Point site in the Shaw Creek region, and the presence of early microblades at the Healy Lake site to the south, leaves open the identity of the users of the Nenana Complex and their relationship to microblade-using peoples. Alternative interpretations—that these complexes represent seasonal or other activity-related facies of early tool industries—must also be resolved.

In addition, it is unclear how the site-use patterns described here for interior Alaska might relate to the earliest sites in northern Alaska, such as the Mesa site. The latter sites apparently show higher ratios of formal artifacts, and fewer extensive lithic workshops, than do the sites from interior Alaska. Whether these sites serve as more than ephemeral "lookout" points for game spotting and interception cannot be clarified without more extensive artifactual, architectural, and, we can hope, faunal data. The same may be said for early sites in southwestern Alaska, which are poorly dated and tend to be dominated by microblade assemblages. These sites are frequently found on river terraces and also appear to be lookout points for game spotting, but little further can be concluded about them at present.

Finally, in southern coastal Alaska, human occupation did not occur until deglaciation of the region. Few early sites are found in the region, although microblade localities are known from areas ranging from the Kenai and Alaska peninsulas to southeastern Alaska. Many are undated, but the earliest are universally early Holocene in age (i.e., 8,000–10,000 BP). Although deglaciation of the southern coastal region was *initiated* by circa 14,000 BP, it clearly was not *completed* until closer to 10,000 BP (the date of basal peats found in coastal sequences from the Aleutian Islands eastward). If coastal location can be a guide, sites such as Anangula in the eastern Aleutian Islands and Ground Hog Bay and Hidden Falls in southeast Alaska represent some of the earliest utilization of coastal environments, although more intensive use of the coast appears to postdate 6,000 BP. Thus, although Laughlin and his colleagues once argued for maritime adaptations on the southern land bridge coast as early as 15,000 BP, it is now clear that the transition to coastal lifeways in the far north was *entirely a Holocene phenomenon*, possibly associated with the availability of ice-free environments along the coast of southern Alaska and with the simultaneous reduction of large-game animal populations in interior Alaska to the north (Yesner 1993).

REFERENCES

Ager, T., 1982, Vegetational History of Western Alaska during the Wisconsin Glacial Interval and the Holocene, in: *Paleoecology of Beringia* (D. M. Hopkins et al., eds.), Academic Press, New York, pp. 75–93.

Ager, T., 1983, Holocene Vegetational History of Alaska, in: *Late Quaternary Environments of the United States*, Vol. 2: The Holocene (H. E. Wright, Jr., ed.), University of Minnesota Press, Minneapolis, pp. 128–141.

Ager, T., and Brubaker, L., 1985, Quaternary Palynology and Vegetational History of Alaska, in: *Pollen Records of Late Quaternary North American Sediments* (V. M. Bryant, Jr. and R. G. Holloway, eds.), American Association of Stratigraphic Palynologists Foundation, Dallas, pp. 353–384.

Alexander, H. L., 1987, *Putu: A Fluted Point Site in Alaska*, Department of Archaeology Publication 17, Simon Fraser University, Burnaby.

Anderson, D. D., 1970, Akmak: An Early Archaeology Assemblage from Onion Portage, Northwest Alaska, *Arcta Arctica 16*.

Anderson, D. D., 1984, Prehistory of north Alaska, in: *Handbook of North American Indians*, vol. 5: Arctic (W. L. Sturdevant and D. Dumas, eds.), Smithsonian Institution Press, Washington, DC, pp. 80–93.

Anderson, D. D., 1988, Onion Portage: The Archaeology of a Stratified Site from the Kobuk River, Northwest Alaska, *Anthropological Papers of the University of Alaska 22(1/2)*.

Barnosky, C. W., Anderson, P. M., and Bartlein, P. J., 1987, The Northwestern US during Deglaciation: Vegetational History and Paleoclimatic Implications, in: *North America and Adjacent Oceans during Deglaciation* (W. F. Ruddiman and H. E. Wright, Jr.), Geological Society of America, Boulder, pp. 289–321.

Bigelow, N. H., Beget, J. E., and Powers, W. R., 1990a, Latest Pleistocene Increase in Wind Intensity Recorded in Aeolian Sediments from Central Alaska, *Quaternary Research* 34:160–168.

Bigelow, N. H., Powers, W. R., and Beget, J. E., 1990b, Increased Sediment Size in the Nenana Valley: A Proxy Record of the Younger Dryas Cold Event? Paper presented at the 17th Annual Meeting of the Alaska Anthropological Association, Fairbanks.

Bigelow, N H., Powers, W. R., and Beget, J. E., 1990c, Holocene Climates in the Nenana and Teklanika Valleys, Central Alaska, Paper presented to the 23rd Annual Meeting of the Canadian Archaeological Association, Whitehorse.

Binford, L. W., 1978a, *Nunamiut Ethnoarchaeology*, Academic Press, New York.

Binford, L. R., 1987b, Dimensional Analysis of Behavior and Site Structure: Learning from an Eskimo Hunting Stand, *American Antiquity* 43(3):330–361.

Cinq-Mars, J., 1979, Bluefish Cave I: A Late Pleistocene Eastern Beringian Cave Deposit in the Northern Yukon, *Canadian Journal of Archaeology* 3:1–32.

Clark, D. W., 1992, The Northern (Alaska–Yukon) Fluted Points, in: *Clovis: Origins and Adaptations* (R. Bonnichsen and K. L. Turnmire, eds.), Center for the Study of the First Americans, Oregon State University, Corvallis, pp. 35–48.

Colinvaux, P., and West, F. H., 1984, The Beringian Ecosystem, *Quarterly Review of Archaeology* 5:10–16.

Cook, J. P., 1969, *The Early Prehistory of Healy Lake, Alaska*, University Microfilms, Ann Arbor.

Cook, J. R., 1975, Archaeology of Interior Alaska, *Western Canadian Journal of Anthropology* 5:125–133.

Crossen, K. J., Yesner, D. R., and Holmes, C. E., 1991, Stratigraphy and Fossil Assemblages from Broken Mammoth, an 11,500-yr BP Archaeological Site in Interior Alaska, *Geological Society of America Abstracts with Programs* 23(5):A235.

Crossen, K. J., Dilley, T. R., Yesner, D. R., and Holmes, C. E., 1992, Late Quaternary Environmental Change and Human Occupation of the Broken Mammoth Site, Delta Junction, East-Central Alaska, *American Quaternary Association Program and Abstracts* 12:37.

Cwynar, L. C., and Ritchie, J. C., 1980, Arctic Steppe–Tundra: A Yukon Perspective, *Science* 208:1375–1377.

Dixon, E. J., Jr., 1993, *Quest for the Origins of the First Americans*, University of New Mexico Press, Albuquerque.

Elias, S. A., Short, S. K., and Phillips, R. L., 1992, Paleoecology of Late-Glacial Peats from the Bering Land Bridge, Chuckchi Sea Shelf Region, Northwestern Alaska, *Quaternary Research* 38:371–378.

Frison, G. C., 1982, Paleoindian Winter Subsistence Strategies on the High Plains, in: *Plains Indian Studies* (D. H. Ubelaker and H. J. Viola, eds.), Smithsonian Contributions to Anthropology, No. 30, Washington, DC, pp. 193–201.

Frison, G. C., 1987, Prehistoric, Plains-Mountain, Large-Mammal, Communal Hunting Strategies, in: *The Evolution of Human Hunting* (M. H. Nitecki and D. V. Nitecki, eds.), Plenum Press, New York, pp. 177–223.

Frison, G. C., 1991, Hunting strategies, Prey Behavior, and Mortality Data, in: *Human Predators and Prey Mortality* (M. C. Stiner, ed.), Westview Press, Boulder, pp. 15–30.

Frison, G. C., 1992, The Goshen Paleoindian Complex: New Data for Paleoindian Research, in: *Clovis: Origins and Adaptations* (R. Bonnichsen and K. L. Turnmire, eds.), Center for the Study of the First Americans, Oregon State University, Corvallis, pp. 133–151.

Frison, G. C., 1993, The North American Paleoindian: A Wealth of New Data but Still So Much to Learn, *Plains Anthropologist* 38:5–16.

Goebel, F. E., Powers, W. R., and Bigelow, N. H., 1991, The Nenana Complex of Alaska and Clovis Origins, in: *Clovis: Origins and Adaptations* (R. Bonnichsen and K. L. Turnmire, eds.), Center for the Study of the First Americans, Oregon State University, Corvallis, pp. 49–79.

Guthrie, R. D., 1966, The Extinct Wapiti of Alaska and the Yukon Territory, *Canadian Journal of Zoology* 44:45–57.

Guthrie, R. D., 1968, Paleoecology of the Large Mammal Community in Interior Alaska during the Late Pleistocene, *American Midland Naturalist* 79:346–363.

Guthrie, R. D., 1970, Bison Evolution and Zoogeography in North America during the Pleistocene, *Quarterly Review of Biology* 45:1–15.

Guthrie, R. D., 1980, Bison and Man in North America, *Canadian Journal of Anthropology* 1:55–73.

Guthrie, R. D., 1982, Mammals of the Mammoth Steppe as Paleoenvironmental Indicators, in: *Palaeoecology of Beringia* (D. M. Hopkins, J. V. Matthews, Jr., C. E. Schweger, and S. B. Young, eds.), Academic Press, New York, pp. 307–326.

Guthrie, R. D., 1983, Paleoecology of the Site and Its Implications for Early Hunters, in: *Dry Creek* (W. R. Powers, R. D. Guthrie, and J. F. Hoffecker, eds.), National Park Service, Washington, DC, pp. 209–287.

Guthrie, R. D., 1985, Woolly Arguments against the Mammoth Steppe: A New Look at the Palynological Data, *Quarterly Review of Archaeology* 6:9–16.

Guthrie, R. D., 1990, *Frozen Fauna of the Mammoth Steppe*, Columbia University Press, New York.

Guthrie, R. D., and Guthrie, M. L., 1990, On the Mammoth's Dusty Trail, *Natural History* 90(7):34–41.

Hamilton, T. D., 1970, Geologic Relations of the Akmak Assemblage, Onion Portage Area, *Acta Arctica* 16:71–80.

Hamilton, T. D., 1996, Late Pleistocene Peopling of Alaska, in: *Peopling of the Americas* (R. Bonnichsen, ed.), Center for the Study of the First Americans, Oregon State University, Corvallis.

Harington, C. R., 1978, *Quaternary Vertebrate Faunas of Canada and Alaska and Their Suggested Chronological Sequence*, Syllogeus No. 15, Canadian National Museum of Natural Sciences, Ottawa.

Harington, C. R., 1980, Pleistocene Mammals from Lost Chicken Creek, Alaska, *Canadian Journal of Earth Sciences* 17:168–198.

Haynes, C. V., 1990, Contributions of Radiocarbon Dating to the Geochronology of the Peopling of the New World, in: *Radiocarbon Dating After Four Decades* (R. E. Taylor et al., eds.), Springer, New York, pp. 355–374.

Hoffecker, J. F., 1985, The Moose Creek Site, *National Geographic Society Research Reports* 19:33–48.

Hoffecker, J. F., 1988, Applied Geomorphology and Archaeological Survey for Sites of Pleistocene Age: An Example from Central Alaska, *Journal of Archaeological Science* 15:683–713.

Hoffecker, J. F., Powers, W. R., and Goebel, F. E., 1993, The Colonization of Beringia and the Peopling of the New World, *Science* 259:46–53.

Holmes, C. E., 1974, New Evidence for a Late Pleistocene Culture in Central Alaska: Preliminary Investigations at Dry Creek, Paper presented to the 7th Annual Meeting of the Canadian Archaeological Association, Whitehorse.

Holmes, C. E., 1991, *The Broken Mammoth Archaeological Project, Heritage*, No. 48, Anchorage: Alaska Office of History and Archaeology.

Holmes, C. E., and Yesner, D. R., 1992, Investigating the Earliest Alaskans: The Broken Mammoth Archaeological Project, *Arctic Research of the United States* 6:6–9.

Hopkins, D. M., Matthews, J. V., Jr., Schweger, C. E., and Young, S. B., 1982, Palaeocoelogy of Beringia—A Synthesis, in: *Palaeoecology of Beringia* (D. M. Hopkins, J. V., Matthews, Jr., C. E. Schweger, and S. B. Young), Academic Press, New York, pp. 425–444.

Jodry, M. A., and Stanford, D. J., 1992, Stewart's Cattle Guard Site: An Analysis of Bison Remains in a Folsom Kill–Butchery Campsite, in: *Ice Age Hunters of the Rockies* (D. J. Stanford and J. S. Day, eds.), University of Colorado Press and Denver Museum of Natural History, Niwot, pp. 101–168.

Kelly, R., and Todd, L., 1988, Coming into the Country: Early Paleoindian Hunting and Mobility, *American Antiquity* 53:231–244.

Kunz, M. L., and Reanier, R. E., 1994, Paleoindians in Beringia: Evidence from Arctic Alaska, *Science* 263:660–662.

Matthews, J. V., Jr., 1982, East Beringia during Late Wisconsin Time: A Review of the Biotic Evidence, in: *Paleoecology of Beringia* (D. M. Hopkins, J. V. Matthews, Jr., C. E. Schweger, and S. B. Young, eds.), Academic Press, New York, 127–150.

Mobley, C. M., 1991, *The Campus Site: A Prehistoric Camp at Fairbanks, Alaska*, University of Alaska Press, Fairbanks.

Morlan, R., and Cinq-Mars, J., 1982, Ancient Beringians: Human Occupation in the Late Pleistocene of Alaska and the Yukon Territory, in: *The Palaeoecology of Beringia* (D. M. Hopkins, J. V. Matthews, Jr., C. E. Schweger, and S. B. Young, eds.), Academic Press, New York, pp. 353–381.

O'Connell, J. F., Hawkes, K. R., and Blurton Jones, N. G., 1988, Hadza Hunting, Butchering, and Bone Transport and Their Archaeological Implications, *Journal of Anthropological Research* 44:113–161.

O'Connell, J. F., Hawkes, K. R., and Blurton Jones, N. G., 1990, Reanalysis of Large Mammal Body Part Transport among the Hadza, *Journal of Archaeological Science* 17:301–316.

Olsen, S. J., 1990, Was Early Man in North America a Big Game Hunter? in: *Hunters of the Recent Past* (L. B. Davis and B. O. K. Reeves, eds.), Unwin and Hyman, Winchester, pp. 103–110.

Phippen, P. G., 1988, *Archaeology at Owl Ridge: A Pleistocene–Holocene Boundary Age Site in Central Alaska*, Unpublished M.A. Thesis, University of Alaska, Fairbanks.

Polyakova, Ye. I., 1990, Stratigraphy of Late-Pleistocene/Holocene Sediments on the Bering Shelf on the Basis of Diatom Complexes, *Polar Geography and Geology* 14:271–278.

Porter, L., 1979, *Ecology of a Late Pleistocene (Wisconsin) Ungulate Community near Jack Wade, East-central Alaska*, unpublished, M.S. thesis, University of Washington, Seattle.

Powers, W. R., and Hamilton, T. D., 1978, Dry Creek: A Late Pleistocene Human Occupation in Central Alaska, in: *Early Man in America from a Circum-Pacific Perspective* (A. L. Bryan, ed.), Occasional Papers No. 1, Department of Anthropology, University of Alberta, Edmonton, pp. 72–77.

Powers, W. R., and Hoffecker, J., 1989, Late Pleistocene settlement in the Nenana Valley, central Alaska, *American Antiquity* 54(2):263–287.

Powers, W. R., and Maxwell, H. E., 1986, *Lithic Remains from Panguingue Creek, an Early Holocene Site in the Northern Foothills of the Alaska Range*, Alaska Historical Commission Studies, No. 189, Anchorage.

Powers, W. R., Guthrie, R. D., and Hoffecker, J. F., eds. 1983, *Dry Creek: Archaeology and Paleoecology of a Late Pleistocene Alaskan Hunting Camp*, National Park Service, Washington, DC.

Powers, W. R., Goebel, F. E., and Bigelow, N. H., 1990, Late Pleistocene Occupation at Walker Road: New data on the Central Alaskan Nenana Complex, *Current Research in the Pleistocene* 7:40–43.

Reanier, R. E., 1982, An Application of Pedological and Palynological Techniques at the Mesa Site, Northern Brooks Range, Alaska, *Anthropological Papers of the University of Alaska* 20:123–129.

Schweger, C. E., 1982, Late Pleistocene Vegetation of Eastern Beringia: Pollen Analysis of Dated Alluvium, in: *Paleoecology of Beringia* (D. M. Hopkins, J. V. Matthews, Jr., C. E. Schweger, and S. B. Young, eds.), Academic Press, New York, pp. 95–112.

Schweger, C. E., 1985, Geoarchaeology of Northern Regions: Lessons from Cryoturbation at Onion Portage, Alaska, in: *Archaeological Sediments in Context* (J. K. Stein and W. A. Farrand, eds.), Center for the Study of the First Americans, Orono, pp. 127–141.

Schweger, C. E., and Habgood, T., 1976, The Late Pleistocene steppe-tundra in Beringia: A critique, *American Quaternary Association Program and Abstracts* 4:157.

Thorson, R. M., 1990, Geologic Contexts of Archaeological Sites in Beringia, in: *Archaeological Geology of North America* (N. P. Lasca and J. Donahue, eds.), Geological Society of America, Centennial Special Volume No. 4, Boulder, pp. 399–420.

Thorson, R. M., and Hamilton, T. D., 1977, Geology of the Dry Creek Site: A Stratified Early Man Site in Interior Alaska, *Quaternary Research* 7:149–176.

Todd, L. C., 1987, Analysis of Kill–Butchery Bonebeds and Interpretation of Paleoindian Hunting, in: *The Evolution of Human Hunting* (M. H. Nitecki and D. V. Nitecki, eds.), Plenum Press, New York, pp. 225–266.

Todd, L. C., 1991, Seasonality Studies and Paleoindian Subsistence Strategies, in: *Human Predators and Prey Mortality* (M. C. Stiner, ed.), Westview Press, Boulder, pp. 217–238.

Vinson, D., 1988, Preliminary Report on Faunal Identifications from Trail Creek Caves, in: *The Bering Land Bridge National Preserve: An Archaeological Survey* (J. Schaaf, ed.), National Park Service, CRM Report No. AR-14, Anchorage, pp. 410–436.

West, F. H., 1967, The Donnelly Ridge Site and the Definition of an Early Core and Blade Complex in Central Alaska, *American Antiquity* 32:360–382.

West, F. H., 1974, The Significance of Typologically Early Site Collections in the Tangle Lakes, Central Alaska, in: *International Conference on the Prehistory and Paleoecology of the Western North American Arctic and Subarctic* (S. Raymond and P. Schlederman, eds.), Chacmool, Calgary, pp. 217–238.

West, F. H., 1975, Dating the Denali Complex, *Arctic Anthropology* 12:76–81.

West, F. H., 1980, Late Palaeolithic Cultures in Alaska, in: *Early Native Americans* (D. L. Browman, ed.), Mouton, The Hague, pp. 161–187.

West, F. H., 1981, *Archaeology of Beringia*, Columbia University Press, New York, pp. 161–187.

Wilnsen, E. N., 1974, *Lindenmeier: A Pleistocene Hunting Society*, Harper and Row, New York.

Wright, H. E., Jr., 1991, Environmental conditions for Paleoindian immigration, in: *The First Americans: Search and Research* (T. D. Dillehay and D. J. Meltzer, eds.), CRC Press, Boca Raton, pp. 113–135.

Yesner, D. R., 1980, Caribou Exploitation in Interior Alaska: Evidence from Two Paxson Lake Sites, *Anthropological Papers of the University of Alaska* 19(2):15–32.

Yesner, D. R., 1989, Moose Hunters of the Boreal Forest? A Re-examination of Subsistence Patterns in the Western Subarctic, *Arctic* 42(2):97–108.

Yesner, D. R., 1993, *Origins and Development of Maritime Adaptations in the Northwest Pacific Region of North America*, Paper presented at the International Seminar on the Origins, Development, and Spread of Prehistoric North Pacific-Bering Sea Maritime Cultures, Honolulu, Hawaii.

Yesner, D. R., 1994, Subsistence Diversity, Faunal Extinction, and Hunter–Gatherer Foraging Strategies in Late Pleistocene/Early Holocene Beringia, in: *Beringia*, special volume of *Current Research in the Pleistocene* (R. L. Bonnichsen, ed.), 11:154–156.

Yesner, D. R., 1996, The Pleistocene/Holocene Transition in Interior Alaska, in: *Bridges of Science* (R. Meehan, ed.), University of Alaska Press, Fairbanks (in press).

Yesner, D. R., and Crossen, K. J., 1994, Prehistoric People of Alaska's Interior, in: *Prehistoric Alaska* (P. Rennick, ed.), *Alaska Geographic* 21(4):90–93.

Yesner, D. R., Holmes, C. E., and Crossen, K. J., 1993, Archaeology and Palaeoecology of the Broken Mammoth Site, Central Tanana Valley, Interior Alaska, USA, *Current Research in the Pleistocene* 9:1–12.

Young, S. B., 1976, Is Steppe Tundra Alive and Well in Alaska? *American Quaternary Association Program and Abstracts* 4:84–88.

Young, S. B., 1982, The Vegetation of Land-Bridge Beringia, in: *Paleoecology of Beringia* (D. M. Hopkins et al., eds.), Academic Press, New York.

Chapter **14**

The Pleistocene–Holocene Transition along the Pacific Coast of North America

Jon M. Erlandson and Madonna L. Moss

From the cool coastal rain forests of southeast Alaska to the parched desert shorelines of Baja California, the Pacific Coast of North America stretches for 6000 km, spans 35 degrees of latitude, and contains a remarkably diverse array of resources and environments. Encompassing the Northwest Coast and California culture areas, this region is critical for understanding the relationships between cultural and environmental changes of the Pleistocene–Holocene transition. During this period, a complex web of environmental changes facilitated the dispersal of Northeast Asian peoples into Beringia and the New World. The Pacific Coast of North America is a pivotal region for tracking the movements and developmental trajectories of these early pioneers and their descendants. Knowledge of the Pacific Coast archaeological record remains uneven, but data acquired during the past 15 years allow us to identify some broad regional trends in the cultural developments of this critical time period (see also Moss and Erlandson 1995).

In this chapter, we examine the evidence for cultural and environmental changes associated with the Pleistocene–Holocene transition along the Pacific Coast of North America. Our focus is on the area from southeast Alaska to southern California, but limited data from the Gulf of Alaska and Baja California areas are also presented. Throughout, we have had to compromise between our mission of sketching broad cultural and environmental patterns characteristic of the entire region and the urge to present potentially endless qualifications of these generalities. We use a number of case studies to illustrate local variability, complexity, and ambiguity. In the sections that follow, we examine the nature of Pacific Coast environments, discuss the scale and scope of environmental changes between

JON M. ERLANDSON and MADONNA L. MOSS • Department of Anthropology, University of Oregon, Eugene, Oregon 97403-1218.

Humans at the End of the Ice Age: The Archaeology of the Pleistocene–Holocene Transition, edited by Lawrence Guy Straus, Berit Valentin Eriksen, Jon M. Erlandson, and David R. Yesner. Plenum Press, New York, 1996.

13,000 and 8,000 years ago,[1] and describe the geographic distribution and contents of known archaeological sites for each millennium. In our final sections, we examine the implications of the existing data for understanding the origins and development of early Pacific Coast societies.

ENVIRONMENTAL BACKGROUND

The entire Pacific Coast of North America is mountainous and tectonically active. From southern Alaska to Baja California, a nearly continuous belt of mountain ranges rises relatively abruptly from the sea. Compared to many regions of the world, the coastal plains and continental shelves of the Pacific Coast are very narrow. The juxtaposition of mountains and the sea tends to "stack" numerous ecological zones within a narrow area and allows access to a variety of marine and terrestrial resources. Such landscapes also confined many coastal groups between significant, although not necessarily impassable, geographic barriers. This confinement is particularly true for southeast Alaska and much of British Columbia, where cultural developments occurred largely within geographically circum-scribed areas, access to terrestrial habitats was limited, and a more intensive focus on coastal resources emerged. Numerous rivers (the Chilkat, Skeena, Nass, Fraser, Columbia, Klamath, and others), along with less formidable mountains like the Oregon Coast Range and the Willapa Hills and low-lying landforms like Puget Sound and San Francisco Bay, all allowed access to interior regions and more extensive riverine or terrestrial habitats. Such travel routes were also important avenues for the exchange of goods and ideas, interaction that went beyond the boundaries of the two culture areas considered here.

Another common feature of Pacific Coast environments was the presence of a multi-tude of marine resources, including sea mammals, marine fish, shellfish, shore birds, and seaweeds. Virtually all of North America's Pacific Coast is characterized by significant marine upwelling, where nutrient-laden oceanic currents support highly productive marine food chains. In recent times—and probably in the distant past as well—some marine ecosystems of the Pacific Coast have been susceptible to periodic crashes, although the impacts of these El Niño–like events on coastal peoples are being debated (see Arnold 1992; Raab et al. 1994). Because a similar suite of marine resources was present along the entire Pacific Coast, however, the economies and technologies of the region's coastal peoples share some general similarities.

Significant local and regional variation existed, however, in the accessibility of marine resources. In the island archipelagos and fjord systems of southeast Alaska and British Columbia, coastlines are highly convoluted, and many are relatively protected from heavy ocean swells. Here, the greater linear extent of protected intertidal and nearshore habitats provided a wealth of microenvironments in which hunting and collecting could be con-ducted for much of the year. On the exposed outer coasts of these island archipelagos, marine travel and subsistence were more limited by stormy weather. On the northern Northwest Coast, the relatively short days of winter further constrained hunting, gathering, and fishing.

South of Puget Sound, coastlines are generally straighter, mostly west-facing, with

---

[1] All dates in this chapter are expressed in uncorrected radiocarbon years before present (RYBP).

broad expanses of outer coast habitats broken by occasional estuaries and river mouths. These outer coast environments are frequently exposed to heavy surf and seasonally to the full force of North Pacific storms, imposing even greater obstacles to marine resource use. Protected bays and estuaries, stretches of south-facing coast, and occasional islands provided sheltered and productive habitats in some areas, and many of these habitats provided havens for concentrations of coastal peoples, even during the early Holocene (see Erlandson 1994).

Pacific Coast vegetation communities range from the coniferous rain forests of the Northwest Coast to the relatively arid mosaics of chaparral, coastal scrub, or desert vegetation of Alta and Baja California. The productivity of terrestrial food plants is generally quite high in the south, but generally decreases to the north. Along much of the California coast, plants that produce edible calorie-rich nuts or seeds are diverse and abundant. In Oregon, Washington, and southern British Columbia, there are fewer seed resources, although root crops like camas and wapato are often present. Farther north, very few potential plant food staples are available, but berries, greens, and roots were significant seasonal foods. Generally, however, people of the northern Northwest Coast relied more on marine foods as sources of both protein *and* calories than did people to the south.

The distribution of salmon and other anadromous fish (e.g., eulachon, lamprey eels, steelhead) is another major axis of variation from north to south along the Pacific Coast. The Northwest Coast is famous for its large historic runs of six Pacific salmon species. There was great variability in the abundance, diversity, and duration of salmon runs along the Northwest Coast, but most scholars agree that the predictable and storable salmon were the most important staple during later prehistory. Anadromous fish runs were very limited, however, south of San Francisco Bay, where most rivers and streams flow only intermittently during the dry months of summer and fall.

Environments of the Pleistocene–Holocene Transition

Between 13,000 and 8,000 years ago, many Pacific Coast ecological communities were in a state of transition. Postglacial warming, deglaciation, sea-level rise, and biotic adjustments had profound effects on early peoples of the Pacific Coast. Local variation in the physical, biological, and cultural responses to environmental change, however, may have been equally dramatic. Mann and Hamilton (1993) recently provided a summary of the Late Quaternary environmental history of the region, a review on which much of the following reconstruction is based. The driving force behind much of the environmental change that occurred along the Pacific Coast at the end of the Pleistocene was Postglacial warming of global climates. Climatic warming during the Pleistocene–Holocene transition was not uniform, however, and some evidence suggests that a major cool period corresponding to the Younger Dryas occurred along the Pacific Coast between about 11,000 and 10,000 years ago.

Global models suggest that deglaciation caused sea levels to rise as much as 75 m between 13,000 and 8,000 years ago, the levels ending about 20–25 m lower than modern sea levels (Fairbanks 1989). At any given point in time, local sea levels varied due to regional or local differences in tectonics, isostasy, and glacial history. South of the Columbia River, most local sea-level histories probably do not depart dramatically from global curves, but the effects of sea-level rise varied according to local differences in offshore topography. Farther north, the complicated interplay of deglaciation, isostasy, and tectonics caused extreme variations in local sea-level histories (e.g., Clague et al. 1982; Mobley 1988).

From Puget Sound northward, glaciation played a major role in the environmental and cultural history of the Pleistocene–Holocene transition. Much of the Northwest Coast was covered in Cordilleran ice during the late Pleistocene, but parts of the Queen Charlotte Islands in British Columbia and Prince of Wales and nearby islands in southeast Alaska now appear to have been ice-free for at least the last 16,000 years (Clague et al. 1982). Glacial retreat along the southeast Alaskan mainland coast and from the higher mountains of the Alexander archipelago occurred between 14,000 and 13,000 years ago. This retreat was followed by marine transgression reaching 50–200 m above present sea level (Mann 1986) and roughly modern sea levels in the early Holocene. Along British Columbia's Coast Mountains, ice had retreated to the inner fjords of the mainland by about 13,000 years ago. By 10,600 BP, lowered sea levels had exposed large areas of the Hecate Plain east of the Queen Charlotte Islands, the bottom of Queen Charlotte Sound, and areas adjacent to the north and west coasts of Vancouver Island (Fladmark 1990; Luternauer et al. 1989). The marine transgression in some of these areas did not peak until 8,000 BP, when sea level was 15 m higher than present (Clague et al. 1982). In Puget Sound and the Straits of Georgia, the Cordilleran ice sheet retreated rapidly after 14,000 BP, with a minor readvance between 11,500 and 11,000 BP. Deglaciation here was followed by lowered sea levels during the early Holocene, with isostatic rebound outstripping eustatic sea level rise.

Changes in Plant and Animal Communities

Responding to general patterns of climatic warming, terrestrial plant communities appear to have shifted northward virtually regionwide, a phenomenon best documented for coniferous forests. Pollen data from the California coast, for instance, suggest that vegetation communities generally shifted northward 300–350 km, with once extensive pine forests of the south coast breaking into limited and widely scattered relict tree stands by about 11,000 years ago (Axelrod 1967:296; Heusser 1978; Johnson 1983; West and Erlandson 1994). By 14,000 BP, ice-free areas of southern British Columbia supported heath, grass, sedge, and herb meadows with patches of conifers (Hebda 1992). Herb tundra vegetation colonized newly deglaciated areas elsewhere in the region, and conifers spread rapidly. In general, tree species migrated northward from southern *refugia*, with arrival times progressively more recent to the north (Peteet 1991). By about 12,000 BP, lodgepole pine and poplar had invaded the Queen Charlotte Islands and lodgepole pine and alder had invaded southeast Alaska (Cwynar 1990; Engstrom et al. 1990; Warner et al. 1982). Sitka spruce arrived in the Queen Charlottes by 11,200 BP (Warner et al. 1982) and somewhat later to the north. Sitka spruce was followed by western hemlock, mountain hemlock, and, during the mid-Holocene, red cedar (Hebda and Mathewes 1984). Similar shifts have been noted around the Gulf of Alaska, where coniferous forests spread northwestward from southeast Alaska into Prince William Sound and the Kodiak Archipelago throughout the Holocene (Haggarty et al. 1991).

The effects of these changes on animal populations are poorly documented. Many of the large land animals of the Rancholabrean fauna disappeared from coastal California, Oregon, and Washington near the end of the Pleistocene. The chronology of this extinction is poorly understood, however, and the lack of clear cultural associations with Rancholabrean fauna suggests that the extinction had little impact on humans. New data on the distribution of land mammals along the northern Northwest Coast are emerging from a series of limestone caves in coastal southeast Alaska (Baichtal 1993; Heaton and Grady 1993). On Prince of Wales Island, the remains of brown bear, black bear, red fox, ermine, otter, and other small mammals have been found in deposits dating between about 12,000 and 8,000 years ago (Baichtal no date). The existence of large omnivores like brown and black bears on Prince of Wales Island at the end of the Pleistocene implies the presence of a relatively diversified suite of resources with the potential to support early coastal peoples. New information suggests the existence of relict land mammal populations on the outer islands during the last Glacial and promises to revise conventional scenarios of land mammal dispersal and distribution (Klein 1965). The presence of endemic subspecies of land mammals on the Queen Charlotte Islands (caribou, black bear, marten, ermine, mice, and shrews), for instance, suggests that these mammals have been separated from mainland populations for a long time (Fladmark 1990:186).

Environmental changes also affected the structure and productivity of marine habitats. Some of the most dramatic changes during the Pleistocene–Holocene transition were in the spatial distribution of intertidal, nearshore, and estuarine habitats. Sea-level rise along the Oregon and California coasts inundated major tracts of land and formed bays or estuaries in the inundated mouths of rivers and streams. Generally, this transgression must have increased the productivity of marine and estuarine resources relative to those found on land—especially in areas of relatively narrow coastal plains. The formation of estuaries also appears to have been widespread, and much of the Pacific Coast appears to have been more convoluted and more productive between 13,000 and 8,000 years ago.

Study of a sediment core recovered off the southern Oregon coast, however, led Sancetta et al. (1992) to propose that reversed late Pleistocene wind patterns weakened coastal upwelling and significantly reduced primary marine productivity. These authors claim that modern oceanographic conditions were not achieved until 9,000 years ago and that from 9,000 to 7,000 BP there were periods of weaker upwelling and reduced productivity. The detailed effects of such changes on various classes of marine fauna have not been investigated (see Hebda and Frederick 1992). If lower marine productivity was a regional phenomenon during the Pleistocene–Holocene transition, however, we might expect that the general productivity of sea mammals, marine fish, seabirds, and shellfish might all have been lower than they were by the late Holocene.

North of Puget Sound, shifts in the relative productivity of marine vs. terrestrial habitats across the Pleistocene–Holocene transition are less well understood. The potential effects of sea-level rise and glaciation on the productivity of salmon runs, for instance, are poorly known. It seems likely that salmon and other anadromous fish were a rich potential resource in some areas, but local or regional distributions of such resources may have been limited in others. The distribution and productivity of shellfish beds also may have been affected in glaciated areas, since productive shellfish populations generally are absent in silt-laden waters around the mouths of glacial streams. It is also not clear what the relative productivity of sea mammals would have been in various areas of the North Pacific Coast. Since pinnipeds and many whales exist relatively high in the food chain, however, it seems likely that their productivity would have mirrored general patterns of coastal productivity during the Pleistocene–Holocene transition.

THE ARCHAEOLOGICAL RECORD

Interpreting the early archaeological record of North America's Pacific Coast is complicated by a variety of factors. Postglacial sea-level rise inundated vast areas of the continental shelves, for instance, dramatically altering the coastal landscape and almost certainly flooding some early sites. Tectonic activity has uplifted much of the California coast, while much of the Oregon and Washington coasts appear to be subsiding. Farther north, the effects of deglaciation, tectonics, sea-level rise, and isostatic rebound deeply submerged some terminal Pleistocene shorelines, dramatically uplifted others, and left still others at or near modern sea level. In addition, the acidic soils typical of most northern coniferous forests may have led to broad regional differences in the preservation of faunal remains and shell middens.

Contemporary and historical factors also structure our knowledge of the archaeological record in different areas, where the intensity of archaeological and paleoenvironmental research has varied tremendously. Systematic excavations along Baja California's Pacific Coast have been very limited, while the coast of Alta California has been studied intensively. Even here, however, the number of investigated sites declines dramatically from south to north, raising questions about the representative nature of the existing record (Jones 1991). On the Oregon and Washington coasts, relatively little research has been done, while British Columbia has seen intermediate levels of archaeological work. Southeast Alaska has seen comparatively little research, but has produced several early sites. These problems suggest the need for caution in interpreting and comparing data from individual sites or areas, in searching for local or regional patterns, and in explaining any similarities or differences identified. On a regional level, however, with a data base of well over 50 sites that seem to date between about 11,500 and 8,000 years ago (Table 1), the amount of data available for analysis is substantial.

13,000–12,000 Years Ago

Despite claims to the contrary, there is no firm evidence for the occupation of North America's Pacific Coast prior to about 12,000 years ago. Claims for Pre-Clovis occupation of the coast (like the interior) have come primarily from California, where several controversial human skeletons or sites previously dated to the Pleistocene have been redated to the Holocene (see Taylor et al. 1985). These remains include several "Pleistocene shell middens" on Santa Rosa Island described by Orr (1968), but recently redated to the early Holocene (Erlandson 1994; Erlandson and Morris 1992).

12,000–11,000 Years Ago

What is probably the earliest evidence for occupation of the Pacific Coast comes from a handful of fluted Clovis-like points found in California, Oregon, and Washington (R. L. Carlson 1990; Erlandson et al. 1987; Hemphill 1990:25; Meltzer and Dunnell 1987; Minor 1989; Simons et al. 1985; Wallmann 1994). Unfortunately, all these finds are isolated point fragments lacking dated stratigraphic contexts or clear associations. Meltzer and Dunnell (1987) suggested that the morphology of many specimens from western Washington and Oregon might indicate a late "backwash" of Paleoindian technology into the Northwest.

Several more recent discoveries, however, seem very similar to classic Clovis points dated elsewhere in the western United States to between about 11,500 and 11,000 years ago. At least three of the fluted point fragments were found with or near more recent archaeological materials, and one or more could be curated items left by more recent peoples (Erlandson et al. 1987). A point fragment from the northern California coast reportedly had Pleistocene sediments adhering to it (Simons et al. 1985), however, and two points from near the southern Oregon coast were made from local cherts (see Hemphill 1990:25; Wallmann 1994).

These finds suggest that Paleoindians occupied at least the southern parts of the Pacific Coast region during Clovis times, a probability supported by fluted points found in mountain passes or on lakeshores only 50–100 km from the coast (Glennan 1971; Moratto 1984). Substantial evidence of Clovis occupation nearest the Pacific Coast is found at Borax Lake in California (Harrington 1948; Meighan and Haynes 1970) and East Wenatchee in central Washington (Mehringer and Foit 1990). While Clovis influence is most probable for areas south of the Cordilleran ice sheet, Clovis material has not been found on the coasts of British Columbia or southeast Alaska. R. L. Carlson (1991:111) believes the Clovis tradition was distinct from the earliest complexes documented on the Northwest Coast north of Puget Sound. To our knowledge, of the Clovis sites in California, Oregon, or Washington, only East Wenatchee in Washington has produced clearly associated faunal remains. Consequently, we have almost no direct evidence for Paleoindian subsistence along the Pacific Coast or nearby interior regions. An apparent Clovis-age level in a stratified rockshelter (SIS-218) at Tule Lake in interior northern California produced fish and waterfowl bones (Beaton 1991), however, suggesting that Clovis peoples relied on aquatic resources to some extent. Until stratified coastal sites of Clovis age are found and investigated, we cannot be sure whether Clovis peoples used marine resources.

11,000–10,000 Years Ago

The distribution of sites and the nature of coastal cultures are little better known for the next millennium. The only archaeological materials dated to this time come from California's Northern Channel Islands. Geologic and oceanographic data show that the Channel Islands have been separated from the California mainland since at least the Pliocene. Consequently, the earliest occupants of the islands must have had seaworthy boats to navigate the often treacherous waters of the Santa Barbara Channel. The impoverished nature of the land flora and fauna on the islands (Johnson 1983) suggests that these early island dwellers must have relied heavily on marine foods (Erlandson 1994).

One of the early Channel Islands sites is Daisy Cave (CA-SMI-261) on San Miguel Island, where a thin cave soil containing red abalone, mussel, turban, chiton, and crab shells has produced a handful of chert and siliceous shale artifacts (Erlandson 1993a). Three uncorrected ^{14}C dates on shell and charcoal from this soil range from 10,180 ± 70 RYBP to 10,390 ± 130 BP. Erlandson (1991a, 1994) cautioned, however, that shellfish remains may have been carried to the site by carrion-feeding seabirds, and the association of artifacts and faunal remains has yet to be unequivocally demonstrated. Nonetheless, it seems quite likely that Daisy Cave was occupied briefly during the terminal Pleistocene.

Possible support for the early presence of humans on the Northern Channel Islands comes from Arlington Springs (CA-SRI-173) on Santa Rosa Island. Here, Orr (1962, 1968)

Table 1. Early Sites of the Pacific Coast of North America

Site name	General location	^{14}C age (RYBP)	Site description or contents	Primary references
			Gulf of Alaska	
Anangula Blade Site	Umnak Island, Aleutian Islands	≈8,700	Unifacial blade industry in site nearly devoid of faunal remains, but coastal focus was essential.	Aigner (1976), Laughlin and Aigner (1966)
AK-KOD-44 (Crag Point)	Kodiak Island	7,790 ± 620	Possible coastal Paleoarctic component?	Jordan (1992)
			Southeast Alaska	
Groundhog Bay 2	Icy Straits	9,200 <8,900	Possible basal bifacial component; Microblade component; no fauna.	Ackerman (1968), Ackerman et al. (1979)
Hidden Falls (SIT-119)	Baranof Island	9,060 ± 260	Microblade assemblage with little or no associated fauna.	Davis (1989)
Chuck Lake 2	Heceta Island	≈8,200	Microblade assemblage with fish, shellfish, and sea mammals.	Ackerman et al. (1985), Okada et al. (1989, 1992)
			British Columbia	
Namu	Central BC mainland	9,700–9,000	Bifacial, "macrolithic," and pebble tool assemblage with no fauna.	R. L. Carlson (1991)
Glenrose	Fraser River mouth	≈8,500	Old Cordilleran assemblage with leaf-shaped bifaces, cobble tools.	Matson (1976)
Queen Charlotte Island	Intertidal sites	8,500–9,500?	Biface, microblade, and pebble tool bearing intertidal site remnants.	Fladmark (1990), Fedje (1993)
Bear Cove	N. Vancouver Island	8,020 ± 110	Old Cordilleran assemblage.	C. Carlson (1979)
			Washington	
Manis Mastodon	Strait of Juan de Fuca	12,000?	Mastodon kill site? Lacks clear cultural associations.	Gustafson and Manis (1984), R. L. Carlson (1990)
Whidbey Island	Puget Sound	None	Isolated fluted point find.	R. L. Carlson (1990)
Olympia	Puget Sound	None	Isolated fluted point find.	Osborne (1956)

Site	Location	Date	Description	Reference
Oregon				
Siltcoos Lake 35-CU-176	Central coast	None	Isolated fluted point.	Minor (1989)
	Winchuck River	None	Fluted point fragment.	Hemphill (1990)
Neptune Site (35-LA-3A)	Lane County coast	8,310 ± 110	Possibly cultural charcoal from below recent midden.	Lyman (1991)
Indian Sands (35-CU-67)	Curry County coast	8,250–8,150	Small, low-density shell midden on outer coast.	Moss and Erlandson (1994)
Tahkenitch Lake (DO-130)	Douglas County	7,960 ± 90 / 6,880 ± 80	Estuarine site with fish and sea mammal remains. 8,000 yr old?	Minor and Toepel (1986)
Northern California				
MEN-1918	Caspar/Ft. Bragg	None	Fluted point fragment from below more recent midden?	Simons et al. (1985)
Duncan's Landing (SON-348/H)	Sonoma coast	8,210 ± 110 / 8,620 ± 420	Lower levels of deep stratified shell midden.	Schwaderer (1992)
Central California				
Scotts Valley (SCR-177)	Santa Cruz area	8,500 ± 250 to 12,520 ± 740	Low-density pericoastal lithic site; early levels probably date to Early Holocene.	Cartier (1993)
Metcalf Site (SCL-178)	South San Francisco Bay	8,500 ± 300 to 9,960 ± 500	Low-density pericoastal site with some fish, shellfish use.	Hildebrandt (1983)
Diablo Canyon (SLO-2)	South of Morro Bay	8,960 ± 190 / 9,320 ± 140	Stratified shell midden with burials in basal levels.	Greenwood (1972)
SLO-177	Cambria	8,290 ± 100 / 8,430 ± 200	Stratified shell midden, basal Early Millingstone component.	Pierce (1979), Rudolph (1983)
SLO-585A	Diablo Canyon	8,410 ± 190 / 7,370 ± 150	Stratified shell midden, basal Early Millingstone component.	Greenwood (1972)
SLO-801	Shell Beach area	8,660 ± 150	Multicomponent shell midden with early basal component.	Breschini and Haversat (1991), Erlandson (1994)
SLO-832	Pismo Beach area	8,520 ± 140	Multicomponent shell midden with Early Millingstone level.	Breschini and Haversat (1991), Erlandson (1994)

(continued)

Table 1. (*Continued*)

Site name	General location	¹⁴C age (RYBP)	Site description or contents	Primary references
			Central California (*continued*)	
SLO-877	Cayucos area	8,080 ± 100	Basal shell midden stratum in multicomponent site.	Breschini and Haversat (1991), Erlandson (1994)
SLO-884	Shell Beach area	8,010 ± 100	Lower levels of multicomponent shell midden site.	Breschini and Haversat (1991), Erlandson (1994)
SBA-931	Santa Ynez River Mouth	8,490 ± 120 to 9,440 ± 150	Pre-Millingstone shell midden strata at base of two loci.	Glassow (1991)
SBA-530	Point Arguello area	8,430 ± 120 to 7,830 ± 350	Early Millingstone shell midden in multicomponent site.	Glassow (1991), Erlandson (1994)
			Southern California	
SBA-1951	Santa Barbara coast	None	Clovis point fragment.	Erlandson et al. (1987)
SBA-1807	Santa Barbara coast	8,000–8,200	Large shell midden, residential base?	Erlandson (1994)
SBA-2057	Santa Barbara coast	8,200	Small shell midden/temporary camp?	Erlandson (1994)
Daisy Cave (SMI-261)	San Miguel Island	10,260 ± 90 8,000–9,000	Ephemeral Terminal Pleistocene shell under dense Early Holocene midden with basketry; bone gorges, fish, and sea mammal remains.	Erlandson (1993a), Connolly et al. (1995)
SRI-173	Arlington Canyon, Santa Rosa Island	10,000 ± 200 10,080 ± 810	Deeply buried isolated human bones in old arroyo fill.	Orr (1962, 1968), Erlandson (1994)
SRI-116	Northeast coast, Santa Rosa Island	8,615 ± 115 8,815 ± 140	Isolated human burial with *Olivella* shell beads.	Morris and Erlandson (1993)
SRI-1	Garanon Canyon, Santa Rosa Island	8,320 ± 105	Small, low-density shell midden.	Erlandson and Morris (1992)
SRI-6	Arlington Canyon, Santa Rosa Island	8,360 ± 80	Deeply buried shell midden.	Erlandson (1994)
VEN-294	Medea Creek	8,250 ± 160	Shell midden in interior valley setting; Millingstone assemblage.	Rosen (1978), Erlandson (1994)
LAN-159	La Brea tar pits	9,000 ± 80	Human burial with shell beads.	Moratto (1984)

ORA-386	Quail Hill	8,960 ± 260	Estuarine shell midden.	Weisbord (1985)
ORA-339	Newport Beach	9,280 ± 90	Multicomponent site with Early Holocene component.	Mason et al. (1991)
ORA-246	Crystal Cove	8,550 ± 80	Multicomponent shell midden.	Mason et al. (1992)
ORA-64 (Irvine Site)	Upper Newport Bay, Orange County	4,900 ± 80	Multicomponent shell midden: Millingstone deposits with possible premilling stratum.	Koerper (1981), Drover et al. (1983)
ORA-5 (ORA-7775?)	Laguna Beach, Orange County	8,445 ± 280; 8,300 ± 80; 8,950 ± 80	Mussel shell lenses bracketing "Laguna Woman" skull.	Berger et al. (1971), Moratto (1984)
Eel Point (SCLI-43B)	San Clemente Island	≈8,200	Stratified 3-m-deep shell midden: basal data dated to 8,200 RYBP. >9,500-year-old dates appear to have been erroneous.	Salls (1988), Meighan (1989), Raab et al. (1994)
Harris Site (SDI-149)	San Dieguito River	8,490 ± 400; 9,030 ± 350	San Dieguito "type" site, with basal bifacial assemblage and no milling tools.	Warren (1966, 1967)
SDI-194	San Dieguito River	≈8,150	San Dieguito–La Jolla shell midden with estuarine fauna.	Norwood and Walker (1980)
SDI-210 (UCLJ-M-15)	Agua Hedionda Lagoon	9,020 ± 500	Basal levels of stratified shell midden lack milling tools.	Moriarty (1967)
SDI-293	San Dieguito River	≈8,000	San Dieguito–La Jolla shell midden with estuarine fauna.	Norwood and Walker (1980)
SDI-685	San Dieguito River	≈8,000	San Dieguito–La Jolla shell midden with estuarine fauna.	Norwood and Walker (1980)
SDI-691	Carlsbad area	8,290 ± 100	Estuarine shell midden.	Cheever et al. (1986)
SDI-4669	U.C. San Diego area	8,330 ± 160; 8,470 ± 140	Two associated and tightly flexed human burials.	Kennedy (1983)
SDI-4850	Batiquitos Lagoon	8,160 ± 360	San Dieguito–La Jolla shell midden with estuarine fauna.	Gallegos (1987)
SDI-5119 (W-1353)	San Dieguito River	8,310 ± 170	Transitional San Dieguito–La Jolla shell midden.	Norwood (1980)
SDI-5369W	San Dieguito River	≈8,200	San Dieguito–La Jolla shell midden with estuarine fauna.	Norwood and Walker (1980)
SDI-10940 (Del Mar)	San Dieguito River	≈8,400	Shell midden, site of "Del Mar Man" skeleton.	Stafford et al. (1987)
SDI-10965	Agua Hedionda Lagoon	8,390 ± 110	San Dieguito–La Jolla shell midden with estuarine fauna.	Gallegos and Carrico (1984)
Baja California				
Unnamed cave	Punta Negra	≈8,500	Turban shells from possible cache in cave shell midden.	Linick (1977:30)

located the scattered bones of a person who appears to have died in a small arroyo on the northwest coast of the island. Found 11 m below the surface in stratified arroyo fill deposits, charcoal, carbon-bearing soil, and human bone collagen from the "Arlington Man" (now thought to have been a woman) skeleton all produced dates of about 10,000 years ago (Berger and Protsch 1989; Orr 1968). The bone collagen sample was not pretreated or dated using sophisticated techniques (i.e., accelerator mass spectrometry [AMS]) designed to avoid contamination problems, but the consistency of the dates suggests that people were present on the Channel Islands around 10,000 years ago (see Erlandson 1994:184–186). A recent effort to radiocarbon-date the Arlington skeleton using AMS has yet to produce definitive results.

10,000–9,000 Years Ago

Between 10,000 and 9,000 years ago, evidence for the occupation of the Pacific Coast is still sparse, but by the end of this period, a number of sites near the southern and northern parts of our study area may have first been occupied. In California, these early "Paleo-Coastal" sites (Moratto 1984:104) appear to be associated with San Dieguito (or Western Pluvial Lakes Tradition) bifacial industries probably derived from Clovis antecedents. The basal levels of a number of shell middens appear to date to this time period, notably CA-SBA-931 near the mouth of the Santa Ynez River (Glassow 1991), CA-SLO-2 at Diablo Canyon in San Luis Obispo County (Greenwood 1972), and CA-SDI-210 at Agua Hedionda Lagoon near San Diego (Moriarty 1967). These mainland sites have produced uncorrected ^{14}C dates of about 9,000 RYBP, and each appears to lack the grinding tools (*manos* and *metates*) prevalent in later sites of the California coast (Erlandson 1994). All have also produced evidence for coastal resource use—primarily shellfish—but little is known about the other contents of these early components or the nature of the broader adaptations they represent.

Another California site widely reported to date to this time period is the Eel Point site (CA-SCLI-43) located on San Clemente Island, 75 km off the San Diego coast (Raab and Yatsko 1992; Salls 1988, 1990). Here, charcoal samples from near the base of a 3-m-deep stratified shell midden were ^{14}C-dated at the UCLA laboratory to between about 8,850 and 9,800 RYBP (Salls 1990:65). On the basis of disparities in the ages of shell and charcoal samples, however, Erlandson (1994:214–216) questioned the accuracy of the earliest ^{14}C dates for Eel Point. More recent research at the site has found no evidence for occupation prior to about 8,000 years ago, and the levels once thought to be over 9,000 years old have been redated to the middle Holocene (Raab et al. 1994).

The earliest sites in the north are Ground Hog Bay 2 (GHB2) in southeast Alaska and Namu in British Columbia. The investigations of Ackerman (1965, 1968) at GHB2 were a milestone in Northwest Coast archaeology. Prior to that time, scholars thought the northern Northwest Coast was covered in glacial ice during much of the Holocene and not inhabited until relatively late in prehistory. GHB2 is located 10–15 m above the shoreline on a marine terrace isostatically uplifted after a glacial advance 11,500–11,000 years ago (Ackerman et al. 1979:198). The oldest component (III) contained two obsidian biface fragments, a chert scraper, and several pieces of debitage dated to between 10,180 and 9,130 years ago. Ackerman (1992:21) recently estimated the age of this component at 9,200 years. No faunal remains were found, but the geographic setting supports the use of boats and a marine economy (Ackerman 1992:22).

Namu contains the earliest large assemblage from the Northwest Coast during this period. The site's oldest component (1A), dating between 9,700 and 9,000 years ago (R. L. Carlson 1991:111), produced an assemblage of almost 1000 "macrolithic" chipped stone artifacts, 32 of which are formal tools, including several bifaces (R. L. Carlson 1996). A few ground and pecked stone tools are present, but a microblade industry reportedly is not. Like GHB2, Namu has no faunal remains associated with its earliest component. Today, Namu is located on the coast, but during its initial occupation, it may have been a kilometer or so up the Namu River. Contemporary coastal sites may have been inundated or destroyed by sea-level rise and coastal erosion (R. L. Carlson 1991:114). The "Pebble Tool Tradition" at Namu, like related coastal and interior assemblages, has been called both Old Cordilleran and Protowestern. Some scholars (e.g., Matson 1976) believe it derives from the interior Northwest south of the ice sheets. R. L. Carlson (1991:114) argued, however, that the Pebble Tool Tradition is an extension of a coastal Beringian culture that expanded south along the coast as these regions became habitable between 11,500 and 10,500 years ago. He believes that this expansion occurred prior to the introduction of microblade technology on the Northwest Coast.

The lack of intact sites older than 9,000 years between southeast Alaska and Namu may be due to sea-level changes. As described earlier, much of the now-submerged Hecate Plain and Queen Charlotte Sound were exposed until the final millennia of the Pleistocene, when sea levels began to rise rapidly (Fladmark 1990). Most outer coast sites from this time period probably have been inundated, while along the mainland, some early Holocene shorelines are now several hundred meters higher than modern coasts (Fladmark 1990:184). Despite these problems, coastal surveys on the Queen Charlotte Islands have documented a number of redeposited intertidal sites (e.g., Fedje 1993; Fladmark 1990). Some of these sites, discussed more fully below, may be older than 9,000 years.

9,000–8,000 Years Ago

By 9,000–8,000 years ago, coastal sites are known from all major Pacific Coast areas, from Anangula in the Aleutians to Baja California. The distribution of these sites is uneven, however, with very few examples in Baja California, from Monterey Bay to the Canadian border, and northwest of southeast Alaska (Figure 1).

The best record of cultural and environmental developments for this period once again comes from the southern and central California coast, where at least 40 sites have produced reasonably reliable ^{14}C dates between 8,000 and 9,000 RYBP (see Erlandson 1994). Between 9,000 and 8,500 years ago, milling tools (*manos* and *metates*) first appear in mainland sites of the California coast. *Manos* and *metates* are rare or absent in early assemblages on the California Islands, however, where the diversity of plant resources was limited. Almost certainly associated primarily with seed collecting and processing, the "Millingstone" tool complex (including many angular hammerstones used to shape and rejuvenate grinding surfaces) may signal an increase in sedentism and a diversification of subsistence among peoples of the southern and central California coast (see Glassow 1991). These changes may be related to environmentally induced shifts in plant and animal productivity. Although "Millingstone" economies appear to have been fairly eclectic, considerable technological and faunal evidence suggests that subsistence focused on shellfish and small seeds (Erlandson 1988, 1991b). Projectile points and fishing gear are rare in most Millingstone sites (Wallace 1955; Warren 1965), and the nutritional yields of all vertebrate remains generally seem to be

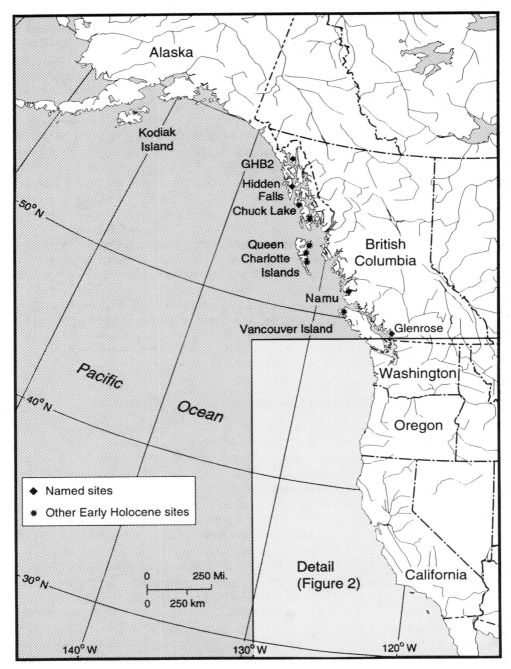

Figure 1. Pacific Coast of North America, showing some early Holocene sites of the Northwest Coast.

surpassed by those of shellfish (Erlandson 1994). During this period, coastal groups traded shell beads and other materials to interior peoples for obsidian from sources 250–300 km away in the Sierras and western Great Basin (Bennyhoff and Hughes 1987).

Daisy Cave (Figure 2) on San Miguel Island provides a remarkable record of early Holocene maritime activity. Daisy Cave, perched directly above the modern coastline, was located only about 200 m from the early Holocene coast. In stratified shell midden deposits dating between 9,000 and 8,000 years ago, several bipointed bone gorges, numerous expedient flake tools, three bifacial points or knives, and several *Olivella* shell beads have been found. Numerous pieces of woven sea grass cordage and two possible twined sandal fragments have also been recovered from these levels, fortuitously preserved in a localized deposit of seabird guano (Connolly et al. 1995). The Daisy Cave artifacts are found in lenses of densely packed mussel, abalone, turban, and other shells, along with smaller quantities of fish, sea mammal, and bird bone.

Several British Columbia and southeast Alaska sites also have produced materials dating to this period. Component II ($\approx$ 8,900–4,200 BP) at Ground Hog Bay contained microblade cores, microblades, macroblade and flake cores, hammerstones, a few broken bifaces, choppers, notches, scrapers, a Donnelly-type burin, and utilized flakes (Ackerman 1992). The earliest component at Hidden Falls also contains microblade and pebble tool industries and possibly a single biface tip (Davis 1989). Radiocarbon dates on unmodified wood from Hidden Falls I range from over 10,000 to 8,000 BP, but a small charcoal sample from a possible hearth dated to 9,060 ± 230 BP suggests that the earliest occupation occurred about 9,000 years ago. A single fish bone and two shell fragments were the only faunal remains found (Erlandson 1989; Moss 1989), and their association with the early component is dubious. Nonetheless, the site's location on an outer island of the Alexander archipelago as well as the presence of exotic obsidian indicate boat travel and marine-oriented subsistence.

Another assemblage dominated by microblades and cobble tools is found at the Chuck Lake site on Heceta Island, with one of the oldest shell-bearing components on the Northwest Coast (Ackerman 1988; Ackerman et al. 1985; Okada et al. 1989). Dated to about 8,200 BP, the site is now 15 m above sea level and 800 m from saltwater. What is now Chuck Lake probably was the upper end of an embayment during the early Holocene. The faunal assemblage is dominated by bottomfish and shellfish, with a few sea mammal, land mammal, and bird bones. Salmon bones make up fewer than 2% of the identified specimens (Ackerman 1992:22). Data from Chuck Lake clearly show that microblade-using people of this period exploited a variety of marine resources.

The oldest cultural material yet described for the Queen Charlotte Islands probably dates to this millennium. At Skoglund's Landing, Fladmark (1990) described six pebble and flake tools found 3–8 m below the surface in a raised beach deposit. The variable depth of these artifacts indicates that they were being incorporated into an active beach as it rose to 4–7 m above its present position (Fladmark 1990:192). In light of the local sea-level history, Fladmark proposed that these artifacts must be at least 8,000 years old, and probably older. Fladmark also found a handful of artifacts at the base of the eroding exposure, a "Paleo-intertidal" assemblage similar to those found on the southern Charlottes and elsewhere in central British Columbia (Hobler 1978). Recent Parks Canada research on the Charlottes promises to significantly expand our understanding of these sites. Here Fedje (1993) and his colleagues (Fedje et al. 1996) have identified a number of intertidal sites containing bifaces,

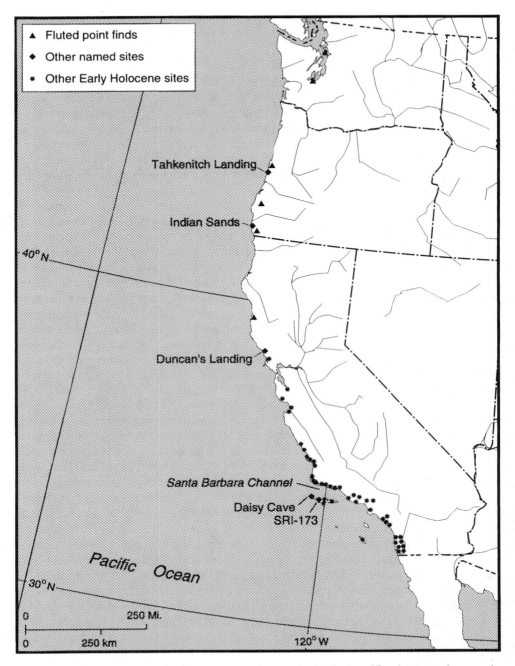

Figure 2. California, Oregon, and Washington coasts, showing the distribution of fluted points and some early Holocene sites.

microblade cores, or both. Detailed study of local sea-level histories and radiocarbon dating of the beach deposits in which the artifacts were found suggest that these sites date to *at least* 8,500 BP, and some appear to be older than 9,000 years (Fedje et al. 1996). At present, the artifact assemblages from these important sites are quite small and the temporal relationships of bifacial and microblade technologies has yet to be sorted out. However, they clearly support the proposal by Fladmark (1990) that maritime peoples were on the Queen Charlotte Islands at least 9,000 years ago.

At Namu, Component 1B dates between 9,000 and 8,000 years ago and lacks faunal remains (Cannon 1995), but produced a large artifact assemblage. R. L. Carlson (1995) described this assemblage as very similar to the earliest Namu materials, except that a microblade technology was added about 8,500 years ago. Also present are unifacial pebble choppers, pebble rasps, and core scrapers that Carlson interprets as the earliest heavy woodworking tools of the Northwest Coast.

Located along the Fraser River, the earliest component at Glenrose is thought to date from 8,500 to 5,500 BP (Matson and Coupland 1995). During this early occupation, the site was closer to the outlet of the Fraser than it is today. The assemblage contains cobble tools, foliate bifaces, and ground stone, along with wedges and a punch of antler, and a barbed bone point. Matson (1976) called this component "Old Cordilleran," but except for the microblade industry, the stone tools seem similar to those from Namu. There are numerous faunal remains associated with this component, but the age of these materials is uncertain (Matson and Coupland 1995).

A key site on the Oregon coast is 35-DO-130 (Tahkenitch Landing), located on the shore of freshwater Tahkenitch Lake, which may have been occupied as much as 8,000 years ago. Prior to Minor and Toepel's (1986) investigations, there was no evidence for coastal settlement or resource use in Oregon prior to 3,000 years ago. Tahkenitch contains a basal component ^{14}C-dated to 7,960 ± 90 and 6,880 ± 80 (Minor and Toepel 1986:40), but these dates appear to be on scattered charcoal, and their precise relationship to the recovered artifacts and faunal remains is unclear. Minor and Toepel (1986:104) estimate that the earlier occupation took place between 8,000 and 5,200 years ago. Only seven tools were recovered from this component: three hammerstones, a chopper, a scraper, a graver, and a sandstone abrader. A total of 971 bone fragments included a variety of marine fish and aquatic birds. Most of the mammal bone was unidentifiable, but single fragments of harbor seal and deer bone were identified (Greenspan 1986). Small amounts of marine shell were also found in the early component (Barner 1986:48; Minor and Toepel 1986:104), but this stratum is sometimes described as a "non-shell facies" (McDowell and Minor 1986:38). Although questions about the age of the early component at Tahkenitch persist, Minor and Toepel demonstrated that dramatic changes in the Oregon coastline have occurred since the early Holocene. Prior to 3,000 years ago, Tahkenitch Lake was an arm of the sea that supported a flourishing estuarine fauna. After 3,000 years ago, vast dune sheets blocked the outlet of Tahkenitch Creek and many other coastal drainages, converting many coastal estuaries into freshwater lakes.

Between Gold Beach and Brookings on the southern Oregon coast, we recently identified another early site (35-CU-67C) near a place called Indian Sands. Here, a virtually continuous scatter of chipped stone tools and debris is exposed in dune blowouts for about a kilometer along the coastal bluffs. On a blown-out surface within this larger site, we identified a localized and low-density scatter of mussel shells covering an area about 20 × 25 m.

Two well-preserved shell samples produced very similar ^{14}C dates of 8,250 ± 80 and 8,150 ± 120 RYBP, and a sample of burned shell was dated to 7,790 ± 70 RYBP. Because the archaeological materials at 35-CU-67C are located on a deflated surface, we cannot be certain which artifacts are associated with these early dates. Within the horizontally discrete shell cluster, however, the most abundant implements are large flaked cobble tools and cores that resemble those from other Old Cordilleran sites to the north (see Matson and Coupland 1995). Also found within this area were a number of small obsidian flakes from volcanic flows located in the Klamath Basin 150–200 km to the east. If these obsidian artifacts are associated with the early Holocene dates, they would seem to suggest the existence of early trade networks much like those documented for early Holocene coastal peoples of Southern California and the northern Northwest Coast (Moss and Erlandson 1995).

A final key site is Duncan's Point Cave (CA-SON-348/H), located a few kilometers south of the Russian River mouth on the Northern California coast. In 1989, archaeologists from California's Department of Parks and Recreation excavated a single test pit in this small sea cave and dug through a shell midden almost 3 m deep. The lower portions of the midden produced ^{14}C dates of 8,620 ± 420, 8,210 ± 110, and 7,850 ± 110 RYBP (Schwaderer 1992:57), quadrupling the known antiquity of shell middens on the Northern California coast. Rodent burrowing has caused some mixing among various strata, but the lower levels of the site contain fish, sea mammal, pinniped, and bird bones. Shellfish remains are dominated by rocky shore species throughout the sequence, but the lower levels contain a significant proportion of estuarine clams and oysters, suggesting that a bay or estuary existed in the vicinity of the site during the early Holocene.

THE ORIGINS AND EARLY DEVELOPMENT OF PACIFIC COAST PEOPLES

Environmental changes play a critical role in structuring the archaeological record of the Pleistocene–Holocene transition. Rising sea levels flooded large tracts of land in some areas, while isostatic rebound raised some former shorelines high above the modern coast. The geographic setting of many early sites has changed dramatically—from estuarine to lacustrine, from riverine to coastal, or from interior to coastal. These changes illustrate the dynamics of coastal environments at the Pleistocene–Holocene transition and emphasize the need for caution in interpreting the record of early Pacific Coast settlement. Indeed, we cannot yet be reasonably certain that the earliest part of the record is not missing in virtually any local area or region.

From Clovis to Old Cordilleran, the earliest coastal peoples seem to have had chipped stone industries featuring lanceolate or leaf-shaped bifaces, but no microblades. The existence of this early bifacial tradition is only hinted at in coastal Alaska, but seems relatively well established from coastal British Columbia to southern California. In fact, the bifaces and chopping tools from the earliest levels at Namu look very similar to contemporaneous assemblages from the southern California coast. Between 9,000 and 8,500 years ago, however, a distinctive microblade technology appears on the northern Northwest Coast. The sequence of these technological developments is similar to that of earlier developments around the North Pacific Rim, where bifacial traditions generally precede microblade technologies (Aikens 1990; Aikens and Dumond 1986; Powers and Hoffecker

1989). These developments are almost certainly related to two or more migrations from northeast Asia to the New World.

Whether these migrations included a migration of maritime peoples down the Pacific Coast (see Easton 1992; Fladmark 1979) is not known. Data from Australia, Melanesia, and Japan now support the idea that coastal peoples have used seaworthy boats for at least 25,000–40,000 years (Dixon 1993; Erlandson 1993b, 1994). From northern Japan, the Kurile Islands could have provided a series of stepping-stones for maritime voyages to the Beringian coast. Paleoenvironmental data also show that unglaciated coastlines of southern and southeast Alaska were more extensive than previously recognized, especially after 13,000 years ago. So far, however, no coastal occupation sites of Clovis age or earlier have been found along the Pacific Coast of North America. While some early coastal sites have undoubtedly been submerged by rising sea levels, we do not know whether such sites are any older than those known on dry land. Although intriguing circumstantial evidence continues to accumulate for the possibility that the New World was first settled by boat, proving that such a coastal migration actually took place will require clear evidence for Pacific Coast sites that are older than their earliest interior counterparts.

What we know today is that Clovis peoples occupied the coastal area south of Puget Sound, probably by 11,000 or more years ago. Traditionally, Clovis economies have been thought of as almost exclusively terrestrial in nature and origin. This may be the case along the Pacific Coast, as well, but we know almost nothing about what Clovis peoples were doing in far western North America. However, the nature of Pacific Coast environments, the location of intermontane sites, and the limited archaeological data available all suggest that Clovis peoples of the Far West had more diversified economies than the "big-game-hunting" Paleoindians of North America's Great Plains and Southwest regions. Moreover, with Clovis points in both coastal and interior areas of California, Oregon, and Washington, there is no longer any clear temporal priority to interior vs. coastal settlement (Erlandson 1994; Jones 1991).

By at least 9,000–10,000 years ago, coastal peoples were using boats in southern California and on the northern Northwest Coast. The bifacial and microblade technologies clearly find analogues not just in adjacent coastal areas, but also in very similar technological traditions in adjacent interior regions. The presence of exotic obsidian in some of the earliest coastal sites in California and southeast Alaska also suggests that long-distance trade networks had been established between coastal and interior peoples by at least 9,000 years ago (Erlandson 1994; Erlandson et al. 1992; Moss 1994). Meighan (1989) suggested that the earliest island sites in California represent an adaptation too different from the "big-game hunters" of the interior to be derivative and that a coastal migration must account for these early maritime peoples. R. L. Carlson (1991) also noted that the earliest bifacial assemblages of the Northwest Coast are found along the north coast and that similar assemblages appear somewhat later to the south and in upriver and interior sites, implying that the initial colonization of the Pacific Coast may have had maritime origins.

When did people first settle various parts of the Pacific Coast? Did a coastal migration lead to the initial colonization of this vast and varied coastal region? If so, what kind of environments did these early coastal peoples encounter? How did they live and what happened to them? Our reading of the evidence, considering the available data from Baja California to Southern Alaska, suggests that there is not yet enough information to clearly indicate whether the earliest settlers of the Pacific Coast had interior origins, maritime origins, or both. More research is necessary before we can answer such questions with confidence. Major progress has been made, however, in reconstructing the complex relationships between environmental and cultural changes that accompany the Pleistocene–Holocene transition along the Pacific Coast. Only a decade ago, there was no firm evidence for a human presence along the Pacific Coast of North America prior to about 9,000 years ago and no coastal sites from San Francisco Bay to the Canadian border that predated about 3,000 years. In the intervening years, a number of Clovis-like fluted points have been found in coastal or pericoastal settings south of Puget Sound, a human presence on California's Channel Islands has been pushed back beyond 9,000 and perhaps 10,000 years, coastally oriented sites of 8,000 years or older have been found on the coasts of northern California and Oregon, and additional early coastal sites have been found in British Columbia and Southeast Alaska. Significant new data have also emerged about the complexity of environmental changes associated with the Pleistocene–Holocene transition along the Pacific Coast. We can only hope that the next ten years of research will be as productive as the last decade.

ACKNOWLEDGMENTS

We thank L. G. Straus, G. Frison, B. Eriksen, D. Yesner, and the other members of INQUA's Pleistocene–Holocene Transition Working Group for inviting us to participate in this volume. A. Mackie, D. Fedje, and B. Wilson kindly shared unpublished data on their recent research on Haida Gwaii, and Richard Hughes identified the geochemical sources of the obsidian artifacts from 35-CU-67C. Our recent work on the Oregon Coast has been supported in part by National Park Service funds administered by the Oregon State Historic Preservation Office. Partial support for our research and travel also was provided by the University of Oregon.

REFERENCES

Ackerman, R. E., 1965, *Archaeological Survey of Glacier Bay National Monument, Southeastern Alaska*, Washington State University, Laboratory of Anthropology Report of Investigations, No. 36, Pullman.

Ackerman, R. E., 1968, *The Archaeology of the Glacier Bay Region, Southeastern Alaska*, Washington State University, Laboratory of Anthropology Report of Investigations, No. 44, Pullman.

Ackerman, R. E., 1988, Early Subsistence Patterns in Southeast Alaska, in: *Diet and Subsistence: Current Archaeological Perspective* (B. V. Kennedy and G. M. LeMoine, eds.), Proceedings of the 19th Annual Conference of the Archaeological Association of the University of Calgary, Alberta, pp. 175–189.

Ackerman, R. E., 1992, Earliest Stone Industries on the North Pacific Coast of North America, in: *Maritime Cultures of Southern Alaska: Papers in Honor of Richard H. Jordan, Arctic Anthropology* 29(2):18–27.

Ackerman, R. E., Hamilton, T. D., and Stuckenrath, R., 1979, Early Culture Complexes of the Northern Northwest Coast, *Canadian Journal of Archaeology* 3:195–209.

Ackerman, R. E., Reid, K. C., Gallison, D., and Roe, M. E., 1985, *Archaeology of Heceta Island: A Survey of 16 Timber Units in the Tongass National Forest, Southeastern Alaska*, Center for Northwest Anthropology Project Report 3, Washington State University, Pullman.

Aigner, J. S., 1976, Early Holocene Evidence for the Aleut Maritime Adaptation, *Arctic Anthropology* 13(2):32–45.

Aikens, C. M., 1990, From Asia to America: The First Peopling of the New World, *Prehistoric Mongoloid Dispersals* 7:1–34.

Aikens, C. M., and Dumond, D. E., 1986, Convergence and Common Heritage: Some Parallels in the Archaeology of Japan and Western North America, in *Windows on the Japanese Past: Studies in Archaeology and Prehistory* (R. J. Pearson, ed.), Center for Japanese Studies, University of Michigan, pp. 163–178.

Arnold, J. E., 1992, Complex Hunter-Gatherer-Fishers of Prehistoric California: Chiefs, Specialists, and Maritime Adaptations on the Channel Islands, *American Antiquity* 57:60–84.

Axelrod, D. I., 1967, Geologic History of the Californian Insular Flora, in: *Proceedings of the Symposium on the Biology of the California Islands* (R. N. Philbrick, ed.), Santa Barbara Botanic Garden, pp. 93–149.

Baichtal, J., 1993, Management of the Karst Areas with the Ketchikan Area of the Tongass National Forest, Southeastern Alaska, in: *Proceedings of the 1991 National Cave Management Symposium*, American Cave Conservation Association, pp. 198–208.

Baichtal, J., no date, *An Update on the Pleistocene and Holocene Fauna Recovered from the Caves on Prince of Wales and the Surrounding Islands*, Manuscript on File, Tongass National Forest, Ketchikan, AK.

Barner, D. C., 1986, Aboriginal Use of Molluscan Resources, in: *The Archaeology of the Tahkenitch Landing Site: Early Prehistoric Occupation on the Oregon Coast* (R. Minor and K. A. Toepel, eds.), Heritage Research Associates Report 46:43–56, Eugene.

Beaton, J., 1991, Paleoindian Occupation Greater than 11,000 Years B.P. at Tule Lake, Northern California, *Current Research in the Pleistocene* 8:5–7.

Bennyhoff, J. A., and Hughes, R. E., 1987, Shell Bead and Ornament Exchange Networks between California and the Western Great Basin, *Anthropological Papers of the American Museum of Natural History* 64(2).

Berger, R., and Protsch, R., 1989, UCLA Radiocarbon Dates XI, *Radiocarbon* 31:55–67.

Berger, R., Protsch, R., Reynolds, R., Rozaire, C., and Sackett, J. R., 1971, New Radiocarbon Dates Based on Bone Collagen of California Indians, *Contributions to the University of California Archaeological Survey* 12:43–49.

Breschini, G. S., and Haversat, T., 1991, Early Holocene Occupation of the Central California Coast, in: *Hunter–Gatherers of Early Holocene Coastal California* (J. M. Erlandson and R. H. Colten, eds.), Perspectives in California Archaeology, Vol. 1, Institute of Archaeology, University of California, Los Angeles, pp. 125–132.

Cannon, A., 1996, The Early Namu Archaeofauna, in: *Early Human Occupation in British Columbia* (R. L. Carlson and L. Dala Bona, eds.), University of British Columbia Press, Vancouver, pp. 103–110.

Carlson, C., 1979, The Early Component at Bear Cove, *Canadian Journal of Archaeology* 3:177–194.

Carlson, R. L., 1990, Cultural Antecedents, in: *Northwest Coast* (W. Suttles, ed.), Handbook of North American Indians, Vol. 7, pp. 60–69.

Carlson, R. L., 1991, The Northwest Coast before A.D. 1600. In *The North Pacific to 1600: Proceedings of the Great Ocean Conference* (E. Crownheart-Vaughan, ed.).

Carlson, R. L., 1995, Early Namu, in: *Early Human Occupation in British Columbia* (R. L. Carlson and L. Dala Bona, eds.), University of British Columbia Press, Vancouver, pp. 83–102.

Cartier, R. (ed.), 1993, *The Scotts Valley Site: CA-SCr-177*, Santa Cruz Archaeological Society, Santa Cruz.

Cheever, D., Gallegos, D., and Carrico, R., 1986, *Cultural and Paleontological Survey and Testing for Pacific Rim, Carlsbad, California*, WESTEC Services, San Diego.

Clague, J. J., Harper, J. R., Hebda, R. J., and Howes, D. E., 1982, Late Quaternary Sea Levels and Crustal Movements, Coastal British Columbia, *Canadian Journal of Earth Sciences* 19:597–618.

Connolly, T. J., Erlandson, J. M., and Norris, S. E., 1995, Early Holocene Basketry from Daisy Cave, San Miguel Island, California, *American Antiquity* 60:309–318.

Cwynar, L. C., 1990, A Late Quaternary Vegetation History for Lily Lake, Chilkat Peninsula, Southeast Alaska, *Canadian Journal of Botany* 68:1106–1112.

Davis, S. D. (ed.), 1989, *The Hidden Falls Site, Baranof Island, Alaska*, Alaska Anthropological Association Monograph Series V, Aurora.

Dixon, E. J., 1993, *Quest for the Origins of the First Americans*, University of New Mexico, Albuquerque.

Drover, C. E., Koerper, H. C., and Langenwalter, P. E., II, 1983, Early Holocene Human Adaptation on the Southern California Coast: A Summary Report of Investigations at the Irvine Site (CA-ORA-64), Newport Bay, Orange County, California. *Pacific Coast Archaeological Society Quarterly* 19:1–84.

Easton, N. A., 1992, Mal de Mer above Terra Incognita, or "What Ails the Coastal Migration Theory?" *Arctic Anthropology* 29(2):28–42.

Engstrom, D. R., Hansen, B. C. S., and Wright, H. E., 1990, A Possible Younger Dryas Record in Southeastern Alaska, *Science* 250:1383–1385.

Erlandson, J. M., 1988, *Of Millingstones and Molluscs: The Cultural Ecology of Early Holocene Hunter–Gatherers on the California Coast*, Unpublished Ph.D. dissertation, University of California, Santa Barbara.

Erlandson, J. M., 1989, Analysis of the Shellfish Assemblage, in: *The Hidden Falls Site, Baranof Island, Alaska* (S. D. Davis, ed.), Alaska Anthropological Association Monograph Series V, Aurora, pp. 131–158.

Erlandson, J. M., 1991a, Early Maritime Adaptations on the Northern Channel Islands, in: *Hunter–Gatherers of*

Early Holocene Coastal California (J. M. Erlandson and R. H. Colten, eds.), Perspectives in California Archaeology, Vol. 1, Institute of Archaeology, University of California, Los Angeles, pp. 101–111.

Erlandson, J. M., 1991b, Shellfish and Seeds as Optimal Resources: Early Holocene Subsistence on the Santa Barbara Coast, in: *Hunter–Gatherers of Early Holocene Coastal California* (J. M. Erlandson and R. H. Colten, eds.), Perspectives in California Archaeology, Vol. 1, Institute of Archaeology, University of California, Los Angeles, pp. 89–100.

Erlandson, J. M., 1993a, Evidence for a Terminal Pleistocene Human Occupation of Daisy Cave, San Miguel Island, California, *Current Research in the Pleistocene* 10:17–21.

Erlandson, J. M., 1993b, California's Coastal Prehistory: A Circum-Pacific Perspective, *Proceedings of the Society for California Archaeology* 6:23–36.

Erlandson, J. M., 1994, *Early Hunter–Gatherers of the California Coast*, Plenum, New York.

Erlandson, J., and Morris, D., 1992, CA-SRI-1: A "Pleistocene" Shell Midden on Santa Rosa Island, California, *Current Research in the Pleistocene* 9:7–10.

Erlandson, J. M., Cooley, T., and Carrico, R., 1987, A Fluted Projectile Point Fragment from the Southern California Coast: Chronology and Context at CA-SBA-1951, *Journal of California and Great Basin Anthropology* 9:120–128.

Erlandson, J. M., Moss, M. L., and Hughes, R. E., 1992, Archaeological Distribution and Trace Element Geochemistry of Volcanic Glass from Obsidian Cove, Suemez Island, Southeast Alaska, *Canadian Journal of Archaeology* 16:80–95.

Fairbanks, R. G., 1989, A 17,000 Year Glacio-Eustatic Sea Level Record: Influence of Glacial Melting Rates on the Younger Dryas Event and Deep-Ocean Circulation, *Nature* 342:637–642.

Fedje, D., 1993, *Sea-Levels and Prehistory in Gwaii Haanas*, Unpublished M.A. thesis, Department of Archaeology, University of Calgary.

Fedje, D. W., Mackie, A., McSporran, J. B., and Wilson, B., 1994, Early Period Archaeology in Gwaii Haanas: Results of the 1993 Field Programme, in: *Early Human Occupation in British Columbia* (R. L. Carlson and L. Dala Bona, eds.), University of British Columbia Press, Vancouver, pp. 133–150.

Fladmark, K., 1979, Routes: Alternate Migration Corridors for Early Man in North America, *American Antiquity* 44:55–69.

Fladmark, K., 1990, Possible Early Human Occupation of the Queen Charlotte Islands, British Columbia, *Canadian Journal of Archaeology* 14:183–197.

Gallegos, D., 1987, A Review and Synthesis of Environmental and Cultural Material for the Batiquitos Lagoon Region, in: *San Dieguito-La Jolla: Chronology and Controversy* (D. Gallegos, ed.), San Diego County Archaeological Society Research Papers Vol. 1, pp. 23–34.

Gallegos, D., and Carrico, R., 1984, *Windsong Shores Data Recovery Program for Site W-131, Carlsbad, California*, WESTEC Services, San Diego.

Glassow, M. A., 1991, Early Holocene Adaptations on Vandenberg Air Force Base, Santa Barbara County, in: *Hunter–Gatherers of Early Holocene Coastal California* (J. M. Erlandson and R. H. Colten, eds.), Perspectives in California Archaeology, Vol. 1, Institute of Archaeology, University of California, Los Angeles, pp. 113–124.

Glennan, W. S., 1971, Concave-Based Lanceolate Fluted Projectile Points from California, *The Masterkey* 45(1):27–32.

Greenspan, R. L., 1986, Aboriginal Exploitation of Vertebrate Fauna, in: *The Archaeology of the Tahkenitch Landing Site: Early Prehistoric Occupation on the Oregon Coast* (R. Minor and K. A. Toepel, eds.), Heritage Research Associates Report, Vol. 46, Eugene, pp. 57–72.

Greenwood, R. S., 1972, *9000 Years of Prehistory at Diablo Canyon*, San Luis Obispo County Archaeological Society Occasional Papers 7.

Gustafson, C. E., and Manis, C., 1984, *The Manis Mastodon Site: An Adventure in Prehistory*, Manis Enterprises, Sequim, Washington.

Haggarty, J. C., Wooley, C. B., Erlandson, J. M., and Crowell, A., 1991, *The 1990 Exxon Cultural Resource Program: Site Protection and Maritime Cultural Ecology in Prince William Sound and the Gulf of Alaska*, Exxon Shipping Company and Exxon Company, U.S.A. Anchorage.

Harrington, M. R., 1948, An Ancient Site at Borax Lake, California, *Southwest Museum Papers* 16:1–126.

Heaton, T. H., and Grady, F., 1993, Fossil Grizzly Bears (*Ursos arctos*) from Prince of Wales Island, Alaska, Offer New Insights into Animal Dispersal, Interspecific Competition, and Age of Deglaciation, *Current Research in the Pleistocene* 10:98–100.

Hebda, R. J., 1992, Fraser-age Environments of Vancouver Island and Adjacent Mainland British Columbia (Abstract), in: *Quaternary Research Center Spring Conference on Chronology and Palaeoenvironments of the*

Western and Southern Margins of the Cordillerian Ice Sheet during the Last Glaciation, University of Washington Press, Seattle.

Hebda, R. J., and Frederick, S. G., 1992, History of Marine Resources of the Northeast Pacific Since the Last Glaciation, *Transactions of the Royal Society of Canada*, Sixth Series 1:319–342.

Hebda, R. J., and Mathewes, R. W., 1984, Holocene History of Cedar and Native Indian Cultures of the North American Pacific Coast, *Science* 225(4663):711–713.

Hemphill, C., 1990, *Test Excavations at the Winchuck Site (35CU176), 1989*, Report prepared for the Chetco Ranger District, Siskyou National Forest, Roseburg, Oregon.

Heusser, L. E., 1978, Pollen in Santa Barbara Basin, California: A 12,000 Year Record, *Geological Society of America Bulletin* 89:673–678.

Hildebrandt, W. R., 1983, *Archaeological Research at the Southern Santa Clara Valley Project*, Manuscript on file, Daniel, Mann, Johnson, and Mendenhall, Caltrans District 4 Information Office, San Francisco.

Hobler, P., 1978, The Relationship of Archaeological Sites to Sea Levels on Moresby Island, Queen Charlotte Islands, *Canadian Journal of Archaeology* 2:1–14.

Johnson, D. L., 1983, The California Continental Borderland: Landbridges, Watergaps, and Biotic Dispersals, in: *Quaternary Coastlines and Marine Archaeology* (P. M. Masters and N. C. Flemming, eds.), Academic Press, New York, pp. 482–527.

Jones, T., 1991, Marine Resource Value and the Priority of Coastal Settlement: A California Perspective, *American Antiquity* 56:419–443.

Jordan, R. H., 1992, A Maritime Paleoarctic Assemblage from Crag Point, Kodiak Island, Alaska, *Anthropological Papers of the University of Alaska* 24(1–2):127–140.

Kennedy, G. E., 1983, An Unusual Burial Practice at an Early California Indian site, *Journal of New World Archaeology* 5(3):4–6.

Klein, D., 1965, Post-glacial Distribution Patterns of Mammals in the Southern Coastal Regions of Alaska, *Arctic* 18(1):7–20.

Koerper, H. C., 1981, *Prehistoric Subsistence and Settlement in the Newport Bay Area and Environs, Orange County, California*, Unpublished Ph.D. dissertation, University of California, Riverside, University Microfilms International, Ann Arbor.

Laughlin, W. S., and Aigner, J. S., 1966, Preliminary Analysis of the Anangula Unifacial Core and Blade Industry, *Arctic Anthropology* 3(2):41–56.

Lightfoot, K., 1993, Long-Term Developments in Complex Hunter-Gatherer Societies: Recent Perspectives from the Pacific Coast of North America, *Journal of Archaeological Research* 1(3):167–201.

Linick, T. W., 1977, La Jolla Natural Radiocarbon Measurements VII, *Radiocarbon* 19:19–48.

Luternauer, J. L., Clague, J. J., Conway, K. W., Barie, J. V., Blaise, B., and Mathewes, R. W., 1989, Late Pleistocene Terrestrial Deposits on the Continental Shelf of Western Canada: Evidence for Rapid Sea-Level Change at the End of the Last Glaciation, *Geology* 17:357–360.

Lyman, R. L., 1991, *Prehistory of the Oregon Coast*, Academic Press, New York.

Mann, D. H., 1986, Wisconsin and Holocene Glaciation of Southeast Alaska, in: *Glaciation in Alaska* (T. D. Hamilton, K. M. Reed, and R. M. Thorson, eds.), Alaska Geological Society, Anchorage, pp. 237–265.

Mann, D. H., and Hamilton, T. D., 1993, *Late Pleistocene and Holocene Paleoenvironments of the North Pacific Coast*, Paper presented at the United States–Japanese International Seminar on the Origins, Development, and Spread of Prehistoric North Pacific–Bering Sea Maritime Cultures, Honolulu.

Mason, R., Brechbiel, B., Peterson, M., Singer, C. A., Langenwalter, P. E., Gibson, R. O., Morgan, T., and Hurd, G. S., 1991, *Newport Coast Archaeological Project: Results of Data Recovery at the Wishbone Hill Sites, CA-ORA-339, CA-ORA-340, CA-ORA-928, CA-ORA-929*, The Keith Companies, Costa Mesa.

Mason, R. D., Peterson, M. L., Brechbiel, B. A., Singer, C. A., Bonner, W. H., Gibson, R. O., and Morgan, T., 1992, *Newport Coast Archaeological Project: Results of Data Recovery from Sites Impacted by Construction of Pacific Coast Highway (Inland Side), CA-ORA-246 and CA-ORA-1208*, The Keith Companies, Costa Mesa.

Matson, R. G., 1976, *The Glenrose Cannery Site*, National Museum of Man, Mercury Series, Archaeological Survey of Canada, No. 52, Ottawa.

Matson, R. G., and Coupland, G., 1995, *The Prehistory of the Northwest Coast*, Academic Press, San Diego.

McDowell, P. F., and Minor, R., 1986, Stratigraphy and Dating, in: *The Archaeology of the Tahkenitch Landing Site: Early Prehistoric Occupation on the Oregon Coast* (R. Minor and K. A. Toepel, eds.), Heritage Research Associates Report, Vol. 46, Eugene, pp. 29–42.

Mehringer, P. H., and Foit, F., 1990, Volcanic Ash Dating of the Clovis Cache at East Wenatchee, Washington, *National Geographic Research* 6(4):495–503.

Meighan, C. W., 1989, *Early Shellmound Dwellers of the Pacific Coast of North America*, Paper presented at the Circum-Pacific Prehistory Conference, Seattle.

Meighan, C. W., and Haynes, C. V., 1970, The Borax Lake Site Revisited, *Science* 167(3922):1213–1221.

Meltzer, D. J., and Dunnell, R. C., 1987, Fluted Points from the Pacific Northwest, *Lithic Studies* 4:64–67.

Minor, R., 1989, *Southern Northwest Coast Prehistory: The Lower Columbia Valley and Oregon Coast*, Paper presented at the Circum-Pacific Prehistory Conference, Seattle.

Minor, R., and Toepel, K. A. (eds.), 1986, *The Archaeology of the Tahkenitch Landing Site: Early Prehistoric Occupation on the Oregon Coast*, Heritage Research Associates Report 46, Eugene.

Mobley, C. M., 1988, Holocene Sea Levels in Southeast Alaska: Preliminary Results, *Arctic* 41(4):261–266.

Moratto, M. J., 1984, *California Archaeology*, Academic Press, New York.

Moriarty, J. R., III, 1967, Transitional Pre-Desert Phase in San Diego County, California, *Science* 155:553–556.

Morris, D. P., and Erlandson, J. M., 1993, A 9500 Year-Old Human Burial from CA-SRI-116, Santa Rosa Island, *Journal of California and Great Basin Anthropology* 15:129–134.

Moss, M. L., 1989, Analysis of the Vertebrate Assemblage, in: *The Hidden Falls Site, Baranof Island, Alaska* (S. D. Davis, ed.), Alaska Anthropological Association Monograph Series V, Aurora, pp. 93–115.

Moss, M. L., 1994, Northern Northwest Coast Regional Overview, in: *The Origins, Development, and Spread of Prehistoric North Pacific–Bering Sea Maritime Cultures* (A. McCartney and W. Workman, eds.), Manuscript submitted for publication.

Moss, M. L., and Erlandson, J. M., 1994, *An Evaluation Survey, and Dating Program for Archaeological Sites on State Lands of the Southern Oregon Coast*, Department of Anthropology, University of Oregon, Eugene.

Moss, M. L., and Erlandson, J. M., 1995, Reflections on North American Pacific Coast Prehistory, *Journal of World Prehistory* 9:1–45.

Norwood, R., 1980, *The Cultural Resources of Fairbanks Ranch, Rancho Sante Fe, California*, Regional Environmental Consultants, San Diego.

Norwood, R., and Walker, C., 1980, *The Cultural Resources of San Dieguito Estates*, Regional Environmental Consultants, San Diego.

Okada, H., Okada, A., Kotani, Y., Yajima, K., Olson, W. M., Nishimoto, T., and Okino, S., 1989, *Heceta Island, Southeastern Alaska: Anthropological Survey in 1987*, Department of Behavioral Science, Hokkaido University, Sapporo, Japan.

Okada, H., Okada, A., Yajima, K., Olson, W. M., Sugita, M., Shionosaki, N., Okino, S., Yoshida, K., and Kaneko, H., 1992, *Heceta Island, Southeastern Alaska: Anthropological Survey in 1989 & 1990*, Department of Behavioral Science, Hokkaido University, Sapporo, Japan.

Orr, P. C., 1962, The Arlington Springs Site, Santa Rosa Island, California, *American Antiquity* 27:417–419.

Orr, P. C., 1968, *Prehistory of Santa Rosa Island*, Santa Barbara Museum of Natural History.

Osborne, D., 1956, Evidence of Early Lithic in the Pacific Northwest, *Washington State College Research Studies* 24(1):38–44.

Peteet, D. M., 1991, Postglacial Migration History of Lodgepole Pine near Yakutat, Alaska, *Canadian Journal of Botany* 69:786–796.

Pierce, A. M., 1979, *Archaeological Investigations at SLO-177 and Vicinity, Cambria, California*, Unpublished M.A. thesis, Stanford University.

Powers, W. R., and Hoffecker, J., 1989, Late Pleistocene Settlement in the Nenana Valley, Central Alaska, *American Antiquity* 54:263–287.

Raab, L. M., and Yatsko, A., 1992, Ancient Maritime Adaptations of the California Bight: A Perspective from San Clemente Island, in: *Essays on the Prehistory of Maritime California* (T. L. Jones, ed.), Center for Archaeological Research at Davis Publication, Vol. 10, University of California, Davis, pp. 173–193.

Raab, L. M., Bradford, K., and Yatsko, A., 1994, Advances in Southern Channel Islands Archaeology: 1983 to 1993, *Journal of California and Great Basin Anthropology* 16:243–270.

Raab, L. M., Bradford, K., Porcasi, J. P., and Howard, W. C., 1995, Return to Little Harbor, Santa Catalina Island, California: A Critique of the Marine Paleotemperature Model, *American Antiquity* 60:287–308.

Rosen, M. D., 1978, Archaeological Investigations at CA-VEN-294, in: *Archaeology of Oak Park, Ventura County, California, Volume II*, Institute of Archaeology Monograph V:7–113, University of California, Los Angeles.

Rudolph, T., 1983, *Archaeological Testing at SLO-177, Cambria, California*, Office of Public Archaeology, Social Process Research Institute, University of California, Santa Barbara.

Salls, R. A., 1988, Prehistoric Fisheries of the California Bight, Unpublished Ph.D. dissertation, University of California, Los Angeles.

Salls, R. A., 1990, The Ancient Mariners: Ten Thousand Years of Marine Exploitations at Eel Point, San Clemente Island, California, *Pacific Coast Archaeological Society Quarterly* 26:61–92.

Sancetta, C., Lyle, M., Heusser, L., Zahn, R., and Bradbury, J. P., 1992, Late-Glacial to Holocene Changes in Winds, Upwelling, and Seasonal Production of the Northern California Current System, *Quaternary Research* 38: 359–370.

Schwaderer, R., 1992, Archaeological Test Excavation at the Duncans Point Cave, CA-SON-348/H, in: *Essays on the Prehistory of Maritime California* (T. L. Jones, ed.), Center for Archaeological Research at Davis Publication, Vol. 10, Department of Anthropology, University of California, pp. 55–71.

Simons, D. D., Layton, T. N., and Knudson, R., 1985, A Fluted Point from the Mendocino County Coast, California, *Journal of California and Great Basin Anthropology* 7:260–269.

Stafford, T. W., Jr., Jull, A. J. T., Brendel, K., Duhamel, R. C., and Donahue, D., 1987, Study of Bone Radiocarbon Dating Accuracy at the University of Arizona Accelerator Facility for Radioisotope Analysis, *Radiocarbon* 29: 24–44.

Taylor, R. E., Payen, L. A., Prior, C. A., Slota, P. J., Jr., Gillespie, R., Gowlett, J. A. J., Hedges, R. E. M., Jull, A. J. T., Zabel, T. H., Donahue, D. J., and Berger, R., 1985, Major Revisions in the Pleistocene Age Assignments for North American Human Skeletons by C-14 Accelerator Mass Spectrometry: None Older than 11,000 C-14 Years BP, *American Antiquity* 50:136–140.

Wallace, W. J., 1995, A Suggested Chronology for Southern California Coastal Archaeology, *Southwest Journal of Anthropology* 11:214–230.

Wallmann, S., 1994, Camas Valley Clovis Projectile Fragment, *Screenings* 43(4):2.

Warner, B. G., Mathewes, R. W., and Carlson, J. J., 1990, Ice-Free Conditions on the Queen Charlotte Islands, British Columbia, at the Height of the Late Wisconsin Glaciation, *Science* 218:675–677.

Warren, C. N. (ed.), 1966, The San Dieguito Type Site: M. J. Rogers' 1938 Excavation on the San Dieguito River, *San Diego Museum Papers* 5:1–39.

Warren, C. N., 1967, The San Dieguito Complex: A Review and Hypothesis, *American Antiquity* 32:233–236.

Warren, C. N., 1968, Cultural Tradition and Ecological Adaptation on the Southern California Coast, *Eastern New Mexico University Contributions to Anthropology* 1(3):1–14.

Weisbord, J., 1985, *Quail Hill: Archaeological Excavation at CA-ORA-386*, Unpublished M.A. thesis, California State University, Dominguez Hills.

West, G. J., and Erlandson, J. M., 1994, A Late Pleistocene and Holocene Pollen Record from San Miguel Island, California: Preliminary Results, *American Quaternary Association Abstracts*.

Chapter 15

The Pleistocene–Holocene Transition on the Plains and Rocky Mountains of North America

GEORGE C. FRISON AND ROBSON BONNICHSEN

PROBLEM STATEMENT

Throughout the last decade, a main focus of Pleistocene–Holocene New World archaeology has been the peopling of the New World. Much controversy has centered around the problem of pre-Clovis or ancestral Clovis or both (e.g., see Adovasio 1993; Marshall 1990; Morlan 1988). Two contrasting models have been developed to explain the initial peopling of the Americas. They can loosely be called the "Clovis-first" and the "Early-entry" models. Many specialists use the term "pre-Clovis" to refer to pre-12,000-year-old populations in the Americas. We prefer not to use the term "pre-Clovis," as it implies that there are only two stages of cultural development in the Americas: Clovis and Pre-Clovis. Clovis does not occur in every region of the New World, however, and clearly is not appropriate as a descriptive term for all of North America and South America. Accordingly, we prefer to use the term "pre-12,000" as a descriptive chronological term that has neither technological nor cultural implications (Bonnichsen and Schneider no date).

Our goal in this chapter is to review some of the most significant data that bracket the late Pleistocene–Holocene transition period in the Northwestern Plains and Rocky Mountains. Knowledge of the cultural sequence found in these two areas has gradually accumulated since the 1926 discovery of the now-famous Folsom site near Folsom, New Mexico. Investigations of deeply stratified Paleoindian sites in our study region by multidisciplinary teams have played a pivotal role in developing a stratigraphic and chronological framework for the placement of late Glacial and early Holocene cultural complexes.

GEORGE C. FRISON • Department of Anthropology, University of Wyoming, Laramie, Wyoming 82071. ROBSON BONNICHSEN • Department of Anthropology, Oregon State University, Corvallis, Oregon 97331.

Humans at the End of the Ice Age: The Archaeology of the Pleistocene–Holocene Transition, edited by Lawrence Guy Straus, Berit Valentin Eriksen, Jon M. Erlandson, and David R. Yesner. Plenum Press, New York, 1996.

We are now at an interesting juncture in the development of our understanding of this region. We propose that at least two alternative models can be used to interpret existing sequences of cultural complexes from the Northwestern Plains. The models are known as the *in situ* model and the *"environmental-response"* model. Each has different predictive implications in respect to how we interpret the past. The in situ developmental model, which has traditionally been adopted in this region, proposes that if evidence of pre-12,000-year-old populations is present, it should be found in stratigraphic contexts that occur below Clovis levels, and preferably will be separated from Clovis by sterile stratigraphic levels. The second proposition of this model is that each succeeding cultural sequence found in stratigraphic context evolved from the preceding cultural complex. This focus has led investigators to characterize the normative behavior patterns that can be inferred from existing cultural and environmental data. Consequently, the dynamics of how these transitions occur from one complex to the next are almost never stated in the literature. This model does not focus scientific attention on understanding how environmental change may have triggered significant shifts in human adaptation that can be studied through the investigation of surviving environmental and archaeological remains.

The environmental-response model is based on several related premises. Basic propositions of this model include: (1) culture and environment are linked; (2) environmental changes can force changes in human adaptive strategies; and (3) cultural complexes found in stratified archaeological sites need not be related to one another (Bonnichsen 1991; Bonnichsen et al. 1987). The environmental-response model envisions that the earth's atmospheric, oceanographic, climatological, geological, biological, and cultural systems represent a series of linked subsystems. The operation of these subsystems can be studied at the local, regional, and global scales. Practically speaking, this model posits that archaeological remains are deposited as part of a complex multidimensional record. Precisely how an individual site record will be decoded and related to its formation processes is in part dependent on what survives the coercive forces of time. A full interpretation of a single site may draw on expertise in the disciplines of paleoclimatology, geology, soil science, paleoecology, and archaeology. A thorough and careful analysis of an individual site can provide important information that will provide insights as to its relationships to local-, regional-, and global-scale cultural and environmental events.

As deglaciation occurred at the end of the last Ice Age and the Laurentide and Cordilleran Ice Sheets receded (Hughes 1987), significant changes occurred in paleoclimatic patterns throughout North America (COHMAP) (Kutzbach et al. 1993). As ice recession progressed, the position of the jet stream moved north; this move in turn influenced temperature, precipitation, and wind patterns, which affected vegetation communities (Whitlock 1993) and animal populations. These changes brought about significant changes in the natural environment. As the snow line, mountain glaciers, and continental glaciers receded, an enormous landmass (the Rocky Mountains and Canada) previously covered by snow and ice became available for colonization by plants, animals, and humans. As these new environments emerged, resident human populations were presented with choices and new opportunities for adapting to new environmental conditions. They could either (1) follow time-transgressive environments altitudinally or latitudinally, (2) modify their adaptive strategies, (3) follow new but structurally altered natural environments altitudinally or longitudinally, or (4) do nothing and become extinct. One of the implications of the environmental-response model is that since stratified sites are stationary, human populations who chose to follow a traditional adaptive system may have followed time-transgressive environments. In this case, there need not be any necessary relationships between cultural complexes found one above the other in a stratified context.

METHODOLOGICAL APPROACHES

The methodological approach for investigating cultural environmental relationships in the Plains–Rocky Mountain region has necessarily been multidisciplinary. We are well aware that if geologic deposits exist that contain pre-12,000-year-old archaeological evidence amenable to acceptable study, they would have to be stratigraphically below and separated by sterile levels from deposits that contain evidence of the known and recognized Paleoindian cultural complexes. We are now well aware also that all sediments of this nature must have their integrity and formation processes well documented and confirmed, and doing so requires expertise from a number of disciplines.

Several symposia, both national and international, have been organized to bring together workers whose research centers around the peopling of the Americas to share and discuss their data. We are well aware that these efforts have not resolved the question of when the initial peopling of the Americas occurred. On the other hand, they have resulted in a number of edited publications that have served to disseminate a wealth of both old and new data. A sampling but not an exhaustive list of these publications would include Agenbroad et al. (1990), Bonnichsen and Sorg (1989), Bonnichsen and Turnmire (1991), Carlisle (1988), Davis and Reeves (1990), Hofman and Enloe (1992), Montet-White and Holen (1991), Nitecki and Nitecki (1987), Soffer and Praslov (1993), and Stanford and Day (1992).

At the same time, there has been a continual accumulation of information from the reanalysis of the old Paleoindian site data and limited excavations in old Paleoindian sites such as Agate Basin (Frison and Stanford 1982), Horner (Frison and Todd 1987), Hanson (Ingbar 1992), and Hell Gap (Sellet and Frison 1994) in Wyoming, and Lindenmeier (Wilmsen and Roberts 1978) in Colorado. New sites with significant data also continue to appear, including Stewart's Cattle Guard (Jodry and Stanford 1992) in Colorado; Indian Creek (Davis and Greiser 1992), Mill Iron (Frison 1991a), and Mammoth Meadow (Bonnichsen et al. 1992a) in Montana; Carter/Kerr-McGee (Frison 1984), Horner (Frison and Todd 1987), and Sunrise Mine (M. Stafford 1990) in Wyoming; and Lange Ferguson (Hannus 1990) in South Dakota. Again, this is not intended to be an exhaustive review of the pertinent literature, since it deals almost exclusively with the northern Plains and central Rocky Mountain region.

This volume is intended to bring together information from a world perspective. From our own perspective, we argue that past climates affected the many and rapidly changing landforms and environments on the plains and in the mountains, creating new opportunities for adaptive strategies. Human groups responded to these changing environments by creating mutually exclusive subsistence strategies to best exploit the different economic possibilities. The resulting human adaptive patterns are reflected in the archaeological record as a series of discrete co-traditions. If the co-traditions concept is further supported, future study will necessarily center around developing an understanding of the causal factors responsible for these regional variants and on the interactions between co-traditions.

In the following discussion, we present an outline of some of the most important adaptive responses to late Glacial and early Holocene environments in the Northwestern Plains and Rocky Mountain region. Archaeological site locations mentioned are shown in Figure 1 and a tentative chronological chart of Paleoindian cultural complexes is presented in Figure 2.

PALEOCLIMATES, ENVIRONMENTS, AND HUMAN RESPONSES

Climate was a strong determining factor in the progress and development of prehistoric High Plains–Rocky Mountain human subsistence strategies. As archaeologists, we have often been more concerned with the results of past climatic episodes than with the actual process. However, understanding the process (e.g., see Kutzbach et al. 1993) of how paleoclimate related to changes in human adaptive systems will be beneficial to any final interpretation of past human adaptations. We know, for example, that environmental conditions on the Northern Plains and Rocky Mountains south of the ice sheets at the Last Glacial Maximum (see Porter 1988) and until the final late Pleistocene extinctions supported a large megafauna. However, the full extent of human exploitation of this megafauna and the combined effects of human and climatic factors on its extinction are far from being resolved.

The ice-free corridor between the Cordilleran and Laurentide Ice Sheets has claimed the attention of archaeologists concerned with the peopling of the New World. Climatic conditions gradually warmed so that by 13,000 years ago, there was a narrow corridor between the Cordilleran and Laurentide Ice Sheets. By 12,000 years ago, the corridor had expanded (see Figure 1), but contained large meltwater lakes (see Dyke and Prest 1987). The millennium from 11,000 to 10,000 years ago witnessed significant and dramatic climatic changes. Rapid ablation of the continental ice sheets, movement of the jet stream, changes in temperature and precipitation, and shifts in vegetation communities forced human populations to continually readapt to changing conditions (e.g., see Bonnichsen et al. 1987; Bryson 1974).

On the High Plains of North America, however, there apparently had been no extinctions of floral species since before Clovis times, but there were shifts in vegetation zones and ratios of plant species within the zones, as documented by pollen and phytolith studies (e.g., see Cummings 1996; Markgraf and Lennon 1986). Further support for these kinds of vegetation shifts can be found in studies of shifts in small-mammal populations (e.g., see Graham et al. 1987; Walker 1982, 1987).

A growing body of evidence indicates that at least by 10,000 years ago, and possibly earlier, there was a definite dichotomy between human subsistence strategies in the foothill–mountain areas and those on the open plains. This dichotomy is proposed to have been the result of differences in resources and consequent development of mutually exclusive procurement strategies (e.g., see Frison 1988, 1992). While bison and pronghorn were the major food animals on the Plains, the mountain sheep and deer were the major food animals in the foothills and mountains. Different vegetable food resources were also found in each area, and all these resources needed constant monitoring in order to effectively schedule procurement activities. The economic infeasibility of one group's monitoring and exploiting the resources of both areas gave rise to the separation between plains and foothill–mountain subsistence strategies. This separation is well documented by different diagnostic tools and weaponry assemblages from sites in each ecological area.

Along with long-term climatic changes that affected human adaptive strategies, there

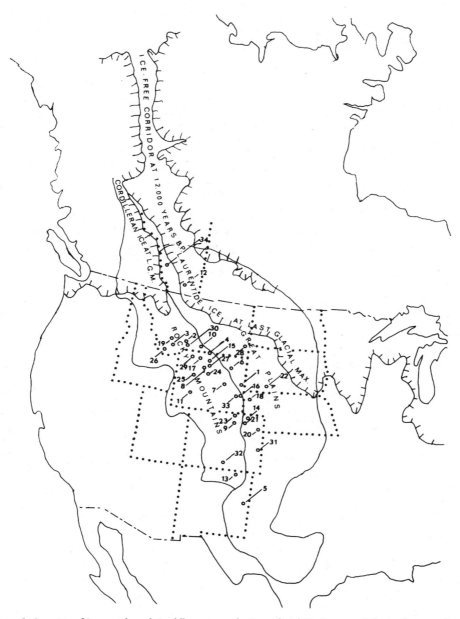

Figure 1. Location of Laurentide and Cordilleran ice at the Last Glacial Maximum and the ice-free corridor at 12,000 years B.P. Archaeological site locations: (1) Agate Basin; (2) Anzick; (3) Barton Gulch; (4) Bighorn Canyon caves; (5) Blackwater Draw; (6) Carter/Kerr-McGee; (7) Casper; (8) Colby; (9) Dent; (10) False Cougar Cave; (11) Finley; (12) Fletcher; (13) Folsom; (14) Frasca; (15) Hanson; (16) Hell Gap; (17) Horner; (18) Hudson-Meng; (19) Indian Creek; (20) Jones-Miller; (21) Jurgens; (22) Lange-Ferguson; (23) Lindenmeier; (24) Little Canyon Creek Cave; (25) Lookingbill; (26) Mammoth Meadow; (27) Medicine Lodge Creek; (28) Mill Iron; (29) Mummy Cave; (30) Myers-Hindman; (31) Olsen-Chubbuck; (32) Stewart's Cattleguard; (33) Sunrise Mine; (34) Varsity and Silver Spring.

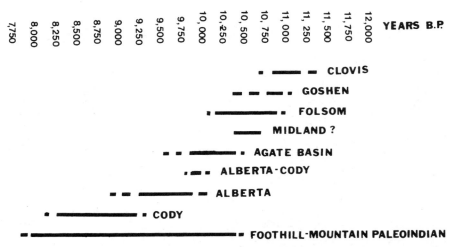

Figure 2. Tentative cultural chronology of Paleoindian cultural complexes in the Plains–Rocky Mountain region.

occurred year-to-year changes that were not predictable and enforced subsistence strategies on hunters–gatherers, who had a very limited cultural buffer between them and the environment. Some kind of short-term storage was necessary to tide the human groups over periods, especially during the cold months, when food procurement involving both faunal and floral resources was not possible. Several site features can be used to argue for this kind of temporary food storage to ensure winter survival (e.g., see Frison 1982).

As brought to our attention in Soffer and Praslov (1993:197), the North American record of human occupation of the late Pleistocene is neither as long nor as rich as it is in Eurasia, but the human inhabitants of both areas were hunters–gatherers living in open environments. Climate played an all-important role in the adaptations of the early New World migrants. The role of humans, if any, in the final extinctions of the late Pleistocene–Holocene megafauna is still hotly debated. Geologic evidence has been presented to indicate that Clovis groups arrived on the scene during a severe drought about 11,000 years ago. The combination of drought and predation by Clovis hunters may have figured prominently in the extinction of several large mammals, at least in the North American Southwest (see Haynes 1993).

These drought conditions were alleviated by an increase in yearly precipitation very soon afterward. Goshen-Plainview (Frison 1996) and Folsom groups appeared on the scene shortly after 11,000 BP (see Haynes 1993). They were unable to exploit the mammoth and other now-extinct large fauna. However, accumulating evidence strongly suggests that *Camelops* may have survived for another millennium on the northern High Plains. Relationships of Goshen-Plainview to both Clovis and Folsom, if any, are open to question, but the former may have appeared just before and, technologically, may also have been a direct precursor of Folsom at least in terms of projectile point manufacture. However, site data concerning Goshen-Plainview and Clovis lithic technology are as yet insufficient to allow adequate conclusions.

Extinct subspecies of bison (*Bison antiquus* or *Bison occidentalis* or both) survived until at least 6,000 years ago on the Northwestern Plains (Frison et al. 1976). They underwent a gradual decrease in size (see Wilson 1978) and were the main target of the post-Clovis Paleoindian hunters. That they were is indicated by evidence from a number of archaeological sites, including, to name a few, Agate Basin (Frison and Stanford 1982), Casper (Frison 1974), and Horner (Frison and Todd 1987) in Wyoming; Hudson-Meng (Agenbroad 1978) in Nebraska; Olsen-Chubbuck (Wheat 1972) and Jones-Miller (Stanford 1978) in Colorado; and Mill Iron (Frison 1996) in Montana. The bison species most intensely predated by humans (*B. antiquus* and *B. occidentalis*) and, to a much lesser extent, pronghorn (*Antilocapra americana*) managed to survive the late Pleistocene extinctions. On the other hand, the less heavily predated ones, such as the horse (*Equus* sp.) and camel (*Camelops* sp.), did not manage to survive. This failure is one of the more puzzling questions pertaining to this time period, especially so since the onset of arid conditions should have favored the latter two. Obviously, the last word on Pleistocene extinctions remains to be spoken by future researchers.

It appears that continually increasing aridity affected the High Plains and the mountains from about 10,000 years ago, and possibly several hundred years earlier, so that by about 8,000 years ago, bison populations were forced either to move or to endure population decline, or both, to such an extent that they were no longer a stable and dependable source of human food. At this time, which is generally regarded as the beginning of the Altithermal climatic episode (Antevs 1948, 1955), human populations in both the High Plains and the mountains had shifted toward a greater dependence on plant foods and had adopted or developed tool assemblages that verify these different subsistence strategies. There is also some evidence to indicate that there were oasis-like areas such as the Black Hills of South Dakota and Wyoming, where the Paleoindian pattern of bison procurement may have continued until at least 6,000 years ago, with bison intermediate in size between Paleoindian-age animals and the modern form present by about 5,000 years ago (see Frison et al. 1976).

THE ARCHAEOLOGICAL RECORD

The search for evidence of pre-12,000-year-old human occupations in the New World has been the theme that captured the most attention both from professionals and from the public. This attraction is understandable, since the evidence has been controversial and not straightforward enough to have been universally accepted. The result has been wrangling, among professionals, providing grist for the media (e.g., see Lynch 1990). Another aspect that has nurtured this continual argument is the claims for sites with pre-12,000-year-old ages that at first appear promising, but fail to withstand the test of careful scientific scrutiny. Nonetheless, some sites have managed to lay stronger claims to authenticity (e.g., see Adovasio 1993; Marshall 1990; Morlan 1988).

Paleoindian studies are increasingly drawing on the full range of Quaternary sciences to interpret late Ice Age and early Holocene sites. Paleoindian archaeologists are beginning to use may independent lines of evidence in their studies of early New World sites. The use of the multidisciplinary approach, coupled with an ever-increasing array of new analytical techniques, has the potential to lead to more accurate and sophisticated models of past human adaptive strategies. The development of new analytical techniques, especially accelerator mass spectrometry (AMS) radiocarbon dating, faunal analysis and taphonomy, and lithic analysis, are certainly among the most significant advances that promise to offer better means of interpreting both old and new data bases.

In addition to these techniques, there is a need to critically assess the model-building procedures that we use to interpret the stratigraphic record from archaeological sites. A case in point is the implicit use of the in situ development model that was prominent in the Northwestern Plains during the 1970s and early 1980s. For example, the goal of the Hell Gap site investigations (Irwin-Williams et al. 1973) was to provide a badly needed Paleoindian chronology supported by radiocarbon dates and geochronology. The interpretation of archaeological sequence information at that time managed to imprint on archaeologists the idea that the genesis of each Paleoindian cultural complex was out of the stratigraphically underlying culture. Such thinking was further advanced by the stratigraphy of the Carter/Kerr-McGee site (Frison 1984) and, to a lesser extent, by the Agate Basin site investigations (Frison and Stanford 1982). However, with a careful evaluation of radiocarbon dates (Haynes 1992, 1993), reanalysis of the Hell Gap site stratigraphy (Sellet and Frison 1994), and the results of the Horner site (Frison and Todd 1987) and Mill Iron site investigations (Frison 1996), some of this chronological picture of Northwestern Plains Paleoindian occupations is now open to question. Added to this evidence is the recognition of a number of foothill–mountain Paleoindian occupations that are contemporaneous with many of the so-called High Plains Paleoindian groups, but not found on the plains and thus believed to be the result of mutually exclusive human subsistence strategies between the two ecological areas (see Frison 1988, 1992; Husted 1969).

In summary, with shifting climatic conditions (temperature, precipitation, wind velocities), changing paleoecological conditions, and human responses to these changes in the Northwestern Plains and Rocky Mountains, it is clear that we can no longer accept the in situ development model at face value. It is imperative that we leave open the possibility that any stratified sequence of archaeological remains could have been deposited by unrelated cultural groups that had overlapping diachronic geographical ranges. Given these considerations, we will briefly review some of the major archaeological complexes and their temporal, geographic, and adaptive patterns.

Evidence of Pre-12,000-Year-Old Occupations: Pre-Clovis or Ancestral Clovis or Both

Cultural groups that managed to reach the New World included both ones that were not the genetic forebears of Clovis and other groups that were "ancestral Clovis." There are numerous possibilities to explore: More than one cultural group may have migrated to North America prior to Clovis, and there may have been more than one access route. Some may have returned; some may have stayed and not survived; others may have coalesced and formed the ancestors of Clovis. Clovis may also have been the results of a discrete New World migration. The archaeological record has as yet yielded little by way of answers to these questions.

The question of "ancestral Clovis" cannot be ignored or brushed aside. There is evidence claimed for human occupation older than Clovis that is not acceptable to all Paleoindian archaeologists, but it has not yet been examined closely enough to be disproved. In both North and South America, there are a few sites that have been carefully investigated (see Marshall 1990) and critically examined, but still can be neither accepted nor disregarded by all (see also Meltzer et al. 1994). In the area described in this chapter, human hair from False Cougar Cave in the Prior Mountains of south-central Montana was found in a level below a radiocarbon date of 10,500 BP and is believed to actually be from a level dated at 14,500 BP (Bonnichsen et al. 1986).

Another situation not yet satisfactorily explained is the occurrence of unquestionable human artifacts and extinct fauna (*Symbos* and *Ovis*) below an unconformity in Little Canyon Creek Cave in the Southern Big Horn Mountains (Frison 1991b:27). A fire hearth above the unconformity is dated at about 10,200 BP. Stone tools and a bone awl, but no chronological diagnostics, were found in association. Higher in the stratigraphic column was a radiocarbon date of about 8,800 years BP with late Paleoindian diagnostics (projectile points) of the type expected for that time period.

Ongoing research at the Mammoth Meadow site, which lies in southwestern Montana at the base of the Beaverhead Mountains, has revealed yet another early complex (Bonnichsen et al. 1992a). The occurrence of high-quality chert used in the manufacture of flaked stone tools apparently attracted people to this locality beginning in late Ice Age times. Systematic excavations of the Mammoth Meadow fan–terrace complex have exposed a long sequence of workshop–habitation occupations. On the surface of a deeply buried terrace at the Mammoth Meadow II excavation, archaeological remains occur in what is known as stratigraphic unit 9C (Beatty et al. in press). This level occurs stratigraphically below Glacier Peak volcanic ash. Glacier Peak, which is located in northwestern Washington, had multiple eruptions that date between 11,200 and 11,800 years ago. Although only small samples of units 9C and 10C have been excavated, it is evident that a biface and blade industry is present. Broken bifaces, flake tools, macroflake-blade cores, true blades, and tools made on blades have been recovered. Additionally, small-scale biological remains have been retrieved, including naturally shed human and animal hair (Bonnichsen et al. 1992b, in press). Ongoing research by Walter Ream and Katharine Field at Oregon State University suggests that it will be possible to extract from the naturally shed human hair ancient DNA that will allow us to characterize the biological populations who resided at Mammoth Meadow.

Claims of percussion-flaked human artifacts with a suggested age of more than 21,000 years BP, based on stratigraphic evidence, are made for two sites, Varsity Estates and Silver Springs, located in the western part of the city of Alberta, Canada. If the stratigraphy of these sites passes the test of close scrutiny and the date proves valid, it would confirm pre-12,000-year-old human occupations in North America (Clachula 1994).

Until these and all other possible but questionable pre-12,000-year-old occurrences are resolved, these kinds of human occupations of the Plains and Rocky Mountain area will continue to remain open questions.

Clovis, Goshen, Folsom

The Anzick Clovis burial site, which occurs beneath a small rock shelter in an intermontane basin between the Crazy and Belt Mountains along a tributary of the Shields River, was accidentally discovered in 1968 by two construction workers. Primarily through a sustained effort by Dr. Larry Lahren over many years, this important and unique collection of red ocher–covered fluted points, bifaces, flake tools, and bone foreshafts is now on exhibit at the Montana Historical Society (Jones and Bonnichsen 1994). T. Stafford (1994:52), by use of ^{14}C dating, has dated human bone from two subadults found associated with the disturbed burial. A red-ocher– stained calvarium yielded several dates averaging 10,680 ± 50 BP. Younger dates averaging 8,610 BP were obtained from a bleached calvarium that had apparently been exposed on the surface. The younger cluster of dates cannot be regarded as reliable, but the older dates match our expectations for a terminal Clovis age.

Other radiocarbon-dated Clovis sites in the region include the Colby mammoth kill site in northern Wyoming (Frison and Todd 1986), with one bone date of nearly 10,900 BP and another bone date of 11,200 BP. The Lange-Ferguson site in western South Dakota (Hannus 1990) produced a charcoal date of 11,100 BP. An average of six bone dates from the Dent site in northern Colorado is 10,800 BP, although an earlier date on bone is 11,200 BP (Haynes 1992:360). It should be noted that the reliability of bone protein or collagen for radiocarbon dating has been seriously questioned (see Haynes 1992:364–365).

If the assessment of radiocarbon dates by Haynes (1992) proves correct, there is a very short window of time between the Clovis and Folsom cultural complexes. The Hell Gap site investigations led the investigators to suggest that the Goshen complex probably dated to between Clovis and Folsom (Irwin-Williams et al. 1973). The Mill Iron site in southeast Montana (Frison 1991a, 1996) yielded two sets of AMS radiocarbon dates that are inconclusive, because the older group would place Goshen contemporaneous with Clovis and the younger group lies in the older range of Folson. An AMS charcoal date from the Goshen level at the Hell Gap site, however, is 10,954 ± 135 BP (AA-14434), which is a strong indicator that the younger group of Mill Iron site AMS dates is most likely to be correct. In terms of lithic projectile point manufacturing technology, Goshen could easily be considered an immediate precursor of Folsom, lacking only fluting instead of basal thinning to be identical.

It is difficult to envision Clovis, with its distinctive percussion technology, as a precursor of Goshen, with its highly developed pressure technology. Further, except for the concept of fluting, it is also difficult to accept Clovis as a precursor of Folsom. These difficulties leave the origins of both Clovis and Goshen in doubt.

A reevaluation of the Hell Gap site suggests similar problems. Instead of the cultural stratigraphy suggested earlier (Irwin-Williams et al. 1973), we could be dealing with palimpsests having Agate Basin and Folsom present in one level and Goshen and Folsom in another (Sellet and Frison 1994). On the basis of an as yet incomplete analysis of past work, the Hell Gap site strongly suggests contemporaneous but not synchronous occupations of the site by different cultural groups. The Hell Gap site investigators proposed a Midland Cultural complex dating from "circa 8700 to 8400 B.C." (Irwin-Williams et al. 1973:52). What was named Midland at Hell Gap, in terms of projectile points, is indistinguishable morphologically and technologically from Goshen. The cultural sequence at Hell Gap may be Goshen–Folsom–Goshen instead of Goshen–Folsom–Midland.

Agate Basin

Although the oldest Folsom dates are believed to be around 10,900 BP, other Folsom dates are as young as about 10,300 BP (see Haynes 1992). An Agate Basin bison bone bed overlies and is separated by a sterile level from a Folsom bison bone bed at the Agate Basin site (see Frison and Stanford 1982). The Agate Basin radiocarbon date is over 10,400 years old. The Hell Gap site investigators suggested a duration from about 10,500 to 10,000 years ago for the Agate Basin complex, although there were no actual radiocarbon dates obtained from an Agate Basin component at Hell Gap. If these Folsom and Agate Basin radiocarbon dates are correct, the two complexes were at least partially contemporaneous; in fact, that they are was suggested as a possibility some time ago by evidence at Blackwater Draw (Haynes and Agogino 1966).

Cody Complex

An important milestone in Paleoindian studies was the order that Wormington (1957) resurrected out of the misused concept of "Yuma." She also coined the term "Cody" and proposed the Horner site in northwest Wyoming as the type site of the Cody cultural complex, because it contained both the Scottsbluff and Eden diagnostic variants. On the basis of the stratigraphy and radiocarbon dates from the Hell Gap site, the Cody complex was dated from "circa 6800 to 6400 BC" and the Alberta complex from "circa 7500 to 7000 BC" (Irwin-Williams et al. 1973). Acceptable radiocarbon dates on the Cody complex from the Horner site range from about 8,700 to 9,300 BP (Frison and Todd 1987:98). Radiocarbon dates from other Wyoming sites include Finley site at about 9,000 BP (Frison 1991b:28; Moss et al. 1951) and a single date from the Medicine Lodge Creek site at just over 8,800 BP (Frison 1991b:26). Two radiocarbon-dated Colorado sites include Frasca at about 8,900 BP (Fulgham and Stanford 1982) and Jurgens at about 9,100 BP (Wheat 1979). The Mammoth Meadow site in southwestern Montana has revealed an extensive Cody complex workshop and habitation level with radiocarbon dates spanning an interval from 8,200 to 9,400 BP (Bonnichsen et al. 1992a).

The first substantial evidence that the linear Plains Paleoindian chronology, as proposed from the Hell Gap site investigation, was not as reliable as previously believed evolved out of the reanalysis of materials and the field notes from the first Horner site investigations and the data recovered from a second site investigation.

Briefly, the first investigations at the Horner site were a joint effort of Princeton University (see Jepsen 1953) and the Smithsonian Institution during the late 1940s and early 1950s. The Princeton–Smithsonian materials, along with those recovered from another site component excavated in 1977–1978 by the University of Wyoming, were analyzed and published (see Frison and Todd 1987). The site component excavated in 1977–1978 was older than the Cody complex and, with radiocarbon dates around 10,000 BP (Frison and Todd 1987:98), compared more favorably in age with the Alberta cultural complex. The diagnostic projectile points, however, while demonstrating some Alberta complex characteristics as seen from the Alberta-type projectile points from the Fletcher site (Forbis 1968), also demonstrated some Cody complex characteristics. Consequently, a compromise was made, and the older Horner site materials were named Alberta-Cody (see Bradley and Frison 1987). The Hell Gap site contained an unmistakable Alberta component as described earlier (Wormington 1957), but the assumption that the Cody complex evolved directly out of the Alberta complex is now open to question.

The Foothill–Mountain Paleoindian

Mummy Cave in the Absaroka Mountains in northwest Wyoming (Wedel et al. 1968) and the Bighorn Canyon caves straddling the Montana–Wyoming boundary between the Big Horn and Absaroka Mountains (Husted 1969) provided the first secure evidence that there were foothill–mountain groups as early as about 9,000 BP that were contemporaneous with those living on the open plains. The Medicine Lodge Creek site (Frison 1976) in the Big Horn Mountains and the Lookingbill site (Frison 1983; Larson et al. 1995) in the southern Absaroka Mountains extended the foothill–mountain Paleoindian occupations back to at least 10,000 BP. Foothill–Mountain Paleoindians are well represented at the Barton Gulch site (Davis et al. 1988) and the Myers-Hindman site (Lahren 1976), both in southwestern Montana.

Studies of the foothill–mountain Paleoindian are still very much in the data-gathering stage. Most of the sites are in caves and rock shelters, with stratigraphy controlled by conditions inside these features allowing limited information on the paleoecology. However, Lookingbill, Myers-Hindman, and Barton Gulch are open, stratified sites. One of the deepest cultural levels at the former site is radiocarbon-dated to 10,400 years BP, and as yet has only been minimally tested. In our present state of knowledge, the Cody cultural complex appears in some foothill–mountain Paleoindian sites and seems to be one exception to the dichotomy in subsistence observed between the foothill–mountains and the open plains.

At this time, the cultural relationships between foothill–mountain Paleoindian groups in the higher altitudes adjacent to the plains and late Paleoindian groups west of the continental divide along the drainages of the Snake River have not been explored (e.g., see Swanson 1972). The same is true of the Plateau and areas still farther to the west (see Bryan 1979; Carlson 1983). There is a bewildering array of Intermountain lanceolate, stemmed, laterally restricted, expanding base, split base, fishtail base, transverse-flaked, and obliquely flaked projectile point types and styles from the southern to the northern Rocky Mountains, for which a reliable chronology is just beginning to emerge. The next decade should see major advances toward a better understanding of the Foothill–Mountain Paleoindian.

CONCLUSIONS

The linear chronology proposed earlier for cultural complexes before and after the Pleistocene–Holocene boundary is now being questioned as a result of AMS dating and better-controlled excavation procedures. This doubt also requires changes in thinking about the relationships between the different cultural groups. Co-traditions during this time period are now a distinct possibility.

The concept of co-traditions during Paleoindian times needs further study. In conducting this study, we may have to consider the genesis of a number of cultural groups besides Clovis. Future directions in research need to first carefully evaluate old site assemblages and the methodology employed and then to evaluate these aspects as guidelines for future research. Both stratified and single-component sites with high integrity are limited in number, and research designs for future data collection in these kinds of sites should be carefully reviewed in order to avoid unnecessary loss of the database, which would deprive future investigators of the opportunity to apply new methodological approaches as they are developed.

It is also too soon to dismiss the possibility of pre-12,000-year-old human occupations in this region, since the archaeological record is still far from complete. Consider for a moment that it took over two decades to satisfactorily confirm the existence of a Goshen cultural complex after it was first proposed from evidence recovered at the Hell Gap site.

REFERENCES

Adovasio, J., 1993, The Ones that Will Not Go Away: A Biased View of Pre-Clovis Populations in the New World, in: *From Kostenki to Clovis* (O. Soffer and N. Praslov, eds.), Plenum, pp. 199–218.

Agenbroad, L., 1978, *The Hudson-Meng Site: An Alberta Bison Kill in the Nebraska High Plains*, University Press of America, Washington, DC.

Agenbroad, L., Mead, J., and Nelson, L. (eds.), 1990, *Megafauna and Man: Discovery of America's Heartland*, The Mammoth Site of Hot Springs, South Dakota, Inc., Scientific Papers, 1.

Antevs, E., 1948, Climatic Change and Pre-White Man, *Bulletin of the University of Utah* 38:168–191.

Antevs, E., 1955, Geologic-Climatic Dating in the West, *American Antiquity* 20(4):317–335.

Beatty, M., Turner, M., and Bonnichsen, R., in press, A Pedo-Archaeology of the Mammoth Meadow Fan/Terrace Workshop Site in Southwestern Montana, in: *Proceedings of the International Conferences on Pedo-Archaeology*, Columbia.

Bonnichsen, R., 1991, Clovis Origins, in: *Clovis Origins and Adaptations* (R. Bonnichsen and K. Turnmire, eds.), Center for the Study of the First Americans, Oregon State University, Corvallis, pp. 309–329.

Bonnichsen, R., and Schneider, A., no date, *Breaking the Impasse on the Peopling of the Americas: Analytical Procedures and Using Ancient DNA*, Unpublished manuscript, Center for the Study of the First Americans, Oregon State University, Corvallis.

Bonnichsen, R., and Sorg, M. (eds.), 1989, *Bone Modification*, A Peopling of the Americas Publication, Center for the Study of the First Americans Institute, University of Maine, Orono.

Bonnichsen, R., and Turnmire, K. (eds.), 1991, *Clovis: Origins and Adaptations*, A Peopling of the Americas Publication, Center for the Study of the First Americans, Oregon State University, Corvallis.

Bonnichsen, R., Graham, R., Geppert, T., Oliver, J., Oliver, S., Schnurrenberger, D., Stuckenrath, R., Tratebas, A., and Young, D., 1986, False Cougar and Shield Trap Caves, Pryor Mountains, Montana, *National Geographic Research* 2:276–290.

Bonnichsen, R., Stanford, D., and Fastook, J., 1987, Environmental Change and Developmental History of Human Adaptive Patterns: The Paleoindian Case, in: *North America and Adjacent Oceans During the Last Deglaciation* (W. Ruddiman and H. E. Wright, Jr., eds.), The Geological Society of America, Boulder, pp. 403–424.

Bonnichsen, R., Beatty, M., Turner, M., Turner, J., and Douglas, D., 1992a, in: *Ice Age Hunters of the Rockies* (D. Stanford and J. Day, eds.), Denver Museum of Natural History and University Press of Colorado, Denver, pp. 285–322.

Bonnichsen, R., Bolen, C., Turner, M., and Beatty, M., 1992b, Hair from Mammoth Meadow II, Southwestern Montana, *Current Research in the Pleistocene* 9:75–78.

Bonnichsen, R., Beatty, M., Turner, M., and Stoneking, M., in press, What Can be Learned from Hair? A Hair Record from the Mammoth Meadow Locus, Southwestern Montana, in: *Prehistoric Mongoloid Dispersions* (T. Akazawa and E. Szathmary, eds.), Oxford University Press, Oxford.

Bradley, B., and Frison, G., 1987, Projectile Points and Specialized Bifaces from the Horner Site, in: *The Horner Site: The Type Site of the Cody Cultural Complex* (G. Frison and L. Todd, eds.), Academic Press, New York, pp. 199–231.

Bryan, A., 1979, The Stemmed Tradition: An Early Technological Tradition in Western North America, in: *Anthropological Papers in Memory of Earl H. Swanson, Jr.* (L. Harten, C. Warren, and D. Touhy, eds.), Special Publication of the Idaho Museum of Natural History, Pocatello, pp. 77–107.

Bryson, R., 1974, A Perspective on Climatic Change, *Science* 184:753–760.

Carlisle, R. (ed.), 1988, Americans before Columbus: Ice-Age Origins, *Ethnology Monographs 12*, University of Pittsburgh.

Carlson, R., 1983, The Far West, in: *Early Man in the New World* (R. Shutler, ed.), Sage Publications, Beverly Hills, pp. 73–96.

Clachula, J., 1994, A Paleo-American (Pre-Clovis) Settlement in Alberta, *Current Research in the Pleistocene* 11:21–23.

COHMAP Members, 1988, Climatic Changes of the Last 18,000 Years: Observations and Model Simulations, *Science* 241:1043–1052.

Cummings, L., 1996, Paleoenvironmental Interpretations for the Mill Iron Site, Based on Stratigraphic Pollen and Phytolith Analysis, in: *The Mill Iron Site 24CT30 and the Goshen–Plainview Cultural Complex on the Northern High Plains* (G. Frison, ed.), University of New Mexico Press, Albuquerque, pp. 177–193.

Davis, L., and Greiser, S., 1992, Indian Creek Paleoindians: Early Occupation of the Elkhorn Mountains' Southeast Flank, West-Central Montana, in: *Ice Age Hunters of the Rockies* (D. Stanford and J. Day, eds.), Denver Museum of Natural History and University Press of Colorado, Denver, pp. 225–283.

Davis, L., and Reeves, B. (eds.), 1990, *Hunters of the Recent Past*, Unwin Hyman, London.

Davis, L., Aaberg, S., and Greiser, S., 1988, Paleoindians in Transmontane Southwestern Montana: The Barton Gulch Occupations, Ruby River Drainage, *Current Research in the Pleistocene* 5:9–11.

Dyke, A., and Prest, V., 1987, Late Wisconsinan and Holocene History of the Laurentide Ice Sheet, *Geographie Physique et Quaternaire* 31:237–263.

Forbis, R., 1968, Fletcher: A Paleo-Indian Site in Alberta, *American Antiquity* 33:1–10.

Frison, G., 1974, *The Casper Site: A Hell Gap Bison Kill on the High Plains*, Academic Press, New York.

Frison, G., 1976, The Chronology of Paleo-Indian and Altithermal Period Groups in the Bighorn Basin, Wyoming, in: *Cultural Change and Continuity: Essays in Honor of James Bennet Griffin* (C. Cleland, ed.), Academic Press, New York, pp. 147–173.

Frison, G., 1982, Paleoindian Winter Subsistence Strategies on the High Plains, in: *Plains Indian Studies: A Collection of Essays in Honor of John C. Ewers and Waldo R. Wedel* (D. Ubelaker and H. Viola, eds.), Smithsonian Contributions to Anthropology 30, Smithsonian Institution Press, Washington, DC.

Frison, G., 1983, The Lookingbill Site, Wyoming, *Tebiwa* 20:1–16.

Frison, G., 1984, The Carter/Kerr-McGee Paleoindian Site: Cultural Resource Management and Archaeological Research, *American Antiquity* 49(2):288–314.

Frison, G., 1988, Paleoindian Subsistence and Settlement During Post-Clovis Times on the Northwestern Plains, the Adjacent Mountains and Intermontane Basins, in: *Americans Before Columbus: Ice-Age Origins* (R. Carlisle, ed.), Ethnology Monographs, No. 12, University of Pittsburgh, Pittsburgh, pp. 83–106.

Frison, G., 1991a, The Goshen Paleoindian Complex: New Data for Paleoindian Research, in: *Clovis Origins and Adaptations* (R. Bonnichsen and K. Turnmire, eds.), Center for the Study of the First Americans Publication, Oregon State University, Corvallis, pp. 133–151.

Frison, G., 1991b, *Prehistoric Hunters of the High Plains*, 2nd ed., Academic Press, San Diego.

Frison, G., 1992, The Foothills–Mountains and the Open Plains: A Dichotomy in Paleoindian Subsistence Strategies between Two Ecosystems, in: *Ice Age Hunters of the Rockies* (D. Stanford and J. Day, eds.), Denver Museum of Natural History and University Press of Colorado, Denver, pp. 323–342.

Frison, G., 1996. *The Mill Iron Site 24CT30 and the Goshen–Plainview Cultural Complex on the Northern High Plains*, University of New Mexico Press, Albuquerque.

Frison, G., and Stanford, D. (eds.), 1982, *The Agate Basin Site: A Record of the Paleoindian Occupation of the Northwestern High Plains*, Academic Press, New York.

Frison, G., and Todd, L., 1986, *The Colby Mammoth Site: Taphonomy and Archaeology of a Clovis Kill in Northern Wyoming*, University of New Mexico Press, Albuquerque.

Frison, G., and Todd, L. (eds.), 1987, *The Horner Site: The Type Site of the Cody Cultural Complex*, Academic Press, Orlando.

Frison, G., Wilson, M., and Wilson, D., 1976, Fossil Bison and Artifacts from an Early Altithermal Period Arroyo Trap in Wyoming, *American Antiquity* 41(1):28–57.

Fulgham, G., and Stanford, D., 1982, The Frasca Site: A Preliminary Report, *Southwestern Lore* 48(1):1–9.

Graham, M., Wilson, M., and Graham, R., 1987, Paleoenvironments and Mammalian Faunas of Montana, Southern Alberta, and Southern Saskatchewan, in: *Late Quaternary Mammalian Biogeography and Environments of the Great Plains and Prairies* (R. Graham, H. Semken, Jr., and M. Graham, eds.), Illinois State Museum Scientific Papers, Vol. 22, Springfield, pp. 410–459.

Hannus, L., 1990, Mammoth Hunting in the New World, in: *Hunters of the Recent Past* (L. Davis and B. Reeves, eds.), Unwin-Hyman, London, pp. 47–67.

Haynes, C. V., Jr., 1992, Contributions of Radiocarbon Dating to the Geochronology of the Peopling of the New World, in: *Radiocarbon After Four Decades* (R. Taylor, A. Long, and R. Kra, eds.), Springer-Verlag, New York, pp. 355–374.

Haynes, C. V., Jr., 1993, Clovis–Folsom Geochronology and Climatic Change, in: *From Kostenki to Clovis: Upper Paleolithic—Paleo-Indian Adaptations* (O. Soffer and N. D. Praslov, eds.), Plenum, New York, pp. 219–236.

Haynes, C. V., Jr., and Agogino, G., 1966, Prehistoric Springs and Geochronology of the Clovis Site, *American Antiquity* 31(6):812–821.

Hofman, J., and Enloe, J. (eds.), 1992, *Piecing Together the Past: Applications of Refitting Studies in Archaeology*, British Archaeological Report, International Series 578, Oxford.

Hughes, T., 1987, Ice Dynamics and Deglaciation Models when Ice Sheets Collapsed, in: *North America and Adjacent Oceans During the Last Deglaciation* (W. Ruddiman and H. Wright, eds.), Geological Society of America, Boulder, pp. 183–220.

Husted, W., 1969, *Bighorn Canyon Archaeology*, Smithsonian Institution River Basin Surveys, Publications in Salvage Archaeology 12, Washington, DC.

Ingbar, E., 1992, The Hanson Site and Folsom on the Northwestern Plains, in: *Ice Age Hunters of the Rockies* (D. Stanford and J. Day, eds.), Denver Museum of Natural History and University Press of Colorado, Denver, pp. 169–192.

Irwin-Williams, C., Irwin, H., Agogino, G., and Haynes, C. V., Jr., 1973, Hell Gap: Paleo-Indian Occupation on the High Plains, *Plains Anthropologist* 18(5):40–53.

Jepsen, G., 1953, Ancient Buffalo Hunters of Northwestern Wyoming, *Southwestern Lore* 19:19–25.

Jodry, M., and Stanford, D., 1992, Stewart's Cattle Guard Site: An Analysis of Bison Remains in a Folsom Kill–Butchery Campsite, in: *Ice Age Hunters of the Rockies* (D. Stanford and J. Day, eds.), Denver Museum of Natural History and University Press of Colorado, Denver, pp. 101–168.

Jones, S., and Bonnichsen, R., 1994, The Anzick Clovis Burial, *Current Research in the Pleistocene* 11:42–44.

Kutzbach, P., Guetter, P., Behling, P., and Selin, R., 1993, Simulated Climate Change: Results of the COHMAP Climate-Model Experiments, in: *Global Climates Since the Last Glacial Maximum* (H. Wright, Jr., J. Kutzbach, T. Webb, III, W. Ruddiman, F. Street-Perrott, and P. Bartlein, eds.), University of Minnesota Press, Minneapolis, pp. 24–93.

Lahren, L., 1976, *The Myers–Hindman Site: An Exploratory Study of Human Occupation Patterns in the Upper Yellowstone Valley from 7000 B.C. to A.D. 1200*, Anthropologos Researches International, Livingston.

Larson, M., Kornfeld, M., Rapson, D., Finley, J., Frison, G., Miller, J., and Scott-Cummings, L., 1995, High Altitude Hunter-Gatherer Adaptations in the Middle Rocky Mountains: 1988–1994 Investigations, Technical Report No. 4, Department of Anthropology, University of Wyoming, Laramie.

Lynch, T., 1990, Glacial-Age Man in South America? A Critical Review, *American Antiquity* 55(1):12–36.

Markgraf, V., and Lennon, T., 1986, Paleoenvironmental History of the Last 13,000 Years of the Eastern Powder River Basin, Wyoming, and Its Implication for Prehistoric Cultural Patterns, *Plains Anthropologist* 31(111):1–12.

Marshall, E., 1990, Clovis Counterrevolution, *Science* 249:738–741.

Meltzer, J., Adovasio, J., and Dillehay, T., 1994, On a Pleistocene Human Occupation at Pedra Furada, Brazil, *Antiquity* 68:695–714.

Montet-White, A., and Holen, S. (eds.), 1991, *Raw Material Economies Among Prehistoric Hunter–Gatherers*, University of Kansas, Publications in Anthology, 19, Lawrence.

Morlan, R., 1988, Pre-Clovis People: Early Discoveries of North America, in: *Americans Before Columbus: Ice-Age Origins* (R. Carlisle, ed.), Ethnology Monographs No. 12, University of Pittsburgh, pp. 31–43.

Moss, J., Bryan, K., Holmes, G., Satterthwaite, L., Jr., Hansen, H., Schultz, C., and Frankforter, W., 1951, *Early Man in the Eden Valley*, University of Pennsylvania, Museum Monographs 6.

Nitecki, M., and Nitecki, D. (eds.), 1987, *The Evolution of Human Hunting*, Plenum, New York.

Porter, S., 1988, Landscapes of the Last Ice Age in North America, in: *Americans before Columbus* (R. Carlisle, ed.), Ethnology Monographs No. 12, University of Pittsburgh, pp. 1–24.

Sellet, F., and Frison, G., 1994, Hell Gap Revisited, Paper presented at the 59th Annual Meeting of the Society for American Archaeology, Anaheim.

Soffer, O., and Praslov, N. (eds.), 1993, *From Kostenki to Clovis: Upper Paleolithic–Paleoindian Adaptations*, Plenum, New York.

Stafford, M., 1990, The Powars II Site (48PL330): A Paleoindian Red Ochre Mine in Eastern Wyoming, Unpublished M.A. thesis, Department of Anthropology, University of Wyoming, Laramie.

Stafford, T., Jr., 1994, Accelerator C-14 Dating of Human Skeletons: Assessing Accuracy and Results on New World Specimens, in: *Method and Theory in the Peopling of the Americas* (R. Bonnichsen and D. Steele, eds.), Center for the Study of the First Americans, Oregon State University, Corvallis, pp. 45–55.

Stanford, D., 1978, The Jones-Miller Site: An Example of Hell Gap Bison Procurement Strategy, in: *Bison Procurement and Utilization: A Symposium* (L. Davis and M. Wilson, eds.), Plains Anthropologist Memoir, No. 14, pp. 90–97.

Stanford, D., and Day, J. (eds.), 1992, *Ice-Age Hunters of the Rockies*, Denver Museum of Natural History and University Press of Colorado, Denver.

Swanson, E., 1972, *Birch Creek: Human Ecology in the Cool Desert of the Northern Rocky Mountains 9,000 B.C.–A.D. 1850*, Idaho State University Press, Pocatello.

Walker, D., 1982, Early Holocene Vertebrate Fauna, in: *The Agate Basin Site: A Record of the Paleoindian Occupation of the Northwestern Plains* (G. Frison and D. Stanford, eds.), Academic Press, New York, pp. 274–308.

Walker, D., 1987, Late Pleistocene/Holocene Environmental Changes in Wyoming: The Mammalian Record, in: *Late Quaternary Mammalian Biogeography and Environments of the Great Plains and Prairies* (R. Graham, H. Semken, Jr., and M. Graham, eds.), Illinois State Museum Scientific Papers, Vol. 22, Springfield, pp. 334–392.

Wedel, W., Husted, W., and Moss, J., 1968, Mummy Cave: Prehistoric Record from the Rocky Mountains of Wyoming, *Science* 160:184–186.

Wheat, J., 1972, The Olsen–Chubbuck Site: A Paleo-Indian Bison Kill. *Society for American Archaeology Memoir*, No. 26.

Wheat, J., 1979, The Jurgens Site, *Plains Anthropologist Memoir*, No. 15.

Whitlock, C., 1993, Postglacial Vegetation and Climate of Grand Teton and Southern Yellowstone National Parks, *Ecological Monographs* 63(2):173–198.

Wilmsen, E., and Roberts, F., 1978, *Lindenmeier, 1934–1974*, Smithsonian Contributions to Anthropology, No. 24, Washington, DC.

Wilson, M., 1978, Archaeological Kill Site Populations and the Holocene Evolution of the Genus Bison, in: *Bison Procurement and Utilization: A Symposium* (L. Davis and M. Wilson, eds.), Plains Anthropologist Memoir, No. 14, pp. 9–22.

Wormington, H., 1957, *Ancient Man in North America*, Denver Museum of Natural History, Popular Series No. 4.

Chapter 16

The Pleistocene–Holocene Transition in the Eastern United States

DAN F. MORSE, DAVID G. ANDERSON, AND ALBERT C. GOODYEAR

We define the eastern United States for the purposes of this chapter as being bordered by the Laurentide Ice Sheet on the north, the ancestral Gulf of Mexico on the south, the Atlantic Ocean on the east, and the Western Plains on the west. These borders enclose most of the area between the latitudes 25–50°N and longitudes 65–90°W, a region of ecological diversity and complexity even today.

In this area, a rich heritage of human occupation extends from the late Paleolithic/late Pleistocene through the present. The indigenous development of horticulture took place by about 5,000 BP[1] (Smith 1995:196), and the development of complex political systems based on intensive maize agriculture began by the 9th century AD. In this chapter, however, we focus on the cultures and environments of the area during the terminal Pleistocene and Early Holocene.

LATE GLACIAL AND POSTGLACIAL ENVIRONMENTS

In the eastern United States, the Last Glacial Maximum circa 20,000–18,000 BP coincided with a sea-level decrease of around 120 m below present (Bloom 1984:42). A cool

---

[1]All dates in this chapter are expressed in radiocarbon years before present (BP).

DAN F. MORSE • Arkansas Archeological Survey, State University, Arkansas 72467.   DAVID G. ANDERSON • National Park Service, Atlanta, Georgia 30303.   ALBERT C. GOODYEAR • Institute of Archaeology and Anthropology, University of South Carolina, Columbia, South Carolina 29208.

Humans at the End of the Ice Age: The Archaeology of the Pleistocene–Holocene Transition, edited by Lawrence Guy Straus, Berit Valentin Eriksen, Jon M. Erlandson, and David R. Yesner. Plenum Press, New York, 1996.

temperate-boreal vegetation ecotone existed at 20,000 BP through Tennessee (Delcourt and Delcourt 1991:103; see also Delcourt and Delcourt 1987b; T. Webb 1987, 1988). During the late glacial, "boreal forest dominated by jack pine (*Pinus banksiana*) and spruce (*Picea*) was replaced progressively by temperate deciduous forest" as climate ameliorated (Delcourt and Delcourt 1991:102–103). Near Memphis, Tennessee, a large male mastodon was recovered with spruce cones, insects, and snails dated to about 17,000 BP (Brister et al. 1981; Delcourt et al. 1980). Other megafaunal mammals of this general region include ground sloth, giant beaver, horse, camel, llama, and tapir.

The terminal Pleistocene deglaciation was a time of rapidly changing landscapes, biota, and climates, the character of which appears to have profoundly shaped the colonization of the region (Figure 1). Deglaciation commenced around 14,000 BP and seas rose slowly from their full glacial minimum stands, although by circa 12,000 BP, when the first human groups may have appeared, sea level was still approximately 60 m below its modern stand. Lake strandlines and other glacial features pose special problems in the north (Ellis 1994). Vast areas of the exposed continental shelf were characterized by a rich floral and faunal record and would have been ideally suited for human habitation, particularly in the southern part of the region, from the Middle Atlantic to the Gulf coasts (Autin et al. 1991:563; Graham and Mead 1987; Ruddiman 1987). At this same time, the Laurentide Ice Sheet had receded sufficiently in the north to clear Niagara Falls and expose and fill the basins of the vast glacial great lakes, while to the south the deltaic plain of the Mississippi River began to form. Glacial retreat and sea-level rise appear to have arrested or even reversed during the Younger Dryas, from roughly 11,100 to 10,500 BP, and it is during this interval that unequivocal evidence for human occupation appears throughout the East. Human populations entering eastern North America from the west—if the so-called "ice-free corridor" was indeed the route of initial entry south of the ice sheets (e.g., Haynes 1964)—or, alternatively, along the continental shelf from the south, if initial colonization occurred along coastal margins (e.g., Fladmark 1979) may, accordingly, have been forced away from coastal areas by the fluctuating sea levels (Faught 1995).

The relationship between early human populations and Pleistocene fauna in the East is likewise not clear at present, with arguments advanced favoring generalist adaptations directed to an array of resources, with a fairly minimal emphasis on megafauna (e.g., Meltzer 1988; Meltzer and Smith 1986), to those arguing for an appreciable focus on large game animals (e.g., Anderson 1995; Kelly and Todd 1988). A late survival of megafauna to shortly after 11,000 BP is clearly indicated, however (Mead and Meltzer 1984). In southeast Missouri, for example, a *Paleolama* was found associated with hazel nuts that were dated to about 10,890 ± 130 BP (Morse and Graham 1991 [NZA-1100]). Direct associations between humans and now-extinct Terminal Pleistocene fauna indicating that hunting was occurring have been found at Little Salt Spring (a giant land tortoise with an embedded sharpened wooden stake [Clausen et al. 1979]) and in the Wacissa River of Florida (a *Bison antiquus* skull with a projectile point embedded in its forehead [S. D. Webb et al. 1984]) (Figure 2). In addition, indisputable associations of humans and mastodon have been found at Kimms-wick in southern Missouri (Graham et al. 1981) and Martins Creek in Ohio (Brush and Smith 1994), and other likely candidates include the Coates-Hindes site in western Tennessee (John Broster 1995 personal communication). Finally, worked mastodon and mammoth green bone and ivory, including foreshafts, have been recovered in a number of locations in Florida (Dunbar and Webb in press; Milanich 1994; S. D. Webb 1995). All these lines of

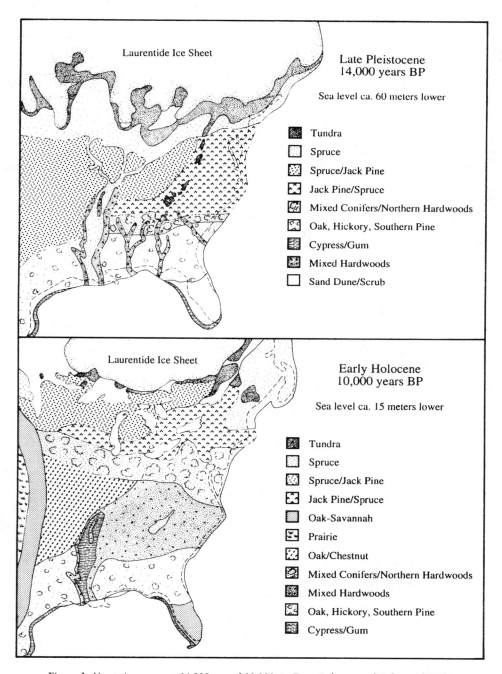

Figure 1. Vegetation zones at 14,000 BP and 10,000 BP. From Delcourt and Delcourt (1981).

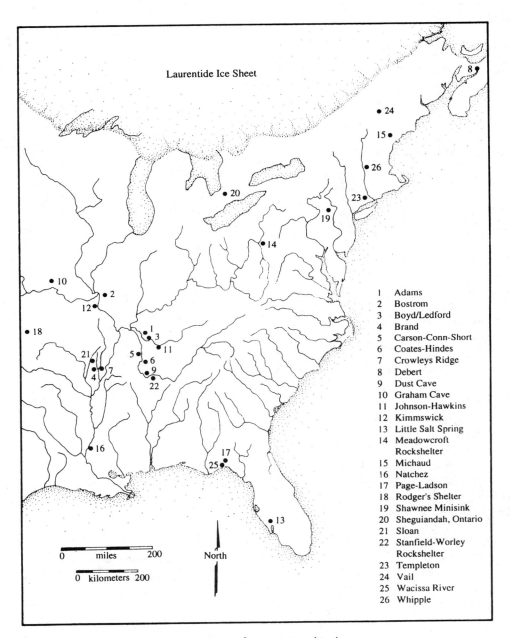

Laurentide Ice Sheet

1   Adams
2   Bostrom
3   Boyd/Ledford
4   Brand
5   Carson-Conn-Short
6   Coates-Hindes
7   Crowleys Ridge
8   Debert
9   Dust Cave
10 Graham Cave
11 Johnson-Hawkins
12 Kimmswick
13 Little Salt Spring
14 Meadowcroft
    Rockshelter
15 Michaud
16 Natchez
17 Page-Ladson
18 Rodger's Shelter
19 Shawnee Minisink
20 Sheguiandah, Ontario
21 Sloan
22 Stanfield-Worley
    Rockshelter
23 Templeton
24 Vail
25 Wacissa River
26 Whipple

0   miles   200
0   kilometers 200

North

Figure 2. Locations of sites mentioned in the text.

evidence indicate that Eastern Paleoindians hunted Pleistocene fauna and megafauna at least some of the time and may have played at least some role in the extinction of some of these species.

By 10,000 BP, the glacial ice had receded north of the Great Lakes, sea level was only 15–20 m below modern tides, and much of the southern two thirds of the eastern United States was covered by deciduous or combined deciduous and pine forests. Prairie-like conditions were characteristic on the west central border (Munson 1990). To the far north, immediately south of the ice, were boreal forests. A possible dichotomy of largest surviving land mammals emerges. White-tailed deer existed throughout much of the hardwood region, but in the north there were moose, elk, and caribou. The smaller deer were most prolific in the south, particularly in hardwood ecotones, where adequate year-round browse was available.

The central Mississippi Valley was mostly a cypress–gum floodplain with surrounding uplands and a central erosional remnant known as Crowley's Ridge characterized by mixed hardwoods (Delcourt and Delcourt 1981). The floodplain itself was made up of active and ponded relict braided stream channels of the Mississippi as well as meandering streams. Forest edges probably including hardwoods lined the streams and ponds, making up a mosaic of vegetation zones probably ideal for white-tailed deer. Acorn mast provided adequate winter food for deer and the huge numbers of waterfowl in the Mississippi River flyway. Fish, small mammals, and plant foods would have been abundant. In much of the eastern United States, the following Hypsithermal Interval (8,000–4,000 BP) was a period of decreased rainfall and increasing warming.

THE ARCHAEOLOGICAL RECORD

The archaeological record is almost entirely lithic in nature. Sites include rock shelters, eroded surface scatters, buried sites, coastal submarine locations, and submerged sinkholes. Frustrating aspects are the general lack of radiocarbon dates and the relative absence of good faunal and floral associations. The research tools either developed or adopted in eastern North America include microwear analysis, fluted point technology, identification of chert sources, and the reconstruction of stone artifact assemblages.

Pre-Clovis Remains

No satisfactory evidence exists at the present for "Pre-Clovis" occupation(s) in the East. While Meadowcroft Rockshelter in southwestern Pennsylvania has yielded a series of Pre-Clovis dates, controversy continues to swirl around their interpretation and context (Haynes 1980, 1992; Mead 1980). The Natchez pelvis, originally found with Late Pleistocene megafaunal remains, was redated using accelerator mass spectrometry (AMS) to 5580 ± 80 BP (e.g., Cotter 1991). The claimed Oldowan nature of the Alabama pebble tool complex (Lively 1965) has never been substantiated, and the "complex" instead appears to be initial stage lithic reduction debris as well as expedient tools associated with Holocene quarrying and wild-plant-gathering activity (Futato in press), a speculative construct rather than an assemblage captured in clear stratigraphic context. The alleged Pre-Clovis occupation at the Sheguiandah site in Ontario has been shown to be Post-glacial in age (Storck et al. 1994).

Outside these examples, there has been little evidence of a pre–12,000 BP occupation of the eastern United States. At Page-Ladson, five dates bracketing the interval from 12,000 to 12,500 BP have been obtained from a level containing a mastodon tusk bearing cut marks (Dunbar and Webb in press; 1995 personal communication), and at Little Salt Springs, a wooden spear associated with the giant tortoise was dated to 12,030 ± 200 BP (Clausen et al. 1979:611). While these dates raise the possibility of early human occupations in the Southeast well before the currently accepted maximum age for western Clovis at 11,200 BP, their acceptance has been limited, because the associated artifacts are few.

Major periods of early human occupation in the eastern United States encompass initial colonization and settlement, identified by the makers of early fluted point forms (≈ 11,500–10,750 BP); the emergence of distinctive subregional cultural traditions, the best known of which are the Dalton horizon in the southern woodlands and the fluted-point-using hunters of the northern Great Lakes and periglacial tundra (≈ 10,750–10,000 BP); the adoption of Initial Holocene or Early Archaic lifeways based on the exploitation of modern flora and fauna identified by side and corner notched point forms (≈ 10,000–9,000 BP); and the decline and eventual disappearance of the formal and highly curated toolkit that characterized occupation in the region up to this time. A pattern of increasingly localized group movement and interaction becomes evident, identified by groups using stemmed and bifurcate-based projectile points (≈ 9,000–8,000 BP). Dramatic changes in population growth, interaction, and adaptation that occurred over this time are best reflected in lithic technology, which remains the primary source of information about the early occupants of the region at this time (Figure 3).

Initial Colonization (11,500–10,750 BP)

Clear evidence for human occupation of the East appears after 11,500 BP, when fluted point forms resembling classic western Clovis projectile points are found in large numbers across the region. Unfortunately, radiocarbon dates from this period are restricted almost exclusively to the northeast (Levine 1990), with the result that age estimates for Clovis assemblages are largely based on cross-dating with well-documented southwestern assemblages, which range from circa 11,200 to 10,900 BP (e.g., Haynes 1987, 1992). Locational or metric data or both have been compiled for almost 5000 fluted points just from the Southeast and on over 8000 fluted points from eastern North America as a whole, almost 80% of the number of fluted points reported from the entire continent (Anderson 1990b; 168, 1991a; Brennan 1982; Dincauze 1993a; Faught et al. 1994). Despite this difference in numbers, the view of New World Paleoindian that has come to dominate thinking is based largely on data from the Southwest and the Great Plains because of where the earliest discoveries of fluted points in superb geological context occurred.

Large numbers of fluted points are found in the major river valleys of the interior Southeast and lower Midwest, along stretches of the Tennessee, Ohio, Cumberland, lower Missouri, Mississippi, Illinois, and Wabash rivers, with particularly dense concentrations near confluences, major chert sources, and areas likely rich in game. These areas are thought to represent areas of initial extended settlement, staging areas from which the exploration and eventual occupation of the larger region may have proceeded (e.g., Anderson 1990a,b; Dincauze 1993b). The numbers of fluted points in these areas suggest appreciable time depth, leading a number of scholars to suggest that Clovis technology itself may have arisen

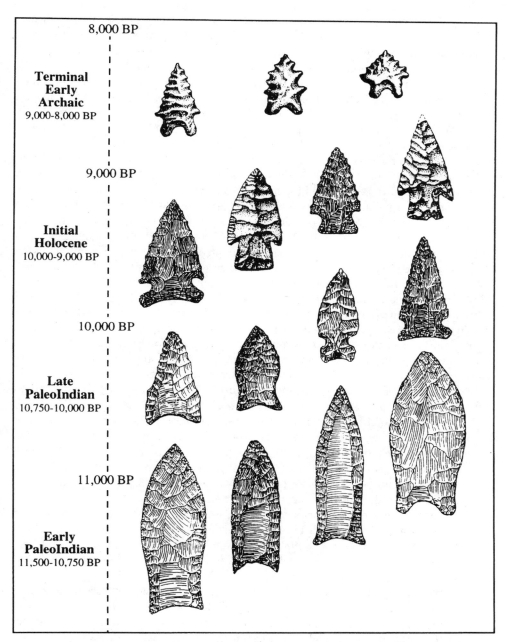

Figure 3. Major artifacts characteristic of the four periods during 11,500–8,000 BP.

in the region (e.g., Faught 1995; Mason 1962; Stanford 1991). In the East, the irregular distribution of fluted points, which occur in large numbers in some areas and are nearly absent in others, such as in portions of the Gulf Coastal Plain, suggests that colonization and subsequent settlement were uneven, proceeding in leapfrog fashion rather than as a continuous wave of advance, as suggested by Martin (1973) in his now classic overkill hypothesis paper (Anderson 1995; Faught 1995; Faught et al. 1994).

Radiocarbon determinations from the East associated with Clovis or Clovis-like fluted points are almost exclusively from the northeast, and even here dating indicates occupation only during the 11th millennium BP and perhaps somewhat later (Levine 1990). Six northeastern sites—Debert, Michaed, Shawnee Minisink, Templeton, Vail, and Whipple, which are fairly well dated, suggest that deeply indented fluted forms occur somewhat later in time than classic Clovis-like lanceolates, to circa 10,600 BP. A number of major eastern Clovis sites remain undated, such as Kimmswick (Graham et al. 1981), where one fluted point appears to have been embedded in mastodon flesh, yet charcoal preservation was poor. A hearth at the Johnson-Hawkins site near Nashville with an associated fluted point preform and spruce fragments has been recently dated to 11,700 ± 980 BP (Broster and Barker 1992; Broster and Norton 1992, in press; Broster et al. 1991, 1994) and, although an early date, has such a large standard deviation as to preclude its use in arguments about the antiquity of fluted points in the region. With few exceptions, then, the radiocarbon dates obtained thus far from fluted point sites in the East are in the 11th and 10th millennia BP (Haynes et al. 1984; Levine 1990). Well-dated sites like Debert (MacDonald 1968) and Vail (Gramley 1982) are contemporaneous with Folsom assemblages from the West and Dalton sites in the Southeast, at least at Rodgers Shelter (Goodyear 1982). The later dates for fluted points from the Northeast are contemporaneous with dates for Early Holocene notched point assemblages in the South, which, whenever found in stratigraphic position, *always* overlay fluted point deposits. Pre–11,000 BP dates from the East are thus comparatively few and equivocal at present, a situation that must be remedied if we are to work out an accurate Paleoindian chronology and occupational history for the region. While one conceptual sequence of fluted points through time sees the development of any or all of longer "waists," narrower stems, and deeper basal concavities from a Clovis-like archetype toward a Dalton-like form (e.g., Perino 1985:100, 1991:91; see also Haynes et al. 1984), until larger samples are discovered in good context, this sequence must remain speculative.

A remarkable artifact assemblage consisting of large single-platform polyhedral cores and large curved blades has been recovered from Adams and Boyd/Ledford in Kentucky (Bostrom 1993; Freeman et al. in press), Carson-Conn-Short in Tennessee (Broster and Norton 1993), the Bostrom site in Illinois (Tankersley and Morrow 1993), and at sites in West Texas (M. Collins personal communication) and at Blackwater Draw in New Mexico (Green 1963). At the Tennessee site, 53 polyhedral cores and 465 true blades have been recovered to date (J. Broster 1994 personal communication).

Eastern fluted points are not expedient tools, but formal, hafted bifaces made mainly for forcible penetration of animal hide, possibly including mastodon, tapir, sloth, horse, caribou, camel, llama, elk, deer, and others. The hafted area is defined and possibly strengthened (Titmus and Woods 1991) by lateral grinding and by surface flutes that extend from the base to about one third of the length of the point. The lanceolate shape and fluting indicate a binding that allowed deep penetration of the spear into an animal. Many exhibit impact fractures, and resharpened points seem to be simply shortened versions of a tip-damaged larger point. Other possible Paleoindian tools found in Florida include bola-like stones and a boomerang (Milanich 1994). Also in northwest Florida, points and scrapers were made from flakes removed from large bifaces. These bifaces functioned as combination core and knife tools, emphasizing the need for a portable toolkit. Unfortunately, little is known of the cultural expression except for base camps, extraction (almost exclusively hunting) camps, quarry locations, and the apparent focus on hunting. Logically, gathering wild plants and fishing must have been as prominent, if not more so, but we are only on the verge of discovering sites that can produce confirmatory data (McNett et al. 1977). Our point of reference remains a combination of western United States sites (mostly kill sites) and our knowledge of the late Upper Paleolithic of Europe.

The movements of Paleoindian populations, specifically the determination of settlement ranges, are being explored throughout the East through detailed lithic raw material source identification analyses (e.g., Ellis and Lothrop 1989; Tankersley 1989, 1990, 1991). Unfortunately, regional and subregional scale analyses are in their infancy, although Geographic Information System (GIS)-based efforts are beginning to emerge encompassing large areas and datasets (Faught 1995; Faught et al. 1994; Gillam 1995). While population *estimates* have yet to be attempted on a regional scale, analyses of sites and artifact incidence over a number of localities in the region indicate that appreciable population *growth* was likely occurring during the Paleoindian period (Anderson 1990b).

The Emergence of Regional Traditions (10,750–10,000 BP)

There are a great many named varieties of fluted and unfluted lanceolate Paleoindian projectile points in the eastern United States, assemblages that are commonly if somewhat arbitrarily placed into Early, Middle, and Late subperiods, with estimated temporal ranges of from circa 11,500 to 10,900 BP, 10,900 to 10,500 BP, and 10,500 to 10,000 BP (Anderson 1990b, 1995a,b; Goodyear in press). These subperiods are thought to correspond to the occurrence of lanceolate fluted points resembling Western Clovis forms that are variously called Eastern Clovis, Gainey, or Clovis Variants; fluted and unfluted forms with broad blades and constricted hafts like the Barnes, Cumberland, Suwannee, Simpson (Daniel and Wisenbaker 1987; Dunbar and Waller 1992), Quad, and Beaver Lake types; and resharpened lanceolate corner- and side-notched forms like Dalton, San Patrice, Hardaway (Coe 1964), Crowfield, Bolen, and Big Sandy. As we have seen, however, absolute dating for the first two of these subperiods is minimal outside the Northeast. The increasingly evident close technological affinities between Clovis and northeast Arkansas/central Mississippi Valley Dalton technology (Bradley in press) suggest, furthermore, that Dalton evolved directly from Clovis in the central Mississippi Valley, perhaps as early as 10,800 years ago. Thus, traditional dates assigned to Dalton, from circa 10,500 to 9,900 BP (Goodyear 1982), may eventually be pushed back.

Accordingly, given the ambiguity that attached to the "Middle Paleoindian" temporal construct as it is presently conceived—Dalton assemblages may well overlap with some or all of the period—in this discussion we have chosen a date of 10,750 BP as a useful dividing line for the Paleoindian period, with the hope that distinct assemblages will be discovered and firmly dated in the near future to help refine the regional sequence and chronology. Because appreciable variability is evident in the initial Clovis occupations in the region, which occur in areas as diverse as the karstic river valleys of Florida, along the major drainages of the midsouth, and along the northern glacial lake and sea margins (Storck 1984), some of the diversity currently attributed to later societies likely began to emerge at a very early time level. Finally, because existing well-dated later fluted point assemblages date to circa 10,600 BP or later in the region (Lepper and Meltzer 1991; Levine 1990), it is unlikely that major stylistic changes indicative of the emergence of subregional cultural traditions occurred precisely at 10,900–10,800 BP. Such changes are evident, however, by 10,750 BP or soon thereafter.

The demise of classic Clovis projectile point forms appears to correspond closely with the extinction of Pleistocene megafauna, suggesting that the two events are closely related. While timing is uncertain, these events appear to have occurred some time around 10,900–10,800 BP (Haynes 1987, 1992; Mead and Meltzer 1984). The emergence of a number of subregional cultural traditions, identified by distinctive stylistic projectile point forms, has been noted at this time and explicitly linked to decreases in group mobility and interaction that occurred with the changeover in hunting from a strategy targeting megafauna to one focused on essentially modern game animals, amid a regional landscape characterized by increasing numbers of people (Anderson 1990b; Anderson et al. 1992; Morse and Morse 1983). That is, populations throughout the East are assumed to have been adopting habitual use areas, precluding the option of group movement into previously unoccupied areas. The disappearance of key target megafauna would have comprised the earlier big game or "high technology foraging" adaptation (*sensu* Kelly and Todd 1988), which was simultaneously under stress given the increase in groups occupying more or less fixed ranges. Such a view of developments in the East does not require massive population growth, only the adoption of fixed ranges by local populations. Furthermore, as subregional cultural traditions emerged, specific adaptations would have varied from area to area, due to differences in climate, physiography, and resource structure.

In the idyllic environment of the middle portion of the Mississippi River Valley, the late Paleoindian expression climaxed in what is called Dalton culture. Dalton culture ($\approx$ 10,700–10,200 BP) existed throughout the southeastern United States and in much of the Midwest (Goodyear in press). However, the richness of the remains, site types, and formal tool assemblages characteristic of the central Mississippi Valley do not seem to have existed elsewhere. In the central Mississippi Valley, over 750 Dalton sites have been plotted and well over 1000 complete Dalton points have been collected; at some sites 100–350 points have been professionally collected. One reconstructed settlement system model (Morse 1971) postulates a base camp with satellite extraction sites including hunting camps similar to the Brand site (Goodyear 1974). The cemetery is also separate from the base camp or village. A base camp represented a local group or microband that was associated with a single watershed that extended from hardwood uplands with raw stone resources into the cypress–gum floodplain. Up to 6 microbands in neighboring watersheds interacted as a band network held together by trade in exotic stone and red ocher and by the marriage exchange of mates. Another settlement model postulated is seasonal nomadic movement of bands across parallel watersheds from one upland to another (Schiffer 1975), a trek that took DeSoto's Spanish army 4 days to accomplish in 1541. Gillam (1995) has demonstrated that group territories likely were oriented along rivers and near lithic sources in northeast Arkansas.

A most unique expression is the cemetery, as exemplified by the Sloan site (Morse in press; Morse and Morse 1983:89–95). The Sloan site excavation (14 m × 14 m × 0.5 m deep) produced 144 points, 30 adzes, 36 endscrapers, and over 200 other tools. A total of 141 fragments of human bone were also recovered (Condon and Rose in press). With very rare exceptions, the points were in pristine unused condition and ranged up to 20 cm in length.

Dalton points are different from earlier points. While still lanceolate, the hafting area attached to the foreshaft is considerably shortened, based on length of lateral grinding. Serrated points were resharpened laterally as knives to cut meat (Yerkes in press). Impact fractures are characteristic of unresharpened points; presumably resharpened points would penetrate deeply only with difficulty owing to the creation of a "shoulder" that would have hindered penetration beyond the haft. Another tool of note was the true woodworking adze (Morse and Goodyear 1973). Adzes hafted in handles by leather and characterized by wear typical of wood and charred wood (Gaertner in press) were evidently used to make dugout canoes. While these technological changes are easily recognized, the effects of these changes, if any, on the later mid-Holocene shift to food production is not readily understood as yet. But it is evident that people before the end of the Pleistocene were very sophisticated technologically in a number of regions of the world, including the eastern United States. The carved wooden objects are now gone, but the stone tools that produced them survive. Other tools include end-scrapers and a variety of other unifaces, abraders, and cobble tools (Morse and Morse 1983). Found at Sloan was an edge-abraded cobble that was probably used to pound wild plant food. In fact, *Chenopodium*, one of the plants destined to be cultivated, was recovered from Dust Cave and dated circa 10,000 BP (Driskell and Goldman-Finn 1994). An eyed bone needle was recovered from the Dalton deposit at Graham Cave in Missouri (Logan 1952:55). Such needles would have been necessary for the production of tailored clothing by the original immigrants, who had to adapt to an Arctic environment.

Paleoindian points are normally manufactured of high-quality chert. These cherts are often traceable to specific outcrops, and there is a clear association of many sites with quarry activities (Goodyear in press). Movements of peoples over a distance of 150–200 km or more have been postulated. At the Arkansas Sloan site, many points were manufactured of Crescent Quarry chert, which outcrops immediately south of St. Louis, Missouri, or about 300 km north of Sloan. Dalton-like points that appear to have been made of Arkansas Pitkin chert (House 1975) have been reported to Morse as found in Alabama and near the Texas–New Mexico border. There is a potential wealth of information in chert-sourcing studies, but better means of identification and closer attention to known hunter–gatherer behavior must accompany these investigations (Binford 1980; Cable 1982, 1992; Ellis and Lothrop 1989; Kelly 1983, 1992; Morse 1975; Tankersley 1989, 1991).

Radiocarbon dates on Dalton deposits tend to be later than expected (Goodyear 1982). Most of these dates were based on charcoal fragments contained within Dalton-bearing levels that also contained early Archaic notched points. It was assumed previously that bioturbation was minimal and that the stratigraphic context was properly interpreted. At Rodgers Shelter, two dates were derived from samples associated with Dalton hearths: 10,530 ± 650 BP and 10,200 ± 300 BP (Wood and McMillan 1976). The 10th millennium BP dates (i.e., 9,000–9,999 BP) supposedly on Dalton deposits at other sites probably date the initial Holocene expression in the East; notched points were also part of the basal deposits of those sites. Samples from Rodgers definitely need to be redated via AMS, but these two dates are considered the best Dalton dates extant (Goodyear 1982).

The Dalton expression is most evident in the central oak–hickory vegetation zone. To the south in the mixed pine and hardwoods section are found fewer sites and artifacts, but the technology is clearly Dalton in character (Goodyear in press). To the north in the boreal forests and the mixed conifer–northern hardwoods, Dalton points decline in number but seem to be replaced by late non-Dalton fluted points. Despite its variable regional distribution, according to distinctive local culture areas, Dalton is significant in that it is the first adaptation since Clovis that has such a large areal distribution, covering in this case the lower half of the eastern United States. Counting the various regional expressions with included Dalton-like points, an area spanning from east Texas to Missouri, and to Virginia and south Georgia can be reconstructed (Goodyear in press).

Typologically, Dalton points really begin the intensive resharpening of the Paleoindian lanceolate for hafted knife usage. Prior to this resharpening, the concern seems to have been with retipping the point. The beveling often seen on the Central Mississippi Valley Dalton, and other subsequent Early Holocene notched and stemmed points, is a by-product of the repeated application of serrations to the knife margins. These resharpened serrations are a functional hallmark of the Early Holocene hafted bifaces that follow in time. Regular resharpening of blade edges that eventually leaves a shoulder because it is covered by the haft is the technological common denominator of a variety of point types within the Dalton horizon.

Initial Holocene Adaptations (10,000–9,000 BP)

After the Dalton horizon, there is a generally recognized sequence of two more projectile point horizons that follow closely in time. Following Tuck (1974), these are the "Big Sandy" (side-notched) and Kirk (corner-notched) horizons. Side-notched points are radiocarbon-dated to the first millennium of the Holocene (Broyles 1966, 1971; Chapman 1976). The side-notched horizon is best represented by Bolen points in Florida, where they have been found in underwater karst deposits (Dunbar et al. 1988), and at Dust Cave in northern Alabama in stratigraphically discrete layers (Driskell 1992).

Dust Cave and Page-Ladson have produced large numbers of logically ordered radio-carbon dates, demonstrating that side-notched point forms (locally described as Big Sandy, Bolen, or Early Side Notched) may have first appeared around 10,200 BP, somewhat earlier than previously thought. Dust Cave yielded only minimal evidence for Dalton occupation or use, in the form of a few badly reworked and fragmentary points that may have been brought in by later occupants. The site is only a few kilometers from the Stanfield-Worley rock shelter, one of the region's major excavated Dalton sites (DeJarnette et al. 1962). Dalton sites in northeast Arkansas and southeast Missouri do not contain early notched points, suggest-ing that Dalton and side notching are temporally and perhaps culturally distinct horizons. There are point forms in the region, however, that appear to reflect a mixture of Dalton and side-notched characteristics, such as Hardaway and San Patrice, suggesting that an evolu-tion between the two forms did occur (Brookes 1979; Morse and Morse 1983; Goodyear in press; C. H. Webb et al. 1971).

The Kirk corner-notched horizon or "cluster" (Chapman 1976) is well-dated through-out most of the eastern United States. Corner-notched Early Archaic points consistently date from 9,500 to 8,800 BP (Broyles 1971; Chapman 1976). The chipped stone tools of the side- and corner-notched complexes are essentially the same, with a strong emphasis on unifacial flake tools, nearly all of which can be traced back to previous fluted point complexes. The Kirk horizon is significant for its areal distribution over the East. Owing to its widespread occurrence, from Florida to Ontario (see Ellis et al. 1991), it represents a large-scale reunification of the East for the first time since the colonial Clovis culture some 1,500 years earlier. No doubt by 9,000 BP, most climatic barriers and biotic limitations had ameliorated such that aboriginal populations or ideas could freely migrate and exist in an effectively modern Holocene environment. Models have been constructed at this time period of band-level local groups occupying individual drainages, or portions of drainages, and loosely tied together into larger entities consisting of a number of bands (Anderson and Hanson 1988; Anderson and Sassaman in press; Kimbal 1992). Similarity in artifact style is evident over the region, suggesting that there were no distinct cultural boundaries and that individual movement was fairly open and unconstrained. Factors shaping Early Archaic settlement included environmental structure, specifically seasonal and geographic variation in food and other resources; the need for maintenance of mating networks; information exchange, notably for mating network maintenance, social interaction, and subsistence resource regulation; and regional demographic structure, evidenced in population size and spacing. Settlement is thought to have been characterized by the use of a logistically provisioned seasonal base camp or camps during the winter and a series of short-term foraging camps throughout the remainder of the year. Fall aggregation events by groups from two or more different drainages are assumed to have occurred at prominent and resource-rich locations.

The decrease in hafting area seen on notched points continues a trend seen in Dalton points. Either the atlatl appeared at this time or this spear thrower underwent a significant technological advance immediately after the Pleistocene. The early Holocene notched horizon in Louisiana and southern Arkansas is known as San Patrice (corner-notched and side-notched) and the expression in Tennessee (north of the southern pine zone) is known as Kirk. Actually, many corner-notched types include side-notched varieties. During almost a millennium, corner-notched points increased in size. Larger points were beveled as knives; however, they were beveled opposite the way classic Dalton points in the Central Mississippi Valley were beveled. A shift in point orientation during the knapping process may have taken place. Dalton points are thought to have been resharpened by right-handed knappers with the tip held toward the knapper and notched points renewed as knives with the point tip held away from the knapper. The foreshaft may have undergone some sort of design change, possibly requiring the knapper to hold it in a different position on the thigh for proper balance during rejuvenation. It is also possible that pressure was applied in opposite directions on a point held in the same position during these respective time periods.

Terminal Early Archaic Adaptations (9,000–8,000 BP)

The western and midwestern parts of the eastern United States are characterized by Hardin Stemmed points during this period. These points seem to have developed from earlier larger corner-notched points called St. Charles. Southward Kirk Stemmed and other stemmed varieties were characteristic. This millennium saw the demise of classic corner notching of the Kirk type and an evolution toward the last horizon of the Early Archaic, that of the Bifurcate horizon in the Appalachian portion of the East (Anderson 1991b; Chapman 1976:5). Such a horizon had been posited by James Fitting (1964) earlier. Bifurcate points are essentially created by removing a notch in the base of a corner- or side-notched point. Toward the end of the 9th millennium BP, bifurcates begin to be replaced by true stemmed points such as Stanly, which ushered in several other changes in the chipped stone inventory. A number of poorly dated phases based on differences in projectile point types comprise the last early Holocene complexes of the East. It is clear, however, that significant regionalization occurred during the post-Kirk period such that geographic lacunae appear to exist. There is the strong possibility of whole regions being abandoned or lightly occupied from 8,500 to 7,500 BP, something evident when regional scale maps showing the distribution of Early and Middle Archaic sites are examined (Anderson and Sassaman in press).

The expansion of pine and cypress forests in the interriverine and riverine zones of the southeastern Coastal Plain at the end of the Early Archaic and the onset of the Middle Holocene, for example, appears to have led to appreciable depopulation of this region, something attributed both to the broad-scale global warming occurring at this time and to an increase in the occurrence of fires accidentally or intentionally set by Indian populations (Delcourt and Delcourt 1981, 1987a). Increased use of interior areas, in the Piedmont and Appalachian Summit, by populations using bifurcate-based projectile points is clearly evident at this time, with major reoccupation of the Coastal Plain not indicated until later in the Middle Archaic (Anderson 1991a; Anderson and Sassaman in press; Chapman 1975).

Over the course of the Paleoindian and subsequent Early Archaic era, group settlement range decreased, regional population densities grew, and mobility over a wide area was no longer feasible or desirable, leading to the abandonment of the formal stone toolkit that so characterizes this period of settlement. There may have been climatic factors at work that were particularly related to the Hypsithermal period (8,000–4,000 BP). This period was one of warmer and drier conditions, the effect of which was most pronounced in the midwest. The climatic situation farther east, north, and south is not as clear. Strong regional differentiation took place both altitudinally and latitudinally within the East.

It is also within this period or immediately afterward or both that we see the final dissolution and loss of an essentially Upper Paleolithic chipped stone technology that had continued from Clovis times in the selection of cryptocrystalline raw materials used to make finely crafted unifacial flake tools and bifaces, most of which were heavily curated. With the onset of early Holocene stemmed point technology in much of the East (Hardin Stemmed is an apparent exception to this rule), there was a decrease in the use of exotic cryptocrystalline lithics in favor of more local and often poorer raw materials and a loss of most of the well-made unifacial tool forms of the previous 2,500 years. As some have noted, the real technological break in lithic traditions in large parts of the East may not be at the Paleoindian–Early Archaic transition (or the Pleistocene–Holocene border), but between early Holocene and middle Holocene lithic technologies.

SUMMARY AND CONCLUSIONS

The eastern United States and southeastern Canada comprise a large and diverse region. At the end of the Pleistocene, there were also major changes in fauna and flora. At one time, spruce forests existed as far south as Memphis, Tennessee. Until about 10,900 BP, mastodon, mammoth, bison, tapir, llama, horse, camel, giant beaver, and ground sloth were present in much of the region. The Great Lakes evolved toward their present configuration, a rising sea level covered large parts of the Coastal Plain and flooded the karst region of Florida, and the plains/prairie in the west began to expand eastward. Deciduous forests expanded within the midsection of the region.

Initial colonization is thought to have begun by about 12,000–11,500 BP and probably was rapidly funneled down the Mississippi drainage into most of the eastern United States. Primary staging areas of small bands of local groups were located in large river valleys within exceptionally rich environments and near excellent chert sources. Over 8000 fluted points have been recorded so far in the eastern portion of North America. The points probably were mainly used as weapons to hunt larger land game. The environments occupied, however, would also have contained abundant waterfowl, fish, and a diverse and rich assemblage of edible flora. Only in the Northeast might there have been limits on edible flora. There is very little evidence of actual big-game hunting, and most investigators interpret this lack to mean that white-tailed deer and caribou contributed the major largest game sought.

Initial colonization is thought to be represented by Clovis-like points. Fluted points that are similar to Folsom are interpreted as representative of a later, post-Clovis occupation. After about 10,750 BP, there was a wide range of locally diverse styles, all of which are only very generally dated. Together, they provide evidence of increased populations, increased geographic occupation, and increased specialization in the exploitation of diverse ecologies. It is at this time (10,750–10,000 BP) that we get a glimpse of the sophistication of these earliest Americans in the East who were responsible for the fluted points. Bone needles are a reflection of the need for tailored clothing to the north. Red ocher reflects the very early use of a color primary to modern Native American life. Sophisticated stone tools interpreted to have been specially manufactured for woodworking are indicative of the possibility that objects such as masks and dugout canoes were made by the earliest colonists. Stone tools interpreted to have been used to grind vegetation for food have helped to defuse a total protein diet hypothesis. Cemeteries can mean that some populations were much less nomadic than thought and that there was a rich religious element to the matrix of what has always been assumed to be family local groups. Expansion of populations beyond the chert sources is an indication of the presence of sophisticated and peaceful trade relations to ensure access by all inhabitants to stone to make tools. That there is widespread similarity in styles of fluted points reflects a Paleoindian world view that encompassed much of the eastern part of the United States and Canada.

In the past, interpretations of the eastern United States Paleoindian have focused on the big-game-hunting model generated by the discoveries of kill sites in the western United States. There are many more points and sites in the east. There is more water, more game, and more vegetation diversity. Chert is universal, much of it in the form of gravel disbursed by glacial meltwater. Marine resources are vast. Populations have traditionally been larger and more advanced technologically in the east. Models of Paleoindian behavior have to be based on internal Eastern data, not tied to being modeled on a single aspect of western Paleoindian cultural reconstruction.

What were the cultural changes during the circa 10,000 BP shift from the Pleistocene to the Holocene? As archaeologists, we see a very significant change in projectile point styles. Fluted lanceolate points terminate and triangular notched points appear. The change is evidently sudden and universal, with a possible transitional period thought to be represented by points that can be classified as intermediate in basic style. If diet has not changed significantly, we can only infer that there was a technological advance in the weaponry used to obtain part of that diet. More significant cultural changes (in settlement and in tool technology), however, seem to have taken place after 8,000 BP. A decline in end scrapers may reflect a decreased emphasis on hide production for example.

What effects have the expansion of the northern land surfaces and the shrinkage of the eastern and southern coastal plain had on Paleoindian populations? Obviously, these effects constitute important aspects of changes in settlement and exploitation. Changing forests also were important aspects. Emphasis must have been on those natural resources that offered a high predictability of reliability and that continued to be hunted and gathered and then domesticated during the ensuing Holocene. No one lives for the distant future, but there is a tradition of the past that guides our futures.

REFERENCES

Anderson, D., 1990a, A North American PaleoIndian Projectile Point Database, *Current Research in the Pleistocene* 7:67–69.

Anderson, D., 1990b, The PaleoIndian Colonization of Eastern North America: A View from the Southeastern United States, in: *Early PaleoIndian Economies of Eastern North America* (B. Isaac and K. Tankersley, eds.), Journal of Economic Anthropology Supplement 5, pp. 163–216.

Anderson, D., 1991a, Examining Prehistoric Settlement Distribution in Eastern North America, *Archaeology of Eastern North America* 19:1–22.

Anderson, D., 1991b, The Bifurcate Tradition in the South Atlantic Region, *Journal of Middle Atlantic Archaeology* 7:91–106.

Anderson, D., 1995a, Recent Advances in Paleoindian and Archaic Period Research in the Southeastern United States, *Archaeology of Eastern North America* 23:145–176.

Anderson, D., 1995b, Paleoindian Interaction Networks in the Eastern Woodlands, in: *Native American Interaction: Multiscalar Analyses and Interpretations in the Eastern Woodlands* (M. S. Nassaney and K. E. Sassaman, eds.), University of Tennessee Press, Knoxville (in press).

Anderson, D. G., and Hanson, G. T., 1988, Early Archaic Settlement in the Southeastern United States: A Case Study from the Savannah River Valley, *American Antiquity* 53:262–286.

Anderson, D. G., and Sassaman, K. E. (eds.), n.d., *The Paleoindian and Early Archaic Southeast*, University of Alabama Press, Tuscaloosa (in press).

Anderson, D. G., Sassaman, K. E., and Judge, C. (eds.), 1992, *Paleoindian and Early Archaic Period Research in the Lower Southeast: A South Carolina Perspective*, Council of South Carolina Professional Archaeologists, Columbia.

Autin, W. J., Burns, S. F., Miller, B. J., Saucier, R. T., and Snead, J. I., 1991, Quaternary Geology of the Lower Mississippi Valley, in: *Quaternary Nonglacial Geology: Conterminous U.S.* (R. B. Morrison, ed.), The Geology of North America, Vol. K-2, Geological Society of America, Boulder, Colorado, pp. 547–580.

Binford, L. R., 1980, Willow Smoke and Dogs' Tails: Hunter–Gatherer Settlement Systems and Archaeological Site Formation, *American Antiquity* 45:4–20.

Bloom, A. L., 1984, Sea Level and Coastal Changes, in: *Late Quaternary Environments of the United States: Volume 2, The Holocene* (H. E. Wright, Jr., ed.), Longman Press, London, pp. 52–51.

Bostrom, P. A., 1993, *Early Paleo-Indian Period*, L.C.L. Press, Troy, Illinois.

Bradley, B., n.d., Sloan Site Biface and Projectile Point Technology, in: *The Sloan Site* (D. F. Morse, ed.), Smithsonian Institution Press, Washington, DC.

Brennan, L., 1982, A Compilation of Fluted Points of Eastern North America by Count and Distribution: An AENA Project, *Archaeology of Eastern North America* 10:27–46.

Brister, R. C., Armon, J. W., and Dye, D. H., 1981, American Mastodon Remains and Late Glacial Conditions at Nonconnah Creek, Memphis, Tennessee, *Anthropological Research Center Occasional Papers* 10.

Brookes, S. O., 1979, The Hester Site: An Early Archaic Occupation in Monroe County, Mississippi, *Mississippi Department of Archives and History*, Archaeology Report 5, Jackson, Mississippi.

Broster, J. B., and Barker, G. L., 1992, Second Report of Investigations at the Johnson Site, 40DV400: The 1991 Field Season, *Tennessee Anthropologist, Journal of the Tennessee Anthropological Association* 17(2):120–130.

Broster, J. B., and Norton, M. R., 1992, PaleoIndian Projectile Point and Site Survey in Tennessee: 1988–1992, in: *PaleoIndian and Early Archaic Period Research in the Lower Southeast: A South Carolina Perspective* (D. G.

Anderson, K. E., Sassaman, and C. Judge, eds.), Council of South Carolina Professional Archaeologists, Columbia, pp. 263–268.

Broster, J. B., and Norton, M. R., 1993, The Carson-Conn-Short Site (40BN190): An Extensive Clovis Habitation in Benton County, Tennessee, *Current Research in the Pleistocene* 10:3–5.

Broster, J. B., and Norton, M. R., in press, Recent Paleoindian Research in Tennessee, in: *The Paleoindian and Early Archaic Southeast* (D. G. Anderson and K. E. Sassaman, eds.), University of Alabama Press, Tuscaloosa.

Broster, J. B., Johnson, D. P., and Norton, M. R., 1991, The Johnson Site: A Dated Clovis–Cumberland Occupation in Tennessee, *Current Research in the Pleistocene* 8:8–10.

Broster, J. B., Norton, M. R., Stanford, D. J., Haynes, C. V., Jr., and Jodry, M. A., 1994, Eastern Clovis Adaptations in the Tennessee River Valley, *Current Research in the Pleistocene* 11:12–14.

Broyles, B. J., 1966, Preliminary Report: The St. Albans Site (46Ka27), Kanawha County, West Virginia, *The West Virginia Archaeologist* 19, West Virginia Archaeological Society, Moundsville.

Broyles, B. J., 1971, Second Preliminary Report: The St. Albans Site, Kanawha County, West Virginia, *West Virginia Geological and Economic Survey Report Archaeological Investigations* 3.

Brush, N., and Smith, F., 1994, The Martins Creek Mastodon: A Paleoindian Butchery Site in Holmes County, Ohio, *Current Research in the Pleistocene* 11:14–15.

Cable, J. S., 1982, Organizational Variability in Piedmont Hunter-Gatherer Lithic Assemblages, in: *The Haw River Sites: Archaeological Investigation at Two Stratified Sites in the North Carolina Piedmont* (S. R. Claggett and J. S. Cable, assemblers), Commonwealth Associates, Inc. Report R-2386, Jackson, MI. U.S. Army Engineer District, Wilmington. Wilmington, pp. 637–688.

Cable, J. S., 1992, The Haw River Sites Revisited: Implications for Modeling Terminal Late Glacial and Early Holocene Hunter-Gatherer Settlement Systems in South Carolina, in: *Paleoindian and Early Archaic Period Research in the Lower Southeast: A South Carolina Perspective* (D. G. Anderson and K. E. Sassaman, eds.), Council of South Carolina Professional Archaeologists, Columbia, pp. 96–142.

Chapman, J., 1975, *The Rose Island Site and the Bifurcate Point Tradition*, Department of Anthropology, University of Tennessee, Reports of Investigations 14.

Chapman, J., 1976, The Archaic Period in the Lower Little Tennessee River Valley: The Radiocarbon Dates, *Tennessee Anthropologist* 1(1):1–12.

Clausen, C. J., Cohen, A. D., Emiliani, C., Holman, J. A., and Stipp, J. J., 1979, Little Salt Spring, Florida: A Unique Underwater Site, *Science* 203(4381):609–614.

Coe, J. L., 1964, The Formative Cultures of the Carolina Piedmont, *Transactions of the American Philosophical Society* 54(5), Philadelphia.

Condon, K. W., and Rose, J. C., n.d., Bioarcheology of the Sloan Site, Chapter 3, in: *The Sloan Site* (D. F. Morse, ed.), Smithsonian Institution Press, Washington, DC.

Cotter, J. L., 1991, Update on Natchez Man, *American Antiquity* 56:36–39.

Curran, M. L., 1984, The Whipple Site and PaleoIndian Tool Assemblage Variation: A Comparison of Intrasite Structuring, *Archaeology of Eastern North America* 12:5–40.

Daniel, I. R., and Wisenbaker, M., 1987, *Harney Flats: A Florida PaleoIndian Site*, Baywood, New York.

DeJarnette, D. L., Kurjack, E. B., and Cambron, J. W., 1962, Stanfield-Worley Bluff Shelter Excavations, *Journal of Alabama Archaeology* 8(1&2).

Delcourt, P. A., and Delcourt, H. R., 1981, Vegetation Maps for Eastern North America: 40,000 YR. B.P. to the Present, in *Geobotany II* (R. C. Romans, ed.), Plenum, New York, pp. 123–165.

Delcourt, P. A., and Delcourt, H. R., 1987a, *Long-Term Forest Dynamics of the Temperate Zone*, Springer-Verlag, New York.

Delcourt, P. A., and Delcourt, H. R., 1987b, Late-Quaternary Dynamics of Temperate Forests: Applications of Paleoecology to Issues of Global Environmental Change, *Quaternary Science Reviews* 6:129–146.

Delcourt, P., and Delcourt, H., 1991, *Quaternary Ecology: A Paleoecological Perspective*, Chapman & Hall, New York.

Delcourt, P., Delcourt, H., Brister, R., and Lackey, L., 1980, Quaternary Vegetation History of the Mississippi Embayment, *Quaternary Research* 13:111–132.

Dincauze, D. F., 1993a, Pioneering in the Pleistocene Large Paleoindian Sites in the Northwest, in: *Archaeology of Eastern North America Papers in Honor of Stephen Williams* (J. B. Stoltman, ed.), Mississippi Department of Archives and History Archaeological Report, No. 25, Jackson, pp. 43–60.

Dincauze, D. F., 1993b, Fluted Points in the Eastern Forests, in: *From Kostenki to Clovis: Upper Paleolithic Paleo-Indian Adaptations* (O. Soffer and N. D. Praslov, eds.), Plenum Press, New York, pp. 279–292.

Driskell, B., 1992, Stratified Early Holocene Remains at Dust Cave, Northwest Alabama, in: *PaleoIndian and Early*

Archaic Period Research in the Lower Southeast: A South Carolina Perspective (D. G. Anderson, K. E. Sassaman, and C. Judge, eds.), Council of South Carolina Professional Archaeologists, pp. 273–278.

Driskell, B., and Goldman-Finn, N., 1994, Preliminary Archaeological Investigations at Dust Cave, Northwest Alabama, *Journal of Alabama Archaeology* 40(1,2).

Dunbar, J. S., and Waller, B. I., 1992, Resource Orientation of Clovis, Suwannee, and Simpson Age PaleoIndian Sites in Florida, in: *PaleoIndian and Early Archaic Period Research in the Lower Southeast: A South Carolina Perspective* (D. G. Anderson, K. E. Sassaman, and C. Judge, eds.), Council of South Carolina Professional Archaeologists, pp. 219–235.

Dunbar, J. S., and Webb, S. D., n.d., Bone and Ivory Tools from Submerged Paleoindian Sites in Florida, in: *The Paleoindian and Early Archaic Southeast*, by D. G. Anderson and K. E. Sassaman, University of Alabama Press, Tuscaloosa (in press).

Dunbar, J. S., Faught, M. K., and Webb, S. D., 1988, Page/Ladson (8Je591): An Underwater Paleo-Indian Site in Northwestern Florida, *The Florida Anthropologist* 41:442–452.

Ellis, C., 1994, Some Unanswered Questions Concerning Early Paleoindian Settlement and Subsistence in Southern Ontario, in: *Great Lakes Archaeology and Paleoecology: Exploring Interdisciplinary Initiatives for the 1990s* (B. G. Warner and R. MacDonald, eds.), Quaternary Sciences Institute, Waterloo, Ontario, pp. 413–429.

Ellis, C. J., and Lothrop, J. C. (eds.), 1989, *Eastern PaleoIndian Lithic Resource Use*, Westview Press, Boulder.

Ellis, C. J., Wortner, S., and Fox, W. A., 1991, Nettling: An Overview of an Early Archaic "Kirk Corner-Notched Cluster" Site in Southwestern Ontario, *Canadian Journal of Archaeology* 15:1–34.

Faught, M. K., 1995, Clovis Origins and Underwater Prehistoric Archaeology in Northwestern Florida, Unpublished Ph.D. dissertation, Department of Anthropology, University of Arizona, Tuscon.

Faught, M. K., Anderson, D. G., and Gisiger, A., 1994, North American Paleoindian Database—An Update, *Current Research in the Pleistocene* 11:32–35.

Fitting, J. E., 1964, Bifurcate-stemmed Projectile Points in the Eastern United States, *American Antiquity* 30(1):92–94.

Fladmark, K. R., 1979, Routes: Alternate Migration Corridors for Early Man in North America, *American Antiquity* 44:55–69.

Freeman, A., Tankersley, K. B., and Smith, E. E., Jr., n.d., A Stone's Throw from Kimmswick: Paleoindian Period Research in Kentucky, in: *The Paleoindian and Early Archaic Southeast*, by D. G. Anderson and K. E. Sassaman, University of Alabama Press, Tuscaloosa (in press).

Futato, E., in press, A Synopsis of Paleoindian and Early Archaic Research in Alabama, in: *The Paleoindian and Early Archaic Southeast*, D. G. Anderson and K. E. Sassaman (ed.), University of Alabama Press, Tuscaloosa (in press).

Gaertner, L., n.d., Microwear Analysis of the Artifacts, Chapter 6, in: *The Sloan Site* (D. F. Morse, ed), Smithsonian Institution Press, Washington, DC.

Gillam, C., 1995, *Paleoindian Settlement in the Mississippi Valley of Arkansas*, Unpublished M.A. Thesis, Department of Anthropology, University of Arkansas, Fayetteville.

Goodyear, A. C., III, 1974, The Brand Site: A Techno-functional Study of a Dalton Site in Northeast Arkansas, *Arkansas Archeological Survey Research Series* 7.

Goodyear, A. C., III, 1982, The Chronological Position of the Dalton Horizon in the Southeastern United States, *American Antiquity* 47:382–395.

Goodyear, A. C., III, n.d., The Early Holocene Occupation of the Southeastern United States: A Geoarchaeological Summary, in: *Ice Age People of North America* (R. Bonnichsen, G. C. Frison, and K. Turnmire, eds.), Center for the Study of the First Americans, Portland.

Graham, R. W., and Mead, J. I., 1987, Environmental Fluctuations and Evolution of Mammalian Faunas During the Last Deglaciation in North America, in: *North America and Adjacent Oceans during the Last Glaciation* (W. F. Ruddiman and H. E. Wright, Jr., eds.), The Geology of North America, Vol. K-3, Geological Society of America, Boulder, Colorado, pp. 371–402.

Graham, R. W., Haynes, C. V., Johnson, D., and Kay, M., 1981, Kimmswick: A Clovis-Mastodon Association in Eastern Missouri, *Science* 213:1115–1117.

Gramley, R. M., 1982, *The Vail Site: A Paleo-Indian Encampment in Maine*, Bulletin of the Buffalo Society of Natural Sciences, No. 30.

Green, F. E., 1963, The Clovis Blades: An Important Addition to the Llano Complex, *American Antiquity* 29(2):145–165.

Haynes, C. V., 1964, Fluted Points: Their Age and Dispersion, *Science* 145:1408–1413.

Haynes, C. V., 1980, PaleoIndian Charcoal from Meadowcroft Rockshelter: Is Contamination a Problem? *American Antiquity* 45(3):582–587.

Haynes, C. V., 1987, Clovis Origin Update, *The Kiva* 52(2):83–93.

Haynes, C. V., 1992, Contributions of Radiocarbon Dating to the Geochronology of the Peopling of the New World, in: *Radiocarbon after Four Decades* (R. E. Taylot and R. S. Kra, eds.), Springer-Verlag, New York, pp. 355–374.

Haynes, C. V., Donahue, D. J., Jull, A. J. T., and Zabel, T. H., 1984, Application of Accelerator C-14 Dating to Fluted Point PaleoIndian Sites, *Archaeology of Eastern North America* 12:184–191.

House, J. H., 1975, Prehistoric Lithic Resource Utilization in the Cache Basin: Crowley's Ridge Chert and Quartzite and Pitkin Chert, in: *The Cache River Archeological Project* (M. B. Schiffer and J. H. House, assemblers), Arkansas Archaeological Survey Research Series No. 8, Fayetteville, pp. 81–91.

Kelly, R. L., 1983, Hunter-Gatherer Mobility Strategies, *Journal of Anthropological Research* 39:277–306.

Kelly, R. L., 1992, Mobility/Sedentism: Concepts, Archaeological Measures, and Effects, *Annual Review of Anthropology* 21:43–66.

Kelly, R. L., and Todd, L. C., 1988, Coming into the Country: Early PaleoIndian Hunting and Mobility, *American Antiquity* 53:231–244.

Kimball, L. R., 1992, Early Archaic Settlement and Technology: Lessons from Tellico, in: *Paleoindian and Early Archaic Period Research in the Lower Southeast: A South Carolina Perspective* (D. G. Anderson, K. E. Sassaman, and C. Judge, eds.), Council of South Carolina Professional Archaeologists, Columbia, pp. 143–181.

Lepper, B. T., and Meltzer, D. J., 1991, Late Pleistocene Human Occupation of the Eastern United States, in: *Clovis: Origins and Adaptations* (R. Bonnichsen and K. Turnmire, eds.), Center for the Study of the First Americans, Oregon State University, Corvallis, pp. 175–184.

Levine, M. A., 1990, Accommodating Age: Radiocarbon Results and Fluted Point Sites in Northeastern North America, *Archaeology of Eastern North America* 18:33–64.

Lively, M., 1965, The Lively Complex: Announcing a Pebble Tool Industry in Alabama, *Journal of Alabama Archaeology* 11(2):104–122.

Logan, W. D., 1952, Graham Cave, An Archaic Site in Montgomery County, Missouri, *Memoir of The Missouri Archaeological Society* 2.

MacDonald, G. F., 1968, *Debert: A Palaeo-Indian Site in Central Nova Scotia*, Anthropology Papers, National Museum of Canada, No. 16.

Martin, P. S., 1973, The Discovery of America, *Science* 179:969–974.

Mason, R. J., 1962, The Paleo-Indian Tradition in Eastern North America, *Current Anthropology* 3:227–283.

Mason, R. J., and Irwin, C., 1960, An Eden-Scottsbluff Burial in Northeastern Wisconsin, *American Antiquity* 26:43–57.

McNett, C. W., McMillan, B. A., and Marshall, S. B., 1977, The Shawnee-Minisink Site, in: *Amerinds and the Paleoenvironments in Northeastern North America* (W. S. Newman and B. Salwen, eds.), *Annals of the New York Academy of Sciences* 288:282–296.

Mead, J. I., 1980, Is It Really That Old? A Comment about the Meadowcroft Rockshelter "Overview," *American Antiquity* 45(3):579–582.

Mead, J. I., and Meltzer, D. J., 1984, North American Late Quaternary Extinctions and the Radiocarbon Record, in: *Quaternary Extinctions: A Prehistoric Revolution* (P. S. Martin and R. G. Klein, eds.), University of Arizona Press, Tucson, pp. 440–450.

Meltzer, D. J., 1988, Late Pleistocene Human Adaptations in Eastern North America, *Journal of World Prehistory* 2:1–53.

Meltzer, D. J., and Smith, B. D., 1986, Paleo-Indian and Early Archaic Subsistence Strategies in Eastern North America, in: *Foraging, Collecting, and Harvesting: Archaic Period Subsistence and Settlement in the Eastern Woodlands* (S. Neusius, ed.), Center for Archaeological Investigations, Southern Illinois University, Carbondale, pp. 1–30.

Milanich, J. T., 1994, *Archaeology of Precolumbian Florida*, University Press of Florida, Gainesville.

Morse, D. F., 1971, Recent Indications of Dalton Settlement Pattern in Northeast Arkansas, *Southeastern Archaeological Conference, Bulletin* 13:5–10.

Morse, D. F., 1975, PaleoIndian in the Land of Opportunity: Preliminary Report on the Excavations at the Sloan Site (3GE94), in: *The Cache River Archaeological Project: An Experiment in Contract Archaeology* (M. B. Schiffer and J. H. House, assemblers), Arkansas Archaeological Survey, Research Series 8, pp. 93–113.

Morse, D. F., in press, *The Sloan Site*, Smithsonian Institution Press, Washington, DC.

Morse, D. F., and Goodyear, A. C., III, 1973, The Significance of the Dalton Adze in Northeast Arkansas, *Plains Anthropologist* 18:316–322.

Morse, D. F., and Graham, R., 1991, Searching for Paleolama, *Field Notes, Newsletter of the Arkansas Archeological Society* 239:10–12.

Morse, D. F., and Morse, P. A., 1983, *Archaeology of the Central Mississippi Valley*, Academic Press, New York.

Munson, P. J., 1990, Folsom Fluted Projectile Points East of the Great Plains and Their Biogeographical Correlates, *North American Archaeologist* 11(3):255–272.

Perino, G., 1985, *Selected Preforms, Points and Knives of the North American Indians*, Volume 1, Points and Barbs Press, Idabel.

Perino, G., 1991, *Selected Preforms, Points and Knives of the North American Indians*, Volume 2, Points and Barbs Press, Idabel.

Ruddiman, W. F., 1987, Synthesis: The Ocean/Ice Sheet Record, in: *North American and Adjacent Oceans During the Last Deglaciation*, Volume K-3 (W. F. Ruddiman and H. E. Wright, eds.), Geological Society of America, Boulder, pp. 463–478.

Schiffer, M. B., 1975, Some Further Comments on the Dalton Settlement Pattern Hypothesis, in: *The Cache River Archaeological Project: An Experiment in Contract Archaeology* (M. B. Schiffer and J. H. House, assemblers), Arkansas Archaeological Research Series 8, Fayetteville, pp. 103–112.

Smith, B. D., 1995, *The Emergence of Agriculture*, Scientific American Library, New York.

Stanford, D., 1991, Clovis Origins and Adaptations: An Introductory Perspective, in: *Clovis Origins and Adaptations* (R. Bonnichsen and K. L. Turnmire, eds.), Center for the Study of the First Americans, Oregon State University, Corvallis, pp. 1–13.

Storck, P., 1984, Glacial Lake Algonquin and Early Palaeo-Indian Settlement Patterns in Southcentral Ontario, *Archaeology of Eastern North America* 12:286–298.

Storck, P. L., Julig, P., Anderson, T., Barnett, P., and Mahaney, W., 1994, *Is There a Pre-Clovis Component at the Sheguiandah Site, Ontario?—New Geoarchaeological Evidence*, Paper presented at the 59th Annual Meeting of the Society for American Archaeology, Anaheim, California.

Tankersley, K. B., *Late Pleistocene Lithic Exploitation and Human Settlement in the Midwestern United States*, Unpublished Ph.D. dissertation, Department of Anthropology, Indiana University, Bloomington.

Tankersley, K. B., 1990, Late Pleistocene Lithic Exploitation in the Midwest and Midsouth: Indiana, Ohio, and Kentucky, in: *Early Paleoindian Economies of Eastern North America* (K. B. Tankersley and B. L. Isaac, eds.), Research in Economic Anthropology, Supplement 5, JAI Press, Greenwich, pp. 259–299.

Tankersley, K. B., 1991, A Geoarcheological Investigation of Distribution and Exchange in the Raw Material Economies of Clovis Groups in Eastern North America, in: *Raw Material Economies among Prehistoric Hunter–Gatherers* (A. Montet-White and S. Holen, eds.), University of Kansas Publications in Anthropology 19, Lawrence, Kansas, pp. 285–303.

Tankersley, K. B., and Morrow, J. E., 1993, Clovis Procurement and Land-Use Patterns in the Confluence Region of the Mississippi, Missouri, and Illinois Rivers, *Highways to the Past: Essays on Illinois Archaeology in Honor of Charles J. Bareis*, Journal of the Illinois Archaeological Survey, 5(1&2):119–129.

Titmus, G. L., and Woods, J. C., 1991, A Closer Look at Margin "Grinding" on Folsom and Clovis Points, *Journal of California and Great Basin Anthropology* 13(2):194–203.

Tuck, J. A., 1974, Early Archaic Horizons in Eastern North America, *Archaeology of Eastern North America* 2(1): 72–80.

Webb, C. H., Shriner, J. L., and Roberts, E. W., 1971, The John Pearce Site (16CD56): A San Patrice Site in Caddo Parish, Louisiana, *Bulletin of the Texas Archaeological Society* 42:1–49.

Webb, S. D., 1995, Status of 1993 Tusk, in: *Aucilla River Times* 8(1):3–4.

Webb, S. D., Milanich, J. T., Alexon, R., and Dunbar, J. S., 1984, A *Bison Antiquus* Kill Site: Wacissa River, Jefferson County, Florida, *American Antiquity* 49(2):384–392.

Webb, T., III, 1987, The Appearance and Disappearance of Major Vegetational Assemblages: Long-term Vegetational Dynamics in Eastern North America, *Vegetation* 69:177–187.

Webb, T., III, 1988, Eastern North America, in: *Vegetation History* (B. Huntley and T. Webb, eds.), Kluwer Academic Publishers, Dordrecht, pp. 383–414.

Wood, W. R., and McMillan, R. B., 1976, *Prehistoric Man and His Environments: A Case Study in the Ozark Highland*, Academic Press, New York.

Yerkes, R., n.d., Microwear Analysis of the Artifacts, Chapter 6, in: *The Sloan Site* (D. F. Morse, ed.), Smithsonian Institution Press, Washington, DC.

Chapter 17

The Pleistocene–Holocene Transition in Southern South America

Luis Alberto Borrero

INTRODUCTION

This chapter explores some of the data and models relevant for an understanding of human adaptations during the Pleistocene–Holocene transition in southern South America, between approximately 13,000 BP and 8,000 BP.

PALEOECOLOGICAL AND PALEOCLIMATIC BACKGROUND

The climate in southern South America witnessed alternating episodes of cooling and warming between 13,000 BP and 8,000 BP (Markgraf 1993). Basically, the southernmost regions saw treeless vegetation, the specific components of which varied with latitude (Heusser 1989; Mancini et al. 1993). Starting circa 14,000 BP, the Pleistocene ice masses covering most of Andean South America began their retreat (Clapperton 1992, 1993; Mercer and Ager 1983; Rabassa and Clapperton 1990), offering new ground for organic colonization. The Ecuadorian *páramo* and the high Punas in Peru were available for the first time for human exploitation (i.e., mining of obsidian), and within 3,000–4,000 years, some of these zones witnessed sustained human use. Alternations between dry and wet climates characterized the Brazilian plateaus (Bombin 1980) and the Argentinian pampas (Tonni et al. 1988) during the transition. On the southern tip of the continent, the Magellanic tundra of

LUIS ALBERTO BORRERO • Prehistoric Studies Program, University of Buenos Aires, 1039 Buenos Aires, Argentina.

Humans at the End of the Ice Age: The Archaeology of the Pleistocene–Holocene Transition, edited by Lawrence Guy Straus, Berit Valentin Eriksen, Jon M. Erlandson, and David R. Yesner. Plenum Press, New York, 1996.

Patagonia was characterized by a low carrying capacity, which probably limited the size of the initial human populations (see Dollenz 1991).

In general, late Pleistocene climates prior to 14,000 BP were colder than today's everywhere in southern South America (Heusser 1987, 1989; Markgraf 1989, 1993), and atmospheric circulation patterns were probably different from those prevalent today (Bombin 1980; Kutzbach and Guetter 1986).

Information derived mostly from pollen profiles and geology shows that lakes substantially larger than today's existed between 13,000 BP and 10,000 BP in the Bolivian Peruvian altiplano (Grosjean 1993; Mourguiart et al. 1993; Véliz Beltrán 1993), circa 13,000 BP in the cordilleran area of Neuquén (del Valle et al. 1993), and before 12,000 BP in Tagua-Tagua (central Chile) (Varela et al. 1993), Laguna del Bebedero (central Argentina) (Markgraf 1989), and Ultima Esperanza (Patagonia) (see Prieto 1991; Stern 1993), and circa 10,000 BP in Lago Cardiel (Patagonia) (Stine and Stine 1990). It has been suggested that these high stands are related to cool conditions (Clapperton 1993:519). Starting after 12,000 BP, lake levels began to fall, in correlation with a warming trend (Markgraf 1989), perhaps interrupted by short cool episodes (Clapperton 1993). Under these conditions, the first indications of human use of lacustrine environments are recorded in different regions (Prieto 1991; Rick 1983; Varela et al. 1993; C. Aschero 1993 personal communication). Nothing in these records can be used to sustain an argument that adaptations were centered on lake resources. On the contrary, terrestrial adaptations are indicated everywhere for this time. Incorporation of lake resources, especially birds, is a late feature in the history of human occupations (see Humphrey et al. 1993).

An important and debated issue is that of the existence in South America of a Younger Dryas cold interval between 12,000 BP and 11,000 BP. Such an interval was initially proposed on the basis of pollen profiles (Heusser and Rabassa 1987), but beetle and additional pollen analysis failed to identify it (Ashworth et al. 1991; Hoganson and Ashworth 1982). Geological information about a Younger Dryas glacial advance is suggestive, but not yet conclusive in South America (Clapperton 1993; Heusser and Rabassa 1987; Rabassa 1990). It is important to solve the Younger Dryas issue, since human populations were already present in that period. In general, after 10,000 BP, temperatures everywhere approached near-modern levels (Heusser 1989; Markgraf 1989).

Explosive volcanic activity was an important component in the cordilleran areas of South America during the last 14,000 years (Stern 1990), with semicontinental-scale events occurring circa 12,500 BP and 7,900 BP (Stern 1992, 1993). Their role in contributing to continental cooling through the production of atmospheric dust veils is still debated (Clapperton 1993). Some of these events may have caused widespread changes in the distribution of fauna, thus indirectly affecting human populations.

HUMAN SETTLEMENT

The absolute dating of hunter–gatherer arrival in southern South America is not a facile matter, but with present information, it is difficult to restrict human settlement to the period after 11,500 BP. This difficulty holds true even when, in some areas like Andean Peru, "the radiocarbon evidence for human presence … prior to 10,500 BP is surprisingly weak" (Rick 1987:64). In fact, acceptable early determinations suggest that a date of at least 12,000 BP to

13,000 BP is required in order to make sense of the available information in South America. Even in Peru, some probability of occupation prior to 10,500 BP is accepted by Rick (1987). To do so is not necessarily to support controversial claims, like those of the Ayacucho sites (MacNeish et al. 1981), where the association between dated materials and human occupation is questionable. Better published information than that currently available is needed in order to judge the Piauí sites (e.g., Pedra Furada) in Brazil, with determinations ranging between 40,000 BP and 14,000 BP (Schmitz 1987:63; see Guidon 1986).

On the other hand, at the Los Toldos site in Patagonia, often invoked to support a Pre-Clovis peopling of South America (Cardich et al. 1973), the entire case rests on a single date on dispersed pieces of charcoal. There are other cases in South America of sites producing chronological results of more than 12,000 BP that have not been supported by subsequent datings (Lavallée 1985; Lynch 1980; Nami 1987; Rick 1983). It is clear that in light of the statistical nature of radiocarbon readings, analysis of several samples is needed to credibly establish the chronology of the initial utilization of an archaeological site. Therefore, the Los Toldos evidence cannot be used as a proof of the early peopling of Patagonia. Monte Verde is the only site producing levels with repeated determinations between 13,000 BP and 12,000 BP (Dillehay and Pino 1989).

Taking into account the low frequencies of artifacts at any of the sites dated between 12,000 BP and 10,000 BP, it is clear that human populations were in general small and dispersed in southern South America at the time of the transition. It is difficult, however, to identify the major zones of human settlement during these times, since enormous areas are still unexplored. Distinctions have been made by several researchers (i.e., for Patagonia [Orquera 1987] and for Brazil [Schmitz 1987]) among different industries, phases, or traditions, but they are difficult to maintain due to the lack of information on variability among the samples. The use of a chronology independent of the cultural content of these units is a better procedure for dealing with the archaeological record. The record can be divided spatially among four different zones: west central South America, east central South America, central Chile and Argentina, and Patagonia. These zones are not defined by their cultural content, but only by geographical proximity of the dated sites.

In the lowlands of Amazonia, evidence for human occupations during the time of the transition is lacking. The "refuge theory" used to explain environmental changes in that region supports the notions that dry savannas were prevalent during glacial periods and that trees were concentrated in wetter *refugia*. Expansion of the forest to the lowlands came only with a more humid climate. Recent developments showed that reality probably was more complex than assumed by supporters of the refuge theory, with many minor fluctuations in the distribution of trees (Colinvaux 1987).

Figures 1–4 present samples of relevant early dates, ordered by periods of 1,000 years each, for the four major archaeological zones (see Tables 1–5).

Rick observed that "the Puna has a relatively constant number of dates after about 10,000 BP" (Rick 1987:67), and the same is true for the few dated sites in the Argentinian and Chilean Punas (Yacobaccio 1991) (Table 3). Associations with Pleistocene megafauna are not frequent, however, especially in the highlands. The diversity of archaeological assemblages is high, with many distinctive artifact forms dominating the different regions within the zone (Bryan 1975; Lynch 1983). These differences can be tied to variation among biotic communities.

Sites in east central South America zone are generally in open-air situations, with

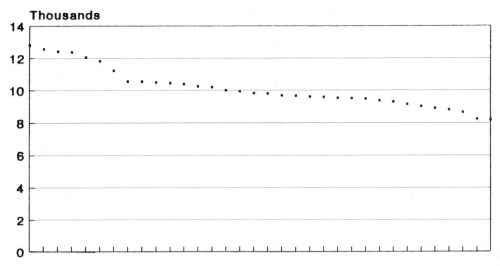

Figure 1. Radiocarbon dates for Peru between 13,000 BP and 8,000 BP.

abundant dates around 10,000 BP. Associations with megafauna, when present, are not always clear. That is the case with sites attributed to the Ibicui Phase in Brazil (see Schmitz 1987:86–87), but cave sites like Lapa Vermelha in northeast Brazil have better preservation of faunal remains, and human coexistence with *Glossotherium* sp. and other Pleistocene species can be supported. Most artifacts recovered in late Pleistocene–early Holocene

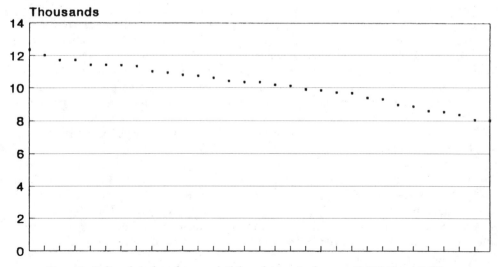

Figure 2. Radiocarbon dates for central Chile and Argentina between 13,000 BP and 8,000 BP.

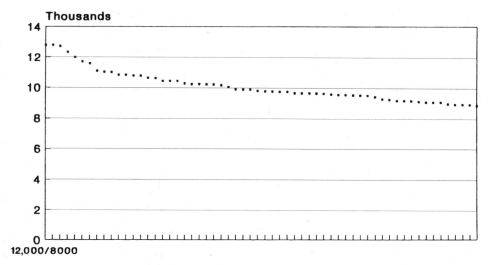

Figure 3. Radiocarbon dates for Brazil between 13,000 BP and 8,000 BP.

deposits lack distinctiveness, except for the importance of lateral retouch in the so-called "Itaparica Tradition" between 11,000 BP and 8,500 BP (Schmitz 1987).

The case in central Chile and Argentina is different, with clear associations between humans and megafauna, dated by radiocarbon between circa 11,000 BP and 8,500 BP (i.e., Politis and Beukens 1991; Varela et al. 1993). Associated artifacts include the so-called

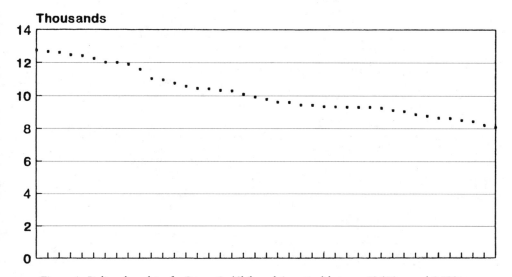

Figure 4. Radiocarbon dates for Patagonia (Chile and Argentina) between 13,000 BP and 8,000 BP.

Table 1. Radiocarbon Dates for the Millennium 13,000–12,000 BP[a]

Brazil

RS-I-50	12,770 ± 220 (SI-801)
Arroio dos Fosseis	12,770 ± 220 (SI-800)
RS-Q-2	12,690 ± 100 (SI-2351)
Abrigo do Sol	12,300 ± 95 (SI-3477)

Central Chile and central Argentina

La Moderna	12,330 ± 370 (TO-1507)
Quereo 1	12,000 ± 195 (N-2965)[b] (see Table 2)

Patagonia (Chile and Argentina)

Monte Verde MV-7	12,740 ± 440 (TX-5375)
Monte Verde MV-7	12,650 ± 130 (TX-4437)
Los Toldos 11	12,600 ± 600 (NR)
Monte Verde MV-6	12,450 ± 150 (OXA-381)
Cueva del Medio 4	12,390 ± 180 (PITT-1343)
Monte Verde MV-6	12,230 ± 140 (Beta-6755)
Monte Verde MV-6	12,000 ± 250 (OXA-105)

[a]From Cardich et al. (1973), Bombin and Bryan (1978), Lavallée (1985), Schmitz (1987), Dillehay and Pino (1989), Politis and Beukens (1991), and Galvez Mora (1992). (NR) No reference.
[b]Half-life = 5730 years.

Table 2. Radiocarbon Dates for the Millennium 12,000–11,000 BP[a]

Peru

Talara	11,200 ± 115 (SI-1415)
Pachamachay	11,800 ± 930 (UCLA-2118A)

Brazil

Abrigo Grande, Sta Ana Riacho	11,960 ± 250 (GIF-5089)
Lapa Vermelha	11,680 ± 500 (NR)
RS-I-68	11,555 ± 230 (SI-3750)
Brejo da Madre de Deus	11,060 ± 90 (SI-6298)
Cha de Caboclo	11,000 ± 250 (MC-1046)

Central Chile and central Argentina

Tagua Tagua	11,000 ± 170 (NR)
Quereo 1	11,700 ± 150 (N-2960) (see Table 1)
Quereo 1	11,700 ± 160 (N-2964) (see Table 1)
Tagua Tagua	11,320 ± 300 (NR)
Quereo 1	11,400 ± 155 (N-2963) (see Table 1)
Quereo 1	11,400 ± 155 (N-2962) (see Table 1)
Tagua Tagua	11,380 ± 320 (GX-1205)

Patagonia (Chile and Argentina)

Monte Verde MV-6	11,990 ± 200 (TX-3760)
Cueva Sofía 1	11,570 ± 60 (PITT-0684)
Tres Arroyos Va-b	11,880 ± 250 (Beta 20219)
Fell	11,000 ± 170 (I-3988)

[a]From Bombin and Bryan (1978), Orquera (1987), Schmitz (1987), and Dillehay and Pino (1989). (NR) No reference.

Table 3.   Radiocarbon Dates for the Millennium 11,000–10,000 BP[a]

Peru		Northern Chile/northwest Argentina	
La Cumbre	10,535 ± 280 (GX-2019)	Inca Cueva 4	10,620 ± 140 (LP-137)
Guitarrero II	10,535 ± 290 (GX-1778)	Tuina 1	10,820 ± 630 (SI-3112)
Guitarrero II	10,475 ± 300 (GX-1780)	San Lorenzo	10,400 ± 130 (N-3423)
Cerro Chivateros	10,430 ± 160 (UCLA 683)	San Lorenzo	10,280 ± 120 (HU-299)
Pampa de los Fósiles	10,380 ± 170 (GIF 5160)	Huachichocana E3	10,200 ± 420 (GAK-5847)
Guitarrero II	10,240 ± 110 (SI-1502)	Central Chile/central Argentina/Uruguay	
Pampa de los Fósiles	10,200 ± 180 (GIF 3781)	Quereo 1	10,925 ± 85 (SI-3391)
Quirihuac	10,005 ± 320 (GX-2004)	La China 1	10,790 ± 120 (AA-1327)
		La China 1	10,730 ± 150 (I-12741)
Brazil		La China 3	10,610 ± 180 (AA-1328)
RS-I-69	10,985 ± 100 (SI-2630)	El Tigre	10,420 ± ? (NR)
RS-I-69	10,800 ± 150 (N-2523)	Agua de la Cueva 46	10,350 ± 220 (NR)
RS-I-66	10,810 ± 275 (SI-2722)	Gruta del Indio	10,350 ± 60 (GRN-5558)
GO-NI 49	10,750 ± 300 (SI-2769)	Tagua Tagua 2	10,190 ± 130 (Beta 45520)
GO-JA-14	10,740 ± 85 (SI-3111)	Ñague Base	10,120 ± 80 (Beta-55279)
Niquelandia	10,605 ± 125 (NR)	El Sombrero	5 dates mentioned in Flegen-
GO-JA-01	10,580 ± 115 (SI-3699)		heimer and Zárate (1993)
Abrigo do Sol	10,405 ± 100 (SI-3476)		
GO-JA-1	10,400 ± 130 (N-2348)	Patagonia (Chile and Argentina)	
RS-I-69	10,400 ± 110 (N-2521)	Cueva del Medio 4	10,930 ± 230 (Beta 39081)
RS-I-69	10,240 ± 80 (SI-3106)	Fell	10,720 ± 300 (W-915)
RS-I-69	10,200 ± 125 (N-2522)	Cueva del Medio 4	10,550 ± 120 (GR-N 14911)
Lapa Vermelha	10,200 ± 220 (NR)		
MG-RP-6	10,190 ± 120 (SI-6837)	Tres Arroyos Vb	10,420 ± 100 (Dic 2733)
RS-I-98	10,180 ± 275 (SI-3752)	Piedra Museo	10,400 ± 80 (NR)
GO-JA-02	10,120 ± 80 (SI-3108)	Cueva del Medio 4	10,310 ± 70 (GR-N 14913)
Touro Passo	10,010 ± 190 (SI-9628)	Tres Arroyos Va	10,280 ± 110 (Dic 2732)
		Fell	10,080 ± 160 (I-5146)

[a]From Fernández Distel (1986), Taddei (1987), García (1990), Flegenheimer (1991), Galvez Mora (1992), Miotti (1993), Jackson (1993), Nami and Menegaz (1991), Orquera (1987), and Schmitz (1987). (NR) No reference.

"fishtail" projectile points at Tagua Tagua, Cerro La China, and several sites in the northern Argentine pampas (Flegenheimer and Zárate 1993; Politis 1991), as well as predominantly unifacial archaeological assemblages in the central pampas (Politis 1984).

In Patagonia and Tierra del Fuego, at sites like Cueva Fell, Cueva del Medio, or Tres Arroyos, there is a redundant pattern of *Mylodon darwini*, *Onohippidium* s.l., and *Lama guanicoe* bones, some showing cut marks and signs of burning, associated with artifacts, and hearths. Human occupations are dated between 11,000 BP and 10,000 BP, indicating some temporal overlap with the Younger Dryas chron.

In general terms, the chronological evidence is patterned. In Peru, "date records of each zone [coast and highlands] begin simultaneously in the range of 12,000 BP, [and] show their first significant number of dates around 10,500 BP" (Rick 1987:70). This is also true of other areas south of the Equator, including various regions of Brazil and Patagonia (Figures 3 and 4 and Table 6). Chronological information, then, fits within a model of slow initial exploration of the different areas of central South America, with a later phase of effective colonization

Table 4.   Radiocarbon Dates for the Millennium 10,000–9,000 BP[a]

Peru

Quirihuac	9,930 ± 820 (GX-2493)
Pampa de los Fósiles	9,810 ± 180 (GIF-4161)
Guitarrero I	9,790 ± 240 (GX-1779)
Ascope	9,670 ± 170 (GIF-4912)
Guitarrero I	9,660 ± 150 (SI-1498)
Lauricocha	9,525 ± 250 (NR)
Guitarrero II	9,580 ± 135 (SI-1499)
Pampa de los Fósiles	9,600 ± 170 (GIF-5162)
Pampa de los Fósiles	9,490 ± 170 (GIF-4914)
Guitarrero I	9,475 ± 130 (SI-1496)
Pampa de los Fósiles	9,300 ± 160 (GIF-4915)
Pampa de los Fósiles	9,360 ± 170 (GIF-5161)
Guitarrero I	9,140 ± 90 (SI-1497)
Quirihuac	9,020 ± 650 (GX-2491)

Brazil

RS-IJ-67	9,855 ± 130 (SI-3749)
Boa Vista II	9,850 ± 120 (MC-2513)
RS-I-67	9,840 ± 105 (N-2519)
GO-JA-03	9,765 ± 75 (SI-3110)
Boa Vista I	9,730 ± 140 (GIF-4629)
Cerca Grande 6	9,720 ± 128 (P-521)
Bojo	9,700 ± 120 (GIF-4624)
Boa Vista II	9,700 ± 120 (MC-2481)
RS-I-69	9,620 ± 110 (SI-2631)
Pilao	9,610 ± 90 (Beta-10015)
RS-I-97	9,605 ± 120 (SI-3754)
RS-IJ-67	9,595 ± 175 (SI-2637)
Lapa Vermelha	9,580 ± 200 (GIF-3208)
Baixao do Perna I	9,540 ± 170 (GIF-5414)
Cha do Caboclo	9,520 ± 160 (MC-1056)
GO-JA-01	9,510 ± 60 (SI-3700)
Caldeirão do Rodrigues	9,480 ± ? (GIF-5650)
Santana do Riacho	9,460 ± 500 (NR)
RS-I-72	9,450 ± 115 (SI-2634)
Abrigo do Sol	9,370 ± 70 (SI-3479)
RS-I-67	9,230 ± 145 (SI-2625)
GO-JA-02	9,155 ± 75 (SI-3107)
MG-VG-II	9,135 ± 105 (SI-5508)
RS-I-70	9,120 ± 340 (SI-2632)
Morro Furado	9,110 ± 100 (SI-7160)
GO-JA-01	9,060 ± 65 (SI-3698)
RS-I-99	9,035 ± 100 (SI-3755)
GO-JA-01	9,020 ± 70 (SI-3697)
Cerca Grande 6	9,020 ± 120 (P-519)

Northern Chile/northwest Argentina

San Lorenzo 1	9,960 ± 125 (N-3424)
Inca Cueva 4	9,900 ± 200 (AC-564)
San Pedro Viejo Pichasca	9,890 ± 80 (IVIC-728)
Tiliviche 1(B)	9,760 ± 365 (SI-3116)
Huachichocana E3	9,620 ± 130 (P-2236)
Inca Cueva 4	9,650 ± 110 (LP-102)
Toconce	9,590 ± 90 (NR)
Inca Cueva 4	9,230 ± 70 (CSIC-498)
Tuina 1	9,080 ± 130 (NR)

Central Chile/central Argentina/Uruguay

Tagua Tagua	9,900 ± 100 (Beta 45519)
Agua de la Cueva 45	9,840 ± 90 (NR)
Tagua Tagua 2	9,710 ± 90 (Beta 45518)
Las Conchas	9,680 ± 160 (P-2702)
Las Conchas	9,400 ± 160 (P-2702)
Calpica	9,320 ± ? (NR)

Patagonia (Chile and Argentina)

Cuyin Manzano	9,920 ± 85 (KN-1432)
Cueva del Medio 4	9,770 ± 70 (Beta 40281)
Cueva del Medio 4	9,595 ± 115 (PITT-0344)
Marazzi Inf.	9,590 ± 210 (GIF-1034)
Traful 18	9,430 ± 230 (Ingeis 2676)
Arroyo Feo 11	9,410 ± 70 (CSIC-514)
Arroyo Feo 11	9,330 ± 80 (CSI-396)
Cueva de las Manos 6 middle	9,320 ± 90 (CSIC-138)
Cueva de las Manos 6 base	9,300 ± 90 (CSIC-385)
Traful 13	9,285 ± 313 (LP-62)
Traful 21	9,285 ± 105 (GX-1711G)
Englefield	9,236 ± 1500 (Sa-20-c)
Fell 13	9,100 ± 150 (I-5144)
Fell 17	9,030 ± 230 (I-5145)

[a]From Cardich (1984–1985), Fernández Distel (1986), Taddei (1987), Nami and Menegaz (1991), Orquera (1987), Schmitz (1987), and Crivelli et al. (1993). (NR) No reference.

Table 5. Radiocarbon Dates for the Millennium 9,000–8,000 BP[a]

Peru		Northern Chile/northwest Argentina	
Guitarrero II	8,910 ± 90 (SI-1500)	Huachichocana E3	8,670 ± 550 (P-2280)
Telarmachay VIIb	8,810 ± 65 (LU-1279)	Quebrada Seca	8,670 ± 350 (AC-1118)
Quirihuac	8,645 ± 370 (GX-2022)	Aragon 1	8,660 ± 230 (GAK-5966)
Guitarrero IV	8,225 ± 90 (SI-1503)	Tambillo 1	8,590 ± 130 (Beta 25536)
Guitarrero II	8,175 ± 95 (SI-1501)	Tulan 67	8,190 ± 120 (NR)
Brazil		Central Chile and central Argentina	
GO-JA-01	8,915 ± 115 (SI-3695)	Arroyo Seco	8,980 ± 100 (TO-1505)
GO-JA-26	8,880 ± 90 (SI-5563)	Arroyo Seco	8,890 ± 90 (TO-1504)
MG-VG-11	8,865 ± 110 (SI-5509)	Casa de Piedra I	8,620 ± 190 (I-12067)
Morro Furado	8,860 ± 115 (SI-5565)	Arroyo Seco	8,560 ± 320 (LP-55)
MG-VG-19	8,845 ± 90 (SI-5511)	Arroyo Seco	8,390 ± 240 (LP-53)
GO-JA-01	8,805 ± 100 (SI-3696)	Inti Huasi	8,060 ± 100 (P-345)
Paraguaio	8,780 ± 120 (MC-2511)	Gruta del Indio	8,045 ± 55 (GRN-5394)
GO-JA-01	8,740 ± 90 (N-2347)		
SC-U-6	8,640 ± 95 (SI-995)	Patagonia	
MG-RP-6	8,620 ± 110 (SI-3210)	Fell	8,480 ± 135 (SI-5143)
Paraguaio	8,600 ± 100 (MC-2510)	Englefield	8,846 ± 1500 (Sa-20-c)
RS-IJ-67	8,585 ± 115 (SI-2636)	Arroyo Feo 11	8,610 ± 70 (CSIC-315)
Breja de Madre de Deus	8,495 ± 70 (SI-6296)	middle	
		Arroyo Feo 11	8,410 ± 70 (CSIC-516)
Pedra do Caboclo	8,400 ± 200 (MC-1003)	Los Toldos 3-(9)	8,755 ± 480 (NR)
GO-JA-26	8,370 ± 85 (SI-5562)	Palli Aike inf.	8,639 ± 450 (C-485)
Lapa Pequena	8,240 ± 160 (Birm-868)	Fell 10	8,180 ± 135 (I-5142)
MG-RP-6	8,215 ± 120 (SI-2373)	La Martita 7b	8,050 ± 50 (CSIC-506)
Cha do Caboclo	8,100 ± 135 (MC-1042)		
Bojo	8,080 ± 170 (GIF-170)		
Boqueirao da Pedra Furada	8,050 ± 170 (GIF-4635)		

[a]From Bird (1988), Cardich et al. (1973), Nuñez (1982), Lavallée (1985), Fernández Distel (1986), Orquera (1987), Schmitz (1987), and Politis and Beukens (1991). (NR) No reference.

circa 10,000 BP. In Fuego–Patagonia, exploration movements probably took longer, and human populations required more time before entering a colonization phase (Borrero 1994).

ADAPTED TO THE TRANSITION: LIVING IN TRANSITION TIMES

Generally speaking, the southern South American late Pleistocene archaeological record is less rich than that of other parts of the world, simply as a result of a lack of chronological depth. Despite its quantitatively small size, a record of variation is clear.

What is interesting about the situation in southern South America is that the transition, at least for most of that huge area, approximately coincides with the initial process of human colonization (Borrero 1990). From that point of view, it is valid to say that in most regions, the transition produced no impact on human populations, since they were slowly beginning their process of adjustment to new environments. Pleistocene fauna certainly was an item in the early colonists' diet (Table 7), but it was not a crucial one (Borrero 1984). A scavenging

Table 6. Number of Radiocarbon Dates/Number of Deposits or Sites
Dated

| | Millennium BP | | | | |
Archaeological zone	13–12	12–11	11–10	10–9	9–8
Brazil	4/4	5/5	17/12	29/22	20/15
Peru	5/4	2/2	8/5	14/5	5/3
Central Chile/Argentina	2/2	7/2	10/9	6/5	7/4
Northern Chile/northwest Argentina	—	—	5/4	9/7	5/5
Patagonia	7/3	4/4	8/4	14/8	8/6

mode of exploitation of *Mylodon darwini* and other large Pleistocene mammals can be
defended (Borrero et al. 1988), but *Hippidion* sp. was surely hunted (Nami and Menegaz
1991). At any rate, the disruption of the trophic chains that included Pleistocene mammals
was probably not of any lasting impact on human populations.

The process of human exploration and colonization was probably one of slow filling of
empty areas, with settlement being discontinuous in time and space (Borrero 1989). The
instability of environments around the times of the transition (Clapperton 1993; Pisano
1975), which were in early successional stages, helps to explain both the paucity of the
early archaeological record and the slowness of the colonization process.

At the hemicontinental scale, a wide variety of contemporary stone tool technologies is
observed (Politis 1991; Rick 1983). A tendency toward the use of local lithic sources (not
necessarily of the best quality) is evident in the older known archaeological sites. Bifacial
work is limited to projectile points. This tendency contrasts with the situation in North
America during Clovis times, where good-quality exotic rocks are abundant (Meltzer 1993).
This means that the archaeological landscapes generated synchronously in North and South
America are dramatically different, inviting one to consider independent trajectories.

There are also indications of the exploitation of a variety of food resources. The list
of subsistence items expanded around transition times (Table 7). The opportunistic use of
large—mainly Pleistocene—mammals and concentration on smaller animals contributed

Table 7. Major Faunal Remains in Pleistocene and Early Holocene Archaeological
Deposits in Fuego–Patagonia

Taxa	Late Pleistocene	Early Holocene	Taxa	Late Pleistocene	Early Holocene
Mylodon darwini	×	—	*Zaedius pichii*	—	×
Hippidion saldiasi	×	—	*Arctocephalus australis*	—	×
Hippocamelus bisulcus	—	×	*Otaria* sp.	—	×
Lama gracilis	×	—	Cetaceae	—	×
Lama guanicoe	×	×	Rheidae	—	×
Dusicyon avus	×	×	*Chloephaga* sp.	—	×
Pseudalopex griseus	—	×	*Anas* sp.	—	×
Pseudalopex culpeus	—	×			

to create this panorama. An absence of mass kills is manifest in all the regions, and whenever intensive use of any given resource is recorded, be it vicuñas (*Lama vicugna*) (Rick 1983), guanacos (*Lama guanicoe*) (Borrero 1991), or horses (*Hippidion* sp) (Nami and Menegaz 1991), it is the result of the averaging of several small events. Exploitation at any given site rarely is monospecific. A varied diet is usually a solution to living in risky environments (i.e., those presenting unpredictable variation). For initial settlers, it is a more adequate solution than storing or sharing. Expansion implies a reduction in hunting efficiency, but it also lowers the variance in the outcome (Hames 1990). It also specifies increments in time spent foraging, thus creating situations of time stress (Franco and Borrero 1993). This situation is explained as the result of slow incorporation of new territories for human exploitation.

The late Pleistocene witnessed the initial human explorations of the majority of these regions, and much of the record is elusive and limited as a consequence. Large human ranges were probably imperative, so a sparse human presence in an unpredictable environment was also part of the picture. The formation of new biogeographical barriers in the early Holocene, such as the Straits of Magellan or the Western Channels in Chile, or processes of intensive aridification in northern Andean environments, prompted fission and probably produced isolation of human populations (Mena 1991). This may also be the case with the borders of Amazonia if aspects of the "refuge theory" can be maintained. For this reason, founder effects were surely operating, probably leading to high rates of innovation in the artifactual repertoires and initiating divergent trajectories for the industries and for the human populations. These conditions also suggest the extinction of local groups as a valid alternative. Phenotypic variation recognized among skeletons in later periods (Cocilovo 1981; Rothhammer and Silva 1990) may be causally related to these processes.

LONG-TERM AND SHORT-TERM CHANGES

At least two kinds of external processes affected human populations in southern South America. Long-term changes, such as retreat of the ice masses, sea-level rise, extinction of the Pleistocene megafauna, reforestation of areas recently abandoned by the glaciers, and the opening of the Straits of Magellan, all took thousands of years, making them imperceptible in the span of a single human generation. These processes do not overlap precisely, and there is a cause–effect relationship between many of them (i.e., climatic change and extinction of the megafauna). Human responses were probably slow, but they should have produced a clear mark on the archaeological record. For example, increasing frequencies of modern faunas in the archaeological middens, including species with high fat content (pinnipeds, South American rheas), may have been related to the extinction of the large Pleistocene mammals. Postglacial reforestation may have caused human responses in midlatitudes, with the radiation of populations with industries attributed to the Itaparica Tradition into the highlands of Brazil (Sales Barbosa 1992), but in most other regions the forest was apparently underexploited. On the negative side, we must take into account the vast strip of coastal Pleistocene plains inundated by the sea in the early Holocene, with its biasing effects against the recovery of a coastal archaeological record.

On the other hand, short-term changes, such as volcanic events or earthquakes (Ocampo and Aspillaga 1991), probably provoked immediate responses. The most important recorded volcanic event, the explosion of Volcan Reclus, took place in 12,500 BP in Ultima Esperanza, probably before any human population arrived in that region (Stern 1992). But later eruptions of the Burney and Hudson volcanoes, dated circa 7,900 BP and 6,700 BP, respectively, may have evinced human responses. The problem is that this kind of phenomenon is very difficult to understand from the archaeological record. It is not sufficient to suggest human migrations as a response to the 6,700 BP eruption of the Hudson, as done by Cardich (1984–1985), or to droughts induced by airborne ash, as done by Miller (Schmitz 1987:89). Short-term impacts of volcanism on human populations probably preclude this kind of response (Baillie 1991; Sheets and Grayson 1979). Earthquakes, on the other hand, may have produced changes in prehistoric settlement patterns by collapsing caves (see Collins 1991) or by destroying coastal resources via tsunamis (Ocampo and Aspillaga 1991), dramatically transforming the cultural geography of the regions.

If a Younger Dryas episode is recognized, even when its duration could have been on the order of several hundreds of years, it probably belongs to the category of "short-term changes." Records of Younger Dryas in the Greenland ice cores suggest that the climatic change was probably abrupt, occurring perhaps within only a few years (Alley et al. 1993; Broecker 1992). The Younger Dryas issue must await resolution. The study of the archaeological record should help in this debate by discussing the presence or absence of human responses to a very cold climatic pulse (Franco and Borrero 1993).

CONCLUSIONS

In sum, except for conditions causing founder effects and the extinction of Pleistocene faunas, many of the changes were of relatively small importance, or very local. As for founder effects, their importance was evident over the long term by imposing divergent trajectories on local populations (Borrero 1989).

A focus on modern fauna was apparent from the beginning of human peopling of South America, and opportunism is a key concept in understanding the exploitation of Pleistocene megafauna (Borrero 1984). The impact of the extinctions on human populations, then, was probably smaller than previously thought.

Finally, an intriguing proposition needs to be considered. The general coincidence between initial sets of radiocarbon dates circa 13,000–12,000 BP with the record of comparatively rapid amelioration in global climate after the Last Glacial Maximum (Clapperton 1993:724) suggests that initial success in the process of human exploration of a variety of regions is intrinsically tied with climatic conditions. Human radiation in the vast hemicontinent may have been part of a wider process of organic recolonization (see Gamble 1993). This opens the possibility of the existence of initial populations inhabiting refuge areas even before 13,000 BP, ready to expand by taking advantage of the milder conditions of the postglacial.

A general cooling trend circa 12,500–10,000 BP recorded in the Vostok ice core of Antarctica (Jouzel et al. 1992), as well as in different parts of the northern Andes, may have retarded this peopling process in many regions, thus explaining why only about 10,500–10,000 BP are there evidences of widespread human presence. A Younger Dryas episode may fit comfortably within this scheme. The subsequent warming trend reached its peak circa 9,000–6,000 BP, a period during which human settlement was achieving some demographic success in several regions.

Whatever the scenario, the fact remains that there is an almost perfect timing between the initial human exploration of southern South America and many of the changes involved in the Pleistocene–Holocene transition. This coincidence reduced the impact of the transition on human populations. Those humans were adapting to constantly changing conditions, over a newly created space. In conclusion, from the very beginning, risk and uncertainty were part of the survival game for southern populations.

ACKNOWLEDGMENTS

I am grateful to Lawrence Straus for his support of my work and for correcting my English, and to Juan B. Belardi, Nora V. Franco, and Fabiana M. Martín for the useful comments they made on the manuscript.

REFERENCES

Alley, R. B., Meese, D. A., Shuman, C. A., Gow, A. J., Taylor, K. C., Grootes, P. M., White, J. W. C., Ram, M., Waddington, E. D., Mayewski, P. A., and Zielinski, G. A., 1993, Abrupt Increase in Greenland Snow Accumulation at the End of the Younger Dryas Event, *Nature* 362:527–529.

Ashworth, A. C., Markgraf, V., and Villagrán, C., 1991, Late Quaternary Climatic History of the Chilean Channels based on Fossil Pollen and Beetle Analysis, with an Analysis of the Modern Vegetation and Pollen Rain, *Journal of Quaternary Science* 6:279–291.

Baillie, M. G. L., 1991, Suck-in and Smear: Two Related Chronological Problems for the 1990s, *Journal of Theoretical Archaeology* 2:12–16.

Bird, J., 1988, *Travels and Archaeology in South Chile*, University of Iowa Press, Iowa City.

Bombin, M., 1980, Southeastern South America Atmospheric Circulation Patterns in the last 20,000 years, *Abstracts of the Biennial Meeting of the American Quaternary Association* 6:41–42.

Bombin, M., and Bryan, A. L., 1978, New Perspectives on Early Man in S. W. Rio Grande do Sul, Brazil, in: *Early Man in America from a Circum-Pacific Perspective* (A. L. Bryan, ed.), University of Alberta, Edmonton, pp. 301–302.

Borrero, L. A., 1984, Pleistocene Extinctions in South America, *Quaternary of South America and Antarctic Peninsula* 2:115–125.

Borrero, L. A., 1989, Evolución Cultural Divergente en la Patagonia Austral, *Anales del Instituto de la Patagonia* 19:133–140.

Borrero, L. A., 1990, Spatial Heterogeneity in Fugeo-Patagonia, in: *Archaeological Approaches to Cultural Identity* (S. Shennan, ed.), pp. 258–266, Unwin Hyman, London.

Borrero, L. A., 1991, Fuego-Patagonian Bone Assemblages and the Problem of Communal Guanaco Hunting, in: *Hunters of the Recent Past* (L. B. Davis and B. O. K. Reeves, eds.), Unwin Hyman, London, pp. 373–399.

Borrero, L. A., 1994, Arqueología de la Patagonia Meridional: Estado de la Cuestión a Fines de 1992, Unpublished manuscript in possession of author.

Borrero, L. A., Lanata, J. L., and Borella, F., 1988, Reestudiando huesos, *Anales del Instituto de la Patagonia.* 18:133-155.

Broecker, W. S., 1992, Defining the Boundaries of the Late-Glacial Isotope Episodes, *Quaternary Research* 38:135–138.

Bryan, A. L., 1975, Palaeoenvironments and Cultural Diversity in Late Pleistocene South America: A Rejoinder to Vance Haynes and a Reply to Thomas Lynch, *Quaternary Research* 5:151–159.

Cardich, A., 1984–85, Una fecha radiocarbónica más de la Cueva 3 de Los Toldos, Santa Cruz, *Relaciones* 16:269–274.

Cardich, A., Cardich, L. A., Hajduk, A., 1973, Secuencia Arqueológica y Cronología Radiocarbónica de la Cueva 3 de Los Toldos, *Relaciones* 7:85–123.

Clapperton, C., 1992, La Última Glaciación y Deglaciación en el Estrecho de Magellanes: Implicaciones para el Poblamiento de Tierra del Fuego, *Anales del Instituto de la Patagonia* 21:113–128.

Clapperton, C., 1993, *Quaternary Geology and Geomorphology of South America*, Elsevier, Amsterdam.

Cocilovo, J., 1981, Estudio Sobre Discriminación y Clasificación de Poblaciones Prehispánicas del N.O. Argentino, *Publicacion Ocasional* 36, Museo Nacional de Historia Natural, Santiago.

Colinvaux, P. A., 1987, Amazon Diversity in Light of the Palaeoecological Record, *Quaternary Science Review* 6:93–114.

Collins, M. B., 1991, Rockshelters and the Early Archaeological Record in the Americas, in: *The First Americans: Search and Research* (T. Dillehay and D. Meltzer, eds.), CRC Press, Boca Raton, pp. 157–182.

Crivelli, E. A., Silveira, M. J., and Curzio, D., 1993, La Estratigrafía de la Cueva Traful 1, *Praehistoria* 1:9–159, CONICET.

Dillehay, T., and Pino, M., 1989, Stratigraphy and Chronology, in: *Monte Verde. A Late Pleistocene Settlement in Chile* (T. D. Dillehay, ed.), Smithsonian Institution, Washington, DC, pp. 133–145.

Dollenz, O., 1991, Sucesión Vegetal en el Sistema Morénico del Glaciar Dickson, Magallanes, Chile, *Anales del Instituto de la Patagonia* 20 (Ciencias Naturales):49–60.

Fernández Distel, A., 1986, Las cuevas de Huachichocana, su Posición Dentro del Precerámico con Agricultura Incipiente del Noroeste Argentino, *Beitrage sur Allgemeinen und Vergleichenden Archäologie* 8:353–430.

Flegenheimer, N., 1991, Bifacialidad y Piedra Pulida en Sitios Pampeanos Tempranos, *Shincal* 3(2):64–78.

Flegenheimer, N., and Zarate, M., 1993, The Archaeological Record in Pampean Loess Deposits, *Quaternary International* 17:95–100.

Franco, N. V., and Borrero, L. A., 1993, Stress Temporal en Artefactos Líticos: El Caso de Santa Cruz. Paper presented at the Segundas Jornadas de Arqueología de la Patagonia.

Galvez Mora, C. A., 1992, Investigaciones Sobre el Paleolítico de la Costa de los Andes Centrales. *II Curso de Prehistoria de America Hispana*, Universidad de Murcia, Murcia, pp. 15–38.

Gamble, C., 1993, People on the Move: Interpretations of Regional Variation in Palaeolithic Europe, in: *Cultural Transformations and Interactions in Eastern Europe* (J. Chapman and P. Dolukhanov, eds.), Avebury, pp. 37–55.

García, A., 1990, Investigaciones arqueológicas en las Pampas Altas de la Precordillera Mendocina (1984–1989): Inserción en el Panorama Prehistórico del Centro-Oeste Argentino, *Revista de Estudios Regionales* 5:7–34.

Grcsjean, M., 1993, Late Glacial and Early Holocene Hydrology and Climate in the Atacama Altiplano 22–24°S, *Resúmenes Taller Internacional "El Cuaternario de Chile,"* Universidad de Chile, Santiago, p. 23.

Guidon, N., 1986, Las Unidades Culturales de Sao Raimundo Nonato–Sudeste del Estado de Piaui, in: *New Evidences for the Pleistocene Peopling of the Americas* (A. L. Bryan, ed.), Center for the Study of Early Man, Orono, pp. 157–171.

Hames, R., 1990, Sharing among the Yanomamo: Part I, The Effects of Risk, in: *Risk and Uncertainty in Tribal and Peasant Economies* (E. Cashdan, ed.), Westview Press, Boulder, pp. 89–105.

Heusser, C. J., 1987, Quaternary Vegetation of Southern South America, *Quaternary of South America and Antarctic Peninsula* 5:197–222.

Heusser, C. J., 1989, Late Quaternary Vegetation and Climate of Southern Tierra del Fuego, *Quaternary Research* 31:396–406.

Heusser, C. J., and Rabassa, J., 1987, Cold Climatic Episode of Younger Dryas Age in Tierra del Fuego, *Nature* 328:609–611.

Hoganson, J. W., and Ashworth, A. C., 1982, The Late Glacial Climate of the Chilean Lake Region implied by Fossil Beetles, *Proceedings of the Third North American Paleontological Convention*, 1:251–256.

Humphrey, P. S., Péfaur, J. E., and Rasmussen, P. C., 1993, Avifauna of Three Holocene Cave Deposits in Southern Chile, *Occasional Papers of the Museum of Natural History* 154:1–37.

Jackson, D., 1993, Datación Radiocarbónica para una Adaptación Costera del Arcaico Temprano en el Norte Chico, Comuna de Los Vilos, *Boletin* 16:28–31.

Jouzel, J., Lorius, C., Merlivat, L., and Petit, J. R., 1992, Abrupt Climatic Changes: The Antarctic Ice Record during the Late Pleistocene, in: *Abrupt Climatic Change* (W. H. Berger and L. D. Labeyrie, eds.), Reidel, Dordrecht, pp. 235–246.

Kutzbach, J. E., and Guetter, P. J., 1986, The Influence of Changing Orbital Parameters and Surface Boundary Conditions on Climate Simulations for the Past 18,000 years, *Journal of Atmospheric Science* 43:1726–1759.

Lavallée, D., 1985, *Telarmachay*, Tome 1, Editions Recherche sur les Civilisations, Paris.

Lynch, T., 1980, *Guitarrero Cave*, Academic Press, New York.

Lynch, T., 1983, The South American Paleoindians, in: *Ancient Native Americans* (J. D. Jennings, ed.), W. H. Freeman, San Francisco, pp. 87–137.

MacNeish, R. S., Cook, A. G., Lumbreras, L. G., Vierra, R. K., and Nelken-Terner, A., 1981, *Prehistory of the Ayacucho Basin*, Volume II, University of Michigan Press, Ann Arbor.

Mancini, M. V., Paéz, M. M., and Prieto, A. R., 1993, Historia de la Vegetación durante los Últimos 13,000 Años en la Estepa Patagónica, Argentina, *Resúmenes Taller Internacional "El Cuaternario de Chile,"* Universidad de Chile, Santiago, p. 38.

Markgraf, V., 1989, Paleoclimates in Central and South America since 18,000 BP Based on Pollen and Lake-Level Records, *Quaternary Sciences Reviews* 8:1–24.

Markgraf, V., 1993, Paleoenvironments and Paleoclimates in Tierra del Fuego and Southernmost Patagonia, South America, *Palaeogeography, Palaeoclimatology, Palaeoecology* 102:53–68.

Meltzer, D., 1993, Is There a Clovis Adaptation?, in: *From Kostenski to Clovis* (O. Soffer and N. D. Praslov, eds.), Plenum Press, New York, pp. 293–309.

Mena, F., 1991, *Prehistoric Resource Space and Settlement in the Río Ibañez Valley (Central Patagonian Andes)*, Ph.D. thesis, University of California, Los Angeles.

Mercer, J. H., and Ager, T., 1983, Glacial and Floral Changes in Southern Argentina since 14,000 Years Ago, *National Geographic Society Research Reports* 15:457–477.

Miotti, L., 1993, Piedra Museo: La Ocupación Diferencial del Espacio como Estrategia Logística Paleoindia en Patagonia, *Resúmenes Taller Internacional "El Cuaternario de Chile,"* Santiago, p. 55.

Mourguiart, Ph., Argollo, J., and Wirrmann, D., 1993, Evolución del Lago Titicaca durante los Últimos 25,000 Años, in *Resúmenes Taller Internacional "El Cuaternario de Chile,"* Santiago, p. 83.

Nami, H. G., Cueva del Medio, Perspectivas Arqueólogicas para la Patagonia Austral, *Anales del Instituto de la Patagonia* 17:73–106.

Nami, H. G., and Menegaz, A., 1991, Cueva del Medio: Aportes para el Conocimiento de la Diversidad Faunística Hacia el Pleistoceno–Holoceno en la Patagonia Austral, *Anales del Instituto de la Patagonia* 20:117–132.

Nuñez, L., 1982, *Paleoindio y Arcaico en Chile: Diversidad, Secuencia y Procesos*, Ediciones Cuicuilco, México.

Ocampo, C., and Aspillaga, E., 1991, Problemas del Registro Arqueológico de los Sitios del Archipiélago de los Chonos y las Guaitecas, in: *Resúmenes XII Congreso Nacional de Arqueología Chilena*, Museo Regional de la Araucanía de Temuco, Temuco, pp. 17–18.

Orquera, L. A., 1987, Advances in the Archaeology of the Pampa and Patagonia, *Journal of World Prehistory* 1:333–413.

Pisano, E., 1975, Caracteristicas de la biota magallánica derivadas de factores especiales, *Anales del Instituto de la Patagonia* 6:126–137.

Politis, G., 1984, Investigaciones Arqueológicas en el Área Interserrana Bonaerense, *Etnía* 32:7–52.

Politis, G., 1991, Fishtail Projectile Points in the Southern Cone of South America: An Overview, in: *Clovis* (R. Bonnichsen and K. L. Turnmikre, eds.), Peopling of the Americas Publications, Corvallis, pp. 287–302.

Politis, G., and Beukens, R., 1991, Cronología Radiocarbónica de la Ocupación Humana del Area Interserrana Bonaerense (Argentina), *Shincal* 3(3):151–157.

Prieto, A., 1991, Cazadores Tempranos y Tardíos en la Cueva 1 del Lago Sofia, *Anales del Instituto de la Patagonia* 20:75–99.

Rabassa, J., 1990, Global Change in Tierra del Fuego, Southernmost South America, during the last 15,000 Years: Glaciers, Sea-level, Neotectonics, Climate, Forest and Man, *Revista de Geofisica* 32:217–222.

Rabassa, J., and Clapperton, C., 1990, Quaternary Glaciations of the Southern Andes, *Quaternary Science Review* 9:153–174.

Rick, J. W., 1983, *Cronología, Clima y Subsistencia en el Precerámico Peruano*, Instituto Andino de Estudios Arueológicos, Lima.

Rick, J. W., 1987, Dates as Data: An Examination of the Peruvian Preceramic Radiocarbon Record, *American Antiquity* 52:55–73.

Rothhammer, F., and Silva, C., 1990, Craniometrical Variation among South American Prehistoric Populations: Climatic, Altitudinal, Chronological and Geographic Contributions, *American Journal of Physical Anthropology* 82:9–17.

Sales Barbosa, A., 1992, A Tradicao Itaparica: Uma Compreunsao Ecologica e Cultural do Povoamento Inicial do Planalto Brasileiro, in: *Prehistoria Sudamericana: Nuevas Perspectivas* (B. J. Meggers, ed.), Taraxacum, Washington, pp. 145–160.

Schmitz, P. I., 1987, Prehistoric Hunters and Gatherers of Brazil, *Journal of World Prehistory* 1:53–126.

Sheets, P., and Grayson, D. (eds.), 1979, *Volcanic Activity and Human Ecology*, Academic Press, New York.

Stern, C., 1990, Tephrochronology of Southernmost Patagonia, *National Geographic Research* 6:110–126.

Stern, C., 1992, Tefrocronología de Magallanes: Nuevos Datos e Implicaciones, *Anales del Instituto de la Patagonia* 21:129–141.

Stern, C., 1993, Tefrocronologia Holocénica de Tierra del Fuego, *Resúmenes Taller Internacional "El Cuaternario de Chile,"* Universidad de Chile, Santiago, p. 37.

Stine, S., and Stine, M., 1990, A Record from Lake Cardiel of Climate Change in southern South America, *Nature* 345(6277):705–708.

Taddei, A., 1987, Algunos aspectos de la arqueología prehistórica del Uruguay, in: *Investigaciones Paleoindias al Sur de la Línea Ecuatorial* (L. Nuñez and B. Meggers, eds.), San Pedro de Atacama, pp. 62–93.

Tonni, E. P., Bargo, M., and Prado, J., 1988, Los Cambios Ambientales en el Pleistoceno Tardío y Holoceno del Sudeste de la Provincia de Buenos Aires a Través de una Secuencia de Mamíferos, *Ameghiniana* 25(2):99–110.

Valle, R. A. del, Tatur, A., Amos, A., Ariztegui, D., Bianchi, M. M., Cusminsky, G., Hsu, K., Lami, A., Miranda, J. M., Martinez Macciavello, J. C., Masaferro, J., Nunez, H. J., Rinaldi, C. A., Roman Ross, G., Vallverdo, R., Vigna, G., Hobis, G., and Wheatley, R. C., 1993, Late Pleistocene–Holocene Sedimentary Core from Mascardi Lake, Nahuel Huapi National Park, Argentina. Paper presented at the XII Congreso Geológico Argentino, Mendoza.

Varela, J., Nuñez, L., and Casamiquela, R., 1993, Geología del Cuaternario de la Depresión Central de Chile entre Santiago y Laguna de Taguatagua, *Guía de Excursión Taller "El Cuaternario de Chile,"* Unversidad de Chile, Santiago.

Véliz Beltrán, Y., 1993, Secuencia Glacial Pleistoceno Tardío–Holoceno en la Cordillera Blanca, Peru, *Resúmenes Taller Internacional "El Cuaternario de Chile,"* Universidad de Chile, Santiago, p. 73.

Yacobaccio, H. D., 1991, *Sistemas de Asentamiento de Cazadores-Recolectores Tempranos de los Andes Centro-Sur*, Ph.D. thesis, Universidad de Buenos Aires.

PART VI

CONCLUSION

Chapter **18**

Surprises, Recurring Themes, and New Questions in the Study of the Late Glacial and Early Postglacial

MICHAEL A. JOCHIM

INTRODUCTION

This volume presents a wealth of new information about a critical period of global history. Only in the dramatic transition at the end of the Pleistocene was there a set of environmental changes of such magnitude over so wide an area at a time when modern humans were about. As a result, this period is an ideal laboratory for investigating human responses to environmental change. As these chapters make clear, the changes were not uniform across the planet. They varied spatially in terms of magnitude, timing, and nature. It is precisely this variability that encourages a comparative study of human adaptations.

Not surprisingly, given the defining, unifying focus of these chapters on a period of environmental transformations, the dominant approach is ecological. This theoretical orientation has several implications, all apparent in most of the chapters. The first is an emphasis on the dynamically changing relationships between people and their natural environments. Changes in climate, habitat, and resources are viewed not simply as a backdrop for cultural change, but as a continually altering set of problems and opportunities, changing the context for survival. The authors attempt to present dynamic pictures of prehistoric people, not lists of artifacts and sites.

Second, the studies are (and must be) multidisciplinary. They draw upon the most

MICHAEL A. JOCHIM • Department of Anthropology, University of California, Santa Barbara, California 93106.

Humans at the End of the Ice Age: The Archaeology of the Pleistocene–Holocene Transition, edited by Lawrence Guy Straus, Berit Valentin Eriksen, Jon M. Erlandson, and David R. Yesner. Plenum Press, New York, 1996.

recent studies in both the natural sciences and archaeology in an attempt to specify the nature of these changing relationships.

Third, these chapters share a clear recognition of the importance of spatiotemporal variability at different scales. Each chapter focuses on a different region, allowing comparison among them, but each in turn stresses the variations within these regions, making broad generalizations difficult. Each region is realistically portrayed as a varying mosaic that is the context for an equally variable mosaic of cultural changes. This rich detail allows investigation of specific environmental–cultural correlations, necessary for an understanding of changing ecological relationships. What emerges from many of these studies as a particular challenge for human ecology is a lack of neat, tight correlations: Changes in the archaeological record are frequently not isomorphic with specific changes in the natural environment. One inevitable conclusion to be drawn is that stone tools, the bulk of the archaeological record for this period, are poor, indirect monitors of adaptive behavior. Another conclusion is that the ultimate distribution of many new behaviors may have little to do with the causes that underlie their origins.

SURPRISES

One of the important revelations from these studies is that world prehistory still presents a number of surprises and challenges to our conventional reconstructions. For example, we have increasingly concrete and detailed evidence for early use of plant resources in regions as far apart as southern and northern Africa, southwestern Asia, Japan, and Thailand. Particularly in the latter region, the diversity of plants used for food or medicine is astounding. Similarly, the early appearance of agriculture in New Guinea is increasingly well documented. The appearance of this evidence during what seems to be a period of environmental amelioration poses challenges to theories of agricultural origins based on environmental stress.

Another result of the accumulating new data is the recognition of greater dietary and cultural diversity than was previously thought. This diversity is most obvious in studies of New World Palaeo-Indians, who have suffered more than most groups from overgeneralized, simplistic stereotypes. We now know these people in greater detail from contexts as different as coastal environments, interior mountains and plains, and temperate woodlands; not surprisingly, their behavior differs considerably from region to region.

A minor surprise is the persistence of some species of prey much later than their supposed local extinction, such as reindeer well into the central European Postglacial. Such evidence underscores the fact that seemingly discrete environmental stages are a product of poor chronological resolution. In reality, environmental changes were generally slow relative to human lifetimes and would have been perceived as gradual changes in relative proportions of habitats and resources, not abrupt replacements. Such a pace should have important implications for the nature of human responses to these changes.

Although it has long been presumed that the abandonment of coastal regions throughout the world occurred during this period of rising sea level, surprisingly, some interior areas were abandoned as well—most notably southwestern Tasmania and the interior of Alaska. Unless these areas became virtually uninhabitable, which is doubtful, their abandonment represents an unexpected lability of occupation of such large regions, in light of documented prior habitation. It might be supposed that both areas became simply less hospitable than neighboring areas (southeastern Tasmania, coastal Alaska), which implies that ecological models of patch use have relevance at this scale as well as within hunting territories.

THEMES

In addition to the common temporal focus and a generally ecological approach, a number of converging themes link these chapters. One of these themes has been mentioned: a recognition of, and emphasis on, the increasingly detailed resolution of spatial diversity, in both environments and behavior. This diversity is important as the raw material for cultural evolution, the source of behavioral innovations and borrowings that may have spread far more widely than their origins in specific, local ecological circumstances.

A second theme, and one certainly related to changes in the distribution of cultural practices, is that large-scale population movements were a common feature of this period. Some areas were abandoned, as mentioned earlier. Others were colonized in the late Glacial or early Postglacial after long periods of little or no occupation. These areas include the deserts of Australia, the Near East and Africa, the northern portions of Eurasia, and probably the entire New World as well. Although migrations—especially by hunter–gatherer populations—have not been a popular topic of archaeological study for a number of decades, they have attracted recent attention (Fagan 1987; Gamble 1993), and for good reason. Population movements and colonization are very real components of history and prehistory. The archaeological record of the late Pleistocene–early Holocene documents the importance of population redistribution as a cross-cultural means of coping with environmental change.

An additional coping mechanism that forms a third major theme of these chapters is technological innovation and change. Ceramics and domesticated plants, dogs, and cattle all appear for the first time during this period. The bow and arrow and composite, microlithic technology are developed or assume much greater importance than previously. All these innovations demonstrate a critical adaptive shift worldwide toward wresting greater control over natural resources—their productivity and distribution, their capture, and their storage and processing. This shift laid the groundwork for the unprecedented population growth and sociopolitical transformations to follow.

QUESTIONS

As these chapters demonstrate, we now know at least the basic outlines of the fundamental changes in environment, human distributions, and economic activities in most parts of the world during this critical transitional period. To achieve further understanding, we clearly need to continue working to gather data and add detail. It is likely that we will encounter a number of additional surprises as we do so. At the same time, however, we should be ready to move beyond this stage to ask particular questions of cross-cultural significance. If the Pleistocene–Holocene transition is to be a laboratory for investigating culture change, we need to specify the research questions, the "experiments," that will guide future work and realize the potential of this remarkable laboratory.

Optimality and Historical Constraints

One of these questions concerns the very nature of how humans adapt to environmental change. One approach to this question, common in archaeology and forming the foundation of evolutionary ecology and its anthropological applications, is to assume optimal responses according to some criteria. In studies based on optimal foraging theory, this criterion is net energetic foraging efficiency, which structures diet choice, patch use, and group size. Such an approach assumes an extreme flexibility of organization and behavior among prehistoric peoples, allowing them to adjust easily to environmental changes in a rational manner. The problem with this approach, even when used simply as a baseline for analysis, is that it ignores history and its constraints (see Trigger 1991). When people confront adaptive challenges, they do so carrying considerable cultural baggage and they fashion responses out of the contents, often trying to minimize the changes they must undergo. Just as is true in biological evolution, change must build upon the past, modifying the raw materials present. As Stone (1993:77) states, and demonstrates with concrete examples, "adaptive strategies result from the interplay between the unique history of a culture and its physical environment." In Chapter 4, Bar-Yosef similarly emphasizes the importance of "cultural filters" in responses to environmental changes in the Near East.

The implication of this view for studies of the late Glacial and early Postglacial is that responses to the environmental changes of this period should vary according to the specific past adaptations of the groups involved. Different groups could have very different trajectories of culture change, regardless of the similarities of their natural environmental contexts. The spread of temperate forests in many parts of the world in the early postglacial, for example, should not be expected to have led to a convergence of behavior among the groups affected. In Japan, the spread of oak forests was accompanied by an increasing emphasis on plant foods and the appearance of pottery; in Europe, a very different suite of cultural changes are correlated with similar patterns of environmental change. In each case, we should look to the preceding cultural patterns of economic activities, settlement patterns, and probable sex roles to gain an understanding of the role of historical precedent in structuring the pathways of change. An economy dominated by hunting, for example, and supporting this emphasis through value systems and norms of role behavior, might not easily accommodate a shift toward plant foods, even if they became extremely abundant and efficient to procure.

Colonization Processes

A second question deserving of more focus and suitable for exploration in this laboratory of environmental change concerns the processes by which colonization occurs. We unfortunately know very little about the means by which expansion into empty lands occurs among hunter–gatherer groups, and there is little ethnographic documentation upon which to draw. Keeping in mind the importance of local, historical particulars, can we see common themes? Are we likely to see strategies of high mobility, with colonizers essentially skimming the most efficient resources from a broad region? Or might we expect immigrants to focus on the richest resource locales and settle in, with later migrants leapfrogging to other rich areas, leaving poorer regions empty until later population growth promotes infilling? Does the colonization represent the wholesale transferral of a group's annual range, or simply a gradual extension of a group's range, first by temporary occupation of special-purpose camps?

The processes of colonization should have important implications for the archaeological record. Some have argued, for example, that movement into new regions should be accompanied by an emphasis on hunting rather than gathering (Hiscock 1994; Kelly and Todd 1988). The basis of this argument is that knowledge of animal behavior is easily transferrable to new areas, whereas successful gathering requires more detailed knowledge of specific landscapes. These authors also argue that initial colonizers should show high mobility, frequent range shifts, and redundant behavior across many sites. It is likely that models of optimal patch use would support these predictions. Archaeological tests could be designed to investigate these expectations by examining site contents and the distribution of lithic raw materials and stylistic indicators across a variety of colonized landscapes.

These authors have also argued that colonization of empty lands should have predictable effects on technology. They emphasize two features of lithic technology: transportability (important in the context of high mobility) and reliability (a necessary adaptation to the uncertainties of new habitats). These features of technology will influence quality of stone raw material used, frequency of resharpening, degree of retouch and standardization, and importance of hafting, all of which are measurable in the archaeological record.

The Pleistocene–Holocene transition provides us with the opportunity to explore such cross-cultural generalizations that are grounded in theories of optimality. We can explore these propositions in a variety of specific habitats that were colonized at this time. We can also investigate the role of historical constraints that may have caused deviations from optimality in the specific adaptations in each case.

Local and Regional Patterns

A third set of research questions that can appropriately be explored in this time period deals with the relationship between local and regional patterns of culture change. As mentioned earlier, many of the chapters point out a lack of congruence between aspects of environmental change and patterns of culture change. Such a pattern challenges any interpretations of behavioral shifts as direct responses to environmental factors. Insight into the basis of such patterning may be provided by the existence of extensive spatial networks of connection among many of the groups examined. These networks are identified through the distribution patterns of raw materials and artifact styles.

Such networks, reflecting mobility patterns, exchange, intermarriage, or other behaviors, represent a means by which new activities, techniques, and ideas can be communicated and transmitted. It is certainly possible, for example, that innovations in technology, such as the bow and arrow or domesticated animals, had local origins as responses to stresses or risks in changing environments. Once present, such innovations might have been rapidly adopted by neighboring groups for other reasons, perhaps because they allowed greater net subsistence efficiency or greater gross productivity that gave some individuals a competitive edge for prestige. In essence, the innovations could have been co-opted for purposes other than the originally perceived advantages, and their spread would have become disconnected from the original environmental context.

If this type of scenario occurred, as I suspect may have been frequently the case, then the preexisting social networks become critical to understanding the spatial distributions of innovations. Any local responses to the environmental changes of the late Glacial would have been thrown into the pool of behaviors available to all participants in these networks, to be observed, evaluated, and perhaps adopted for various reasons. We must therefore devote more attention to understanding the extent and behavioral basis of these networks in the late Glacial, in order not only to better understand this period, but also to contribute to more general investigations of the relationship between local and regional scales of archaeological patterning.

Warfare

A fourth set of research questions for which this period is an appropriate laboratory concerns the causes and role of warfare. The anthropological literature abounds with different approaches to this complex topic, variously emphasizing political, materialist, and evolutionary factors. The late Glacial–early Postglacial provides a context in which we can at least explore the materialist approaches. Throughout this period, there were dramatic changes in "man–land" relationships. In some cases, environmental shifts opened up new ares for exploitation and led to extremely low population densities in the colonized regions. In other cases, people were gradually compressed into *refugia* by changes in sea level and rainfall. These changes should reflect similarly dramatic changes in the potential for conflict over resources: low in newly colonized areas and high in circumscribed *refugia*.

If materialist approaches to warfare are correct, we should be able to predict corresponding patterns in the likelihood for conflict and warfare. Only Chapter 3 in this volume discusses this topic. Remarking upon a mortality rate of at least 40% from violent injuries in an Egyptian cemetery, Close suggests that conflict was one direct result of the local economic devastation of the "Wild Nile" within the circumscribed environment of the arid desert surroundings. Tacon and Chippindale (1994:224) suggest a similar phenomenon for the late Pleistocene of Australia. They link the appearance of fighting scenes in rock art at this time to increased competition due to "climate change and forced migrations and land redistribution that resulted from the rise in world sea levels at the end of the last glaciation." Again, here is a topic for which the cross-cultural laboratory of late Glacial environmental change can offer real potential.

CONCLUSION

There is no conclusion: I see, rather, continuation and new beginnings. It is clear to me that this period of world prehistory is inherently interesting because it witnessed so many profound changes in human distributions and lifeways. I anticipate that archaeological research will continue in each area to reveal the diversity of cultures and patterns of culture change during this period. At the same time, I hope that we will embark upon a new stage, systematically comparing regional histories to test and refine ecological theories and to explore the role of social interaction and historical constraint in culture change.

REFERENCES

Fagan, B., 1987, *The Great Journey*, Thames and Hudson, London.
Gamble, C., 1993, *Timewalkers*, Alan Sutton Publishing, London.

Hiscock, P., 1994, Technological Responses to Risk in Holocene Australia, *Journal of World Prehistory* 8:267–292.

Kelly, R., and Todd, L., 1988, Coming into the Country: Early Paleoindian Hunting and Mobility, *American Antiquity* 53:231–244.

Stone, G., 1993, Agricultural Abandonment: A Comparative Study in Historical Ecology, in: *Abandonment of Settlements and Regions* (C. Cameron and S. Tomka, eds.), Cambridge University Press, Cambridge, pp. 74–81.

Tacon, P., and Chippindale, C., 1994, Australia's Ancient Warriors: Changing Depictions of Fighting in the Rock Art of Arnhem Land, N. T., *Cambridge Archaeological Journal* 4:211–248.

Trigger, B., 1991, Constraint and Freedom—A New Synthesis for Archaeological Explanation, *American Anthropologist* 93:551–569.

Index

INTERDISCIPLINARY CONTRIBUTIONS TO ARCHAEOLOGY
Chronological Listing of Volumes

THE ARCHAEOLOGY OF GENDER
Separating the Spheres in Urban America
Diana diZerega Wall

ORIGINS OF ANATOMICALLY MODERN HUMANS
Edited by Matthew H. Nitecki and Doris V. Nitecki

PREHISTORIC EXCHANGE SYSTEMS IN NORTH AMERICA
Edited by Timothy G. Baugh and Jonathon E. Ericson

STYLE, SOCIETY, AND PERSON
Archaeological and Ethnological Perspectives
Edited by Christopher Carr and Jill E. Neitzel

REGIONAL APPROACHES TO MORTUARY ANALYSIS
Edited by Lane Anderson Beck

DIVERSITY AND COMPLEXITY IN PREHISTORIC MARITIME SOCIETIES
A Gulf of Maine Perspective
Bruce J. Bourque

CHESAPEAKE PREHISTORY
Old Traditions, New Directions
Richard J. Dent. Jr.

PREHISTORIC CULTURAL ECOLOGY AND EVOLUTION
Insights from Southern Jordan
Donald O. Henry

STONE TOOLS
Theoretical Insights into Human Prehistory
Edited by George H. Odell

THE ARCHAEOLOGY OF WEALTH
Consumer Behavior in English America
James G. Gibb

STATISTICS FOR ARCHAEOLOGISTS
A Commonsense Approach
Robert D. Drennan

DARWINIAN ARCHAEOLOGIES
Edited by Herbert Donald Graham Maschner

CASE STUDIES IN ENVIRONMENTAL ARCHAEOLOGY
Edited by Elizabeth J. Reitz, Lee A. Newsom, and Sylvia J. Scudder

HUMANS AT THE END OF THE ICE AGE
The Archaeology of the Pleistocene–Holocene Transition
Edited by Lawrence Guy Straus, Berit Valentin Eriksen, Jon M. Erlandson, and
David R. Yesner